Microsoft® Office Word 2003

ILLUSTRATED, CourseCard Edition

COMPLETE

Expert

Jennifer A. Duffy • Carol M. Cram

THOMSON
COURSE TECHNOLOGY

Australia • Canada • Mexico • Singapore • Spain • United Kingdom • United States

Microsoft® Office Word 2003—Illustrated Complete, CourseCard Edition

Jennifer A. Duffy, Carol M. Cram

Managing Editor:
Marjorie Hunt

Production Editors:
Melissa Panagos, Summer Hughes

QA Manuscript Reviewers:
John Freitas, Holly Schabowski, Christian Kunciw, Susan Whalen, Ashlee Welz, Harris Bierhoff

Product Managers:
Christina Kling Garrett, Jane Hosie-Bounar, Jeanne Herring

Developmental Editor:
Pamela Conrad

Text Designer:
Joseph Lee, Black Fish Design

Associate Product Manager:
Emilie Perreault

Editorial Assistant:
Shana Rosenthal

Composition House:
GEX Publishing Services

The Illustrated Series Vision

Teaching and writing about computer applications can be extremely rewarding and challenging. How do we engage students and keep their interest? How do we teach them skills that they can easily apply on the job? As we set out to write this book, our goals were to develop a textbook that:

- works for a beginning student

- provides varied, flexible, and meaningful exercises and projects to reinforce skills

- serves as a reference tool

- makes your job as an educator easier, by providing resources above and beyond the textbook to help you teach your course

Our popular, streamlined format is based on advice from instructional designers and customers. This flexible design presents each lesson on a two-page spread, with step-by-step instructions on the left, and screen illustrations on the right. This signature style, coupled with high-caliber content, provides a comprehensive yet manageable introduction to Microsoft Office Word 2003—it is a teaching package for the instructor and a learning experience for the student.

About This Edition

New to this edition is a free, tear-off Word 2003 CourseCard that provides students with a great way to have Word skills at their fingertips!

Acknowledgments

Many talented people at Course Technology helped to shape this book — thank you all. I am especially indebted to Pam Conrad for her precision editing and endless good cheer throughout the many months of writing. On the home front, I am ever grateful to my family for their patience, and to Nancy Macalaster, who so lovingly cared for my babies when I needed to be at my desk.

Jennifer A. Duffy

I wish to thank Pam Conrad, who provided so much encouragement, support, and intelligence throughout the editorial process. She is truly beyond compare! I also wish to thank my husband, Gregg Simpson, for his ongoing support and encouragement, and our daughter Julia for her enthusiastic help. Finally, I'd like to thank my students at Capilano College in North Vancouver. They are what it's all about.

Carol M. Cram

Preface

Welcome to *Microsoft® Office Word 2003—Illustrated Complete, CourseCard Edition*. Each lesson in this book contains elements pictured to the right.

How is the book organized?

Two units on Windows XP introduce students to basic operating system skills. The book is then organized into sixteen units and an appendix on Word, covering creating, editing and formatting text and documents. Students also learn how to create tables and Web sites, merge Word documents, and work with graphics, styles, charts, forms, macros, and XML.

What kinds of assignments are included in the book? At what level of difficulty?

The lessons use MediaLoft, a fictional chain of bookstores, as the case study. The assignments on the light purple pages at the end of each unit increase in difficulty. Data Files and case studies, with many international examples, provide a great variety of interesting and relevant business applications. Assignments include:

- **Concepts Reviews** include multiple choice, matching, and screen identification questions.
- **Skills Reviews** provide additional hands-on, step-by-step reinforcement.
- **Independent Challenges** are case projects requiring critical thinking and application of the unit skills. The Independent Challenges increase in difficulty, with the first one in each unit being the easiest (most step-by-step with detailed instructions). Independent Challenges 2 and 3 become increasingly more open-ended, requiring more independent problem solving.
- **E-Quest Independent Challenges** are case projects with a Web focus. E-Quests require the use of the World Wide Web to conduct research to complete the project.
- **Advanced Challenge Exercises** set within the Independent Challenges provide optional steps for more advanced students.
- **Visual Workshops** are practical, self-graded capstone projects that require independent problem solving.

iv

Each 2-page spread focuses on a single skill.

Concise text introduces the basic principles in the lesson and integrates a real-world case study.

UNIT A — Word 2003

Saving a Document

To store a document permanently so you can open it and edit it in the future, you must save it as a **file**. When you **save** a document you give it a name, called a **filename**, and indicate the location where you want to store the file. Files can be saved to your computer's internal hard disk, to a floppy disk, or to a variety of other locations. You can save a document using the Save button on the Standard toolbar or the Save command on the File menu. Once you have saved a document for the first time, you should save it again every few minutes and always before printing so that the saved file is updated to reflect your latest changes. You save your memo with the filename Marketing Memo.

STEPS

TROUBLE
If you don't see the extension .doc on the filename in the Save As dialog box, don't worry. Windows can be set to display or not to display the file extensions.

1. **Click the Save button on the Standard toolbar**
   The first time you save a document, the Save As dialog box opens, as shown in Figure A-7. The default filename, Memorandum, appears in the File name text box. The default filename is based on the first few words of the document. The .doc extension is assigned automatically to all Word documents to distinguish them from files created in other software programs. To save the document with a different filename, type a new filename in the File name text box, and use the Save in list arrow to select where you want to store the document file. You do not need to type .doc when you type a new filename. Table A-3 describes the functions of the buttons in the Save As dialog box.

2. **Type Marketing Memo in the File name text box**
   The new filename replaces the default filename. It's a good idea to give your documents brief filenames that describe the contents.

TROUBLE
This book assumes your Data Files for Unit A are stored in a folder titled UnitA. Substitute the correct drive or folder if this is not the case.

3. **Click the Save in list arrow, then navigate to the drive or folder where your Data Files are located**
   The drive or folder where your Data Files are located appears in the Save in list box. Your Save As dialog box should resemble Figure A-8.

4. **Click Save**
   The document is saved to the location you specified in the Save As dialog box, and the title bar displays the new filename, "Marketing Memo.doc."

5. **Place the insertion point before August in the second sentence, type early, then press [Spacebar]**
   You can continue to work on a document after you have saved it with a new filename.

6. **Click **
   Your change to the memo is saved. Saving a document after you give it a filename saves the changes you make to the document. You also can click File on the menu bar, and then click Save to save a document.

Clues to Use

Recovering lost document files

Sometimes while you are working on a document, Word might freeze, making it impossible to continue working, or you might experience a power failure that shuts down your computer. Should this occur, Word has a built-in recovery feature that allows you to open and save the files that were open at the time of the interruption. When you restart Word after an interruption, the Document Recovery task pane opens on the left side of your screen and lists both the original and the recovered versions of the Word files. If you're not sure which file to open (original or recovered), it's usually better to open the recovered file because it includes your latest changes to the document. You can, however, open and review all the versions of the file that were recovered and select the best one to save. Each file listed in the Document Recovery task pane has a list arrow with options that allow you to open the file, save the file, delete the file, or show repairs made to the file.

WORD A-10 GETTING STARTED WITH WORD 2003

OFFICE-102

Tips, as well as troubleshooting advice, are located right where you need them—next to the steps themselves.

Clues to Use boxes provide concise information that either expands on the major lesson skill or describes an independent task that in some way relates to the major lesson skill.

Every lesson features large, full-color representations of what the screen should look like as students complete the numbered steps.

Brightly colored tabs indicate which section of the book you are in.

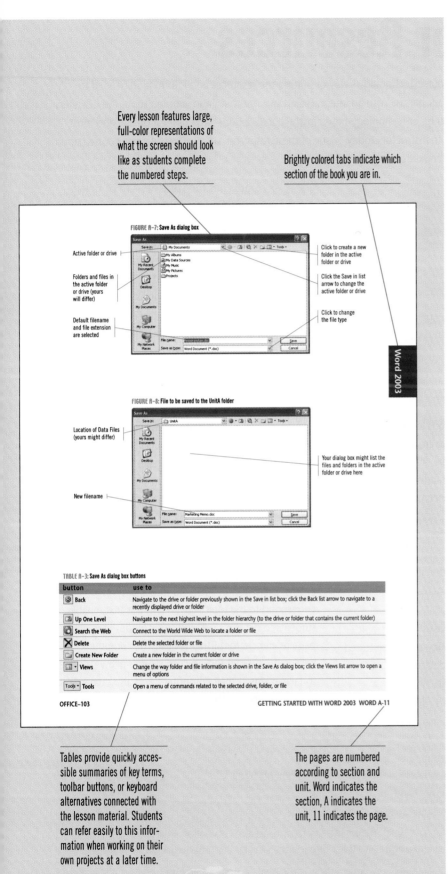

FIGURE A-7: Save As dialog box

Active folder or drive

Folders and files in the active folder or drive (yours will differ)

Default filename and file extension are selected

Click to create a new folder in the active folder or drive

Click the Save in list arrow to change the active folder or drive

Click to change the file type

Word 2003

FIGURE A-8: File to be saved to the UnitA folder

Location of Data Files (yours might differ)

New filename

Your dialog box might list the files and folders in the active folder or drive here

TABLE A-3: Save As dialog box buttons

button		use to
	Back	Navigate to the drive or folder previously shown in the Save in list box; click the Back list arrow to navigate to a recently displayed drive or folder
	Up One Level	Navigate to the next highest level in the folder hierarchy (to the drive or folder that contains the current folder)
	Search the Web	Connect to the World Wide Web to locate a folder or file
X	Delete	Delete the selected folder or file
	Create New Folder	Create a new folder in the current folder or drive
	Views	Change the way folder and file information is shown in the Save As dialog box; click the Views list arrow to open a menu of options
Tools	Tools	Open a menu of commands related to the selected drive, folder, or file

OFFICE-103

GETTING STARTED WITH WORD 2003 WORD A-11

Tables provide quickly accessible summaries of key terms, toolbar buttons, or keyboard alternatives connected with the lesson material. Students can refer easily to this information when working on their own projects at a later time.

The pages are numbered according to section and unit. Word indicates the section, A indicates the unit, 11 indicates the page.

What online content solutions are available to accompany this book?

Visit www.course.com for more information on our online content for Illustrated titles. Options include:

MyCourse 2.0

Need a quick, simple tool to help you manage your course? Try MyCourse 2.0, the most flexible syllabus and content management tool available. MyCourse 2.0 offers you brand new content, including Topic Reviews, Extra Case Projects, and Quizzes to accompany this book.

WebCT

Course Technology and WebCT have partnered to provide you with the highest quality online resources and Web-based tools for your class. Course Technology offers content for this book to help you create your WebCT class, such as a suggested Syllabus, Lecture Notes, Practice Test questions, and more.

Blackboard

Course Technology and Blackboard have also partnered to provide you with the highest quality online resources and Web-based tools for your class. Course Technology offers content for this book to help you create your Blackboard class, such as a suggested Syllabus, Lecture Notes, Practice Test questions, and more.

Is this book Microsoft Office Specialist Certified?

Microsoft Office Word 2003—Illustrated Complete, CourseCard Edition covers the objectives for Microsoft Office Word 2003 and Microsoft Office Word 2003 Expert and has received certification approval as courseware for the Microsoft Office Specialist program. See the last page of this book for more information on other Illustrated titles meeting Microsoft Office Specialist certification.

The first page of each unit indicates which objectives in the unit are Microsoft Office Specialist skills. If an objective is set in red, it meets a Microsoft Office Specialist skill. A document in the Review Pack cross-references the skills with the lessons and exercises.

Instructor Resources

The Instructor Resources CD is Course Technology's way of putting the resources and information needed to teach and learn effectively into your hands. With an integrated array of teaching and learning tools, the CD offers you and your students a broad range of technology-based instructional options—the highest quality and most cutting–edge resources available to instructors today. Many of these resources are available at www.course.com. The resources available with this book are:

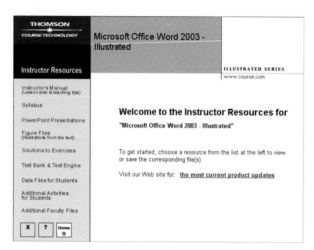

- **Data Files for Students**—To complete most of the units in this book, your students will need Data Files, which you can put on a file server for students to copy. The Data Files are available on the Instructor Resources CD-ROM and in the Review Pack, and can also be downloaded from www.course.com.

  Direct students to use the **Data Files List** located in the Review Pack and on the Instructor Resources CD. This list provides instructions on copying and organizing files.

- **Solutions to Exercises**—Solutions to Exercises contains every file students are asked to create or modify in the lessons and End-of-Unit material. A Help file on the Instructor Resources CD includes information for using the Solution Files. There is also a document outlining the solutions for the End-of-Unit Concepts Review, Skills Review, and Independent Challenges.

- **PowerPoint Presentations**—Each unit has a corresponding PowerPoint presentation that you can use in a lecture, distribute to your students, or customize to suit your course.

- **Instructor's Manual**—Available as an electronic file, the Instructor's Manual is quality-assurance tested and includes unit overviews and detailed lecture topics with teaching tips for each unit.

- **Sample Syllabus**—Prepare and customize your course easily using this sample course outline.

- **Figure Files**—The figures in the text are provided on the Instructor Resources CD to help you illustrate key topics or concepts. You can create traditional overhead transparencies by printing the figure files, or you can create electronic slide shows by using the figures in a presentation program such as PowerPoint.

- **ExamView**—ExamView is a powerful testing software package that allows you to create and administer printed, computer (LAN-based), and Internet exams. ExamView includes hundreds of questions that correspond to the topics covered in this text, enabling students to generate detailed study guides that include page references for further review. The computer-based and Internet testing components allow students to take exams at their computers, and also save you time by grading each exam automatically.

SAM 2003 Assessment & Training

SAM 2003 helps you energize your class exams and training assignments by allowing students to learn and test important computer skills in an active, hands-on environment.

With SAM 2003 Assessment, you create powerful interactive exams on critical applications such as Word, Outlook, PowerPoint, Windows, the Internet, and much more. The exams simulate the application environment, allowing your students to demonstrate their knowledge and think through the skills by performing real-world tasks.

Designed to be used with the Illustrated series, SAM 2003 Assessment & Training includes built-in page references so students can create study guides that match the Illustrated textbooks you use in class. Powerful administrative options allow you to schedule exams and assignments, secure your tests, and run reports with almost limitless flexibility.

Brief Contents

Contents

WORD 2003

Formatting Text and Paragraphs C-1

WORD 2003

Formatting Documents D-1

WORD 2003

Creating and Formatting Tables E-1

WORD 2003

Illustrating Documents with Graphics F-1

WORD 2003

Creating a Web Page G-1

WORD 2003

Merging Word Documents   H-1

WORD 2003

Working with Styles and Templates   I-1

WORD 2003

Developing Multipage Documents   J-1

WORD 2003

Integrating Word with Other Programs   K-1

WORD 2003

Exploring Advanced Graphics   L-1

WORD 2003

Building Forms   M-1

WORD 2003

Working with Charts and Diagrams   N-1

WORD 2003

Collaborating with Workgroups   O-1

WORD 2003

Customizing Word   P-1

WORD 2003

Working with XML   APPENDIX-1

Glossary   1

Index   7

Read This Before You Begin

Software Information and Required Installation

This book was written and tested using Microsoft Office 2003—Professional Edition (which includes Microsoft Office Word 2003), with a typical installation on Microsoft Windows XP, including installation of the most recent Windows XP Service Pack and with Internet Explorer 6.0 or higher. Some of the exercises in this book assume that your computer is connected to the Internet. If you are not connected to the Internet, see your instructor.

Tips for Students

What are Data Files?

To complete many of the units in this book, you need to use Data Files. A Data File contains a partially completed document, so that you don't have to type all the information in the document yourself. Your instructor will either provide you with copies of the Data Files or ask you to make your own copies. Your instructor also can give you instructions on how to organize your files, as well as a complete file listing, or you can find the list and the instructions for organizing your files in the Review Pack. In addition, because Unit A does not have supplied Data Files, you will need to create a Unit A directory at the same level as all of the other unit directories in order to save the files you create in Unit A.

Also, if you are saving your work on floppy disks as you complete the exercises in this book, then you may need to use multiple disks to complete all of the work in Unit K, depending on the size of graphics files that you use.

Why is my screen different from the book?

Your desktop components and some dialog box options might be different if you are using an operating system other than Windows XP.

Depending on your computer hardware and the Display settings on your computer, you may notice the following differences:

- Your screen may look larger or smaller because of your screen resolution (the height and width of your screen).

- Your title bars and dialog boxes may not display file extensions. To display file extensions, click Start on the taskbar, click Control Panel, click Appearance and Themes, then click Folder Options. Click the View tab if necessary, click Hide extensions for known file types to deselect it, then click OK. Your Office dialog boxes and title bars should now display file extensions.

- Depending on your Office settings, your Standard and Formatting toolbars may be displayed on a single row and your menus may display a shortened list of frequently used commands. Office menus and toolbars can modify themselves to your working style by displaying only the most frequently used buttons and menu commands. To view buttons not currently displayed, click a Toolbar Options button ⬇ at the right end of either the Standard or Formatting toolbar. To view the full list of menu commands, click the double arrow at the bottom of the menu.

Toolbars in one row

Toolbars in two rows

This book assumes you are displaying toolbars in two rows and displaying full menus. In order to have your toolbars displayed on two rows, showing all buttons, and to have the full menus displayed, you must turn off the personalized menus and toolbars feature. Click Tools on the menu bar, click Customize, select the show Standard and Formatting toolbars on two rows and Always show full menus check boxes on the Options tab, and then click Close.

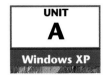

Getting Started with Windows XP

OBJECTIVES

| Start Windows and view the desktop |
| Use the mouse |
| Start a program |
| Move and resize windows |
| Use menus, keyboard shortcuts, and toolbars |
| Use dialog boxes |
| Use scroll bars |
| Use Windows Help and Support Center |
| Close a program and shut down Windows |

If you have a SAM user profile, you may have access to hands-on instruction, practice, and assessment of the skills covered in this unit. Log in to your SAM account and go to your assignments page to see what your instructor has assigned.

Microsoft Windows XP, or simply Windows, is an operating system. An **operating system** is a kind of computer program that controls how a computer carries out basic tasks such as displaying information on your computer screen and running other programs. Windows helps you save and organize the results of your work as **files**, which are electronic collections of data, with each collection having a unique name (called the **filename**). Windows also coordinates the flow of information among the programs, printers, storage devices, and other components of your computer system, as well as among other computers on a network. When you work with Windows, you use **icons**, small pictures intended to be meaningful symbols of the items they represent. You will also use rectangular-shaped work areas known as windows, thus the name of the operating system. ▰▰▰ This unit introduces you to basic skills that you can use in all Windows programs.

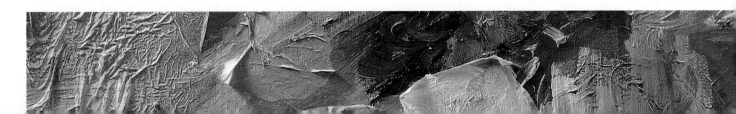

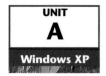

Starting Windows and Viewing the Desktop

When you turn on your computer, Windows XP automatically starts and the desktop appears (you may be prompted to select your user name and/or enter your password first). The desktop, shown in Figure A-1, is where you can organize all the information and tools you need to accomplish your computer tasks. On the desktop, you can access, store, share, and explore information seamlessly, whether it resides on your computer, a network, or on the **Internet**, a worldwide collection of over 40 million computers linked together to share information. When you start Windows for the first time, the desktop appears with the **default** settings, those preset by the operating system. For example, the default color of the desktop is blue. If any of the default settings have been changed on your computer, your desktop will look different from the one in the figures, but you should be able to locate the items you need. The bar at the bottom of the screen is the **taskbar**, which shows what programs are currently running. You click the **Start button** at the left end of the taskbar to perform such tasks as starting programs, finding and opening files, and accessing Windows Help. The **Quick Launch toolbar** often appears next to the Start button; it contains several buttons you can click to start Internet-related programs quickly, and another that you can click to show the desktop when it is not currently visible. Table A-1 identifies the icons and other elements you see on your desktop. If Windows XP is not currently running on your computer, follow the steps below to start it now.

STEPS

TROUBLE
If a Welcome to Microsoft Windows tour opens, move your mouse pointer over the Next button in the lower-right corner of the dialog box and click the left mouse button once; when you see the Do you want to activate Windows now? dialog box, click the No, remind me every few days option. See your instructor or technical support person for further assistance.

1. **Turn on your computer and monitor**

   When Windows starts, you may see an area where you can click your user name or a Log On to Windows dialog box. If so, continue to Step 2. If not, view Figure A-1, then continue on to the next lesson.

2. **Click the correct user name, if necessary, type your password, then press [Enter]**

   Once the password is accepted, the Windows desktop appears on your screen. See Figure A-1.

   If you don't know your password, see your instructor or technical support person.

Clues to Use

Accessing the Internet from the Desktop

Windows XP provides a seamless connection between your desktop and the Internet with Internet Explorer. Internet Explorer is an example of a **browser**, a program designed to access the **World Wide Web** (also known as the **WWW**, or simply the **Web**). Internet Explorer is included with the Windows XP operating system. You can access it on the Start menu or by clicking its icon if it appears on the desktop or on the Quick Launch toolbar. You can use it to access Web pages and to place Web content such as weather or stock updates on the desktop for instant viewing. This information is updated automatically whenever you connect to the Internet.

FIGURE A-1: Windows desktop

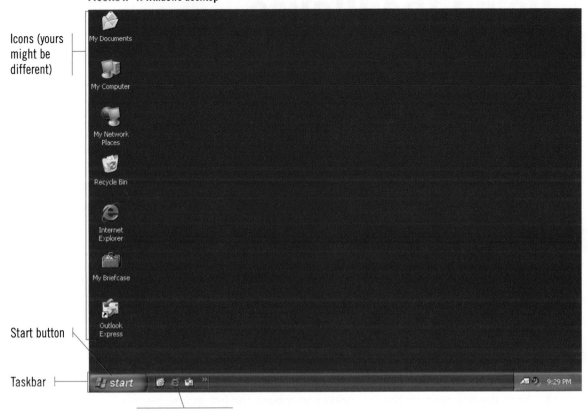

Icons (yours might be different)

Start button

Taskbar

Quick Launch toolbar

TABLE A-1: Elements of a typical Windows desktop

desktop element	icon	allows you to
My Computer		Work with different disk drives, folders, and files on your computer
My Documents folder		Store documents, graphics, video and sound clips, and other files
Internet Explorer		Start the Internet Explorer browser to access the Internet
Recycle Bin		Delete and restore files
My Network Places		Open files and folders on other computers and install network printers
My Briefcase		Synchronize files when you use two computers
Outlook Express		Send and receive e-mail and participate in newsgroups
Start button	start	Start programs, open documents, search for files, and more
Taskbar		Start programs and switch among open programs and files
Quick Launch toolbar		Display the desktop, start Internet Explorer, and start Outlook Express

Using the Mouse

A **mouse** is a handheld **input** or **pointing device** that you use to interact with your computer. Input or pointing devices come in many shapes and sizes; some, like a mouse, are directly attached to your computer with a cable; others function like a TV remote control and allow you to access your computer without being right next to it. Figure A-2 shows examples of common pointing devices. Because the most common pointing device is a mouse, this book uses that term. If you are using a different pointing device, substitute that device whenever you see the term "mouse." When you move the mouse, the **mouse pointer** on the screen moves in the same direction. You use the **mouse buttons** to select icons and commands, which is how you communicate with the computer. Table A-2 shows some common mouse pointer shapes that indicate different activities. Table A-3 lists the five basic mouse actions. ▅▅▅▅ Begin by experimenting with the mouse now.

STEPS

1. **Locate the mouse pointer on the desktop, then move the mouse across your desk or mouse pad**

   Watch how the mouse pointer moves on the desktop in response to your movements; practice moving the mouse pointer in circles, then back and forth in straight lines.

2. **Position the mouse pointer over the Recycle Bin icon 🗑**

   Positioning the mouse pointer over an item is called **pointing**.

3. **With the pointer over the 🗑, press and release the left mouse button**

   Pressing and releasing the left mouse button is called **clicking** (or single-clicking, to distinguish it from double-clicking, which you'll do in Step 7). When you position the mouse pointer over an icon or any item and click, you select that item. When an item is **selected**, it is **highlighted** (shaded differently from other items), and the next action you take will be performed on that item.

4. **With 🗑 selected, press and hold down the left mouse button, move the mouse down and to the right, then release the mouse button**

   The icon becomes dimmed and moves with the mouse pointer; this is called **dragging**, which you do to move icons and other Windows elements. When you release the mouse button, the item is positioned at the new location (it may "snap" to another location, depending on the settings on your computer).

5. **Position the mouse pointer over the 🗑, then press and release the right mouse button**

   Clicking the right mouse button is known as **right-clicking**. Right-clicking an item on the desktop produces a **shortcut menu**, as shown in Figure A-3. This menu lists the commands most commonly used for the item you have clicked. A **command** is a directive that provides access to a program's features.

6. **Click anywhere outside the menu to close the shortcut menu**

7. **Position the mouse pointer over the 🗑, then quickly press and release the left mouse button twice**

   Clicking the mouse button twice quickly is known as **double-clicking**; in this case, double-clicking the Recycle Bin icon opens the Recycle Bin window, which displays files that you have deleted.

8. **Click the Close button ☒ in the upper-right corner of the Recycle Bin window**

FIGURE A-2: **Common pointing devices**

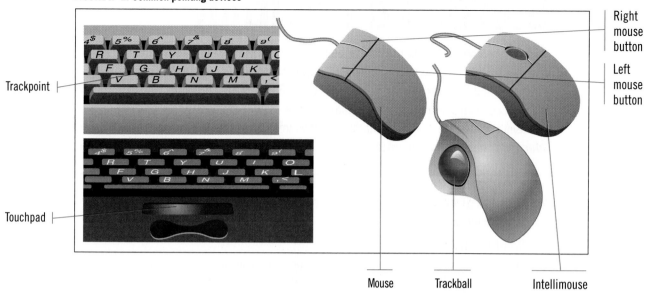

Trackpoint

Touchpad

Right mouse button

Left mouse button

Mouse   Trackball   Intellimouse

FIGURE A-3: **Displaying a shortcut menu**

Selected icon

Pointer positioned over icon

Shortcut menu

TABLE A-2: **Common mouse pointer shapes**

shape	used to
▻	Select items, choose commands, start programs, and work in programs
I	Position mouse pointer for editing or inserting text; called the insertion point or Text Select pointer
⧖	Indicate Windows is busy processing a command
↔	Change the size of a window; appears when mouse pointer is on the border of a window
ᗞ	Select and open Web-based data and other links

TABLE A-3: **Basic mouse techniques**

technique	what to do
Pointing	Move the mouse to position the mouse pointer over an item on the desktop
Clicking	Press and release the left mouse button
Double-clicking	Press and release the left mouse button twice quickly
Dragging	Point to an item, press and hold the left mouse button, move the mouse to a new location, then release the mouse button
Right-clicking	Point to an item, then press and release the right mouse button

Starting a Program

Clicking the Start button on the taskbar opens the **Start menu**, which lists submenus for a variety of tasks described in Table A-4. As you become familiar with Windows, you might want to customize the Start menu to include additional items that you use most often. Windows XP comes with several built-in programs, called **accessories**. Although not as feature-rich as many programs sold separately, Windows accessories are useful for completing basic tasks. In this lesson, you start a Windows accessory called **WordPad**, which is a word-processing program you can use to create and edit simple documents.

STEPS

1. **Click the** Start button **on the taskbar**

   The Start menu opens.

2. **Point to** All Programs

   The All Programs submenu opens, listing the programs and categories for programs installed on your computer. WordPad is in the category called Accessories.

QUICK TIP
The left side of the Windows XP Start menu lists programs you've used recently, so the next time you want to open WordPad, most likely it will be handy in this list of recently opened programs.

3. **Point to** Accessories

   The Accessories menu, shown in Figure A-4, contains several programs to help you complete common tasks. You want to start WordPad.

4. **Click** WordPad

   WordPad starts and opens a blank document window, as shown in Figure A-5. Don't worry if your window does not fill the screen; you'll learn how to maximize it in the next lesson. Note that a program button appears on the taskbar and is highlighted, indicating that WordPad is open.

TABLE A–4: Start menu categories

category	description
Default	Displays the name of the current user; different users can customize the Start menu to fit their work habits
Internet Explorer / Outlook Express	The two programs many people use for a browser and e-mail program; you can add programs you use often to this list (called the "pinned items list")
Frequently used programs list	Located below Internet Explorer and Outlook Express, contains the last six programs used on your computer; you can change the number listed
All Programs	Displays a menu of most programs installed on your computer
My Documents, etc.	The five items in this list allow you to quickly access files you've saved in the three folders listed (My Documents, My Pictures, and My Music), as well as access My Computer, which you use to manage files, folders, and drives on your computer; the My Recent Documents list contains the last 15 files that have been opened on your computer
Control Panel / Connect To / Printers and Faxes	Control Panel displays tools for selecting settings on your computer; Connect To lists Internet connections that have been set up on your computer; and Printers and Faxes lists the printers and faxes connected to your computer
Help and Support / Search / Run	Help and Support provides access to Help topics and other support services; Search locates files, folders, computers on your network, and Web pages on the Internet; Run opens a program, file, or Web site by letting you type commands or names in a dialog box
Log Off / Turn Off Computer	End your Windows session; used when you are done using the computer and don't expect to use it again soon

FIGURE A-4: Cascading menus

Arrow indicates
submenu

Click to open
WordPad

Submenu

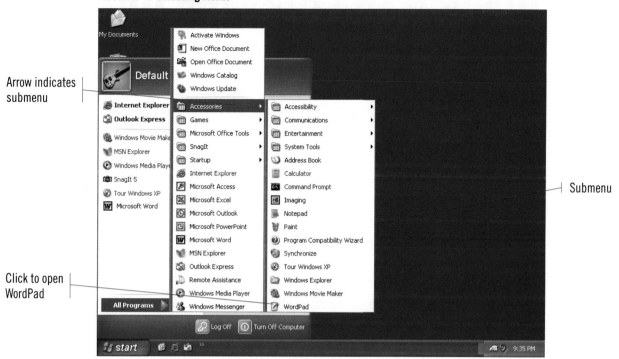

FIGURE A-5: WordPad program window

Document
window

Program button
indicates open
program

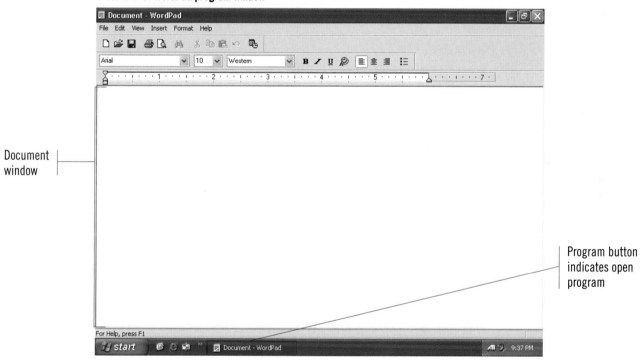

Clues to Use

Customizing the Start Menu

With Windows XP, you can change the way the Start menu looks and behaves by opening the Control Panel (click the Start button and then click Control Panel), switching to Classic view, if necessary, then double-clicking Taskbar and Start Menu. To get the look and feel of the classic Start menu from earlier versions of Windows, click the Start Menu tab and then click the Classic Start menu option

button. You can then click the Customize button to add shortcuts to the Start menu for desired programs and documents, or change the order in which they appear. To preserve the Windows XP look of the Start menu but modify how it behaves, click the Customize button next to the Start menu and select the options you want.

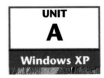

Moving and Resizing Windows

One of the powerful features of Windows is the ability to open more than one window or program at once. This means, however, that the desktop can get cluttered with the various programs and files you are using. You can keep your desktop organized by changing the size of a window or moving it. You can do this by clicking the sizing buttons in the upper-right corner of any window or by dragging a corner or border of any window that does not completely fill the screen. ▚▚▚▚ Practice sizing and moving the WordPad window now.

STEPS

1. **If the WordPad window does not already fill the screen, click the** Maximize button ◻ **in the WordPad window**
   When a window is **maximized**, it takes up the whole screen.

2. **Click the** Restore button ▣ **in the WordPad window**
   To **restore** a window is to return it to its previous size, as shown in Figure A-6. The Restore button only appears when a window is maximized.

3. **Position the pointer on the right edge of the WordPad window until the pointer changes to ↔, then drag the border to the right**
   The width of the window increases. You can change the height or width of a window by dragging any of the four sides.

> **QUICK TIP**
> You can resize windows by dragging any corner. You can also drag any border to make the window taller, shorter, wider, or narrower.

4. **Position the pointer in the lower-right corner of the WordPad window until the pointer changes to ↖, as shown in Figure A-6, then drag down and to the right**
   The height and width of the window increase proportionally when you drag a corner instead of a side. You can also position a restored window wherever you want on the desktop by dragging its title bar. The **title bar** is the area along the top of the window that displays the filename and program used to create it.

5. **Drag the** title bar **on the WordPad window up and to the left, as shown in Figure A-6**
   The window is repositioned on the desktop. At times, you might want to close a program window, yet keep the program running and easily accessible. You can accomplish this by minimizing a window.

> **QUICK TIP**
> If you have more than one window open and you want to quickly access something on the desktop, you can click the Show Desktop button 🗗 on the Quick Launch toolbar. All open windows are minimized so the desktop is visible. If your Quick Launch toolbar isn't visible, right-click the taskbar, point to Toolbars, and then click Quick Launch.

6. **In the WordPad window, click the** Minimize button ▬
   When you **minimize** a window, it shrinks to a program button on the taskbar, as shown in Figure A-7. WordPad is still running, but it is out of your way.

7. **Click the** WordPad program button **on the taskbar to reopen the window**
   The WordPad program window reopens.

8. **Click the** Maximize button ◻ **in the upper-right corner of the WordPad window**
   The window fills the screen.

FIGURE A-6: Restored program window

Title bar

Sizing buttons

Drag to
resize height
and width
proportionally

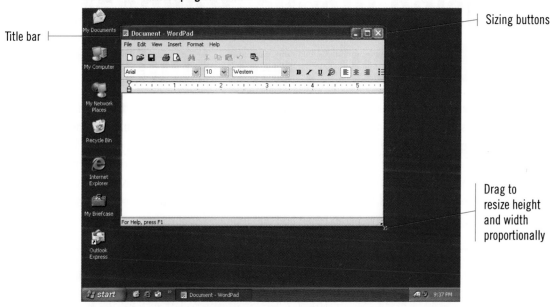

FIGURE A-7: Minimized program window

Indicates
program is
running but
not in use

Clues to Use

More about sizing windows

Keep in mind that some programs contain two sets of sizing buttons: one that controls the program window itself and another that controls the window for the file with which you are working. The program sizing buttons are located in the title bar and the file sizing buttons are located below them. See Figure A-8. When you minimize a file window within a program, the file window is reduced to an icon in the lower-left corner of the program window, but the size of the program window remains intact. (*Note:* WordPad does not use a second set of window sizing buttons.)

Also, to see the contents of more than one window at a time, you can open the desired windows, right-click a blank area on the taskbar, and then click either Tile Windows Vertically or Tile Windows

Horizontally. With the former, you see the windows side by side, and with the latter, the windows are stacked one above the other. You can also click Cascade Windows to layer any open windows in the upper-left corner of the desktop, with the title bar of each clearly visible.

FIGURE A-8: Program and file sizing buttons

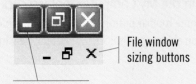

File window
sizing buttons

Program window
sizing buttons

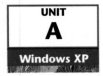
Using Menus, Keyboard Shortcuts, and Toolbars

A **menu** is a list of commands that you use to accomplish certain tasks. Each Windows program also has its own set of menus, which are located on the **menu bar** under the title bar. The menus organize commands into groups of related tasks. See Table A-5 for a description of items on a typical menu. **Toolbar buttons** offer another method for executing menu commands; instead of clicking the menu and then the menu command, you click the button for the command. A **toolbar** is a set of buttons usually positioned below the menu bar. ▰▰▰ You will open My Computer, use a menu and toolbar button to change how the contents of the window appear, and then add and remove a toolbar button.

STEPS

1. **Minimize WordPad, if necessary, then double-click the My Computer icon ▨ on the desktop**

   The My Computer window opens. You now have two windows open: WordPad and My Computer. My Computer is the **active window** (or active program) because it is the one with which you are currently working. WordPad is **inactive** because it is open but you are not working with it.

   > **TROUBLE**
   > If you don't see the My Computer icon on your desktop, right-click the desktop, click Properties, click the Desktop tab, click the Customize Desktop button, click the My Computer check box, then click OK twice.

2. **Click View on the menu bar**

   The View menu appears, listing the View commands, as shown in Figure A-9. On a menu, a **check mark** identifies a feature that is currently enabled or "on." To disable or turn "off" the feature, you click the command again to remove the check mark. A **bullet mark** can also indicate that an option is enabled.

3. **Click List**

   The icons are now listed one after the other rather than as larger icons.

4. **Press [Alt][V] to open the View menu, then press [T] to open the Toolbars submenu**

   The View menu appears again, and then the Toolbars submenu appears, with check marks next to the selected commands. Notice that a letter in each command on the View menu is underlined. These are **keyboard navigation indicators**, indicating that you can press the underlined letter, known as a **keyboard shortcut**, instead of clicking to execute the command.

   > **TROUBLE**
   > [Alt][V] means that you should press and hold down the Alt key, press the V key, and then release both simultaneously.

5. **Press [C] to execute the Customize command**

   The Customize Toolbar dialog box opens. A **dialog box** is a window in which you specify how you want to perform a task; you'll learn more about working in a dialog box shortly. In the Customize Toolbar dialog box, you can add toolbar buttons to the current toolbar, or remove buttons already on the toolbar. The list on the right shows which buttons are currently on the toolbar, and the list on the left shows which buttons are available to add.

6. **Click the Home button in the Available toolbar buttons section, then click the Add button (located between the two lists)**

   As shown in Figure A-10, the Home button is added to the Standard toolbar.

7. **Click the Home button in the Current toolbar buttons section, click the Remove button, then click Close on the Customize Toolbar dialog box**

   The Home button disappears from the Standard toolbar, and the Customize Toolbar dialog box closes.

8. **On the My Computer toolbar, click the Views button list arrow ▦▾, then click Details**

   Some toolbar buttons have an arrow, which indicates the button contains several choices. Clicking the button shows the choices. The Details view includes a description of each item in the My Computer window.

   > **QUICK TIP**
   > When you rest the pointer over a button without clicking, a ScreenTip often appears with the button's name.

FIGURE A-9: Opening a menu

Menu bar

Check mark

Bullet

Commands
in View
menu

Arrow
indicates
submenu

FIGURE A-10: Customize Toolbar dialog box

Buttons
you can
add to the
toolbar

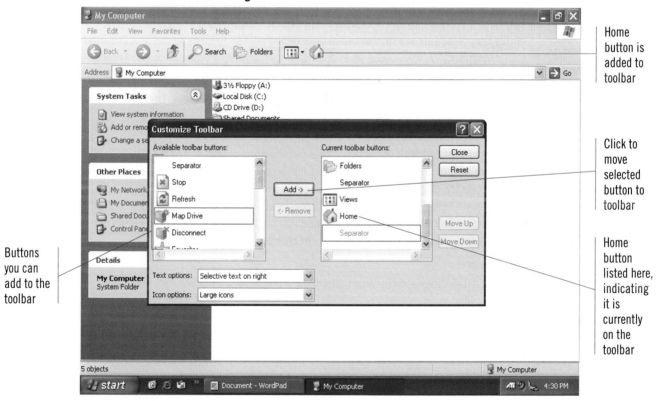

Home
button is
added to
toolbar

Click to
move
selected
button to
toolbar

Home
button
listed here,
indicating
it is
currently
on the
toolbar

TABLE A-5: Typical items on a menu

item	description	example
Dimmed command	Indicates the menu command is not currently available	Recent File
Ellipsis	Indicates that a dialog box will open that allows you to select additional options	Save As...
Triangle	Opens a cascading menu containing an additional list of commands	Toolbars ▶
Keyboard shortcut	Executes a command using the keyboard instead of the mouse	Print... Ctrl+P
Underlined letter	Indicates the letter to press for the keyboard shortcut	Exit

Using Dialog Boxes

A **dialog box** is a window that opens when you choose a menu command that needs more information before the program can carry out the command you selected. Dialog boxes open in other situations as well, such as when you open a program in the Control Panel. See Figure A-11 and Table A-6 for some of the typical elements of a dialog box. 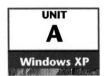 Practice using a dialog box to control your mouse settings.

STEPS

1. **In the left side of the My Computer window, click Control Panel; in the Control Panel window, click Printers and Other Hardware, then click the Mouse icon** 🖱

   The Mouse Properties dialog box opens, as shown in Figure A-12. **Properties** are characteristics of a computer element (in this case, the mouse) that you can customize. The options in this dialog box allow you to control the way the mouse buttons are configured, select the types of pointers that appear, choose the speed and behavior of the mouse movement on the screen, and specify what type of mouse you are using. **Tabs** at the top of the dialog box separate these options into related categories.

2. **Click the Pointer Options tab if necessary to make it the frontmost tab**

   This tab contains three options for controlling the way your mouse moves. Under Motion, you can set how fast the pointer moves on the screen in relation to how you move the mouse. You drag a **slider** to specify how fast the pointer moves. Under Snap To is a **check box**, which is a toggle for turning a feature on or off—in this case, for setting whether you want your mouse pointer to move to the default button in dialog boxes. Under Visibility, you can choose three options for easily finding your cursor and keeping it out of the way when you're typing.

3. **Under Motion, drag the slider all the way to the left for Slow, then move the mouse pointer across your screen**

   Notice how slowly the mouse pointer moves. After you select the options you want in a dialog box, you need to click a **command button**, which carries out the options you've selected. The two most common command buttons are OK and Cancel. Clicking OK accepts your changes and closes the dialog box; clicking Cancel leaves the original settings intact and closes the dialog box. The third command button in this dialog box is Apply. Clicking the Apply button accepts the changes you've made and keeps the dialog box open so that you can select additional options. Because you might share this computer with others, you should close the dialog box without making any permanent changes.

4. **Click Cancel**

   The original settings remain intact, the dialog box closes, and you return to the Printers and Other Hardware window.

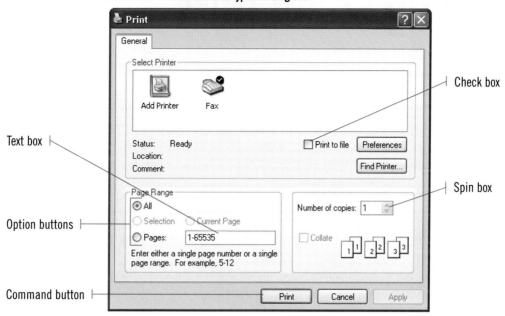
FIGURE A-11: Elements of a typical dialog box

Check box

Text box

Spin box

Option buttons

Command button

FIGURE A-12: Mouse Properties dialog box

Tabs

Slider

TABLE A-6: Typical items in a dialog box

item	description
Tab	A place in a dialog box that organizes related commands and options
Check box	A box that turns an option on (when the box is checked) and off (when it is unchecked)
Command button	A rectangular button with the name of the command on it
List box	A box containing a list of items; to choose an item, click the list arrow, then click the desired item
Option button	A small circle that you click to select a single dialog box option; you cannot select more than one option button in a list
Text box	A box in which you type text
Slider	A shape that you drag to set the degree to which an option is in effect
Spin box	A box with two arrows and a text box; allows you to scroll in numerical increments or type a number

UNIT
A
Windows XP

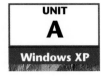

Using Scroll Bars

When you cannot see all of the items available in a window, scroll bars appear on the right and/or bottom edges of the window. **Scroll bars** are the vertical and horizontal bars along the right and bottom edges of a window and contain elements that you click and drag so you can view the additional contents of the window. When you need to scroll only a short distance, you can use the scroll arrows. To scroll the window in larger increments, click in the scroll bar above or below the scroll box. Dragging the scroll box moves you quickly to a new part of the window. See Table A-7 for a summary of the different ways to use scroll bars. With the Control Panel window in Details view, you can use the scroll bars to view all of the items in this window.

STEPS

TROUBLE
Your window might be called Printers and Faxes or something similar, and the Printing link may appear as Troubleshoot printing, but you should still be able to complete the steps.

TROUBLE
If you don't see scroll bars, drag the lower-right corner of the Help and Support Center window up and to the left until scroll bars appear.

1. **In the left side of the Printers and Other Hardware window, under Troubleshooters, click Printing**
   The Help and Support Center window opens, which you'll work with further in the next lesson. For now, you'll use the window to practice using the scroll bars.

2. **If the Help and Support Center window fills the screen, click the Restore button in the upper-right corner so the scroll bars appear, as shown in Figure A-13**

3. **Click the down scroll arrow, as shown in Figure A-13**
   Clicking this arrow moves the view down one line.

4. **Click the up scroll arrow in the vertical scroll bar**
   Clicking this arrow moves the view up one line.

5. **Click anywhere in the area below the scroll box in the vertical scroll bar**
   The view moves down one window's height. Similarly, you can click in the scroll bar above the scroll box to move up one window's height. The size of the scroll box changes to reflect how much information does not fit in the window. A larger scroll box indicates that a relatively small amount of the window's contents is not currently visible; you need to scroll only a short distance to see the remaining items. A smaller scroll box indicates that a relatively large amount of information is currently not visible.

6. **Drag the scroll box all the way up to the top of the vertical scroll bar**
   This view shows the items that appear at the top of the window.

7. **In the horizontal scroll bar, click the area to the right of the scroll box**
   The far right edge of the window comes into view. The horizontal scroll bar works the same as the vertical scroll bar.

8. **Click the area to the left of the scroll box in the horizontal scroll bar**

9. **Click the Close button to close the Help and Support Center window**
   You'll reopen the Help and Support Center window from the Start menu in the next lesson.

FIGURE A-13: Scroll bars

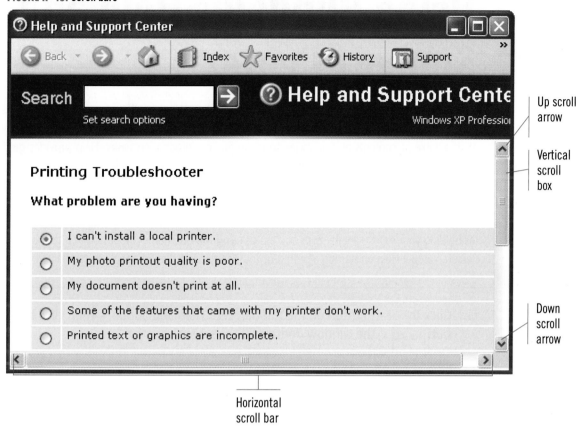

Up scroll arrow

Vertical scroll box

Down scroll arrow

Horizontal scroll bar

TABLE A-7: Using scroll bars

to	do this
Move down one line	Click the down arrow at the bottom of the vertical scroll bar
Move up one line	Click the up arrow at the top of the vertical scroll bar
Move down one window height	Click in the area below the scroll box in the vertical scroll bar
Move up one window height	Click in the area above the scroll box in the vertical scroll bar
Move up a large distance in the window	Drag the scroll box up in the vertical scroll bar
Move down a large distance in the window	Drag the scroll box down in the vertical scroll bar
Move a short distance side-to-side in a window	Click the left or right arrows in the horizontal scroll bar
Move to the right one window width	Click in the area to the right of the scroll box in the horizontal scroll bar
Move to the left one window width	Click in the area to the left of the scroll box in the horizontal scroll bar
Move left or right a large distance in the window	Drag the scroll box in the horizontal scroll bar

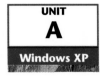

Using Windows Help and Support Center

When you have a question about how to do something in Windows XP, you can usually find the answer with a few clicks of your mouse. The Windows Help and Support Center works like a book stored on your computer, with a table of contents and an index to make finding information easier. Help provides guidance on many Windows features, including detailed steps for completing procedures, definitions of terms, lists of related topics, and search capabilities. You can browse or search for information in the Help and Support Center window, or you can connect to a Microsoft Web site on the Internet for the latest technical support on Windows XP. You can also access **context-sensitive help**, help specifically related to what you are doing, using a variety of methods such as holding your mouse pointer over an item or using the question mark button in a dialog box. In this lesson, you get Help on starting a program. You also get information about the taskbar.

STEPS

1. **Click the Start button on the taskbar, click Help and Support, then click the Maximize button if the window doesn't fill the screen**

    The Help and Support Center window opens, as shown in Figure A-14. This window has a toolbar at the top of the window, a Search box below where you enter keywords having to do with your question, a left pane where the items matching your keywords are listed, and a right pane where the specific steps for a given item are listed.

    QUICK TIP
    Scroll down the left pane, if necessary, to view all the topics. You can also click Full-text Search Matches to view more topics containing the search text you typed or Microsoft Knowledge Base for relevant articles from the Microsoft Web site.

2. **Click in the Search text box, type start a program, press [Enter], then view the Help topics displayed in the left pane**

    The left pane contains a selection of topics related to starting a program. The Suggested Topics are the most likely matches for your search text.

3. **Click Start a program**

    Help information for this topic appears in the right pane, as shown in Figure A-15. At the bottom of the text in the right pane, you can click Related Topics to view a list of topics that are related to the current topic. Some Help topics also allow you to view additional information about important words; these words are underlined, indicating that you can click them to display a pop-up window with the additional information.

4. **Click the underlined word taskbar, read the definition, then click anywhere outside the pop-up window to close it**

5. **On the toolbar at the top of the window, click the Index button**

    The Index provides an alphabetical list of all the available Help topics, like an index at the end of a book. You can type a topic in the text box at the top of the pane. You can also scroll down to the topic. In either case, you click the topic you're interested in and the details about that topic appear in the right pane.

    QUICK TIP
    You can click the Favorites button to view a list of Help pages that you've saved as you search for answers to your questions. You can click the History button to view a list of Help pages that you've viewed during the current Help session.

6. **In the left pane, type tiling windows**

    As you type, the list of topics automatically scrolls to try to match the word or phrase you type.

7. **Double-click tiling windows in the list in the left pane and read the steps and notes in the right pane**

    You can also click the Related Topics link for more information.

8. **Click the Support button on the toolbar**

    Information on the Web sites for Windows XP Help appears in the right pane (a **Web site** is a document or related documents that contain highlighted words, phrases, and graphics that link to other sites on the Internet). To access online support or information, you would click one of the available options in the left pane.

9. **Click the Close button in the upper-right corner of the Help and Support Center window**

    The Help and Support Center window closes.

FIGURE A-14: Windows Help and Support Center

Help toolbar

Type keyword
or phrase
to search
for topics

Links for
popular
Help topics

FIGURE A-15: Viewing a Help topic

Type search
text here

Left pane
contains
list of
Help topics
matching
your search
text

Click this
topic

Right pane
contains
information
on the topic
you select

Clues to Use

Other forms of Help

The Help and Support Center offers information on Windows itself, not on all the other programs you can run on your computer. To get help on a specific Windows program, click Help on that program's menu bar. Also, to receive help in a dialog box (whether you are in Windows or another program), click the Help button ⬚ in the upper-right corner of the dialog box; the mouse pointer changes to ⬚. Click any item in the dialog box that you want to learn more about. If information is available on that item, a pop-up window appears with a brief explanation of the selected feature.

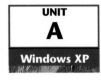

UNIT
A
Windows XP

Closing a Program and Shutting Down Windows

When you are finished working on your computer, you need to make sure you shut it down properly. This involves several steps: saving and closing all open files, closing all the open programs and windows, shutting down Windows, and finally, turning off the computer. If you turn off the computer while Windows is running, you could lose important data. To **close** a program, you can click the Close button in the window's upper-right corner or click File on the menu bar and choose either Close or Exit. To shut down Windows after all your files and programs are closed, click Turn Off Computer on the Start menu, then select the desired option in the Turn off computer dialog box, shown in Figure A-16. See Table A-8 for a description of shut down options. ▰▰▰▰▰ Close all your open files, windows, and programs, then exit Windows.

STEPS

1. **In the Control Panel window, click the** Close button ☒ **in the upper-right corner of the window**

    The Control Panel window closes.

2. **Click** File **on the WordPad menu bar, then click** Exit

    If you have made any changes to the open file, you will be asked to save your changes before the program closes. Some programs also give you the option of choosing the Close command on the File menu in order to close the active file but leave the program open, so you can continue to work in it with a different file. Also, if there is a second set of sizing buttons in the window, the Close button on the menu bar will close the active file only, leaving the program open for continued use.

3. **If you see a message asking you to save changes to the document, click** No

    WordPad closes and you return to the desktop.

QUICK TIP
Complete the remaining steps to shut down Windows and your computer only if you have been told to do so by your instructor or technical support person. If you have been told to Log Off instead of exiting Windows, click Log Off instead of Turn Off Computer, and follow the directions from your instructor or technical support person.

4. **Click the** Start button **on the taskbar, then click** Turn Off Computer

    The Turn off computer dialog box opens, as shown in Figure A-16. In this dialog box, you have the option to stand by, turn off the computer, or restart the computer.

5. **If you are working in a lab, click** Cancel **to leave the computer running; if you are working on your own machine or if your instructor told you to shut down Windows, click** Turn Off, **then click** OK

6. **If you see the message "It is now safe to turn off your computer," turn off your computer and monitor**

    On some computers, the power shuts off automatically, so you may not see this message.

FIGURE A-16: Turn off computer dialog box

Click to leave Windows running but reduce computer's power mode

Click to exit Windows safely and turn off your computer

Click to exit Windows and automatically restart it

Click to return to the desktop without taking any action

Clues to Use

The Log Off command

To change users on the same computer quickly, you can choose the Log Off command from the Start menu. When you click this command, you can choose to switch users, so that the current user is logged off and another user can log on, or you can simply log off. Windows XP shuts down partially, stopping at the point where you click your user name. When you or a new user clicks a user name (and enters a password, if necessary), Windows restarts and the desktop appears as usual.

TABLE A-8: Turn off options

Turn off option	function	when to use it
Stand By	Leaves Windows running but on minimal power	When you are finished working with Windows for a short time and plan to return before the end of the day
Turn Off	Exits Windows completely and safely	When you are finished working with Windows and want to shut off your computer for an extended time (such as overnight or longer)
Restart	Exits Windows safely, turns off the computer automatically, and then restarts the computer and Windows	When your programs might have frozen or stopped working correctly

Practice

▼ CONCEPTS REVIEW

Identify each of the items labeled in Figure A-17.

FIGURE A-17

Match each of the statements with the term it describes.

14. Shrinks a window to a button on the taskbar
15. Shows the name of the window or program
16. The taskbar item you first click to start a program
17. Requests more information for you to supply before carrying out command
18. Shows the Start button, Quick Launch toolbar, and any currently open programs
19. An input device that lets you point to and make selections
20. Graphic representation of program

a. dialog box
b. program button
c. taskbar
d. Minimize button
e. icon
f. mouse
g. Start button

Select the best answer from the list of choices.

21. The term "file" is best defined as

   a. a set of instructions for a computer to carry out a task.   **c.** a collection of icons.

   b. an electronic collection of data.   **d.** an international collection of computers.

22. Which of the following is NOT provided by Windows XP?

   a. The ability to organize files

   b. Instructions to coordinate the flow of information among the programs, files, printers, storage devices, and other components of your computer system

   c. Programs that allow you to specify the operation of the mouse

   d. Spell checker for your documents

23. All of the following are examples of using a mouse, EXCEPT

   a. clicking the Maximize button.   **c.** double-clicking to start a program.

   b. pressing [Enter].   **d.** dragging the My Computer icon.

24. The term for moving an item to a new location on the desktop is

   a. pointing.   **c.** dragging.

   b. clicking.   **d.** restoring.

25. The Maximize button is used to

   a. return a window to its previous size.   **c.** scroll slowly through a window.

   b. expand a window to fill the computer screen.   **d.** run programs from the Start menu.

26. What appears if a window contains more information than can be viewed in the window?

   a. Program icon   **c.** Scroll bars

   b. Cascading menu   **d.** Check boxes

27. A window is active when

   a. you can only see its program button on the taskbar.   **c.** it is open and you are currently using it.

   b. its title bar is dimmed.   **d.** it is listed in the Programs submenu.

28. You can exit Windows by

   a. double-clicking the Control Panel application.

   b. double-clicking the Program Manager control menu box.

   c. clicking File, then clicking Exit.

   d. selecting the Turn Off Computer command from the Start menu.

▼ SKILLS REVIEW

1. Start Windows and view the desktop.

   a. Turn on the computer, select your user name, then enter a password, if necessary.

   b. After Windows starts, identify as many items on the desktop as you can, without referring to the lesson material.

   c. Compare your results to Figure A-1.

2. Use the mouse.

   a. Double-click the Recycle Bin icon, then click the Restore button if the window fills the screen.

   b. Drag the Recycle Bin window to the upper-right corner of the desktop.

   c. Right-click the title bar of the Recycle Bin, then click Close.

3. Start a program.

   a. Click the Start button on the taskbar, then point to All Programs.

   b. Point to Accessories, then click Calculator.

   c. Minimize the Calculator window.

4. Move and resize windows.

   a. Drag the Recycle Bin icon to the top of the desktop.

   b. Double-click the My Computer icon to open the My Computer window (if you don't see the My Computer icon, read the Trouble in the lesson on menus and toolbars for how to display it).

   c. Maximize the My Computer window, if it is not already maximized.

    d. Restore the window to its previous size.

    e. Resize the window until you see the vertical scroll bar.

    f. Minimize the My Computer window.

    g. Drag the Recycle Bin icon back to its original position.

5. Use menus, keyboard shortcuts, and toolbars.

    a. Click the Start button on the taskbar, then click Control Panel.

    b. Click View on the menu bar, point to Toolbars, then click Standard Buttons to deselect the option and hide the toolbar.

    c. Redisplay the toolbar.

    d. Press [Alt][V] to display the View menu, then press [B] to hide the status bar at the bottom of the window.

    e. Note the change, then use keyboard shortcuts to change the view back.

    f. Click the Up button to view My Computer.

    g. Click the Back button to return to the Control Panel.

    h. Click View, point to Toolbars, then click Customize.

    i. Add a button to the toolbar, remove it, then close the Customize Toolbar dialog box.

6. Use dialog boxes.

    a. With the Control Panel in Category view, click Appearance and Themes, click Display, then click the Screen Saver tab.

    b. Click the Screen saver list arrow, click any screen saver in the list, then view it in the preview monitor above the list.

    c. Click the Appearance tab in the Display Properties dialog box, then click the Effects button.

    d. In the Effects dialog box, click the Use large icons check box to select it, click the OK button to close the Effects dialog box, then click OK to close the Display Properties dialog box.

    e. Note the change in the icons on the desktop, minimizing windows if necessary.

    f. Right-click a blank area on the desktop, click Properties on the shortcut menu, click the Appearance tab, click the Effects button, click the Use large icons check box to deselect it, click OK, click the Screen Saver tab, return the screen saver to its original setting, then click Apply.

    g. Click the OK button in the Display Properties dialog box, but leave the Control Panel open and make it the active program.

7. Use scroll bars.

    a. In the left side of the Control Panel window, click Switch to Classic View, if necessary, click the Views button on the toolbar, then click Details.

    b. Drag the vertical scroll box down all the way.

    c. Click anywhere in the area above the vertical scroll box.

    d. Click the down scroll arrow until the scroll box is back at the bottom of the scroll bar.

    e. Click the right scroll arrow twice.

    f. Click in the area to the right of the horizontal scroll box.

    g. Drag the horizontal scroll box all the way back to the left.

8. Get Help.

    a. Click the Start button on the taskbar, then click Help and Support.

    b. Click Windows basics under Pick a Help topic, then click Tips for using Help in the left pane.

    c. In the right pane, click Add a Help topic or page to the Help and Support Center Favorites list.

    d. Read the topic contents, click Related Topics, click Print a Help topic or page, then read the contents. Leave the Help and Support Center open.

9. Close a program and shut down Windows.

    a. Click the Close button to close the Help and Support Center window.

    b. Click File on the menu bar, then click Close to close the Control Panel window.

    c. Click the Calculator program button on the taskbar to restore the window.

    d. Click the Close button in the Calculator window to close the Calculator program.

    e. If you are instructed to do so, shut down Windows and turn off your computer.

▼ INDEPENDENT CHALLENGE 1

You can use the Help and Support Center to learn more about Windows XP and explore Help on the Internet.

a. Open the Help and Support Center window and locate help topics on adjusting the double-click speed of your mouse and displaying Web content on your desktop.

If you have a printer, print a Help topic for each subject. Otherwise, write a summary of each topic.

b. Follow these steps below to access help on the Internet. If you don't have Internet access, you can't do this step.

   i.   Click a link under "Did you know?" in the right pane of the Help and Support Home page.

   ii. In the left pane of the Microsoft Web page, click Using Windows XP, click How-to Articles, then click any link.

   iii. Read the article, then write a summary of what you find.

   iv. Click the browser's Close button, disconnect from the Internet, and close Help and Support Center.

▼ INDEPENDENT CHALLENGE 2

You can change the format and the actual time of the clock and date on your computer.

a. Open the Control Panel window; in Category view, click Date, Time, Language, and Regional Options; click Regional and Language Options; then click the Customize button under Standards and formats.

b. Click the Time tab, click the Time format list arrow, click H:mm:ss to change the time to show a 24-hour clock, then click the Apply button to view the changes, if any.

c. Click the Date tab, click the Short date format list arrow, click dd-MMM-yy, then click the Apply button.

d. Click the Cancel button twice to close the open dialog boxes.

e. Change the time to one hour later using the Date and Time icon in the Control Panel.

f. Return the settings to the original time and format, then close all open windows.

▼ INDEPENDENT CHALLENGE 3

Calculator is a Windows accessory that you can use to perform calculations.

a. Start the Calculator, click Help on the menu bar, then click Help Topics.

b. Click the Calculator book in the left pane, click Perform a simple calculation to view that help topic, then print it if you have a printer connected.

c. Open the Perform a scientific calculation topic, then view the definition of a number system.

d. Determine how many months you have to work to earn an additional week of vacation if you work for a company that provides one additional day of paid vacation for every 560 hours you work. (*Hint:* Divide 560 by the number of hours you work per month.)

e. Close all open windows.

▼ INDEPENDENT CHALLENGE 4

You can customize many Windows features, including the appearance of the taskbar on the desktop.

a. Right-click the taskbar, then click Lock the Taskbar to uncheck the command, if necessary.

b. Position the pointer over the top border of the taskbar. When the pointer changes shape, drag up an inch.

c. Resize the taskbar back to its original size.

d. Right-click the Start button, then click Properties. Click the Taskbar tab.

e. Click the Help button (a question mark), then click each check box to view the pop-up window describing it.

f. Click the Start Menu tab, then click the Classic Start menu option button and view the change in the preview. (*Note:* Do not click OK.) Click Cancel.

▼ VISUAL WORKSHOP

Use the skills you have learned in this unit to customize your desktop so it looks like the one in Figure A-18. Make sure you include the following:

- Calculator program minimized
- Vertical scroll bar in Control Panel window
- Large icons view in Control Panel window
- Rearranged icons on desktop; your icons may be different. (*Hint*: If the icons snap back to where they were, they are set to be automatically arranged. Right-click a blank area of the desktop, point to Arrange Icons By, then click Auto Arrange to deselect this option.)

Use the Print Screen key to make a copy of the screen, then print it from the Paint program. (To print from the Paint program, click the Start button on the taskbar, point to All Programs, point to Accessories, then click Paint; in the Paint program window, click Edit on the menu bar, then click Paste; click Yes to fit the image on the bitmap, click the Print button on the toolbar, then click Print in the Print dialog box. See your instructor or technical support person for assistance.)

When you have completed this exercise, be sure to return your settings and desktop back to their original arrangement.

FIGURE A-18

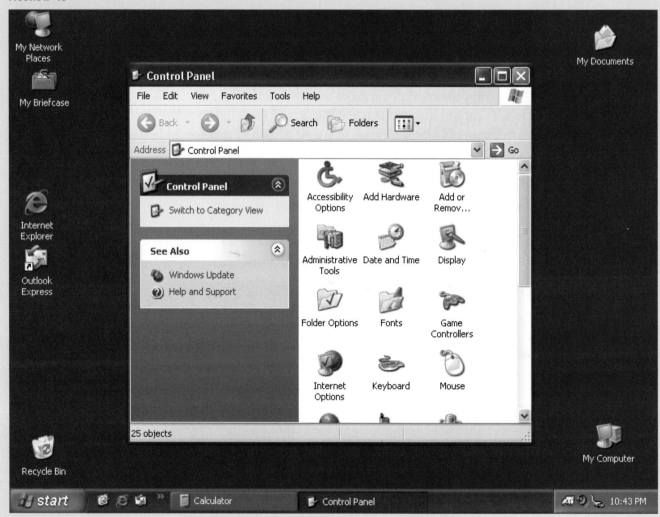

Working with Programs, Files, and Folders

OBJECTIVES

Create and save a WordPad document
Open, edit, and save an existing Paint file
Work with multiple programs
Understand file management
View files and create folders with My Computer
Move and copy files with My Computer
Manage files with Windows Explorer
Search for files
Delete and restore files

If you have a SAM user profile, you may have access to hands-on instruction, practice, and assessment of the skills covered in this unit. Log in to your SAM account and go to your assignments page to see what your instructor has assigned.

Most of your work on a computer involves using programs to create files. For example, you might use WordPad to create a resumé or Microsoft Excel to create a budget. The resumé and the budget are examples of **files**, electronic collections of data that you create and save on a disk. ▇▇▇ In this unit, you learn how to work with files and the programs you use to create them. You create new files, open and edit an existing file, and use the Clipboard to copy and paste data from one file to another. You also explore the file management features of Windows XP, using My Computer and Windows Explorer. Finally, you learn how to work more efficiently by managing files directly on your desktop.

Creating and Saving a WordPad Document

As with most programs, when you start WordPad, a new, blank document opens. To create a new file, such as a memo, you simply begin typing. Your work is automatically stored in your computer's random access memory (RAM) until you turn off your computer, at which point anything stored in the computer's RAM is erased. To store your work permanently, you must save your work as a file on a disk. You can save files either on an internal **hard disk**, which is built into your computer, usually the C: drive, or on a removable 3½" **floppy disk**, which you insert into a drive on your computer, usually the A: or B: drive, or on a **CD-ROM** or **Zip disk**, two other kinds of removable storage devices. (Before you can save a file on a floppy disk, the disk must be formatted; see the Appendix, "Formatting a Floppy Disk.") When you name a file, you can use up to 255 characters, including spaces and punctuation, using either upper- or lowercase letters. ▓▓▒▒ In this lesson, you start WordPad and create a file that contains the text shown in Figure B-1 and save the file to the drive and folder where your Project Files are stored.

STEPS

QUICK TIP

If you make a mistake, press [Backspace] to delete the character to the left of the insertion point.

1. **Click the Start button on the taskbar, point to All Programs, point to Accessories, click WordPad, then click the Maximize button ▣ if the window does not fill your screen**
   The WordPad program window opens. The blinking insertion point indicates where the text you type will appear.

2. **CType Memo, then press [Enter] to move the insertion point to the next line**

3. **Press [Enter] again, then type the remaining text shown in Figure B-1, pressing [Enter] at the end of each line**

4. **Click File on the menu bar, then click Save As**
   The Save As dialog box opens, as shown in Figure B-2. In this dialog box, you specify where you want your file saved and give your document a name.

TROUBLE

This unit assumes that you are using the A: drive for your Project Files. If not, substitute the correct drive when you are instructed to use the 3 1/2 Floppy (A:) drive. See your instructor or technical support person for help.

5. **Click the Save in list arrow, then click 3½ Floppy (A:), or whichever drive contains your Project Files**
   The drive containing your Project Files is now active, meaning that the contents of the drive appear in the Save in dialog box and that the file will now be saved in this drive.

6. **Click in the File name text box, type Memo, then click the Save button**
   Your memo is now saved as a WordPad file with the name "Memo" on your Project Disk. The WordPad title bar contains the name of the file. Now you can **format** the text, which changes its appearance to make it more readable or attractive.

QUICK TIP

You can double-click to select a word or triple-click to select a paragraph.

7. **Click to the left of the word Memo, drag the mouse to the right to highlight the word, then release the mouse button**
   Now the text is highlighted, indicating that it is **selected**. This means that any action you make will be performed on the highlighted text.

8. **Click the Center button ≣ on the Formatting toolbar, then click the Bold button Ⓑ on the Formatting toolbar**
   The text is centered and bold.

9. **Click the Font Size list arrow ⑩▾, click 16 in the list, then click the Save button ⬛**
   A **font** is a set of letters and numbers sharing a particular shape of type. The **font size** is measured in points; one **point** is 1/72 of an inch in height.

FIGURE B-1: Text to enter in WordPad

Press [Enter] three and four times (respectively) to insert blank lines

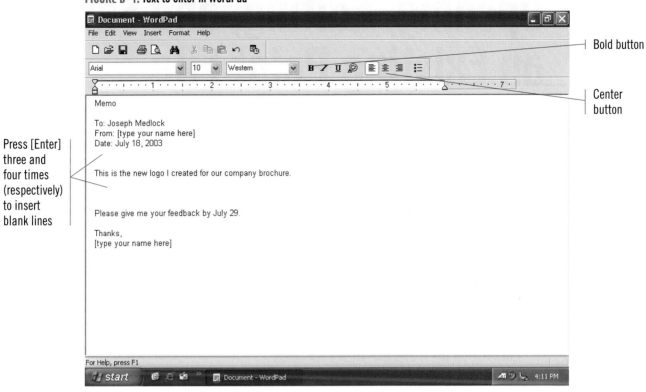

Bold button

Center button

FIGURE B-2: Save As dialog box

Type new filename here

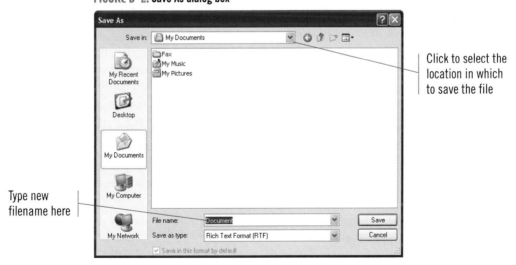

Click to select the location in which to save the file

Opening, Editing, and Saving an Existing Paint File

Sometimes you create files from scratch, as you did in the previous lesson, but often you may want to work with a file you or someone else has already created. To do so, you need to open the file. Once you open a file, you can **edit** it, or make changes to it, such as adding or deleting text or changing the formatting. After editing a file, you can save it with the same filename, which means that you no longer will have the file in its original form, or you can save it with a different filename, so that the original file remains unchanged. ▀▀▀▀▀ In this lesson, you use Paint (a graphics program that comes with Windows XP) to open a file, edit it by changing a color, and then save the file with a new filename to leave the original file unchanged.

STEPS

1. **Click the** Start button **on the taskbar, point to** All Programs, **point to** Accessories, **click** Paint, **then click the** Maximize button ☐ **if the window doesn't fill the screen**

   The Paint program opens with a blank work area. If you wanted to create a file from scratch, you would begin working now. However, you want to open an existing file, located on your Project Disk.

2. **Click** File **on the menu bar, then click** Open

   The Open dialog box works similarly to the Save As dialog box that you used in the previous lesson.

3. **Click the** Look in list arrow, **then click** 3½ Floppy (A:)

   The Paint files on your Project Disk are listed in the Open dialog box, as shown in Figure B-3.

QUICK TIP

You can also open a file by double-clicking it in the Open dialog box.

4. **Click** Win B-1 **in the list of files, and then click the** Open button

   The Open dialog box closes and the file named Win B-1 opens. Before you change this file, you should save it with a new filename, so that the original file is unchanged.

5. **Click** File **on the menu bar, then click** Save As

6. **Make sure** 3½ Floppy (A:) **appears in the Save in text box, select the text** Win B-1 **in the File name text box, type** Logo, **click the** Save as type list arrow, **click** 256 Color Bitmap, **then click the** Save button

   The Logo file appears in the Paint window, as shown in Figure B-4. Because you saved the file with a new name, you can edit it without changing the original file. You saved the file as a 256 Color Bitmap to conserve space on your floppy disk. You will now modify the logo by using buttons in the **Tool Box**, a toolbar of drawing tools, and the **Color Box**, a palette of colors from which you can choose.

7. **Click the** Fill With Color button 🖌 **in the Tool Box, then click the** Light blue color box, **which is the fourth from the right in the bottom row**

   Notice how clicking a button in the Tool Box changes the mouse pointer. Now when you click an area in the image, it will be filled with the color you selected in the Color Box. See Table B-1 for a description of the tools in the Tool Box.

8. **Move the pointer into the white area that represents the sky until the pointer changes to 🖌, then click**

   The sky is now blue.

9. **Click** File **on the menu bar, then click** Save

   The change you made is saved to disk, using the same Logo filename.

FIGURE B-3: Open dialog box

List of files ——

FIGURE B-4: Paint file saved with new filename

Name of file
appears in
title bar

Tool Box —

Sky area to
fill with
light blue

Color Box —

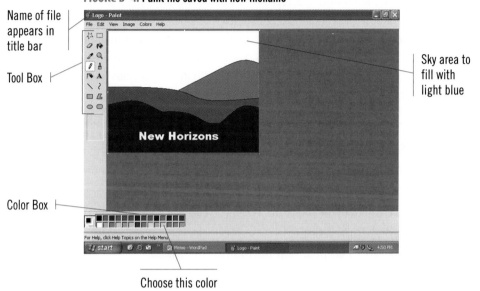

Choose this color

TABLE B-1: Paint Tool Box buttons

tool	description
Free-Form Select button	Selects a free-form section of the picture to move, copy, or edit
Select button	Selects a rectangular section of the picture to move, copy, or edit
Eraser button	Erases a portion of the picture using the selected eraser size and foreground color
Fill With Color button	Fills a closed shape or area with the current drawing color
Pick Color button	Picks up a color from the picture to use for drawing
Magnifier button	Changes the magnification; lists magnifications under the toolbar
Pencil button	Draws a free-form line one pixel wide
Ellipse button	Draws an ellipse with the selected fill style; hold down [Shift] to draw a circle
Brush button	Draws using a brush with the selected shape and size
Airbrush button	Produces a circular spray of dots
Text button	Inserts text into the picture
Line button	Draws a straight line with the selected width and foreground color
Curve button	Draws a wavy line with the selected width and foreground color
Rectangle button	Draws a rectangle with the selected fill style; hold down [Shift] to draw a square
Polygon button	Draws polygons from connected straight-line segments
Rounded Rectangle button	Draws rectangles with rounded corners using the selected fill style; hold down [Shift] to draw a rounded square

Working with Multiple Programs

A powerful feature of Windows is its capability to run more than one program at a time. For example, you might be working with a document in WordPad and want to search the Internet to find the answer to a question. You can start your **browser**, a program designed to access information on the Internet, without closing WordPad. When you find the information, you can leave your browser open and switch back to WordPad. Each open program is represented by a program button on the taskbar that you click to switch between programs. You can also copy data from one file to another (whether or not the files were created with the same Windows program) using the Clipboard, an area of memory on your computer's hard drive, and the Cut, Copy, and Paste commands. See Table B-2 for a description of these commands. In this lesson, you copy the logo graphic you worked with in the previous lesson into the memo you created in WordPad.

STEPS

1. **Click Edit on the menu bar, then click Select All to select the entire picture**
   A dotted rectangle surrounds the picture, indicating it is selected, as shown in Figure B-5.

2. **Click Edit on the menu bar, then click Copy**
   The logo is copied to the Clipboard. When you **copy** an object onto the Clipboard, the object remains in its original location and is also available to be pasted into another location.

QUICK TIP
To switch between programs using the keyboard, press and hold down [Alt], press [Tab] until you select the program you want, then release [Alt].

3. **Click the WordPad program button on the taskbar**
   WordPad becomes the active program.

4. **Click in the first line below the line that ends "for our company brochure."**
   The insertion point indicates where the logo will be pasted.

5. **Click the Paste button 📋 on the WordPad toolbar**
   The contents of the Clipboard, in this case the logo, are pasted into the WordPad file, as shown in Figure B-6.

6. **Click the WordPad Close button; click Yes to save changes**
   Your WordPad document and the WordPad program close. Paint is now the active program.

7. **Click the Paint Close button; if you are prompted to save changes, click Yes**
   Your Paint document and the Paint program close. You return to the desktop.

Clues to Use

Other Programs that Come with Windows XP

WordPad and Paint are just two of many programs that come with Windows XP. From the All Programs menu on the Start menu, you can access everything from games and entertainment programs to powerful communications software and disk maintenance programs without installing anything other than Windows XP. For example, from the Accessories menu, you can open a simple calculator; start Windows Movie Maker to create, edit, and share movie files; and use the Address Book to keep track of your contacts. From the Communications submenu, you can use NetMeeting to set up a voice and/or video conference over the Internet, or use the Remote Desktop Connection to allow another person to access your computer for diagnosing and solving computer problems. Several other menus and submenus display programs and tools that come with Windows XP. You can get a brief description of each by holding your mouse pointer over the name of the program in the menu. You might have to install some of these programs from the Windows CD if they don't appear on the menus.

FIGURE B-5: Selecting the logo to copy and paste into the Memo file

Dotted line
indicates
selected area

FIGURE B-6: Memo with pasted logo

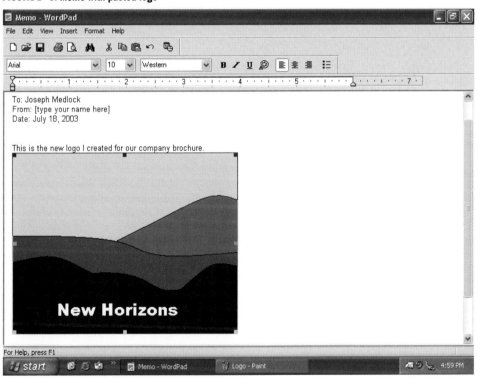

TABLE B-2: Overview of cutting, copying, and pasting

toolbar button	function	keyboard shortcut
✂ Cut	Removes selected information from a file and places it on the Clipboard	[Ctrl][X]
📋 Copy	Places a copy of the selected information on the Clipboard, leaving the file intact	[Ctrl][C]
📋 Paste	Inserts whatever is currently on the Clipboard into another location within the same file or into another file (depending on where you place the insertion point)	[Ctrl][V]

Understanding File Management

After you have created and saved numerous files, the process of organizing and keeping track of all of your files (referred to as **file management**) can be a challenge. Fortunately, Windows provides tools to keep everything organized so you can easily locate the files you need, move files to new locations, and delete files you no longer need. There are two main tools for managing your files: My Computer and Windows Explorer. ◼◼▦ In this lesson, you preview the ways you can use My Computer and Windows Explorer to manage your files.

DETAILS

Windows XP gives you the ability to:

QUICK TIP

To browse My Computer using multiple windows, click Tools on the menu bar, and then click Folder Options. In the Folder Options dialog box, click the General tab, and then under Browse Folders, click the Open each folder in its own window option button. Each time you open a new folder, a new window opens, leaving the previous folder's window open so that you can view both at the same time.

- **Create folders in which you can save and organize your files**

  Folders are areas on a floppy disk (or other removable storage medium) or hard disk that help you organize your files, just as folders in a filing cabinet help you store and organize your papers. For example, you might create a folder for your work documents and another folder for your personal files. Folders can also contain other folders, which creates a more complex structure of folders and files, called a **file hierarchy**. See Figure B-7 for an example of how files can be organized.

- **Examine and organize the hierarchy of files and folders**

  You can use either My Computer or Windows Explorer to see and manipulate the overall structure of your files and folders. By examining your file hierarchy with these tools, you can better organize the contents of your computer and adjust the hierarchy to meet your needs. Figures B-8 and B-9 illustrate how My Computer and Windows Explorer list folders and files.

- **Copy, move, and rename files and folders**

  If you decide that a file belongs in a different folder, you can move it to another folder. You can also rename a file if you decide a different name is more descriptive. If you want to keep a copy of a file in more than one folder, you can copy it to new folders.

- **Delete files and folders you no longer need and restore files you delete accidentally**

  Deleting files and folders you are sure you don't need frees up disk space and keeps your file hierarchy more organized. The **Recycle Bin**, a space on your computer's hard disk that stores deleted files, allows you to restore files you deleted by accident. To free up disk space, you should occasionally check to make sure you don't need the contents of the Recycle Bin and then delete the files permanently from your hard drive.

- **Locate files quickly with the Windows XP Search feature**

  As you create more files and folders, you may forget where you placed a certain file or you may forget what name you used when you saved a file. With Search, you can locate files by providing only partial names or other facts you know about the file, such as the file type (for example, a WordPad document or a Paint graphic) or the date the file was created or modified.

- **Use shortcuts**

  If a file or folder you use often is located several levels down in your file hierarchy (in a folder within a folder, within a folder), it might take you several steps to access it. To save time accessing the files and programs you use frequently, you can create shortcuts to them. A **shortcut** is a link that gives you quick access to a particular file, folder, or program.

FIGURE B-7: Sample file hierarchy

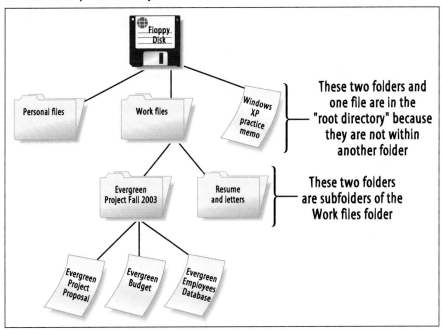

These two folders and one file are in the "root directory" because they are not within another folder

These two folders are subfolders of the Work files folder

FIGURE B-8: Evergreen Project folder shown in My Computer

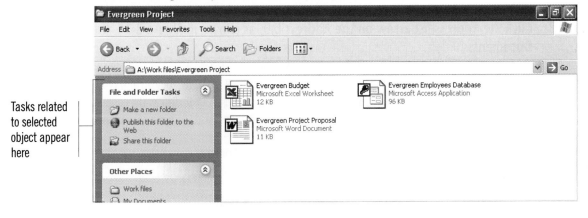

Tasks related to selected object appear here

FIGURE B-9: Evergreen Project folder shown in Windows Explorer

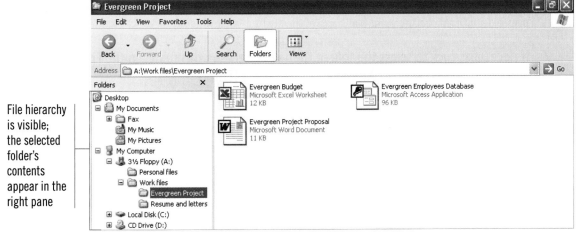

File hierarchy is visible; the selected folder's contents appear in the right pane

Viewing Files and Creating Folders with My Computer

My Computer shows the contents of your computer, including files, folders, programs, disk drives, and printers. You can click the icons to view that object's contents or properties. You use the My Computer Explorer Bar, menu bar, and toolbar to manage your files. See Table B-3 for a description of the toolbar buttons. In this lesson, you use My Computer to look at your computer's file hierarchy, then you create two new folders on your Project Disk.

STEPS

TROUBLE
If you do not see My Computer, click the Start button, and click My Computer. If you do not see the toolbar, click View, point to Toolbars, and click Standard Buttons. If you do not see Address bar, click View, point to Toolbar, and click Address Bar.

1. **Double-click the My Computer icon on your desktop, then click the Maximize button if the My Computer window does not fill the screen**

   My Computer displays the contents of your computer, as shown in Figure B-10. The left pane, called the **Explorer Bar**, displays tasks related to whatever is selected in the right pane.

2. **Make sure your Project Disk is in the floppy disk drive, then double-click the 3½ Floppy (A:) icon**

   The contents of your Project Disk appear in the window. Each file is represented by an icon, which varies in appearance depending on the program that was used to create the file. If Microsoft Word is installed on your computer, the Word icon appears for the WordPad files; if not, the WordPad icon appears.

TROUBLE
If you are in a lab you may not have access to the My Documents folder. See your instructor for assistance.

3. **Click the Address list arrow on the Address bar, as shown in Figure B-10, then click My Documents**

   The window changes to show the contents of the My Documents folder on your computer's hard drive. The Address bar allows you to open and view a drive, folder, or even a Web page. You can also type in the Address bar to go to a different drive, folder, or Web page. For example, typing "C:\" will display the contents of your C: drive, and typing "http://www.microsoft.com" opens Microsoft's Web site if your computer is connected to the Internet.

QUICK TIP
You can click the list arrow next to the Back or Forward buttons to quickly view locations you've viewed recently.

4. **Click the Back button on the Standard Buttons toolbar**

   The Back button displays the previous location, in this case, your Project Disk.

5. **Click the Views button list arrow on the Standard Buttons toolbar, then click Details**

   Details view shows not only the files and folders, but also the sizes of the files, the types of files, folders, or drives and the date the files were last modified.

6. **In the File and Folder Tasks pane, click Make a new folder**

   A new folder called "New Folder" is created on your Project Disk, as shown in Figure B-11. You can also create a new folder by right-clicking in the blank area of the My Computer window, clicking New, then clicking Folder.

QUICK TIP
You can also rename a folder or file by pressing [F2], typing the new name, then pressing [Enter].

7. **If necessary, click to select the folder, then click Rename this folder in the File and Folder Tasks pane; type Windows XP Practice, then press [Enter]**

   Choosing descriptive names for your folders helps you remember their contents.

8. **Double-click the Windows XP Practice folder, repeat Steps 6 and 7 to create a new folder in the Windows XP Practice folder, name the folder Brochure, then press [Enter]**

9. **Click the Up button to return to the root directory of your Project Disk**

FIGURE B-10: My Computer window

Menu bar

Address bar

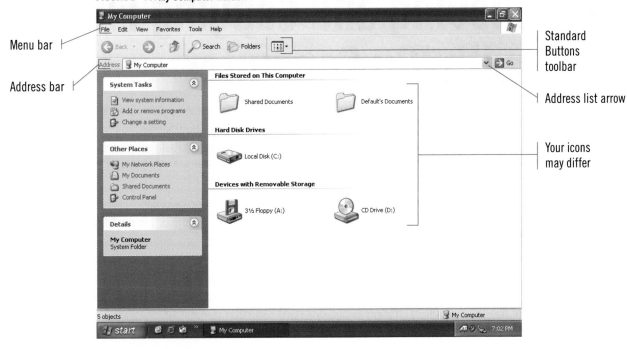

Standard
Buttons
toolbar

Address list arrow

Your icons
may differ

FIGURE B-11: Creating a new folder

Back button

Folder is
located on
the A: drive

You'll rename
the new
folder; yours
might appear
selected

TABLE B-3: Buttons on the Standard Buttons toolbar in My Computer

button	function
Back button	Moves back one location in the list of locations you have recently viewed
Forward button	Moves forward one location in the list of locations you have recently viewed
Up button	Moves up one level in the file hierarchy
Search button	Opens the Search Companion task pane, where you can choose from various options to search for files, computers, Web pages, or people on the Internet
Folders button	Opens the Folders task pane, where you can easily view and manage your computer's file hierarchy
Views button	Lists the contents of My Computer using different views

WORKING WITH PROGRAMS, FILES, AND FOLDERS WINDOWS XP B-11

Moving and Copying Files with My Computer

You can move a file or folder from one location to another using a variety of methods in My Computer. If the file or folder and the location to which you want to move it are both visible, you can simply drag the item from one location to another. You can also use the Cut, Copy, and Paste commands on the Edit menu, or right-click a file or folder and click the appropriate option on the menu that appears. Perhaps the most powerful file management tool in My Computer is the Common Tasks pane. When you select any item in My Computer, the Common Tasks pane changes to the File and Folder Tasks pane, listing tasks you can typically perform with the selected item. For example, if you select a file, the options in the Files and Folders task pane include "Rename this file," "Move this file," and "Delete this file," among many others. If you select a folder, file management tasks for folders appear. If you select more than one object, tasks appear that relate to manipulating multiple objects. You can also right-click any file or folder and choose the Send To command to "send" it to another location – most often a floppy disk or other removable storage medium. This **backs up** the files, making copies of them in case you have computer trouble (which can cause you to lose files from your hard disk). In this lesson, you move your files into the folder you created in the last lesson.

STEPS

1. **Click the** Win B-1 file, **hold down the mouse button and drag the file onto the** Windows XP Practice folder, **as shown in Figure B-12, then release the mouse button**
   Win B-1 is moved into the Windows XP Practice folder.

2. **Double-click the** Windows XP Practice folder **and confirm that the folder contains the** Win B-1 file as well as the Brochure folder

3. **Click the** Up button 🗁 **on the Standard Buttons toolbar, as shown in Figure B-12**
   You return to the root directory of your Project Disk. The Up button shows the next level up in the folder hierarchy.

4. **Click the** Logo file, **press and hold down [Shift], then click the** Memo file
   Both files are selected. Table B-4 describes methods for selecting multiple objects.

5. **Click** Move the selected items **in the File and Folder Tasks pane**
   The filenames turn gray, and the Move Items dialog box opens, as shown in Figure B-13.

6. **Click the plus sign next to My Computer if you do not see 3½ Floppy (A:) listed, click the** 3½ Floppy (A:) **drive, click the** Windows XP Practice folder, **click the** Brochure folder, **then click** Move
   The two files are moved to the Brochure folder. Only the Windows XP Practice folder and the Win B-2 file remain in the root directory.

7. **Click the** Close button **in the 3½ Floppy (A:) (My Computer) window**

> **QUICK TIP**
>
> It is easy to confuse the Back button with the Up button. The Back button returns you to the last location you viewed, no matter where it is in your folder hierarchy. The Up button displays the next level up in the folder hierarchy, no matter what you last viewed.

FIGURE B-12: Dragging a file from one folder to another

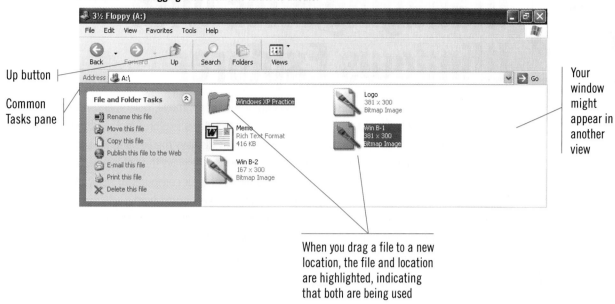

Up button

Common Tasks pane

Your window might appear in another view

When you drag a file to a new location, the file and location are highlighted, indicating that both are being used

FIGURE B-13: Moving files

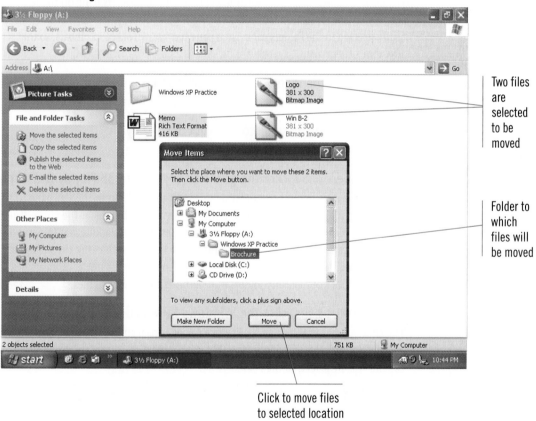

Two files are selected to be moved

Folder to which files will be moved

Click to move files to selected location

TABLE B-4: Techniques for selecting multiple files and folders

to select	do this
Individual objects not grouped together	Click the first object you want to select, then press and hold down [Ctrl] as you click each additional object you want to add to the selection
Objects grouped together	Click the first object you want to select, then press and hold down [Shift] as you click the last object in the list of objects you want to select; all the objects listed between the first and last objects are selected

Managing Files with Windows Explorer

As with My Computer, you can use Windows Explorer to copy, move, delete, and rename files and folders. However, in their default settings, My Computer and Windows Explorer look a little different and work in slightly different ways. In My Computer, the Explorer Bar displays the File and Folder Tasks pane when you select files or folders. In Windows Explorer, the Explorer Bar displays the Folders pane, which allows you to see and manipulate the overall structure of the contents of your computer or network while you work with individual files and folders within that structure. This allows you to work with more than one computer, folder, or file at once. Note that you can change the view in My Computer to show the Folders pane, and in Windows Explorer to view the File and Folder Tasks pane. ▰▰▰▰ In this lesson, you copy a folder from your Project Disk into the My Documents folder on your hard disk and then rename the folder.

STEPS

TROUBLE

If you do not see the toolbar, click View on the menu bar, point to Toolbars, then click Standard Buttons. If you do not see the Address bar, click View, point to Toolbars, then click Address Bar.

1. **Click the Start button, point to All Programs, point to Accessories, click Windows Explorer, then maximize the window if necessary**

   Windows Explorer opens, as shown in Figure B-14. The Folders pane on the left displays the drives and folders on your computer in a hierarchy. The right pane displays the contents of whatever drive or folder is currently selected in the Folders pane. Each pane has its own set of scroll bars, so that scrolling in one pane won't affect the other.

2. **Click View on the menu bar, then click Details if it is not already selected**

   Remember that a bullet point or check mark next to a command on the menu indicates that it's selected.

TROUBLE

If you cannot see the A: drive, you may have to click the plus sign (+) next to My Computer to view the available drives on your computer.

3. **In the Folders pane, scroll to and click 3½ Floppy (A:)**

   The contents of your Project Disk appear in the right pane.

4. **In the Folders pane, click the plus sign (+) next to 3½ Floppy (A:), if necessary**

   You click the plus sign (+) or minus sign (-) next to any item in the left pane to show or hide the different levels of the file hierarchy, so that you don't always have to look at the entire structure of your computer or network. A plus sign (+) next to an item indicates there are additional folders within that object. A minus sign (-) indicates the next level of the hierarchy is shown. Clicking the + displays (or "expands") the next level; clicking the – hides (or "collapses") it. When neither a + nor a – appears next to an icon, it means that the object does not have any folders in it, although it may have files.

5. **In the Folders pane, click the Windows XP Practice folder**

   The contents of the Windows XP Practice folder appear in the right pane, as shown in Figure B-15. Double-clicking an item in the Folders pane that has a + next to it displays its contents in the right pane and also expands the next level in the Folders pane.

TROUBLE

If you are working in a lab setting, you may not be able to add items to your My Documents folder. Skip, but read carefully, Steps 6, 7, and 8 if you are unable to complete them.

6. **In the Folders pane, drag the Windows XP Practice folder on top of the My Documents folder, then release the mouse button**

   When you drag files or folders from one drive to a different drive, they are copied rather than moved.

7. **In the Folders pane, click the My Documents folder**

   The Windows XP Practice folder should now appear in the list of folders in the right pane. You may have to scroll to see it. Now you should rename the folder so you can distinguish the original folder from the copy.

8. **Right-click the Windows XP Practice folder in the right pane, click Rename in the shortcut menu, type Windows XP Copy, then press [Enter]**

FIGURE B-14: Windows Explorer window

Left pane, known as the Folders list or the Explorer Bar

Your list of devices, folders, and files will differ

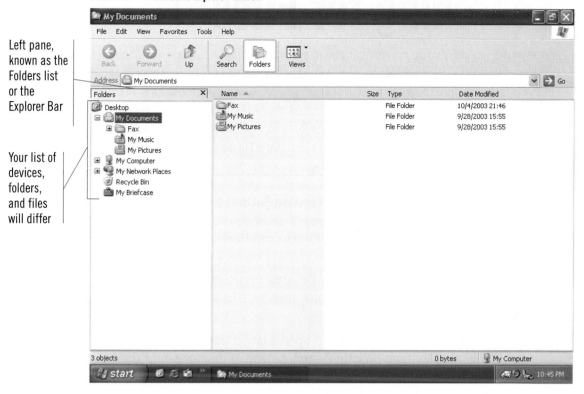

FIGURE B-15: Contents of Windows XP Practice folder

Windows XP Practice folder selected in left pane

Contents of Windows XP Practice folder appear in right pane

Your window might appear in a different view

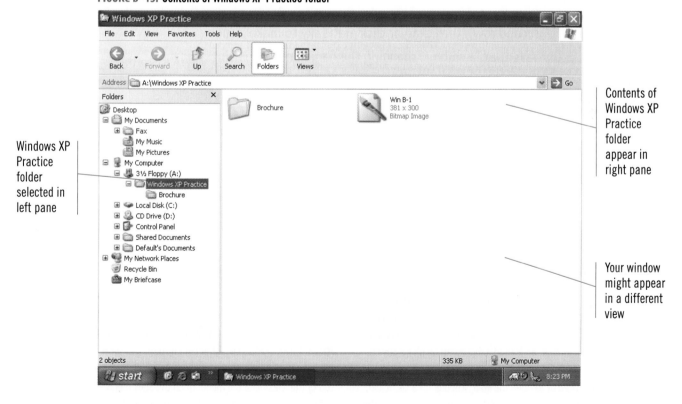

Searching for Files

After you've worked a while on your computer, saving, deleting, and modifying files and folders, you may forget where you've saved an item or what you named it. Or, you may want to send an e-mail to someone, but you can't remember how the name is spelled. You can use the **Windows XP Search** feature to quickly find any kind of object, from a Word document or a movie file to a computer on your network or a person in your address book. If you're connected to the Internet, you can use Search to locate Web pages and people on the Internet. ▄▄▄▄ In this lesson, you search for a file on your Project Disk.

STEPS

QUICK TIP

You can also start the Search Companion by clicking the Start button and then clicking Search. To change the way the Search tool works (such as whether the animated dog appears), click Change preferences at the bottom of the Search Companion pane.

1. **Click the Search button 🔎 on the Standard Buttons toolbar**

   The Explorer Bar changes to display the Search Companion pane, as shown in Figure B-16. Let's assume you can't remember where you placed the Logo file you created earlier. You know that it is a picture file and that it is somewhere on your floppy disk.

2. **In the Search Companion pane, click Pictures, music, or video; in the list that appears, click the Pictures and Photos check box, then type Logo in the All or part of the file name text box, as shown in Figure B-17**

3. **Click Use advanced search options to open a larger pane, click the Look in list arrow, click 3½ Floppy (A:), then click the Search button at the bottom of the Search Companion pane**

   The search results are displayed in the right pane and options for further searching are displayed in the Search Companion pane.

4. **Click the Logo icon in the right pane, click File on the menu bar, point to Open With, and then click Paint**

TROUBLE

If you don't like the way your clouds look, click Edit on the menu bar, click Undo, then repeat Step 5.

5. **Click the Airbrush tool 🖌, click the white color box in the Color box (the first one in the second row), then drag or click in the sky to make clouds**

6. **Save the file without changing the name and close Paint**

Clues to Use

Accessing files, folders, programs, and drives you use often

As you continue to use your computer, you will probably find that you use certain files, folders, programs, and disk drives almost every day. You can create a **shortcut**, an icon that represents an object stored somewhere else, and place it on the desktop. From the desktop, you double-click the shortcut to open the item, whether it's a file, folder, program, or disk drive. To create a shortcut on the desktop, view the object in My Computer or Windows Explorer, size the window so you can see both the object and part of the desktop at the same time, use the *right* mouse button to drag the object to the desktop, and then click Create Shortcuts Here. To delete the shortcut, select it and press [Delete]. The original file, folder, or program will not be affected. To **pin** a program to the Start menu, which places it conveniently at the top of the left side of the menu, open the Start menu as far as needed to view the program you want to pin, right-click the program name, and then click Pin to Start menu. To remove it, right-click it in its new position and then click Unpin from Start menu.

FIGURE B-16: Getting ready to search

Search button

Search Companion pane

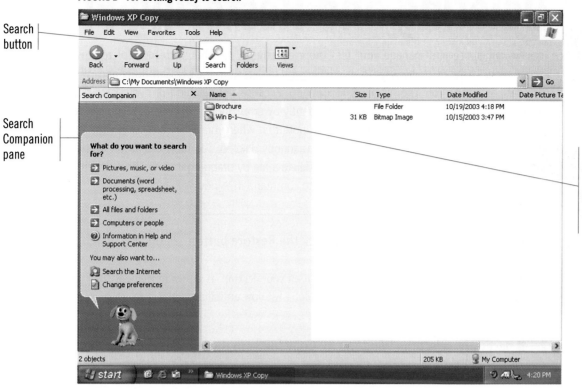

Contents of right pane won't change until you begin a search

FIGURE B-17: Specifying search options

Select this check box

Enter search text here

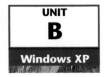
Deleting and Restoring Files

To save disk space and manage your files more effectively, you should **delete** (or remove) files you no longer need. There are many ways to delete files and folders from the My Computer and Windows Explorer windows, as well as from the Windows XP desktop. Because files deleted from your hard disk are stored in the Recycle Bin until you remove them permanently by emptying the Recycle Bin, you can restore any files you might have deleted accidentally. However, note that when you delete files from your floppy disk, they are not stored in the Recycle Bin – they are permanently deleted. See Table B-5 for an overview of deleting and restoring files. ▓▓▓▓▓ In this lesson, you delete a file by dragging it to the Recycle Bin, you restore it, and then you delete a folder by using the Delete command in Windows Explorer.

STEPS

1. **Click the Folders button** 📂**, then click the Restore button** 🗗 **on the Search Results (Windows Explorer) title bar**

    You should be able to see the Recycle Bin icon on your desktop, as shown in Figure B-18. If you can't see the Recycle Bin, resize or move the Windows Explorer window until it is visible.

2. **If necessary, select the Windows XP Copy folder in the left pane of Windows Explorer**

QUICK TIP

If you are unable to delete the file, it might be because your Recycle Bin is full or the properties have been changed so that files are deleted right away. See your instructor or technical support person for assistance.

3. **Drag the Windows XP Copy folder from the left pane to the Recycle Bin on the desktop, as shown in Figure B-18, then click Yes to confirm the deletion, if necessary**

    The folder no longer appears in Windows Explorer because you have moved it to the Recycle Bin.

4. **Double-click the Recycle Bin icon on the desktop, then scroll if necessary until you can see the Windows XP Copy folder**

    The Recycle Bin window opens, as shown in Figure B-19. Depending on the number of files already deleted on your computer, your window might look different.

TROUBLE

If the Recycle Bin window blocks your view of Windows Explorer, minimize the Recycle Bin window. You might need to scroll the right pane to find the restored folder in Windows Explorer.

5. **Click the Windows XP Copy folder, then click Restore this item in the Recycle Bin Tasks pane**

    The Windows XP Copy folder is restored and should now appear in the Windows Explorer window.

6. **Right-click the Windows XP Copy folder in the right pane of Windows Explorer, click Delete on the shortcut menu, then click Yes**

    When you are sure you no longer need files you've moved into the Recycle Bin, you can empty the Recycle Bin. You won't do this now, in case you are working on a computer that you share with other people. But when you're working on your own machine, open the Recycle Bin window, verify that you don't need any of the files or folders in it, then click Empty the Recycle Bin in the Recycle Bin Tasks pane.

7. **Close the Recycle Bin and Windows Explorer**

    If you minimized the Recycle Bin in Step 5, click its program button to open the Recycle Bin window, and then click the Close button.

FIGURE B-18: Dragging a folder to delete it

Your desktop background and icons might differ

Drag the folder here

Folder located in the My Documents folder

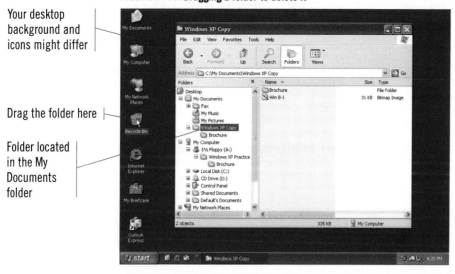

FIGURE B-19: Recycle Bin window

Deleted folder

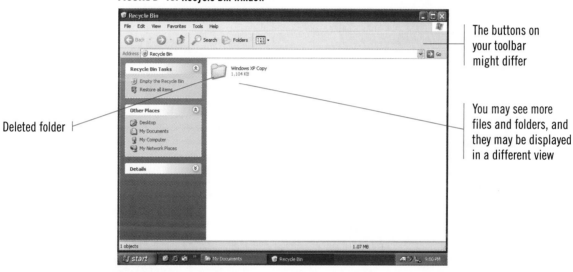

The buttons on your toolbar might differ

You may see more files and folders, and they may be displayed in a different view

TABLE B-5: Methods for deleting and restoring files

ways to delete a file	ways to restore a file from the Recycle Bin
If File and Folder Tasks pane is open, click the file, then click Delete this file	Click Edit, then click Undo Delete
Select the file, then press [Delete]	Select the file in the Recycle Bin window, then click Restore this file
Right-click the file, then click Delete on the shortcut menu	Right-click the file in the Recycle Bin window, then click Restore
Drag the file to the Recycle Bin	Drag the file from the Recycle Bin to any other location

Clues to Use

Customizing your Recycle Bin

You can set your Recycle Bin according to how you like to delete and restore files. For example, if you do not want files to go to the Recycle Bin but rather want them to be immediately and permanently deleted, right-click the Recycle Bin, click Properties, then click the Do Not Move Files to the Recycle Bin check box. If you find that the Recycle Bin fills up too fast and you are not ready to delete the files permanently, you can increase the amount of disk space devoted to the Recycle Bin by moving the Maximum Size of Recycle Bin slider to the right. This, of course, reduces the amount of disk space you have available for other things. Also, you can choose not to have the Confirm File Delete dialog box open when you send files to the Recycle Bin. See your instructor or technical support person before changing any of the Recycle Bin settings.

Practice

▼ CONCEPTS REVIEW

Label each of the elements of the Windows Explorer window shown in Figure B-20.

FIGURE B-20

Match each of the statements with the term it describes.

6. Electronic collections of data
7. Your computer's temporary storage area
8. Temporary location of information you wish to paste into another location
9. Storage areas on your hard drive for files, folders, and programs
10. Structure of files and folders

a. RAM
b. Folders
c. Files
d. File hierarchy
e. Clipboard

Select the best answer from the list of choices.

11. To prepare a floppy disk to save your files, you must first make sure
   a. files are copied to the disk.
   b. the disk is formatted.
   c. all the files that might be on the disk are erased.
   d. the files are on the Clipboard.

12. You can use My Computer to
   a. create a drawing of your computer.
   b. view the contents of a folder.
   c. change the appearance of your desktop.
   d. add text to a WordPad file.

13. Which of the following best describes WordPad?
   a. A program for organizing files
   b. A program for performing financial analysis
   c. A program for creating basic text documents
   d. A program for creating graphics

14. **Which of the following is NOT a way to move a file from one folder to another?**
    a. Open the file and drag its program window to the new folder.
    b. In My Computer or Windows Explorer, drag the selected file to the new folder.
    c. Use the Move this file command in the File and Folder Tasks pane.
    d. Use the [Ctrl][X] and [Ctrl][V] keyboard shortcuts while in the My Computer or the Windows Explorer window.

15. **In which of the following can you, by default, view the hierarchy of drives, folders, and files in a split pane window?**
    a. Windows Explorer
    b. All Programs
    c. My Computer
    d. WordPad

16. **To restore files that you have sent to the Recycle Bin,**
    a. click File, then click Empty Recycle Bin.
    b. click Edit, then click Undo Delete.
    c. click File, then click Undo.
    d. You cannot retrieve files sent to the Recycle Bin.

17. **To select files that are not grouped together, select the first file, then**
    a. press [Shift] while selecting the second file.
    b. press [Alt] while selecting the second file.
    c. press [Ctrl] while selecting the second file.
    d. click the second file.

18. **Pressing [Backspace]**
    a. deletes the character to the right of the cursor.
    b. deletes the character to the left of the cursor.
    c. moves the insertion point one character to the right.
    d. deletes all text to the left of the cursor.

19. **The size of a font is measured in**
    a. centimeters.
    b. points.
    c. places.
    d. millimeters.

20. **The Back button on the My Computer toolbar**
    a. starts the last program you used.
    b. displays the next level of the file hierarchy.
    c. backs up the currently selected file.
    d. displays the last location you visited.

▼ SKILLS REVIEW

1. **Create and save a WordPad file.**
    a. Start Windows, then start WordPad.
    b. Type **My Drawing Ability**, then press [Enter] three times.
    c. Save the document as **Drawing Ability** to your Project Disk, but do not close it.

2. **Open, edit, and save an existing Paint file.**
    a. Start Paint and open the file Win B-2 on your Project Disk.
    b. Save the picture with the filename **First Unique Art** as a 256-color bitmap file to your Project Disk.
    c. Inside the picture frame, use [Shift] with the Ellipse tool to create a circle, fill it with purple, switch to yellow, then use [Shift] with the Rectangle tool to place a square inside the circle. Fill the square with yellow.
    d. Save the file, but do not close it. (Click Yes, if necessary to replace the file.)

3. **Work with multiple programs.**
    a. Select the entire graphic and copy it to the Clipboard, then switch to WordPad.
    b. Place the insertion point in the last blank line, paste the graphic into your document, then deselect the graphic.
    c. Save the changes to your WordPad document. Switch to Paint.
    d. Using the Fill With Color tool, change the color of a filled area of your graphic.
    e. Save the revised graphic with the new name **Second Unique Art** as a 256-color bitmap on your Project Disk.
    f. Select the entire graphic and copy it to the Clipboard.
    g. Switch to WordPad, move the insertion point to the line below the graphic by clicking below the graphic and pressing [Enter], type **This is another version of my graphic:** below the first picture, then press [Enter].
    h. Paste the second graphic under the text you just typed.
    i. Save the changed WordPad document as **Two Drawing Examples** to your Project Disk. Close Paint and WordPad.

▼ SKILLS REVIEW (CONTINUED)

4. **View files and create folders with My Computer.**
   a. Open My Computer. Double-click the drive that contains your Project Disk.
   b. Create a new folder on your Project Disk by clicking File, pointing to New, then clicking Folder, and name the new folder **Review**.
   c. Open the folder to display its contents (it is empty).
   d. Use the Address bar to view the My Documents folder.
   e. Create a folder in the My Documents folder called **Temporary**, then use the Back button to view the Review folder.
   f. Create two new folders in the Review folder, one named **Documents** and the other named **Artwork**.
   g. Click the Forward button as many times as necessary to view the contents of the My Documents folder.
   h. Change the view to Details if necessary.

5. **Move and copy files with My Computer.**
   a. Use the Address bar to view your Project Disk. Switch to Details view, if necessary.
   b. Press the [Shift] key while selecting First Unique Art and Second Unique Art, then cut and paste them into the Artwork folder.
   c. Use the Back button to view the contents of Project Disk.
   d. Select the two WordPad files, Drawing Ability and Two Drawing Examples, then move them into the Review folder.
   e. Open the Review folder, select the two WordPad files again, move them into the Documents folder, then close My Computer.

6. **Manage files with Windows Explorer.**
   a. Open Windows Explorer and view the contents of the Artwork folder in the right pane.
   b. Select the two Paint files.
   c. Drag the two Paint files from the Artwork folder to the Temporary folder in the My Documents folder to copy – not move – them.
   d. View the contents of the Documents folder in the right pane, then select the two WordPad files.
   e. Repeat Step c to copy the files to the Temporary folder in the My Documents folder.
   f. View the contents of the Temporary folder in the right pane to verify that the four files are there.

7. **Search for files.**
   a. Open the Search companion from Windows Explorer.
   b. Search for the First Unique Art file on your Project Disk.
   c. Close the Search Results window.

8. **Delete and restore files and folders.**
   a. If necessary, open and resize the Windows Explorer window so you can see the Recycle Bin icon on the desktop, then scroll in Windows Explorer so you can see the Temporary folder in the left pane.
   b. Delete the Temporary folder from the My Documents folder by dragging it to the Recycle Bin.
   c. Click Yes to confirm the deletion, if necessary.
   d. **Open the Recycle Bin, restore the Temporary folder and its files to your hard disk, and then close the Recycle Bin.** (*Note*: If your Recycle Bin is empty, your computer is set to automatically delete items in the Recycle Bin.)
   e. Delete the Temporary folder again by clicking to select it and then pressing [Delete]. Click Yes to confirm the deletion.

▼ INDEPENDENT CHALLENGE 1

You have decided to start a bakery business and you want to use Windows XP to create and organize the files for the business.

   a. Create two new folders on your Project Disk, one named **Advertising** and one named **Customers**.
   b. Use WordPad to create a letter inviting new customers to the open house for the new bakery, then save it as **Open House Letter** in the Customers folder.
   c. Use WordPad to create a new document that lists five tasks that need to get done before the business opens (such as purchasing equipment, decorating the interior, and ordering supplies), then save it as **Business Plan** to your Project Disk, but don't place it in a folder.

▼ INDEPENDENT CHALLENGE 1 (CONTINUED)

d. Use Paint to create a simple logo for the bakery, save it as a 256-color bitmap named **Bakery Logo**, then place it in the Advertising folder.

e. Print the three files.

▼ INDEPENDENT CHALLENGE 2

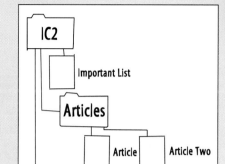

FIGURE B-21

To complete this Independent Challenge, you will need a second formatted, blank floppy disk. Write **IC2** on the disk label, then complete the steps below. Follow the guidelines listed here to create the file hierarchy shown in Figure B-21.

a. In the My Documents folder on your hard drive, create one folder named IC2 and a second named Project Disk 1.

b. Copy the contents of your first Project Disk into the new Project Disk 1 folder. This will give you access to your files as you complete these steps.

c. Place your blank IC2 disk into the floppy drive.

d. Start WordPad, then create a new file that contains a list of things to get done. Save the file as **To Do List** to your IC2 Disk.

e. Start My Computer and copy the To Do List from your IC2 Disk to the IC2 folder and rename the file in the IC2 folder **Important List**.

f. Copy the Open House Letter file from your Project Disk 1 folder to the IC2 folder. Rename the file **Article**.

g. Copy the Memo file from your Project Disk 1 folder to the IC2 folder in the My Documents folder and rename it **Article Two**.

h. Copy the Logo file from your Project Disk 1 folder to the IC2 folder and rename the file **Sample Logo**.

i. Move the files into the folders shown in Figure B-21.

j. Copy the IC2 folder to your IC2 Disk, then delete the Project Disk 1 and IC2 folders from the My Documents folder.

▼ INDEPENDENT CHALLENGE 3

With Windows XP, you can access the Web from My Computer and Windows Explorer, allowing you to search for information located not only on your computer or network but also on any computer on the Internet.

a. Start Windows Explorer, then click in the Address bar so the current location is selected, type **www.microsoft.com**, then press [Enter].

b. Connect to the Internet if necessary. The Microsoft Web page appears in the right pane of Windows Explorer.

c. Click in the Address bar, then type **www.course.com**, press [Enter], and then wait a moment while the Course Technology Web page opens.

d. Make sure your Project Disk is in the floppy disk drive, then click 3½ Floppy (A:) in the left pane.

e. Click the Back button list arrow, then click Microsoft's home page.

f. Capture a picture of your desktop by pressing [Print Screen] (usually located on the upper-right side of your keyboard). This stores the picture on the Clipboard. Open the Paint program, paste the contents of the Clipboard into the drawing window, clicking No if asked to enlarge the Bitmap, then print the picture.

g. Close Paint without saving your changes.

h. Close Windows Explorer, then disconnect from the Internet if necessary.

▼ INDEPENDENT CHALLENGE 4

Open Windows Explorer, make sure you can see the drive that contains your Project Disk listed in the left pane, use the right mouse button to drag the drive to a blank area on the desktop, then click Create Shortcuts Here. Then capture a picture of your desktop showing the new shortcut: press [Print Screen], located on the upper-right side of your keyboard. Then open the Paint program and paste the contents of the Clipboard into the drawing window. Print the screen, close Paint without saving your changes, then delete the shortcut when you are finished.

▼ VISUAL WORKSHOP

Recreate the screen shown in Figure B-22, which shows the Search Results window with the Memo file listed, one shortcut on the desktop, and one open (but minimized) file. Press [Print Screen] to make a copy of the screen, (a copy of the screen is placed on the Clipboard), open Paint, click Paste to paste the screen picture into Paint, then print the Paint file. Close Paint without saving your changes, and then return your desktop to its original state. Your desktop might have different icons and a different background.

FIGURE B-22

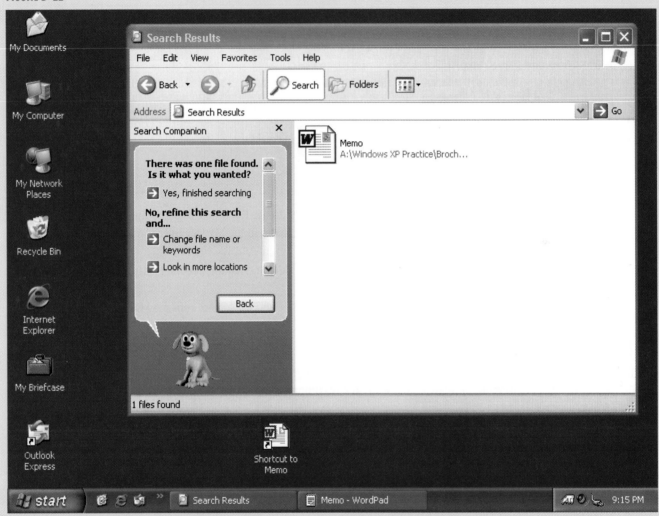

Formatting a Floppy Disk

A **disk** is a device on which you can store electronic data. Disks come in a variety of sizes and have varying storage capacities. Your computer's **hard disk**, one of its internal devices, can store large amounts of data. **Floppy disks**, on the other hand, are smaller, inexpensive, and portable. Most floppy disks that you buy today are 3 ½-inch disks (the diameter of the inside, circular part of the disk) and are already formatted. Check the package that your disk came in for the word "formatted" or "pre-formatted;" such disks do not require further formatting. If your package says "unformatted," then you should follow the steps in this appendix. In this appendix, you will prepare a floppy disk for use.

Formatting a Floppy Disk

In order for an operating system to be able to store data on a disk, the disk must be formatted. **Formatting** prepares a disk so it can store information. Usually, floppy disks are formatted when you buy them, but if not, you can format them yourself using Windows XP. To complete the following steps, you need a blank floppy disk or a disk containing data you no longer need. Do not use your Project Disk for this lesson, as all information on the disk will be erased.

STEPS

TROUBLE

This appendix assumes that the drive that will contain your floppy disks is drive A. If not, substitute the correct drive when you are instructed to use the 3 ½ Floppy (A:) drive.

1. **Start your computer and** Windows XP **if necessary, then place a 3 ½-inch floppy disk in drive A**

2. **Double-click the** My Computer icon 💾 **on the desktop**

   My Computer opens, as shown in Figure AP-1. This window lists all the drives and printers that you can use on your computer. Because computers have different drives, printers, programs, and other devices installed, your window will probably look different.

3. **Right-click the** 3 ½ Floppy (A:) icon

   When you click with the right mouse button, a shortcut menu of commands that apply to the item you right-clicked appears. Because you right-clicked a drive, the Format command is available.

TROUBLE

Windows cannot format a disk if it is write-protected; therefore, you may need to slide the write-protect tab over until it clicks to continue. See Figure AP-3 to locate the write-protect tab on your disk.

4. **Click** Format **on the shortcut menu**

   The Format dialog box opens, as shown in Figure AP-2. In this dialog box, you specify the capacity of the disk you are formatting, the File system, the Allocation unit size, the kind of formatting you want to do, and if you want, a volume label. You are doing a standard format, so you will accept the default settings.

5. **Click** Start, **then, when you are warned that formatting will erase all data on the disk, click** OK **to continue**

   Windows formats your disk. After the formatting is complete, you might see a summary about the size of the disk.

6. **Click** OK **when the message telling you that the format is complete appears, then click** Close **in the Format dialog box**

QUICK TIP

Once a disk is formatted, you do not need to format it again. However, some people use the Quick Format option to erase the contents of a disk quickly, rather than having to select the files and then delete them.

7. **Click the** Close button ☒ **in the My Computer window**

   My Computer closes and you return to the desktop.

FIGURE AP-1: My Computer window

The drive containing your disk

FIGURE AP-2: Format dialog box

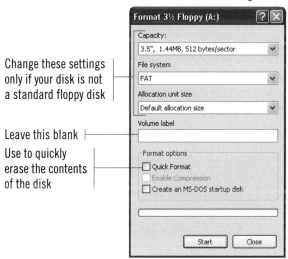

Change these settings only if your disk is not a standard floppy disk

Leave this blank

Use to quickly erase the contents of the disk

FIGURE AP-3: Write-protect tab

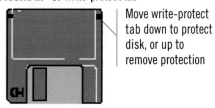

Move write-protect tab down to protect disk, or up to remove protection

3.5" disk

Clues to Use

More about disks

Disks are sometimes called **drives**, but this term really refers to the name by which the operating system recognizes the disk (or a portion of the disk). The operating system typically assigns a drive letter to a drive (which you can reassign if you want). For example, on most computers the hard disk is identified by the letter "C" and the floppy drive by the letter "A." The amount of information a disk can hold is called its capacity, usually measured in megabytes (MB). The most common floppy disk **capacity** is 1.44 MB. Computers also come with other disk drives, such as a **CD drives** and **Zip drives**. Such drives handle CDs and Zip disks, respectively. Both are portable like floppy disks, but they can contain far more data than floppy disks.

Data Files

Read the following information carefully!

It is very important to organize and keep track of the files you need for this book.

---

1. **Find out from your instructor the location of the Data Files you need and the location where you will store your files.**

   - To complete many of the units in this book, you need to use Data Files. Your instructor will either provide you with a copy of the Data Files or ask you to make your own copy.
   - If you need to make a copy of the Data Files, you will need to copy a set of files from a file server, stand-alone computer, or the Web to the drive and folder where you will be storing your Data Files.
   - Your instructor will tell you which computer, drive letter, and folders contain the files you need, and where you will store your files.
   - You can also download the files by going to www.course.com. A copy of a Data Files list is provided on the Review Pack for this book or may be provided by your instructor.

2. **Copy and organize your Data Files.**

   Floppy disk users

   - If you are using floppy disks to store your Data Files, the Data Files List shows which files you'll need to copy onto your disk(s).
   - Unless noted in the Data Files List, you will need one formatted, high-density disk for each unit. For each unit you are assigned, copy the files listed in the **Data File Supplied column** onto one disk.
   - Make sure you label each disk clearly with the unit name (e.g., Word Unit A).
   - When working through the unit, save all your files to this disk.

   Users storing files in other locations

   - If you are using a zip drive, network folder, hard drive, or other storage device, use the Data Files List to organize your files.
   - Create a subfolder for each unit in the location where you are storing your files, and name it according to the unit title (e.g., Word Unit A).
   - For each unit you are assigned, copy the files listed in the **Data File Supplied column** into that unit's folder.
   - Store the files you modify or create for each unit in the unit folder.

3. **Find and keep track of your Data Files and completed files.**

   - Use the **Data File Supplied column** to make sure you have the files you need before starting the unit or exercise indicated in the **Unit and Location column**.
   - Use the **Student Saves File As column** to find out the filename you use when saving your changes to a Data File that was provided.
   - Use the **Student Creates File column** to find out the filename you use when saving a file you create new for the exercise.

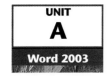

UNIT A — Word 2003

Getting Started with Word 2003

OBJECTIVES

Understand word processing software
Start Word 2003
Explore the Word program window
Start a document
Save a document
Print a document
Use the Help system
Close a document and exit Word

Microsoft Office Word 2003 is a word processing program that makes it easy to create a variety of professional-looking documents, from simple letters and memos to newsletters, research papers, Web pages, business cards, resumes, financial reports, and other documents that include multiple pages of text and sophisticated formatting. In this unit, you will explore the editing and formatting features available in Word, learn how to start Word, and create a document. You have just been hired to work in the Marketing Department at MediaLoft, a chain of bookstore cafés that sells books, music, and videos. Shortly after reporting to your new office, Alice Wegman, the marketing manager, asks you to familiarize yourself with Word and use it to create a memo to the marketing staff.

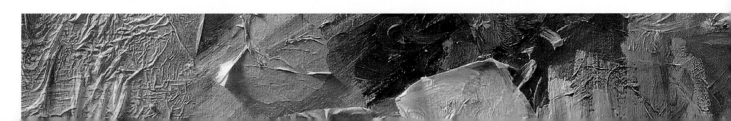

Understanding Word Processing Software

A **word processing program** is a software program that includes tools for entering, editing, and formatting text and graphics. Microsoft Word is a powerful word processing program that allows you to create and enhance a wide range of documents quickly and easily. Figure A-1 shows the first page of a report created using Word and illustrates some of the Word features you can use to enhance your documents. The electronic files you create using Word are called **documents**. One of the benefits of using Word is that document files can be stored on a disk, making them easy to transport, exchange, and revise. 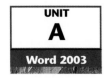 You need to write a memo to the marketing staff to inform them of an upcoming meeting. Before beginning your memo, you explore the editing and formatting capabilities available in Word.

DETAILS

You can use Word to accomplish the following tasks:

- **Type and edit text**

  The Word editing tools make it simple to insert and delete text in a document. You can add text to the middle of an existing paragraph, replace text with other text, undo an editing change, and correct typing, spelling, and grammatical errors with ease.

- **Copy and move text from one location to another**

  Using the more advanced editing features of Word, you can copy or move text from one location and insert it in a different location in a document. You also can copy and move text between documents. Being able to copy and move text means you don't have to retype text that is already entered in a document.

- **Format text and paragraphs with fonts, colors, and other elements**

  The sophisticated formatting tools available in Word allow you to make the text in your documents come alive. You can change the size, style, and color of text, add lines and shading to paragraphs, and enhance lists with bullets and numbers. Formatting text creatively helps you highlight important ideas in your documents.

- **Format and design pages**

  The Word page-formatting features give you power to design attractive newsletters, create powerful resumes, and produce documents such as business cards, CD labels, and books. You can change the paper size and orientation of your documents, add headers and footers to pages, organize text in columns, and control the layout of text and graphics on each page of a document.

- **Enhance documents with tables, charts, diagrams, and graphics**

  Using the powerful graphic tools available in Word, you can spice up your documents with pictures, photographs, lines, shapes, and diagrams. You also can illustrate your documents with tables and charts to help convey your message in a visually interesting way.

- **Create Web pages**

  The Word Web page design tools allow you to create documents that others can read over the Internet or an intranet. You can enhance Web pages with themes and graphics, add hyperlinks, create online forms, and preview Web pages in your Web browser.

- **Use Mail Merge to create form letters and mailing labels**

  The Word Mail Merge feature allows you to easily send personalized form letters to many different people. You can also use Mail Merge to create mailing labels, directories, e-mail messages, and many other types of documents.

FIGURE A-1: A report created using Word

Format the size and appearance of text

Insert graphics

Create columns of text

Add bullets to lists

Create tables

Add headers to every page

Align text in paragraphs evenly

Add lines

Create charts

Add page numbers in footers

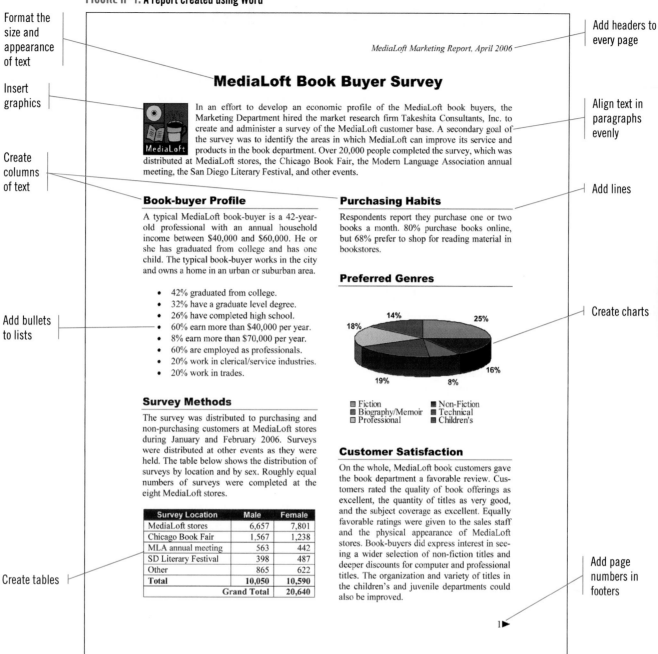

MediaLoft Marketing Report, April 2006

MediaLoft Book Buyer Survey

In an effort to develop an economic profile of the MediaLoft book buyers, the Marketing Department hired the market research firm Takeshita Consultants, Inc. to create and administer a survey of the MediaLoft customer base. A secondary goal of the survey was to identify the areas in which MediaLoft can improve its service and products in the book department. Over 20,000 people completed the survey, which was distributed at MediaLoft stores, the Chicago Book Fair, the Modern Language Association annual meeting, the San Diego Literary Festival, and other events.

Book-buyer Profile

A typical MediaLoft book-buyer is a 42-year-old professional with an annual household income between $40,000 and $60,000. He or she has graduated from college and has one child. The typical book-buyer works in the city and owns a home in an urban or suburban area.

- 42% graduated from college.
- 32% have a graduate level degree.
- 26% have completed high school.
- 60% earn more than $40,000 per year.
- 8% earn more than $70,000 per year.
- 60% are employed as professionals.
- 20% work in clerical/service industries.
- 20% work in trades.

Survey Methods

The survey was distributed to purchasing and non-purchasing customers at MediaLoft stores during January and February 2006. Surveys were distributed at other events as they were held. The table below shows the distribution of surveys by location and by sex. Roughly equal numbers of surveys were completed at the eight MediaLoft stores.

Survey Location	Male	Female
MediaLoft stores	6,657	7,801
Chicago Book Fair	1,567	1,238
MLA annual meeting	563	442
SD Literary Festival	398	487
Other	865	622
Total	**10,050**	**10,590**
	Grand Total	**20,640**

Purchasing Habits

Respondents report they purchase one or two books a month. 80% purchase books online, but 68% prefer to shop for reading material in bookstores.

Preferred Genres

14% 25% 18% 16% 19% 8%

■ Fiction ■ Non-Fiction
■ Biography/Memoir ■ Technical
□ Professional ■ Children's

Customer Satisfaction

On the whole, MediaLoft book customers gave the book department a favorable review. Customers rated the quality of book offerings as excellent, the quantity of titles as very good, and the subject coverage as excellent. Equally favorable ratings were given to the sales staff and the physical appearance of MediaLoft stores. Book-buyers did express interest in seeing a wider selection of non-fiction titles and deeper discounts for computer and professional titles. The organization and variety of titles in the children's and juvenile departments could also be improved.

1▶

Clues to Use

Planning a document

Before you create a new document, it's a good idea to spend time planning it. Identify the message you want to convey, the audience for your document, and the elements, such as tables or charts, you want to include. You should also think about the tone and look of your document—is it a business letter, which should be written in a pleasant, but serious tone and have a formal appearance, or are you creating a flyer that must be colorful, eye-catching, and fun to read?

The purpose and audience for your document determines the appropriate design. Planning the layout and design of a document involves deciding how to organize the text, selecting the fonts to use, identifying the graphics to include, and selecting the formatting elements that will enhance the document's message and appeal. For longer documents, such as newsletters, it can be useful to sketch the layout and design of each page before you begin.

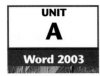

UNIT A · Word 2003

Starting Word 2003

Before starting Word, you must start Windows by turning on your computer. Once Windows is running, you can start Word or any other application by using the Start button on the Windows taskbar. You can also start Word by clicking the Word icon on the Windows desktop or the Word icon on the Microsoft Office Shortcut bar, if those items are available on your computer. ▰▰▰ You use the Start button to start Word so you can familiarize yourself with its features.

STEPS

1. **Click the Start button 🔲 start on the Windows taskbar**

   The Start menu opens on the desktop. The left pane of the Start menu includes shortcuts to the most frequently used programs on the computer.

2. **Point to All Programs on the Start menu**

   The All Programs menu opens. The All Programs menu displays the list of programs installed on your computer.

> **TROUBLE**
> If Microsoft Office is not on your All Programs menu, ask your technical support person for assistance.

3. **Point to Microsoft Office**

   A menu listing the Office programs installed on your computer opens, as shown in Figure A-2.

4. **Click Microsoft Office Word 2003 on the Microsoft Office menu**

   The **Word program window** opens and displays a blank document in the document window and the Getting Started task pane, as shown in Figure A-3. The blank document opens in the most recently used view. **Views** are different ways of displaying a document in the document window. Figure A-3 shows a blank document in Print Layout view. The lessons in this unit will use Print Layout view.

5. **Click the Print Layout View button 🔲 as shown in Figure A-3**

   If your blank document opened in a different view, the view changes to Print Layout view.

> **TROUBLE**
> If your toolbars are on one row, click the Toolbar Options button at the end of the Formatting toolbar, then click Show Buttons on Two Rows.

6. **Click the Zoom list arrow on the Standard toolbar as shown in Figure A-3, then click Page Width**

   The blank document fills the document window. Your screen should now match Figure A-3. The blinking vertical line in the upper-left corner of the document window is the **insertion point**. It indicates where text appears as you type.

7. **Move the mouse pointer around in the Word program window**

   The mouse pointer changes shape depending on where it is in the Word program window. In the document window in Print Layout view, the mouse pointer changes to an **I-beam pointer** I or a **click and type pointer** $\mathrm{I}^{\equiv}$. You use these pointers to move the insertion point in the document or to select text to edit. Table A-1 describes common Word pointers.

8. **Place the mouse pointer over a toolbar button**

   When you place the pointer over a button or some other element of the Word program window, a ScreenTip appears. A **ScreenTip** is a label that identifies the name of the button or feature.

TABLE A-1: Common Word pointers

pointer	use to
I	Move the insertion point in a document or to select text
$\mathrm{I}^{\equiv}$ or $\underset{\equiv}{\mathrm{I}}$	Move the insertion point in a blank area of a document in Print Layout or Web Layout view; automatically applies the paragraph formatting required to position text at that location in the document
▷	Click a button, menu command, or other element of the Word program window; appears when you point to elements of the Word program window
◁	Select a line or lines of text; appears when you point to the left edge of a line of text in the document window
🖑	Open a hyperlink; appears when you point to a hyperlink in the task pane or a document

FIGURE A-2: Starting Word from the All Programs menu

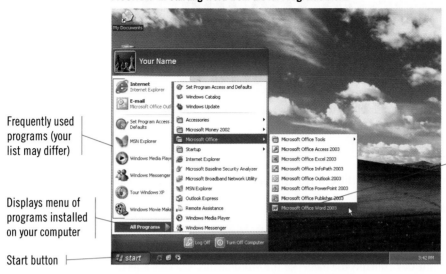

Frequently used programs (your list may differ)

Displays menu of programs installed on your computer

Start button

Click to start Word (the order of the programs listed may differ)

FIGURE A-3: Word program window in Print Layout view

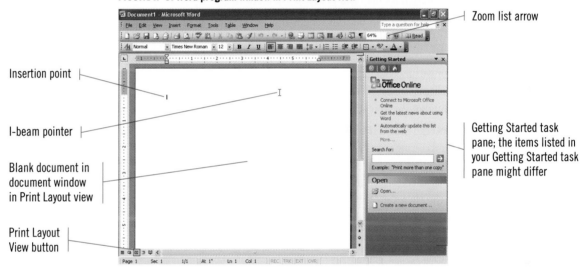

Insertion point

I-beam pointer

Blank document in document window in Print Layout view

Print Layout View button

Zoom list arrow

Getting Started task pane; the items listed in your Getting Started task pane might differ

Clues to Use

Using Word document views

Each Word view provides features that are useful for working on different types of documents. The default view, **Print Layout view**, displays a document as it will look on a printed page. Print Layout view is helpful for formatting text and pages, including adjusting document margins, creating columns of text, inserting graphics, and formatting headers and footers. Also useful is **Normal view**, which shows a simplified layout of a document, without margins, headers and footers, or graphics. When you want to quickly type, edit, and format text, it's often easiest to work in Normal view. **Web Layout view** allows you to accurately format Web pages or documents that will be viewed on a computer screen. In Web Layout view, a document appears just as it will when viewed with a Web browser. **Outline view** is useful for editing and formatting longer documents that include multiple headings. Outline view allows you to reorganize text by moving the headings. You switch between these views by clicking the view buttons to the left of the horizontal scroll bar or by using the commands on the View menu.

Two additional views make it easier to read documents on the screen. **Reading Layout view** displays document text so that it is easy to read and annotate. When you are working with highlighting or comments in a document, it's useful to use Reading Layout view. You switch to Reading Layout view by clicking the Read button on the Standard toolbar or the Reading Layout button to the left of the horizontal scroll bar. You return to the previous view by clicking the Close button on the Reading Layout toolbar. **Full Screen view** displays only the document window on screen. You switch to Full Screen view by using the Full Screen command on the View menu; you return to the previous view by pressing [Esc].

Changing views does not affect how the printed document will appear. It simply changes the way you view the document in the document window.

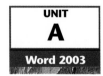
Exploring the Word Program Window

When you start Word, a blank document appears in the document window and the Getting Started task pane appears. You examine the elements of the Word program window.

DETAILS

Using Figure A-4 as a guide, find the elements described below in your program window.

- The **title bar** displays the name of the document and the name of the program. Until you give a new document a different name, its temporary name is Document1. The title bar also contains resizing buttons and the program Close button, buttons that are common to all Windows programs.

- The **menu bar** contains the names of the Word menus. Clicking a menu name opens a list of commands. The menu bar also contains the **Type a question for help box** and the Close Window button. You use the Type a question for help box to access the Word Help system.

- The **toolbars** contain buttons for the most commonly used commands. The **Standard toolbar** contains buttons for frequently used operating and editing commands, such as saving a document, printing a document, and cutting, copying, and pasting text. The **Formatting toolbar** contains buttons for commonly used formatting commands, such as changing font type and size, applying bold to text, and changing paragraph alignment. The Clues to Use in this lesson provides more information about working with toolbars and menus in Word.

- The **Getting Started task pane** contains shortcuts for opening a document, for creating new documents, and for accessing information on the Microsoft Web site. The blue words in the Open section of the task pane are **hyperlinks** that provide quick access to existing documents and the New Document task pane. If your computer is connected to the Internet, you can use the Microsoft Office Online section of the task pane to search the Microsoft Web site for information related to Office programs. As you learn more about Word, you will work with other task panes that provide shortcuts to Word formatting, editing, and research features. Clicking a hyperlink in a task pane can be quicker than using menu commands and toolbar buttons to accomplish a task.

- The **document window** displays the current document. You enter text and format your document in the document window.

- The horizontal and vertical rulers appear in the document window in Print Layout view. The **horizontal ruler** displays left and right document margins as well as the tab settings and paragraph indents, if any, for the paragraph in which the insertion point is located. The **vertical ruler** displays the top and bottom document margins.

- The **vertical and horizontal scroll bars** are used to display different parts of the document in the document window. The scroll bars include **scroll boxes** and **scroll arrows**, which you can use to easily move through a document.

- The **view buttons** to the left of the horizontal scroll bar allow you to display the document in Normal, Web Layout, Print Layout, Outline, or Reading Layout view.

- The **status bar** displays the page number and section number of the current page, the total number of pages in the document, and the position of the insertion point in inches, lines, and characters. The status bar also indicates the on/off status of several Word features, including tracking changes, overtype mode, and spelling and grammar checking.

FIGURE A-4: Elements of the Word program window

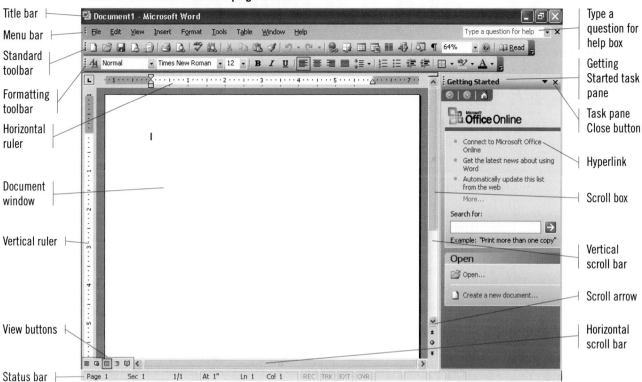

Title bar
Menu bar
Standard toolbar
Formatting toolbar
Horizontal ruler
Document window
Vertical ruler
View buttons
Status bar

Type a question for help box
Getting Started task pane
Task pane Close button
Hyperlink
Scroll box
Vertical scroll bar
Scroll arrow
Horizontal scroll bar

Clues to Use

Working with toolbars and menus in Word 2003

The lessons in this book assume you are working with full menus and toolbars visible, which means the Standard and Formatting toolbars appear on two rows and display all the buttons, and the menus display the complete list of menu commands.

You can also set Word to use personalized toolbars and menus that modify themselves to your working style. When you use personalized toolbars, the Standard and Formatting toolbars appear on the same row and display only the most frequently used buttons. To use a button that is not visible on a toolbar, click the Toolbar Options button at the end of the toolbar, and then click the button you want on the Toolbar Options list. As you work, Word adds the buttons you use to the visible toolbars, and moves the buttons

you haven't used recently to the Toolbar Options list. Similarly, Word menus adjust to your work habits, so that the commands you use most often appear on shortened menus. You double-click the menu name or click the double arrow at the bottom of a menu to view additional menu commands.

To work with full toolbars and menus visible, you must turn off the personalized toolbars and menus features. To turn off personalized toolbars and menus, double-click Tools on the menu bar, click Customize, click the Options tab, select the Show Standard and Formatting toolbars on two rows and Always show full menus check boxes, and then click Close.

Starting a Document

You begin a new document by simply typing text in a blank document in the document window. Word includes a **word-wrap** feature, so that as you type Word automatically moves the insertion point to the next line of the document when you reach the right margin. You only press [Enter] when you want to start a new paragraph or insert a blank line. You can easily edit text in a document by inserting new text or by deleting existing text. You type a quick memo to the marketing staff to inform them of an upcoming meeting.

STEPS

1. **Click the Close button in the Getting Started task pane**
   The task pane closes and the blank document fills the screen.

   QUICK TIP
   If you press the wrong key, press [Backspace] to erase the mistake, then try again.

2. **Type Memorandum, then press [Enter] four times**
   Each time you press [Enter] the insertion point moves to the start of the next line.

3. **Type DATE:, then press [Tab] twice**
   Pressing [Tab] moves the insertion point several spaces to the right. You can use the [Tab] key to align the text in a memo header or to indent the first line of a paragraph.

   QUICK TIP
   Smart tags and other automatic feature markers appear on screen but do not print.

4. **Type April 21, 2006, then press [Enter]**
   When you press [Enter], a purple dotted line appears under the date. This dotted underline is a **smart tag**. It indicates that Word recognizes the text as a date. If you move the mouse pointer over the smart tag, a **Smart Tag Actions button** ⑤ appears above the date. Smart tags are one of the many automatic features you will encounter as you type. Table A-2 describes other automatic features available in Word. You can ignore the smart tags in your memo.

5. **Type:**   TO: [Tab] [Tab] Marketing Staff [Enter]
                 FROM: [Tab] Your Name [Enter]
                 RE: [Tab] [Tab] Marketing Meeting [Enter] [Enter]
   Red or green wavy lines may appear under the words you typed. A red wavy line means the word is not in the Word dictionary and might be misspelled. A green wavy line indicates a possible grammar error. You can correct any typing errors you make later.

   QUICK TIP
   To reverse an AutoCorrect adjustment, immediately click the Undo button ↺ on the Standard toolbar.

6. **Type The next marketing meeting will be held May 6th at 10 a.m. in the Bloomsbury room on the ground floor., then press [Spacebar]**
   As you type, notice that the insertion point moves automatically to the next line of the document. You also might notice that Word corrects typing errors or makes typographical adjustments as you type. This feature is called **AutoCorrect**. AutoCorrect automatically detects and adjusts typos, certain misspelled words (such as "taht" for "that"), and incorrect capitalization as you type. For example, Word automatically changed "6th" to "6th" in the memo.

   QUICK TIP
   Type just one space after a period at the end of a sentence when typing with a word processor.

7. **Type Heading the agenda will be a discussion of our new cafe music series, scheduled for August. Please bring ideas for promoting this exciting new series to the meeting.**
   When you type the first few characters of "August," the Word AutoComplete feature displays the complete word in a ScreenTip. **AutoComplete** suggests text to insert quickly into your documents. You can ignore AutoComplete for now. Your memo should resemble Figure A-5.

8. **Position the I pointer after for (but before the space) in the second sentence, then click**
   Clicking moves the insertion point after "for."

9. **Press [Backspace] three times, then type to debut in**
   Pressing [Backspace] removes the character before the insertion point.

10. **Move the insertion point before marketing in the first sentence, then press [Delete] ten times to remove the word marketing and the space after it**
    Pressing [Delete] removes the character after the insertion point. Figure A-6 shows the revised memo.

FIGURE A-5: Memo text in the document window

Blank lines between paragraphs

Purple dotted underline indicates a smart tag

Green wavy underline indicates a possible grammar error (your memo will show your name)

Text wraps to the next line (yours might wrap differently)

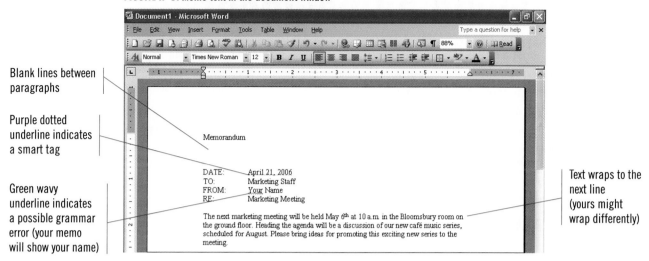

FIGURE A-6: Edited memo text

Text inserted in the memo

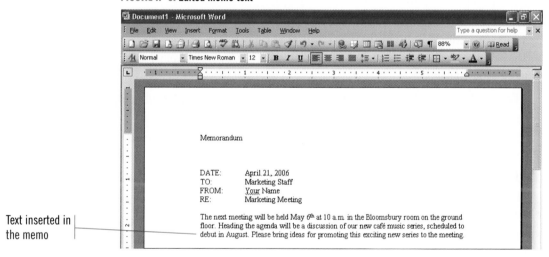

TABLE A-2: Automatic features in Word

feature	what appears	to use
AutoComplete	A ScreenTip suggesting text to insert appears	Press [Enter] to insert the text suggested by the ScreenTip; continue typing to reject the suggestion
Spelling and Grammar	A red wavy line under a word indicates a possible misspelling; a green wavy line under text indicates a possible grammar error	Right-click red- or green-underlined text to display a shortcut menu of correction options; click a correction to accept it and remove the wavy underline
AutoCorrect	A small blue box appears when you place the pointer under text corrected by AutoCorrect; an AutoCorrect Options button appears when you point to the corrected text	Word automatically corrects typos, minor spelling errors, and capitalization, and adds typographical symbols (such as © and ™) as you type; to reverse an AutoCorrect adjustment, click the AutoCorrect Options button, then click Undo or the option that will undo the action
Smart tag	A purple dotted line appears under text Word recognizes as a date, name, address, or place; a Smart Tag Actions button appears when you point to a smart tag	Click the Smart Tag Actions button to display a shortcut menu of options (such as adding a name to your address book in Outlook or opening your Outlook calendar); to remove a smart tag, click Remove this Smart Tag on the shortcut menu

Saving a Document

To store a document permanently so you can open it and edit it in the future, you must save it as a **file**. When you **save** a document you give it a name, called a **filename**, and indicate the location where you want to store the file. Files can be saved to your computer's internal hard disk, to a floppy disk, or to a variety of other locations. You can save a document using the Save button on the Standard toolbar or the Save command on the File menu. Once you have saved a document for the first time, you should save it again every few minutes and always before printing so that the saved file is updated to reflect your latest changes. You save your memo with the filename Marketing Memo.

STEPS

TROUBLE
If you don't see the extension .doc on the filename in the Save As dialog box, don't worry. Windows can be set to display or not to display the file extensions.

1. **Click the** Save button **on the Standard toolbar**
   The first time you save a document, the Save As dialog box opens, as shown in Figure A-7. The default filename, Memorandum, appears in the File name text box. The default filename is based on the first few words of the document. The .doc extension is assigned automatically to all Word documents to distinguish them from files created in other software programs. To save the document with a different filename, type a new filename in the File name text box, and use the Save in list arrow to select where you want to store the document file. You do not need to type .doc when you type a new filename. Table A-3 describes the functions of the buttons in the Save As dialog box.

2. **Type** Marketing Memo **in the File name text box**
   The new filename replaces the default filename. It's a good idea to give your documents brief filenames that describe the contents.

TROUBLE
This book assumes your Data Files for Unit A are stored in a folder titled UnitA. Substitute the correct drive or folder if this is not the case.

3. **Click the** Save in list arrow**, then navigate to the drive or folder where your Data Files are located**
   The drive or folder where your Data Files are located appears in the Save in list box. Your Save As dialog box should resemble Figure A-8.

4. **Click** Save
   The document is saved to the location you specified in the Save As dialog box, and the title bar displays the new filename, "Marketing Memo.doc."

5. **Place the insertion point before** August **in the second sentence, type** early**, then press [Spacebar]**
   You can continue to work on a document after you have saved it with a new filename.

6. **Click**
   Your change to the memo is saved. Saving a document after you give it a filename saves the changes you make to the document. You also can click File on the menu bar, and then click Save to save a document.

Clues to Use

Recovering lost document files

Sometimes while you are working on a document, Word might freeze, making it impossible to continue working, or you might experience a power failure that shuts down your computer. Should this occur, Word has a built-in recovery feature that allows you to open and save the files that were open at the time of the interruption. When you restart Word after an interruption, the Document Recovery task pane opens on the left side of your screen and lists both the original and the recovered versions of the Word files. If you're not sure which file to open (original or recovered), it's usually better to open the recovered file because it includes your latest changes to the document. You can, however, open and review all the versions of the file that were recovered and select the best one to save. Each file listed in the Document Recovery task pane has a list arrow with options that allow you to open the file, save the file, delete the file, or show repairs made to the file.

FIGURE A-7: Save As dialog box

Active folder or drive

Folders and files in the active folder or drive (yours will differ)

Default filename and file extension are selected

Click to create a new folder in the active folder or drive

Click the Save in list arrow to change the active folder or drive

Click to change the file type

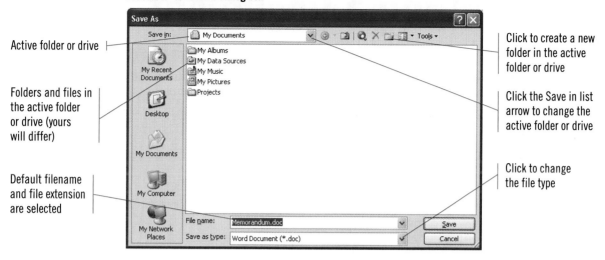

FIGURE A-8: File to be saved to the UnitA folder

Location of Data Files (yours might differ)

New filename

Your dialog box might list the files and folders in the active folder or drive here

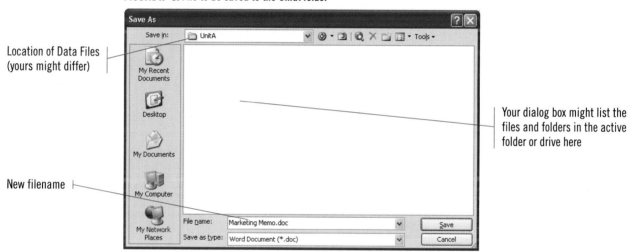

TABLE A-3: Save As dialog box buttons

button	use to
Back	Navigate to the drive or folder previously shown in the Save in list box; click the Back list arrow to navigate to a recently displayed drive or folder
Up One Level	Navigate to the next highest level in the folder hierarchy (to the drive or folder that contains the current folder)
Search the Web	Connect to the World Wide Web to locate a folder or file
Delete	Delete the selected folder or file
Create New Folder	Create a new folder in the current folder or drive
Views	Change the way folder and file information is shown in the Save As dialog box; click the Views list arrow to open a menu of options
Tools	Open a menu of commands related to the selected drive, folder, or file

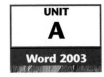

Printing a Document

Before you print a document, it's a good habit to examine it in **Print Preview** to see what it will look like when printed. When a document is ready to print, you can print it using the Print button on the Standard toolbar or the Print command on the File menu. When you use the Print button, the document prints using the default print settings. If you want to print more than one copy of a document or select other printing options, you must use the Print command. ▪▪▪▪▪ You display your memo in Print Preview and then print a copy.

STEPS

1. **Click the** Print Preview button 🔍 **on the Standard toolbar**

   The document appears in Print Preview. It is useful to examine a document carefully in Print Preview so that you can correct any problems before printing it.

2. **Move the pointer over the memo text until it changes to** 🔍 **, then click**

   Clicking with the 🔍 pointer magnifies the document in the Print Preview window and changes the pointer to 🔍. The memo appears in the Print Preview window exactly as it will look when printed, as shown in Figure A-9. Clicking with the 🔍 pointer reduces the size of the document in the Print Preview window.

3. **Click the** Magnifier button 🔍 **on the Print Preview toolbar**

   Clicking the Magnifier button turns off the magnification feature and allows you to edit the document in Print Preview. In edit mode, the pointer changes to I. The Magnifier button is a **toggle button**, which means you can use it to switch back and forth between magnification mode and edit mode.

4. **Compare the text on your screen with the text in Figure A-9, examine your memo carefully for typing or spelling errors, correct any mistakes, then click the** Close Preview **button** Close **on the Print Preview toolbar**

   Print Preview closes and the memo appears in the document window.

5. **Click the** Save button 💾 **on the Standard toolbar**

   If you made any changes to the document since you last saved it, the changes are saved.

6. **Click** File **on the menu bar, then click** Print

   The Print dialog box opens, as shown in Figure A-10. Depending on the printer installed on your computer, your print settings might differ slightly from those in the figure. You can use the Print dialog box to change the current printer, change the number of copies to print, select what pages of a document to print, and modify other printing options.

7. **Click** OK

   The dialog box closes and a copy of the memo prints using the default print settings. You can also click the Print button 🖨 on the Standard toolbar or the Print Preview toolbar to print a document using the default print settings.

FIGURE A-9: Memo in the Print Preview window

Print Preview toolbar

Magnifier button

Close Preview button

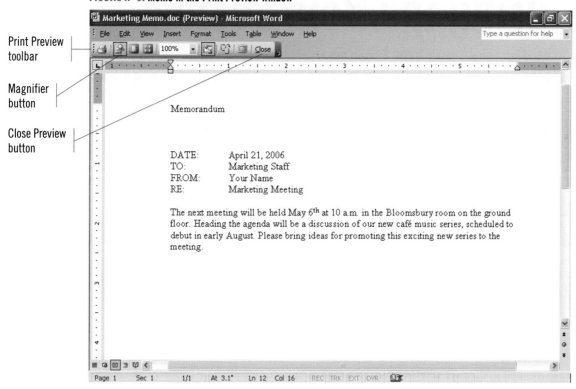

FIGURE A-10: Print dialog box

Change document properties for printing, such as orientation, page order, and paper source

Default printer (yours might differ)

Select the range of pages to print

Select the special aspects of the document to print

Change the number of copies to print

Change the number of pages to print on a sheet of paper

Print using the current settings

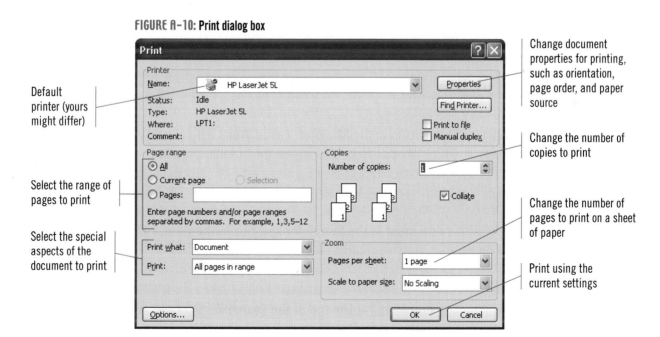

Using the Help System

Word includes an extensive Help system that provides immediate access to definitions, instructions, and useful tips for working with Word. You can quickly access the Help system by typing a question in the Type a question for help box on the menu bar, by clicking the Microsoft Office Word Help button on the Standard toolbar, or by selecting an option from the Help menu. If you are working with an active Internet connection, your queries to the Help system will also return information from the Microsoft Office Online Web site. Table A-4 describes the many ways to get help while using Word. You are curious to learn more about typing with AutoCorrect and viewing and printing documents. You search the Word Help system to discover more about these features.

STEPS

TROUBLE
The figures in this lesson reflect an active Internet connection. If you are not connected to the Internet, then connect if possible.

1. **Type AutoCorrect in the Type a question for help box on the menu bar, then press [Enter]**
   The Search Results task pane opens. Help topics related to AutoCorrect are listed in blue in the task pane. Notice that the pointer changes to 🖑 when you move it over the blue hyperlink text. If you are working online, it may take a few seconds for information to appear in the task pane.

2. **Click About automatic corrections in the Search Results task pane**
   The Microsoft Office Word Help window opens, as shown in Figure A-11. The Help window displays the "About automatic corrections" Help topic you selected. The colored text in the Help window indicates a link to a definition or to more information about the topic. Like all windows, you can maximize the Help window by clicking the Maximize button on its title bar, or you can resize the window by dragging a top, bottom, or side edge.

TROUBLE
If the hyperlink is not visible in your Help window, click the down scroll arrow until it appears.

3. **Read the information in the Help window, then click the colored text hyperlinks**
   Clicking the link expands the Help topic to display more detailed information. A definition of the word "hyperlink" appears in colored text in the Help window.

4. **Read the definition, then click hyperlinks again to close the definition**

5. **Click Using AutoCorrect to correct errors as you type in the Help window, then read the expanded information, clicking the down scroll arrow as necessary to read the entire Help topic**
   Clicking the up or down scroll arrow allows you to navigate through the Help topic when all the text does not fit in the Help window. You can also **scroll** by clicking the scroll bar above and below the scroll box, or by dragging the scroll box up or down in the scroll bar.

6. **Click the Close button in the Microsoft Office Word Help window title bar, then click the Microsoft Office Word Help button 🔘 on the Standard toolbar**
   The Word Help task pane opens, as shown in Figure A-12. You use this task pane to search for Help topics related to a keyword or phrase, to browse the Table of Contents for the Help system, or to connect to the Microsoft Office Online Web site, where you can search for more information on a topic.

7. **Type print a document in the Search for text box in the Word Help task pane, then click the green Start searching button →**
   When you click the green Start searching button, a list of Help topics related to your query appears in the Search Results task pane. You can also press [Enter] to return a list of Help topics.

8. **Click the Back button 🔘 at the top of the Search Results task pane, then click Table of Contents in the Word Help task pane**
   The table of contents for the Help system appears in the Word Help task pane. To peruse the table of contents, you simply click a category in the list to expand it and see a list of subcategories and Help topics. Categories are listed in black text in the task pane and are preceded by a book icon. Help topics are listed in blue text and are preceded by a question mark icon.

QUICK TIP
Click the Back and Forward buttons on the Word Help window toolbar to navigate between the Help topics you have viewed.

9. **Click Viewing and Navigating Documents, click a blue Help topic, read the information in the Microsoft Office Word Help window, then click the Close button in the Help window**

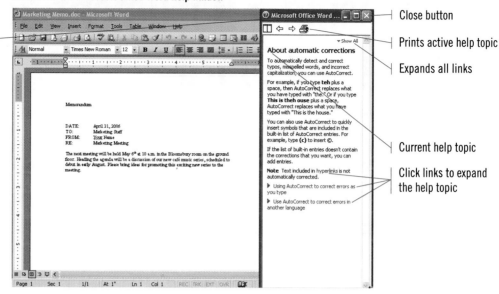

Microsoft Office Word Help window

Close button

Prints active help topic

Expands all links

Current help topic

Click links to expand the help topic

FIGURE A-12: Word Help task pane

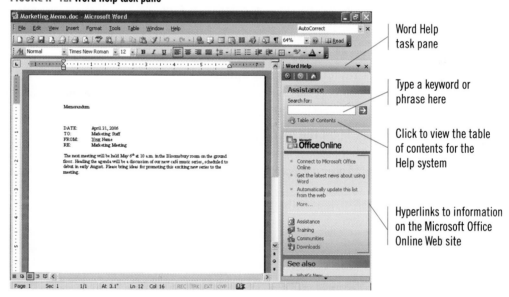

Word Help task pane

Type a keyword or phrase here

Click to view the table of contents for the Help system

Hyperlinks to information on the Microsoft Office Online Web site

TABLE A-4: Word resources for getting Help

resource	function	to use
Type a question for help box	Provides quick access to the Help system	Type a word or question in the Type a question for help box, then press [Enter]
Word Help task pane	Displays the table of contents for the Help system, provides access to a search function, and includes hyperlinks to Help information on the Microsoft Office Online Web site	Press [F1] or click the Microsoft Office Word Help button on the Standard toolbar; in the Word Help task pane, type a word or phrase in the Search for text box to return a list of possible Help topics, click Table of Contents to browse the complete list of Help topics, or click a link to access information on the Microsoft Office Online Web site
Microsoft Office Online Web site	Connects to the Microsoft Office Online Web site, where you can search for information on a topic	Click the Microsoft Office Online command on the Help menu, or click a link in the Word Help task pane
Office Assistant	Displays tips related to your current task and provides access to the Help system	Click Show the Office Assistant on the Help menu to display the Office Assistant; click Hide the Office Assistant on the Help menu to hide the Office Assistant

Word 2003

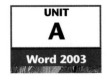
Closing a Document and Exiting Word

When you have finished working on a document and have saved your changes, you can close the document using the Close Window button on the menu bar or the Close command on the File menu. Closing a document closes the document only, it does not close the Word program window. To close the Word program window and exit Word, you can use the Close button on the title bar or the Exit command on the File menu. Using the Exit command closes all open documents. It's good practice to save and close your documents before exiting Word. Figure A-13 shows the Close buttons on the title bar and menu bar. ⬛⬛⬛ You close the memo and exit Word.

STEPS

1. **Click the Close button on the Word Help task pane**

   The task pane closes. It is not necessary to close the task pane before closing a file or the program, but it can be helpful to reduce the amount of information displayed on the screen. Table A-5 describes the functions of the Word task panes.

2. **Click File on the menu bar, then click Close**

   If you saved your changes to the document before closing it, the document closes. If you did not save your changes, an alert box opens asking if you want to save the changes.

3. **Click Yes if the alert box opens**

   The document closes, but the Word program window remains open, as shown in Figure A-14. You can create or open another document, access Help, or close the Word program window.

4. **Click File on the menu bar, then click Exit**

   The Word program window closes. If any Word documents were still open when you exited Word, Word closes all open documents, prompting you to save changes to those documents if necessary.

TABLE A-5: Word task panes

task pane	use to
Getting Started	Open a document, create a new blank document, or search for information on the Microsoft Office Online Web site
Word Help	Access Help topics and connect to Help on the Microsoft Office Online Web site
Search Results	View the results of a search for Help topics and perform a new search
Clip Art	Search for clip art and insert clip art in a document
Research	Search reference books and other sources for information related to a word, such as for synonyms
Clipboard	Cut, copy, and paste items within and between documents
New Document	Create a new blank document, XML document, Web page, or e-mail message, or create a new document using a template
Shared Workspace	Create a Web site (called a document workspace) that allows a group of people to share files, participate in discussions, and work together on a document
Document Updates	View information on a document that is available in a document workspace
Protect Document	Apply formatting and editing restrictions to a shared document
Styles and Formatting	Apply styles to text
Reveal Formatting	Display the formatting applied to text
Mail Merge	Perform a mail merge
XML Structure	Apply XML elements to a Word XML document

FIGURE A-13: Close and Close Window buttons

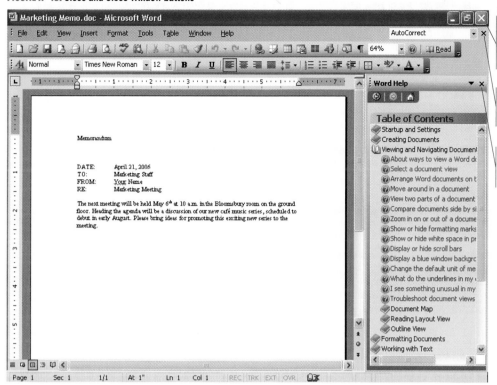

Close button on title bar closes all open documents and exits Word

Close Window button closes the current document

Close button closes the task pane

FIGURE A-14: Word program window with no documents open

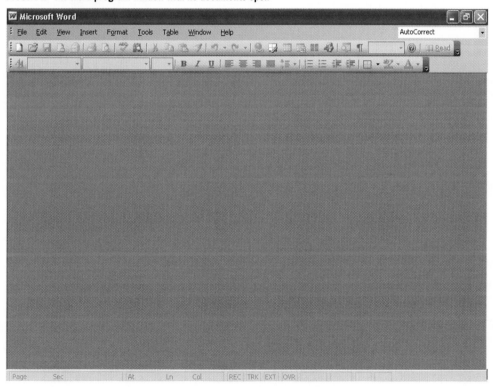

Practice

▼ CONCEPTS REVIEW

Label the elements of the Word program window shown in Figure A-15.

FIGURE A-15

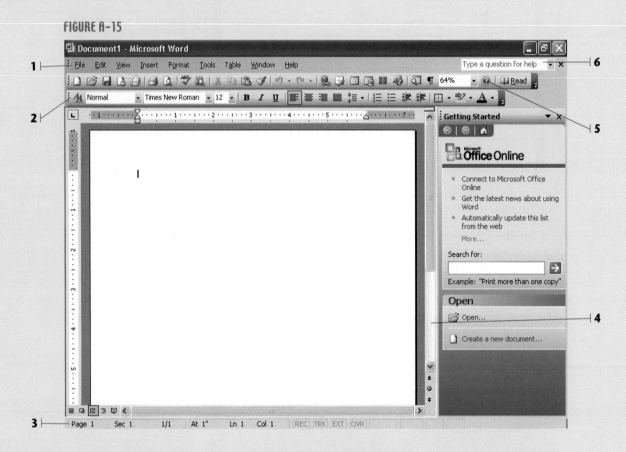

Match each term with the statement that best describes it.

7. **Print Preview**
8. **Office Assistant**
9. **Status bar**
10. **Menu bar**
11. **AutoComplete**
12. **Horizontal ruler**
13. **AutoCorrect**
14. **Normal view**

a. Displays a simple layout view of a document
b. Displays tips on using Word
c. Displays the document exactly as it will look when printed
d. Suggests text to insert into a document
e. Fixes certain errors as you type
f. Displays the number of pages in the current document
g. Displays tab settings and document margins
h. Provides access to Word commands

Select the best answer from the list of choices.

15. Which task pane opens automatically when you start Word?

   a. Document Updates

   b. Getting Started

   c. Word Help

   d. New Document

16. Which element of the Word program window shows the settings for the left and right document margins?

   a. Formatting toolbar

   b. Status bar

   c. Horizontal ruler

   d. Getting Started task pane

17. What is the function of the Exit command on the File menu?

   a. To close the current document without saving changes

   b. To close all open documents and the Word program window

   c. To save changes to and close the current document

   d. To close all open programs

18. Which view do you use when you want to adjust the margins in a document?

   a. Outline view

   b. Web Layout view

   c. Normal view

   d. Print Layout view

19. Which of the following does not appear on the status bar?

   a. The current page number

   b. The current tab settings

   c. The Overtype mode status

   d. The current line number

20. Which of the following is not used to access the Help system?

   a. Type a question for help box

   b. The Office Assistant

   c. Microsoft Office Online

   d. The Research task pane

▼ SKILLS REVIEW

1. Start Word 2003.

   a. Start Word.

   b. Switch to Print Layout view if your blank document opened in a different view.

   c. Change the zoom level to Page Width.

2. Explore the Word program window.

   a. Identify as many elements of the Word program window as you can without referring to the unit material.

   b. Click each menu name on the menu bar and drag the pointer through the menu commands.

   c. Point to each button on the Standard and Formatting toolbars and read the ScreenTips.

   d. Point to each hyperlink in the Getting Started task pane.

▼ SKILLS REVIEW (CONTINUED)

    e. Click the view buttons to view the blank document in Normal, Web Layout, Print Layout, Outline, and Reading Layout view.

    f. Click the Close button in Reading Layout view, then return to Print Layout view.

3. Start a document.

    a. Close the Getting Started task pane.

    b. In a new blank document, type **FAX** at the top of the page, then press [Enter] four times.

    c. Type the following, pressing [Tab] as indicated and pressing [Enter] at the end of each line:

        To: [Tab] **Dr. Beatrice Turcotte**

        From: [Tab] **Your Name**

        Date: [Tab] **Today's date**

        Re: [Tab] **Travel arrangements**

        Pages: [Tab] **1**

        Fax: [Tab] **(514) 555-3948**

    d. Press [Enter], then type **I have reserved a space for you on the March 4-18 Costa Rica Explorer tour. You are scheduled to depart Montreal's Dorval Airport on Plateau Tours and Travel charter flight 234 at 7:45 a.m. on March 4th, arriving in San Jose at 4:30 p.m. local time.**

    e. Press [Enter] twice, then type **Please call me at (514) 555-4983 or stop by our offices on rue St-Denis.**

    f. Insert this sentence at the beginning of the second paragraph: **I must receive full payment within 48 hours to hold your reservation.**

    g. Using the [Backspace] key, delete **Travel** in the Re: line, then type **Costa Rica tour.**

    h. Using the [Delete] key, delete **48** in the last paragraph, then type **72.**

4. Save a document.

    a. Click File on the menu bar, then click Save.

    b. Save the document as **Turcotte Fax** to the drive and folder where your Data Files are located.

    c. After your name, type a comma, press [Spacebar], then type **Plateau Tours and Travel**.

    d. Click the Save button to save your changes to the document.

5. Print a document.

    a. Click the Print Preview button to view the document in Print Preview.

    b. Click the word FAX to zoom in on the document, then proofread the fax.

    c. Click the Magnifier button to switch to edit mode, then correct any typing errors in your document.

    d. Close Print Preview, then save your changes to the document.

    e. Print the fax using the default print settings.

6. Use the Help system.

    a. Click the Microsoft Office Word Help button to open the Word Help task pane.

    b. Type **open a document** in the Search text box, then press [Enter].

    c. Click the topic Open a file.

    d. Read about opening documents in Word by clicking the links to expand the Help topic.

    e. Close the Help window, type **viewing documents** in the Type a question for help box, then press [Enter].

    f. Click the link Zoom in on or out of a document in the Search Results task pane, then read the Help topic.

    g. Close the Help window, then close the Search Results task pane.

7. Close a document and exit Word.

    a. Close the Turcotte Fax document, saving your changes if necessary.

    b. Exit Word.

▼ INDEPENDENT CHALLENGE 1

You are a performance artist, well known for your innovative work with computers. The Missoula Arts Council president, Sam McCrum, has asked you to be the keynote speaker at an upcoming conference in Missoula, Montana, on the role of technology in the arts. You are pleased at the invitation, and write a letter to Mr. McCrum accepting the invitation and confirming the details. Your letter to Mr. McCrum should reference the following information:

- The conference will be held October 10–12, 2006, at the civic center in Missoula.
- You have been asked to speak for one hour on Saturday, October 11, followed by a half hour for questions.
- Mr. McCrum suggested the lecture topic "Technology's Effect on Art and Culture."
- Your talk will include a 20-minute slide presentation.
- The Missoula Arts Council will make your travel arrangements.
- Your preference is to arrive in Missoula on Friday, October 10, and depart on Sunday, October 12.
- You want to fly in and out of the airport closest to your home.

a. Start Word.

b. Save a new blank document as **McCrum Letter** to the drive and folder where your Data Files are located.

c. Model your letter to Mr. McCrum after the sample business letter shown in Figure A-16. Use the following formatting guidelines: 3 blank lines after the date, 1 blank line after the inside address, 1 blank line after the salutation, 1 blank line after each body paragraph, and 3 blank lines between the closing and your typed name.

d. Begin the letter by typing today's date.

e. Type the inside address. Be sure to include Mr. McCrum's title and the name of the organization. Make up a street address and zip code.

f. Type a salutation.

g. Using the information listed above, type the body of the letter:

- In the first paragraph, accept the invitation to speak and confirm the important conference details.
- In the second paragraph, confirm your lecture topic and provide any relevant details.
- In the third paragraph, state your travel preferences.
- Type a short final paragraph.

h. Type a closing, then include your name in the signature block.

Advanced Challenge Exercise

- View the letter in Normal view, then correct your spelling and grammar errors, if any, by right-clicking any red- or green-underlined text and then choosing from the options on the shortcut menu.
- View the letter in Print Layout view, then remove any smart tags.
- View the letter in Reading Layout view, then click the Close button on the Reading Layout toolbar to close Reading Layout view.

i. Proofread your letter, make corrections as needed, then save your changes.

j. Preview the letter, print the letter, close the document, then exit Word.

FIGURE A-16

June 12, 2006

Dr. Leslie Morris
Professor of American Literature
Department of Literature
Manchester State College
Manchester, NH 03258

Dear Dr. Morris:

Thank you very much for your kind invitation to speak at your upcoming conference on the literature of place. I will be happy to oblige. I understand the conference will be held September 16 and 17 in the Sanders Auditorium.

I will address my remarks to the topic you suggested, "Writers of the Monadnock region." I understand you would like me to speak at 2:30 p.m. on September 16 for forty minutes, with twenty minutes of questions to follow. My talk will include a slide show. I presume you will have the necessary equipment—a slide projector and viewing screen—on hand.

My preference is to arrive in Manchester on the morning of September 16, and to depart that evening. It is easiest for me to use New York's LaGuardia Airport. I am grateful that your office will be taking care of my travel arrangements.

I look forward to meeting you in September.

Sincerely,

Jessica Grange

▼ INDEPENDENT CHALLENGE 2

Your company has recently installed Word 2003 on its company network. As the training manager, it's your responsibility to teach employees how to use the new software productively. Now that they have begun working with Word 2003, several employees have asked you about smart tags. In response to their queries, you decide to write a memo to all employees explaining how to use the smart tag feature. You know that smart tags are designed to help users perform tasks in Word that normally would require opening a different program, such as Microsoft Outlook (a desktop information-management program that includes e-mail, calendar, and address book features). Before writing your memo, you'll learn more about smart tags by searching the Word Help system.

a. Start Word and save a new blank document as **Smart Tags Memo** to the drive and folder where your Data Files are located.

b. Type **WORD TRAINING MEMORANDUM** at the top of the document, press [Enter] four times, then type the memo heading information shown in Figure A-17. Make sure to include your name in the From line and the current date in the Date line.

c. Press [Enter] twice to place the insertion point where you will begin typing the body of your memo.

d. Search the Word Help system for information on working with smart tags.

e. Type your memo after completing your research. In your memo, define smart tags, then explain what they look like, how to use smart tags, and how to remove smart tags from a document.

FIGURE A-17

> WORD TRAINING MEMORANDUM
>
>
> To: All employees
> From: Your Name, Training Manager
> Date: Today's date
> Re: Smart tags in Microsoft Word

Advanced Challenge Exercise

- Search the Help system for information on how to check for new smart tags developed by Microsoft and third-party vendors.
- Print the information you find.
- Add a short paragraph to your memo explaining how to find new smart tags.

f. Save your changes, preview and print the memo, then close the document and exit Word.

▼ INDEPENDENT CHALLENGE 3

Yesterday you interviewed for a job as marketing director at Komata Web Designs. You spoke with several people at Komata, including Shige Murata, Director of Operations, whose business card is shown in Figure A-18. You need to write a follow-up letter to Mr. Murata, thanking him for the interview and expressing your interest in the company and the position. He also asked you to send him some samples of your marketing work, which you will enclose with the letter.

a. Start Word and save a new blank document as **Komata Letter** to the drive and folder where your Data Files are located.

b. Begin the letter by typing today's date.

c. Four lines below the date, type the inside address, referring to Figure A-18 for the address information. Be sure to include the recipient's title, company name, and full mailing address in the inside address. (*Hint*: When typing a foreign address, type the name of the country in capital letters by itself on the last line.)

d. Two lines below the inside address, type the salutation.

FIGURE A-18

> **Komata Web Designs**
>
> 5-8, Edobori 4-chome
> Minato-ku
> Tokyo 108-0034
> Japan
>
> **Shige Murata**   Phone: (03) 5555-3299
> *Director of Operations*   Fax: (03) 5555-7028
>   Email: smurata@komata.co.jp

▼ INDEPENDENT CHALLENGE 3 (CONTINUED)

e. Two lines below the salutation, type the body of the letter according to the following guidelines:

- In the first paragraph, thank him for the interview. Then restate your interest in the position and express your desire to work for the company. Add any specific details you think will enhance the power of your letter.
- In the second paragraph, note that you are enclosing three samples of your work and explain something about the samples you are enclosing.
- Type a short final paragraph.

f. Two lines below the last body paragraph, type a closing, then four lines below the closing, type the signature block. Be sure to include your name in the signature block.

g. Two lines below the signature block, type an enclosure notation. (*Hint*: An enclosure notation usually includes the word "Enclosures" or the abbreviation "Enc." followed by the number of enclosures in parentheses.)

h. Save your changes.

i. Preview and print the letter, then close the document and exit Word.

▼ INDEPENDENT CHALLENGE 4

Unlike personal letters or many e-mail messages, business letters are formal in tone and format. The World Wide Web is one source for information on writing styles, proper document formatting, and other business etiquette issues. In this independent challenge, you will research guidelines and tips for writing effective and professional business letters. Your online research should seek answers to the following questions: What is important to keep in mind when writing a business letter? What are the parts of a business letter? What are some examples of business letter types? What are some useful tips for writing business letters?

a. Use your favorite search engine to search the Web for information on writing and formatting business letters. Use the keywords **business letters** to conduct your search.

b. Review the Web sites you find. Print at least two Web pages that offer useful guidelines for writing business letters.

c. Start Word and save a new blank document as **Business Letters** to the drive and folder where your Data Files are located.

d. Type your name at the top of the document, then press [Enter] twice.

e. Type a brief report on the results of your research. Your report should answer the following questions:

- What are the URLs of the Web sites you visited to research guidelines for writing a business letter? (*Hint*: A URL is a Web page's address. An example of a URL is www.eHow.com.)
- What is important to keep in mind when writing a business letter?
- What are the parts of a business letter?
- In what situations do people write business letters? Provide at least five examples.

f. Save your changes to the document, preview and print it, then close the document and exit Word.

Create the cover letter shown in Figure A-19. Save the document with the name **Publishing Cover Letter** to the drive and folder where your Data Files are stored, print a copy of the letter, then close the document and exit Word.

FIGURE A-19

July 17, 2006

Ms. Charlotte Janoch
Managing Editor
Sunrise Press
6354 Baker Street
Townsend, MA 02181

Dear Ms. Janoch:

I read of the opening for an editorial assistant on the July 15 edition of Boston.com, and I would like to be considered for the position. A recent graduate of Merrimack College, I am interested in pursuing a career in publishing.

My desire for a publishing career springs from my interest in writing and editing. At Merrimack College, I was a frequent contributor to the student newspaper and was involved in creating a Web site for student poetry and short fiction.

I have a wealth of experience using Microsoft Word in professional settings. For the past several summers I worked as an office assistant for Packer Investment Consultants, where I used Word to create newsletters and financial reports for clients. During the school year, I also worked part-time in the Merrimack College admissions office. Here I used Word's mail merge feature to create form letters and mailing labels.

My enclosed resume details my talents and experience. I would welcome the opportunity to discuss the position and my qualifications with you. I can be reached at 617-555-3849.

Sincerely,

Your Name

Enc.

UNIT B
Word 2003

Editing Documents

OBJECTIVES

Open a document
Select text
Cut and paste text
Copy and paste text
Use the Office Clipboard
Find and replace text
Check spelling and grammar
Use the Thesaurus
Use wizards and templates

If you have a SAM user profile, you may have access to hands-on instruction, practice, and assessment of the skills covered in this unit. Log in to your SAM account and go to your assignments page to see what your instructor has assigned.

The sophisticated editing features in Word make it easy to revise and polish your documents. In this unit, you learn how to open an existing file, revise it by replacing, copying, and moving text, and then save the document as a new file. You also learn how to perfect your documents using proofing tools and how to quickly create attractive, professionally designed documents using wizards and templates. ⬛⬛ You have been asked to create a press release about a new MediaLoft lecture series in New York. The press release should provide information about the series so that newspapers, radio stations, and other media outlets can announce it to the public. MediaLoft press releases are disseminated by fax, so you also need to create a fax coversheet to use when you fax the press release to your list of press contacts.

Opening a Document

Sometimes the easiest way to create a document is to edit an existing document and save it with a new file-name. To modify a document, you must first **open** it so that it displays in the document window. Word offers several methods for opening documents, described in Table B-1. Once you have opened a file, you can use the Save As command to create a new file that is a copy of the original. You can then edit the new file without making changes to the original. ⬛⬛⬛⬛ Rather than write your press release from scratch, you decide to modify a press release written for a similar event. You begin by opening the press release document and saving it with a new filename.

STEPS

TROUBLE
If the task pane is not open, click View on the menu bar, then click Task Pane.

1. **Start Word**

   Word opens and a blank document and the Getting Started task pane appear in the program window, as shown in Figure B-1. The Getting Started task pane contains links for opening existing documents and for creating new documents.

2. **Click the Open or More hyperlink at the bottom of the Getting Started task pane**

   The Open dialog box opens. You use the Open dialog box to locate and select the file you want to open. The Look in list box displays the current drive or folder. You also can use the Open button 🖻 on the Standard toolbar or the Open command on the File menu to open the Open dialog box.

3. **Click the Look in list arrow, click the drive containing your Data Files, then double-click the folder containing your Data Files**

   A list of the Data Files for this unit appears in the Open dialog box, as shown in Figure B-2.

QUICK TIP
You also can double-click a filename in the Open dialog box to open the file.

4. **Click the filename WD B-1.doc in the Open dialog box to select it, then click Open**

   The document opens. Notice that the filename WD B-1.doc appears in the title bar. Once you have opened a file, you can edit it and use the Save or the Save As command to save your changes. You use the **Save** command when you want to save the changes you make to a file, overwriting the file that is stored on a disk. You use the **Save As** command when you want to create a new file with a different filename, leaving the original file intact.

5. **Click File on the menu bar, then click Save As**

   The Save As dialog box opens. By saving a file with a new filename, you create a document that is identical to the original document. The original filename is selected (highlighted) in the File name text box. Any text you type replaces the selected text.

6. **Type NY Press Release in the File name text box, then click Save**

   The original file closes and the NY Press Release file is displayed in the document window. Notice the new filename in the title bar. You can now make changes to the press release file without affecting the original file.

Clues to Use

Managing files and folders

The Open and Save As dialog boxes include powerful tools for navigating, creating, deleting, and renaming files and folders on your computer, a network, or the Web. By selecting a file or folder and clicking the Delete button ✖, you can delete the item and send it to the Recycle Bin. You can also create a new folder for storing files by clicking the Create New Folder button 🗀 and typing a name for the folder. The new folder is created in the current folder. To rename a file or folder, simply right-click it in the dialog box, click Rename, type a new name, and then press [Enter].

Using the Save As dialog box, you can create new files that are based on existing files. To create a new file, you can save an existing file with a different filename or save it in a different location on your system. You also can save a file in a different file format so that it can be opened in a different software program. To save a file in a different format, click the Save as type list arrow, then click the type of file you want to create. For example, you can save a Word document (which has a .doc file extension) as a plain text file (.txt), as a Web page file (.htm), or in a variety of other file formats.

FIGURE B-1: Getting Started task pane

Open button ⊢

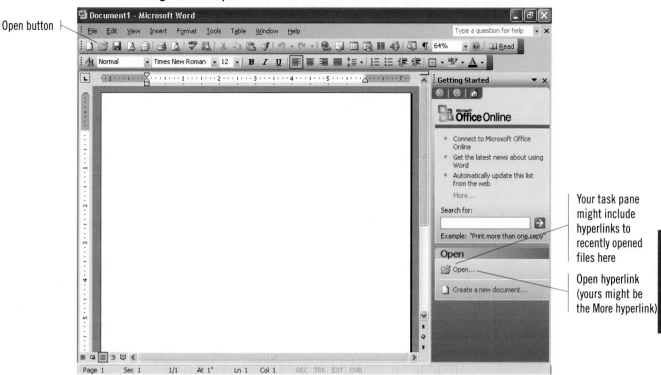

Your task pane
might include
hyperlinks to
recently opened
files here

Open hyperlink
(yours might be
the More hyperlink)

FIGURE B-2: Open dialog box

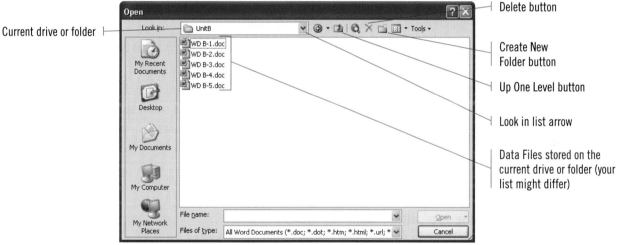

Current drive or folder ⊢

Delete button

Create New
Folder button

Up One Level button

Look in list arrow

Data Files stored on the
current drive or folder (your
list might differ)

TABLE B-1: Methods for opening documents

use	to	if you want to
The Open button 📂 on the Standard toolbar, the Open command on the File menu, the Open or More hyperlink in the Getting Started task pane, or [Ctrl][O]	Open the Open dialog box	Open an existing file
A filename hyperlink in the Getting Started task pane	Open the file in the document window	Open the file; a fast way to open a file that was recently opened on your computer
The From existing document hyperlink in the New Document task pane	Open the New from Existing Document dialog box	Create a copy of an existing file; a fast way to open a document you intend to save with a new filename

Selecting Text

Before deleting, editing, or formatting text, you must **select** the text. Selecting text involves clicking and dragging the I-beam pointer across text to highlight it. You also can click with the ⅍ pointer in the blank area to the left of text to select lines or paragraphs. Table B-2 describes the many ways to select text. You revise the press release by selecting text and replacing it with new text.

STEPS

TROUBLE
If you make a mistake, you can deselect the text by clicking anywhere in the document window.

1. **Click the** Zoom list arrow **on the Standard toolbar, click** Page Width, **click before** April 14, 2006, **then drag the** I **pointer over the text to select it**

   The date is selected, as shown in Figure B-3.

2. **Type** May 1, 2006

   The text you type replaces the selected text.

3. **Double-click** James, **type your first name, double-click** Callaghan, **then type your last name**

   Double-clicking a word selects the entire word.

4. **Place the pointer in the margin to the left of the phone number so that the pointer changes to** ⅍, **click to select the phone number, then type** (415) 555-8293

   Clicking to the left of a line of text with the ⅍ pointer selects the entire line.

5. **Click the** down scroll arrow **at the bottom of the vertical scroll bar until the headline Alex Fogg to Speak... is at the top of your document window**

   The scroll arrows or scroll bars allow you to scroll through a document. You scroll through a document when you want to display different parts of the document in the document window.

6. **Select** SAN FRANCISCO, **then type** NEW YORK

QUICK TIP
If you delete text by mistake, immediately click the Undo button ↻ on the Standard toolbar to restore the deleted text to the document.

7. **In the fourth body paragraph, select the sentence** All events will be held at the St. James Hotel., **then press** [Delete]

   Selecting text and pressing [Delete] removes the text from the document.

8. **Select and replace text in the second and last paragraphs using the following table:**

select	type
May 12	June 14
St. James Hotel in downtown San Francisco	Waldorf-Astoria Hotel
National Public Radio's Helen DeSaint	New York Times literary editor Janet Richard

   The edited press release is shown in Figure B-4.

9. **Click the** Save button 🖫 **on the Standard toolbar**

   Your changes to the press release are saved. Always save before and after editing text.

TABLE B-2: Methods for selecting text

to select	use the mouse pointer to
Any amount of text	Drag over the text
A word	Double-click the word
A line of text	Click with the ⅍ pointer to the left of the line
A sentence	Press and hold [Ctrl], then click the sentence
A paragraph	Triple-click the paragraph or double-click with the ⅍ pointer to the left of the paragraph
A large block of text	Click at the beginning of the selection, press and hold [Shift], then click at the end of the selection
Multiple nonconsecutive selections	Select the first selection, then press and hold [Ctrl] as you select each additional selection
An entire document	Triple-click with the ⅍ pointer to the left of any text, click Select All on the Edit menu, or press [Ctrl][A]

FIGURE B-3: Date selected in the press release

Selected text

Left document margin

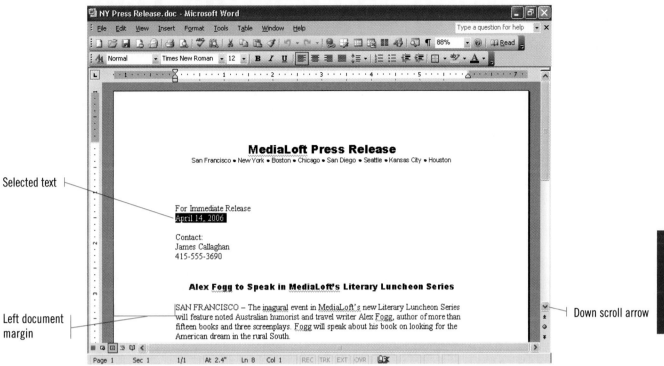

Down scroll arrow

FIGURE B-4: Edited press release

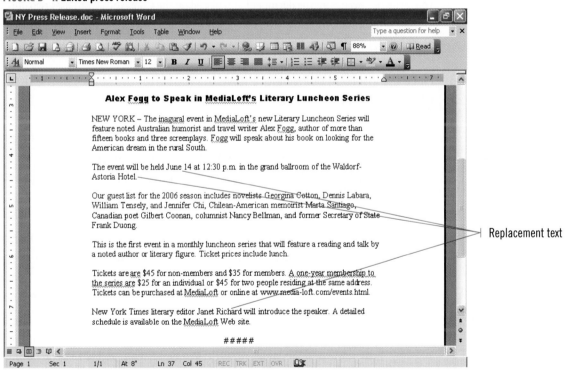

Replacement text

Clues to Use

Replacing text in Overtype mode

Normally you must select text before typing to replace the existing characters, but by turning on **Overtype mode** you can type over existing characters without selecting them first. To turn Overtype mode on and off on your computer, double-click OVR in the status bar. On some computers you also can turn Overtype mode on and off by pressing [Insert]. When Overtype mode is on, OVR appears in black in the status bar. When Overtype mode is off, OVR is dimmed.

Cutting and Pasting Text

The editing features in Word allow you to move text from one location to another in a document. The operation of moving text is often called **cut and paste**. When you cut text from a document, you remove it from the document and add it to the **Clipboard**, a temporary storage area for text and graphics that you cut or copy from a document. You cut text by selecting it and using the Cut command on the Edit menu or the Cut button. To insert the text from the Clipboard into the document, you place the insertion point where you want to insert the text, and then use the Paste command on the Edit menu or the Paste button to paste the text at that location. You also can move text by dragging it to a new location using the mouse. This operation is called **drag and drop**. ▓▓▓▓▒ You reorganize the information in the press release using the cut-and-paste and drag-and-drop methods.

STEPS

1. **Click the** Show/Hide ¶ **button** ¶ **on the Standard toolbar**

   Formatting marks appear in the document window. **Formatting marks** are special characters that appear on your screen and do not print. Common formatting marks include the paragraph symbol (¶), which shows the end of a paragraph—wherever you press [Enter]; the dot symbol (•), which represents a space—wherever you press [Spacebar]; and the arrow symbol (➔), which shows the location of a tab stop—wherever you press [Tab]. Working with formatting marks turned on can help you to select, edit, and format text with precision.

2. **In the third paragraph, select** Canadian poet Gilbert Coonan, **(including the comma and the space after it), then click the** Cut button ✂ **on the Standard toolbar**

   The text is removed from the document and placed on the Clipboard. Word uses two different clipboards: the **system Clipboard** (the Clipboard), which holds just one item, and the **Office Clipboard**, which holds up to 24 items. The last item you cut or copy is always added to both clipboards. You'll learn more about the Office Clipboard in a later lesson.

3. **Place the insertion point before** novelists **(but after the space) in the first line of the third paragraph, then click the** Paste button 📋 **on the Standard toolbar**

   The text is pasted at the location of the insertion point, as shown in Figure B-5. The Paste Options button 📋 appears below text when you first paste it in a document. You'll learn more about the Paste Options button in the next lesson. For now, you can ignore it.

4. **Press and hold [Ctrl], click the sentence** Ticket prices include lunch. **in the fourth paragraph, then release [Ctrl]**

   The entire sentence is selected.

5. **Press and hold the mouse button over the selected text until the pointer changes to** ▨, **then drag the pointer's vertical line to the end of the fifth paragraph (between the period and the paragraph mark) as shown in Figure B-6**

   The pointer's vertical line indicates the location the text will be inserted when you release the mouse button.

6. **Release the mouse button**

   The selected text is moved to the location of the insertion point. It's convenient to move text using the drag-and-drop method when the locations of origin and destination are both visible on the screen. Text is not removed to the Clipboard when you move it using drag-and-drop.

7. **Deselect the text, then click the** Save button 💾 **on the Standard toolbar**

   Your changes to the press release are saved.

FIGURE B-5: Moved text with Paste Options button

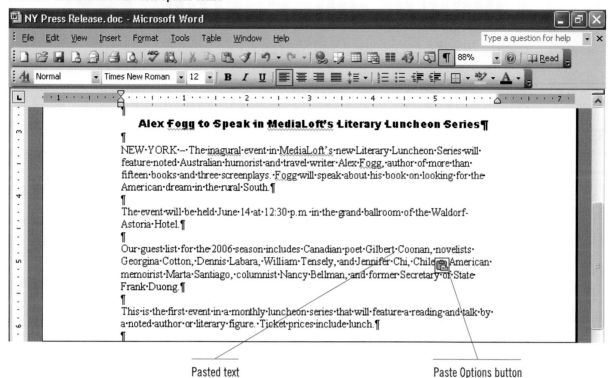

Pasted text   Paste Options button

FIGURE B-6: Text being dragged to a new location

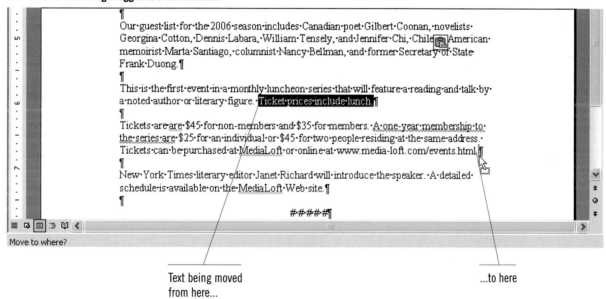

Text being moved   ...to here
from here...

Clues to Use

Using keyboard shortcuts

Instead of using the Cut, Copy, and Paste commands to edit text in Word, you can use the **keyboard shortcuts** [Ctrl][X] to cut text, [Ctrl][C] to copy text, and [Ctrl][V] to paste text. A **shortcut key** is a function key, such as [F1], or a combination of keys, such as [Ctrl][S], that you press to perform a command. For example, pressing [Ctrl][S] saves changes to a document just as clicking the Save button or using the Save command on the File menu saves a document. Becoming skilled at using keyboard shortcuts can help you to quickly accomplish many of the tasks you perform frequently in Word. If a keyboard shortcut is available for a menu command, then it is listed next to the command on the menu.

Copying and Pasting Text

Copying and pasting text is similar to cutting and pasting text, except that the text you copy is not removed from the document. Rather, a copy of the text is placed on the Clipboard, leaving the original text in place. You can copy text to the Clipboard using the Copy command on the Edit menu or the Copy button, or you can copy text by pressing [Ctrl] as you drag the selected text from one location to another. You continue to edit the press release by copying text from one location to another.

STEPS

1. **In the headline, select Literary Luncheon, then click the Copy button ▣ on the Standard toolbar**

   A copy of the text is placed on the Clipboard, leaving the text you copied in place.

2. **Place the insertion point before season in the third body paragraph, then click the Paste button ▣ on the Standard toolbar**

   "Literary Luncheon" is inserted before "season," as shown in Figure B-7. Notice that the pasted text is formatted differently than the paragraph in which it was inserted.

3. **Click the Paste Options button ▣, then click Match Destination Formatting**

   The Paste Options button allows you to change the formatting of pasted text. The formatting of "Literary Luncheon" is changed to match the rest of the paragraph. The options available on the Paste Options menu depend on the format of the text you are pasting and the format of the surrounding text.

4. **Scroll down if necessary so that the last two paragraphs are visible on your screen**

5. **In the fifth paragraph, select www.media-loft.com, press and hold [Ctrl], then press the mouse button until the pointer changes to ▣**

6. **Drag the pointer's vertical line to the end of the last paragraph, placing it between site and the period, release the mouse button, then release [Ctrl]**

   The text is copied to the last paragraph. Since the formatting of the text you copied is the same as the formatting of the paragraph in which you inserted it, you can ignore the Paste Options button. Text is not copied to the Clipboard when you copy it using the drag-and-drop method.

7. **Place the insertion point before www.media-loft.com in the last paragraph, type at followed by a space, then click the Save button ▣ on the Standard toolbar**

   Compare your document with Figure B-8.

Clues to Use

Copying and moving items in a long document

If you want to copy or move items between parts of a long document, it can be useful to split the document window into two panes so that the item you want to copy or move is displayed in one pane and the destination for the item is displayed in the other pane. To split a window, click the Split command on the Window menu, drag the horizontal split bar that appears to the location you want to split the window, and then click. Once the document window is split into two panes, you can drag the split bar to resize the panes and use the scroll bars in each pane to display different parts of the document. To copy or move an item from one pane to another, you can use the Cut, Copy, and Paste commands, or you can drag the item between the panes. When you are finished editing the document, double-click the split bar to restore the window to a single pane.

FIGURE B-7: Text pasted in document

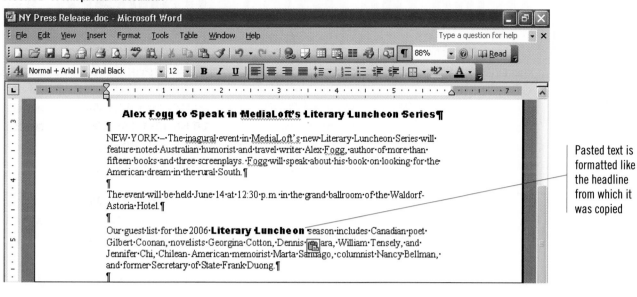

Pasted text is formatted like the headline from which it was copied

FIGURE B-8: Copied text in press release

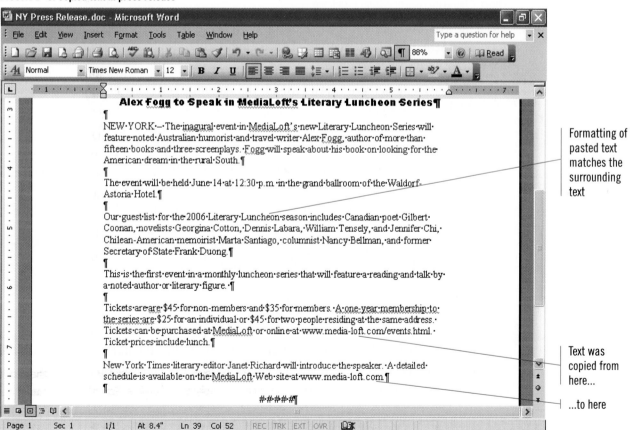

Formatting of pasted text matches the surrounding text

Text was copied from here...

...to here

Using the Office Clipboard

The Office Clipboard allows you to collect text and graphics from files created in any Office program and insert them into your Word documents. It holds up to 24 items and, unlike the system Clipboard, the items on the Office Clipboard can be viewed. By default, the Office Clipboard opens automatically when you cut or copy two items consecutively. You can also use the Office Clipboard command on the Edit menu to manually display the Office Clipboard if you prefer to work with it open. You add items to the Office Clipboard using the Cut and Copy commands. The last item you collect is always added to both the system Clipboard and the Office Clipboard. ▰▰▰▰ You use the Office Clipboard to move several sentences in your press release.

STEPS

1. **In the last paragraph, select the sentence** New York Times literary editor... **(including the space after the period), then click the** Cut button ✂ **on the Standard toolbar**

   The sentence is cut to the Clipboard.

2. **Select the sentence** A detailed schedule is... **(including the ¶ mark), then click** ✂

   The Office Clipboard opens in the Clipboard task pane, as shown in Figure B-9. It displays the items you cut from the press release. The icon next to each item indicates the items are from a Word document.

3. **Place the insertion point at the end of the second paragraph (after Hotel. but before the ¶ mark), then click the** New York Times literary editor... **item on the Office Clipboard**

   Clicking an item on the Office Clipboard pastes the item in the document at the location of the insertion point. Notice that the item remains on the Office Clipboard even after you pasted it. Items remain on the Office Clipboard until you delete them or close all open Office programs. Also, if you add a 25th item to the Office Clipboard, the first item is deleted.

4. **Place the insertion point at the end of the third paragraph (after Duong.), then click the** A detailed schedule is... **item on the Office Clipboard**

   The sentence is pasted in the document.

5. **Select the fourth paragraph, which contains the sentence** This is the first event... **(including the ¶ mark), then click** ✂

   The sentence is cut to the Office Clipboard. Notice that the last item collected displays at the top of the Clipboard task pane. The last item collected is also stored on the system Clipboard.

6. **Place the insertion point at the beginning of the third paragraph (before Our...), click the** Paste button 🖺 **on the Standard toolbar, then press** [Backspace]

   The "This is the first..." sentence is pasted at the beginning of the "Our guest list..." paragraph. You can paste the last item collected using either the Paste command or the Office Clipboard.

7. **Place the insertion point at the end of the third paragraph (after www.media-loft.com and before the ¶ mark), then press** [Delete] **twice**

   The ¶ symbols and the blank line between the third and fourth paragraphs are deleted.

8. **Click the** Show/Hide ¶ button ¶ **on the Standard toolbar**

   Compare your press release with Figure B-10.

9. **Click the** Clear All button **on the Office Clipboard to remove the items from it, close the Clipboard task pane, press** [Ctrl][Home], **then click the** Save button 🖫

   Pressing [Ctrl][Home] moves the insertion point to the top of the document.

FIGURE B-9: Office Clipboard in Clipboard task pane

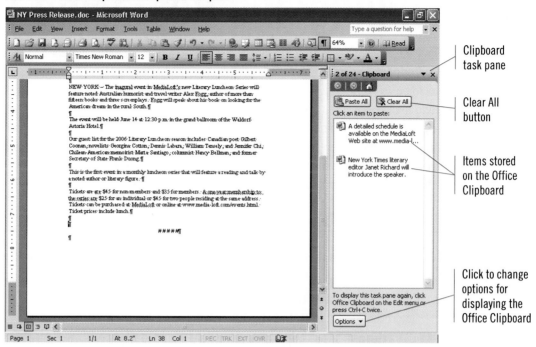

Clipboard task pane

Clear All button

Items stored on the Office Clipboard

Click to change options for displaying the Office Clipboard

FIGURE B-10: Revised press release

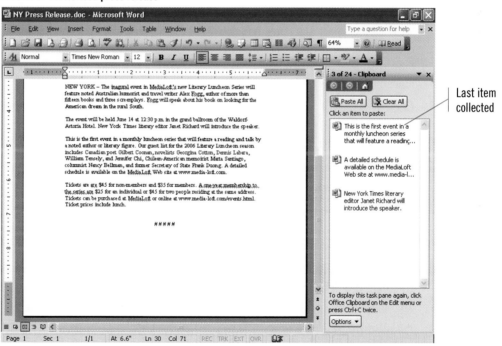

Last item collected

Clues to Use

Copying and moving items between documents

The system and Office Clipboards also can be used to copy and move items between Word documents. To copy or cut items from one Word document and paste them into another, first open both documents and the Clipboard task pane in the program window. With multiple documents open, you can copy and move items between documents by copying or cutting the item(s) from one document and then switching to another document and pasting the item(s). To switch between open documents, click the button on the taskbar for the document you want to appear in the document window. You can also display both documents at the same time by clicking the Arrange All command on the Window menu. The Office Clipboard stores all the items collected from all documents, regardless of which document is displayed in the document window. The system Clipboard stores the last item collected from any document.

Finding and Replacing Text

The Find and Replace feature in Word allows you to automatically search for and replace all instances of a word or phrase in a document. For example, you might need to substitute "bookstore" for "store," and it would be very time-consuming to manually locate and replace each instance of "store" in a long document. Using the Replace command you can automatically find and replace all occurrences of specific text at once, or you can choose to find and review each occurrence individually. You also can use the Find command to locate and highlight every occurrence of a specific word or phrase in a document. ██████ MediaLoft has decided to change the name of the New York series from "Literary Luncheon Series" to "Literary Limelight Series." You use the Replace command to search the document for all instances of "Luncheon" and replace them with "Limelight."

STEPS

1. **Click Edit on the menu bar, click Replace, then click More in the Find and Replace dialog box**
   The Find and Replace dialog box opens, as shown in Figure B-11.

2. **Click the Find what text box, then type Luncheon**
   "Luncheon" is the text that will be replaced.

3. **Press [Tab], then type Limelight in the Replace with text box**
   "Limelight" is the text that will replace "Luncheon."

4. **Click the Match case check box in the Search Options section to select it**
   Selecting the Match case check box tells Word to find only exact matches for the uppercase and lowercase characters you entered in the Find what text box. You want to replace all instances of "Luncheon" in the proper name "Literary Luncheon Series." You do not want to replace "luncheon" when it refers to a lunchtime event.

5. **Click Replace All**
   Clicking Replace All changes all occurrences of "Luncheon" to "Limelight" in the press release. A message box reports three replacements were made.

6. **Click OK to close the message box, then click Close to close the Find and Replace dialog box**
   Word replaced "Luncheon" with "Limelight" in three locations, but did not replace "luncheon."

7. **Click Edit on the menu bar, then click Find**
   The Find and Replace dialog box opens with the Find tab displayed. The Find command allows you to quickly locate all instances of text in a document. You can use it to verify that Word did not replace "luncheon."

8. **Type luncheon in the Find what text box, click the Highlight all items found in check box to select it, click Find All, then click Close**
   The Find and Replace dialog box closes and "luncheon" is selected in the document, as shown in Figure B-12.

9. **Deselect the text, press [Ctrl][Home], then click the Save button 🖫 on the Standard toolbar**

Clues to Use

Inserting text with AutoCorrect

As you type, AutoCorrect automatically corrects many commonly misspelled words. By creating your own AutoCorrect entries, you also can set Word to quickly insert text that you type often, such as your name or contact information, or to correct words you frequently misspell. For example, you could create an AutoCorrect entry so that the name "Alice Wegman" is automatically inserted whenever you type "aw" followed by a space. To create an AutoCorrect entry, click AutoCorrect Options on the Tools menu. On the AutoCorrect tab in the AutoCorrect dialog box, type the text you want to be automatically corrected in the Replace text box (such as "aw"), type the text you want to be automatically inserted in its place in the With text box (such as "Alice Wegman"), then click Add. The AutoCorrect entry is added to the list. Note that Word inserts an AutoCorrect entry in a document only when you press [Spacebar] after typing the text you want Word to correct. For example, Word will insert "Alice Wegman" when you type "aw" followed by a space, but not when you type "awful."

FIGURE B-11: Find and Replace dialog box

Replace only exact matches of uppercase and lowercase characters

Find only complete words

Use wildcards (*) in a search string

Find words that sound like the Find what text

Find and replace all forms of a word

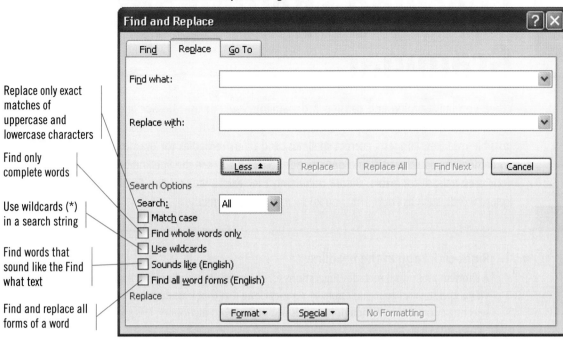

Word 2003

FIGURE B-12: Found text highlighted in document

Found text is highlighted

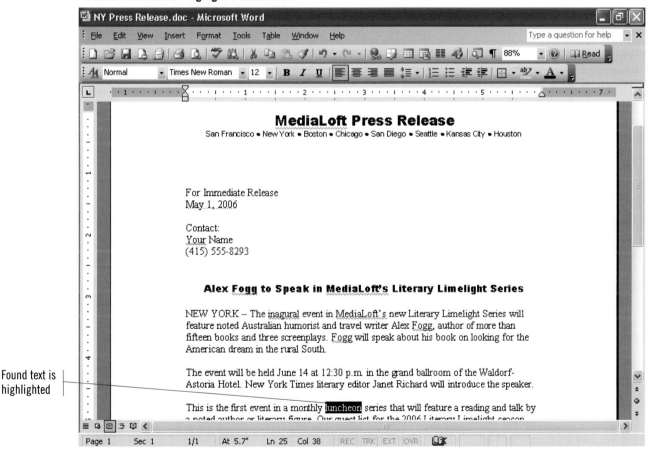

Checking Spelling and Grammar

When you finish typing and revising a document, you can use the Spelling and Grammar command to search the document for misspelled words and grammar errors. The Spelling and Grammar checker flags possible mistakes, suggests correct spellings, and offers remedies for grammar errors such as subject-verb agreement, repeated words, and punctuation. ████▓▓ You use the Spelling and Grammar checker to search your press release for errors. Before beginning the search, you set the Spelling and Grammar checker to ignore words, such as Fogg, that you know are spelled correctly.

STEPS

TROUBLE

If Word flags your name as misspelled, right-click it, then click Ignore All.

1. **Right-click Fogg in the headline**

   A shortcut menu that includes suggestions for correcting the spelling of "Fogg" opens. You can correct individual spelling and grammar errors by right-clicking text that is underlined with a red or green wavy line and selecting a correction. Although "Fogg" is not in the Word dictionary, it is spelled correctly in the document.

2. **Click Ignore All**

   Clicking Ignore All tells Word not to flag "Fogg" as misspelled.

TROUBLE

If "MediaLoft" and "MediaLoft's" are not flagged as misspelled, skip this step.

3. **Right-click MediaLoft at the top of the document, click Ignore All, right-click MediaLoft's in the headline, then click Ignore All**

   The red wavy underline is removed from all instances of "MediaLoft" and "MediaLoft's."

QUICK TIP

To change the language used by the Word proofing tools, click Tools on the menu bar, point to Language, then click Set Language.

4. **Press [Ctrl][Home], then click the Spelling and Grammar button 🔤 on the Standard toolbar**

   The Spelling and Grammar: English (U.S.) dialog box opens, as shown in Figure B-13. The dialog box identifies "inagural" as misspelled and suggests possible corrections for the error. The word selected in the Suggestions box is the correct spelling.

5. **Click Change**

   Word replaces the misspelled word with the correctly spelled word. Next, the dialog box indicates "are" is repeated in a sentence.

TROUBLE

You might need to correct other spelling and grammar errors.

6. **Click Delete**

   Word deletes the second occurrence of the repeated word. Next, the dialog box flags a subject-verb agreement error and suggests using "is" instead of "are," as shown in Figure B-14. The phrase selected in the Suggestions box is correct.

QUICK TIP

If Word does not offer a valid correction, correct the error yourself.

7. **Click Change**

   The word "is" replaces the word "are" in the sentence and the Spelling and Grammar dialog box closes. Keep in mind that the Spelling and Grammar checker identifies many common errors, but you cannot rely on it to find and correct all spelling and grammar errors in your documents. Always proofread your documents carefully.

8. **Click OK to complete the spelling and grammar check, press [Ctrl][Home], then click the Save button 🖫 on the Standard toolbar**

FIGURE B-13: Spelling and Grammar: English (U.S.) dialog box

Word identified as misspelled

Suggested corrections

Adds the misspelled word and the correction to the AutoCorrect list

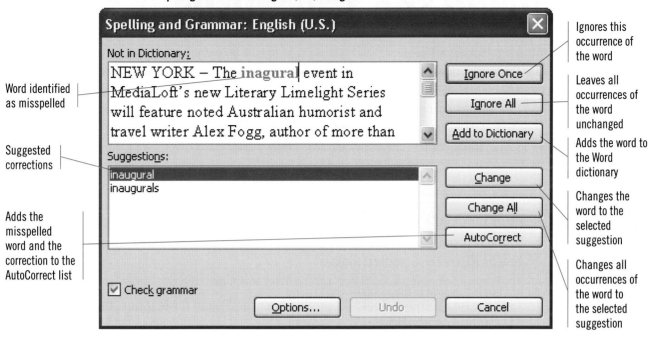

Ignores this occurrence of the word

Leaves all occurrences of the word unchanged

Adds the word to the Word dictionary

Changes the word to the selected suggestion

Changes all occurrences of the word to the selected suggestion

FIGURE B-14: Grammar error identified in Spelling and Grammar dialog box

Grammar error identified

Possible corrections

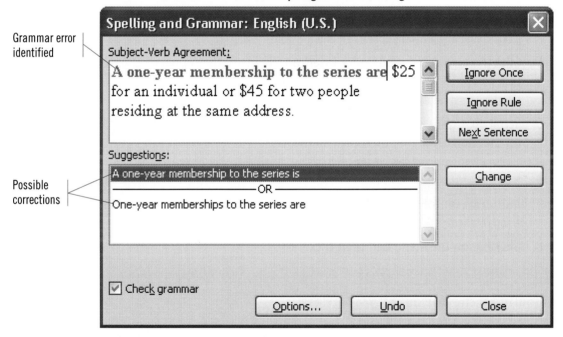

Clues to Use

Using the Undo, Redo, and Repeat commands

Word remembers the editing and formatting changes you make so that you can easily reverse or repeat them. You can reverse the last action you took by clicking the Undo button on the Standard toolbar, or you can undo a series of actions by clicking the Undo list arrow and selecting the action you want to reverse. When you undo an action using the Undo list arrow, you also undo all the actions above it in the list; that is, all actions that were performed after the action you selected. Similarly, you can keep the changes you just reversed by using the Redo button and the Redo list arrow.

If you want to repeat a change you just made, use the Repeat command on the Edit menu. The name of the Repeat command changes depending on the last action you took. For example, if you just typed "thank you," the name of the command is Repeat Typing. Clicking the Repeat Typing command inserts "thank you" at the location of the insertion point. You also can repeat the last action you took by pressing [F4].

Using the Thesaurus

Word also includes a Thesaurus, which you can use to look up synonyms for awkward or repetitive words. The Thesaurus is one of the reference sources available in the Research task pane. This task pane allows you to quickly search reference sources for information related to a word or phrase. When you are working with an active Internet connection, the Research task pane provides access to dictionary, encyclopedia, translation, and other reference sources and research services. ▰▰▰▰ After proofreading your document for errors, you decide the press release would read better if several adjectives were more descriptive. You use the Thesaurus to find synonyms for "noted" and "new".

STEPS

1. **Scroll down until the headline is displayed at the top of your screen**

2. **In the first sentence of the third paragraph, select noted, then click the Research button 🔍 on the Standard toolbar**

   The Research task pane opens. "Noted" appears in the Search for text box.

QUICK TIP
You can also select a word, click Tools on the menu bar, point to Language, and then click Thesaurus to open the Research task pane and display a list of synonyms for the word.

3. **Click the All Reference Books list arrow under the Search for text box, then click Thesaurus: English (U.S.)**

   Possible synonyms for "noted" are listed under the Thesaurus: English (U.S.) heading in the task pane, as shown in Figure B-15.

4. **Point to distinguished in the list of synonyms**

   A box containing an arrow appears around the word.

QUICK TIP
Right-click a word, then click Look up to open the Research task pane.

5. **Click the arrow in the box, click Insert on the menu that appears, then close the Research task pane**

   "Distinguished" replaces "noted" in the press release.

6. **Scroll up, right-click new in the first sentence of the first paragraph, point to Synonyms on the shortcut menu, then click innovative**

   "Innovative" replaces "new" in the press release.

7. **Press [Ctrl][Home], click the Save button 💾 on the Standard toolbar, then click the Print button 🖨 on the Standard toolbar**

   A copy of the finished press release prints. Compare your document to Figure B-16.

8. **Click File on the menu bar, then click Close**

Clues to Use

Viewing and modifying the document properties

Document properties are details about a file that can help you to organize and search your files. The author name, the date the file was created, the title, and keywords that describe the contents of the file are examples of document property information. You can view and modify the properties of an open document by clicking Properties on the File menu to open the Properties dialog box. The General, Statistics, and Contents tabs of the Properties dialog box display information about the file that is automatically created and updated by Word. The General tab shows the file type, location, size, and date and time the file was created and last modified; the Statistics tab displays information about revisions to the document along with the number of pages, words, lines, paragraphs, and characters in the file; and the Contents tab shows the title of the document.

You can define other document properties using the Summary and Custom tabs of the Properties dialog box. The Summary tab includes identifying information about the document such as the title, subject, author, and keywords. Some of this information is entered by Word when the document is first saved, but you can modify or add to the summary details by typing new information in the text boxes on the Summary tab. The Custom tab allows you to create new document properties, such as client, project, or date completed. To create a custom property, select a property name in the Name list box on the Custom tab, use the Type list arrow to select the type of data you want for the property, and then type the identifying detail (such as a project name) in the Value text box. When you are finished viewing or modifying the document properties, click OK to close the Properties dialog box.

FIGURE B-15: Research task pane

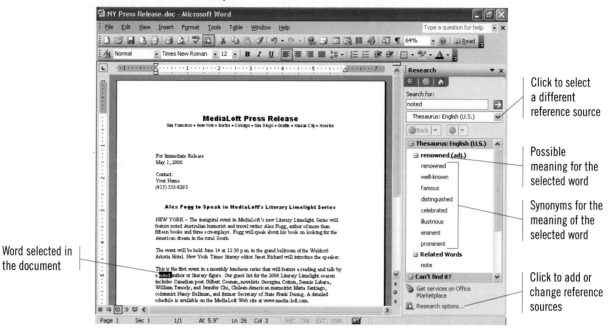

Click to select a different reference source

Possible meaning for the selected word

Synonyms for the meaning of the selected word

Word selected in the document

Click to add or change reference sources

FIGURE B-16: Completed press release

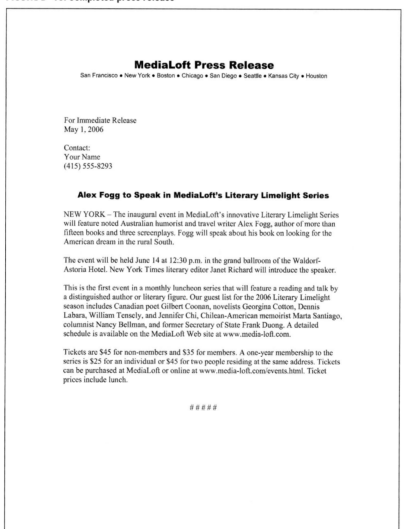

Using Wizards and Templates

Word includes many templates that you can use to quickly create memos, faxes, letters, reports, brochures, and other professionally designed documents. A **template** is a formatted document that contains placeholder text. To create a document that is based on a template, you replace the placeholder text with your own text and then save the document with a new filename. A **wizard** is an interactive set of dialog boxes that guides you through the process of creating a document. A wizard prompts you to provide information and select formatting options, and then it creates the document for you based on your specifications. You can create a document with a wizard or template using the New command on the File menu. ▰▰▰ You will fax the press release to your list of press contacts, beginning with the *New York Times*. You use a template to create a fax coversheet for the press release.

STEPS

1. **Click File on the menu bar, then click New**
   The New Document task pane opens.

2. **Click the On my computer hyperlink in the New Document task pane**
   The Templates dialog box opens. The tabs in the dialog box contain icons for the Word templates and wizards.

3. **Click the Letters & Faxes tab, then click the Professional Fax icon**
   A preview of the Professional Fax template appears in the Templates dialog box, as shown in Figure B-17.

   > **QUICK TIP**
   > Double-clicking an icon in the Templates dialog box also opens a new document based on the template.

4. **Click OK**
   The Professional Fax template opens as a new document in the document window. It contains placeholder text, which you can replace with your own information.

5. **Drag to select Company Name Here, then type MediaLoft**

6. **Click the Click here and type return address and phone and fax numbers placeholder**
   Clicking the placeholder selects it. When a placeholder says Click here... you do not need to drag to select it.

7. **Type MediaLoft San Francisco, press [Enter], then type Tel: (415) 555-8293**
   The text you type replaces the placeholder text.

   > **QUICK TIP**
   > Delete any placeholder text you do not want to replace.

8. **Replace the remaining placeholder text with the text shown in Figure B-18**
   Word automatically inserted the current date in the document. You do not need to replace the current date with the date shown in the figure.

9. **Click File on the menu bar, click Save As, use the Save in list arrow to navigate to the drive or folder where your Data Files are located, type NYT Fax in the File name text box, then click Save**
   The document is saved with the filename NYT Fax.

10. **Click the Print button 🖨 on the Standard toolbar, click File on the menu bar, then click Exit**
    A copy of the fax coversheet prints and the document and Word close.

FIGURE B-17: Letters & Faxes tab in Templates dialog box

Preview of selected template

FIGURE B-18: Completed fax coversheet

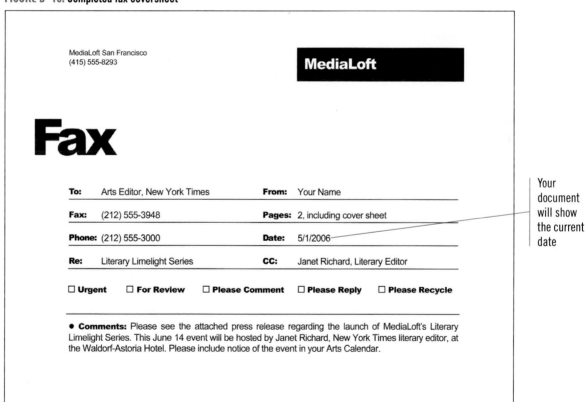

Your document will show the current date

Practice

▼ CONCEPTS REVIEW

Label the elements of the Open dialog box shown in Figure B-19.

FIGURE B-19

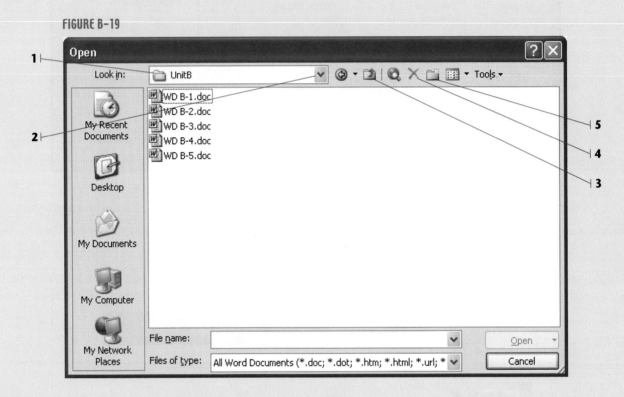

Match each term with the statement that best describes it.

6. **System Clipboard**
7. **Show/Hide**
8. **Select**
9. **Thesaurus**
10. **Undo**
11. **Template**
12. **Office Clipboard**
13. **Paste**
14. **Replace**

a. Command used to insert text stored on the Clipboard into a document
b. Document that contains placeholder text
c. Feature used to suggest synonyms for words
d. Temporary storage area for only the last item cut or copied from a document
e. Command used to display formatting marks in a document
f. Command used to locate and replace occurrences of specific text in a document
g. Command used to reverse the last action you took in a document
h. Temporary storage area for up to 24 items collected from any Office file
i. Action that must be taken before text can be cut, copied, or deleted

Select the best answer from the list of choices.

15. **Which of the following is *not* used to open an existing document?**
    a. Blank document hyperlink in the New Document task pane
    b. Open button on the Standard toolbar
    c. Open or More hyperlink in the Getting Started task pane
    d. Open command on the File menu

16. **To locate and change all instances of a word in a document, which menu command do you use?**
    a. Find
    b. Search
    c. Paste
    d. Replace

17. **Which of the following statements is *not* true?**
    a. The last item cut or copied from a document is stored on the system Clipboard.
    b. You can view the contents of the Office Clipboard.
    c. When you move text by dragging it, a copy of the text you move is stored on the system Clipboard.
    d. The Office Clipboard can hold more than one item.

18. **Which Word feature corrects errors as you type?**
    a. Thesaurus
    b. AutoCorrect
    c. Spelling and Grammar
    d. Undo and Redo

19. **Which command is used to display a document in two panes in the document window?**
    a. Split
    b. New Window
    c. Arrange All
    d. Compare Side by Side with…

20. **What does the symbol ¶ represent when it is displayed in the document window?**
    a. Hidden text
    b. A space
    c. A tab stop
    d. The end of a paragraph

▼ SKILLS REVIEW

1. **Open a document.**
   a. Start Word, click the Open button, then open the file WD B-2.doc from the drive and folder where your Data Files are located.
   b. Save the document with the filename **CAOS Press Release**.

2. **Select text.**
   a. Select **Today's Date** and replace it with the current date.
   b. Select **Your Name** and **Your Phone Number** and replace them with the relevant information.
   c. Scroll down, then select and replace text in the body of the press release using the following table as a guide:

in paragraph	select	replace with
1	13 and 14	**16 and 17**
1	eighth	**eleventh**
4	open his renovated Pearl St studio for the first time this year	**offer a sneak-preview of his Peace sculpture commissioned by the city of Prague**

   d. In the fourth paragraph, delete the sentence **Exhibiting with him will be sculptor Francis Pilo**.
   e. Save your changes to the press release.

3. **Cut and paste text.**
   a. Display paragraph and other formatting marks in your document if they are not already displayed.
   b. Use the Cut and Paste buttons to switch the order of the two sentences in the fourth paragraph (which begins New group shows…).
   c. Use the drag-and-drop method to switch the order of the second and third paragraphs.
   d. Adjust the spacing if necessary so that there is one blank line between paragraphs, then save your changes.

4. **Copy and paste text.**
   a. Use the Copy and Paste buttons to copy **CAOS 2003** from the headline and paste it before the word **map** in the third paragraph.
   b. Change the formatting of the pasted text to match the formatting of the third paragraph, then insert a space between **2003** and **map** if necessary.
   c. Use the drag-and-drop method to copy **CAOS** from the third paragraph and paste it before the word **group** in the second sentence of the fourth paragraph, then save your changes.

5. **Use the Office Clipboard.**

   a. Use the Office Clipboard command on the Edit menu to open the Clipboard task pane.

   b. Scroll so that the first body paragraph is displayed at the top of the document window.

   c. Select the fifth paragraph (which begins Studio location maps...) and cut it to the Office Clipboard.

   d. Select the third paragraph (which begins Cambridgeport is easily accessible...) and cut it to the Office Clipboard.

   e. Use the Office Clipboard to paste the Studio location maps... item as the new fourth paragraph.

   f. Use the Office Clipboard to paste the Cambridgeport is easily accessible... item as the new fifth paragraph.

   g. Use any method to switch the order of the two sentences in the fourth paragraph (which begins Studio location maps...).

   h. Adjust the spacing if necessary so that there is one blank line between each of the six body paragraphs.

   i. Turn off the display of formatting marks, clear and close the Office Clipboard, then save your changes.

6. **Find and replace text.**

   a. Using the Replace command, replace all instances of **2003** with **2006**.

   b. Replace all instances of the abbreviation **st** with **street**, taking care to replace whole words only when you perform the replace. (*Hint*: Click More to expand the Find and Replace dialog box, and then deselect Match case if it is selected.)

   c. Use the Find command to find all instances of **st** in the document, and make sure no errors occurred when you replaced st with street. (*Hint*: Deselect the Find whole words only check box.)

   d. Save your changes to the press release.

7. **Check Spelling and Grammar and use the Thesaurus.**

   a. Set Word to ignore the spelling of Cambridgeport, if it is marked as misspelled. (*Hint*: Right-click Cambridgeport.)

   b. Move the insertion point to the top of the document, then use the Spelling and Grammar command to search for and correct any spelling and grammar errors in the press release.

   c. Use the Thesaurus to replace **thriving** in the second paragraph with a different suitable word.

   d. Proofread your press release, correct any errors, save your changes, print a copy, then close the document.

8. **Use wizards and templates.**

   a. Use the New command to open the New Document task pane.

   b. Use the On my computer hyperlink to open the Templates dialog box.

   c. Create a new document using the Business Fax template.

   d. Replace the placeholder text in the document using Figure B-20 as a guide. Delete any placeholders that do not apply to your fax. The date in your fax will be the current date.

   e. Save the document as **CAOS Fax**, print a copy, close the document, then exit Word.

FIGURE B-20

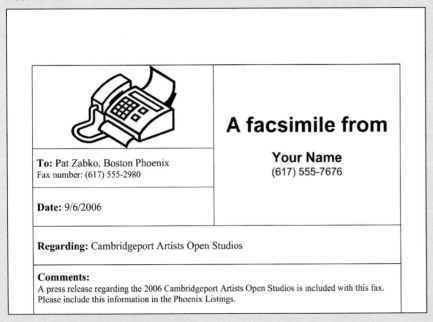

WORD B-22 EDITING DOCUMENTS

▼ INDEPENDENT CHALLENGE 1

Because of your success in revitalizing an historic theatre in Hobart, Tasmania, you were hired as the director of The Auckland Lyric Theatre in Auckland, New Zealand, to breathe life into its theatre revitalization efforts. After a year on the job, you are launching your first major fund-raising drive. You'll create a fund-raising letter for the Lyric Theatre by modifying a letter you wrote for the theatre in Hobart.

a. Start Word, open the file WD B-3.doc from the drive and folder where your Data Files are located, then save it as **Lyric Theatre Letter**.

b. Replace the theatre name and address, the date, the inside address, and the salutation with the text shown in Figure B-21.

c. Use the Replace command to replace all instances of **Hobart** with **Auckland**.

d. Use the Replace command to replace all instances of **Tasmanians** with **New Zealanders**.

e. Use the Find command to locate the word **considerable**, then use the Thesaurus to replace the word with a synonym.

f. Create an AutoCorrect entry that inserts **Auckland Lyric Theatre** whenever you type **alt**.

g. Select each XXXXX, then type **alt** followed by a space.

h. Move the fourth body paragraph so that it becomes the second body paragraph.

i. Replace Your Name with your name in the signature block.

j. Use the Spelling and Grammar command to check for and correct spelling and grammar errors.

FIGURE B-21

> # The Auckland Lyric Theatre
> 64-70 Queen Street, Auckland, New Zealand
>
> September 24, 2006
>
> Ms. Keri Marshall
> 718 Elliott Street
> Auckland
>
> Dear Ms. Marshall,

Advanced Challenge Exercise

- Open the Properties dialog box, then review the paragraph, line, word, and character count on the Statistics tab.
- On the Summary tab, change the title to **Auckland Lyric Theatre** and add the keyword **fund-raising**.
- On the Custom tab, add a property named Project with the value **Capital Campaign**, then close the dialog box.

k. Proofread the letter, correct any errors, save your changes, print a copy, close the document, then exit Word.

▼ INDEPENDENT CHALLENGE 2

An advertisement for job openings in London caught your eye and you have decided to apply. The ad, shown in Figure B-22, was printed in last weekend's edition of your local newspaper. You'll use the Letter Wizard to create a cover letter to send with your resume.

a. Read the ad shown in Figure B-22 and decide which position to apply for. Choose the position that most closely matches your qualifications.

b. Start Word and open the Templates dialog box.

c. Double-click Letter Wizard on the Letters & Faxes tab, then select Send one letter in the Letter Wizard dialog box.

d. In the Letter Wizard—Step 1 of 4 dialog box, choose to include a date on your letter, select Elegant Letter for the page design, select Modified block for the letter style, include a header and footer with the page design, then click Next.

e. In the Letter Wizard—Step 2 of 4 dialog box, enter the recipient's name (Ms. Katherine Winn) and the delivery address, referring to the ad for the address information. Also enter the salutation **Dear Ms. Winn** using the business style, then click Next.

f. In the Letter Wizard—Step 3 of 4 dialog box, include a reference line in the letter, enter the appropriate position code (see Figure B-22) in the Reference line text box, then click Next.

g. In the Letter Wizard—Step 4 of 4 dialog box, enter your name as the sender, enter your return address (including your country), and select an appropriate complimentary closing. Then, because you will be including your resume with the letter, include one enclosure. Click Finish when you are done.

h. Save the letter with the filename **Global Dynamics Letter** to the drive and folder where your Data Files are located.

i. Replace the placeholder text in the body of the letter with three paragraphs that address your qualifications for the job:

- In the first paragraph, specify the job you are applying for, indicate where you saw the position advertised, and briefly state your qualifications and interest in the position.

- In the second paragraph, describe your work experience and skills. Be sure to relate your experience and qualifications to the position requirements listed in the ad.

- In the third paragraph, politely request an interview for the position and provide your phone number and e-mail address.

j. When you are finished typing the letter, check it for spelling and grammar errors and correct any mistakes.

k. Save your changes to the letter, print a copy, close the document, then exit Word.

FIGURE B-22

*Global*Dynamics

Career Opportunities in London

Global Dynamics, an established software development firm with offices in North America, Asia, and Europe, is seeking candidates for the following positions in its London facility:

Instructor
Responsible for delivering software training to our expanding European customer base. Duties include delivering hands-on training, keeping up-to-date with product development, and working with the Director of Training to ensure the high quality of course materials. Successful candidate will have excellent presentation skills and be proficient in Microsoft PowerPoint and Microsoft Word. **Position B12C6**

Administrative Assistant
Proficiency with Microsoft Word a must! Administrative office duties include making travel arrangements, scheduling meetings, taking notes and publishing meeting minutes, handling correspondence, and ordering office supplies. Must have superb multi-tasking abilities, excellent communication, organizational, and interpersonal skills, and be comfortable working with e-mail and the Internet. **Position B16F5**

Copywriter
The ideal candidate will have marketing or advertising writing experience in a high tech environment, including collateral, newsletters, and direct mail. Experience writing for the Web, broadcast, and multimedia is a plus. Fluency with Microsoft Word required. **Position C13D4**

Positions offer salary, excellent benefits, moving expenses, and career growth opportunities.

Send resume and cover letter referencing position code to:

Katherine Winn
Director of Recruiting
Global Dynamics
483 Briar Terrace
London LH3 9JH
United Kingdom

▼ INDEPENDENT CHALLENGE 3

As administrative director of continuing education, you drafted a memo to instructors asking them to help you finalize the course schedule for next semester. Today you'll examine the draft and make revisions before printing it.

a. Start Word and open the file WD B-4.doc from the drive and folder where your Data Files are located.

b. Open the Save As dialog box, navigate to the drive and folder where your Data Files are located, then use the Create New Folder button to create a new folder called **Memos.**

c. Click the Up One Level button in the dialog box, rename the Memos folder **Spring Memos**, then save the document as **Instructor Memo** in the Spring Memos folder.

d. Replace Your Name with your name in the From line, then scroll down until the first body paragraph is at the top of the screen.

Advanced Challenge Exercise

- Use the Split command on the Window menu to split the window under the first body paragraph, then scroll until the last paragraph of the memo is displayed in the bottom pane.
- Use the Cut and Paste buttons to move the sentence **If you are planning to teach...** from the first body paragraph to become the first sentence in the last paragraph of the memo.
- Double-click the split bar to restore the window to a single pane.

e. Use the [Delete] key to merge the first two paragraphs into one paragraph.

f. Use the Office Clipboard to reorganize the list of twelve-week courses so that the courses are listed in alphabetical order. (*Hint*: Use the Zoom list arrow to enlarge the document as needed.)

g. Use the drag-and-drop method to reorganize the list of one-day seminars so that the seminars are listed in alphabetical order.

h. Use the Spelling and Grammar command to check for and correct spelling and grammar errors.

i. Clear and close the Office Clipboard, save your changes, print a copy, close the document, then exit Word.

▼ INDEPENDENT CHALLENGE 4

Reference sources—dictionaries, thesauri, style and grammar guides, and guides to business etiquette and procedure—are essential for day-to-day use in the workplace. Much of this reference information is available on the World Wide Web. In this independent challenge, you will locate reference sources on the Web and use some of them to look up definitions, synonyms, and antonyms for words. Your goal is to familiarize yourself with online reference sources so you can use them later in your work.

a. Start Word, open the file WD B-5.doc from the drive and folder where your Data Files are located, and save it as **Web References**. This document contains the questions you will answer about the Web reference sources you find. You will type your answers to the questions in the document.

b. Replace the placeholder text at the top of the Web References document with your name and the date.

c. Use your favorite search engine to search the Web for grammar and style guides, dictionaries, and thesauri. Use the keywords **grammar**, **usage**, **dictionary**, **glossary**, and **thesaurus** to conduct your search.

d. Complete the Web References document, then proofread it and correct any mistakes.

e. Save the document, print a copy, close the document, then exit Word.

▼ VISUAL WORKSHOP

Using the Elegant Letter template, create the letter shown in Figure B-23. Save the document as **Visa Letter**. Check the letter for spelling and grammar errors, then print a copy.

YOUR NAME

March 17, 2006

Embassy of Australia
Suite 710
50 O'Connor Street
Ottawa, Ontario K1P 6L2

Dear Sir or Madam:

I am applying for a long-stay (six-month) tourist visa to Australia, valid for four years. I am scheduled to depart for Sydney on July 1, 2006, returning to Vancouver on December 23, 2006.

While in Australia, I plan to conduct research for a book I am writing on coral reefs. I am interested in a multiple entry visa valid for four years so that I can return to Australia after this trip to follow-up on my initial research. I will be based in Cairns, but will be traveling frequently to other parts of Australia to meet with scientists, policy-makers, and environmentalists.

Enclosed please find my completed visa application form, my passport, a passport photo, a copy of my return air ticket, and the visa fee. Please let me know if I can provide further information.

Sincerely,

Your Name

35 HARDY STREET • VANCOUVER, BC • V6C 3K4
PHONE: (604) 555-8989 • FAX: (604) 555-8981

UNIT C
Word 2003

Formatting Text and Paragraphs

OBJECTIVES

Format with fonts
Change font styles and effects
Change line and paragraph spacing
Align paragraphs
Work with tabs
Work with indents
Add bullets and numbering
Add borders and shading

If you have a SAM user profile, you may have access to hands-on instruction, practice, and assessment of the skills covered in this unit. Log in to your SAM account and go to your assignments page to see what your instructor has assigned.

Formatting can enhance the appearance of a document, create visual impact, and help illustrate a document's structure. The formatting of a document can also add personality to it and lend it a degree of professionalism. In this unit you learn how to format text using different fonts and font-formatting options. You also learn how to change the alignment, indentation, and spacing of paragraphs, and how to spruce up documents with borders, shading, bullets, and other paragraph-formatting effects. You have finished drafting the quarterly marketing report for the MediaLoft Chicago store. You now need to format the report so it is attractive and highlights the significant information.

Formatting with Fonts

Formatting text with different fonts is a quick and powerful way to enhance the appearance of a document. A **font** is a complete set of characters with the same typeface or design. Arial, Times New Roman, Comic Sans, Courier, and Tahoma are some of the more common fonts, but there are hundreds of others, each with a specific design and feel. Another way to alter the impact of text is to increase or decrease its **font size**, which is measured in points. A **point** is ¹⁄₇₂ of an inch. When formatting a document with fonts, it's important to pick fonts and font sizes that augment the document's purpose. You apply fonts and font sizes to text using the Font and Font Size list arrows on the Formatting toolbar. You change the font and font size of the title and headings in the report, selecting a font that enhances the business tone of the document. By formatting the title and headings in a font different from the body text, you help to visually structure the report for readers.

STEPS

1. **Start Word, open the file** WD C-1.doc **from the drive and folder where your Data Files are located, then save it as** Chicago Marketing Report

   The file opens in Print Layout view.

2. **Click the** Normal View button ≡ **on the horizontal scroll bar, click the** Zoom list arrow **on the Standard toolbar, then click** 100% **if necessary**

   The document switches to Normal view, a view useful for simple text formatting. The name of the font used in the document, Times New Roman, is displayed in the Font list box on the Formatting toolbar. The font size, 12, appears next to it in the Font Size list box.

3. **Select the title** MediaLoft Chicago Quarterly Marketing Report, **then click the** Font list arrow **on the Formatting toolbar**

   The Font list, which shows the fonts available on your computer, opens as shown in Figure C-1. Fonts you have used recently appear above the double line. All the fonts on your computer are listed in alphabetical order below the double line. You can click the font name in either location on the Font list to apply the font to the selected text.

4. **Click** Arial

   The font of the report title changes to Arial.

5. **Click the** Font Size list arrow **on the Formatting toolbar, then click** 20

   The font size of the title increases to 20 points.

6. **Click the** Font Color list arrow ▲▾ **on the Formatting toolbar**

   A palette of colors opens.

7. **Click** Plum **on the Font Color palette as shown in Figure C-2, then deselect the text**

   The color of the report title text changes to plum. The active color on the Font Color button also changes to plum.

8. **Scroll down until the heading Advertising is at the top of your screen, select** Advertising, **press and hold** [Ctrl], **select the heading** Events, **then release** [Ctrl]

   The Advertising and Events headings are selected. Selecting multiple items allows you to format several items at once.

9. **Click the** Font list arrow, **click** Arial, **click the** Font Size list arrow, **click** 14, **click the** Font Color button ▲, **then deselect the text**

   The headings are formatted in 14-point Arial with a plum color.

10. **Press** [Ctrl][Home], **then click the** Save button 🖫 **on the Standard toolbar**

    Pressing [Ctrl][Home] moves the insertion point to the beginning of the document. Compare your document to Figure C-3.

FIGURE C-1: **Font list**

Font list arrow

Font Size list arrow

Font names are
formatted in the
font (your list of
fonts might differ)

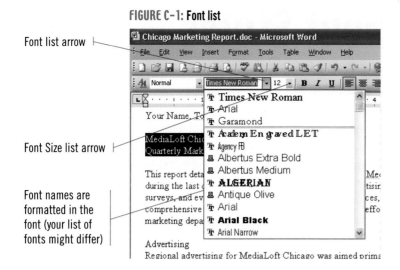

FIGURE C-2: **Font Color palette**

Font Color list arrow

Name of color
appears as a
ScreenTip

Click to create a
custom color

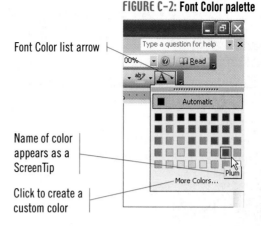

FIGURE C-3: **Document formatted with fonts**

Title formatted
in 20-point
Arial, plum

Headings
formatted in
14-point
Arial, plum

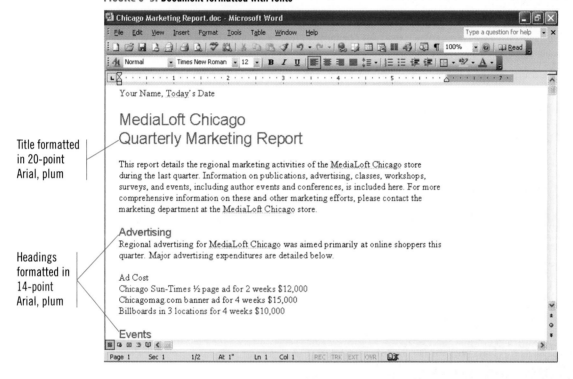

Clues to Use

Adding a drop cap

A fun way to illustrate a document with fonts is to add a drop cap to a paragraph. A **drop cap** is a large
initial capital letter, often used to set off the first paragraph of an article. To create a drop cap, place the
insertion point in the paragraph you want to format, and then click Drop Cap on the Format menu to
open the Drop Cap dialog box. In the Drop Cap dialog box, shown in Figure C-4, select the position,
font, number of lines to drop, and the distance you want the drop cap to be from the paragraph text,
and then click OK to create the drop cap. The drop cap is added to the paragraph as a graphic object.

    Once a drop cap is inserted in a paragraph, you can modify it by selecting it and then changing the
settings in the Drop Cap dialog box. For even more interesting effects, try enhancing a drop cap with
font color, font styles, or font effects, or try filling the graphic object with shading or adding a border
around it. To enhance a drop cap, first select it, and then experiment with the formatting options available in the Font dialog box and in the Borders and Shading dialog box.

FIGURE C-4: **Drop Cap dialog box**

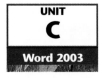

UNIT
C
Word 2003

Changing Font Styles and Effects

You can dramatically change the appearance of text by applying different font styles, font effects, and character-spacing effects. For example, you can use the buttons on the Formatting toolbar to make text darker by applying **bold**, or to slant text by applying *italic*. You can also use the Font command on the Format menu to apply font effects and character-spacing effects to text. ▓▓▓▓ You spice up the appearance of the text in the document by applying different font styles and effects.

STEPS

QUICK TIP

Click the Underline button **U** on the Formatting toolbar to underline text.

1. **Select MediaLoft Chicago Quarterly Marketing Report, then click the Bold button** **B** **on the Formatting toolbar**

   Applying bold makes the characters in the title darker and thicker.

2. **Select Advertising, click** **B**, **select Events, then press [F4]**

   Pressing [F4] repeats the last action you took, in this case applying bold. The Advertising and Events headings are both formatted in bold.

3. **Select the paragraph under the title, then click the Italic button** **I** **on the Formatting toolbar**

   The paragraph is formatted in italic.

4. **Scroll down until the subheading Author Events is at the top of your screen, select Author Events, click Format on the menu bar, then click Font**

   The Font dialog box opens, as shown in Figure C-5. You can use options on the Font tab to change the font, font style, size, and color of text, and to add an underline and apply font effects to text.

QUICK TIP

To hide the selected text, click the Hidden check box on the Font tab. Hidden text is displayed when formatting marks are turned on.

5. **Scroll up the Font list, click Arial, click Bold Italic in the Font style list box, select the Small caps check box, then click OK**

   The subheading is formatted in Arial, bold, italic, and small caps. When you change text to small caps, the lowercase letters are changed to uppercase letters in a smaller font size.

6. **Select the subheading Travel Writers & Photographers Conference, then press [F4]**

   Because you formatted the previous subheading in one action (using the Font dialog box), the Travel Writers subheading is formatted in Arial, bold, italic, and small caps. If you apply formats one by one, then pressing [F4] repeats only the last format you applied.

7. **Under Author Events, select the book title Just H2O Please: Tales of True Adventure on the Environmental Frontline, click** **I**, **select 2 in the book title, click Format on the menu bar, click Font, click the Subscript check box, click OK, then deselect the text**

   The book title is formatted in italic and the character 2 is subscript, as shown in Figure C-6.

QUICK TIP

To animate the selected text, click the Text Effects tab in the Font dialog box, then select an animation style. The animation appears only when a document is viewed in Word; animation effects do not print.

8. **Press [Ctrl][Home], select the report title, click Format on the menu bar, click Font, then click the Character Spacing tab in the Font dialog box**

   You use the Character Spacing tab to change the scale, or width, of the selected characters, to alter the spacing between characters, or to raise or lower the position of the characters.

9. **Click the Scale list arrow, click 150%, click OK, deselect the text, then click the Save button** 🖫 **on the Standard toolbar**

   Increasing the scale of the characters makes them wider and gives the text a short, squat appearance, as shown in Figure C-7.

FIGURE C-5: Font tab in Font dialog box

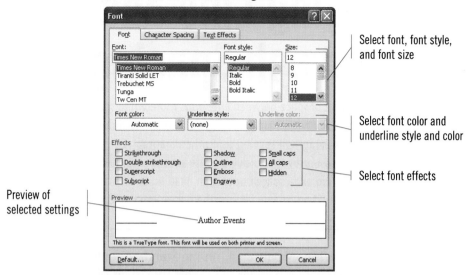

Select font, font style, and font size

Select font color and underline style and color

Select font effects

Preview of selected settings

FIGURE C-6: Font effects applied to text

Subhead formatted in 12-point Arial, bold, italic, and small caps

Book title formatted in italic

Subscript text

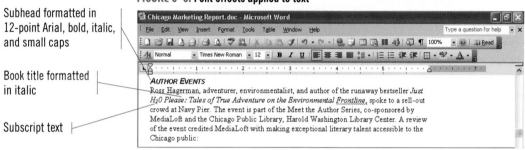

FIGURE C-7: Character spacing effects applied to text

Report title formatted in bold with a character scale of 150%

Paragraph formatted in italic

Headings formatted in bold

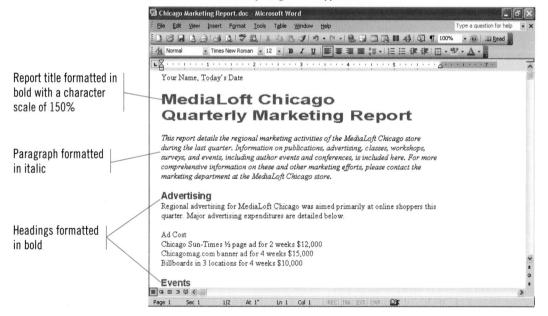

Clues to Use

Changing the case of letters

The Change Case command on the Format menu allows you to quickly change letters from uppercase to lowercase—and vice versa—saving you the time it takes to retype text you want to change. To change the case of selected text, use the Change Case command to open the Change Case dialog box, then select the case style you want to use. Sentence case capitalizes the first letter of a sentence, title case capitalizes the first letter of each word, and toggle case switches all letters to the opposite case.

Changing Line and Paragraph Spacing

UNIT C
Word 2003

Increasing the amount of space between lines adds more white space to a document and can make it easier to read. Adding space between paragraphs can also open up a document and improve its appearance. You can change line and paragraph spacing using the Paragraph command on the Format menu. You can also use the Line Spacing list arrow to quickly change line spacing. You increase the line spacing of several paragraphs and add extra space under each heading to give the report a more open feel. You work with formatting marks turned on, so you can see the paragraph marks (¶).

STEPS

QUICK TIP

The check mark on the Line Spacing list indicates the current line spacing.

1. **Click the Show/Hide ¶ button ¶ on the Standard toolbar, place the insertion point in the italicized paragraph under the report title, then click the Line Spacing list arrow ≣▾ on the Formatting toolbar**

   The Line Spacing list opens. This list includes options for increasing the space between lines.

2. **Click 1.5**

   The space between the lines in the paragraph increases to 1.5 lines. Notice that you do not need to select an entire paragraph to change its paragraph formatting; simply place the insertion point in the paragraph you want to format.

QUICK TIP

Word recognizes any string of text that ends with a paragraph mark as a paragraph, including titles, headings, and single lines in a list.

3. **Scroll down until the heading Advertising is at the top of your screen, select the four-line list that begins with Ad Cost, click ≣▾, then click 1.5**

   The line spacing between the selected paragraphs changes to 1.5. To change the paragraph-formatting features of more than one paragraph, you must select the paragraphs.

4. **Place the insertion point in the heading Advertising, click Format on the menu bar, then click Paragraph**

   The Paragraph dialog box opens, as shown in Figure C-8. You can use the Indents and Spacing tab to change line spacing and the spacing above and below paragraphs. Spacing between paragraphs is measured in points.

QUICK TIP

Adjusting the space between paragraphs is a more precise way to add white space to a document than inserting blank lines.

5. **Click the After up arrow in the Spacing section so that 6 pt appears, then click OK**

   Six points of space are added below the Advertising heading paragraph.

6. **Select Advertising, then click the Format Painter button ✅ on the Standard toolbar**

   The pointer changes to ▨I. The **Format Painter** is a powerful Word feature that allows you to copy all the format settings applied to the selected text to other text that you want to format the same way. The Format Painter is especially useful when you want to copy multiple format settings, but you can also use it to copy individual formats.

QUICK TIP

Using the Format Painter is not the same as using [F4]. Pressing [F4] repeats only the last action you took. You can use the Format Painter at any time to copy multiple format settings.

7. **Select Events with the ▨I pointer, then deselect the text**

   Six points of space are added below the Events heading paragraph and the pointer changes back to the I-beam pointer. Compare your document with Figure C-9.

8. **Select Events, then double-click ✅**

   Double-clicking the Format Painter button allows the Format Painter to remain active until you turn it off. By keeping the Format Painter turned on you can apply formatting to multiple items.

9. **Scroll down, select the headings Classes & Workshops, Publications, and Surveys with the ▨I pointer, then click ✅ to turn off the Format Painter**

   The headings are formatted in 14-point Arial, bold, plum, with six points of space added below each heading paragraph.

10. **Press [Ctrl][Home], click ¶, then click the Save button 💾 on the Standard toolbar**

FIGURE C-8: Indents and Spacing tab in Paragraph dialog box

Change the spacing above and below paragraphs

Change line spacing

Spacing After up arrow

Preview of selected settings

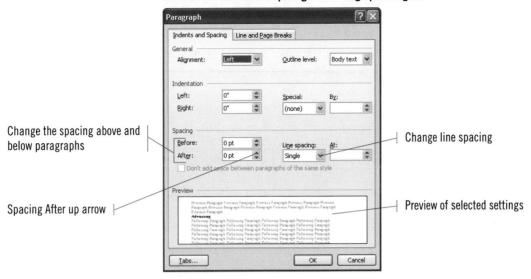

FIGURE C-9: Line and paragraph spacing applied to document

Format Painter button

Style list arrow

Line Spacing list arrow

Line spacing is 1.5

6 points of space added below heading paragraphs

Line spacing is 1

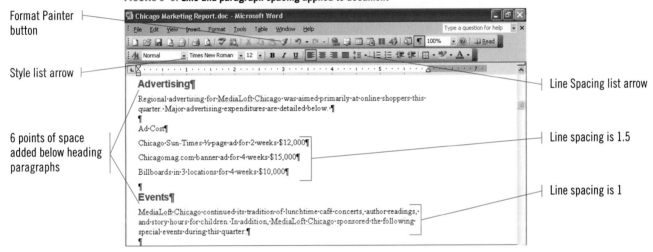

Clues to Use

Formatting with styles

You can also apply multiple format settings to text in one step by applying a style. A **style** is a set of formats, such as font, font size, and paragraph alignment, that are named and stored together. Styles can be applied to text, paragraphs, lists, and tables. To work with styles, click the Styles and Formatting button 🖼 on the Formatting toolbar to open the Styles and Formatting task pane, shown in Figure C-10. The task pane displays the list of available styles and the formats you have created for the current document. To view all the styles available in Word, click the Show list arrow at the bottom of the task pane, then click All Styles.

A **character style**, indicated by **a** in the list of styles, includes character format settings, such as font and font size. A **paragraph style**, indicated by **¶** in the list, is a combination of character and paragraph formats, such as font, font size, paragraph alignment, paragraph spacing, indents, and bullets and numbering. A **table style** indicated by ⊞ in the list, includes format settings for text in tables, as well as for table borders, shading, and alignment. Finally, a **list style**, indicated by ☰ in the list, includes indent and numbering format settings for an outline numbered list.

To apply a style, select the text, paragraph, or table you want to format, then click the style name in the Pick formatting to apply list box. To remove styles from text, select the text, then click Clear Formatting in the Pick formatting to apply list box. You can also apply and remove styles using the Style list arrow on the Formatting toolbar.

FIGURE C-10: Styles and Formatting task pane

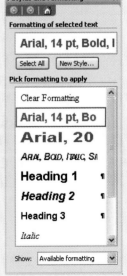

Aligning Paragraphs

Changing paragraph alignment is another way to enhance a document's appearance. Paragraphs are aligned relative to the left and right margins in a document. By default, text is **left-aligned**, which means it is flush with the left margin and has a ragged right edge. Using the alignment buttons on the Formatting toolbar, you can **right-align** a paragraph—make it flush with the right margin—or **center** a paragraph so that it is positioned evenly between the left and right margins. You can also **justify** a paragraph so that both the left and right edges of the paragraph are flush with the left and right margins. You change the alignment of several paragraphs at the beginning of the report to make it more visually interesting.

STEPS

1. **Replace** Your Name, Today's Date **with your name, a comma, and the date**

2. **Select your name, the comma, and the date, then click the** Align Right button **on the Formatting toolbar**

   The text is aligned with the right margin. In Normal view, the junction of the white and shaded sections of the horizontal ruler indicates the location of the right margin. The left end of the ruler indicates the left margin.

3. **Place the insertion point between your name and the comma, press** [Delete] **to delete the comma, then press** [Enter]

   The new paragraph containing the date is also right-aligned. Pressing [Enter] in the middle of a paragraph creates a new paragraph with the same text and paragraph formatting as the original paragraph.

4. **Select the** report title, **then click the** Center button **on the Formatting toolbar**

   The two paragraphs that make up the title are centered between the left and right margins.

> **QUICK TIP**
> Click the Align Left button on the Formatting toolbar to left-align a paragraph.

5. **Place the insertion point in the** Advertising **heading, then click**

   The Advertising heading is centered.

6. **Place the insertion point in the italicized paragraph under the report title, then click the** Justify button

   The paragraph is aligned with both the left and right margins, as shown in Figure C-11. When you justify a paragraph, Word adjusts the spacing between words so that each line in the paragraph is flush with the left and the right margins.

7. **Place the insertion point in** MediaLoft **in the report title, click** Format **on the menu bar, then click** Reveal Formatting

   The Reveal Formatting task pane opens in the Word program window, as shown in Figure C-12. The Reveal Formatting task pane shows the formatting applied to the text and paragraph where the insertion point is located. You can use the Reveal Formatting task pane to check or change the formatting of any character, word, paragraph, or other aspect of a document.

8. **Select** Advertising, **then click the** Alignment **hyperlink in the Reveal Formatting task pane**

   The Paragraph dialog box opens with the Indents and Spacing tab displayed. It shows the settings for the selected text.

9. **Click the** Alignment list arrow, **click** Left, **click** OK, **then deselect the text**

   The Advertising heading is left-aligned.

10. **Close the Reveal Formatting task pane, then click the** Save button **on the Standard toolbar**

FIGURE C-11: Modified paragraph alignment

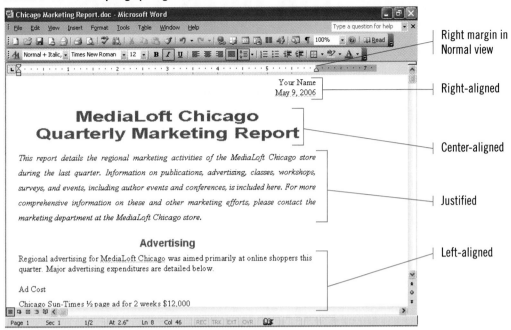

Right margin in Normal view

Right-aligned

Center-aligned

Justified

Left-aligned

FIGURE C-12: Reveal Formatting task pane

Insertion point indicates selected text

Click the minus sign to hide information

Click the plus sign to display information

Reveal Formatting task pane

Format settings for selected text

Click hyperlinks to change format settings

Select to show underlying style

Select to show formatting marks in document

Clues to Use

Comparing formatting

When two words or paragraphs in a document do not look exactly the same but you are not sure how they are formatted differently, you can use the Reveal Formatting task pane to compare the two selections to determine the differences. To compare the formatting of two text selections, select the first instance, select the Compare to another selection check box in the Reveal Formatting task pane, and then select the second instance. Differences in formatting between the two selections are listed in the Formatting differences section in the Reveal Formatting task pane. You can then use the hyperlinks in the Formatting differences section to make changes to the formatting of the second selection. If you want to format the second selection so that it matches the first, you can click the list arrow next to the second selection in the Selected text section, and then click Apply Formatting of Original Selection on the menu that appears. On the same menu, you can also click Select All Text with Similar Formatting to select all the text in the document that is formatted the same, or Clear Formatting to return the formatting of the selected text to the default.

Working with Tabs

Tabs allow you to align text vertically at a specific location in a document. A **tab stop** is a point on the horizontal ruler that indicates the location at which to align text. By default, tab stops are located every ½" from the left margin, but you can also set custom tab stops. Using tabs, you can align text to the left, right, or center of a tab stop, or you can align text at a decimal point or bar character. You set tabs using the horizontal ruler or the Tabs command on the Format menu. You use tabs to format the information on advertising expenditures so it is easy to read.

STEPS

1. **Scroll down until the heading Advertising is at the top of your screen, then select the four-line list beginning with Ad Cost**

   Before you set tab stops for existing text, you must select the paragraphs for which you want to set tabs.

2. **Point to the tab indicator ⌊ at the left end of the horizontal ruler**

   The icon that appears in the tab indicator indicates the active type of tab; pointing to the tab indicator displays a ScreenTip with the name of the active tab type. By default, left tab is the active tab type. Clicking the tab indicator scrolls through the types of tabs and indents.

3. **Click the tab indicator to see each of the available tab and indent types, make left tab ⌊ the active tab type, then click the 1" mark on the horizontal ruler**

   A left tab stop is inserted at the 1" mark on the horizontal ruler. Clicking the horizontal ruler inserts a tab stop of the active type for the selected paragraph or paragraphs.

4. **Click the tab indicator twice so the Right Tab icon ⌋ is active, then click the 4½" mark on the horizontal ruler**

   A right tab stop is inserted at the 4½" mark on the horizontal ruler, as shown in Figure C-13.

5. **Place the insertion point before Ad in the first line in the list, press [Tab], place the insertion point before Cost, then press [Tab]**

   Inserting a tab before Ad left-aligns the text at the 1" mark. Inserting a tab before Cost right-aligns Cost at the 4½" mark.

6. **Insert a tab at the beginning of each remaining line in the list, then insert a tab before each $ in the list**

   The paragraphs left-align at the 1" mark. The prices right-align at the 4½" mark.

7. **Select the four lines of tabbed text, drag the right tab stop to the 5" mark on the horizontal ruler, then deselect the text**

   Dragging the tab stop moves it to a new location. The prices right-align at the 5" mark.

8. **Select the last three lines of tabbed text, click Format on the menu bar, then click Tabs**

   The Tabs dialog box opens, as shown in Figure C-14. You can use the Tabs dialog box to set tab stops, change the position or alignment of existing tab stops, clear tab stops, and apply tab leaders to tabs. **Tab leaders** are lines that appear in front of tabbed text.

9. **Click 5" in the Tab stop position list box, click the 2 option button in the Leader section, click OK, deselect the text, then click the Save button ⊟ on the Standard toolbar**

   A dotted tab leader is added before each 5" tab stop, as shown in Figure C-15.

FIGURE C-13: Left and right tab stops on the horizontal ruler

Right Tab icon in tab indicator

Left tab stop

Right tab stop

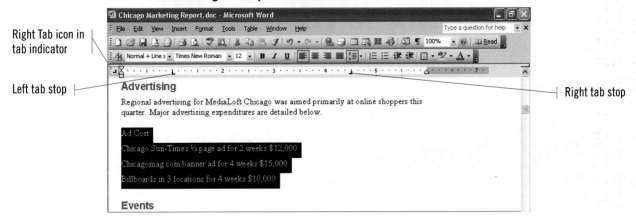

FIGURE C-14: Tabs dialog box

Select the tab stop you want to modify

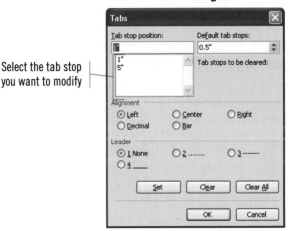

FIGURE C-15: Tab leaders

Tabbed text left-aligned with left tab stop

Tabbed text right-aligned with right tab stop

Tab leader

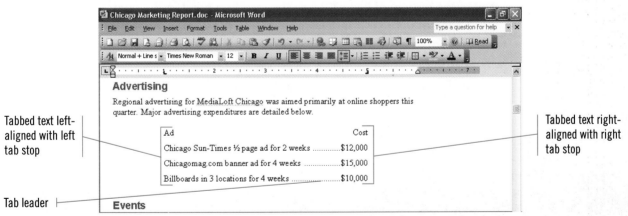

Clues to Use

Working with Click and Type

The **Click and Type** feature in Word allows you to automatically apply the paragraph formatting (alignment and indentation) necessary to insert text, graphics, or tables in a blank area of a document in Print Layout or Web Layout view. As you move the pointer around in a blank area of a document, the pointer changes depending on its location. Double-clicking with a click and type pointer in a blank area of a document automatically applies the appropriate alignment and indentation for that location, so that when you begin typing, the text

is already formatted. The pointer shape indicates which formatting is applied at each location when you double-click. For example, if you click with the $\underline{\text{I}}$ pointer, the text you type is center-aligned. Clicking with I⁼ creates a left tab stop at the location of the insertion point so that the text you type is left-aligned at the tab stop. Clicking with ⁼I right-aligns the text you type. The I⁼ pointer creates left-aligned text with a first line indent. The best way to learn how to use Click and Type is to experiment in a blank document.

Working with Indents

When you **indent** a paragraph, you move its edge in from the left or right margin. You can indent the entire left or right edge of a paragraph, just the first line, or all lines except the first line. The **indent markers** on the horizontal ruler indicate the indent settings for the paragraph in which the insertion point is located. Dragging the indent markers to a new location on the ruler is one way to change the indentation of a paragraph; using the indent buttons on the Formatting toolbar is another. You can also use the Paragraph command on the Format menu to indent paragraphs. Table C-1 describes different types of indents and the methods for creating each. ◼◼◼◼ You indent several paragraphs in the report.

STEPS

1. **Press [Ctrl][Home], click the Print Layout View button ▣ on the horizontal scroll bar, click the Zoom list arrow on the Standard toolbar, then click Page Width**
   The document is displayed in Print Layout view, making it easier to see the document margins.

2. **Place the insertion point in the italicized paragraph under the title, then click the Increase Indent button ▣ on the Formatting toolbar**
   The entire paragraph is indented ½" from the left margin, as shown in Figure C-16. The indent marker ⧖ also moves to the ½" mark on the horizontal ruler. Each time you click the Increase Indent button, the left edge of a paragraph moves another ½" to the right.

3. **Click the Decrease Indent button ▣ on the Formatting toolbar**
   The left edge of the paragraph moves ½" to the left, and the indent marker moves back to the left margin.

4. **Drag the First Line Indent marker ▽ to the ¼" mark on the horizontal ruler as shown in Figure C-17**
   The first line of the paragraph is indented ¼". Dragging the first line indent marker indents only the first line of a paragraph.

5. **Scroll to the bottom of page 1, place the insertion point in the quotation (the last paragraph), then drag the Left Indent marker ▢ to the ½" mark on the horizontal ruler**
   When you drag the Left Indent marker, the First Line and Hanging Indent markers move as well. The left edge of the paragraph is indented ½" from the left margin.

6. **Drag the Right Indent marker △ to the 5½" mark on the horizontal ruler**
   The right edge of the paragraph is indented ½" from the right margin, as shown in Figure C-18.

7. **Click the Save button ▣ on the Standard toolbar**

TABLE C-1: Types of indents

indent type	description	to create
Left indent	The left edge of a paragraph is moved in from the left margin	Drag the Left Indent marker ▢ right to the position where you want the left edge of the paragraph to align, or click the Increase Indent button ▣ to indent the paragraph in ½" increments
Right indent	The right edge of a paragraph is moved in from the right margin	Drag the Right Indent marker △ left to the position where you want the right edge of the paragraph to end
First-line indent	The first line of a paragraph is indented more than the subsequent lines	Drag the First Line Indent marker ▽ right to the position where you want the first line of the paragraph to start
Hanging indent	The subsequent lines of a paragraph are indented more than the first line	Drag the Hanging Indent marker ⬠ right to the position where you want the hanging indent to start
Negative indent (or Outdent)	The left edge of a paragraph is moved to the left of the left margin	Drag the Left Indent marker ▢ left to the position where you want the negative indent to start

FIGURE C-16: Indented paragraph

First Line Indent marker

Hanging Indent marker

Left Indent marker

Indented paragraph

Right Indent marker

Increase Indent button

Decrease Indent button

FIGURE C-17: Dragging the First Line Indent marker

First Line Indent marker being dragged to the ¼" mark

Dotted line shows positon of First Line Indent marker

FIGURE C-18: Paragraph indented from the left and right

Paragraph indented ½" from left margin

Paragraph indented ½" from right margin

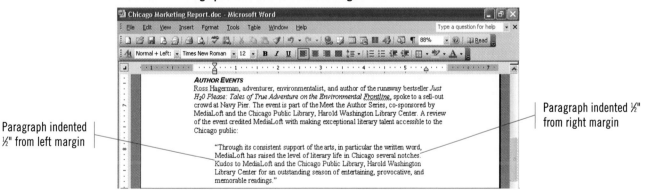

Clues to Use

Clearing formatting

If you are unhappy with the way text is formatted, you can use the Clear Formats command to return the text to the default format settings. By default, text is formatted in 12-point Times New Roman and paragraphs are left-aligned and single-spaced with no indents.

To clear formatting from text, select the text you want to clear, point to Clear on the Edit menu, then click Formats. Alternately, click the Styles list arrow on the Formatting toolbar, then click Clear Formatting.

UNIT
C
Word 2003

Adding Bullets and Numbering

Formatting a list with bullets or numbering can help to organize the ideas in a document. A **bullet** is a character, often a small circle, that appears before the items in a list to add emphasis. Formatting a list as a numbered list helps illustrate sequences and priorities. You can quickly format a list with bullets or numbering by using the Bullets and Numbering buttons on the Formatting toolbar. You can also use the Bullets and Numbering command on the Format menu to change or customize bullet and numbering styles. You format the lists in your report with numbers and bullets.

STEPS

1. **Scroll down until the first paragraph on the second page (Authors on our...) is at the top of your screen**

2. **Select the three-line list of names under the paragraph, then click the Numbering button on the Formatting toolbar**
   The paragraphs are formatted as a numbered list.

> **QUICK TIP**
> To change the numbers to letters, Roman numerals, or another numbering style, right-click the list, click Bullets and Numbering, then select a new numbering style on the Numbered tab.

3. **Place the insertion point after Jack Seneschal, press [Enter], then type Polly Flanagan**
   Pressing [Enter] in the middle of the numbered list creates a new numbered paragraph and automatically renumbers the remainder of the list. Similarly, if you delete a paragraph from a numbered list, Word automatically renumbers the remaining paragraphs.

4. **Click 1 in the list**
   Clicking a number in a list selects all the numbers, as shown in Figure C-19.

5. **Click the Bold button B on the Formatting toolbar**
   The numbers are all formatted in bold. Notice that the formatting of the items in the list does not change when you change the formatting of the numbers. You can also use this technique to change the formatting of bullets in a bulleted list.

> **QUICK TIP**
> To remove a bullet or number, select the paragraph(s), then click ≣ or ≣.

6. **Select the list of classes and workshops under the Classes & Workshops heading, scrolling down if necessary, then click the Bullets button ≣ on the Formatting toolbar**
   The five paragraphs are formatted as a bulleted list.

7. **With the list still selected, click Format on the menu bar, then click Bullets and Numbering**
   The Bullets and Numbering dialog box opens with the Bulleted tab displayed, as shown in Figure C-20. You use this dialog box to apply bullets and numbering to paragraphs, or to change the style of bullets or numbers.

8. **Click the Square bullets box or select another style if square bullets are not available to you, click OK, then deselect the text**
   The bullet character changes to a small square, as shown in Figure C-21.

9. **Click the Save button 🖫 on the Standard toolbar**

Clues to Use

Creating outlines

You can create lists with hierarchical structures by applying an outline numbering style to a list. To create an outline, begin by applying an outline numbering style from the Outline Numbered tab in the Bullets and Numbering dialog box, then type your outline, pressing [Enter] after each item. To demote items to a lower level of importance in the outline, place the insertion point in the item, then click the Increase Indent button 🔲 on the Formatting toolbar. Each time you indent a paragraph, the item is demoted to a lower lever in the outline. Similarly, you can use the Decrease Indent button 🔲 to promote an item to a higher level in the outline. You can also create a hierarchical structure in any bulleted or numbered list by using 🔲 and 🔲 to demote and promote items in the list. To change the outline numbering style applied to a list, select a new style from the Outline Numbered tab in the Bullets and Numbering dialog box.

FIGURE C-19: Numbered list

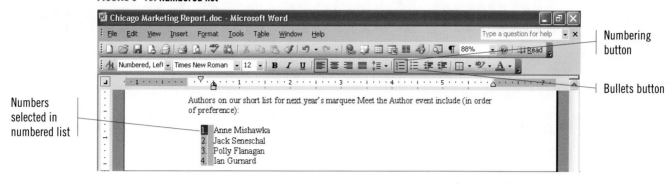

Numbering button

Bullets button

Numbers selected in numbered list

FIGURE C-20: Bulleted tab in the Bullets and Numbering dialog box

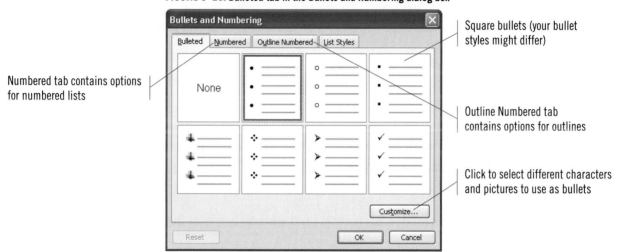

Numbered tab contains options for numbered lists

Square bullets (your bullet styles might differ)

Outline Numbered tab contains options for outlines

Click to select different characters and pictures to use as bullets

FIGURE C-21: Square bullets applied to list

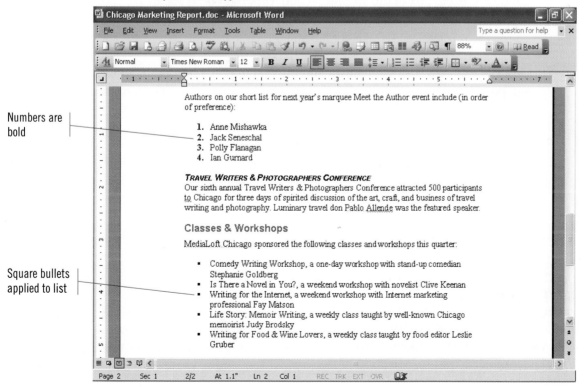

Numbers are bold

Square bullets applied to list

Adding Borders and Shading

Borders and shading can add color and splash to a document. **Borders** are lines you add above, below, to the side, or around words or a paragraph. You can format borders using different line styles, colors, and widths. **Shading** is a color or pattern you apply behind words or paragraphs to make them stand out on a page. You apply borders and shading using the Borders and Shading command on the Format menu. You enhance the advertising expenses table by adding shading to it. You also apply a border under every heading to visually punctuate the sections of the report.

STEPS

1. **Scroll up until the heading Advertising is at the top of your screen**

2. **Select the four paragraphs of tabbed text under the Advertising heading, click Format on the menu bar, click Borders and Shading, then click the Shading tab**
   The Shading tab in the Borders and Shading dialog box is shown in Figure C-22. You use this tab to apply shading to words and paragraphs.

3. **Click the Lavender box in the bottom row of the Fill section, click OK, then deselect the text**
   Lavender shading is applied to the four paragraphs. Notice that the shading is applied to the entire width of the paragraphs, despite the tab settings.

4. **Select the four paragraphs, drag the Left Indent marker ▢ to the ¾" mark on the horizontal ruler, drag the Right Indent marker △ to the 5¼" mark, then deselect the text**
   The shading for the paragraphs is indented from the left and right, making it look more attractive.

5. **Select Advertising, click Format on the menu bar, click Borders and Shading, then click the Borders tab**
   The Borders tab is shown in Figure C-23. You use this tab to add boxes and lines to words or paragraphs.

> **QUICK TIP**
> When creating custom borders, it's important to select the style, color, and width settings before applying the borders in the Preview section.

6. **Click the Custom box in the Setting section, click the Width list arrow, click ¾ pt, click the Bottom Border button ▦ in the Preview section, click OK, then deselect the text**
   A ¾-point black border is added below the Advertising paragraph.

7. **Click Events, press [F4], scroll down and use [F4] to add a border under each plum heading, press [Ctrl] [Home], then click the Save button 🖫 on the Standard toolbar**
   The completed document is shown in Figure C-24.

8. **Click the Print button 🖨, close the document, then exit Word**
   A copy of the report prints. Depending on your printer, colors might appear differently when you print. If you are using a black-and-white printer, colors will print in shades of gray.

Clues to Use

Highlighting text in a document

The Highlight tool allows you to mark and find important text in a document. **Highlighting** is transparent color that is applied to text using the Highlight pointer 🖉. To highlight text, click the Highlight list arrow ⟨ab▾⟩ on the Formatting toolbar, select a color, then use the I-beam part of the 🖉 pointer to select the text. Click ⟨ab⟩ to turn off the Highlight pointer. To remove highlighting, select the highlighted text, click ⟨ab▾⟩, then click None. Highlighting prints, but it is used most effectively when a document is viewed on screen.

FIGURE C-22: Shading tab in Borders and Shading dialog box

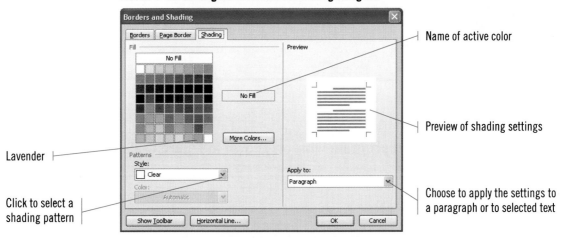

Name of active color

Preview of shading settings

Lavender

Click to select a shading pattern

Choose to apply the settings to a paragraph or to selected text

FIGURE C-23: Borders tab in Borders and Shading dialog box

Select border formats before applying them in the Preview area

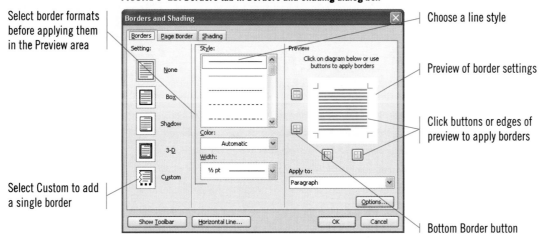

Choose a line style

Preview of border settings

Click buttons or edges of preview to apply borders

Select Custom to add a single border

Bottom Border button

FIGURE C-24: Borders and shading applied to the document

Border under headings

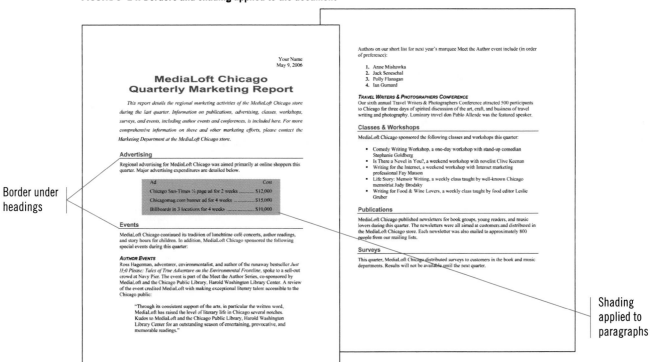

Shading applied to paragraphs

Practice

▼ CONCEPTS REVIEW

Label each element of the Word program window shown in Figure C-25.

FIGURE C-25

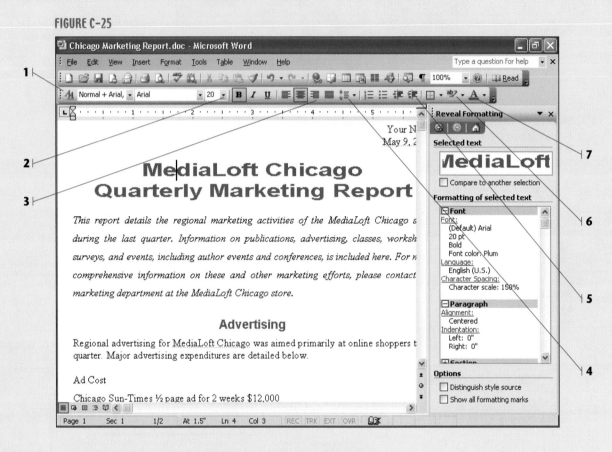

Match each term with the statement that best describes it.

8. Bold	**a.** A character that appears at the beginning of a paragraph to add emphasis
9. Shading	**b.** Transparent color that is applied to text to mark it in a document
10. Point	**c.** A text style in which characters are slanted
11. Style	**d.** Color or a pattern that is applied behind text to make it look attractive
12. Italic	**e.** A set of format settings
13. Highlight	**f.** A unit of measurement equal to ½ of an inch
14. Bullet	**g.** A line that can be applied above, below, or to the sides of a paragraph
15. Border	**h.** A text style in which characters are darker and thicker

Select the best answer from the list of choices.

16. Which button is used to align a paragraph with both the left and right margins?

a. ▤

b. ▤

c. ▤

d. ▤

17. What is Arial?

a. A style

b. A character format

c. A text effect

d. A font

18. What is the most precise way to increase the amount of white space between two paragraphs?

a. Insert an extra blank line between the paragraphs.

b. Change the line spacing of the paragraphs.

c. Indent the paragraphs.

d. Use the Paragraph command to change the spacing below the first paragraph.

19. What element of the Word program window can be used to check the tab settings applied to text?

a. Formatting toolbar

b. Standard toolbar

c. Reveal Formatting task pane

d. Styles and Formatting task pane

20. Which command would you use to apply color behind a paragraph?

a. Background

b. Styles and Formatting

c. Borders and Shading

d. Paragraph

▼ SKILLS REVIEW

1. Format with fonts.

a. Start Word, open the file WD C-2.doc from the drive and folder where your Data Files are located, save it as **EDA Report**, then scroll through the document to get a feel for its contents.

b. Press [Ctrl][Home], format the report title **Richmond Springs Economic Development Report Executive Summary** in 26-point Tahoma. Choose a different font if Tahoma is not available to you.

c. Change the font color of the report title to Teal, then press [Enter] after Springs in the title.

d. Place the insertion point in the first body paragraph under the title, then add a two-line drop cap to the paragraph using the Dropped position.

e. Format each of the following headings in 14-point Tahoma with the Teal font color: **Mission Statement**, **Guiding Principles**, **Issues**, **Proposed Actions**.

f. Press [Ctrl][Home], then save your changes to the report.

2. Change font styles and effects.

a. Apply bold to the report title and to each heading in the report.

b. Show formatting marks, then format the paragraph under the Mission Statement heading in italic.

c. Format **Years Population Growth**, the first line in the four-line list under the Issues heading, in bold, small caps, with a Teal font color.

d. Change the font color of the next two lines under Years Population Growth to Teal.

e. Format the line **Source: Office of State Planning** in italic.

f. Scroll to the top of the report, change the character scale of **Richmond Springs Economic Development Report** to 80%, then save your changes.

3. **Change line and paragraph spacing.**

   a. Change the line spacing of the three-line list under the first body paragraph to 1.5 lines.

   b. Add 12 points of space before the Executive Summary line in the title.

   c. Add 12 points of space after each heading in the report (but not the title).

   d. Add 6 points of space after each paragraph in the list under the Guiding Principles heading.

   e. Add 6 points of space after each paragraph under the Proposed Actions heading.

   f. Press [Ctrl][Home], then save your changes to the report.

4. **Align paragraphs.**

   a. Press [Ctrl][A] to select the entire document, then justify all the paragraphs.

   b. Center the three-line report title.

   c. Press [Ctrl][End], type your name, press [Enter], type the current date, then right-align your name and the date.

   d. Save your changes to the report.

5. **Work with tabs.**

   a. Scroll up and select the four-line list of population information under the Issues heading.

   b. Set left tab stops at the 1¾" mark and the 3" mark.

   c. Insert a tab at the beginning of each line in the list.

   d. In the first line, insert a tab before Population. In the second line, insert a tab before 4.5%. In the third line, insert a tab before 53%.

   e. Select the first three lines, then drag the second tab stop to the 2¾" mark on the horizontal ruler.

   f. Press [Ctrl][Home], then save your changes to the report.

6. **Work with indents.**

   a. Indent the paragraph under the Mission Statement heading ½" from the left and ½" from the right.

   b. Indent the first line of the paragraph under the Guiding Principles heading ½".

   c. Indent the first line of the three body paragraphs under the Issues heading ½".

   d. Press [Ctrl][Home], then save your changes to the report.

7. **Add bullets and numbering.**

   a. Apply bullets to the three-line list under the first body paragraph.

   b. Change the bullet style to small black circles (or choose another bullet style if small black circles are not available to you).

   c. Change the font color of the bullets to Teal.

   d. Scroll down until the Guiding Principles heading is at the top of your screen.

   e. Format the six-paragraph list under Guiding Principles as a numbered list.

   f. Format the numbers in 12-point Tahoma bold, then change the font color to Teal.

   g. Scroll down until the Proposed Actions heading is at the top of your screen, then format the paragraphs under the heading as a bulleted list using check marks as the bullet style. If checkmarks are not available, click Reset or choose another bullet style.

   h. Change the font color of the bullets to Teal, press [Ctrl][Home], then save your changes to the report.

8. **Add borders and shading.**

   a. Change the font color of the report title to Light Yellow, then apply Teal shading.

   b. Add a 1-point Teal border below the Mission Statement heading.

   c. Use the Format Painter to copy the formatting of the Mission Statement heading to the other headings in the report.

   d. Under the Issues heading, select the first three lines of tabbed text, which are formatted in Teal.

e. Apply Light Yellow shading to the paragraphs, then add a 1-point Teal box border around the paragraphs.

f. Indent the shading and border around the paragraphs 1½" from the left and 1½" from the right.

g. Press [Ctrl][Home], save your changes to the report, view the report in Print Preview, then print a copy. The formatted report is shown in Figure C-26.

h. Close the file and exit Word.

FIGURE C-26

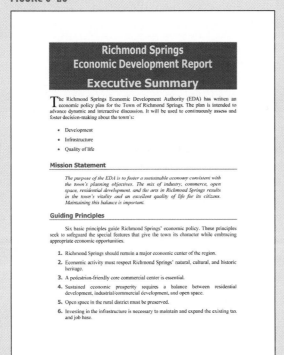
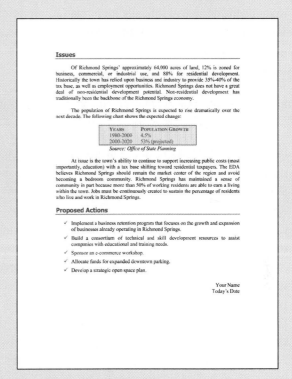

▼ INDEPENDENT CHALLENGE 1

You are an estimator for Zephir Construction in the Australian city of Wollongong. You have drafted an estimate for a home renovation job, and need to format it. It's important that your estimate have a clean, striking design, and reflect your company's professionalism.

a. Start Word, open the file WD C-3.doc from the drive and folder where your Data Files are located, save it as **Zephir Construction**, then read the document to get a feel for its contents. Figure C-27 shows how you will format the letterhead.

FIGURE C-27

b. In the first paragraph, format **ZEPHIR** in 24-point Arial Black, then apply bold. (*Hint*: Select a similar font if Arial Black is not available to you.)

c. Format **Construction** in 24-point Arial, then change the character scale to 90%.

d. Format the next two lines in 9-point Arial bold, center the three-line letterhead, then add a 1-point black border below the last line.

e. Format the title **Proposal of Renovation** in 16-point Arial Black, then center the title.

f. Format the following headings (including the colons) in 12-point Arial Black: **Date**, **Work to be performed for and at**, **Scope of work**, **Payment schedule**, and **Agreement**.

g. Format the 14-line list under **Scope of work** that begins with **Demo of all ...** as a numbered list, then apply bold to the numbers.

▼ INDEPENDENT CHALLENGE 1 (CONTINUED)

h. Change the paragraph spacing to add 4 points of space after each paragraph in the list. (*Hint*: Select 0 pt in the After text box, then type 4.)

i. With the list selected, set a right tab stop at the 5¾" mark, then insert tabs before every price in the list.

j. Apply bold to the two lines, **Total estimated job cost...** and **Approximate job time**... below the list.

k. Replace Your Name with your name in the signature block, select the signature block (Respectfully submitted through your name), set a left tab stop at the 3½" mark, then indent the signature block.

l. Examine the document carefully for formatting errors and make any necessary adjustments.

m. Save and print the document, then close the file and exit Word.

▼ INDEPENDENT CHALLENGE 2

Your employer, The Lange Center for Contemporary Arts in Halifax, Nova Scotia, is launching a membership drive. Your boss has written the text for a flyer advertising Lange membership, and asks you to format it so that it is eye catching and attractive.

a. Open the file WD C-4.doc from the drive and folder where your Data Files are located, save it as **Membership Flyer**, then read the document. Figure C-28 shows how you will format the first several paragraphs of the flyer.

b. Select the entire document and format it in 10-point Arial Narrow.

c. Center the first line, **Membership Drive**, and apply indigo shading to the paragraph. Format the text in 26-point Arial Narrow, bold, with a white font color. Expand the character spacing by 7 points.

d. Format the second line, **2006**, in 36-point Arial Black. Expand the character spacing by 25 points and change the character scale to 200%. Center the line.

FIGURE C-28

e. Format each **What we do for...** heading in 12-point Arial, bold, with an indigo font color. Add a single line ½-point border under each heading.

f. Format each subheading (**Gallery**, **Lectures**, **Library**, **All members...**, and **Membership Levels**) in 10-point Arial, bold. Add 3 points of spacing before each paragraph.

g. Indent each body paragraph ¼", except for the lines under the **What we do for YOU** heading.

h. Format the four lines under the All members... subheading as a bulleted list. Use a bullet symbol of your choice and format the bullets in the indigo color.

i. Indent the five lines under the Membership Levels heading ¼". For these five lines, set left tab stops at the 1¼" mark and the 2" mark on the horizontal ruler. Insert tabs before the price and before the word **All** in each of the five lines.

j. Format the name of each membership level (**Artistic**, **Conceptual**, etc.) in 10-point Arial, bold, italic, with an indigo font color.

k. Format the **For more information** heading in 14-point Arial, bold, with an indigo font color, then center the heading.

l. Format the last two lines in 11-point Arial Narrow, and center the lines. In the contact information, replace Your Name with your name, then apply bold to your name.

Advanced Challenge Exercise

- Change the font color of **2006** to 80% gray and add a shadow effect.
- Add an emboss effect to each subheading.
- Add a 3-point dotted black border above the **For more information** heading.

m. Examine the document carefully for formatting errors and make any necessary adjustments.

n. Save and print the flyer, then close the file and exit Word.

▼ INDEPENDENT CHALLENGE 3

FIGURE C-29

One of your responsibilities as program coordinator at Solstice Mountain Sports is to develop a program of winter outdoor learning and adventure workshops. You have drafted a memo to your boss to update her on your progress. You need to format the memo so it is professional looking and easy to read.

a. Start Word, open the file WD C-5.doc from the drive and folder where your Data Files are located, then save it as **Solstice Memo**.

b. Select the heading **Solstice Mountain Sports Memorandum**, then apply the paragraph style Heading 1 to it. (*Hint:* Open the Styles and Formatting task pane, click the Show list arrow, click Available Styles if necessary, then click Heading 1.)

c. In the memo header, replace Today's Date and Your Name with the current date and your name.

d. Select the four-line memo header, set a left tab stop at the ¾" mark, then insert tabs before the date, the recipient's name, your name, and the subject of the memo.

e. Double-space the four lines in the memo header, then apply the character style Strong to **Date:**, **To:**, **From:**, and **Re:**.

f. Apply a 1½-point double line border below the blank line under the memo header. (*Hint*: Turn on formatting marks, select the paragraph symbol below the memo header, then apply a border below it.)

g. Apply the paragraph style Heading 3 to the headings **Overview**, **Workshops**, **Accommodation**, **Fees**, and **Proposed winter programming**.

h. Under the Fees heading, format the words **Workshop fees** and **Accommodation fees** in bold italic.

i. Add 6 points of space after the Workshop fees paragraph.

Advanced Challenge Exercise

- Format **Fees** as animated text using the Las Vegas Lights animation style.
- After Fees, type **Verify prices with the Moose Lodge**, then format the text as hidden text.
- In the Fees section, apply yellow highlighting to the prices.

j. On the second page of the document, format the list under the **Proposed winter programming** heading as an outline. Figure C-29 shows the hierarchical structure of the outline. (*Hint:* Format the list as an outline numbered list, then use the Increase Indent and Decrease Indent buttons to change the level of importance of each item.)

k. Change the outline numbering style to the bullet numbering style shown in Figure C-29, if necessary.

l. Save and print the document, then close the file and exit Word.

▼ INDEPENDENT CHALLENGE 4

The fonts you choose for a document can have a major effect on the document's tone. Not all fonts are appropriate for use in a business document, and some fonts, especially those with a definite theme, are appropriate only for specific purposes. The World Wide Web includes hundreds of Web sites devoted to fonts and text design. Some Web sites sell fonts, others allow you to download fonts for free and install them on your computer. In this Independent Challenge, you will research Web sites related to fonts and find examples of fonts you can use in your work.

a. Start Word, open the file WD C-6.doc from the drive and folder where your Data Files are located, and save it as **Fonts**. This document contains the questions you will answer about the fonts you find.

b. Use your favorite search engine to search the Web for Web sites related to fonts. Use the keyword **font** to conduct your search.

c. Explore the fonts available for downloading. As you examine the fonts, notice that fonts fall into two general categories: serif fonts, which have a small stroke, called a serif, at the ends of each character, and sans serif fonts, which do not have a serif. Times New Roman is an example of a serif font and Arial is an example of a sans serif font.

d. Replace Your Name and Today's Date with the current date and your name, type your answers in the Fonts document, save it, print a copy, then close the file and exit Word.

Proposed winter programming

- ❖ Skiing, Snowboarding, and Snowshoeing
  - ➢ Skiing and Snowboarding
    - ▪ Cross-country skiing
      - • Cross-country skiing for beginners
      - • Intermediate cross-country skiing
      - • Inn-to-inn ski touring
      - • Moonlight cross-country skiing
    - ▪ Telemarking
      - • Basic telemark skiing
      - • Introduction to backcountry skiing
      - • Exploring on skis
    - ▪ Snowboarding
      - • Backcountry snowboarding
  - ➢ Snowshoeing
    - ▪ Beginner
      - • Snowshoeing for beginners
      - • Snowshoeing and winter ecology
    - ▪ Intermediate and Advanced
      - • Intermediate snowshoeing
      - • Guided snowshoe trek
      - • Above tree line snowshoeing
- ❖ Winter Hiking, Camping, and Survival
  - ➢ Hiking
    - ▪ Beginner
      - • Long-distance hiking
      - • Winter summits
      - • Hiking for women
  - ➢ Winter camping and survival
    - ▪ Beginner
      - • Introduction to winter camping
      - • Basic winter mountain skills
      - • Building snow shelters
    - ▪ Intermediate
      - • Basic winter mountain skills II
      - • Ice climbing
      - • Avalanche awareness and rescue

Word 2003

Using the file WD C-7.doc found in the drive and folder where your Data Files are located, create the menu shown in Figure C-30. (*Hints*: Use Centaur or a similar font. Change the font size of the heading to 56 points, scale the font to 90%, and expand the spacing by 1 point. For the rest of the text, change the font size of the daily specials to 18 points and the descriptions to 14 points. Format the prices using tabs. Use paragraph spacing to adjust the spacing between paragraphs so that all the text fits on one page.) Save the menu as **Melting Pot Specials**, then print a copy.

FIGURE C-30

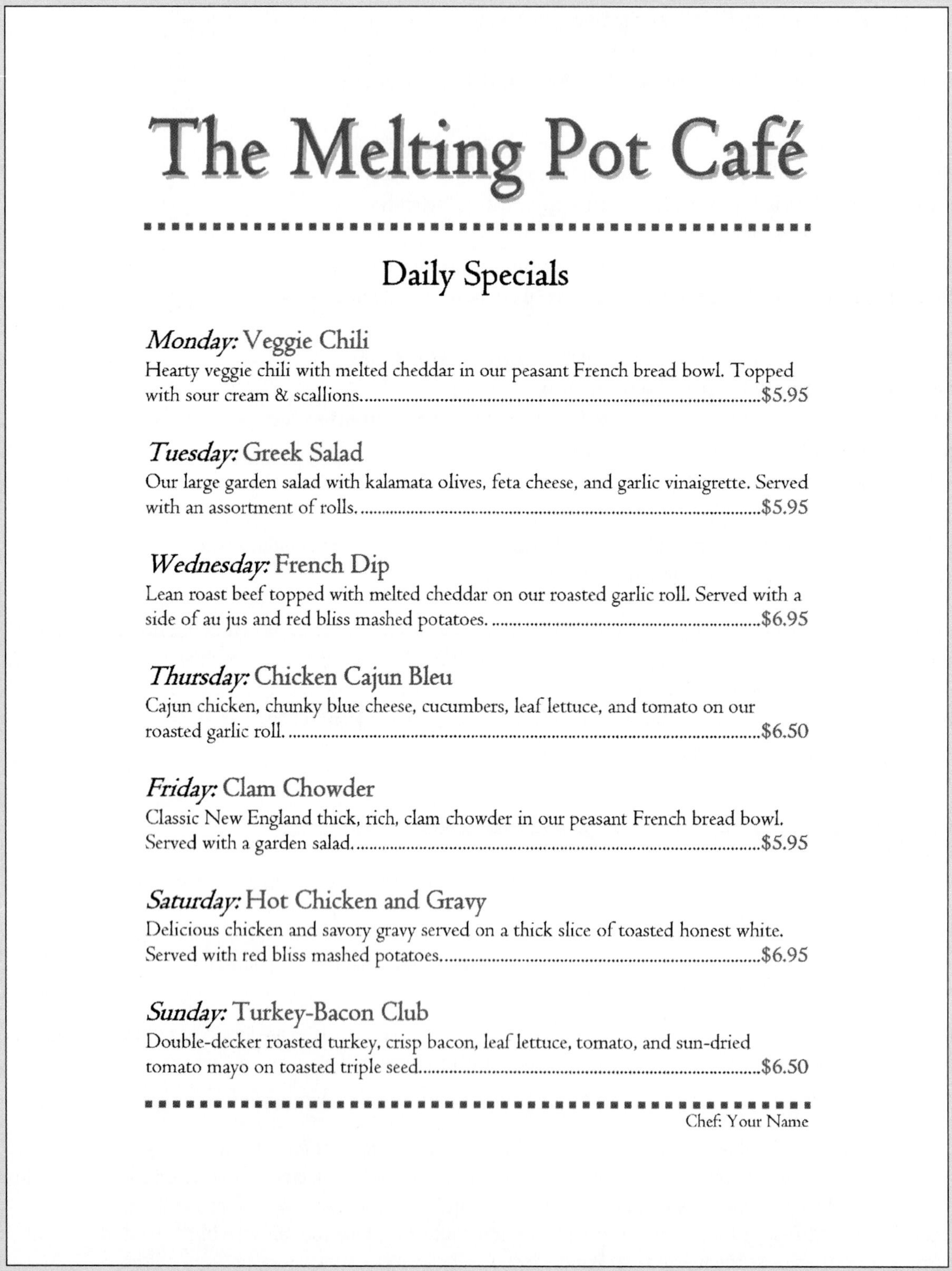

The Melting Pot Café

••

Daily Specials

Monday: Veggie Chili
Hearty veggie chili with melted cheddar in our peasant French bread bowl. Topped with sour cream & scallions..$5.95

Tuesday: Greek Salad
Our large garden salad with kalamata olives, feta cheese, and garlic vinaigrette. Served with an assortment of rolls..$5.95

Wednesday: French Dip
Lean roast beef topped with melted cheddar on our roasted garlic roll. Served with a side of au jus and red bliss mashed potatoes. $6.95

Thursday: Chicken Cajun Bleu
Cajun chicken, chunky blue cheese, cucumbers, leaf lettuce, and tomato on our roasted garlic roll. $6.50

Friday: Clam Chowder
Classic New England thick, rich, clam chowder in our peasant French bread bowl. Served with a garden salad...$5.95

Saturday: Hot Chicken and Gravy
Delicious chicken and savory gravy served on a thick slice of toasted honest white. Served with red bliss mashed potatoes...$6.95

Sunday: Turkey-Bacon Club
Double-decker roasted turkey, crisp bacon, leaf lettuce, tomato, and sun-dried tomato mayo on toasted triple seed...$6.50

••
Chef: Your Name

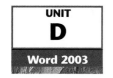

UNIT
D
Word 2003

Formatting Documents

OBJECTIVES

Set document margins
Divide a document into sections
Insert page breaks
Insert page numbers
Add headers and footers
Edit headers and footers
Format columns
Insert a table
Insert WordArt
Insert clip art

If you have a SAM user profile, you may have access to hands-on instruction, practice, and assessment of the skills covered in this unit. Log in to your SAM account and go to your assignments page to see what your instructor has assigned.

The page-formatting features of Word allow you to creatively lay out and design the pages of your documents. In this unit, you learn how to change the document margins, determine page orientation, add page numbers, and insert headers and footers. You also learn how to format text in columns and how to illustrate your documents with tables, clip art, and WordArt. You have written and formatted the text for the quarterly newsletter for the marketing staff. You are now ready to lay out and design the newsletter pages. You plan to organize the articles in columns and to illustrate the newsletter with a table, clip art, and WordArt.

Setting Document Margins

Changing a document's margins is one way to change the appearance of a document and control the amount of text that fits on a page. The **margins** of a document are the blank areas between the edge of the text and the edge of the page. When you create a document in Word, the default margins are 1" at the top and bottom of the page, and 1.25" on the left and right sides of the page. You can adjust the size of a document's margins using the Page Setup command on the File menu, or using the rulers. The newsletter should be a four-page document when finished. You begin formatting the pages by reducing the size of the document margins so that more text fits on each page.

STEPS

1. **Start Word, open the file** WD D-1.doc **from the drive and folder where your Data Files are located, then save it as** MediaLoft Buzz

   The newsletter opens in Print Layout view.

2. **Scroll through the newsletter to get a feel for its contents, then press** [Ctrl][Home]

   The newsletter is currently five pages long. Notice the status bar indicates the page where the insertion point is located and the total number of pages in the document.

3. **Click** File **on the menu bar, click** Page Setup, **then click the** Margins tab **in the Page Setup dialog box if it is not already selected**

   The Margins tab in the Page Setup dialog box is shown in Figure D-1. You can use the Margins tab to change the top, bottom, left, or right document margins, to change the orientation of the pages from portrait to landscape, and to alter other page layout settings. **Portrait orientation** means a page is taller than it is wide; **landscape orientation** means a page is wider than it is tall. This newsletter uses portrait orientation.

QUICK TIP
The minimum allowable margin settings depend on your printer and the size of the paper you are using. Word displays a warning message if you set margins that are too narrow for your printer.

4. **Click the** Top down arrow **three times until 0.7" appears, then click the** Bottom down arrow **until 0.7" appears**

   The top and bottom margins of the newsletter will be .7". Notice that the margins in the Preview section of the dialog box change as you adjust the margin settings.

5. **Press** [Tab], **type** .7 **in the Left text box, press** [Tab], **then type** .7 **in the Right text box**

   The left and right margins of the newsletter will also be .7". You can change the margin settings by using the arrows or by typing a value in the appropriate text box.

6. **Click** OK

   The document margins change to .7", as shown in Figure D-2. The bar at the intersection of the white and shaded areas on the horizontal and vertical rulers indicates the location of the margin. You can also change a document's margins by dragging the bar to a new location.

QUICK TIP
Use the Reveal Formatting task pane to quickly check the margin, orientation, paper size, and other page layout settings for a document.

7. **Click the** Zoom list arrow **on the Standard toolbar, then click** Two Pages

   The first two pages of the document appear in the document window.

8. **Scroll down to view all five pages of the newsletter, press** [Ctrl][Home], **click the** Zoom list arrow, **click** Page Width, **then click the** Save button **on the Standard toolbar to save the document**

FIGURE D-1: Margins tab in Page Setup dialog box

Default margin settings

Set gutter margin

Select page orientation

Select part of document to apply settings to

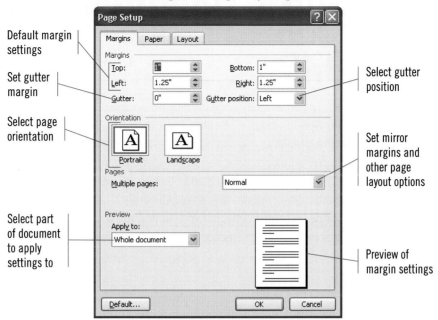

Select gutter position

Set mirror margins and other page layout options

Preview of margin settings

FIGURE D-2: Newsletter with smaller margins

Ruler shows location of left margin

Ruler shows location of top margin

Document margins are narrower than the original default margins

Document is five pages long

Page 1 is the active page

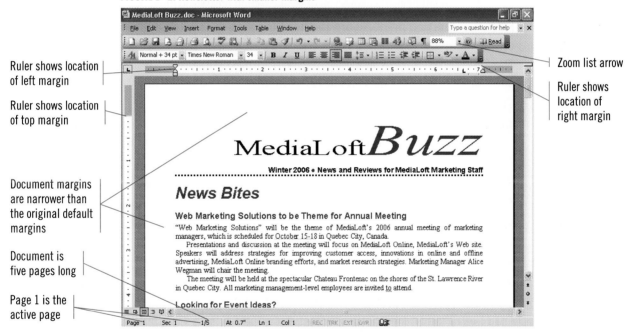

Zoom list arrow

Ruler shows location of right margin

Clues to Use

Changing orientation, margin settings, and paper size

By default, the documents you create in Word use an 8½" × 11" paper size in portrait orientation with the default margin settings. You can adjust these settings in the Page Setup dialog box to create documents that are a different size, shape, or layout. On the Margins tab, change the orientation of the pages by selecting Portrait or Landscape. To change the layout of multiple pages, use the Multiple pages list arrow to create pages that use mirror margins, that include two pages per sheet of paper, or that are formatted like a folded booklet. **Mirror margins** are used in documents with facing pages, such as a magazine, where the margins on the left page of the document are a mirror image of the margins on the right page. Documents with mirror margins have inside and outside margins, rather than right and left margins. Another type of margin is a gutter margin, which is used in documents that are bound, such as books. A **gutter** adds extra space to the left, top, or inside margin to allow for the binding. Add a gutter to a document by adjusting the setting in the Gutter text box on the Margins tab. If you want to change the size of the paper used in a document, use the Paper tab in the Page Setup dialog box. Use the Paper size list arrow to select a standard paper size, or enter custom measurements in the Width and Height text boxes.

Dividing a Document into Sections

Dividing a document into sections allows you to format each section of the document with different page layout settings. A **section** is a portion of a document that is separated from the rest of the document by section breaks. **Section breaks** are formatting marks that you insert in a document to show the end of a section. Once you have divided a document into sections, you can format each section with different column, margin, page orientation, header and footer, and other page layout settings. By default, a document is formatted as a single section, but you can divide a document into as many sections as you like. ▰▰▱▰ You want to format the body of the newsletter in two columns, but leave the masthead and the headline "News Bites" as a single column. You insert a section break before the body of the newsletter to divide the document into two sections, and then change the number of columns in the second section to two.

STEPS

1. **Click the** Show/Hide ¶ **button** ¶ **on the Standard toolbar to display formatting marks if they are not visible**

   Turning on formatting marks allows you to see the section breaks you insert in a document.

QUICK TIP

When you insert a section break at the beginning of a paragraph, Word inserts the break at the end of the previous paragraph. A section break stores the formatting information for the preceding section.

2. **Place the insertion point before the headline** Web Marketing Solutions to be..., **click** Insert **on the menu bar, then click** Break

   The Break dialog box opens, as shown in Figure D-3. You use this dialog box to insert different types of section breaks. Table D-1 describes the different types of section breaks.

3. **Click the** Continuous option button, **then click** OK

   Word inserts a continuous section break, shown as a dotted double line, above the headline. A continuous section break begins a new section of the document on the same page. The document now has two sections. Notice that the status bar indicates that the insertion point is in section 2.

4. **With the insertion point in section 2, click the** Columns button ▦ **on the Standard toolbar**

   A grid showing four columns opens. You use the grid to select the number of columns you want to create.

5. **Point to the** second column **on the grid, then click**

   Section 2 is formatted in two columns, as shown in Figure D-4. The text in section 1 remains formatted in a single column. Notice the status bar now indicates the document is four pages long. Formatting text in columns is another way to increase the amount of text that fits on a page.

6. **Click the** Zoom list arrow **on the Standard toolbar, click** Two Pages, **then scroll down to examine all four pages of the document**

   The text in section 2—all the text below the continuous section break—is formatted in two columns. Text in columns flows automatically from the bottom of one column to the top of the next column.

7. **Press [Ctrl][Home], click the** Zoom list arrow, **click** Page Width, **then save the document**

TABLE D-1: Types of section breaks

section	function
Next page	Begins a new section and moves the text following the break to the top of the next page
Continuous	Begins a new section on the same page
Even page	Begins a new section and moves the text following the break to the top of the next even-numbered page
Odd page	Begins a new section and moves the text following the break to the top of the next odd-numbered page

FIGURE D-3: Break dialog box

FIGURE D-4: Continuous section break and columns

Text in section 1 is formatted in one column

Insertion point in section 2

Text in section 2 is formatted in two columns

Section 2 is the active section

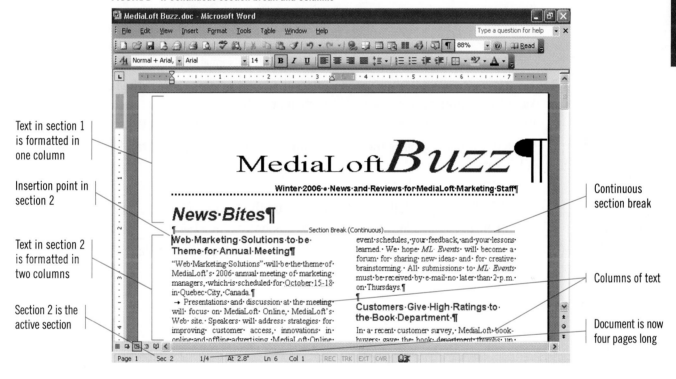

Continuous section break

Columns of text

Document is now four pages long

Clues to Use

Changing page layout settings for a section

Dividing a document into sections allows you to vary the layout of a document. In addition to applying different column settings to sections, you can apply different margins, page orientation, paper size, vertical alignment, header and footer, page numbering, and other page layout settings. For example, if you are formatting a report that includes a table with many columns, you might want to change the table's page orientation to landscape so that it is easier to read. To do this, you would insert a section break before and after the table to create a section that contains only the table. Then you would use the Margins tab in the Page Setup dialog box to change the page orientation of the section that contains the table to landscape.

To change the page layout settings for an individual section, place the insertion point in the section, open the Page Setup (or Columns) dialog box, select the options you want to change, click the Apply to list arrow, click This section, then click OK. When you select This section in the Apply to list box, the settings are applied to the current section only. If you select Whole document in the Apply to list box, the settings are applied to all the sections in the document.

Inserting Page Breaks

As you type text in a document, Word automatically inserts an **automatic page break** (also called a soft page break) when you reach the bottom of a page, allowing you to continue typing on the next page. You can also force text onto the next page of a document by using the Break command to insert a **manual page break** (also called a hard page break). You insert manual page breaks where you know you want to begin each new page of the newsletter.

STEPS

1. **Scroll down to the bottom of page 1, place the insertion point before the headline** Career Corner, **click** Insert **on the menu bar, then click** Break

   The Break dialog box opens. You also use this dialog box to insert page, column, and text-wrapping breaks. Table D-2 describes these types of breaks.

   QUICK TIP
   To delete a break, double-click the break to select it, then press [Delete].

2. **Make sure the** Page break option button **is selected, then click** OK

   Word inserts a manual page break before "Career Corner" and moves all the text following the page break to the beginning of the next page, as shown in Figure D-5. The page break appears as a dotted line in Print Layout view when formatting marks are displayed. Page break marks are visible on the screen but do not print. Manual and automatic page breaks are always visible in Normal view.

3. **Scroll down to the bottom of page 2, place the insertion point before the headline** Webcasts Slated for Spring, **press and hold** [Ctrl], **then press** [Enter]

   Pressing [Ctrl][Enter] is a fast way to insert a manual page break. The headline is forced to the top of the third page.

   QUICK TIP
   To fit more text on the screen in Print Layout view, you can hide the white space on the top and bottom of each page and the gray space between pages. To toggle between hiding and showing white space, move the pointer to the top of a page until the pointer changes to ⊞, then click.

4. **Scroll down page 3, place the insertion point before the headline** Staff News, **then press** [Ctrl][Enter]

   The headline is forced to the top of the fourth page.

5. **Press** [Ctrl][Home], **click the** Zoom list arrow **on the Standard toolbar, then click** Two Pages

   The first two pages of the document are displayed, as shown in Figure D-6.

6. **Scroll down to view pages 3 and 4, click the** Zoom list arrow, **click** Page Width, **then save the document**

Clues to Use

Vertically aligning text on a page

By default, text is vertically aligned with the top margin of a page, but you can change the vertical alignment of text so that it is centered between the top and bottom margins, justified between the top and bottom margins, or aligned with the bottom margin of the page. You vertically align text on a page only when the text does not fill the page; for example, if you are creating a flyer or a title page for a report. To change the vertical alignment of text in a section (or a document), place the insertion point in the section you want to align, open the Page Setup dialog box, use the Vertical alignment list arrow on the Layout tab to select the alignment you want—top, center, justified, or bottom—use the Apply to list arrow to select the part of the document you want to align, and then click OK.

FIGURE D-5: Manual page break in document

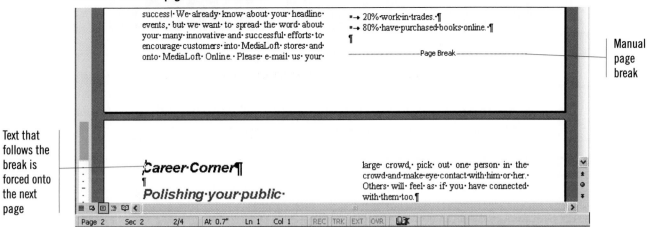

Manual page break

Text that follows the break is forced onto the next page

FIGURE D-6: Pages 1 and 2

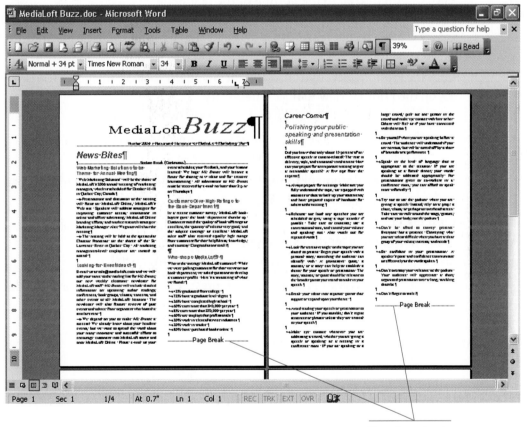

Manual page breaks

TABLE D-2: Types of breaks

break	function
Page break	Forces the text following the break to begin at the top of the next page
Column break	Forces the text following the break to begin at the top of the next column
Text wrapping break	Forces the text following the break to begin at the beginning of the next line

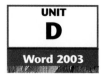

Inserting Page Numbers

If you want to number the pages of a multiple-page document, you can insert a page number field at the top or bottom of each page. A **field** is a code that serves as a placeholder for data that changes in a document, such as a page number or the current date. When you use the Page Numbers command on the Insert menu to add page numbers to a document, Word automatically numbers the pages for you. ▰▰▰ You insert a page number field so that page numbers will appear at the bottom of each page in the document.

STEPS

1. **Click Insert on the menu bar, then click Page Numbers**

   The Page Numbers dialog box opens, as shown in Figure D-7. You use this dialog box to specify the position—top or bottom of the page—and the alignment for the page numbers. Bottom of page (Footer) is the default position.

QUICK TIP
You can also align page numbers with the left, right, inside, or outside margins of a document.

2. **Click the Alignment list arrow, then click Center**

   The page numbers will be centered between the left and right margins at the bottom of each page.

3. **Click OK, then scroll to the bottom of the first page**

   The page number 1 appears in gray at the bottom of the first page, as shown in Figure D-8. The number is gray, or dimmed, because it is located in the Footer area. When the document is printed, the page numbers appear as normal text. You will learn more about headers and footers in the next lesson.

4. **Click the Print Preview button 🔍 on the Standard toolbar, then click the One Page button 📄 on the Print Preview toolbar if necessary**

   The first page of the newsletter appears in Print Preview. Notice the page number.

5. **Click the page number with the 🔍 pointer to zoom in on the page**

   The page number is centered at the bottom of the page, as shown in Figure D-9.

6. **Scroll down the document to see the page number at the bottom of each page**

   Word automatically numbered each page of the newsletter.

QUICK TIP
To display more than six pages of a document in Print Preview, drag to expand the Multiple Pages grid.

7. **Click the Multiple Pages button 🔲 on the Print Preview toolbar, point to the second box in the bottom row on the grid to select 2 × 2 pages, then click**

   All four pages of the newsletter appear in the Print Preview window.

8. **Click Close on the Print Preview toolbar, press [Ctrl][Home], then save the document**

Clues to Use

Inserting the date and time

Using the Date and Time command on the Insert menu, you can insert the current date or the current time into a document, either as a field or as static text. Word uses the clock on your computer to compute the current date and time. To insert the current date or time at the location of the insertion point, click Date and Time on the Insert menu, then select the date or time format you want to use from the list of available formats in the Date and Time dialog box. If you want to insert the date or time as a field that is updated automatically each time you open or print the document, select the Update automatically check box, and then click OK. If you want the current date or time to remain in the document as static text, deselect the Update automatically check box, and then click OK.

FIGURE D-7: Page Numbers dialog box

Set location for page number (header or footer)

Set alignment of page number

Clear to hide the page number on the first page

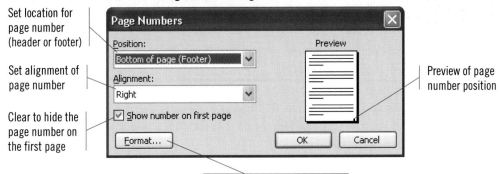

Preview of page number position

Click to change numbering format

FIGURE D-8: Page number in document

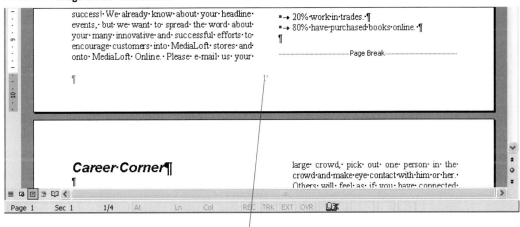

Page number is dimmed

FIGURE D-9: Page number in Print Preview

One Page button

Multiple Pages button

Page number in Print Preview

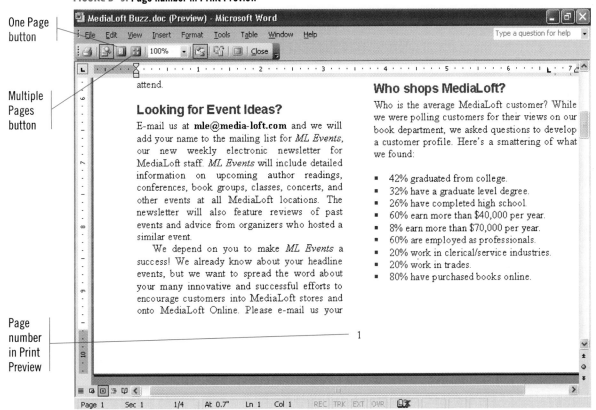

Adding Headers and Footers

A **header** is text or graphics that appears at the top of every page of a document. A **footer** is text or graphics that appears at the bottom of every page. In longer documents, headers and footers often contain information such as the title of the publication, the title of the chapter, the name of the author, the date, or a page number. You can add headers and footers to a document by using the Header and Footer command on the View menu to open the Header and Footer areas, and then inserting text and graphics in them. ▨▨▨▨ You create a header that includes the name of the newsletter and the current date.

STEPS

1. **Click View on the menu bar, then click Header and Footer**

   The Header and Footer areas open and the document text is dimmed, as shown in Figure D-10. When the document text is dimmed, it cannot be edited. The Header and Footer toolbar also opens. It includes buttons for inserting standard text into headers and footers and for navigating between headers and footers. See Table D-3. The Header and Footer areas of a document are independent of the document itself and must be formatted separately. For example, if you select all the text in a document and then change the font, the header and footer font does not change.

   > **QUICK TIP**
   >
   > You can change the date format by right-clicking the field, clicking Edit Field on the shortcut menu, and then selecting a new date format in the Field properties list in the Field dialog box.

2. **Type Buzz in the Header area, press [Spacebar] twice, then click the Insert Date button 🗓 on the Header and Footer toolbar**

   Clicking the Insert Date button inserts a date field into the header. The date is inserted using the default date format (usually month/date/year, although your default date format might be different). The word "Buzz" and the current date will appear at the top of every page in the document.

3. **Select Buzz and the date, then click the Center button ☰ on the Formatting toolbar**

   The text is centered in the Header area. In addition to the alignment buttons on the Formatting toolbar, you can use tabs to align text in the Header and Footer areas. Notice the tab stops shown on the ruler. The tab stops are the default tab stops for the Header and Footer areas and are based on the default margin settings. If you change the margins in a document, you can adjust the tab stops in the Header or Footer area to align with the new margin settings.

   > **QUICK TIP**
   >
   > Unless you set different headers and footers for different sections, the information you insert in any Header or Footer area appears on every page in the document.

4. **With the text still selected, click the Font list arrow on the Formatting toolbar, click Arial, click the Bold button B, then click in the Header area to deselect the text**

   The header text is formatted in 12-point Arial bold.

5. **Click the Switch Between Header and Footer button 🖳 on the Header and Footer toolbar**

   The insertion point moves to the Footer area, where a page number field is centered in the Footer area.

6. **Double-click the page number to select the field, click the Font list arrow, click Arial, click B, then click in the Footer area to deselect the field**

   The page number is formatted in 12-point Arial bold.

   > **QUICK TIP**
   >
   > To change the distance between the header and footer and the edge of the page, change the From edge settings on the Layout tab in the Page Setup dialog box.

7. **Click Close on the Header and Footer toolbar, save the document, then scroll down until the bottom of page 1 and the top of page 2 appear in the document window**

   The Header and Footer areas close and the header and footer text is dimmed, as shown in Figure D-11. The header text—"Buzz" and the current date—appear at the top of every page in the document, and a page number appears at the bottom of every page.

FIGURE D-10: Header area

Header area is open

Tab stops for the header are set for the default document margins

Header and Footer toolbar (yours may open in a different location)

Header ·Section 1·

Document text is dimmed

Winter·2006· ·News·and·Reviews·for·MediaLoft·Marketing·Staff¶

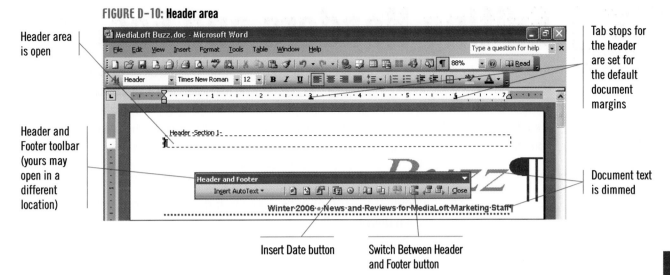

Insert Date button

Switch Between Header and Footer button

FIGURE D-11: Header and footer in document

events,· but· we· want· to· spread· the· word· about· your· many· innovative· and· successful· efforts· to· encourage· customers· into· MediaLoft· stores· and· onto· MediaLoft· Online. · Please· e-mail· us· your·

■ → 20%·work·in·trades.·
■ → 80%·have·purchased·books·online. ·
¶

Page number appears in the footer on every page

Page Break

1

Header text appears centered in the header area on every page (your date will differ)

Career·Corner¶

Buzz·:·1/14/2006¶

large· crowd,· pick· out· one· person· in· the· crowd·and·make·eye·contact·with·him·or·her. ·

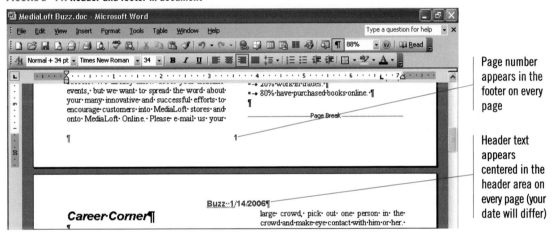

TABLE D-3: Buttons on the Header and Footer toolbar

button	function
Insert AutoText ▾	Inserts an AutoText entry, such as a field for the filename, or the author's name
Insert Page Number	Inserts a field for the page number so that the pages are numbered automatically
Insert Number of Pages	Inserts a field for the total number of pages in the document
Format Page Number	Opens the Page Number Format dialog box; use to change the numbering format or to begin automatic page numbering with a specific number
Insert Date	Inserts a field for the current date
Insert Time	Inserts a field for the current time
Page Setup	Opens the Page Setup dialog box
Show/Hide Document Text	Hides and displays the document text
Link to Previous	Switches the link between headers and footers in adjoining sections on and off; use to make headers and footers in adjoining sections the same or different
Switch Between Header and Footer	Moves the insertion point between the Header and Footer areas
Show Previous	Moves the insertion point to the header or footer in the next section
Show Next	Moves the insertion point to the header or footer in the previous section

Editing Headers and Footers

To change header and footer text or to alter the formatting of headers and footers, you must first open the Header and Footer areas. You open headers and footers by using the Header and Footer command on the View menu or by double-clicking a header or footer in Print Layout view. ▓▓▓▓▓ You modify the header by adding a small circle symbol between "Buzz" and the date. You also add a border under the header text to set it off from the rest of the page. Finally, you remove the header and footer text from the first page of the document.

STEPS

1. **Place the insertion point at the top of page 2, position the pointer over the header text at the top of page 2, then double-click**
   The Header and Footer areas open.

2. **Place the insertion point between the two spaces after Buzz, click Insert on the menu bar, then click Symbol**
   The Symbol dialog box opens and is similar to Figure D-12. **Symbols** are special characters, such as graphics, shapes, and foreign language characters, that you can insert into a document. The symbols shown in Figure D-12 are the symbols included with the (normal text) font. You can use the Font list arrow on the Symbols tab to view the symbols included with each font on your computer.

3. **Scroll the list of symbols if necessary to locate the black circle symbol shown in Figure D-12, select the black circle symbol, click Insert, then click Close**
   A circle symbol is added at the location of the insertion point.

4. **With the insertion point in the header text, click Format on the menu bar, then click Borders and Shading**
   The Borders and Shading dialog box opens.

5. **Click the Borders tab if it is not already selected, click Custom in the Setting section, click the dotted line in the Style scroll box (the second line style), click the Width list arrow, click 2¼ pt, click the Bottom border button in the Preview section, make sure Paragraph is selected in the Apply to list box, click OK, click Close on the Header and Footer toolbar, then scroll as needed to see the top of page 2**
   A dotted line border is added below the header text, as shown in Figure D-13.

6. **Press [Ctrl][Home] to move the insertion point to the beginning of the document**
   The newsletter already includes the name of the document at the top of the first page, making the header information redundant. You can modify headers and footers so that the header and footer text does not appear on the first page of a document or a section.

7. **Click File on the menu bar, click Page Setup, then click the Layout tab**
   The Layout tab of the Page Setup dialog box includes options for creating a different header and footer for the first page of a document or a section, and for creating different headers and footers for odd- and even-numbered pages. For example, in a document with facing pages, such as a magazine, you might want the publication title to appear in the left-page header and the publication date to appear in the right-page header.

8. **Click the Different first page check box to select it, click the Apply to list arrow, click Whole document, then click OK**
   The header and footer text is removed from the Header and Footer areas on the first page.

9. **Scroll to see the header and footer on pages 2, 3, and 4, then save the document**

FIGURE D-12: Symbol dialog box

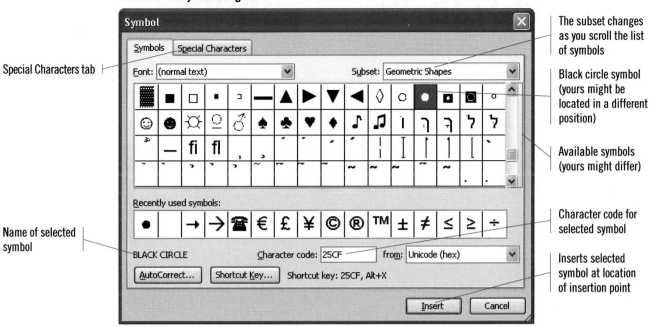

Special Characters tab

The subset changes as you scroll the list of symbols

Black circle symbol (yours might be located in a different position)

Available symbols (yours might differ)

Character code for selected symbol

Name of selected symbol

Inserts selected symbol at location of insertion point

FIGURE D-13: Symbol and border added to header

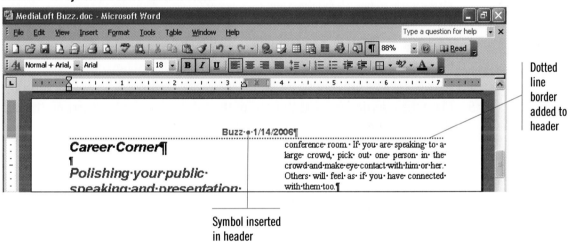

Dotted line border added to header

Symbol inserted in header

Clues to Use

Inserting and creating AutoText entries

Word includes a number of built-in AutoText entries, including salutations and closings for letters, as well as information for headers and footers. To insert a built-in AutoText entry at the location of the insertion point, point to AutoText on the Insert menu, point to a category on the AutoText menu, then click the AutoText entry you want to insert. You can also use the Insert AutoText button on the Header and Footer toolbar to insert an AutoText entry from the Header/Footer category into a header or footer.

The Word AutoText feature also allows you to store text and graphics that you use frequently so that you can easily insert them in a document. To create a custom AutoText entry, enter the text or graphic you want to store—such as a company name or logo—in a document, select it, point to AutoText on the Insert menu, and then click New. In the Create AutoText dialog box, type a name for your AutoText entry, then click OK. The text or graphic is saved as a custom AutoText entry. To insert a custom AutoText entry in a document, point to AutoText on the Insert menu, click AutoText, select the entry name on the AutoText tab in the AutoCorrect dialog box, click Insert, then click OK.

Formatting Columns

Formatting text in columns often makes the text easier to read. You can apply column formatting to a whole document, to a section, or to selected text. The Columns button on the Standard toolbar allows you to quickly create columns of equal width. In addition, you can use the Columns command on the Format menu to create columns and to customize the width and spacing of columns. To control the way text flows between columns, you can insert a **column break**, which forces the text following the break to move to the top of the next column. You can also balance columns of unequal length on a page by inserting a continuous section break at the end of the last column on the page. ◼◼◼◼ You format the Staff News page in three columns, and then adjust the flow of text.

STEPS

1. **Scroll to the top of page 4, place the insertion point before** Boston, **click** Insert **on the menu bar, click** Break, **click the** Continuous option button, **then click** OK

    A continuous section break is inserted before Boston. The newsletter now contains three sections.

    > **QUICK TIP**
    > To change the width and spacing of existing columns, you can use the Columns dialog box or drag the column markers on the horizontal ruler.

2. **Refer to the status bar to confirm that the insertion point is in section 3, click** Format **on the menu bar, then click** Columns

    The Columns dialog box opens, as shown in Figure D-14.

3. **Select** Three **in the Presets section, click the** Spacing down arrow **twice until 0.3" appears, select the** Line between check box, **then click** OK

    All the text in section 3 is formatted in three columns of equal width with a line between the columns, as shown in Figure D-15.

    > **QUICK TIP**
    > To create a banner headline that spans the width of a page, select the headline text, click the Columns button, then click 1 Column.

4. **Click the** Zoom list arrow **on the Standard toolbar, then click** Whole Page

    Notice that the third column of text is much shorter than the first two columns. Page 4 would look better if the three columns were balanced—each the same length.

5. **Place the insertion point at the end of the third column, click** Insert **on the menu bar, click** Break, **click the** Continuous option button, **then click** OK

    The columns in section 3 adjust to become roughly the same length.

6. **Scroll up to page 3**

    The two columns on page 3 are also uneven. You want the information about Jack Niven to appear at the top of the second column.

    > **QUICK TIP**
    > If a section contains a column break, you cannot balance the columns by inserting a continuous section break.

7. **Click the** Zoom list arrow, **click** Page Width, **scroll down page 3, place the insertion point before the heading** Jack Niven, **click** Insert **on the menu bar, click** Break, **click the** Column break option button, **then click** OK

    The text following the column break is forced to the top of the next column.

8. **Click the** Zoom list arrow, **click** Two Pages, **then save the document**

    The columns on pages 3 and 4 are formatted as shown in Figure D-16.

Clues to Use

Hyphenating text in a document

Hyphenating a document is another way to control the flow of text in columns. Hyphens are small dashes that break words that fall at the end of a line. Hyphenation diminishes the gaps between words in justified text and reduces ragged right edges in left-aligned text. If a document includes narrow columns, hyphenating the text can help give the pages a cleaner look. To hyphenate a document automatically, point to Language on the Tools menu, click Hyphenation, select the Automatically hyphenate document check box in the Hyphenation dialog box, and then click OK. You can also use the Hyphenation dialog box to change the hyphenation zone—the distance between the margin and the end of the last word in the line. A smaller hyphenation zone results in a greater number of hyphenated words and a cleaner look to columns of text.

FIGURE D-14: Columns dialog box

Select a preset format for columns

Change the number of columns

Select to add a line between columns

Set custom width and spacing for columns

Preview of current settings

Select to create columns of equal width

Select part of document to apply format to

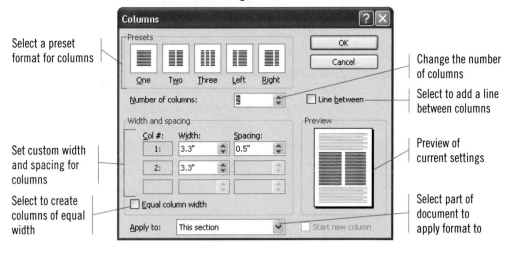

FIGURE D-15: Text formatted in three columns

Column markers show the width and spacing of columns

Text in section 3 is formatted in three columns

Section break is at end of section 2

Line added between columns

FIGURE D-16: Columns on pages 3 and 4 of the newsletter

Text following column break is forced to top of next column

Column break

Continuous section break

Columns in section are balanced

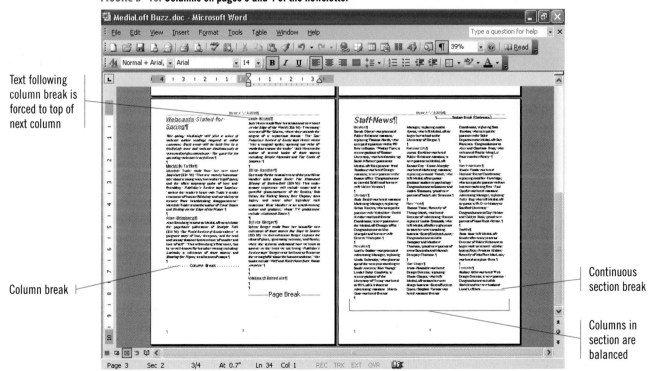

Inserting a Table

Adding a table to a document is a useful way to illustrate information that is intended for quick reference and analysis. A **table** is a grid of columns and rows of cells that you can fill with text and graphics. A **cell** is the box formed by the intersection of a column and a row. The lines that divide the columns and rows of a table and help you see the grid-like structure of the table are called **borders**. A simple way to insert a table into a document is to use the Insert command on the Table menu. This command allows you to determine the dimensions and format of a table before it is inserted. 〓〓〓 You add a table showing the schedule for Webcasts to the bottom of page 3.

STEPS

1. **Click the** Zoom list arrow **on the Standard toolbar, click** Page Width, **then scroll down page 3 until the heading** Webcast Schedule **is at the top of your screen**
   The bottom of page three is displayed.

2. **Place the insertion point before the heading** Webcast Schedule, **click** Insert **on the menu bar, click** Break, **click the** Continuous option button, **then click** OK
   A continuous section break is inserted before the heading Webcast Schedule. The document now includes four sections, with the heading Webcast Schedule in the third section.

3. **Click the** Columns button 〓 **on the Standard toolbar, point to the** first column **on the grid, then click**
   Section 3 is formatted as a single column.

4. **Place the insertion point before the second paragraph mark below the heading Webcast Schedule, click** Table **on the menu bar, point to** Insert, **then click** Table
   The Insert Table dialog box opens, as shown in Figure D-17. You use this dialog box to create a blank table with a set number of columns and rows, and to choose an option for sizing the width of the columns in the table.

5. **Type** 4 **in the Number of columns text box, press** [Tab], **type** 6 **in the Number of rows text box, make sure the** Fixed column width option button **is selected, then click** AutoFormat
   The Table AutoFormat dialog box opens. You use this dialog box to apply a table style to the table. Table styles include format settings for the text, borders, and shading in a table. A preview of the selected style appears in the Preview section of the dialog box.

QUICK TIP
To apply a different table style to a table once it is created, place the insertion point in the table, click Table Auto-Format on the Table menu, and then modify the selections in the Table Auto-Format dialog box.

6. **Scroll down the list of table styles, click** Table Grid 8, **clear the** First column, Last row, **and** Last column check boxes **in the Apply special formats to section, then click** OK twice
   A blank table with four columns and six rows is inserted in the document at the location of the insertion point. The table is formatted in the Table Grid 8 style, with blue shading in the header row and blue borders that define the table cells. The insertion point is in the upper-left cell of the table, the first cell in the header row.

7. **Type** Date **in the first cell in the first row, press** [Tab], **type** Time, **press** [Tab], **type** Guest, **press** [Tab], **type** Store, **then press** [Tab]
   Pressing [Tab] moves the insertion point to the next cell in the row. At the end of a row, pressing [Tab] moves the insertion point to the first cell in the next row. You can also click in a cell to move the insertion point to it.

TROUBLE
If you pressed [Tab] after the last row, click the Undo button 〓 on the Standard toolbar to remove the blank row.

8. **Type the text shown in Figure D-18 in the table cells, pressing** [Tab] **to move from cell to cell**
   You can edit the text in a table by placing the insertion point in a cell and then typing. You can also select the text in a table and then format it using the buttons on the Formatting toolbar. If you want to modify the structure of a table, you can use the Insert and Delete commands on the Table menu to add and remove rows and columns. You can also use the AutoFit command on the Table menu to change the width of table columns and the height of table rows. To select a column, row, or table before performing an action, place the insertion point in the row, column, or table you want to select, and then use the Select command on the Table menu.

9. **Save the document**

FIGURE D-17: **Insert Table dialog box**

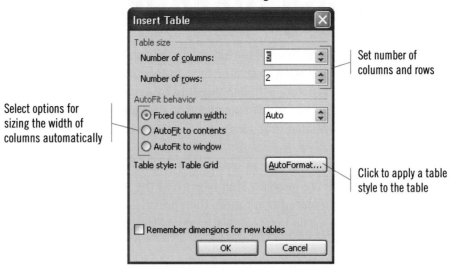

Set number of columns and rows

Select options for sizing the width of columns automatically

Click to apply a table style to the table

FIGURE D-18: **Completed table**

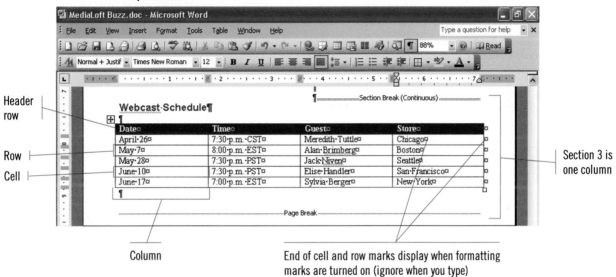

Header row

Row

Cell

Column

Section 3 is one column

End of cell and row marks display when formatting marks are turned on (ignore when you type)

Clues to Use

Moving around in a long document

Rather than scrolling to move to a different place in a long document, you can use the Browse by Object feature, the Go To command, or the Document Map to quickly move the insertion point to a specific location. Browse by Object allows you to browse to the next or previous page, section, line, table, graphic, or other item of the same type in a document. To do this, first click the Select Browse Object button below the vertical scroll bar to open a palette of object types. On this palette, click the button for the type of item by which you want to browse, and then click the Next or Previous buttons to scroll through the items of that type in the document.

To move a specific page, section, or other item in a document,

you can click the Go To command on the Edit menu. On the Go To tab in the Find and Replace dialog box, select the type of item in the Go to what list box, type the item number in the text box, and then click Go To to move the insertion point to the item.

If your document is formatted with heading styles, you can also use the Document Map to navigate a document. The Document Map is a separate pane in the document window that displays a list of headings in the document. You click a heading in the Document Map to move the insertion point to that heading in the document. To open and close the Document Map, click Document Map on the View menu or click the Document Map button on the Standard toolbar.

Inserting WordArt

Illustrating a document with WordArt is a fun way to spice up the layout of a page. **WordArt** is an object that contains specially formatted, decorative text. The text in a WordArt object can be skewed, rotated, stretched, shadowed, patterned, or fit into shapes to create interesting effects. To insert a WordArt object into a document, you use the WordArt command on the Insert menu. ◼◼◼◼◼ You decide to format the Staff News headline as WordArt to add some zest to the final page of the newsletter.

STEPS

1. **Scroll down until the heading** Staff News **is at the top of your screen, select** Staff News **(not including the paragraph mark), then press** [Delete]

   The insertion point is at the top of page 4 in the third section of the document. The third section is formatted as a single column.

2. **Click** Insert **on the menu bar, point to** Picture, **then click** WordArt

   The WordArt Gallery dialog box opens, as shown in Figure D-19. You use the WordArt Gallery to select a style for the WordArt object.

3. **Click the** fourth style in the third row, **then click** OK

   The Edit WordArt Text dialog box opens. You type the text you want to format as WordArt in this dialog box. You can also use the Edit WordArt Text dialog box to change the font and font size of the WordArt text.

> **QUICK TIP**
> Use the Text Wrapping button on the WordArt toolbar to convert the object to a floating graphic.

4. **Type** Staff News, **then click** OK

   The WordArt object appears at the location of the insertion point. The object is an **inline graphic**, or part of the line of text in which it was inserted.

5. **Click the** WordArt object **to select it**

   The black squares that appear on the corners and sides of the object are the **sizing handles**. Sizing handles appear when a graphic object is selected. You can drag a sizing handle to change the size of the object. The WordArt toolbar also appears when a WordArt object is selected. You use the buttons on the WordArt toolbar to edit and modify the format of WordArt objects.

6. **Position the pointer over the** lower-right sizing handle, **when the pointer changes to** ↖ **drag down and to the right to make the object about** 1½" **tall and** 5½" **wide**

   Refer to the vertical and horizontal rulers for guidance as you drag the sizing handle to resize the object. When you release the mouse button, the WordArt object is enlarged, as shown in Figure D-20.

7. **Click the** Center button ▤ **on the Formatting toolbar**

   The WordArt object is centered between the margins.

8. **Click the** WordArt Shape button ◭ **on the WordArt toolbar, then click the** Wave 1 shape **(the fifth shape in the third row)**

   The shape of the WordArt text changes.

> **TROUBLE**
> If the newsletter is five pages instead of four, reduce the height of the WordArt object.

9. **Click outside the WordArt object to deselect it, click the** Zoom list arrow **on the Standard toolbar, click** Two Pages, **then save the document**

   The completed pages 3 and 4 are displayed, as shown in Figure D-21.

FIGURE D-19: WordArt Gallery dialog box

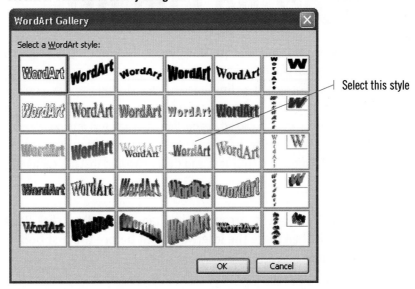

Select this style

FIGURE D-20: Resized WordArt object

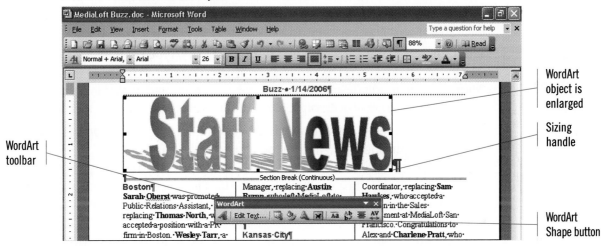

WordArt object is enlarged

Sizing handle

WordArt toolbar

WordArt Shape button

FIGURE D-21: Completed pages 3 and 4

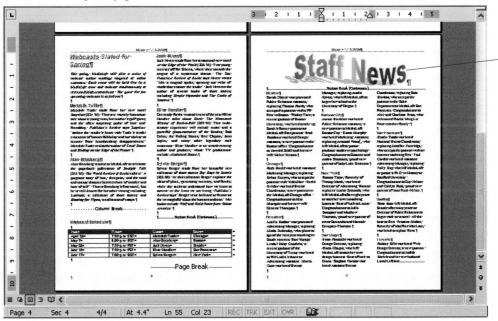

WordArt centered with the Wave 1 shape applied

Inserting Clip Art

Illustrating a document with clip art images can give it visual appeal and help to communicate your ideas. **Clip art** is a collection of graphic images that you can insert into a document. Clip art images are stored in the **Clip Organizer**, a library of the **clips**—media files, including graphics, photographs, sounds, movies, and animations—that come with Word. You can add a clip to a document using the Clip Art command on the Insert menu. Once you insert a clip art image, you can wrap text around it, resize it, and move it to a different location. ▨▨▨▨▨ You illustrate the second page of the newsletter with a clip art image. After you insert the image, you wrap text around it, enlarge it, and then move it so that it is centered between the two columns of text.

1. **Click the** Zoom list arrow **on the Standard toolbar, click** Page Width, **scroll to the top of page 2, then place the insertion point before the first body paragraph, which begins** Did you know...
   You insert the clip art graphic at the location of the insertion point.

2. **Click** Insert **on the menu bar, point to** Picture, **then click** Clip Art
   The Clip Art task pane opens. You can use this task pane to search for clips related to a keyword. If you are working with an active Internet connection, your search results will include clip art from the Microsoft Office Online Web site.

3. **Select the text in the Search for text box if necessary, type** communication, **then click** Go
   Clips that include the keyword "communication" appear in the Clip Art task pane, as shown in Figure D-22. When you point to a clip, a ScreenTip showing the first few keywords applied to the clip (listed alphabetically), the width and height of the clip in pixels, and the file size and file type for the clip appears.

4. **Point to the** clip called out in Figure D-22, **click the** list arrow **that appears next to the clip, click** Insert **on the menu, then close the Clip Art task pane**
   The clip is inserted at the location of the insertion point. You want to center the graphic on the page. Until you apply text wrapping to a graphic, it is part of the line of text in which it was inserted (an **inline graphic**). To move a graphic independently of text, you must wrap the text around it to make it a **floating graphic**, which can be moved anywhere on a page.

5. **Double-click the** clip art image, **click the** Layout tab **in the Format Picture dialog box, click** Tight, **then click** OK
   The text in the first body paragraph wraps around the irregular shape of the clip art image. The white circles that appear on the square edges of the graphic are the sizing handles. The white sizing handles indicate the graphic is a floating graphic.

6. **Position the pointer over the** lower-right sizing handle, **when the pointer changes to** ↘ **drag down and to the right until the graphic is about 2½" wide and 2½" tall**
   As you drag a sizing handle, the dotted lines show the outline of the graphic. Refer to the dotted lines and the rulers as you resize the graphic. When you release the mouse button, the image is enlarged.

7. **With the graphic still selected, position the pointer over the graphic, when the pointer changes to** ⊹ **drag the graphic down and to the right so it is centered on the page as shown in Figure D-23, release the mouse button, then deselect the graphic**
   The graphic is now centered between the two columns of text.

8. **Click the** Zoom list arrow, **then click** Two Pages
   The completed pages 1 and 2 are displayed, as shown in Figure D-24.

9. **Click the** Zoom list arrow, **click** Page Width, **press** [Ctrl][End], **press** [Enter] **twice, type your name, save your changes, print the document, then close the document and exit Word**

FIGURE D-22: Clip Art task pane

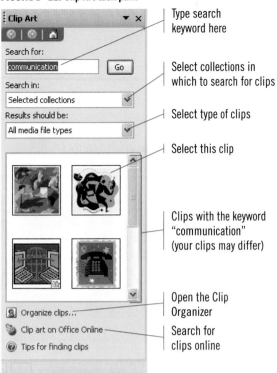

Type search keyword here

Select collections in which to search for clips

Select type of clips

Select this clip

Clips with the keyword "communication" (your clips may differ)

Open the Clip Organizer

Search for clips online

FIGURE D-23: Graphic being moved to a new location

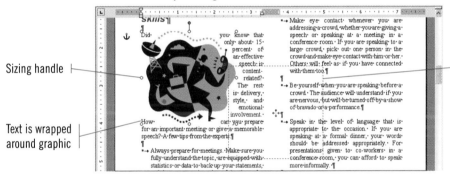

Sizing handle

Text is wrapped around graphic

Dotted line shows square outline of graphic as it is being dragged; position top of square between the last two lines of the first paragraph in column 2

FIGURE D-24: Completed pages 1 and 2 of newsletter

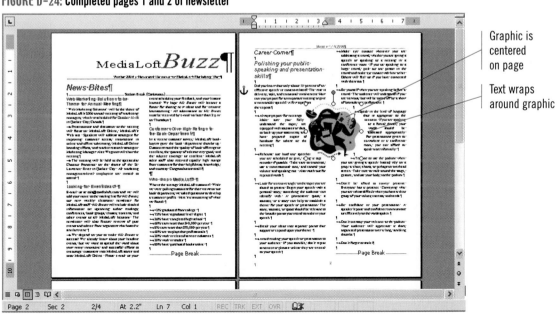

Graphic is centered on page

Text wraps around graphic

FORMATTING DOCUMENTS WORD D-21

Practice

▼ CONCEPTS REVIEW

Label each element shown in Figure D-25.

FIGURE D-25

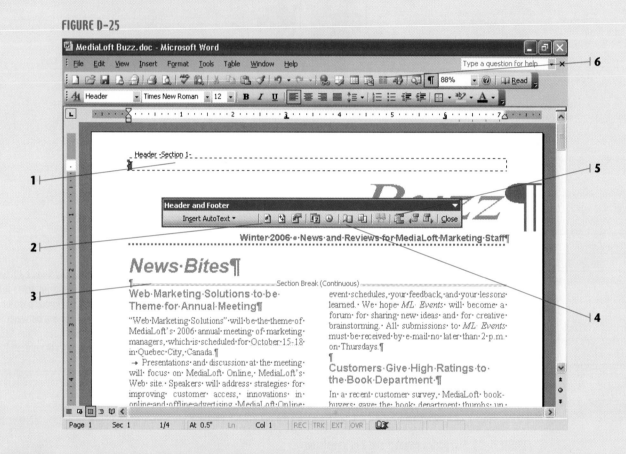

Match each term with the statement that best describes it.

7. **Section break**

8. **Header**

9. **Footer**

10. **Field**

11. **Manual page break**

12. **Margin**

13. **Inline graphic**

14. **Floating graphic**

a. A placeholder for information that changes

b. A formatting mark that divides a document into parts that can be formatted differently

c. The blank area between the edge of the text and the edge of the page

d. A formatting mark that forces the text following the mark to begin at the top of the next page

e. An image that is inserted as part of a line of text

f. An image to which text wrapping has been applied

g. Text or graphics that appear at the bottom of every page in a document

h. Text or graphics that appear at the top of every page in a document

Select the best answer from the list of choices.

15. **Which of the following do documents with mirror margins always have?**

    a. Inside and outside margins

    b. Different first page headers and footers

    c. Gutters

    d. Landscape orientation

16. **Which button is used to insert a field into a header or footer?**

    a. 🖼️   **c.** 🖼️

    b. 🖼️   **d.** 🖼️

17. **Which type of break do you insert if you want to force text to begin on the next page?**

    a. Text wrapping break   **c.** Automatic page break

    b. Manual page break   **d.** Continuous section break

18. **Which type of break do you insert if you want to balance the columns in a section?**

    a. Text wrapping break   **c.** Continuous section break

    b. Column break   **d.** Automatic page break

19. **What must you do to change an inline graphic to a floating graphic?**

    a. Move the graphic   **c.** Anchor the graphic

    b. Resize the graphic   **d.** Apply text wrapping to the graphic

20. **Pressing [Ctrl][Enter] does which of the following?**

    a. Inserts a manual page break

    b. Moves the insertion point to the beginning of the document

    c. Inserts a continuous section break

    d. Inserts an automatic page break

▼ SKILLS REVIEW

1. Set document margins.

    a. Start Word, open the file WD D-2.doc from the drive and folder where your Data Files are located, then save it as **Happy Valley Fitness**.

    b. Change the top and bottom margins to 1.2" and the left and right margins to 1".

    c. Save your changes to the document.

2. Divide a document into sections.

    a. Hide the white space in the document by moving the pointer to the top of a page, then clicking the Hide White Space pointer that appears.

    b. Scroll down, then insert a continuous section break before the **Facilities** heading.

    c. Format the text in section 2 in two columns, then save your changes to the document.

3. Insert page breaks.

    a. Insert a manual page break before the heading **Welcome to the Happy Valley Fitness Center!**.

    b. Scroll down and insert a manual page break before the heading **Services**.

    c. Scroll down and insert a manual page break before the heading **Membership**.

    d. Show the white space in the document by moving the pointer over the thick black line that separates the pages, then clicking the Show White Space pointer that appears.

    e. Press [Ctrl][Home], then save your changes to the document.

4. Insert page numbers.

    a. Insert page numbers in the document. Center the page numbers at the bottom of the page.

    b. View the page numbers on each page in Print Preview, close Print Preview, then save your changes to the document.

5. Add headers and footers.

   a. Change the view to Page Width, then open the Header and Footer areas.

   b. Type your name in the Header area, press [Tab] twice, then use the Insert Date button on the Header and Footer toolbar to insert the current date.

   c. On the horizontal ruler, drag the right tab stop from the 6" mark to the 6½" mark so that the date aligns with the right margin of the document.

   d. Move the insertion point to the Footer area.

   e. Double-click the page number to select it, then format the page number in bold italic.

   f. Close headers and footers, preview the header and footer on each page in Print Preview, close Print Preview, then save your changes to the document.

6. Edit headers and footers.

   a. Open headers and footers, then apply italic to the text in the header.

   b. Move the insertion point to the Footer area, double-click the page number to select it, then press [Delete].

   c. Click the Align Right button on the Formatting toolbar.

   d. Use the Symbol command on the Insert menu to open the Symbol dialog box.

   e. Insert a black right-pointing triangle symbol (character code: 25BA), then close the Symbol dialog box.

   f. Use the Insert Page Number button on the Header and Footer toolbar to insert a page number.

   g. Use the Page Setup button on the Header and Footer toolbar to open the Page Setup dialog box.

   h. Use the Layout tab to create a different header and footer for the first page of the document.

   i. Scroll to the beginning of the document, type your name in the First Page Header area, then apply italic to your name.

   j. Close headers and footers, preview the header and footer on each page in Print Preview, close Print Preview, then save your changes to the document.

7. Format columns.

   a. On page 2, select **Facilities** and the paragraph mark below it, use the Columns button to format the selected text as one column, then center **Facilities** on the page.

   b. Balance the columns on page 2 by inserting a continuous section break at the bottom of the second column.

   c. On page 3, select **Services** and the paragraph mark below it, format the selected text as one column, then center the text.

   d. Balance the columns on page 3.

   e. On page 4, select **Membership** and the paragraph mark below it, format the selected text as one column, then center the text.

   f. Insert a column break before the **Membership Cards** heading, press [Ctrl][Home], then save your changes to the document.

8. Insert a table.

   a. Click the Document Map button on the Standard toolbar to open the Document Map.

   b. In the Document Map, click the heading Membership Rates, then close the Document Map. (*Hint*: The Document Map button is a toggle button.)

   c. Select the word Table at the end of the Membership Rates section, press [Delete], then open the Insert Table dialog box.

   d. Create a table with two columns and five rows, open the AutoFormat dialog box, and then apply the Table Classic 3 style to the table, clearing the Last row check box. Close the dialog box.

   e. Press [Tab] to leave the first cell in the header row blank, then type **Rate**.

   f. Press [Tab], then type the following text in the table, pressing [Tab] to move from cell to cell.

Enrollment/Individual	$100
Enrollment/Couple	$150
Monthly membership/Individual	$35
Monthly membership/Couple	$60

▼ SKILLS REVIEW (CONTINUED)

g. With the insertion point in the table, right-click the table, point to AutoFit on the shortcut menu, then click AutoFit to Contents.

h. With the insertion point in the table, right-click again, point to AutoFit, then click AutoFit to Window.

i. Save your changes to the document.

9. Insert WordArt.

a. Scroll to page 3, place the insertion point before the **Personal Training** heading, then insert a WordArt object.

b. Select any horizontal WordArt style, type **Get Fit!**, then click OK.

c. Click the WordArt object to select it, click the Text Wrapping button on the WordArt toolbar, then apply the Tight text-wrapping style to the object so that it is a floating object.

d. Move the object so that it is centered below the text at the bottom of the page (below the page break mark).

e. Adjust the size and position of the object so that the page looks attractive. (*Hint*: The sizing handles on floating objects are white circles.)

f. Apply a different WordArt shape to the object, preview the page, adjust the size and position if necessary, then save your changes to the document.

FIGURE D-26

The Happy Valley Fitness Center

A Rehabilitation and Exercise Facility

Member Services

10. Insert clip art.

a. On page 1, place the insertion point in the second blank paragraph below **A Rehabilitation and Exercise Facility**. (*Hint*: Place the insertion point to the left of the paragraph mark.)

b. Open the Clip Art task pane. Search for clips related to the keyword **fitness**.

c. Insert the clip shown in Figure D-26. (*Note*: An active Internet connection is needed to select the clip shown in the figure. Select a different clip if this one is not available to you. If you are working offline, you might need to search using a keyword such as sports.)

d. Select the graphic, then drag the lower-right sizing handle down and to the right so that the graphic is about 2.5" wide and 3" tall. Size the graphic so that all the text and the manual page break fit on page 1. (*Hint*: The sizing handles on inline graphics are black squares.)

e. Save your changes to the document. Preview the document, print a copy, then close the document and exit Word.

▼ INDEPENDENT CHALLENGE 1

You are the owner of a small business in Latona, Ontario, called Small World Catering. You have begun work on the text for a brochure advertising your business and are now ready to lay out the pages and prepare the final copy. The brochure will be printed on both sides of an 8½" × 11" sheet of paper, and folded in thirds.

a. Start Word, open the file WD D-3.doc from the drive and folder where your Data Files are located, then save it as **Small World**. Read the document to get a feel for its contents.

b. Change the page orientation to landscape, and change all four margins to .6".

c. Format the document in three columns of equal width.

d. Insert a manual page break before the heading **Catering Services**.

e. On page 1, insert column breaks before the headings **Sample Indian Banquet Menu** and **Sample Tuscan Banquet Menu**.

f. On page 1, insert a continuous section break at the end of the third column to create separate sections on pages one and two.

g. Add lines between the columns on the first page, then center the text in the columns.

h. Create a different header and footer for the first page. Type **Call for custom menus designed to your taste and budget** in the First Page Footer area.

FIGURE D-27

i. Center the text in the footer area, format it in 20-point Comic Sans MS, all caps, with a violet font color, then close headers and footers.

j. On page 2, insert a column break before Your Name. Press [Enter] as many times as necessary to move the contact information to the bottom of the second column. Be sure all five lines of the contact information are in column 2 and do not flow to the next column.

k. Replace Your Name with your name, then center the contact information in the column.

l. Insert a column break at the bottom of the second column. Then, type the text shown in Figure D-27 in the third column. Refer to the figure as you follow the instructions for formatting the text in the third column.

m. Use the Font dialog box to format Small World Catering in 32-point Comic Sans MS, bold, with a violet font color.

n. Format the remaining text in 12-point Comic Sans MS, with a violet font color. Center the text in the third column.

o. Insert the clip art graphic shown in Figure D-27 or another appropriate clip art graphic. Do not wrap text around the graphic.

p. Resize the graphic and add and remove blank paragraphs in the third column of your brochure so that the spacing between elements roughly matches the spacing shown in Figure D-27.

Small World

Catering

Complete catering services available for all types of events. Menus and estimates provided upon request.

Advanced Challenge Exercise

- Format Small World as a WordArt object using a WordArt style and shape of your choice.
- Format Catering as a WordArt object using a WordArt style and shape of your choice.
- Adjust the size, position, and spacing of the WordArt objects, clip art graphic, and text in the third column so that the brochure is attractive and eye-catching.

q. Save your changes, preview the brochure in Print Preview, then print a copy. If possible, print the two pages of the brochure back to back so that the brochure can be folded in thirds.

r. Close the document and exit Word.

▼ INDEPENDENT CHALLENGE 2

You work in the Campus Safety Department at Hudson State College. You have written the text for an informational flyer about parking regulations on campus and now you need to format the flyer so it is attractive and readable.

a. Start Word, open the file WD D-4.doc from the drive and folder where your Data Files are located, then save it as **Hudson Parking FAQ**. Read the document to get a feel for its contents.

b. Change all four margins to .7".

c. Insert a continuous section break before **1. May I bring a car to school?** (*Hint*: Place the insertion point before May.)

d. Scroll down and insert a next page section break before **Sample Parking Permit**.

e. Format the section 2 text in three columns of equal width with .3" of space between the columns.

f. Hyphenate the document using the automatic hyphenation feature. (*Hint*: If the Hyphenation feature is not installed on your computer, skip this step.)

g. Add a 3-point dotted-line bottom border to the blank paragraph under Hudson State College. (*Hint*: Place the insertion point before the paragraph mark under Hudson State College, then apply a bottom border to the paragraph.)

h. Add your name to the header. Right-align your name and format it in 10-point Arial.

i. Add the following text to the footer, inserting symbols between words as indicated: **Parking and Shuttle Service Office • 54 Buckley Street • Hudson State College • 942-555-2227**.

j. Format the footer text in 9-point Arial Black and center it in the footer. Use a different font if Arial Black is not available to you. If necessary, adjust the font and font size so that the entire address fits on one line.

k. Apply a 3-point dotted-line border above the footer text. Make sure to apply the border to the paragraph.

l. Balance the columns in section 2.

m. Add the clip art graphic shown in Figure D-28 or another appropriate clip art graphic to the upper-right corner of the document, above the border. Make sure the graphic does not obscure the border. (*Hint*: Apply text wrapping to the graphic before positioning it.)

FIGURE D-28

Frequently Asked Questions (FAQ)
of the Department of Campus Safety
Parking & Shuttle Service Office
Hudson State College

n. Place the insertion point on page 2 (which is section 4). Change the left and right margins in section 4 to 1". Also change the page orientation of section 4 to landscape.

o. Change the vertical alignment of section 4 to Center.

p. Save your changes, preview the flyer in Print Preview, then print a copy. If possible, print the two pages of the flyer back to back.

q. Close the document and exit Word.

Word 2003

▼ INDEPENDENT CHALLENGE 3

A book publisher would like to publish an article you wrote on stormwater pollution in Australia as a chapter in a forthcoming book called *Environmental Issues for the New Millennium*. The publisher has requested that you format your article like a book chapter before submitting it for publication, and has provided you with a style sheet.

a. Start Word, open the file WD D-5.doc from the drive and folder where your Data Files are located, then save it as **Stormwater**.

b. Change the font of the entire document to 11-point Book Antiqua. If this font is not available to you, select a different font suitable for the pages of a book. Change the alignment to justified.

c. Change the paper size to 6" × 9".

d. Create mirror margins. (*Hint*: Use the Multiple Pages list arrow.) Change the top and bottom margins to .8", change the inside margin to .4", change the outside margin to .6", and create a .3" gutter to allow room for the book's binding.

e. Change the Zoom level to Two Pages, then apply the setting to create different headers and footers for odd- and even-numbered pages.

f. Change the Zoom level to Page Width. In the odd-page header, type **Chapter 5**, insert a symbol of your choice, then type **Stormwater Pollution in the Fairy Creek Catchment**.

g. Format the header text in 9-point Book Antiqua italic, then right-align the text.

h. In the even-page header, type your name, insert a symbol of your choice, then insert the current date. (*Hint*: Scroll down or use the Show Next button to move the insertion point to the even-page header.)

i. Change the format of the date to include just the month and the year. (*Hint*: Right-click the date field, then click Edit Field.)

j. Format the header text in 9-point Book Antiqua italic. The even-page header should be left-aligned.

k. Insert page numbers that are centered in the footer. Format the page number in 10-point Book Antiqua. Make sure to insert a page number field in both the odd- and even-page footer areas.

l. Format the page numbers so that the first page of your chapter, which is Chapter 5 in the book, begins on page 53. (*Hint*: Select a page number field, then use the Format Page Number button.)

m. Go to the beginning of the document, press [Enter] 10 times, type **Chapter 5: Stormwater Pollution in the Fairy Creek Catchment**, press [Enter] twice, type your name, then press [Enter] twice.

n. Format the chapter title in 16-point Book Antiqua bold, format your name in 14-point Book Antiqua using small caps, then left-align the title text and your name.

Advanced Challenge Exercise

■ Use the Browse by Object feature to move the insertion point to page 4 in the document, scroll down, place the insertion point at the end of the paragraph above the Potential health effects... heading, press [Enter] twice, type **Table 1: Total annual pollutant loads per year in the Fairy Creek Catchment**, format the text as bold, then press [Enter] twice.

■ Insert a table with four columns and four rows that is formatted in the Table Professional style.

■ Type the text shown in Figure D-29 in the table. Do not be concerned when the text wraps to the next line in a cell.

■ Format the text as bold in the header row, then remove the bold formatting from the text in the remaining rows.

■ Place the insertion point in the table, point to AutoFit on the Table menu, click Distribute Rows Evenly, point to AutoFit on the Table menu a second time, then click AutoFit to Contents.

o. Save your changes, preview the chapter in Print Preview, print the first four pages of the chapter, then close the document and exit Word.

FIGURE D-29

Area	Nitrogen	Phosphorus	Suspended solids
Fairy Creek	9.3 tonnes	1.2 tonnes	756.4 tonnes
Durras Arm	6.2 tonnes	.9 tonnes	348.2 tonnes
Cabbage Tree Creek	9.8 tonnes	2.3 tonnes	485.7 tonnes

▼ INDEPENDENT CHALLENGE 4

One of the most common opportunities to use the page layout features of Word is when formatting a research paper. The format recommended by the *MLA Handbook for Writers of Research Papers*, a style guide that includes information on preparing, writing, and formatting research papers, is the standard format used by many schools, colleges, and universities. In this independent challenge, you will research the MLA (Modern Language Association) guidelines for formatting a research paper and use the guidelines you find to prepare a sample first page of a research report.

a. Start Word, open the file WD D-6.doc from the drive and folder where your Data Files are located, then save it as **MLA Style**. This document contains the questions you will answer about MLA style guidelines.

b. Use your favorite search engine to search the Web for information on the MLA guidelines for formatting a research report. Use the keywords **MLA Style** and **research paper format** to conduct your search.

c. Look for information on the proper formatting for the following aspects of a research paper: paper size, margins, title page or first page of the report, line spacing, paragraph indentation, page numbers, and works cited.

d. Type your answers to the questions in the MLA Style document, save it, print a copy, then close the document.

e. Using the information you learned, start a new document and create a sample first page of a research report. Use **MLA Format for Research Papers** as the title for your sample report, and make up information about the course and instructor, if necessary. For the body of the report, type several sentences about MLA style. Make sure to format the page exactly as the MLA style dictates.

f. Save the document as **MLA Sample Format** to the drive and folder where your Data Files are located, print a copy, close the document, then exit Word.

Use the file WD D-7.doc, found on the drive and folder where your Data Files are located, to create the article shown in Figure D-30. (*Hint*: Change all four margins to .6". To locate the flower clip art image, search using the keyword **flower**, and be sure only the Photographs check box in the Results should be in list box in the Clip Art task pane has a check mark. Select a different clip if the clip shown in the figure is not available to you.) Save the document with the filename **Gardener's Corner**, then print a copy.

FIGURE D-30

GARDENER'S CORNER

Putting a Perennial Garden to Bed

By Your Name

A certain sense of peace descends when a perennial garden is put to bed for the season. The plants are safely tucked in against the elements, and the garden is ready to welcome the first signs of life. When the work is done, you can sit back and anticipate the bright blooms of spring. Many gardeners are uncertain of how to close a perennial garden. This week's column demystifies the process.

Clean up

Garden clean up can be a gradual process—plants will deteriorate at different rates, allowing you to do a little bit each week.

1. Edge beds and borders and remove stakes and other plant supports.
2. Dig and divide irises, daylilies, and other early bloomers.
3. Cut back plants when foliage starts to deteriorate.
4. Rake all debris out of the garden and pull any weeds that remain.

Plant perennials

Fall is the perfect time to plant perennials! The warm, sunny days and cool nights provide optimal conditions for new root growth.

1. Dig deeply and enhance soil with organic matter.
2. Use a good starter fertilizer to speed up new root growth.
3. Untangle the roots of new plants before planting them.
4. Water deeply after planting as the weather dictates.

Add compost

Organic matter is the key ingredient to healthy soil. If you take care of the soil, your plants will become strong and disease resistant.

1. Use an iron rake to loosen the top few inches of soil.
2. Spread a one to two inch layer of compost over the entire garden.
3. Refrain from stepping on the area and compacting the soil.

To mulch or not to mulch?

Winter protection for perennial beds can only help plants survive the winter. Here's what works and what doesn't:

1. Always apply mulch after the ground is frozen.
2. Never apply generic hay because is contains billions of weed seeds. Also, whole leaves and bark mulch hold too much moisture.
3. Straw and salt marsh hay are excellent choices for mulch.

For copies of earlier Gardener's Corner columns, call 1-800-555-3827.

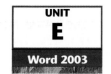

Creating and Formatting Tables

OBJECTIVES

Insert a table

Insert and delete rows and columns

Modify table rows and columns

Sort table data

Split and merge cells

Perform calculations in tables

Use Table AutoFormat

Create a custom format for a table

If you have a SAM user profile, you may have access to hands-on instruction, practice, and assessment of the skills covered in this unit. Log in to your SAM account and go to your assignments page to see what your instructor has assigned.

Tables are commonly used to display information for quick reference and analysis. In this unit, you learn how to create and modify a table in Word, how to sort table data and perform calculations, and how to format a table with borders and shading. You also learn how to use a table to structure the layout of a page. You are preparing a summary budget for an advertising campaign aimed at the Boston market. The goal of the ad campaign is to promote MediaLoft Online, the MediaLoft Web site. You decide to format the budget information as a table so that it is easy to read and analyze.

Inserting a Table

A **table** is a grid made up of rows and columns of cells that you can fill with text and graphics. A **cell** is the box formed by the intersection of a column and a row. The lines that divide the columns and rows and help you see the grid-like structure of a table are called **borders**. You can create a table in a document by using the Insert Table button on the Standard toolbar or the Insert command on the Table menu. Once you have created a table, you can add text and graphics to it. You begin by inserting a blank table into the document and then adding text to it.

STEPS

1. **Start Word, close the Getting Started task pane, click the Print Layout View button on the horizontal scroll bar if it is not already selected, click the Zoom list arrow on the Standard toolbar, then click Page Width**

   A blank document appears in Print Layout view.

2. **Click the Insert Table button on the Standard toolbar**

   A grid opens below the button. You move the pointer across this grid to select the number of columns and rows you want the table to contain. If you want to create a table with more than five columns or more than four rows, then expand the grid by dragging the lower-right corner.

3. **Point to the second box in the fourth row to select 4x2 Table, then click**

   A table with two columns and four rows is inserted in the document, as shown in Figure E-1. Black borders surround the table cells. The insertion point is in the first cell in the first row.

4. **Type Location, then press [Tab]**

   Pressing [Tab] moves the insertion point to the next cell in the row.

5. **Type Cost, press [Tab], then type Boston Sunday Globe**

   Pressing [Tab] at the end of a row moves the insertion point to the first cell in the next row.

6. **Press [Tab], type 27,600, press [Tab], then type the following text in the table, pressing [Tab] to move from cell to cell**

Boston.com	25,000
Taxi tops	18,000

7. **Press [Tab]**

   Pressing [Tab] at the end of the last cell of a table creates a new row at the bottom of the table, as shown in Figure E-2. The insertion point is located in the first cell in the new row.

TROUBLE
If you pressed [Tab] after the last row, click the Undo button on the Standard toolbar to remove the new blank row.

8. **Type the following, pressing [Tab] to move from cell to cell and to create new rows**

Boston Herald	18,760
Townonline.com	3,250
Bus stops	12,000
Boston Magazine	12,400

9. **Click the Save button on the Standard toolbar, then save the document with the filename Boston Ad Budget to the drive and folder where your Data Files are located**

   The table is shown in Figure E-3.

FIGURE E-1: Blank table

Column

Table move handle

Insertion point

Row

Insert Table button

Cell

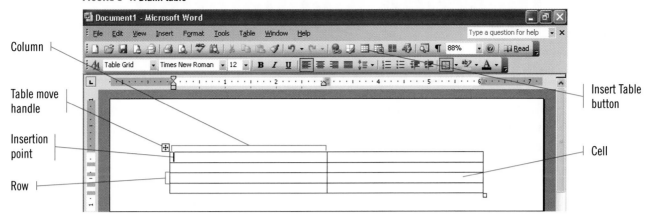

FIGURE E-2: New row in table

New row

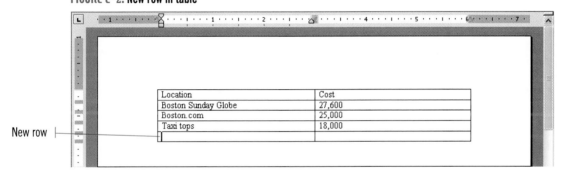

Location	Cost
Boston Sunday Globe	27,600
Boston.com	25,000
Taxi tops	18,000

FIGURE E-3: Text in the table

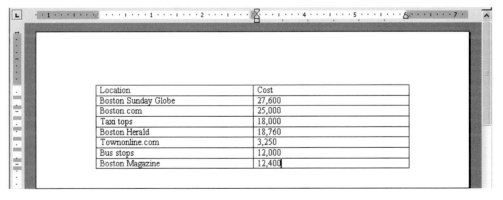

Location	Cost
Boston Sunday Globe	27,600
Boston.com	25,000
Taxi tops	18,000
Boston Herald	18,760
Townonline.com	3,250
Bus stops	12,000
Boston Magazine	12,400

Clues to Use

Converting text to a table and a table to text

Another way to create a table is to convert text that is separated by a tab, a comma, or another separator character into a table. For example, if you want to create a two-column table of last and first names, you could type the names as a list with a comma separating the last and first name in each line, and then convert the text to a table. The separator character—a comma in this example—indicates where you want to divide the table into columns, and a paragraph mark indicates where you want to begin a new row. To convert tabbed or comma-delimited text to a table, select the text, point to

Convert on the Table menu, and then click Text to Table. In the Text to Table dialog box, select from the options for structuring and formatting the table, and then click OK to create the table. You can also select the text and then click the Insert Table button on the Standard toolbar to convert the text to a table.

Conversely, you can convert a table to text that is separated by tabs, commas, or some other character by selecting the table, pointing to Convert on the Table menu, and then clicking Table to Text.

Inserting and Deleting Rows and Columns

You can easily modify the structure of a table by adding and removing rows and columns. First, you must select an existing row or column in the table to indicate where you want to insert or delete information. You can select any element of a table using the Select command on the Table menu, but it is often easier to select rows and columns using the mouse: click in the margin to the left of a row to select the row; click the top border of a column to select the column. Alternatively, you can drag across a row or down a column to select it. To insert rows and columns, use the Insert command on the Table menu or the Insert Rows and Insert Columns buttons on the Standard toolbar. To delete rows and columns, use the Delete command on the Table menu. You add a new row to the table and delete an unnecessary row. You also add new columns to the table to provide more detailed information.

STEPS

1. **Click the Show/Hide ¶ button on the Standard toolbar to display formatting marks**

   An end of cell mark appears at the end of each cell and an end of row mark appears at the end of each row.

2. **Place the pointer in the margin to the left of the Townonline.com row until the pointer changes to ⌐, then click**

   The entire row is selected, including the end of row mark. If the end of row mark is not selected, you have selected only the text in a row, not the row itself. When a row is selected, the Insert Table button changes to the Insert Rows button.

3. **Click the Insert Rows button on the Standard toolbar**

   A new row is inserted above the Townonline.com row, as shown in Figure E-4.

4. **Click the first cell of the new row, type Boston Phoenix, press [Tab], then type 15,300**

   Clicking in a cell moves the insertion point to that cell.

5. **Select the Boston Herald row, right-click the selected row, then click Delete Rows on the shortcut menu**

   The selected row is deleted. If you select a row and press [Delete], you delete only the contents of the row, not the row itself.

6. **Place the pointer over the top border of the Location column until the pointer changes to ↓, then click**

   The entire column is selected. When a column is selected, the Insert Table button changes to the Insert Columns button.

7. **Click the Insert Columns button on the Standard toolbar, then type Type**

   A new column is inserted to the left of the Location column, as shown in Figure E-5.

8. **Click in the Location column, click Table on the menu bar, point to Insert, click Columns to the Right, then type Details in the first cell of the new column**

   A new column is added to the right of the Location column. You can also use the Insert command to add columns to the left of the active column or to insert rows above or below the active row.

9. **Press [↓] to move the insertion point to the next cell in the Details column, enter the text shown in Figure E-6 in each cell in the Details and Type columns, click ¶ to turn off the display of formatting marks, then save your changes**

   You can use the arrow keys to move the insertion point from cell to cell. Notice that text wraps to the next line in the cell as you type. Compare your table to Figure E-6.

FIGURE E-4: Inserted row

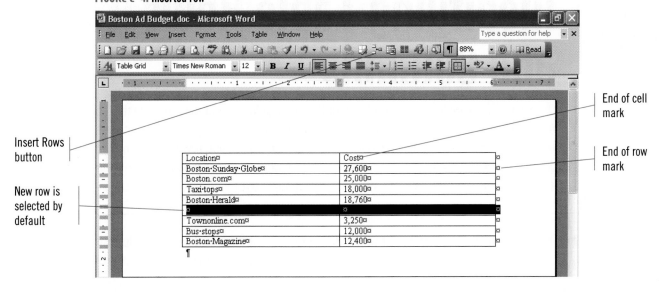

Insert Rows button

End of cell mark

End of row mark

New row is selected by default

FIGURE E-5: Inserted column

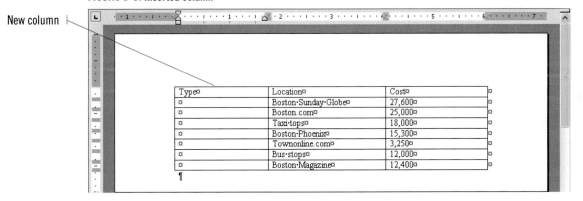

New column

FIGURE E-6: Text in Type and Details columns

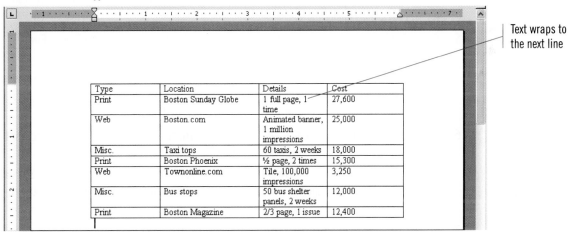

Text wraps to the next line

Clues to Use

Copying and moving rows and columns

You can copy and move rows and columns within a table in the same manner you copy and move text. Select the row or column you want to move, then use the Copy or Cut button to place the selection on the Clipboard. Place the insertion point in the location you want to insert the row or column, then click the Paste button to paste the selection. Rows are inserted above the row containing the insertion point; columns are inserted to the left of the column containing the insertion point. You can also copy or move columns and rows by selecting them and using the 🖱 pointer to drag them to a new location in the table.

Modifying Table Rows and Columns

Once you create a table, you can easily adjust the size of columns and rows to make the table easier to read. You can change the size of columns and rows by dragging a border, by using the AutoFit command on the Table menu, or by setting exact measurements for column width and row height using the Table Properties dialog box. ░░░░░░ You adjust the size of the columns and rows to make the table more attractive and easier to read. You also center the text vertically in each table cell.

STEPS

1. **Position the pointer over the border between the first and second columns until the pointer changes to +‖+, then drag the border to approximately the ½" mark on the horizontal ruler**

   The dotted line that appears as you drag represents the border. Dragging the column border changes the width of the first and second columns: the first column is narrower and the second column is wider. When dragging a border to change the width of an entire column, make sure no cells are selected in the column. You can also drag a row border to change the height of the row above it.

2. **Position the pointer over the right border of the Location column until the pointer changes to +‖+, then double-click**

   Double-clicking a column border automatically resizes the column to fit the text.

3. **Double-click the right border of the Details column with the +‖+ pointer, then double-click the right border of the Cost column with the +‖+ pointer**

   The widths of the Details and Cost columns are adjusted.

4. **Move the pointer over the table, then click the table move handle ⊞ that appears outside the upper-left corner of the table**

   Clicking the table move handle selects the entire table. You can also use the Select command on the Table menu to select an entire table.

5. **Click Table on the menu bar, point to AutoFit, click Distribute Rows Evenly, then deselect the table**

   All the rows in the table become the same height, as shown in Figure E-7. You can also use the commands on the AutoFit menu to make all the columns the same width, to make the width of the columns fit the text, and to adjust the width of the columns so the table is justified between the margins.

6. **Click in the Details column, click Table on the menu bar, click Table Properties, then click the Column tab in the Table Properties dialog box**

   The Column tab, shown in Figure E-8, allows you to set an exact width for columns. You can specify an exact height for rows and an exact size for cells using the Row and Cell tabs. You can also use the Table tab to set a precise size for the table, to change the alignment of the table on a page, and to wrap text around a table.

7. **Select the measurement in the Preferred width text box, type 3, then click OK**

   The width of the Details column changes to 3".

8. **Click ⊞ to select the table, click Table on the menu bar, click Table Properties, click the Cell tab, click the Center box in the Vertical alignment section, click OK, deselect the table, then save your changes**

   The text is centered vertically in each table cell, as shown in Figure E-9.

FIGURE E-7: Resized columns and rows

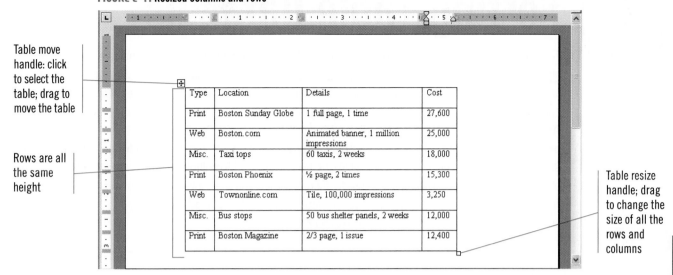

Table move handle: click to select the table; drag to move the table

Rows are all the same height

Table resize handle; drag to change the size of all the rows and columns

FIGURE E-8: Table Properties dialog box

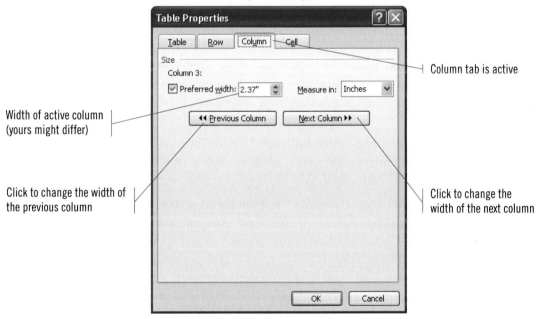

Column tab is active

Width of active column (yours might differ)

Click to change the width of the previous column

Click to change the width of the next column

FIGURE E-9: Text centered vertically in cells

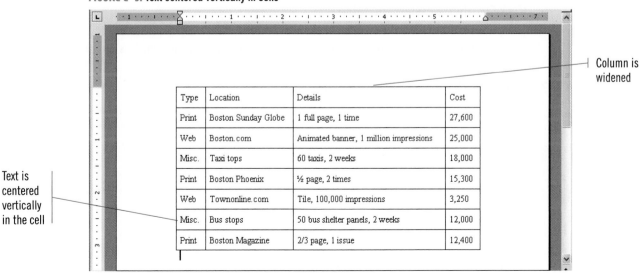

Column is widened

Text is centered vertically in the cell

Sorting Table Data

Tables are often easier to interpret and analyze when the data is **sorted**, which means the rows are organized in alphabetical or sequential order based on the data in one or more columns. When you sort a table, Word arranges all the table data according to the criteria you set. You set sort criteria by specifying the column (or columns) by which you want to sort, and indicating the sort order—ascending or descending—you want to use. **Ascending order** lists data alphabetically or sequentially (from A to Z, 0 to 9, or earliest to latest). **Descending order** lists data in reverse alphabetical or sequential order (from Z to A, 9 to 0, or latest to earliest). You can sort using the data in one column or multiple columns. When you sort by multiple columns you must select primary, secondary, and tertiary sort criteria. You use the Sort command on the Table menu to sort a table. ▟▟▟▟ You sort the table so that all ads of the same type are listed together. You also add secondary sort criteria so that the ads within each type are listed in descending order by cost.

STEPS

QUICK TIP
To quickly sort a table by a single column, click in the column, then click the Sort Ascending 2↓ or Sort Descending button Z↓ on the Tables and Borders toolbar. When you use these buttons, Word does not include the header row in the sort.

1. **Place the insertion point anywhere in the table**

   To sort an entire table, you simply need to place the insertion point anywhere in the table. If you want to sort specific rows only, then you must select the rows you want to sort.

2. **Click Table on the menu bar, then click Sort**

   The Sort dialog box opens, as shown in Figure E-10. You use this dialog box to specify the column or columns by which you want to sort, the type of information you are sorting (text, numbers, or dates), and the sort order (ascending or descending). Column 1 is selected by default in the Sort by list box. Since you want to sort your table first by the information in the first column—the type of ad (Print, Web, or Misc.)—you don't change the Sort by criteria.

3. **Click the Descending option button in the Sort by area**

   The ad type information will be sorted in descending—or reverse alphabetical—order, so that the "Web" ads will be listed first, followed by the "Print" ads, and then the "Misc." ads.

4. **In the first Then by section click the Then by list arrow, click Column 4, click the Type list arrow, click Number if it is not already selected, then click the Descending option button**

   Within the Web, Print, and Misc. groups, the rows will be sorted by the cost of the ad—the information contained in the fourth column, which is numbers, not dates or text. The rows will appear in descending order within each group, with the most expensive ad listed first.

5. **Click the Header row option button in the My list has section to select it**

   The table includes a header row that you do not want included in the sort. A **header row** is the first row of a table that contains the column headings.

6. **Click OK, then deselect the table**

   The rows in the table are sorted first by the information in the Type column and second by the information in the Cost column, as shown in Figure E-11. The first row of the table, which is the header row, is not included in the sort.

7. **Save your changes to the document**

FIGURE E-10: Sort dialog box

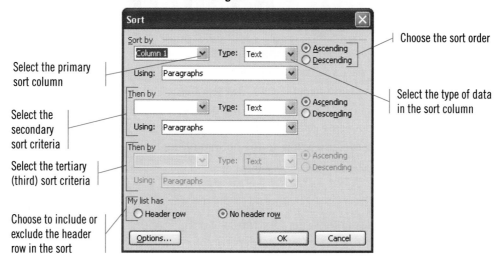

Select the primary sort column

Select the secondary sort criteria

Select the tertiary (third) sort criteria

Choose to include or exclude the header row in the sort

Choose the sort order

Select the type of data in the sort column

FIGURE E-11: Sorted table

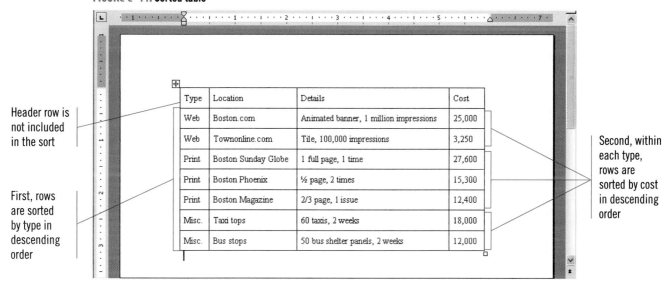

Header row is not included in the sort

First, rows are sorted by type in descending order

Second, within each type, rows are sorted by cost in descending order

Type	Location	Details	Cost
Web	Boston.com	Animated banner, 1 million impressions	25,000
Web	Townonline.com	Tile, 100,000 impressions	3,250
Print	Boston Sunday Globe	1 full page, 1 time	27,600
Print	Boston Phoenix	½ page, 2 times	15,300
Print	Boston Magazine	2/3 page, 1 issue	12,400
Misc.	Taxi tops	60 taxis, 2 weeks	18,000
Misc.	Bus stops	50 bus shelter panels, 2 weeks	12,000

Clues to Use

Sorting lists and paragraphs

In addition to sorting table data, you can use the Sort command on the Table menu to sort lists and paragraphs. For example, you might want to sort a list of names alphabetically. To sort lists and paragraphs, select the items you want included in the sort, click Table on the menu bar, and then click Sort. In the Sort Text dialog box, use the Sort by list arrow to select the sort by criteria (paragraphs or fields), use the Type list arrow to select the type of data (text, numbers, or dates), and then click the Ascending or Descending option button to choose a sort order.

When sorting text information in a document, the term "fields" refers to text or numbers that are separated by a character, such as a tab or a comma. For example, if the names you want to sort are listed in "Last name, First name" order, then last name and first name are each considered a field. You can choose to sort the list in alphabetical order by last name or by first name. Use the Options button in the Sort Text dialog box to specify the character that separates the fields in your lists or paragraphs, along with other sort options.

Splitting and Merging Cells

A convenient way to change the format and structure of a table is to merge and split the table cells. When you **merge** cells, you combine adjacent cells into a single larger cell. When you **split** a cell, you divide an existing cell into multiple cells. You can merge and split cells using the Merge Cells and Split Cells commands on the Table menu, or the Merge Cells and Split Cells buttons on the Tables and Borders toolbar. ▓▓▓▓ You merge cells in the first column to create a single cell for each ad type—Web, Print, and Misc. You also add a new row to the bottom of the table, and split the cells in the row to create three new rows with a different structure.

STEPS

TROUBLE
To move the Tables and Borders toolbar, click its title bar and drag it to a new location.

1. **Click the** Tables and Borders button 🔲 **on the Standard toolbar, then click the** Draw Table button 🔲 **on the Tables and Borders toolbar to turn off the Draw pointer** ✏ **if necessary**

   The Tables and Borders toolbar, which includes buttons for formatting and working with tables, opens. See Table E-1.

2. **Select the two** Web cells **in the first column of the table, click the** Merge Cells button 🔲 **on the Tables and Borders toolbar, then deselect the text**

   The two Web cells merge to become a single cell. When you merge cells, Word converts the text in each cell into a separate paragraph in the merged cell.

3. **Select the first** Web **in the cell, then press** [Delete]

4. **Select the three** Print cells **in the first column, click** 🔲, **type** Print, **select the two** Misc. cells, **click** 🔲, **then type** Misc.

   The three Print cells merge to become one cell and the two Misc. cells merge to become one cell.

5. **Click the** Bus stops cell, **click the** Insert Table list arrow 🔲▾ **on the Tables and Borders toolbar, then click** Insert Rows Below

   A row is added to the bottom of the table. The Insert Table button on the Tables and Borders toolbar also changes to the Insert Rows Below button. The active buttons on the Tables and Borders toolbar reflect the most recently used commands. You can see a menu of related commands by clicking the list arrow next to a button.

6. **Select the** first three cells **in the new last row of the table, click** 🔲, **then deselect the cell**

   The three cells in the row merge to become a single cell.

QUICK TIP
To split a table in two, click the row you want to be the first row in the second table, click Table on the menu bar, then click Split Table.

7. **Click the** first cell in the last row, **then click the** Split Cells button 🔲 **on the Tables and Borders toolbar**

   The Split Cells dialog box opens, as shown in Figure E-12. You use this dialog box to split the selected cell or cells into a specific number of columns and rows.

8. **Type** 1 **in the Number of columns text box, press** [Tab], **type** 3 **in the Number of rows text box, click** OK, **then deselect the cells**

   The single cell is divided into three rows of equal height. When you split a cell into multiple rows and/or columns, the width of the original column does not change. If the cell you split contains text, all the text appears in the upper-left cell.

9. **Click the** last cell in the Cost column, **click** 🔲, **repeat Step 8, then save your changes**

   The cell is split into three rows, as shown in Figure E-13. The last three rows of the table now have only two columns.

FIGURE E-12: Split Cells dialog box

Tables and Borders button

Insert Rows Below button

Cells created by merging other cells

Draw Table button

Split Cells button

Merge Cells button

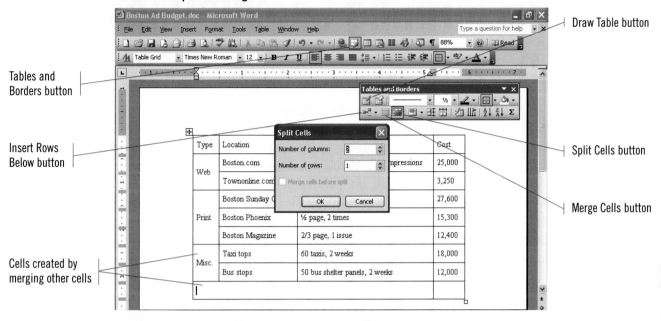

FIGURE E-13: Cells split into three rows

Cells are split into three rows

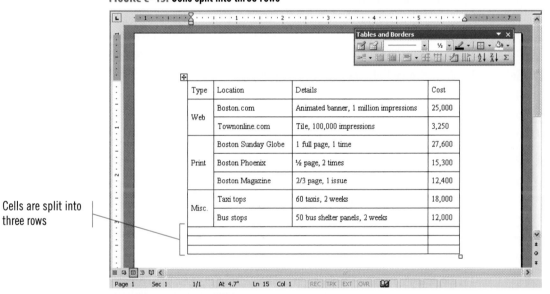

TABLE E-1: Buttons on the Tables and Borders toolbar

button	use to	button	use to
	Draw a table or cells		Divide a cell into multiple cells
	Remove a border between cells		Change the alignment of text in cells
	Change border line style		Make rows the same height
½	Change the thickness of borders		Make columns the same width
	Change the border color		Format the table with a Table AutoFormat table style
	Add or remove individual borders		Change the orientation of text
	Change the shading color of cells		Sort rows in ascending order
	Insert rows, columns, cells, or a table, and AutoFit columns		Sort rows in descending order
	Combine the selected cells into a single cell	Σ	Calculate the sum of values above or to the left of the active cell

Performing Calculations in Tables

If your table includes numerical information, you can perform simple calculations in the table. The Word AutoSum feature allows you to quickly total the numbers in a column or row. In addition, you can use the Formula command to perform other standard calculations, such as averages. When you calculate data in a table using formulas, you use cell references to refer to the cells in the table. Each cell has a unique **cell reference** composed of a letter and a number; the letter represents its column and the number represents its row. For example, the cell in the third row of the fourth column is cell D3. Figure E-14 shows the cell references in a simple table. You use AutoSum to calculate the total cost of the Boston ad campaign. You also add information about the budgeted cost and create a formula to calculate the difference between the actual and budgeted costs.

STEPS

1. **Click the first blank cell in column 1, type Total Cost, press [Tab], then click the AutoSum button Σ on the Tables and Borders toolbar**

   Word totals the numbers in the cells above the active cell and inserts the sum as a field. You can use the AutoSum button to quickly total the numbers in a column or a row. If the cell you select is at the bottom of a column of numbers, AutoSum totals the column. If the cell is at the right end of a row of numbers, AutoSum totals the row.

2. **Select 12,000 in the cell above the total, then type 13,500**

   If you change a number that is part of a calculation, you must recalculate the field result.

3. **Press [↓], then press [F9]**

   When the insertion point is in a cell that contains a formula, pressing [F9] updates the field result.

4. **Press [Tab], type Budgeted, press [Tab], type 113,780, press [Tab], type Difference, then press [Tab]**

   The insertion point is in the last cell of the table.

5. **Click Table on the menu bar, then click Formula**

   The Formula dialog box opens, as shown in Figure E-15. The SUM formula appears in the Formula text box. Word proposes to sum the numbers above the active cell, but you want to insert a formula that calculates the difference between the actual and budgeted costs. You can type simple custom formulas using a plus sign (+) for addition, a minus sign (-) for subtraction, an asterisk (*) for multiplication, and a slash (/) for division.

6. **Select =SUM(ABOVE) in the Formula text box, then type =B9-B10**

   You must type an equal sign (=) to indicate that the text following it is a formula. You want to subtract the budgeted cost in the second column of row 10 from the actual cost in the second column of row 9; therefore, you type a formula to subtract the value in cell B10 from the value in cell B9.

7. **Click OK, then save your changes**

   The difference appears in the cell, as shown in Figure E-16.

FIGURE E-14: Cell references in a table

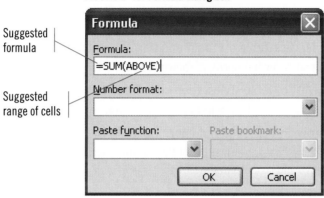

	A	B	C	D
1	A1	B1	C1	D1
2	A2	B2	C2	D2
3	A3	B3	C3	D3

Column D (fourth column)

Cell reference indicates the cell's column and row

Row 3

FIGURE E-15: Formula dialog box

Suggested formula

Suggested range of cells

Formula

Formula:
=SUM(ABOVE)

Number format:

Paste function: Paste bookmark:

OK   Cancel

FIGURE E-16: Difference calculated in table

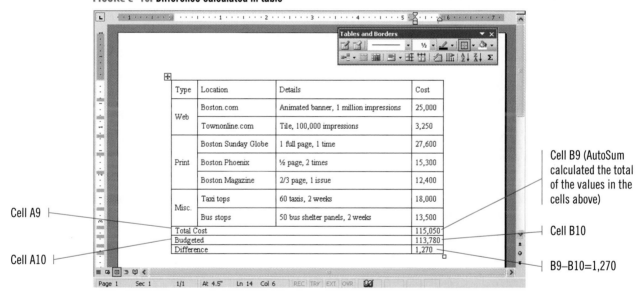

Type	Location	Details	Cost
Web	Boston.com	Animated banner, 1 million impressions	25,000
	Townonline.com	Tile, 100,000 impressions	3,250
Print	Boston Sunday Globe	1 full page, 1 time	27,600
	Boston Phoenix	½ page, 2 times	15,300
	Boston Magazine	2/3 page, 1 issue	12,400
Misc.	Taxi tops	60 taxis, 2 weeks	18,000
	Bus stops	50 bus shelter panels, 2 weeks	13,500
Total Cost			115,050
Budgeted			113,780
Difference			1,270

Cell B9 (AutoSum calculated the total of the values in the cells above)

Cell A9

Cell A10

Cell B10

B9–B10=1,270

Clues to Use

Working with formulas

In addition to the SUM function, Word includes formulas for averaging, counting, and rounding data, to name a few. To use a Word formula, click the Paste function list arrow in the Formula dialog box, select a function, and then insert the cell references of the cells you want included in the calculation in parentheses after the name of the function. When entering formulas, you must separate cell references by a comma. For example, if you want to average the values in cells A1, B3, and C4, enter the formula =AVERAGE(A1,B3,C4). You must also separate cell ranges by a colon. For example, to total the values in cells A1 through A9, enter the formula =SUM(A1:A9). To display the result of a calculation in a particular number format, such as a decimal percentage (0.00%), click the Number format list arrow in the Formula dialog box and select a number format. Word inserts the result of a calculation as a field in the selected cell.

Using Table AutoFormat

Adding shading and other design elements to a table can help give it a polished appearance and make the data easier to read. The Word Table AutoFormat feature allows you to quickly apply a table style to a table. Table styles include borders, shading, fonts, alignment, colors, and other formatting effects. You can apply a table style to a table using the Table AutoFormat command on the Table menu or the Table AutoFormat button on the Tables and Borders toolbar. ▰▰▰▰ You want to enhance the appearance of the table with shading, borders, and other formats. You use the Table AutoFormat feature to quickly apply a table style to the table.

STEPS

1. **Click in the table, click** Table **on the menu bar, then click** Table AutoFormat
   The Table AutoFormat dialog box opens, as shown in Figure E-17.

2. **Scroll down the list of table styles, then click** Table List 7
   A preview of the Table List 7 style appears in the Preview area.

3. **Clear the** Last row **and** Last column check boxes **in the Apply special formats to section**
   The Preview area shows that the formatting of the last row and column of the table now match the formatting of the other rows and columns in the table.

   QUICK TIP
Use the Reveal Formatting task pane to view the format settings applied to tables and cells.

4. **Click** Apply
   The Table List 7 style is applied to the table, as shown in Figure E-18. Because of the structure of the table, this style neither enhances the table nor helps make the data more readable.

5. **With the insertion point in the table, click the** Table AutoFormat button 🔲 **on the Tables and Borders toolbar, scroll down the list of table styles in the Table AutoFormat dialog box, click** Table Professional, **then click** Apply
   The Table Professional style is applied to the table. This style works with the structure of the table.

   TROUBLE
When you select the Type column, the first column in the last three rows is also selected.

6. **Select the** Type column, **click the** Center button ▤ **on the Formatting toolbar, select the** Cost column, **then click the** Align Right button ▤ **on the Formatting toolbar**
   The data in the Type column is centered, and the data in the Cost column is right-aligned.

7. **Select the** last three rows **of the table, click** ▤, **then click the** Bold button **B** **on the Formatting toolbar**
   The text in the last three rows is right-aligned and bold is applied.

8. **Select the** first row **of the table, click** ▤, **click the** Font Size list arrow **on the Formatting toolbar, click** 16, **deselect the row, then save your changes**
   The text in the header row is centered and enlarged, as shown in Figure E-19.

Clues to Use

Using tables to lay out a page

Tables are often used to display information for quick reference and analysis, but you can also use tables to structure the layout of a page. You can insert any kind of information in the cell of a table—including graphics, bulleted lists, charts, and other tables (called **nested tables**). For example, you might use a table to lay out a resume, a newsletter, or a Web page. When you use a table to lay out a page, you generally remove the table borders to hide the table structure from the reader. After you remove borders, it can be helpful to display the table gridlines onscreen while you work. **Gridlines** are light gray lines that show the boundaries of cells, but do not print. If your document will be viewed online—for example, if you are planning to e-mail your resume to potential employers—you should turn off the display of gridlines before you distribute the document so that it looks the same online as it looks when printed. To turn gridlines off or on, click the Hide Gridlines or Show Gridlines command on the Table menu.

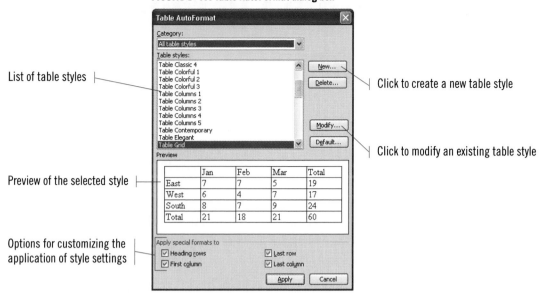

List of table styles

Click to create a new table style

Click to modify an existing table style

Preview of the selected style

Options for customizing the
application of style settings

FIGURE E-18: Table List 7 style applied to table

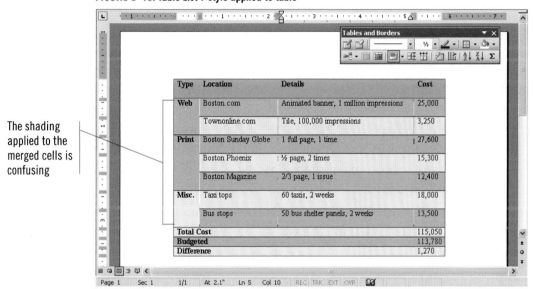

The shading
applied to the
merged cells is
confusing

FIGURE E-19: Table Professional style applied to table

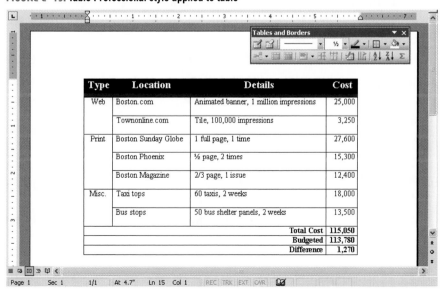

Creating a Custom Format for a Table

You can also use the buttons on the Tables and Borders toolbar to create your own table designs. For example, you can add or remove borders and shading, vary the line style, thickness, and color of borders, change the orientation of text from horizontal to vertical, and change the alignment of text in cells. You adjust the text direction, shading, and borders in the table to make it easier to understand at a glance.

STEPS

1. **Select the** Type **and** Location cells **in the first row, click the** Merge Cells button ⊞ **on the Tables and Borders toolbar, then type** Ad Location

   The two cells are combined into a single cell containing the text "Ad Location."

2. **Select the** Web, Print, **and** Misc. cells **in the first column, click the** Change Text Direction button ⊞ **on the Tables and Borders toolbar twice, then deselect the cells**

   The text is rotated 270 degrees.

3. **Position the pointer over the** right border **of the Web cell until the pointer changes to** ◄‖►, **then drag the border to approximately the ¼" mark on the horizontal ruler**

   The width of the column containing the vertical text narrows.

4. **Place the insertion point in the** Web cell, **then click the** Shading Color list arrow ⊞ **on the Tables and Borders toolbar**

   The Shading Color palette opens, as shown in Figure E-20.

5. **Click** Gold **on the palette, click the** Print cell, **click the** Shading Color list arrow ⊞, **click** Pink, **click the** Misc. cell, **click the** Shading Color list arrow ⊞, **then click** Aqua

   Shading is applied to each cell.

6. **Drag to select the** six white cells **in the Web rows (rows 2 and 3), click the** Shading Color list arrow ⊞, **then click** Light Yellow

7. **Repeat Step 6 to apply** Rose **shading to the Print rows and** Light Turquoise **shading to the Misc. rows**

   Shading is applied to all the cells in rows 1–8.

8. **Select the** last three rows **of the table, click the** Outside Border list arrow ⊞ **on the Tables and Borders toolbar, click the** No Border button ⊞ **on the menu that appears, then deselect the rows**

   The top, bottom, left, and right borders are removed from each cell in the selected rows.

9. **Select the** Total Cost row, **click the** No Border list arrow ⊞, **click the** Top Border button ⊞, **click the** 113,780 cell, **click the** Top Border list arrow ⊞, **then click the** Bottom Border button ⊞

   A top border is added to each cell in the Total Cost row, and a bottom border is added below 113,780. The completed table is shown in Figure E-21.

10. **Press** [Ctrl][Home], **press** [Enter], **type your name, save your changes, print a copy of the document, close the document, then exit Word**

   Press [Enter] at the beginning of a table to move the table down one line in a document.

Merged cell

Text is rotated in the cell

Pink
Gold
Aqua

No Fill

More Fill Colors...

Light Turquiose
Light Yellow
Rose

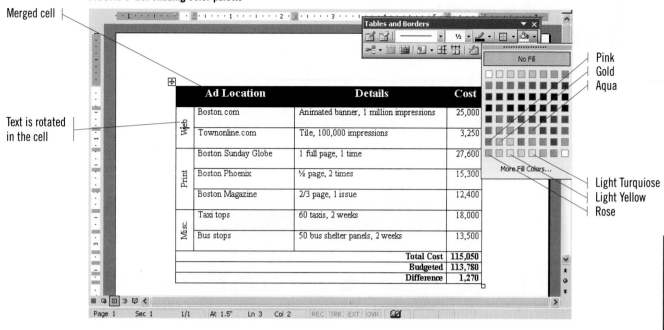

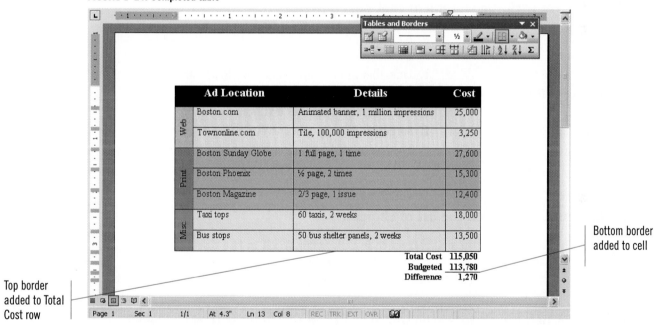

Bottom border added to cell

Top border added to Total Cost row

Word 2003

Clues to Use

Drawing a table

The Word Draw Table feature allows you to draw table cells exactly where you want them. To draw a table, click the Draw Table button on the Tables and Borders toolbar to turn on the Draw pointer, and then click and drag to draw a cell. Using the same method, you can draw borders within the cell to create columns and rows, or draw additional cells attached to the first cell. Click the Draw Table button to turn off the draw feature.

If you want to remove a border from a table, click the Eraser button on the Tables and Borders toolbar to activate the Eraser pointer, and then click the border you want to remove. Click the Eraser button to turn off the erase feature. You can use the Draw pointer and the Eraser pointer to change the structure of any table, not just the tables you draw from scratch.

Practice

▼ CONCEPTS REVIEW

Label each element of the Tables and Borders toolbar shown in Figure E-22.

FIGURE E-22

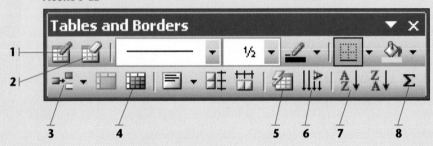

Match each term with the statement that best describes it.

9. Cell
10. Nested table
11. Ascending order
12. Descending order
13. Borders
14. Gridlines
15. Cell reference

a. A cell address composed of a column letter and a row number
b. Lines that separate columns and rows in a table and that print
c. Lines that show columns and rows in a table, but do not print
d. An object inserted in a table cell
e. Sort order that organizes text from A to Z
f. Sort order that organizes text from Z to A
g. The box formed by the intersection of a column and a row

Select the best answer from the list of choices.

16. **Which of the following is the cell reference for the second cell in the third column?**
    a. C2
    b. 2C
    c. 3B
    d. B3

17. **Which of the following is *not* a valid way to add a new row to the bottom of a table?**
    a. Click in the bottom row, then click the Insert Rows Below button on the Tables and Borders toolbar
    b. Click in the bottom row, point to Insert on the Table menu, then click Rows Below
    c. Place the insertion point in the last cell of the last row, then press [Tab]
    d. Click in the bottom row, then click the Insert Rows button on the Standard toolbar

18. **Which button do you use to change the orientation of text in a cell?**
    a. ▢
    b. ▢
    c. ▢
    d. ▢

19. Which of the following is *not* a correct formula for adding the values in cells A1, A2, and A3?

   a. =SUM(A1:A3)   **c.** =SUM(A1~A3)

   b. =SUM(A1, A2, A3)   **d.** =A1+A2+A3

20. What happens when you double-click a column border?

   a. A new column is added to the left

   b. The column width is adjusted to fit the text

   c. The columns in the table are distributed evenly

   d. A new column is added to the right

▼ SKILLS REVIEW

1. Insert a table.

   a. Start Word, close the Getting Started task pane, then save the new blank document as **Mutual Funds** to the drive and folder where your Data Files are located.

   b. Type your name, press [Enter] twice, type **Mutual Fund Performance**, then press [Enter].

   c. Insert a table that contains four columns and four rows.

   d. Type the text shown in Figure E-23, pressing [Tab] to add rows as necessary.

   e. Save your changes.

FIGURE E-23

Fund Name	1 Year	5 Year	10 Year
Computers	16.47	25.56	27.09
Europe	-6.15	13.89	10.61
Natural Resources	19.47	12.30	15.38
Health Care	32.45	24.26	23.25
Financial Services	22.18	21.07	24.44
500 Index	9.13	15.34	13.69

2. Insert and delete rows and columns.

   a. Insert a row above the Health Care row, then type the following text in the new row:

      Canada 8.24   8.12   8.56

   b. Delete the Europe row.

   c. Insert a column to the right of the 10 Year column, type **Date Purchased** in the header row, then enter a date in each cell in the column using the format MM/DD/YY (for example, 11/27/98).

   d. Move the Date Purchased column to the right of the Fund Name column, then save your changes.

3. Modify table rows and columns.

   a. Double-click the border between the first and second columns to resize the columns.

   b. Drag the border between the second and third columns to the 2¼" mark on the horizontal ruler.

   c. Double-click the right border of the 1 Year, 5 Year, and 10 Year columns.

   d. Select the 1 Year, 5 Year, and 10 Year columns, then distribute the columns evenly.

   e. Select rows 2–7, use the Table Properties dialog box to set the row height to exactly .3", then save your changes.

4. Sort table data.

   a. Sort the table data in descending order by the information in the 1 Year column.

   b. Sort the table data in ascending order by date purchased.

   c. Sort the table data by fund name in alphabetical order, then save your changes.

▼ SKILLS REVIEW (CONTINUED)

5. Split and merge cells.

a. Insert a row above the header row.

b. Merge the first cell in the new row with the Fund Name cell.

c. Merge the second cell in the new row with the Date Purchased cell.

d. Merge the three remaining blank cells in the first row into a single cell, then type **Average Annual Returns** in the merged cell.

e. Add a new row to the bottom of the table.

f. Merge the first two cells in the new row, then type **Average Return** in the merged cell.

g. Select the first seven cells in the first column (from Fund Name to Natural Resources), open the Split Cells dialog box, clear the Merge cells before split check box, then split the cells into two columns.

h. Type **Trading Symbol** as the heading for the new column, then enter the following text in the remaining cells in the column: **FINX, CAND, COMP, FINS, HCRX, NARS.**

i. Double-click the right border of the first column to resize the column, double-click the right border of the last column, then save your changes.

6. Perform calculations in tables.

a. Place the insertion point in the last cell in the 1 Year column, then open the Formula dialog box.

b. Delete the text in the Formula text box, type **=average(above)**, click the Number Format list arrow, click 0.00%, then click OK.

c. Repeat Step b to insert the average return in the last cell in the 5 Year and 10 Year columns.

d. Change the value of the 1-year average return for the Natural Resources fund to **10.35.**

e. Use [F9] to recalculate the average return for 1 year, then save your changes.

7. Using Table AutoFormat.

a. Open the Table AutoFormat dialog box, select an appropriate table style for the table, then apply the style to the table. Was the style you chose effective?

b. Using Table AutoFormat, apply the Table List 3 style to the table.

c. Change the font of all the text in the table to 10-point Arial. (*Hint*: Select the entire table.)

d. Apply bold to the 1 Year, 5 Year, and 10 Year column headings, and to the bottom row of the table.

e. Center the table between the margins, center the table title **Mutual Fund Performance**, format the title in 14-point Arial, apply bold, then save your changes.

8. Create a custom format for a table.

a. Select the entire table, then use the Align Center button on the Tables and Borders toolbar to center the text in every cell vertically and horizontally.

b. Right-align the dates in column 3 and the numbers in columns 4–6.

c. Left-align the fund names and trading symbols in columns 1 and 2.

d. Right-align the text in the bottom row. Make sure the text in the header row is still centered.

e. Select all the cells in the header row, including the 1 Year, 5 Year, and 10 Year column headings, change the shading color to indigo, then change the font color to white.

f. Apply rose shading to the cells containing the fund names and trading symbols.

g. Apply pale blue, light yellow, and lavender shading to the cells containing the 1 Year, 5 Year, and 10 Year data, respectively. Do not apply shading to the bottom row of the table.

h. Remove all the borders in the table.

i. Add a ½-point white bottom border to the Average Annual Returns cell. (*Hint*: Use the Tables and Borders toolbar.)

j. Add a 2¼-point black border around the outside of the table. Also add a top border to the last row of the table.

k. Examine the table, make any necessary adjustments, then save your changes.

l. Preview the table in Print Preview, print a copy, close the file, then exit Word.

▼ INDEPENDENT CHALLENGE 1

You are the director of sales for a publishing company with branch offices in six cities around the globe. In preparation for the upcoming sales meeting, you create a table showing your sales projections for the fiscal year 2006.

a. Start Word, then save the new blank document as **2006 Sales** to the drive and folder where your Data Files are located.

b. Type the table heading **Projected Sales in Millions, Fiscal Year 2006** at the top of the document, then press [Enter] twice.

c. Insert a table with five columns and four rows, then enter the data shown in Figure E-24 into the table, adding rows as necessary.

d. Resize the columns to fit the text.

e. Sort the table rows in alphabetical order by Office.

f. Add a new row to the bottom of the table, type **Total** in the first cell, then enter a formula in each remaining cell in the new row to calculate the sum of the cells above it.

FIGURE E-24

Office	Q1	Q2	Q3	Q4
Paris	9500	5800	3900	9800
Tokyo	6700	8900	4500	4900
Berlin	8800	8500	6800	7400
Shanghai	5800	7200	4700	8200
New York	8500	7800	9800	9400
Melbourne	7900	6800	3800	6200

g. Add a new column at the right end of the table, type **Total** in the first cell, then enter a formula in each remaining cell in the new column to calculate the sum of the cells to the left of it. (*Hint*: Make sure the formula you insert in each cell sums the cells to the left, not the cells above.)

h. Using Table AutoFormat, apply a table style to the table. Select a style that enhances the information contained in the table.

i. Center the text in the header row, left-align the remaining text in the first column, then right-align the numerical data in the table.

j. Enhance the table with fonts, font colors, shading, and borders to make the table attractive and easy to read at a glance.

k. Increase the font size of the table heading to 18 points, then center the table heading and the table on the page.

l. Press [Ctrl][End], press [Enter], type your name, save your changes, print the table, close the file, then exit Word.

▼ INDEPENDENT CHALLENGE 2

You have been invited to speak to your local board of realtors about the economic benefits of living in your city. To illustrate some of your points, you want to distribute a handout comparing the cost of living and other economic indicators in the U.S. cities that offer features similar to your city. You decide to format the data as a table.

a. Start Word, open the file WD E-1.doc, then save it as **US Cities** to the drive and folder where your Data Files are located.

b. Format the table heading in 18-point Arial, apply bold, then center the heading.

c. Turn on formatting marks, select the tabbed text in the document, then convert the text to a table.

d. Add a row above the first row in the table, then enter the following column headings in the new header row: **City**, **Cost of Living**, **Median Income**, **Average House Cost**, **Bachelor Degree Rate**.

e. Format the table text in 10-point Arial.

f. Apply an appropriate Table AutoFormat style to the table. Apply bold to the header row if necessary.

g. Adjust the column widths so that the table is attractive and readable. (*Hint*: Put the column headings on two lines.)

h. Make the height of each row at least .25".

i. Center Left align the text in each cell in the first column, including the column head.

j. Center Right align the text in each cell in the remaining columns, including the column heads.

k. Center the entire table on the page.

l. Sort the table by cost of living in descending order. (*Hint*: Use the Sort dialog box.)

▼ INDEPENDENT CHALLENGE 2 (CONTINUED)

Advanced Challenge Exercise

- Add a new row to the bottom of the table, then type **Average** in the first cell in the new row.
- In each subsequent cell in the Average row, insert a formula that calculates the averages of the cells above it. (*Hint:* For each cell, replace SUM with AVERAGE in the Formula text box, but do not make other changes.)
- Change the font color of the text in the Average row to a color of your choice.

m. On the blank line below the table, type **Note: The average cost of living in the United States is 100.**, italicize the text, then use a tab stop and indents to align the text with the left side of the table if it is not aligned.

n. Enhance the table with borders, shading, fonts, and other formats, if necessary to make it attractive and readable.

o. Type your name at the bottom of the document, save your changes, print a copy of the table, close the document, then exit Word.

▼ INDEPENDENT CHALLENGE 3

You work in the advertising department at a magazine. Your boss has asked you to create a fact sheet on the ad dimensions for the magazine. The fact sheet should include the dimensions for each type of ad. As a bonus, you could also add a visual representation of the different ad shapes and sizes, shown in Figure E-25. You'll use tables to lay out the fact sheet, present the dimension information, and, if you are performing the ACE steps, illustrate the ad shapes and sizes.

a. Start Word, open the file WD E-2.doc from the drive and folder where your Data Files are located, then save it as **Ad Dimensions**. Read the document to get a feel for its contents.

b. Drag the border between the first and second column to approximately the 2¾" mark on the horizontal ruler, resize the second and third columns to fit the text, then use the Table Properties dialog box to make each row in the table at least .5".

c. Change the alignment of the text in the first column to center left, then change the alignment of the text in the second and third columns to center right.

d. Remove all the borders from the table, then apply a 2¼-point, red, dotted line, inside horizontal border to the entire table. This creates a red dotted line between each row.

e. In the second blank paragraph under the table heading, insert a new table with three columns and four rows, then merge the cells in the third column of the new blank table.

f. Drag the border between the first and second columns of the new blank table to the 1¼" mark on the horizontal ruler. Drag the border between the second and third columns to the 1½" mark.

g. Select the table that contains text, cut it to the Clipboard, then paste it in the merged cell in the blank table. The table with text is now a nested table in the main table.

h. Split the nested table above the Unit Size (Bleed) row. (*Hint:* Place the insertion point in the Unit Size (Bleed) row, then use the Split Table command on the Table menu.)

i. Scroll up, merge the four cells in the first column of the main table, then merge the four cells in the second column.

j. Split the first column into one column and seven rows.

k. Using the Row tab in the Table Properties dialog box, change the row height of each cell in the first column so that the rows alternate between exactly 1.8" and .25" in height. Make the height of the first, third, fifth, and seventh rows 1.8".

l. Add red shading to the first, third, fifth, and seventh cells in the first column, then remove all the borders from the main table.

▼ INDEPENDENT CHALLENGE 3 (CONTINUED)

Advanced Challenge Exercise

- In the first red cell, type **Full Page**, change the font color to white, then center the text vertically in the cell.
- On the Tables and Borders toolbar, change the Line Style to a single line, change the Line Weight to 1, then change the Border Color to white.
- Activate the Draw Table pointer, then, referring to Figure E-25, draw a vertical border that divides the second red cell into ⅔ and ⅓. (*Hint*: You can also divide the cell using the Split Cells and Merge Cells buttons.)
- Label the cells and align the text as shown in the figure. (*Hint*: Change the text direction and alignment before typing text. Take care not to change the size of the cells when you type. If necessary, press [Enter] to start a new line of text in a cell, or reduce the font size of the text.)
- Referring to Figure E-25, divide the third and fourth red cells, then label the cells as shown in the figure.

m. Examine the document for errors, then make any necessary adjustments.

n. Press [Ctrl][End], type your name, save your changes to the document, preview it, print a copy, close the file, then exit Word.

FIGURE E-25

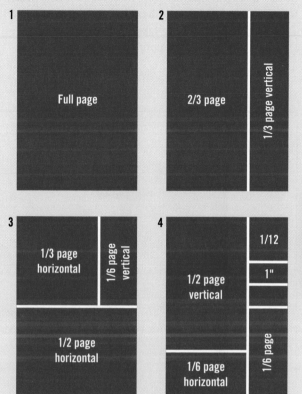

▼ INDEPENDENT CHALLENGE 4

A well-written and well-formatted resume gives you a leg up on getting a job interview. In a winning resume, the content and format support your career objective and effectively present your background and qualifications. One simple way to create a resume is to lay out the page using a table. In this exercise you research guidelines for writing and formatting resumes. You then create your own resume using a table for its layout.

a. Use your favorite search engine to search the Web for information on writing and formatting resumes. Use the keywords **resume templates**.

b. Print helpful advice on writing and formatting resumes from at least two Web sites.

c. Think about the information you want to include in your resume. The header should include your name, address, telephone number, and e-mail address. The body should include your career objective and information on your education, work experience, and skills. You may want to add additional information.

d. Sketch a layout for your resume using a table as the underlying grid. Include the table rows and columns in your sketch.

e. Start Word, open a new blank document, then save it as **My Resume** to the drive and folder where your Data Files are located.

f. Set appropriate margins, then insert a table to serve as the underlying grid for your resume. Split and merge cells and adjust the size of the table columns as necessary.

g. Type your resume in the table cells. Take care to use a professional tone and keep your language to the point.

h. Format your resume with fonts, bullets, and other formatting features. Adjust the spacing between sections by resizing the table columns and rows.

i. When you are satisfied with the content and format of your resume, remove the borders from the table, then hide the gridlines if they are visible.

j. Check your resume for spelling and grammar errors.

k. Save your changes, preview your resume, print a copy, close the file, then exit Word.

Create the calendar shown in Figure E-26 using a table to lay out the entire page. (*Hints*: The top and bottom margins are .7", the left and right margins are 1", and the font is Century Gothic. The clip art image is inserted in the table. The clip art image is found using the keyword **beach**. Use a different clip art image or font if the ones shown in the figure are not available.) Type your name in the last table cell, save the calendar with the filename **August 2006** to the drive and folder where your Data Files are located, then print a copy.

FIGURE E-26

August 2006

Sunday	Monday	Tuesday	Wednesday	Thursday	Friday	Saturday
		1	2	3	4	5
6	7	8	9	10	11	12
13	14	15	16	17	18	19
20	21	22	23	24	25	26
27	28	29	30	31		

Illustrating Documents with Graphics

OBJECTIVES

Add graphics
Resize graphics
Position graphics
Create text boxes
Create AutoShapes
Use the drawing canvas
Format WordArt
Create charts

 If you have a SAM user profile, you may have access to hands-on instruction, practice, and assessment of the skills covered in this unit. Log in to your SAM account and go to your assignments page to see what your instructor has assigned.

Graphics can help illustrate the ideas in your documents, provide visual interest on a page, and give your documents punch and flair. In addition to clip art, you can add graphics created in other programs to a document, or you can use the drawing features of Word to create your own images. In this unit, you learn how to insert, modify, and position graphics, how to draw your own images, and how to illustrate a document with WordArt and charts. You are preparing materials for a workshop for new members of the MediaLoft marketing staff. You use the graphic features of Word to illustrate three handouts on marketing issues of interest to MediaLoft.

Adding Graphics

Graphic images you can insert in a document include the clip art images that come with Word, photos taken with a digital camera, scanned art, and graphics created in other graphics programs. When you first insert a graphic it is an **inline graphic**—part of the line of text in which it is inserted. You move an inline graphic just as you would move text. To be able to move a graphic independently of text, you must apply a text-wrapping style to it to make it a **floating graphic**, which can be moved anywhere on a page. To insert clip art or another graphic file into a document, you use the Picture command on the Insert menu.  You have written a handout containing tips for writing and designing ads. You want to illustrate the handout with the MediaLoft logo, a graphic created in another graphics program. You use the Picture, From File command to insert the logo in the document, and then wrap the text around the logo.

STEPS

1. **Start Word, open the file** WD F-1.doc **from the drive and folder where your Data Files are located, save it as** Ad Tips, **then read the document to get a feel for its contents**
   The document opens in Print Layout view.

> **QUICK TIP**
> The Drawing button is a toggle button that you can use to display and hide the Drawing toolbar.

2. **Click the** Show/Hide ¶ **button** ¶ **on the Standard toolbar to display formatting marks, then click the** Drawing **button** ✎ **on the Standard toolbar to display the Drawing toolbar if it is not already displayed**
   The Drawing toolbar, located below the document window, includes buttons for inserting, creating, and modifying graphics.

3. **Click before the heading** Create a simple layout, **click** Insert **on the menu bar, point to** Picture, **then click** From File
   The Insert Picture dialog box opens. You use this dialog box to locate and insert graphic files. Most graphic files are **bitmap graphics**, which are composed of a series of small dots, called **pixels**, that define color and intensity. Bitmap graphics are often saved with a .bmp, .png, .jpg, .wmf, .tif, or .gif file extension. To view all the graphic files in a particular location, use the Files of type list arrow to select All Pictures. To view a particular type of graphic, use the Files of type list arrow to select the graphic type.

4. **Click the** Files of type list arrow, **click** All Pictures **if it is not already selected, use the** Look in list arrow **to navigate to the drive and folder where your Data Files are located, click the file** MLoft.jpg, **then click** Insert
   The logo is inserted as an inline graphic at the location of the insertion point. Unless you want a graphic to be part of a line of text, usually the first thing you do after inserting it is to wrap text around it so it becomes a floating graphic. To be able to position a graphic anywhere on a page, you must apply a text-wrapping style to it even if there is no text on the page.

> **TROUBLE**
> If your Picture tool-bar does not open, click View on the menu bar, point to Toolbars, then click Picture.

5. **Click the** logo graphic **to select it**
   Squares, called **sizing handles**, appear on the sides and corners of the graphic when it is selected, as shown in Figure F-1. The Picture toolbar also opens. The Picture toolbar includes buttons for modifying graphics.

6. **Click the** Text Wrapping button ▧ **on the Picture toolbar**
   A menu of text-wrapping styles opens.

7. **Click** Tight
   The text wraps around the sides of the graphic, as shown in Figure F-2. Notice that the sizing handles change to circles, indicating the graphic is a floating graphic, and an anchor and a green rotate handle appear. The anchor indicates the floating graphic is **anchored** to the nearest paragraph, so that the graphic moves with the paragraph if the paragraph is moved. The anchor symbol appears only when formatting marks are displayed.

8. **Click** ¶, **deselect the graphic, then click the** Save button ▦ **on the Standard toolbar to save your changes**

FIGURE F-1: Inline graphic

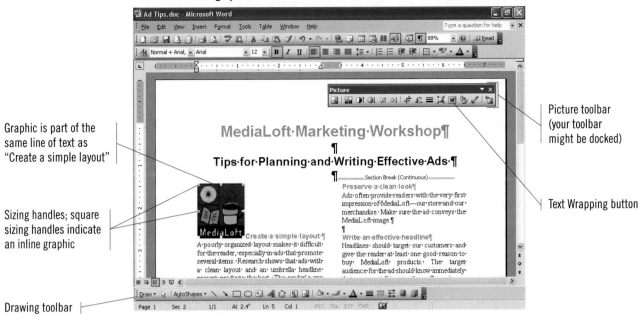

Graphic is part of the same line of text as "Create a simple layout"

Sizing handles; square sizing handles indicate an inline graphic

Drawing toolbar

Picture toolbar (your toolbar might be docked)

Text Wrapping button

FIGURE F-2: Floating graphic

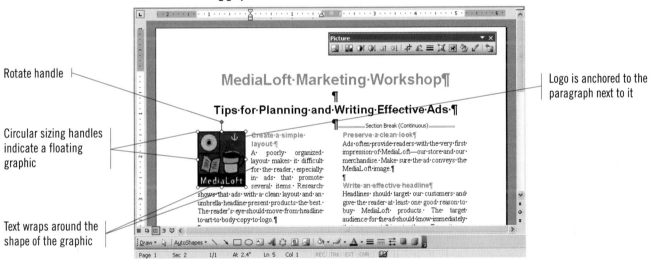

Rotate handle

Circular sizing handles indicate a floating graphic

Text wraps around the shape of the graphic

Logo is anchored to the paragraph next to it

Clues to Use

Narrowing a search for clip art

Searching for clip art with an active Internet connection gives you access to the thousands of clips available on the Microsoft Office Online Web site. With so many clips to choose from, your search can be more productive if you set specific search criteria. To perform an initial search for a clip, type a word or words that describe the clip you want to find in the Search text box in the Clip Art task pane, shown in Figure F-3, and then click Go. If the clips returned in the Results box are too numerous or don't match the criteria you set, you can try using more keywords. For example, rather than "family," you might type "mother father baby" to return only clips associated with all three keywords. You can also narrow your search by reducing the number of collections to search, or by limiting your search to a specific media type, such as photographs. To search specific collections, click the Search in list arrow in the task pane, and then deselect the check box next to each collection you want to omit from the search. To search a specific media type, click the Results should be list arrow, and then deselect the check box next to each type of clip you want to omit from the search. In both lists, you can click a plus sign next to a collection name or media type to expand the list of options. To read more hints on searching for clips, click the Tips for finding clips hyperlink in the Clip Art task pane.

FIGURE F-3: Clip Art task pane

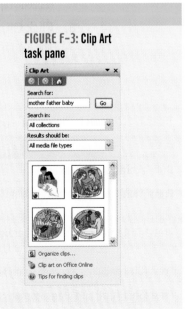

Resizing Graphics

Once you insert a graphic into a document, you can change its shape or size by using the mouse to drag a sizing handle or by using the Picture command on the Format menu to specify an exact height and width for the graphic. Resizing a graphic with the mouse allows you to see how the image looks as you modify it. Using the Picture command to alter a graphic's shape or size allows you to set precise measurements.  You enlarge the MediaLoft logo.

STEPS

QUICK TIP
Click Ruler on the View menu to display the rulers.

1. **Click the logo graphic to select it, place the pointer over the middle-right sizing handle, when the pointer changes to ↔, drag to the right until the graphic is about 1¾" wide**

   As you drag, the dotted outline indicates the size and shape of the graphic. You can refer to the ruler to gauge the measurements as you drag. When you release the mouse button, the image is stretched to be wider. Dragging a side, top, or bottom sizing handle changes only the width or height of a graphic.

QUICK TIP
If you enlarge a bitmap graphic too much, the dots that make up the picture become visible and the graphic is distorted.

2. **Click the Undo button ↩ on the Standard toolbar, place the pointer over the upper-right sizing handle, when the pointer changes to ↗ drag up and to the right until the graphic is about 2" tall and 1¾" wide as shown in Figure F-4, then release the mouse button**

   The image is enlarged. Dragging a corner sizing handle resizes the graphic proportionally so that its width and height are reduced or enlarged by the same percentage. Table F-1 describes other ways to resize objects using the mouse.

3. **Double-click the logo graphic**

   The Format Picture dialog box opens. It includes options for changing the coloring, size, scale, text wrapping, and position of a graphic. You can double-click any graphic object or use the Picture command on the Format menu to open the Format Picture dialog box.

4. **Click the Size tab**

   The Size tab, shown in Figure F-5, allows you to enter precise height and width measurements for a graphic or to scale a graphic by entering the percentage by which you want to reduce or enlarge it. When a graphic is sized to **scale**, its height to width ratio remains the same.

TROUBLE
Your height measurement might differ slightly.

5. **Select the measurement in the Width text box in the Size and rotate section, type 1.5, then click the Height text box in the Size and rotate section**

   The height measurement automatically changes to 1.68". When the Lock aspect ratio check box is selected, you need to enter only a height or width measurement. Word calculates the other measurement so that the resized graphic is proportional.

6. **Click OK, then save your changes**

   The logo is resized to be precisely 1.5" wide and approximately 1.68" tall.

TABLE F-1: Methods for resizing an object using the mouse

do this	to
Drag a corner sizing handle	Resize a clip art or bitmap graphic proportionally from a corner
Press [Shift] and drag a corner sizing handle	Resize a drawing object, such as an AutoShape or a WordArt object, proportionally from a corner
Press [Ctrl] and drag a side, top, or bottom sizing handle	Resize any graphic object vertically or horizontally while keeping the center position fixed
Press [Ctrl] and drag a corner sizing handle	Resize any graphic object diagonally while keeping the center position fixed
Press [Shift][Ctrl] and drag a corner sizing handle	Resize any graphic object proportionally while keeping the center position fixed

FIGURE F-4: Dragging to resize an image

Dotted outline shows the size of the graphic as you drag

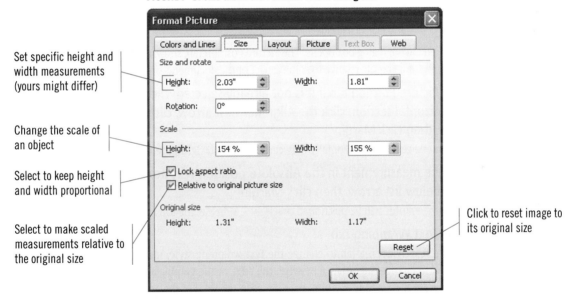

FIGURE F-5: Size tab in the Format Picture dialog box

Set specific height and width measurements (yours might differ)

Change the scale of an object

Select to keep height and width proportional

Select to make scaled measurements relative to the original size

Click to reset image to its original size

Clues to Use

Cropping graphics

If you want to use only part of a picture in a document, you can crop the graphic to trim the parts you don't want to use. To crop a graphic, select it, then click the Crop button ⊹ on the Picture toolbar. The pointer changes to the cropping pointer ⌖, and cropping handles (solid black lines) appear on all four corners and sides of the graphic. To crop one side of a graphic, drag a side cropping handle inward to where you want to trim the graphic. To crop two adjacent sides at once, drag a corner cropping handle inward to the point where you want the corner of the cropped image to be. When you drag a cropping handle, the shape of the cropping pointer changes to correspond to the shape of the cropping handle you are dragging. When you finish adjusting the parameters of the graphic, click the Crop button again to turn off the crop feature. You can also crop a graphic by entering precise crop measurements on the Picture tab in the Format Picture dialog box.

Positioning Graphics

Once you insert a graphic into a document and make it a floating graphic, you can move it by dragging it with the mouse, nudging it with the arrow keys, or setting an exact location for the graphic using the Picture command on the Format menu. Dragging an object with the mouse or using the arrow keys allows you to position a graphic visually. Using the Picture command to position a graphic allows you to place an object precisely on a page. You experiment with different positions for the MediaLoft logo to determine which position enhances the document the most.

To move an object only horizontally or vertically, press [Shift] as you drag.

1. **Select the** logo graphic **if it is not already selected, move the pointer over the graphic, when the pointer changes to** ⌖, **drag the graphic down and to the right as shown in Figure F-6 so its top aligns with the top of the** Create a simple layout **heading**

   As you drag, the dotted outline indicates the position of the graphic. When you release the mouse button, the graphic is moved and the text wraps around the graphic. Notice that the Create a simple layout heading is now above the graphic.

2. **With the graphic selected, press [◄] four times, then press [▲] three times**

   Each time you press an arrow key the graphic is **nudged**—moved a small amount—in that direction. You can also press [Ctrl] and an arrow key to nudge an object in even smaller (one pixel) increments. Nudging the graphic did not position it exactly where you want it to be.

You can place a floating graphic anywhere on a page, including outside the margins.

3. **Double-click the** graphic, **click the** Layout tab **in the Format Picture dialog box, then click** Advanced

   The Advanced Layout dialog box opens. The Picture Position tab, shown in Figure F-7, allows you to specify an exact position for a graphic relative to some aspect of the document, such as a margin, column, or paragraph.

4. **Click the** Picture Position tab **if it is not already selected, click the** Alignment option button **in the Horizontal section, click the** Alignment list arrow, **click** Centered, **click the** relative to list arrow, **then click** Margin

   The logo will be centered horizontally between the left and right page margins.

5. **Change the measurement in the Absolute position text box in the Vertical section to** 1.5, **click the** below list arrow, **then click** Margin

   The top of the graphic will be positioned precisely 1.5" below the top margin.

6. **Click the** Text Wrapping tab

   You use the Text Wrapping tab to change the text-wrapping style, to wrap text around only one side of a graphic, and to change the distance between the edge of the graphic and the edge of the wrapped text. You want to increase the amount of white space between the sides of the graphic and the wrapped text.

7. **Select** Square, **select** 0.13 **in the Left text box, type** .3, **press [Tab], then type** .3 **in the Right text box**

   The distance between the graphic and the edge of the wrapped text will be .3" on either side.

If the Picture toolbar remains open after you deselect the graphic, close the toolbar.

8. **Click** OK **to close the Advanced Layout dialog box, click** OK **to close the Format Picture dialog box, deselect the graphic, then save your changes**

   The logo is centered between the margins, the top of the graphic is positioned 1.5" below the top margin, and the amount of white space between the left and right sides of the graphic and the wrapped text is increased to .3", as shown in Figure F-8.

FIGURE F-6: Dragging a graphic to move it

Top of graphic aligns with the top of the text

Dotted outline shows the position as you drag

FIGURE F-7: Picture Position tab in the Advanced Layout dialog box

Select to horizontally align a graphic relative to an aspect of the document

Select to position a graphic a precise distance from an aspect of the document (your measurements might differ)

Select the aspect of the document you want to position the graphic relative to

FIGURE F-8: Repositioned logo

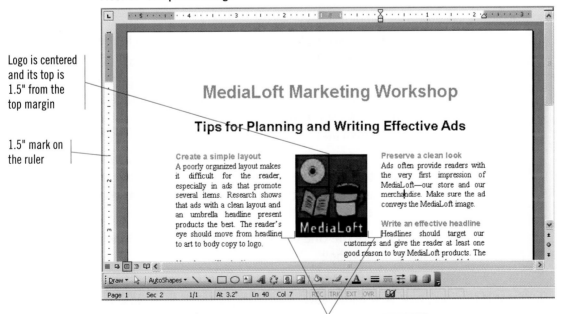

Logo is centered and its top is 1.5" from the top margin

1.5" mark on the ruler

Space between the graphic and the text is increased

Creating Text Boxes

When you want to illustrate your documents with text, you can create a text box. A **text box** is a container that you can fill with text and graphics. Like other drawing objects, text boxes can be resized, formatted with colors, lines, and text-wrapping, and positioned anywhere on a page. You create a text box using the Text Box button on the Drawing toolbar or the Text Box command on the Insert menu. When you insert a text box or another drawing object, a drawing canvas opens in the document. A **drawing canvas** is a workspace for creating your own graphics. You can choose to draw the text box directly in the document, or to draw it in the drawing canvas. You want to add a pull quote to call attention to the main point of the handout. You draw a text box, add the pull quote text to it, format the text, and then position the text box on the page.

STEPS

QUICK TIP

To draw a text box around existing text, select the text, then click the Text Box button.

1. **Scroll down, click before the** Use large illustrations **heading, then click the** Text Box button **on the Drawing toolbar**

   A drawing canvas opens in the document, as shown in Figure F-9, and the pointer changes to +. You'll draw a text box outside the drawing canvas.

2. **Move the** + **pointer directly under the lower-left corner of the MediaLoft logo, then click and drag down and to the right to draw a text box that is about 1½" wide and 2¾" tall**

   When you release the mouse button, the drawing canvas disappears and the insertion point is located in the text box, as shown in Figure F-10. The Text Box toolbar also opens.

3. **Type** The reader's eye should move from headline to art to body copy to logo

TROUBLE

If the text does not fit in the text box, drag the bottom sizing handle down to enlarge the text box.

4. **Select the text, click the** Font list arrow **on the Formatting toolbar, click** Arial, **click the** Font Size list arrow, **click** 14, **click the** Bold button **, click the** Center button **, click the** Line Spacing list arrow **, click** 2.0, **then click outside the text box**

   The text is formatted. Notice that the body text does not wrap around the text box. By default, text boxes are inserted with the In front of text-wrapping style applied.

QUICK TIP

Use the Text Box tab to change the margins in a text box.

5. **Click the** text box, **double-click the** text box frame, **click the** Size tab **in the Format Text Box dialog box, then change the height to** 2.75" **and the width to** 1.5" **in the Size and rotate section, if necessary**

   When you click a text box with the I pointer, the insertion point moves inside the text box and sizing handles appear. Clicking the frame of a text box with the pointer selects the text box object itself. Double-clicking the frame opens the Format Text Box dialog box.

6. **Click the** Layout tab, **click** Advanced, **click the** Picture Position tab, **click the** Alignment option button **in the Horizontal section, click the** Alignment list arrow, **click** Centered, **click the** relative to list arrow, **click** Margin, **make sure the** Absolute position option button **in the Vertical section is selected, change the measurement in the Absolute position text box to** 3.4, **click the** below list arrow, **then click** Margin

   The text box will be centered between the left and right margins, and its top will be precisely 3.4" below the top margin.

7. **Click the** Text Wrapping tab, **click** Square, **change the Top, Bottom, Left, and Right measurements to** .3" **in the Distance from text section, click** OK **twice, then deselect the text box**

   The text is wrapped in a square around the text box.

8. **Click inside the text box, click the** Line Color list arrow **on the Drawing toolbar, click** No Line, **then deselect the text box**

   The thin black border around the text box is removed, as shown in Figure F-11.

9. **Press** [Ctrl][End], **type your name, save your changes, print, then close the file**

FIGURE F-9: Drawing canvas

Drawing canvas

Drawing Canvas toolbar

FIGURE F-10: Text box

Insertion point in text box

Text box frame

Text Box toolbar

Text Box button

Line Color list arrow

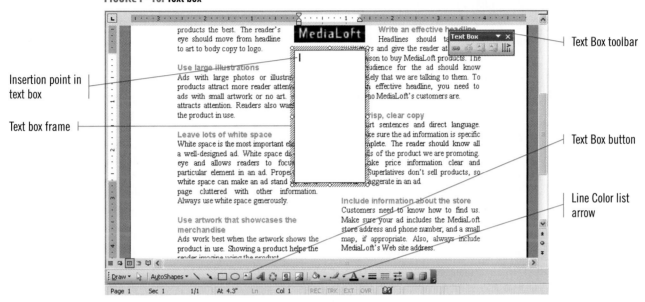

FIGURE F-11: Completed handout with text box

Formatted text in text box

Text wraps around the text box

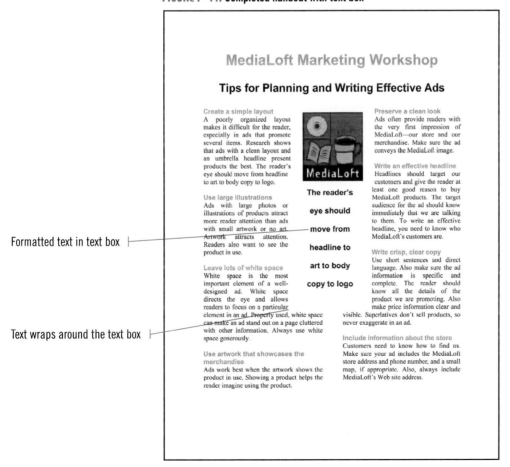

Creating AutoShapes

One way you can create your own graphics in Word is to use AutoShapes. **AutoShapes** are the rectangles, ovals, triangles, lines, block arrows, stars, banners, lightning bolts, hearts, suns, and other drawing objects you can create using the tools on the Drawing toolbar. The Drawing toolbar also includes tools for adding colors, shadows, fills, and three-dimensional effects to your graphics. Table F-2 describes the buttons on the Drawing toolbar. You can choose to draw a line or shape exactly where you want it in a document, or you can create a graphic in a drawing canvas. It's helpful to use a drawing canvas if your graphic includes multiple items.  Your second handout needs to illustrate MediaLoft book sales by genre. You use AutoShapes to create a picture of a stack of books, and then add the text to the picture.

STEPS

1. **Click the** New Blank Document button 🗋 **on the Standard toolbar, then save the document as** Genre Sales **to the drive and folder where your Data Files are located**

2. **Click the** Rectangle button 🔲 **on the Drawing toolbar**

   When you click an AutoShape button, a drawing canvas opens and the pointer changes to ╋. Depending on your computer settings, the Drawing Canvas toolbar might also open. The Drawing Canvas toolbar contains buttons for sizing the graphics you create in the drawing canvas, and for wrapping text around the drawing canvas. You'll learn more about resizing and positioning the drawing canvas in the next lesson.

   > **QUICK TIP**
   > To draw a square, click the Rectangle button, then press [Shift] while you drag the pointer. Similarly, to draw a circle, click the Oval button, then press [Shift] while you drag the pointer.

3. **Scroll down until the entire drawing canvas is visible on your screen, place the pointer about ¾" above the lower-left corner of the drawing canvas, then drag down and to the right to create a rectangle that is about 5" wide and ½" tall**

   You do not need to be exact in your measurements as you drag. When you release the mouse button, sizing handles appear around the rectangle to indicate it is selected. Cropping handles also appear around the edges of the drawing canvas.

4. **Click** AutoShapes **on the Drawing toolbar, point to** Basic Shapes, **then click the** Sun

   The AutoShapes menu contains categories of shapes and lines that you can draw.

5. **Place the ╋ pointer in the upper-left corner of the drawing canvas, then drag down and to the right to create a sun that is about ½" wide**

   The sun shape includes a yellow diamond-shaped adjustment handle. You can drag an **adjustment handle** to change the shape, but not the size, of many AutoShapes.

6. **Position the pointer over the adjustment handle until it changes to ▷, drag the handle to the right about ¼", click the** Fill Color list arrow 🎨▾ **on the Drawing toolbar, click** Gold, **click the** rectangle **to select it, click** 🎨▾, **then click** Rose

   The sun shape becomes narrower and the shapes are filled with color. Notice that when you select a color, the active color changes on the Fill Color button.

   > **QUICK TIP**
   > Double-click the Rectangle, Oval, Line, or Arrow button to activate the ╋ pointer and draw more than one shape or line. When you are finished drawing, click the button again.

7. **Refer to Figure F-12 to draw three more rectangles, then fill the rectangles with color**

   After all four rectangles are drawn, use the sizing handles to resize the rectangles if necessary.

8. **Press and hold [Shift], click each** rectangle **to select it, click the** 3-D Style button 🔲 **on the Drawing toolbar, then click** 3-D Style 1 **(the first style in the top row)**

   The rectangles appear three-dimensional, making the group look like a stack of books.

   > **QUICK TIP**
   > To edit text in an AutoShape, right-click it, then click Edit Text.

9. **Deselect the books, right-click the** top book, **click** Add Text, **click the** Font Size list arrow **on the Formatting toolbar, click** 20, **then type** Children's - 17%

   The 3-D rectangle changes to a text box. You can convert any shape to a text box by right-clicking it and clicking Add Text.

10. **Add the 20-point text as shown in Figure F-13, then save your changes**

FIGURE F-12: AutoShapes in the drawing canvas

Shape of sun is narrower than original shape, but size is the same

Sizing handles indicate rectangle is selected

Cropping handles

Draw three rectangles in Step 7 and fill them with aqua, lavender, and gold

Rose fill

Active color on the Fill Color button is gold (yours might differ)

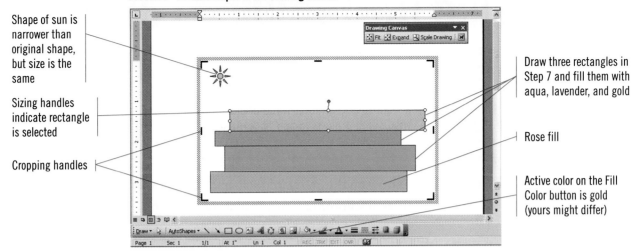

FIGURE F-13: Text added to AutoShapes

Add text in Step 10

Children's – 17%
Nonfiction – 15%
Technical – 23%
Fiction – 19%

Rectangles appear three-dimensional

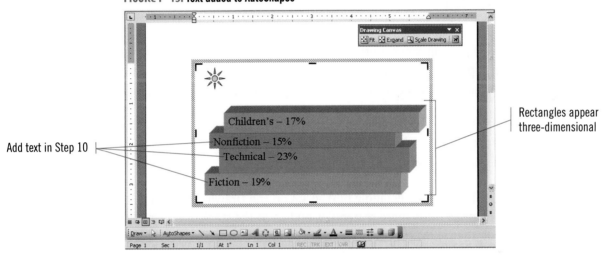

TABLE F-2: Buttons on the Drawing toolbar

button	use to	button	use to
Draw ▾	Open a menu of commands for grouping, positioning, rotating, and wrapping text around graphics, and for changing an AutoShape to a different shape	🖼	Insert a clip art graphic
		🖼	Insert a picture from a file
▸	Select graphic objects	◇ ▾	Fill a shape with a color, a texture, a gradient, or a pattern
AutoShapes ▾	Open a menu of drawing options for lines, shapes, and callouts	🖌 ▾	Change the color of a line, an arrow, or a line around a shape
＼	Draw a straight line	A ▾	Change the color of text
↘	Draw a straight line with an arrowhead	≡	Change the style and weight of a line, an arrow, or a line around a shape
▭	Draw a rectangle or square	⋮⋮⋮	Change the dash style of a line, an arrow, or a line around a shape
○	Draw an oval or circle		
🄰	Insert a text box	⇄	Change a line to an arrow; change the style of an arrow
◢	Insert a WordArt graphic	▢	Add a shadow to a graphic object
🔀	Insert a diagram or an organization chart	▣	Make a graphic object three-dimensional

ILLUSTRATING DOCUMENTS WITH GRAPHICS WORD F-11

Using the Drawing Canvas

When multiple shapes are contained in a drawing canvas, you can resize and move them as a single graphic object. The Drawing Canvas toolbar includes buttons for sizing a drawing canvas and for wrapping text around it. Once you apply a text-wrapping style to a drawing canvas, you can position it anywhere in a document. ⬛▨▨ You want to add another three books to the stack. You enlarge the drawing canvas, add the shapes, size the drawing as a single object, and then move it to the bottom of the page.

STEPS

1. **Click the Zoom list arrow on the Standard toolbar, click 75%, then click the stack of books graphic to make the drawing canvas visible if it is not visible**
   Cropping handles appear around the edges of the drawing canvas.

2. **Place the pointer over the top-middle cropping handle, when the pointer changes to ⊥, drag the handle to the top of the page, then release the mouse button**
   The drawing canvas is enlarged from the top, but the size of the graphic does not change. Dragging a cropping handle resizes the drawing canvas, but not the graphic.

3. **Select the sun, position the pointer over it until the pointer changes to 🕂, drag the sun on top of the right end of the Technical book, then release the mouse button**
   The sun shape is moved to the spine of the book, but is hidden beneath the rectangle shape.

> **TROUBLE**
> If the sun is not selected, click Undo Move Object on the Edit menu, and then repeat Step 3.

4. **With the sun shape selected, click the Draw button on the Drawing toolbar, point to Order, then click Bring to Front**
   The sun shape is moved on top of the rectangle shape.

5. **Double-click the Rectangle button ▢ on the Drawing toolbar to activate the rectangle tool, draw three more rectangles on top of the stack of books, click ▢ to turn off the tool, then right-click each rectangle and add the 20-point text shown in Figure F-14**

6. **Select each rectangle, fill it with any color, then apply the 3-D Style 1**

> **TROUBLE**
> If your Drawing Canvas toolbar is not open, right-click the drawing canvas frame, then click Show Drawing Canvas toolbar on the shortcut menu.

7. **Click the Fit Drawing to Contents button 🔲Fit on the Drawing Canvas toolbar**
   The drawing canvas is automatically resized to fit the graphic within it.

8. **Click the Zoom list arrow, click Whole Page, then click the Scale Drawing button 🔲 Scale Drawing on the Drawing Canvas toolbar**
   The cropping handles on the drawing canvas change to sizing handles. You can now use the drawing canvas frame to resize the contents of the drawing canvas as a single graphic.

> **QUICK TIP**
> To precisely size or position a drawing canvas, double-click the drawing canvas frame to open the Format Drawing Canvas dialog box.

9. **Drag the bottom-middle sizing handle down until the graphic is about 6" tall**
   Resizing the drawing canvas resizes all the shapes within it. Dragging a top, bottom, or side handle stretches the graphic. Dragging a corner handle resizes the graphic proportionally.

10. **Click the Text Wrapping button 🔲 on the Drawing Canvas toolbar, click Square, place the pointer over the drawing canvas frame so it changes to 🕂, drag the drawing canvas down and position it so it is centered in the bottom part of the page, deselect the drawing canvas, then save your changes**
    Compare your document to Figure F-15. You must wrap text around a drawing canvas to be able to position it anywhere on a page.

FIGURE F-14: New rectangles in drawing canvas

Draw rectangles and add text in Step 5

Scale Drawing button

Fit Drawing to Contents button

Sun shape moved to the spine of the book

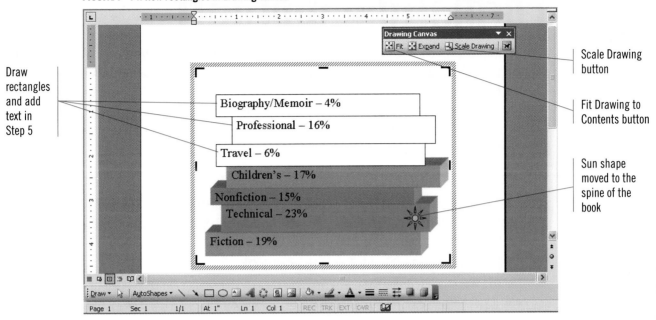

FIGURE F-15: Resized and repositioned graphic

Graphic is stretched to be taller and narrower

Graphic is centered at the bottom of the page

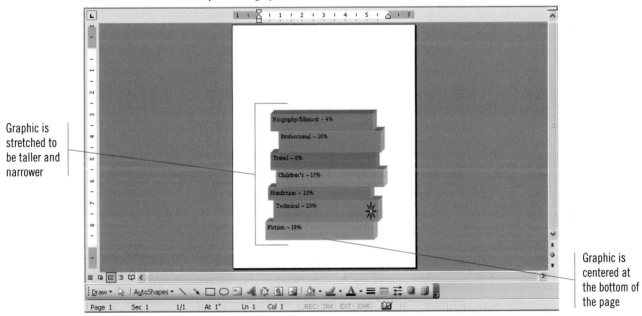

Clues to Use

Drawing lines

In addition to drawing straight lines and arrows, you can use the Lines tools on the AutoShapes menu to draw curved, freeform, and scribble lines. Click AutoShapes on the Drawing toolbar, point to Lines, then select the type of line you want to draw. Choose Curve to draw an object with smooth curves, choose Freeform to draw an object with both freehand and straight-line segments, or choose Scribble to draw a freehand object that looks like it was drawn with a pencil. The lines you draw include vertexes—a **vertex** is either a point where two straight lines meet or the highest point in a curve. To create a curve or freeform line, click the location you want the line to begin, move the mouse, click to insert a vertex, move the mouse, and so on. Double-click to end a curve or freeform line or click near the starting point to close a shape, if that's what you have drawn. Drawing scribble lines is similar to drawing with a pencil: drag the pointer to draw the line, and then release the mouse button when you are finished. The best way to learn about drawing curve, freeform, and scribble lines is to experiment. Once you draw a line, you can modify its shape by right-clicking it, clicking Edit Points, and then dragging a vertex to a different location.

Formatting WordArt

Another way to give your documents punch and flair is to use WordArt. **WordArt** is a drawing object that contains text formatted with special shapes, patterns, and orientations. You create WordArt using either the WordArt button on the Drawing toolbar or the Picture, WordArt command on the Insert menu. Once you have created a WordArt object, you can use the buttons on the WordArt toolbar to format it with different shapes, fonts, colors, and other effects to create the impact you desire. ▰▰▰ You use WordArt to create a fun heading for your handout.

1. **Press [Ctrl][Home], press [Enter], click the** Zoom list arrow **on the Standard toolbar, click** Page Width, **then click the** Insert WordArt button ▰ **on the Drawing toolbar**

   The WordArt Gallery opens. It includes the styles you can choose for your WordArt.

2. **Click the** first style in the third row, **then click** OK

   The Edit WordArt Text dialog box opens. You type the text you want to format as WordArt in this dialog box and, if you wish, change the font and font size of the WordArt text.

3. **Type** Genre Sales, **then click** OK

   The WordArt object appears at the location of the insertion point. Like other graphic objects, the WordArt object is an inline graphic until you wrap text around it.

4. **Click the** WordArt object **to select it**

   The WordArt toolbar opens when a WordArt object is selected. It includes buttons for editing and modifying WordArt.

5. **Drag the** lower-right corner sizing handle **down and to the right to make the object about** 2" **tall and** 6" **wide**

   The WordArt is enlarged to span the page between the left and right margins, as shown in Figure F-16.

6. **Click the** WordArt Character Spacing button ▰ **on the WordArt toolbar, click** Tight, **click the** WordArt Shape button ▰ **on the WordArt toolbar, then click the** Can Up **shape (the third shape in the third row)**

   The spacing between the characters is decreased and the shape of the WordArt text changes.

7. **Click the** Format WordArt button ▰ **on the WordArt toolbar, then click the** Colors and Lines tab

   The Format WordArt dialog box opens. You use the Colors and Lines tab to change the fill color of WordArt, to change the transparency of the fill color, and to change the color or style of the line surrounding the WordArt characters.

8. **Click the** Color list arrow **in the Fill section, then click** Fill Effects

   The Fill Effects dialog box opens, as shown in Figure F-17. You use this dialog box to change the fill colors and effects of the WordArt object. Using the Gradient tab, you can select a preset gradient effect or choose colors and shading styles to create your own gradient effect. You can also apply a preset texture using the Texture tab, design a two-color pattern using the Pattern tab, or fill the object with a graphic using the Picture tab.

9. **Make sure the** Two colors option button **is selected in the Colors section on the Gradient tab, click the** Color 1 list arrow, **click** Indigo, **click the** Color 2 list arrow, **click** Pink, **click the** Diagonal up option button **in the Shading styles section, click the** lower-right box **in the Variants section, then click** OK **twice**

   The new fill effects are applied to the WordArt. The completed handout is shown in Figure F-18.

10. **Press [Ctrl][Home], type your name, save your changes, print the document, then close the file**

FIGURE F-16: **Resized WordArt**

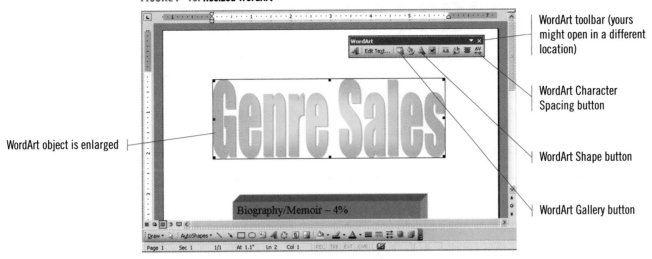

WordArt toolbar (yours might open in a different location)

WordArt Character Spacing button

WordArt object is enlarged

WordArt Shape button

WordArt Gallery button

FIGURE F-17: **Fill Effects dialog box**

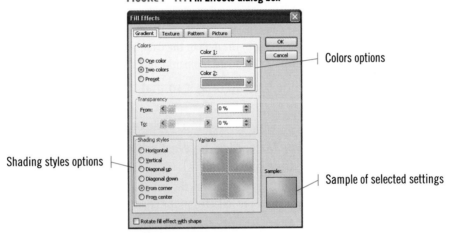

Colors options

Shading styles options

Sample of selected settings

FIGURE F-18: **Completed handout with WordArt**

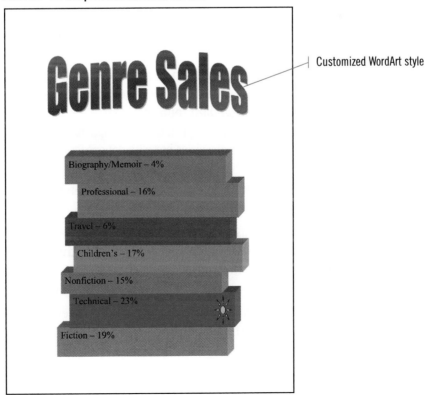

Customized WordArt style

ILLUSTRATING DOCUMENTS WITH GRAPHICS WORD F-15

Creating Charts

Adding a chart can be an attractive way to illustrate a document that includes numerical information. A **chart** is a visual representation of numerical data and usually is used to illustrate trends, patterns, or relationships. The Word chart feature allows you to create many types of charts, including bar, column, pie, area, and line charts. You can add a chart to a document using the Picture, Chart command on the Insert menu. ✦✦✦✦ You create a handout that includes a chart showing the distribution of MediaLoft customers by age and gender.

STEPS

1. **Open the file** WD F-2.doc **from the drive and folder where your Data Files are located, save it as** Age and Gender, **then press** [Ctrl][End]
   The insertion point is centered under the title.

QUICK TIP
To show the toolbars on two rows, click the Toolbar Options button at the end of the Formatting toolbar, then click Show Buttons on Two Rows.

2. **Click** Insert **on the menu bar, point to** Picture, **then click** Chart
   A table opens in a datasheet window and a column chart appears in the document. The datasheet and the chart contain placeholder data that you replace with your own data. The chart is based on the data in the datasheet. Any change you make to the data in the datasheet is made automatically to the chart. Notice that when a chart object is open, the Standard toolbar includes buttons for working with charts.

3. **Click the** datasheet title bar **and drag it so that the chart is visible, then move the pointer over the** datasheet
   The pointer changes to ✛. You use this pointer to select the cells in the datasheet.

QUICK TIP
Click the Chart Type list arrow 📊 ▾ on the Standard toolbar to change the type of chart.

4. **Click the** East cell, **type** Male, **click the** West cell, **type** Female, **click the gray** 3 cell **to select the third row, then press** [Delete]
   When you click a cell and type, the data in the cell is replaced with the text you type. As you edit the datasheet, the changes you make are reflected in the chart.

5. **Replace the remaining placeholder text with the data shown in Figure F-19, then click outside the chart to deselect it**

6. **Click the** chart **to select the object, press** [Ctrl], **then drag the** lower-right corner sizing handle **down and to the right until the outline of the chart is approximately 7" wide**
   The chart is enlarged and still centered.

QUICK TIP
Point to any part of a chart to see a ScreenTip that identifies the part. You can also use the Chart Objects list arrow on the Standard toolbar to select a part of a chart.

7. **Double-click the** chart **to open it, click the** View Datasheet button 📊 **on the Standard toolbar to close the datasheet, click the** legend **to select it, then click the** Format Legend button 📊 **on the Standard toolbar**
   The Format Legend dialog box opens. It includes options for modifying the legend. Select any part of a chart object and use 📊 to open a dialog box with options for formatting that part of the chart. In this case, the name of the button is Format Legend because the legend is selected.

8. **Click the** Placement tab, **click the** Bottom option button, **then click** OK
   The legend moves below the chart.

9. **Click the** Value Axis (the y-axis), **click** 📊, **click the** Number tab **in the Format Axis dialog box, click** Percentage **in the Category list, click the** Decimal places down arrow **twice so** 0 **appears, click** OK, **then deselect the chart**
   Percent signs are added to the y-axis. The completed handout is shown in Figure F-20.

10. **Type** Prepared by **followed by your name centered in the document footer, save your changes, print the handout, close the document, then exit Word**

FIGURE F-19: Datasheet and chart object

Format button

Datasheet window

Chart reflects data in datasheet after all data is entered

Value axis (y-axis)

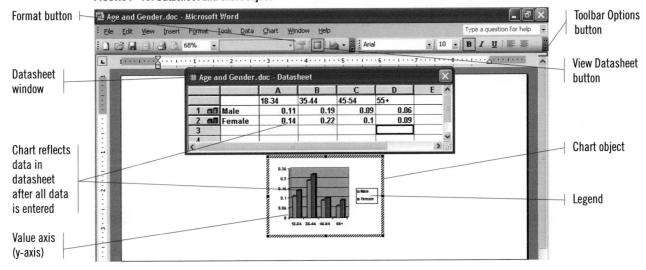

Toolbar Options button

View Datasheet button

Chart object

Legend

FIGURE F-20: Completed handout with chart

Percent signs added to the value axis

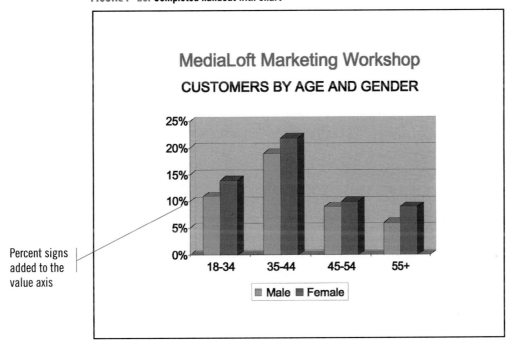

Clues to Use

Creating diagrams and organization charts

Diagrams are another way to illustrate concepts in your documents. Word includes a diagram feature that allows you to quickly create and format several types of diagrams, including pyramid, Venn, target, cycle, and radial diagrams, as well as organization charts. To insert a diagram or an organization chart, click the Insert Diagram or Organization Chart button 🔄 on the Drawing toolbar or use the Diagram command on the Insert menu to open the Diagram Gallery, shown in Figure F-21. Select a diagram type in the Diagram Gallery, then click OK. The diagram appears in a drawing canvas with placeholder text, and the Diagram toolbar opens. The Diagram toolbar contains buttons for customizing and formatting the diagram, and for sizing and positioning the drawing canvas. Use the AutoFormat button on the Diagram toolbar to apply colors and shading to your diagram.

FIGURE F-21: Diagram Gallery

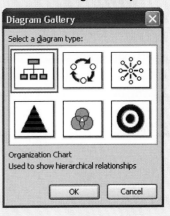

Practice

▼ CONCEPTS REVIEW

Label the elements shown in Figure F-22.

FIGURE F-22

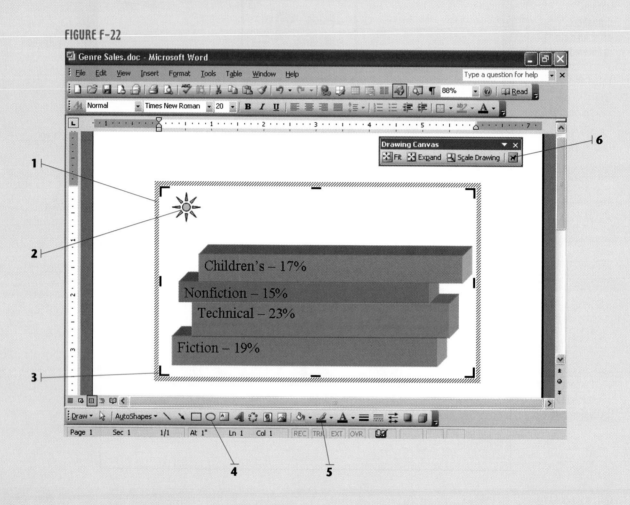

Match each term with the statement that best describes it.

7. Text box   **a.** A graphic object drawn using the tools on the Drawing toolbar

8. Drawing canvas   **b.** A workspace for creating graphics

9. AutoShape   **c.** A graphic that is composed of a series of small dots

10. Bitmap graphic   **d.** A graphic object that is a container for text and graphics

11. Chart   **e.** Dots that define color and intensity in a graphic

12. WordArt   **f.** A visual representation of numerical data

13. Pixels   **g.** A graphic object composed of specially formatted text

14. Vertex   **h.** The intersection of two line sections or the highest point on a curve

Select the best answer from the list of choices.

15. **Which button can be used to create a text box?**

    a. ▣   **c.** ◀

    b. **A**   **d.** ▣

16. **What must you do to a drawing canvas before moving it to a different location?**

    a. Scale the drawing canvas.

    b. Enter a precise position for the drawing canvas in the Format Drawing Canvas dialog box.

    c. Fit the drawing canvas to the contents.

    d. Wrap text around the drawing canvas.

17. **What do you drag to change an AutoShape's shape, but not its size or dimensions?**

    a. Sizing handle

    b. Rotate handle

    c. Cropping handle

    d. Adjustment handle

18. **Which method do you use to nudge a picture?**

    a. Select the picture, then press an arrow key.

    b. Select the picture, then drag a top, bottom, or side sizing handle.

    c. Select the picture, then drag a corner sizing handle.

    d. Select the picture, then drag it to a new location.

19. **If you want to create an oval that contains formatted text, what kind of graphic object would you create?**

    a. A text box

    b. WordArt

    c. A pie chart

    d. An AutoShape

20. **What style of text wrapping is applied to a text box by default?**

    a. Square

    b. In line with text

    c. In front of text

    d. Tight

▼ SKILLS REVIEW

1. **Add graphics.**

    a. Start Word, open the file WD F-3.doc from the drive and folder where your Data Files are located, then save it as **Farm Flyer**.

    b. Press [Ctrl][End], then insert the file **Farm.jpg** from the drive and folder where your Data Files are located.

    c. Select the photo, apply the Square text-wrapping style to it, then save your changes.

2. **Resize graphics.**

    a. Scroll down so that the graphic is at the top of your screen.

    b. Drag the lower-right sizing handle to enlarge the graphic proportionally so that it is about 4" wide and 3" high.

    c. Click the Crop button on the Picture toolbar.

    d. Drag the bottom-middle cropping handle up approximately 1", then click the Crop button again.

    e. Double-click the photo, click the Size tab, then change the width of the photo to 6". (*Hint*: Make sure the Lock aspect ratio check box is selected.)

    f. Save your changes.

3. Position graphics.

a. Drag the photo up so that its top is aligned with the top margin.

b. Double-click the photo, click the Layout tab, then click Advanced.

c. On the Picture Position tab, change the horizontal alignment to centered relative to the margins.

d. In the Vertical section, change the absolute position to 2" below the margin.

e. On the Text Wrapping tab, change the wrapping style to Top and bottom, change the Top measurement to 2", then change the Bottom measurement to .3".

f. Click OK to close the Advanced Layout and Format Picture dialog boxes, then save your changes.

4. Create text boxes.

a. Change the zoom level to Whole Page, then draw a 1.5" x 6" text box at the bottom of the page. (*Note*: Do not draw the text box in the drawing canvas if it opens.)

b. Change the zoom level to Page Width, type **Mountain Realty** in the text box, format the text in 18-point Arial, bold, then center it in the text box.

c. Press [Enter], type **603-555-3466**, press [Enter], type **www.mountainrealty.com**, then format the two lines of text in 11-point Arial, bold.

d. Resize the text box to be 1" high and 4" wide, then move it to the lower-left corner of the page, aligned with the left and bottom margin.

e. Fill the text box with Blue-Gray, change the font color of the text to White, then remove the line from around the text box.

f. With the text box selected, click Draw on the Drawing toolbar, point to Change AutoShape, point to Basic Shapes, then click the Oval. (*Note*: Adjust the text size or oval size if necessary.)

g. Deselect the text box, then save your changes.

5. Create AutoShapes.

a. Place the insertion point in the paragraph of text above the oval, click AutoShapes on the Drawing toolbar, point to Basic Shapes, then click the Isosceles Triangle shape.

b. Draw an isosceles triangle in the drawing canvas, then fill it with Violet. (*Note*: The drawing canvas appears on a new page 2. You resize and position the drawing canvas after you finish drawing in it.)

c. Draw three more isosceles triangles in the drawing canvas, then fill them with Lavender, Blue-Gray, and Indigo.

d. Drag the triangles to position them so they overlap each other to look like mountains.

e. Draw a sun shape in the drawing canvas, fill it with Gold, then position it so it overlaps the tops of the mountains. Resize the sun if necessary.

f. Select the sun, click Draw on the Drawing toolbar, point to Order, then click Send to Back.

g. Use the Order commands to change the order of the triangles and the sun so that the shapes look like a mountain range with the sun setting behind it. Resize and reposition the shapes as necessary to create a mountain effect, then save your changes.

6. Use the drawing canvas.

a. Fit the drawing canvas to the mountain range graphic. (*Hint*: You might need to scroll the document to locate the drawing canvas after you fit the drawing canvas to it.)

b. Apply the Square text-wrapping style to the drawing canvas.

c. Click the Scale Drawing button, then resize the drawing canvas so the graphic is approximately 1.5" wide and 1" tall. Adjust the shapes in the drawing canvas if the graphic looks awkward after resizing it.

d. Change the zoom level to Whole Page, move the drawing canvas to the lower-right corner of the page, aligned with the right and bottom margins, then deselect the drawing canvas.

e. Save your changes, then press [Ctrl][Home] to move the insertion point to the top of the document (the beginning of the text).

7. Format WordArt.

  a. Insert a WordArt object, select any horizontal WordArt style, type **Farmhouse**, then click OK.

  b. Apply Square text wrapping to the WordArt object, then move it above the photograph if necessary.

  c. Resize the WordArt object to be 6" wide and 1.25" tall, then position it so it is centered between the margins and 1" below the top of the page.

  d. Open the WordArt Gallery, then change the style to the fifth style in the second row.

  e. Open the Format WordArt dialog box, open the Fill Effects dialog box, select the Preset color Nightfall, select any Shading style and Variant, then apply the settings to the WordArt object.

  e. Type **Contact** followed by your name in the document footer, center the text, then format it in 12-point Arial.

  f. Save your changes to the flyer, print a copy, then close the file.

8. Create charts.

  a. Open a new, blank document, then save it as **Realty Sales** to the drive and folder where your Data Files are located.

  b. Click the Center button, type **Mountain Realty 2006 Sales**, then format the text in 26-point Arial, bold.

  c. Press [Enter] twice, then insert a chart.

  d. Click the Chart Type list arrow on the Standard toolbar, then click Pie Chart. (*Hint*: Use the Toolbar Options button as needed to locate the Chart Type button.)

  e. Select the second and third rows in the datasheet, then press [Delete].

  f. Replace the data in the datasheet with the data shown in Figure F-23, then close the datasheet. (*Hint*: If the label in your datasheet is East, replace it with **Pie 1**.)

  g. Select the legend, click the Format Legend button, then change the placement of the legend to Bottom.

  h. Use the Chart Objects list arrow to select the Plot Area, open the Format Plot Area dialog box, then change the Border and Area patterns to None.

FIGURE F-23

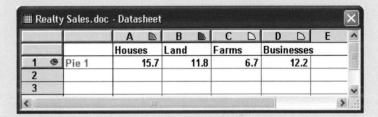

		A Houses	B Land	C Farms	D Businesses	E
1	Pie 1	15.7	11.8	6.7	12.2	
2						
3						

  i. Use the Chart Objects list arrow to select Series "Pie 1," open the Format Data Series dialog box, click the Data Labels tab, then make the data labels show the percentage.

  j. Resize the chart object proportionally so it is about 5" wide and 3" tall.

  k. Type **Prepared by** followed by your name centered in the document footer, save your changes, print the document, close the file, then exit Word.

▼ INDEPENDENT CHALLENGE 1

You are starting a business and need to design a letterhead. Your letterhead needs to include a logo, which you design using AutoShapes, as well as your name and contact information. Figure F-24 shows a sample letterhead.

  a. Start Word, open a new blank document, then save it as **Letterhead** to the drive and folder where your Data Files are located.

FIGURE F-24

Georgia J. McQueeney
Architect/Planner
54 Erie Street • Syracuse, NY 13219 • 315-555-3288 • gjmcq@earthlink.net

  b. Identify the nature of your business, then examine the shapes available on the AutoShapes menus and decide what kind of logo to create.

  c. Using pencil and paper, sketch a design for your letterhead. Determine the positions for your logo, name, address, and any other design elements you want to include. You will create and organize all the elements of your letterhead in a drawing canvas.

▼ INDEPENDENT CHALLENGE 1 (CONTINUED)

d. Using AutoShapes, create your logo in a drawing canvas. Use the buttons on the Drawing toolbar to enhance the logo with color, text, lines, shadows, and other effects.

e. Resize the logo and position it in the drawing canvas.

f. In the drawing canvas, create a text box that includes your name, address, and other important contact information. Format the text and the text box using the buttons on the Formatting and Drawing toolbars.

g. Resize the text box as necessary and position it in the drawing canvas.

h. Add to the drawing canvas any other design elements you want to include.

i. When you are satisfied with the layout of your letterhead in the drawing canvas, fit the drawing canvas to its contents, then resize the drawing canvas as necessary.

j. Wrap text around the drawing canvas, then position it on the page.

k. Save your changes, preview the letterhead, print a copy, close the file, then exit Word.

▼ INDEPENDENT CHALLENGE 2

You design ads for GoTroppo.com, a company that specializes in discounted travel to tropical destinations. Your next assignment is to design a full-page ad for a travel magazine. Your ad needs to contain a photograph of a vacation scene, shown in Figure F-25, the text "Your vacation begins here and now," and the Web address "www.gotroppo.com." If you are performing the ACE steps, your ad will also include a company logo.

FIGURE F-25

a. Start Word, open a new, blank document, then save it as **GoTroppo Ad** to the drive and folder where your Data Files are located.

b. Change all four page margins to .7".

c. Insert the file **Vacation.jpg** from the drive and folder where your Data Files are located, then examine the photo. Think about how you can use this photo effectively in your ad.

d. Using pencil and paper, sketch the layout for your ad. You can use AutoShapes, lines, text boxes, WordArt, and any other design elements in your ad to make it powerful and eye-catching.

e. Apply a text-wrapping style to the photograph to make it a floating graphic, then format the photograph as you planned. You can crop it, resize it, move it, and combine it with other design elements.

f. Using text boxes or WordArt, add the text **Your vacation begins here and now** and the Web address **www.gotroppo.com** to the ad.

g. Use the buttons on the Drawing and Formatting toolbars to format the graphic objects.

Advanced Challenge Exercise

- Using AutoShapes and a text box in a drawing canvas, create a logo that includes a sun setting over the ocean and the company name **gotroppo.com**. Figure F-26 shows a sample logo.
- Using the Fill Effects dialog box, fill the AutoShapes with color, gradients, patterns, or textures.
- Resize the drawing canvas to suit your needs, then move the logo to where you want it in the ad.

FIGURE F-26

h. Adjust the layout and design of the ad: adjust the colors, add or remove design elements, and resize and reposition the objects as necessary.

i. When you are satisfied with your ad, type your name in the document header, save your changes, print a copy, close the document, then exit Word.

▼ INDEPENDENT CHALLENGE 3

You are a graphic designer. The public library has hired you to design a bookmark for Literacy Week. Their only request is that the bookmark includes the words Literacy Week. You'll create three different bookmarks for the library.

a. Start Word, open a new, blank document, then save it as **Bookmarks** to the drive and folder where your Data Files are located.

b. Change all four page margins to .7", change the page orientation to landscape, and change the zoom level to Whole Page.

c. Draw three rectangles in a drawing canvas. Resize the rectangles to be 2.5" x 6.5" and move them so they do not overlap. Each rectangle will become a bookmark. (*Hint*: If you use the Format AutoShape dialog box to resize the rectangles, make sure the Lock aspect ratio check box is not selected.)

d. In the first rectangle, design a bookmark using AutoShapes.

e. In the second rectangle, design a bookmark using WordArt.

f. In the third rectangle, design a bookmark using clip art.

Advanced Challenge Exercise

- Fill one bookmark with a gradient, one with a texture, and one with a pattern. You might need to revise some aspects of the bookmarks you created in the previous steps.
- To one bookmark, add a photograph.
- To one bookmark, add curved, scribble, or freeform lines.

g. Use the buttons on the Drawing toolbar to format the bookmarks with fills, colors, lines, and other effects. Be sure to add the words Literacy Week to each bookmark.

h. Type your name in the document header, save your changes, print, close the document, then exit Word.

▼ INDEPENDENT CHALLENGE 4

One way to find graphic images to use in your documents is to download them from the Web. Many Web sites feature images that are in the public domain, which means they have no copyright restrictions and permission is not required to use the images. You are free to download these images and use them in your documents, although you must acknowledge the artist or identify the source. Other Web sites include images that are copyrighted and require written permission, and often payment, to use. Before downloading and using graphics from the Web, it's important to research and establish their copyright status and permission requirements. In this exercise you download photographs from the Web and research their copyright restrictions.

a. Start Word, open the file WD F-4.doc from the drive and folder where your Data Files are located, then save it as **Copyright Info**. This document contains a table that you will fill with the photos you find on the Web and the copyright restrictions for those photos.

b. Use your favorite search engine to search the Web for photographs. Use the keywords **photo archives** to conduct your search.

c. Find at least three Web sites that contain photos you could use in a document. Save a photo from each Web site to your computer, and note the URL and copyright restrictions. To save an image from a Web page, right-click the image, then click the appropriate command on the shortcut menu.

d. Insert the photos you saved from the Web in the Photo column of the table. Resize the photos proportionally so that they are no more than 1.5" tall or 1.5" wide. Wrap text around the photos and center them in the table cells.

e. For each photo, enter the URL and the copyright restrictions for the photo in the table. In the Copyright Restrictions column, indicate if the photo is copyrighted or in the public domain, and note the requirements for using that photo in a document.

f. Type your name in the document header, save your changes, print a copy, close the file, then exit Word.

Using the files WD F-5.doc and Surfing.jpg (found in the drive and folder where your Data Files are located), create the flyer shown in Figure F-27. Type your name in the header, save the flyer as **Surf Safe**, then print a copy.

FIGURE F-27

Surf safe

NEVER SURF ALONE

Follow the rules
All beginning surfers need to follow basic safety rules before heading into the waves. The key to safe surfing is caution and awareness.

Wear sunscreen
Sunscreen helps prevent skin cancer and aging of the skin. 30+ SPF broad spectrum sunscreen screens out both UVA and UVB rays and provides more than 30 times your natural sunburn protection. Apply sunscreen at least 15 minutes before exposing yourself to the sun, and reapply it every two hours or after swimming, drying with a towel, or excessive perspiration. Zinc cream also helps prevent sunburn and guards against harmful UV rays.

Dress appropriately
Wear a wet suit or a rash vest. Choose a wet suit that is appropriate for the water temperature. Rash vests help protect against UV rays.

Use a safe surfboard
A safe surfboard is a surfboard that suits your ability. Beginners need a big, thick surfboard for stability.

Learn how to escape rips
A rip current is a volume of water moving out to sea: the bigger the surf, the stronger the rips associated with it. Indicators of rips include:

- Brown water caused by stirred up sand
- Foam on the surface of the water that trails past the break
- Waves breaking on both sides of a rip current
- A rippled appearance between calm water
- Debris floating out to sea

If you are dragged out by a rip, don't panic! Stay calm and examine the rip conditions before trying to escape the current. Poor swimmers should ride the rip out from the beach and then swim parallel to the shore for 30 or 40 meters. Once you have escaped the rip, swim toward the shore where the waves are breaking. You can also probe with your feet to see if a sand bar has formed near the edge of the rip. Strong swimmers should swim at a 45 degree angle across the rip.

Study the surf
Always study the surf before going in. Select a safe beach with waves under 1 meter, and pick waves that are suitable for your ability.

Creating a Web Page

OBJECTIVES

Plan a Web page

Create a Web page

Format a Web page with themes

Illustrate a Web page with graphics

Save a document as a Web page

Add hyperlinks

Modify hyperlinks

Preview a Web page in a browser

If you have a SAM user profile, you may have access to hands-on instruction, practice, and assessment of the skills covered in this unit. Log in to your SAM account and go to your assignments page to see what your instructor has assigned.

Creating a Web page and posting it on the World Wide Web or an intranet is a powerful way to share information with other people. The Web page formatting features of Word allow you to easily create professional looking Web pages from scratch or to save an existing document in HTML format so it can be viewed using a browser. In this unit, you learn how to create a new Web page and how to save an existing document as a Web page. You also learn how to edit and format Web pages, create and modify hyperlinks, and preview a Web page in a browser. ▓▓▓▓ MediaLoft is sponsoring the Seattle Writers Festival, a major public event featuring prominent writers from around the world. You need to create a Web site for the Seattle Writers Festival to promote the event and provide information to the public. You plan to post the Web site on the World Wide Web.

Planning a Web Page

A **Web page** is a document that can be stored on a computer called a Web server and viewed on the World Wide Web or on an intranet using a **browser**, a software program used to access and display Web pages. A **Web site** is a group of associated Web pages that are linked together with hyperlinks. Before creating a Web page or a Web site, it's important to plan its content and organization. The **home page** is the main page of a Web site, and the first Web page viewers see when they visit a site. Usually, it is the first page you plan and create. ◼◼◼◼◼ The Seattle Writers Festival Web site will include a home page that serves both as an introduction to the festival and as a table of contents for the other Web pages in the site. Before creating the home page, you identify the content you want to include, plan the organization of the Web site, and sketch the design for each Web page.

DETAILS

- **Identify the goal of the Web site**

  A successful Web site has a clear purpose. For example, it might promote a product, communicate information, or facilitate a transaction. Your Web site will communicate information about the Seattle Writers Festival to the public.

QUICK TIP

Take care to limit the text and graphics on each Web page to those that help you meet your specific goal.

- **Sketch the Web site**

  Identify the information you want to include on each Web page, sketch the layout and design of each Web page, and map the links between the pages in the Web site. A well-designed Web site is visually interesting and easy for viewers to use. Figure G-1 shows a sketch of the Seattle Writers Festival Web site.

- **Create each Web page and save it in HTML format**

  You can create a Web page from scratch in Word or convert an existing document to a Web page. When you create a Web page in Word, you save it in HTML format. **HTML** (Hypertext Markup Language) is the programming language used to describe how each element of a Web page should appear when viewed with a browser. You will use a blank Web page template to create the home page. You will create the Program of Events Web page by saving an existing document in HTML format. Files saved in HTML format can be recognized by their .htm, .html, .mht, or .mhtml file extension.

QUICK TIP

If you intend to publish to the Web, filenames should use all lowercase letters and include no special characters or blank spaces. Valid characters include letters, numbers, and the underscore character.

- **Determine the file-naming convention to use**

  Different operating systems place various restrictions on Web site filenames. Many Web page designers follow the standard eight-dot-three file-naming convention, which specifies that a filename have a maximum of eight characters followed by a period and a three-letter file extension—mypage.htm or chap_1.htm, for example. You will use the eight-dot-three naming convention for your Web pages.

- **Format each Web page**

  You can use the standard Word formatting features to enhance Web pages with fonts, backgrounds, graphics, lines, tables, and other format effects. Word also includes visual themes that you can apply to Web pages to format them quickly. The look of a Web page has as much of an impact on the viewer as its content, so it's important to select fonts, colors, and graphics that complement the goal of your Web site. You plan to apply a theme that expresses the spirit of the writers festival to each Web page. A consistent look between Web pages is an important factor in Web site design.

- **Create the hyperlinks between Web pages**

  Hyperlinks are text or graphics that viewers can click to open a file, another Web page, or an e-mail message, or that viewers can click to jump to a specific location in the same file. Hyperlinks are commonly used to link the pages of a Web site to each other. You will add hyperlinks that link the home page to other Web pages in your Web site. You will also add links from the home page to other Web sites on the Internet and to an e-mail message to MediaLoft.

- **View the Web site using a browser**

  Before publishing your Web site to the Web or an intranet, it's important to view your Web pages in a browser to make sure they look and work as you intended. You will use the Web Page Preview feature to check the formatting of each Web page in your browser and to test the hyperlinks.

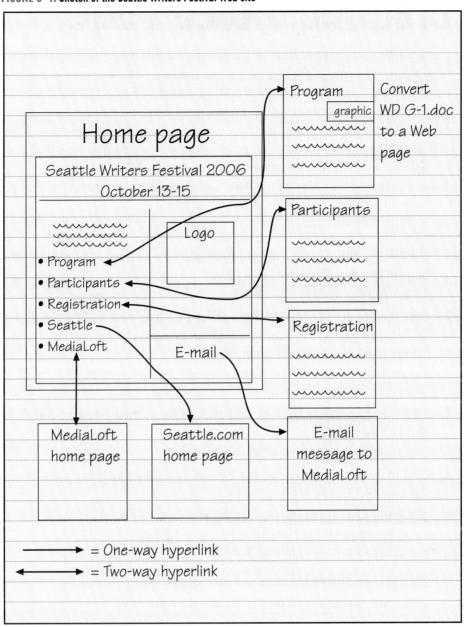

Clues to Use

Choosing a Web page file format

When you save a document as a Web page in Word, you save it in one of several HTML formats, which ensures the HTML codes are embedded in the file. You have the option of saving the document in Single File Web Page (.mht or .mhtml) format or in Web Page (.htm or .html) format. In a single file Web page, all the elements of the Web page, including the text and graphics, are saved together in a single MIME encapsulated aggregate HTML (MHTML) file, making it simple to publish your Web page or send it via e-mail. By contrast, if you choose to save a Web page as an .htm file, Word automatically creates a supporting folder in the same location as the .htm file. This folder has the same name as the .htm file plus the suffix _files, and it houses the supporting files associated with the Web page. For example, when you create a new Web page or save an existing document as an .htm file, each graphic—including the bullets, background textures, horizontal lines, and other graphics included on the Web page—is automatically converted to a GIF or JPEG format file and saved in the supporting folder. Be aware that if you copy or move a Web page saved in .htm format to a different location, it's important that you copy or move the supporting folder (and all the files in it) along with the .htm file, otherwise the links between the .htm file and the supporting files may be broken. If a browser cannot locate the graphic files associated with a Web page, the browser displays a placeholder (often a red X) instead of a graphic. By default, Word saves a Web page as a single file Web page using the .mht file extension.

Creating a Web Page

Creating a Web page involves creating a document that uses HTML formatting. HTML places codes, called **tags**, around the elements of a Web page to describe how each element should appear when viewed with a browser. When you create a Web page in Word, you use the usual Word buttons and commands to edit and format the text, graphics, and other elements, and Word automatically inserts the HTML tags for you. A quick way to create a new Web page is to start with the blank Web page template and add text and graphics to it. Because text and graphics align and position differently on Web pages than in Word documents, it's helpful to use a table to structure the layout of a Web page. ██████ You begin by creating the home page. You start with a new blank Web page, insert a table to structure the layout of the home page, add text, and then save the Web page in single file Web Page format.

STEPS

1. **Start** Word, **click** Create a new document **in the Getting Started task pane, then click** Web page **in the New Document task pane**
   A blank Web page opens in the document window in Web Layout view.

2. **Click the** Zoom list arrow **on the Standard toolbar, click** 100% **if necessary, click the** Insert Table button ▦ **on the Standard toolbar, point to the** second box **in the third row of the grid to create a 3 x 2 Table, then click**
   A table with three rows and two columns is inserted. After you finish using the table to help lay out the design of the Web page, you will remove the table borders.

3. **Select the** two cells **in the first row, click** Table **on the menu bar, click** Merge Cells, **then deselect the row**
   Two cells in the first row merge to become a single cell.

4. **Click in the first row, type** Seattle Writers Festival 2006, **press** [Enter] **twice, type** October 13-15, **then press** [Enter]

5. **Select the** two cells **in the second and third rows of the first column, click** Table **on the menu bar, click** Merge Cells, **then deselect the cell**
   The two cells in the first column merge to become a single cell.

6. **Type the text shown in Figure G-2 in the table cells**

7. **Click the** Save button 🖫 **on the Standard toolbar**
   The Save As dialog box opens. Word assigns a default page title and filename for the Web page and indicates Single File Web Page (*.mht; *mhtml) as the Save as type. If you prefer to save the Web page as an .htm file with a supporting folder for the associated files, click the Save as type list arrow, and then click Web Page (*.htm, *.html).

8. **Click** Change Title, **type** Seattle Writers Festival - Home (Your Name) **in the Set Page Title dialog box, then click** OK
   The page title appears in the title bar when the Web page is viewed with a browser. It's important to assign a page title that describes the Web page for visitors.

9. **Drag to select** Seattle Writers Festival 2006.mht **in the File name text box, type** swfhome, **use the** Save in list arrow **to navigate to the drive and folder where your Data Files are located, then compare your Save As dialog box with Figure G-3**
   The filename appears in the title bar when the Web page is viewed in Word.

10. **Click** Save
    The filename swfhome.mht appears in the title bar. Depending on your Windows settings, the file extension may or may not appear after the filename.

FIGURE G-2: Web page in Web Layout view

New Web
Page
button

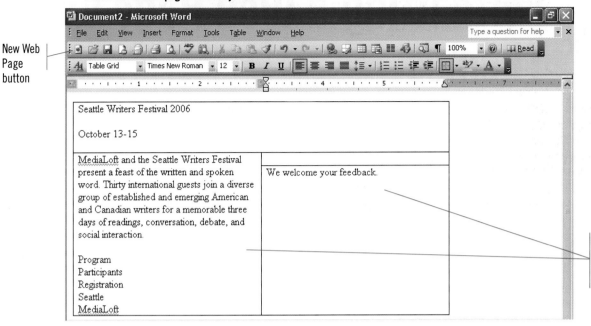

Type the text
in these
table cells in
your table

FIGURE G-3: Save As dialog box

Page title of Web
page (yours will
include your name)

Filename of
Web page

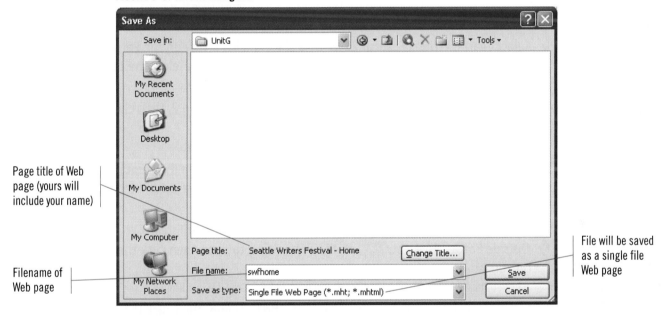

File will be saved
as a single file
Web page

Clues to Use

Adding frames to a Web page

Many Web pages you visit on the Internet include frames for display-ing fixed information. A **frame** is a section of a Web page window in which a separate Web page can be displayed. Frames commonly contain hyperlinks and other navigation elements that help visitors browse a Web site. A header that remains at the top of the screen while visitors browse a Web site is one example of a frame; a left col-umn that contains hyperlinks to each page in the Web site and stays on the screen while readers visit different pages is another example. You can add a frame to a Web page by pointing to Frames on the Format menu, and then clicking the type of frame you want to add.

Click New Frames Page to open the Frames toolbar, which you can use to select a location (left, right, above, or below) for a new, empty frame. Alternately, if you have applied heading styles to text in the current Web page, you can click Table of Contents in Frame to create a frame that includes hyperlinks to each heading in the Web page. Once you have created a frames page, you can resize the frames by dragging a frame border. To hide or show the frame bor-ders or specify which page first appears in a frame, point to Frames on the Format menu, click Frame Properties, and then change the settings in the Frame Properties dialog box.

Formatting a Web Page with Themes

Word includes a multitude of themes that you can apply to Web pages to quickly give them an attractive and consistent look. A **theme** is a set of complementary design elements that you can apply to Web pages, e-mail messages, and other documents that are viewed on screen. Themes include Web page backgrounds, styles for headings and hyperlinks, picture bullets, horizontal lines, table borders, and other specially designed formats that work well together. To apply a theme to a Web page, you use the Theme command on the Format menu. ▀▀▀▀▀ You apply a theme to the Web page, format the text using the theme styles, and add a horizontal line and bullets. You then experiment with alternate themes to find a design that more closely matches the character of the Writers Festival.

STEPS

1. **Click Format on the menu bar, click Theme, then click Blends in the Choose a Theme list box**
   A preview of the Blends theme appears in the Theme dialog box, as shown in Figure G-4. The theme includes a background and styles for text, hyperlinks, bullet characters, and horizontal lines.

2. **Click OK**
   The theme background is added to the Web page and the Normal style that comes with the theme is applied to the text.

QUICK TIP

To create a custom background, point to Background on the Format menu. For a solid color background, select a standard color or click More Colors. For a background with a gradient, texture, pattern, or picture, click Fill Effects.

3. **Select Seattle Writers Festival 2006, click the Style list arrow on the Formatting toolbar, click Heading 1 in the Style list, then click the heading to deselect the text**
   The Heading 1 style—16-point Trebuchet MS bold—is applied to the heading text.

4. **Select October 13-15, click the Style list arrow, click Heading 2, then click the date to deselect the text**
   The Heading 2 style—14-point Trebuchet MS—is applied to the date text.

5. **Select the heading and the date, click the Center button ≣ on the Formatting toolbar, move the pointer over the table, click the table move handle ⊞ to select the table, then click ≣**
   The heading, date, and table are centered on the Web page.

QUICK TIP

To change the size or alignment of a line, double-click the line to open the Format Horizontal Line dialog box, then adjust the settings on the Horizontal Line tab.

6. **Place the insertion point in the blank line between the heading and the date, click the Outside Border list arrow ▦▾ on the Formatting toolbar, then click the Horizontal Line button ≣**
   A horizontal line formatted in the theme design is added below the heading.

7. **Select the five-line list at the bottom of the first column, then click the Bullets button ☰ on the Formatting toolbar**
   The list is formatted using bullets from the Blends theme design.

QUICK TIP

Backgrounds are visible only in Web Layout view and do not print.

8. **Click Format on the menu bar, click Theme, scroll down the Choose a Theme list box, click Pixel, then click OK**
   The background and the text, line, and bullet styles applied to the Web page change to the designs used in the Pixel theme. You do not need to reapply the styles to a Web page when you change its theme.

9. **Select Seattle Writers Festival 2006, click the Font Size list arrow on the Formatting toolbar, click 26, click the Font Color list arrow ▲▾ on the Formatting toolbar, click Indigo, deselect the text, then save your changes**
   The font size of the heading is increased and the color changes to Indigo. Once you have applied styles to text you can customize the format to suit your purpose. Compare your Web page with Figure G-5.

FIGURE G-4: Blends theme in the Theme dialog box

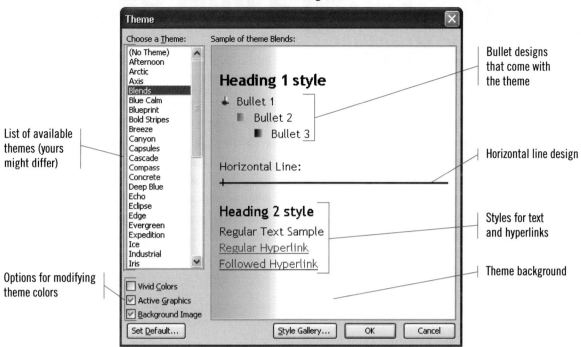

List of available themes (yours might differ)

Options for modifying theme colors

Bullet designs that come with the theme

Horizontal line design

Styles for text and hyperlinks

Theme background

FIGURE G-5: Pixel theme applied to the Web page

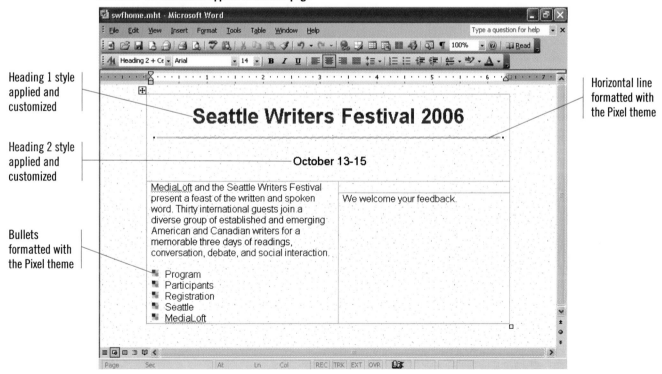

Heading 1 style applied and customized

Heading 2 style applied and customized

Bullets formatted with the Pixel theme

Horizontal line formatted with the Pixel theme

Illustrating a Web Page with Graphics

You can illustrate your Web pages with pictures, clip art, WordArt, text boxes, AutoShapes, and other graphic objects. When you insert a graphic on a Web page, it is inserted as an inline graphic and you must apply text wrapping to be able to move it independently of the line of text. Floating graphics align and position differently on Web pages than in Word documents, however, because browsers do not support the same graphic-formatting options as Word. For example, a floating graphic with square text wrapping can only be left- or right-aligned on a Web page, whereas you can position a floating graphic anywhere in a Word document. For this reason, it's important to use Web Layout view to position graphics on a Web page. If you want to position floating graphics or text precisely on a Web page, you can create a table and then insert the text or graphics in the table cells. ![icon] You want the MediaLoft logo to appear to the right of center on the Web page. You insert the logo in the blank cell in the table, and then adjust the table formatting to make the Web page attractive.

STEPS

1. **Place the insertion point in the blank cell in the second column of the table, click** Insert **on the menu bar, point to** Picture**, then click** From File
   The Insert Picture dialog box opens.

2. **Use the** Look in list arrow **to navigate to the drive and folder where your Data Files are located, click the file** mloft.jpg**, then click** Insert
   The logo is inserted in the cell as an inline graphic.

3. **Click the** logo **to select it, click the** Center button ![icon] **on the Formatting toolbar, press** [→]**, then press** [Enter]
   The graphic is centered in the table cell and a blank line is inserted under the logo.

4. **Position the pointer over the** border **between the first and second columns until the pointer changes to** ++++**, then drag the border to approximately the** 4 ¼" mark **on the horizontal ruler**
   The first column widens and the second column narrows. The logo remains centered in the table cell.

5. **Select** We welcome your feedback.**, click** ![icon]**, then click in the table to deselect the text**
   The text is centered in the table cell, as shown in Figure G-6. In Web Layout view, text and graphics are positioned as they are in a Web browser.

6. **Click the** table move handle ![icon] **to select the table, click the** Horizontal Line list arrow ![icon] **on the Formatting toolbar, click the** No Border button ![icon]**, deselect the table, then save your changes**
   Removing the table borders masks that the underlying structure of the Web page is a table, as shown in Figure G-7. The text on the left is now a wide column and the logo and text under the logo are positioned to the right of center. By inserting text and graphics in a table, you can position them exactly where you want.

FIGURE G-6: Logo and text centered in the second column

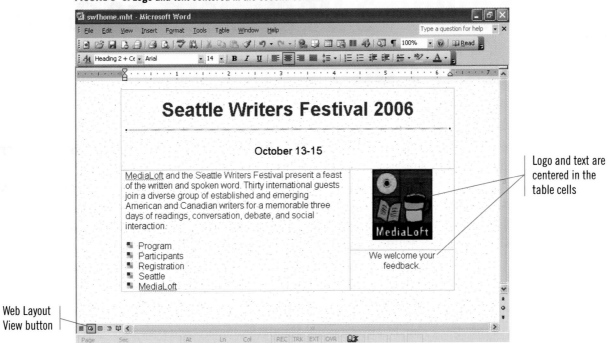

Logo and text are centered in the table cells

Web Layout View button

FIGURE G-7: Web page with table borders removed

Table move handle

Clues to Use

Adding alternate text for graphics

Graphics can take a long time to appear on a Web page. Some people turn off the display of graphics in their browsers so that they can download and view Web pages more quickly. If you don't want visitors to your Web page to see empty space in place of a graphic, you can add alternate text to appear on the Web page instead of the graphic. Alternate text appears in some browsers while the graphic is loading, and is used by search engines to find Web pages. To add alternate text to a Web page, select the graphic, and then click the Picture command on the Format menu. On the Web tab in the Format Picture dialog box, type the text you want to appear in lieu of the graphic, and then click OK.

Saving a Document as a Web Page

When you save an existing document as a Web page, Word converts the content and formatting of the Word file to HTML and displays the Web page as it will appear in a browser. Any formatting that is not supported by Web browsers is either converted to similar supported formatting or removed from the Web page. For example, if you save a document that contains a floating graphic in HTML format, the graphic will be left- or right-aligned on the Web page. Table G-1 describes several common formatting elements that are not supported by Web browsers. To save a document as a Web page, you use the Save as Web Page command on the File menu. You want to add a Web page that includes the festival program of events to your Web site. Rather than create the Web page from scratch, you convert an existing document to HTML format. You then adjust the formatting of the new Web page and apply the Pixel theme.

STEPS

QUICK TIP

To create a Web page that is compatible with a specific browser, click Tools on the menu bar, click Options, click the General tab, click Web Options, then select from the options on the Browsers tab in the Web Options dialog box.

1. **Open the file WD G-1.doc from the drive and folder where your Data Files are located, click the Zoom list arrow on the Standard toolbar, then click Two Pages**

   The document opens in Print Layout view, as shown in Figure G-8. Notice that the document is two pages long, the text is formatted in three columns, and the graphic on the first page is centered.

2. **Click File on the menu bar, click Save as Web Page, click Change Title, type Seattle Writers Festival – Program of Events (Your Name) in the Set Page Title dialog box, click OK, select WD G-1.mht in the Filename text box, type swfevent, then click Save**

   A dialog box opens and informs you that browsers do not support some of the formatting features of the document, including that the floating graphic will be left- or right-aligned in the Web page.

TROUBLE

If the Web page appears in a different view, click the Web Layout View button on the horizontal scroll bar.

3. **Click Continue**

   A copy of the document is saved in HTML format with the filename "swfevent" and the page title "Seattle Writers Festival – Program of Events (Your Name)." The Web page appears in Web Layout view. Notice that the graphic is now left-aligned on the Web page.

4. **Click the Zoom list arrow on the Standard toolbar, click 100% if necessary, then scroll to the bottom of the Web page**

   The text is now formatted in a single column, there are no margins on the Web page, and the document is one long page.

5. **Press [Ctrl][Home], double-click the graphic to open the Format Picture dialog box, click the Size tab, select 3.76 in the Height text box, type 2, then click OK**

   The size of the graphic is reduced.

QUICK TIP

To be able to position a graphic precisely on a Web page, you must insert the graphic in a table or make it an inline graphic.

6. **Drag the graphic to the upper-right corner of the Web page, then deselect the graphic**

   The graphic jumps into place in the upper-right corner when you release the mouse button.

7. **Click Format on the menu bar, click Theme, click Pixel in the Choose a Theme list box, click OK, then save your changes**

   The Pixel theme is applied to the Web page, giving it a look that is consistent with the home page. Notice that the bullet characters change to the bullet design included with the theme. The font of the body text also changes to the Normal style font used in the theme (12-point Arial). Compare your Web page with Figure G-9.

FIGURE G-8: Word document in Print Layout view

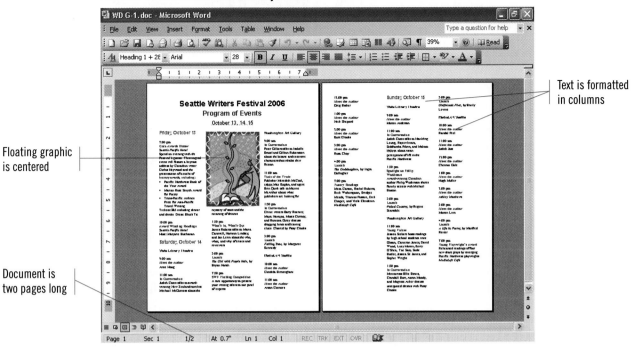

Floating graphic is centered

Document is two pages long

Text is formatted in columns

FIGURE G-9: Web page in Web Layout view

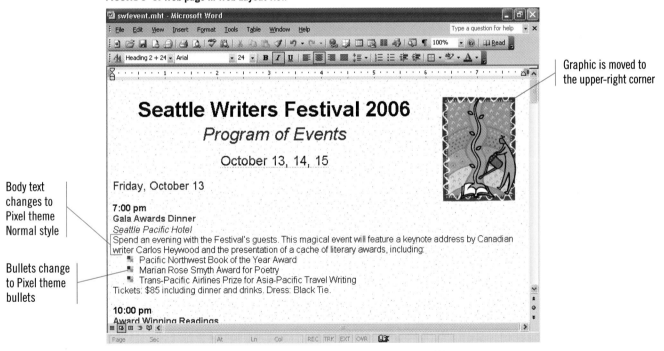

Graphic is moved to the upper-right corner

Body text changes to Pixel theme Normal style

Bullets change to Pixel theme bullets

TABLE G-1: Word features that are not supported by Web browsers

feature	result when viewed with a browser
Character formatting	Shadow text becomes bold; small caps become all caps; embossed, engraved, and outline text becomes solid; character scale changes to 100%; and drop caps are removed
Paragraph formatting	Indents are removed, tabs might not align correctly, and border and shading styles might change
Page layout	Margins, columns, page numbers, page borders, and headers and footers are removed; all footnotes are moved to the end of the document
Graphics	Floating graphics, including pictures, AutoShapes, text boxes, and WordArt, are left- or right-aligned
Tables	Decorative cell borders become box borders, diagonal borders are removed, vertical text is changed to horizontal

Adding Hyperlinks

Hyperlinks allow readers to link (or "jump") to a Web page, an e-mail address, a file, or a specific location in a document. When you create a hyperlink in a document, you select the text or graphic you want to use as a hyperlink and then specify the location you want to jump to when the hyperlink is clicked. You create hyperlinks using the Insert Hyperlink button on the Standard toolbar. Text that is formatted as a hyperlink appears as colored, underlined text. To make navigating the Events Web page easier, you create hyperlinks that jump from the dates in the third line of the Web page to the schedule for those dates farther down the Web page. You then insert several hyperlinks on your home page: one to link to the Events Web page, one to link to the Seattle.com Web site on the Internet, and one to link to an e-mail message to MediaLoft.

STEPS

1. **Select 15 in the third line of the Events Web page, then click the Insert Hyperlink button** 🖳 **on the Standard toolbar**

   The Insert Hyperlink dialog box opens. You use this dialog box to specify the location of the Web page, file, e-mail address, or position in the current document you want to jump to when the hyperlink—in this case, the text "15"—is clicked.

2. **Click Place in This Document in the Link to section**

   All the headings in the Web page are displayed in the dialog box, as shown in Figure G-10. In this context, a "heading" is any text to which a heading style has been applied.

> **QUICK TIP**
> Press [Ctrl] and click any hyperlink in Word to follow the hyperlink.

3. **Click Sunday, October 15 in the Select a place in this document section, then click OK**

   The selected text, "15", is formatted in blue and underlined, the hyperlink style when the Pixel theme is applied. When the Web page is viewed in a browser, clicking the 15 hyperlink jumps the viewer to the heading "Sunday, October 15" farther down the Web page.

4. **Select 14, click** 🖳, **click Saturday, October 14 in the Insert Hyperlink dialog box, click OK, select 13, click** 🖳, **click Friday, October 13, click OK, save your changes, then close the file**

   The numbers 14 and 13 are formatted as hyperlinks to the headings for those dates in the Web page. After you save and close the file, the home page appears in the document window.

5. **Select Program in the bulleted list, click** 🖳, **click Existing File or Web Page in the Link to section, use the Look in list arrow to navigate to the drive and folder where your Data Files are located, then click swfevent.mht**

   The filename swfevent.mht appears in the Address text box, as shown in Figure G-11.

> **QUICK TIP**
> To create a ScreenTip that appears in a browser, click ScreenTip in the Insert Hyperlink dialog box, then in the Set Hyperlink ScreenTip dialog box, type the text you want to appear.

6. **Click OK**

   "Program" is formatted as a hyperlink to the Program of Events Web page. If you point to a hyperlink in Word, the address of the file or Web page it links to appears in a ScreenTip.

7. **Select Seattle in the list, click** 🖳, **type www.seattle.com in the Address text box in the Insert Hyperlink dialog box, then click OK**

   As you type the Web address, Word automatically adds "http://" in front of "www." A Web address is also called a **URL**, which stands for Uniform Resource Locator. The word "Seattle" is formatted as a hyperlink to the Seattle.com Web site on the Internet.

> **QUICK TIP**
> By default, Word automatically creates a hyperlink to an e-mail address or URL when you type the address or URL in a document or Web page.

8. **Select feedback under the logo, click** 🖳, **then click E-mail Address in the Link to section of the Insert Hyperlink dialog box**

   The Insert Hyperlink dialog box changes so you can create a link to an e-mail message.

9. **Type swf@media-loft.com in the E-mail address text box, type Seattle Writers Festival in the Subject text box, click OK, then save your changes**

   The word "feedback" is formatted as a hyperlink, as shown in Figure G-12.

FIGURE G-10: Creating a hyperlink to a heading

Create a hyperlink to a Web page or file

Create a hyperlink to a location in the current file

Create a hyperlink to a new blank document

Create a hyperlink to an e-mail address

Text selected to be formatted as a hyperlink

These headings in the document are formatted with heading styles

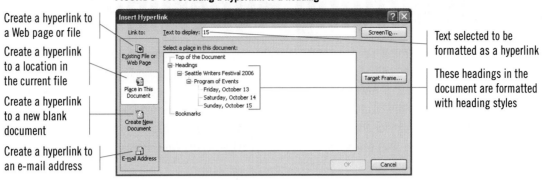

FIGURE G-11: Creating a hyperlink to a file

Click to change the default ScreenTip for the hyperlink

Click to browse the Internet for a specific URL to link to

File to jump to when the hyperlink is clicked

Files in the active drive or folder (yours might differ)

FIGURE G-12: Hyperlinks in the Web page

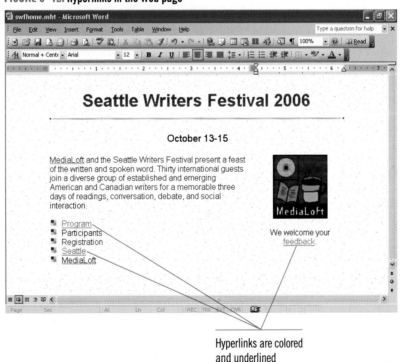

Hyperlinks are colored and underlined

Clues to Use

Pasting text as a hyperlink

You can quickly create a hyperlink to a specific location in any document by copying text from the destination location and pasting it as a hyperlink. To copy and paste text as a hyperlink, select the text you want to jump to, copy it to the Clipboard, place the insertion point in the location you want to insert the hyperlink, click Edit on the menu bar, then click Paste as Hyperlink. The text you copied is pasted and formatted as a hyperlink.

Modifying Hyperlinks

Over time, you might need to edit the hyperlinks on your Web pages with new information or remove them altogether. When you edit a hyperlink, you can change the hyperlink destination, the hyperlink text, or the ScreenTip that appears when a viewer points to the hyperlink. You can easily update or remove a hyperlink by right-clicking it and selecting the Edit Hyperlink or Remove Hyperlink command on the shortcut menu. ▄▄▄▄ You change the hyperlink text for the Program and Seattle hyperlinks to make them more descriptive. You also add a ScreenTip to the Seattle hyperlink so that visitors to the Seattle Writers Festival 2006 home page will better understand what the link offers.

STEPS

1. **Right-click Program, then click Edit Hyperlink on the shortcut menu**
   The Edit Hyperlink dialog box opens.

2. **Click after Program in the Text to display text box, press [Spacebar], type of Festival Events, then click OK**
   The hyperlink text changes to "Program of Festival Events" on the Web page.

3. **Right-click Seattle, click Edit Hyperlink, then click ScreenTip in the Edit Hyperlink dialog box**
   The Set Hyperlink ScreenTip dialog box opens, as shown in Figure G-13. Any text you type in this dialog box appears as a ScreenTip when a viewer points to the hyperlink.

4. **Type Hotels, dining, and entertainment in Seattle in the ScreenTip text box, then click OK**

5. **Click in front of Seattle in the Text to display text box in the Edit Hyperlink dialog box, type Visiting, press [Spacebar], click OK, then save your changes**
   The hyperlink text changes to "Visiting Seattle."

6. **Point to Visiting Seattle**
   The ScreenTip you added appears, as shown in Figure G-14.

Clues to Use

E-mailing a document from Word

Another way to share information online is to e-mail a Word document to others. Using the Send To command on the File menu, you can send a document directly from Word, either as an e-mail message or as an attachment to an e-mail message. To e-mail a document as a message, open the document, point to Send To on the File menu, and then click Mail Recipient. A message header opens above the document window. You can also click the E-mail button 📧 on the Standard toolbar to open a message header. Type the e-mail address(es) of the recipient(s) in the To and Cc text boxes in the message header, separating multiple addresses with a comma or a semicolon. When you are ready to send the file, click Send a Copy on the e-mail header toolbar.

To send a file as an attachment to an e-mail message, open the file, point to Send To on the File menu, and then click Mail Recipient (for Review) or Mail Recipient (as Attachment). When you select Mail Recipient (for Review), a message window opens that includes the request "Please review the attached document" in the body of the message. When you click Mail Recipient (as Attachment), a blank message window opens. Type the e-mail addresses in the To and Cc text boxes, any message you want in the message window, and then click the Send button on the message window toolbar to send the message. When you send a document from Word, your default e-mail program sends a copy of the document to each recipient.

FIGURE G-13: Set Hyperlink ScreenTip dialog box

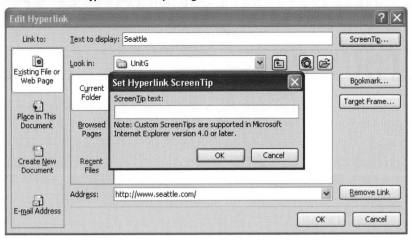

FIGURE G-14: ScreenTip and edited hyperlinks

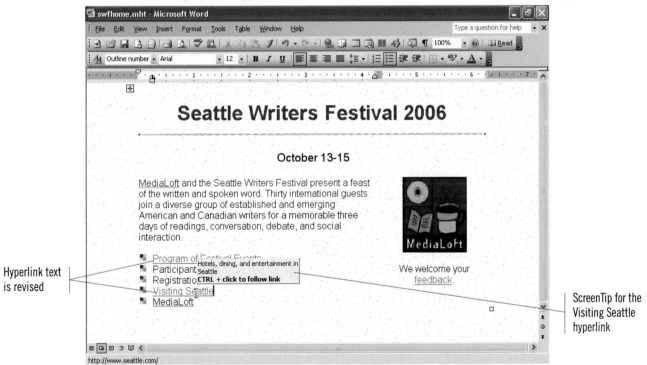

Hyperlink text is revised

ScreenTip for the Visiting Seattle hyperlink

Previewing a Web Page in a Browser

Before you publish Web pages to the Web or an intranet, it's important to preview the pages in a browser to make sure they look as you intended. You can use the Web Page Preview command on the File menu to open a copy of a Web page in your default browser. When previewing a Web page, you should check for formatting errors and test each hyperlink. To complete this lesson, you must have a Web browser installed on your computer. ████ You preview the Web pages in your browser and test the hyperlinks. After viewing the Program Web page, you use Word to adjust its formatting.

STEPS

1. **Click File on the menu bar, click Web Page Preview, then click the Maximize button on the browser title bar if necessary**
   The browser opens and the home page is displayed in the browser window, as shown in Figure G-15. Notice that the page title—Seattle Writers Festival - Home—appears in the browser title bar. Your page title will also include your name.

2. **Click the Program of Festival Events hyperlink**
   The Seattle Writers Festival – Program of Events Web page opens in the browser window.

3. **Click the 15 hyperlink**
   The browser jumps down the page and displays the program for Sunday, October 15 in the browser window.

4. **Click the Back button [⊙ Back] on the browser toolbar**
   The top of the Program of Events Web page is displayed in the browser window. The browser toolbar includes buttons for navigating between Web pages, searching the Internet, and printing and editing the current Web page.

5. **Click the Edit with Microsoft Office Word button [W] on the browser toolbar**
   The Program of Events Web page appears in a Word document window.

6. **Click the Zoom list arrow on the Standard toolbar, click 100% if necessary, select Tickets under the bulleted list, press and hold [Ctrl], select Dress in the same line, release [Ctrl], click the Bold button [B] on the Formatting toolbar, save your changes, then close the file**
   The home page appears in the Word document window. You want to check that your changes to the Program of Events Web page will preview correctly in the browser.

7. **Click File on the menu bar, click Web Page Preview, click the Program of Festival Events hyperlink, then click the Refresh button [⌐] on the browser toolbar**
   The revised Program of Events Web page appears in the browser, as shown in Figure G-16.

8. **Click the Print button [⌐] on the browser toolbar to print a copy of the swfevent Web page, click [⊙ Back], then point to the Visiting Seattle hyperlink**
   The ScreenTip you created for the hyperlink appears. The URL of the Seattle.com Web site also appears in the status bar. If you are connected to the Internet you can click the Visiting Seattle hyperlink to open the Seattle.com Web site in your browser window. Click the Back button on the browser toolbar to return to the Seattle Writers Festival home page when you are finished.

9. **Click the feedback hyperlink**
   An e-mail message that is automatically addressed to swf@media-loft.com with the subject "Seattle Writers Festival" opens in your default e-mail program.

10. **Close the e-mail message, click [⌐] to print the swfhome Web page, exit your browser, then exit Word**

Page title (yours
will include
your name)

If your default
browser is not
Internet Explorer 6,
your screens
might differ

Edit with Microsoft
Office Word button

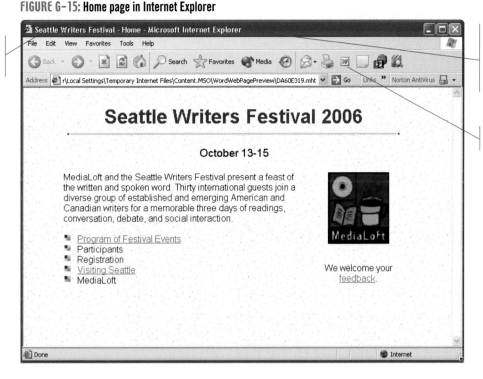

Word 2003

Print button

Text is bold

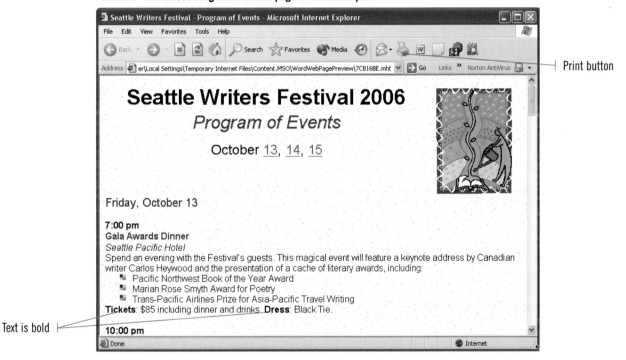

Clues to Use

Posting a Web site to the World Wide Web or an intranet

To make your Web site available to others, you must post (or publish) it to the Web or to a local intranet. Publishing a Web site involves copying the HTML files and any supporting folders and files to a Web server—either your Internet service provider's (ISPs) server, if you want to publish it to the Internet, or the server for your local intranet. Check with your ISP or your network administrator for instructions on how to post your Web pages to the correct server.

Practice

▼ CONCEPTS REVIEW

Label each element shown in Figure G-17.

FIGURE G-17

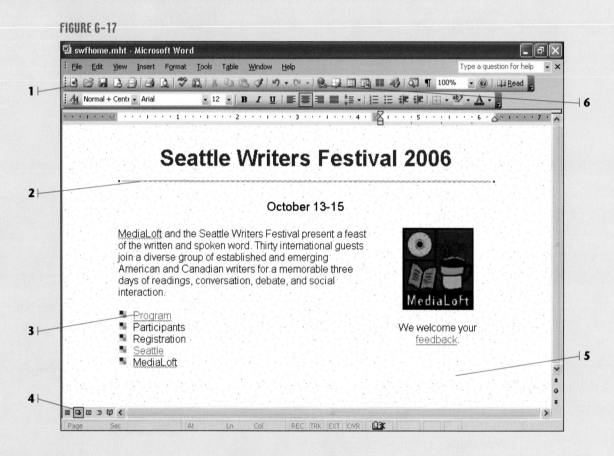

Match each term with the statement that best describes it.

7. **Hyperlink**
8. **Web page**
9. **Home page**
10. **HTML**
11. **Theme**
12. **Web site**
13. **Browser**
14. **URL**

a. A document that can be viewed using a browser

b. A group of associated Web pages

c. The address of a Web page on the World Wide Web

d. A programming language used to create Web pages

e. Text or a graphic that jumps the viewer to a different location when clicked

f. A set of common design elements that can be applied to a Web page

g. The main page of a Web site

h. A software program used to access and display Web pages

Select the best answer from the list of choices.

15. Which of the following is *not* a design element included in a theme?

  a. Bullet design

  b. Frame design

  c. Horizontal line style

  d. Web page background

16. Which of the following *cannot* be opened using a hyperlink?

  a. Files

  b. E-mail messages

  c. Web pages

  d. Support folders

17. Which of the following formats is supported by Web browsers?

  a. Inline graphics

  b. Columns of text

  c. Page numbers

  d. Headers and footers

18. What does using the Save as Web Page command accomplish?

  a. Converts the current file to HTML format

  b. Opens the current file in a browser

  c. Converts floating graphics to inline graphics

  d. Applies a Web theme to the current file

19. Where does the page title of a Web page appear?

  a. In the Word title bar

  b. On the home page

  c. In the browser title bar

  d. In the name of the supporting folder

20. Which of the following statements is false?

  a. A Web page saved as an .mht file does not need a supporting folder.

  b. When you save a document as a Web page, Word adds HTML tags to the file.

  c. You can use the Center button to center a floating graphic in Web Layout view.

  d. Hyperlink text is underlined.

▼ SKILLS REVIEW

1. Create a Web page.

  a. Study the sketch for the Web site devoted to literacy issues shown in Figure G-18.

  b. Start Word and create a blank Web page.

  c. Create a table with two columns and three rows, select the table, then AutoFit the table to fit the window. (*Hint:* Click Table on the menu bar, point to AutoFit, then click AutoFit to Window.)

  d. Type **Literacy Facts** in column 2, cell 1.

  e. Merge cells 2 and 3 in column 2, click Insert on the menu bar, click File, navigate to the drive and folder where your Data Files are located, select WD G-2.doc, then click Insert.

  f. In column 1, cell 3, type the following three-item list: **What you can do, ProLiteracy Worldwide, Contact us**.

  g. Save the file as a single file Web page to the drive and folder where your Data Files are located with the page title **Literacy Facts – Home** and the filename **literacy**.

2. Format a Web page with themes.

  a. Apply the Network theme to the Web page. (*Note:* Select a different theme if Network is not available to you.)

  b. Format Literacy Facts in the Heading 1 style, center the text, then press [Enter].

FIGURE G-18

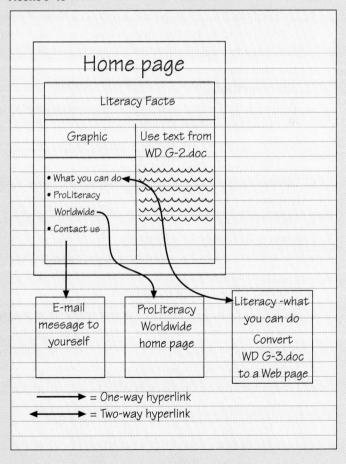

   c. Insert a horizontal line below the heading.

   d. Apply bullets to the list in column 1, cell 3, then save your changes.

3. Illustrate a Web page with graphics.

   a. In the blank cell in the first column, second row, insert the graphic file reader.gif from the drive and folder where your Data Files are located.

   b. Center the graphic in the cell, press [Enter], type **Literacy is not just reading and writing; the ability to perform basic math and solve problems is also important.**, press [Enter], then change the font size of the text to 10.

   c. Click Format on the menu bar, point to Background, click Fill Effects, click the Gradient tab, select the Two colors option button in the Colors section, click the Color 1 list arrow, click Gold, click the Color 2 list arrow, click Light Yellow, select any shading style and variant, then click OK.

   d. Select the table, remove the table borders, hide the gridlines, then save your changes.

4. Save a document as a Web page.

   a. Open the file WD G-3.doc from the drive and folder where your Data Files are located.

   b. Examine the document, then save it as a single file Web page with the page title **Literacy – what you can do** and the filename **whattodo**.

   c. Read the message about formatting changes, then click Continue.

   d. Apply the Network theme (or the theme you used with the Literacy page) to the Web page, then apply the Heading 1 style to the heading.

   e. Double-click the graphic, click the Layout tab, change its text-wrapping style to In line with text, then move it before Literacy in the heading.

   f. Change the background to a gold and light yellow gradient. (*Hint:* See Step 3c).

   g. Save your changes, then close the file.

5. Add hyperlinks.

   a. In the Literacy Facts file, select What you can do, then format it as a hyperlink to the whattodo.mht file.

   b. Format ProLiteracy Worldwide as a hyperlink to the Web address **www.proliteracy.org**.

   c. Format Contact us as a hyperlink to your e-mail address with the message subject **Literacy information**. (*Note:* If you do not have an e-mail address, skip this step.)

   d. Save your changes.

6. Modify hyperlinks.

   a. Right-click the Contact us hyperlink, click Edit Hyperlink, change the Text to display to your name, click OK, then type **For more information on literacy, contact** in front of your name on the Web page.

   b. Edit the ProLiteracy Worldwide hyperlink so that the ScreenTip says **Information on ProLiteracy Worldwide and links to literacy Web sites**.

   c. Edit the What you can do hyperlink so that the ScreenTip says **Simple actions you can take to help eliminate illiteracy**.

   d. Save your changes.

7. Preview a Web page in a browser.

   a. Preview the Literacy Facts Web page in your browser, test all the hyperlinks, print a copy of the Literacy Facts Web page, then close the browser.

   b. Open the whattodo.mht file in Word.

   c. Press [Ctrl][End], press [Enter], type **For more information, contact** followed by your name and a period, format your name as a hyperlink to your e-mail address with the subject line **Literacy Information**, then save your changes.

   d. Preview the Literacy - what you can do Web page in your browser, test the hyperlink, then print the page.

   e. Close the browser, close all open Word files, then exit Word.

▼ INDEPENDENT CHALLENGE 1

You have written a story about a recent hiking expedition you took and want to share it and some photos with your family and friends. You decide to create a Web page. Figure G-19 shows how you will arrange the photos.

a. Start Word, open a blank Web page, save the Web page as a single file Web page with the page title **Conquering Rising Wolf** and the filename **risewolf** to the drive and folder where your Data Files are located, then change the zoom level to 100% if necessary.

b. Insert a table with two columns and four rows, merge the two cells in the first row, merge the three cells in the second column, select the table, then AutoFit the table to fit the window. (*Hint*: Use the AutoFit command on the Table menu.)

c. Type **Conquering Rising Wolf** in the first row of the table, then press [Enter].

d. Click in the second column, then insert the file WD G-4.doc from the drive and folder where your Data Files are located. (*Hint:* Use the File command on the Insert menu.)

e. Click in the first blank cell in the first column, then insert the graphic file rwolf.jpg from the drive and folder where your Data Files are located.

Rising Wolf Mountain (elev. 9513 feet)

Derek enjoying the view

f. Press [Enter], then type **Rising Wolf Mountain (elev. 9513 feet)**.

g. In the last blank cell in the first column, insert the graphic file Derek.jpg from the drive and folder where your Data Files are located, then resize the photo proportionally to be the same width as the Rising Wolf Mountain photo.

h. Press [Enter], then type **Derek enjoying the view**.

i. Drag the border between the first and second columns left to approximately the 3¼" mark.

j. Apply a theme, then format the Web page using theme elements and other formatting features.

k. Select Glacier National Park in the first paragraph in the second column, format it as a hyperlink to the URL **www.nps.gov/glac/home.htm** with the ScreenTip **Glacier National Park Website Visitor Center**.

l. Press [Ctrl][End], press [Enter], type **E-mail** followed by your name, center the text, then format your name as a hyperlink to your e-mail address, if you have one. Type **Conquering Rising Wolf** as the message subject.

m. Resize the table rows and columns as necessary to make the Web page attractive, remove the borders from the table, save your changes, preview the Web page in your browser, then test the hyperlinks.

n. Switch to Word, make any necessary adjustments, save your changes, preview the Web page in your browser, print a copy, close the browser, close the file in Word, then exit Word.

INDEPENDENT CHALLENGE 2

You and your business partner have just started a mail-order business called Monet's Garden. You create a home page for your business. As your business grows, you plan to add additional pages to the Web site.

a. Start Word, then create a new frames page. (*Hint:* Point to Frames on the Format menu, then click New Frames Page.)

b. Click the New Frame Left button on the Frames toolbar, close the toolbar, then drag the frame border to the left so that the left frame is about one quarter the width of the Web page.

c. Save the frames page as a single file Web Page with the page title **Welcome to Monet's Garden** and the filename **monet**.

d. In the left frame, type **Welcome to Monet's Garden**, press [Enter] four times, then type **1-800-555-2837**.

e. Insert an appropriate clip art graphic between the two lines of text in the left frame. Resize the graphic to fit the frame. (*Hint:* You might need to enlarge the frame temporarily to resize the graphic.)

f. In the right frame, insert the text file WD G-5.doc from the drive and folder where your Data Files are located. (*Hint:* Click File on the Insert menu.)

g. Insert an appropriate clip art graphic in the empty cell in the right frame.

h. Add a solid color background to the right frame, then format the frame with lines, fonts, colors, shading, and any other formatting features.

INDEPENDENT CHALLENGE 2 (CONTINUED)

i. Resize the graphic and table as needed, then remove the table borders. (*Note:* You do not need to remove the borders from the nested table.)

j. At the bottom of the right frame, replace Your Name with your name, then format it as a hyperlink to the e-mail address **info@monetsgarden.com** with the subject **Product Information**.

k. Add a different solid color background to the left frame, then format the frame with lines, fonts, colors, and any other formatting features.

l. Adjust the formatting of the Web page to make it attractive and readable, then save your changes.

Advanced Challenge Exercise

■ Place the insertion point in the left frame, then open the Frame Properties dialog box. (*Hint:* Point to Frames on the Format menu.)

■ On the Borders tab, click the No borders option button, click the Show scroll bars in browser list arrow, click Never, then click OK.

■ Place the insertion point in the right frame, open the Frame Properties dialog box, set the scroll bar to show if needed, then save your changes.

m. Preview the Web page in your browser, test the hyperlink, adjust the formatting of the Web page as needed, then save your changes. (*Note:* Depending on your browser settings, the frames page might not preview correctly in your browser.)

n. Print a copy of the Web page, exit your browser, close the file, then exit Word.

▼ INDEPENDENT CHALLENGE 3

You are in charge of publicity for the Sydney Triathlon 2006 World Cup. One of your responsibilities is to create a Web site to provide details of the event. You have created the content for the Web pages as Word documents, and now need to save and format them as Web pages. Your Web site will include a home page and three other Web pages. One of the Web pages is shown in Figure G-20.

a. Start Word, open the file WD G-6.doc from the drive and folder where your Data Files are located, then save it as a single file Web page with the page title **Sydney Triathlon 2006 World Cup - Home** and the filename **tri_home**.

b. Apply the Slate or Breeze theme. (*Note:* Use a different theme if neither of these themes is available to you.)

c. Press [Ctrl][A], then change the font size to 10.

d. Apply the Heading 1 style to the heading Sydney Triathlon 2006 World Cup in the first row of the table, right-align the text, apply italic, select Triathlon 2006, then change the font color to a different color.

e. Apply the Heading 3 style to Welcome to the Sydney Triathlon 2006 World Cup! in the upper-left cell of the table, apply bold, then center the text.

f. Read the remaining text on the Web page, then format it with heading styles, fonts, font colors, and other formatting effects to make it look attractive. Preview the Web page in your browser.

FIGURE G-20

g. Remove the table borders, press [Ctrl][End], type your name, save your changes, then close the file.

▼ INDEPENDENT CHALLENGE 3

h. Open each file listed in Table G-2 from the drive and folder where your Data Files are located, save it as a single file Web Page with the page title and filename listed in the table, follow Steps b–g to format it using the same theme

and other formatting features you used to format the home page, then close the file.

i. In Word, open the tri_home.mht file, then change the zoom level to 100% if necessary.

j. Select Best Views, then format it as a hyperlink to the tri_view.mht file. Format Getting There and The Athletes as hyperlinks to the tri_get.mht and tri_athl.mht files, then save your changes.

k. Open each of the remaining three files—tri_view.mht, tri_get.mht, and tri_athl.mht—and format the text in the left column of each Web page as a hyperlink to the appropriate file. Save your changes, then close each Web page.

l. Be sure tri_home.mht is the active document. Preview the home page in your browser. Test each hyperlink on the home page and on the other Web pages. (If the hyperlinks do not work in your browser, test them in Word.)

m. Examine each Web page in your browser, make any necessary formatting adjustments in Word, print a copy of each Web page from your browser, then close your browser, close all open files, and exit Word.

▼ INDEPENDENT CHALLENGE 4

In this Independent Challenge you will create a Web page that provides information about you and your interests. Your Web page will include text, a graphic, and links to Web sites that you think will be useful to people who visit your Web page.

a. Start Word, open the file WD G-10.doc from the drive and folder where your Data Files are stored, save it as a single file Web page, include your name in the page title, and save it with the filename **my_page**.

b. At the top of the Web page, replace Your Name with your name.

c. Under the heading Contents, format each item in the list as a hyperlink to that heading in the Web page.

d. Under the heading Biographical Information, type at least one paragraph about your background and interests.

e. Under the heading Personal Interests, type a list of your hobbies and interests. Format this list as a bulleted list.

f. Use your favorite search engine to search for Web sites related to your interests. Write down the page titles and URLs of at least three Web sites that you think are worth visiting.

g. Under the heading Favorite Links, type the names of the three Web sites you liked. Format each name as a hyperlink to the Web site, and create a ScreenTip that explains why you think it's a good Web site.

h. Under the heading Contact Information, enter your e-mail address, Web site address, and telephone numbers, if any. Delete any headings that do not apply. Format your e-mail and Web addresses as hyperlinks to those addresses.

i. In each section, format the text Back to top as a hyperlink to your name at the top of the Web page.

j. Illustrate the Web page with a photo of yourself or another graphic. Use a clip art graphic if another graphic is not available to you. Create a table to position the graphic if necessary.

k. Apply a theme, then format the Web page with different formatting features such as bullets and colors.

l. Save your changes, preview the Web page, test each hyperlink, make adjustments, then save again.

Advanced Challenge Exercise

■ In Word, send a copy of the Web page to someone in an e-mail message.

■ In Word, send a copy of the Web page to someone for review as an attachment to an e-mail message.

■ Using the Web Options dialog box, save the Web page for a target browser, then post the Web page to the Web or an intranet if instructed to do so by your instructor.

m. Print a copy of the Web page, close the browser, close the file, then exit Word.

▼ VISUAL WORKSHOP

Create the Web pages shown in Figure G-21 using the graphic files rest.jpg, bridge.jpg, and studlamp.jpg, found on the drive and folder where your Data Files are located. Save the home page with the page title **Gallery Azul Home (Your Name)** and the filename **azulhome.mht**. Save the exhibit page with the page title **Gallery Azul Exhibit (Your Name)** and the filename **azulexhb.mht**. On the home page, create a hyperlink to the exhibit page and a hyperlink to the e-mail address **GalleryAzul@ptown.net**. On the Exhibit page, create a hyperlink to the home page. View the Web pages in your browser, then print a copy of each Web page.

FIGURE G-21

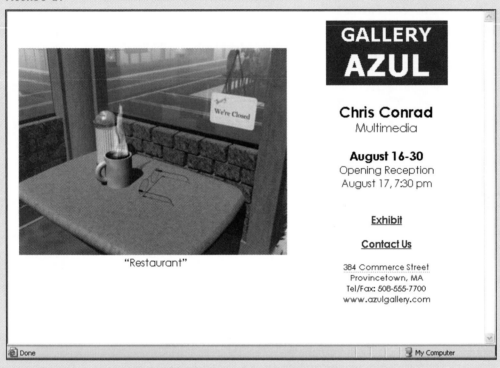

Merging Word Documents

OBJECTIVES

| Understand mail merge |
| Create a main document |
| Design a data source |
| Enter and edit records |
| Add merge fields |
| Merge data |
| Create labels |
| Sort and filter records |

If you have a SAM user profile, you may have access to hands-on instruction, practice, and assessment of the skills covered in this unit. Log in to your SAM account and go to your assignments page to see what your instructor has assigned.

A mail merge operation combines a standard document, such as a form letter, with customized data, such as a set of names and addresses, to create a set of personalized documents. You can perform a mail merge to create documents used in mass mailings, such as letters and labels. You also can use mail merge to create documents that include customized information, such as business cards. In this unit you learn how to use the Mail Merge task pane to set up and perform a mail merge. You need to send a welcome letter to the new members of the MediaLoft Coffee Club, a program designed to attract customers to the MediaLoft Café. You also need to send a brochure to all the members of the club. You use mail merge to create a personalized form letter and mailing labels for the brochure.

Understanding Mail Merge

When you perform a mail merge, you merge a standard Word document with a file that contains customized information for many individuals or items. The standard document is called the **main document**. The file with the unique data for individual people or items is called the **data source**. Merging the main document with a data source results in a merged document that contains customized versions of the main document, as shown in Figure H-1. The Mail Merge task pane steps you through the process of setting up and performing a mail merge. ▰▰▰ You use the Mail Merge task pane to create your form letters and mailing labels. Before beginning, you explore the steps involved in performing a mail merge.

DETAILS

- **Create the main document**

  The main document contains the text—often called **boilerplate text**—that appears in every version of the merged document. The main document also includes the merge fields, which indicate where the customized information is inserted when you perform the merge. You insert the merge fields in the main document after you have created or selected the data source. You use the Mail Merge task pane to create a main document using either the current document, a template, or an existing document.

- **Create a data source or select an existing data source**

  The data source is a file that contains the unique information for each individual or item. It provides the information that varies in every version of the merged document. A data source is composed of data fields and data records. A **data field** is a category of information, such as last name, first name, street address, city, or postal code. A **data record** is a complete set of related information for an individual or an item, such as one person's name and address. It is easiest to think of a data source file as a table: the header row contains the names of the data fields (the **field names**), and each row in the table is an individual data record. You can use the Mail Merge task pane to create a new data source, or you can merge a main document with an existing data source, such as a data source created in Word, an Outlook contact list, or an Access database.

- **Identify the fields to include in the data source and enter the records**

  When you create a new data source, you must first identify the fields to include. It's important to think of and include all the fields before you begin to enter data. For example, if you are creating a data source that includes addresses, you might need to include fields for a person's middle name, title, department name, or country, even though every address in the data source does not include that information. Once you have identified the fields and set up your data source, you are ready to enter the data for each record.

- **Add merge fields to the main document**

  A merge field is a placeholder that you insert in the main document to indicate where the data from each record should be inserted when you perform the merge. For example, in the location you want to insert a zip code, you insert a zip code merge field. The merge fields in a main document must correspond with the field names in the associated data source. Merge fields must be inserted, not typed, in the main document. The Mail Merge task pane provides access to the dialog boxes you use to insert merge fields.

- **Merge the data from the data source into the main document**

  Once you have established your data source and inserted the merge fields in the main document, you are ready to perform the merge. You can merge to a new file, which contains a customized version of the main document for each record in the data source, or you can merge directly to a printer, fax, or e-mail message.

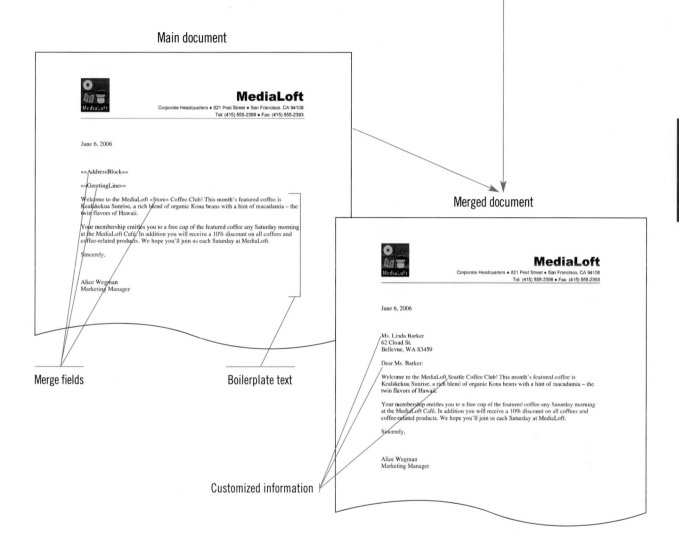

Data source document

Store	Title	First Name	Last Name	Address Line 1	City	State	Zip Code	Country
Seattle	Ms.	Linda	Barker	62 Cloud St.	Bellevue	WA	83459	US
Boston	Mr.	Bob	Cruz	23 Plum St.	Boston	MA	02483	US
Chicago	Ms.	Joan	Yateo	456 Elm St.	Chicago	IL	60603	US
Seattle	Ms.	Anne	Butler	48 East Ave.	Vancouver	BC	V6F 1AH	CANADA
Boston	Mr.	Fred	Silver	56 Pearl St.	Cambridge	MA	02139	US

Field name

Data record

Main document

MediaLoft
Corporate Headquarters • 821 Post Street • San Francisco, CA 94108
Tel: (415) 555-2398 • Fax: (415) 555-2393

June 6, 2006

««AddressBlock»»

««GreetingLine»»

Welcome to the MediaLoft «Store» Coffee Club! This month's featured coffee is Kealakekua Sunrise, a rich blend of organic Kona beans with a hint of macadamia – the twin flavors of Hawaii.

Your membership entitles you to a free cup of the featured coffee any Saturday morning at the MediaLoft Café. In addition you will receive a 10% discount on all coffees and coffee-related products. We hope you'll join us each Saturday at MediaLoft.

Sincerely,

Alice Wegman
Marketing Manager

Merge fields

Boilerplate text

Merged document

MediaLoft
Corporate Headquarters • 821 Post Street • San Francisco, CA 94108
Tel: (415) 555-2398 • Fax: (415) 555-2393

June 6, 2006

Ms. Linda Barker
62 Cloud St.
Bellevue, WA 83459

Dear Ms. Barker:

Welcome to the MediaLoft Seattle Coffee Club! This month's featured coffee is Kealakekua Sunrise, a rich blend of organic Kona beans with a hint of macadamia – the twin flavors of Hawaii.

Your membership entitles you to a free cup of the featured coffee any Saturday morning at the MediaLoft Café. In addition you will receive a 10% discount on all coffees and coffee-related products. We hope you'll join us each Saturday at MediaLoft.

Sincerely,

Alice Wegman
Marketing Manager

Customized information

Word 2003

Creating a Main Document

The first step in performing a mail merge is to create the main document—the file that contains the boiler-plate text. You can create a main document from scratch, save an existing document as a main document, or use a mail merge template to create a main document. The Mail Merge task pane walks you through the process of selecting the type of main document to create. ▓▓▓▓ You use an existing form letter for your main document. You begin by opening the Mail Merge task pane.

STEPS

1. **Start Word, click** Tools **on the menu bar, point to** Letters and Mailings, **then click** Mail Merge

   The Mail Merge task pane opens, as shown in Figure H-2, and displays information for the first step in the mail merge process: selecting the type of merge document to create.

2. **Make sure the** Letters option button **is selected, then click** Next: Starting document **to continue with the next step**

   The task pane displays the options for the second step: selecting the main document. You can use the current document, start with a mail merge template, or use an existing file.

3. **Select the** Start from existing document option button, **make sure** More files **is selected in the Start from existing list box, then click** Open

   The Open dialog box opens.

4. **Use the** Look in list arrow **to navigate to the drive and folder where your Data Files are located, select the file** WD H-1.doc, **then click** Open

   The letter that opens contains the boilerplate text for the main document. Notice the filename in the title bar is Document1. When you create a main document that is based on an existing document, Word gives the main document a default temporary filename.

5. **Click the** Save button 🖫 **on the Standard toolbar, then save the main document with the filename** Coffee Letter Main **to the drive and folder where your Data Files are located**

   It's a good idea to include "main" in the filename so that you can easily recognize the file as a main document.

6. **Click the** Zoom list arrow **on the Standard toolbar, click** Text Width, **select** April 9, 2006 **in the letter, type today's date, scroll down, select** Alice Wegman, **type your name, press** [Ctrl][Home], **then save your changes**

   The edited main document is shown in Figure H-3.

7. **Click** Next: Select recipients **to continue with the next step**

   You continue with Step 3 of 6 in the next lesson.

Clues to Use

Using a mail merge template

If you are creating a letter, fax, or directory, you can use a mail merge template to start your main document. Each template includes boiler-plate text, which you can customize, and merge fields, which you can match to the field names in your data source. To create a main document that is based on a mail merge template, click the Start from a template option button in the Step 2 of 6 Mail Merge task pane, then click Select template. In the Select Template dialog box, select a template on the Mail Merge tab, then click OK to create the document. Once you have created the main document, you can customize it with your own information: edit the boilerplate text, change the document format, or add, remove, or modify the merge fields. Before performing the merge, make sure to match the names of the address merge fields used in the template with the field names used in your data source. To match the field names, click the Match Fields button 🔳 on the Mail Merge toolbar, and then use the list arrows in the Match Fields dialog box to select the field name in your data source that corresponds to each address field component in the main document.

FIGURE H-2: Step 1 of 6 Mail Merge task pane

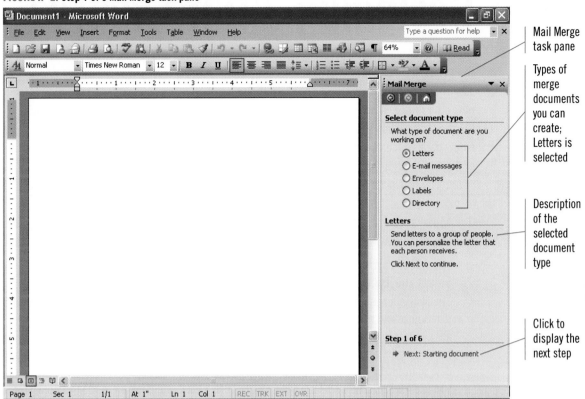

Mail Merge task pane

Types of merge documents you can create; Letters is selected

Description of the selected document type

Click to display the next step

FIGURE H-3: Main document with the Step 2 of 6 Mail Merge task pane

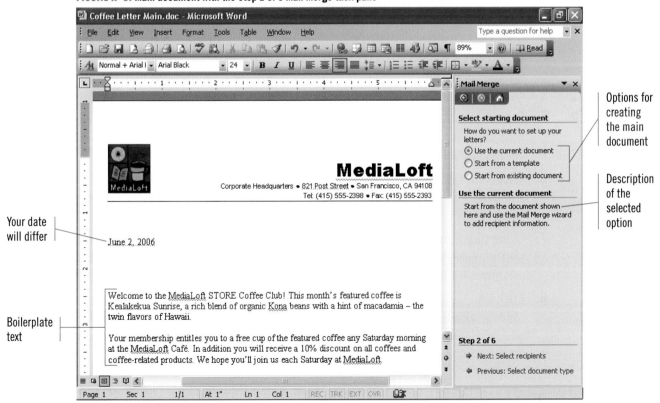

Your date will differ

Boilerplate text

Options for creating the main document

Description of the selected option

Word 2003

Designing a Data Source

Once you have identified the main document, the next step in the mail merge process is to identify the data source, the file that contains the information that differs in each version of the merge document. You can use an existing data source that already contains the records you want to include in your merge, or you can create a new data source. When you create a new data source you must determine the fields to include—the categories of information, such as a first name, last name, city, or zip code—and then add the records. 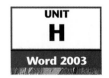 You create a new data source that includes fields for the name, address, and MediaLoft store location of each new member of the Coffee Club.

STEPS

1. **Make sure Step 3 of 6 is displayed at the bottom of the Mail Merge task pane**

   Step 3 of 6 involves selecting a data source to use for the merge. You can use an existing data source, a list of contacts created in Microsoft Outlook, or a new data source.

2. **Select the** Type a new list option button, **then click** Create

   The New Address List dialog box opens, as shown in Figure H-4. You use this dialog box both to design your data source and to enter records. The Enter Address information section of the dialog box includes fields that are commonly used in form letters, but you can customize your data source by adding and removing fields from this list. A data source can be merged with more than one main document, so it's important to design a data source to be flexible. The more fields you include in a data source, the more flexible it is. For example, if you include separate fields for a person's title, first name, middle name, and last name, you can use the same data source to create an envelope addressed to "Mr. John Montgomery Smith" and a form letter addressed to "Dear John."

3. **Click** Customize

   The Customize Address List dialog box opens, as shown in Figure H-5. You use this dialog box to add, delete, rename, and reorder the fields in the data source.

4. **Click** Company Name **in the list of field names, click** Delete, **then click** Yes **in the warning dialog box that opens**

   Company Name is removed from the list of field names. The Company Name field is no longer a part of the data source.

5. **Repeat Step 4 to delete the** Address Line 2, Home Phone, Work Phone, **and** E-mail Address **fields**

   The fields are removed from the data source.

6. **Click** Add, **type** Store **in the Add Field dialog box, then click** OK

   A field called "Store," which you will use to indicate the location of the MediaLoft store where the customer joined the Coffee Club, is added to the data source.

7. **Make sure** Store **is selected in the list of field names, then click** Move Up **eight times**

   The field name "Store" is moved to the top of the list. Although the order of field names does not matter in a data source, it's convenient to arrange the field names logically to make it easier to enter and edit records.

8. **Click** OK

   The New Address List dialog box shows the customized list of fields, with the Store field first in the list. The next step is to enter each record you want to include in the data source. You add records to the data source in the next lesson.

FIGURE H-4: New Address List dialog box

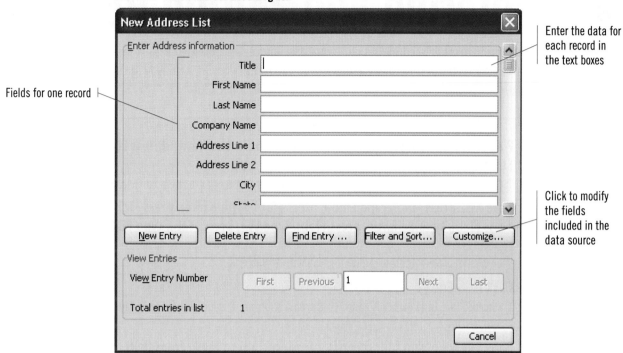

Fields for one record

Enter the data for each record in the text boxes

Click to modify the fields included in the data source

FIGURE H-5: Customize Address List dialog box

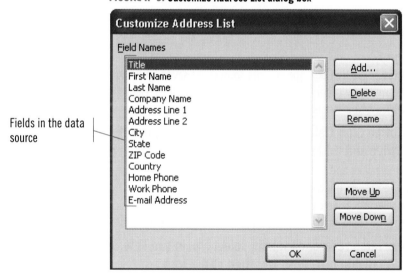

Fields in the data source

Clues to Use

Merging with an Outlook data source

If you maintain lists of contacts in Microsoft Outlook, you can use one of your Outlook contact lists as a data source for a merge. To merge with an Outlook data source, click the Select from Outlook contacts option button in the Step 3 of 6 Mail Merge task pane, then click Choose Contacts Folder to open the Select Contact List Folder dialog box. In this dialog box, select the contact list you want to use as the data source, and then click OK. All the contacts included in the selected folder appear in the Mail Merge Recipients dialog box. Here you can refine the list of recipients to include in the merge by sorting and filtering the records. When you are satisfied, click OK in the Mail Merge Recipients dialog box.

Entering and Editing Records

Once you have established the structure of a data source, the next step is to enter the records. Each record includes the complete set of information for each individual or item you include in the data source. You create a record for each new member of the Coffee Club.

STEPS

1. **Place the insertion point in the Store text box in the New Address List dialog box, type Seattle, then press [Tab]**

   "Seattle" appears in the Store field and the insertion point moves to the next field in the list, the Title field.

2. **Type Ms., press [Tab], type Linda, press [Tab], type Barker, press [Tab], type 62 Cloud St., press [Tab], type Bellevue, press [Tab], type WA, press [Tab], type 83459, press [Tab], then type US**

   Compare your New Address List dialog box with Figure H-6.

3. **Click New Entry**

   The record for Linda Barker is added to the data source and the dialog box displays empty fields for the next record, record 2.

4. **Enter the following four records, pressing [Tab] to move from field to field, and clicking New Entry at the end of each record except the last:**

Store	Title	First Name	Last Name	Address Line 1	City	State	ZIP Code	Country
Boston	Mr.	Bob	Cruz	23 Plum St.	Boston	MA	02483	US
Chicago	Ms.	Joan	Yatco	456 Elm St.	Chicago	IL	60603	US
Seattle	Ms.	Anne	Butler	48 East Ave.	Vancouver	BC	V6F 1AH	CANADA
Boston	Mr.	Fred	Silver	56 Pearl St.	Cambridge	MA	02139	US

5. **Click Close**

   The Save Address List dialog box opens. Data sources are saved by default in the My Data Sources folder so that you can easily locate them to use in other merge operations. Data sources you create in Word are saved in Microsoft Office Address Lists (*.mdb) format.

6. **Type New Coffee Club Data in the File name text box, use the Save in list arrow to navigate to the drive and folder where your Data Files are located, then click Save**

   The data source is saved, and the Mail Merge Recipients dialog box opens, as shown in Figure H-7. The dialog box shows the records in the data source in table format. You can use the dialog box to edit, sort, and filter records, and to select the recipients to include in the mail merge. You will learn more about sorting and filtering in a later lesson. The check marks in the first column indicate the records that will be included in the merge.

7. **Click the Joan Yatco record, click Edit, select Ms. in the Title text box in the New Coffee Club Data.mdb dialog box, type Dr., then click Close**

   The data in the Title field for Joan Yatco changes from "Ms." to "Dr." and the New Coffee Club Data.mdb dialog box closes.

8. **Click OK in the Mail Merge Recipients dialog box**

   The dialog box closes. The file type and filename of the data source attached to the main document now appear under Use an existing list in the Mail Merge task pane, as shown in Figure H-8. The Mail Merge toolbar also appears in the program window when you close the data source. You learn more about the Mail Merge toolbar in later lessons.

FIGURE H-6: Record in New Address List dialog box

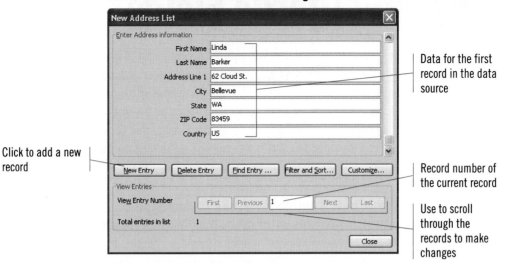

Data for the first record in the data source

Click to add a new record

Record number of the current record

Use to scroll through the records to make changes

FIGURE H-7: Mail Merge Recipients dialog box

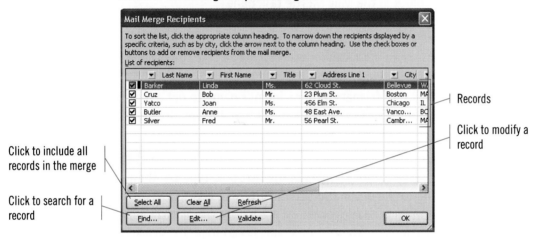

Records

Click to modify a record

Click to include all records in the merge

Click to search for a record

FIGURE H-8: Data source attached to the main document

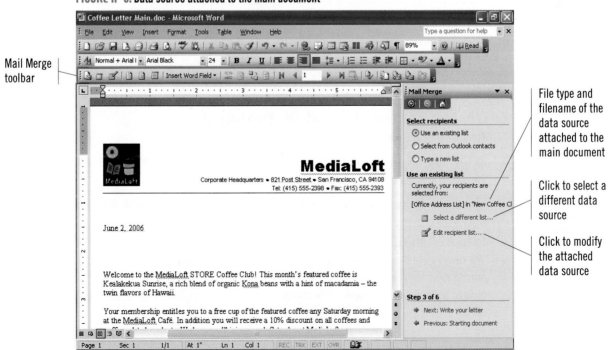

Mail Merge toolbar

File type and filename of the data source attached to the main document

Click to select a different data source

Click to modify the attached data source

Adding Merge Fields

After you have created and identified the data source, the next step is to insert the merge fields in the main document. Merge fields serve as placeholders for text that is inserted when the main document and the data source are merged. The names of merge fields correspond to the field names in the data source. You can insert merge fields using the Mail Merge task pane or the Insert Merge Field button on the Mail Merge toolbar. You cannot type merge fields into the main document. You use the Mail Merge task pane to insert merge fields for the inside address and greeting of the letter. You also insert a merge field for the store location in the body of the letter.

STEPS

1. **Click the Show/Hide ¶ button ¶ on the Standard toolbar to display formatting marks, then click Next: Write your letter in the Mail Merge task pane**

   The Mail Merge task pane shows the options for Step 4 of 6, writing the letter and inserting the merge fields in the main document. Since your form letter is already written, you are ready to add the merge fields to it.

   > **QUICK TIP**
   > You can also click the Insert Address Block button 🔳 on the Mail Merge toolbar to insert an address block.

2. **Place the insertion point in the blank line above the first body paragraph, then click Address block in the Mail Merge task pane**

   The Insert Address Block dialog box opens, as shown in Figure H-9. You use this dialog box to specify the fields you want to include in an address block. In this merge, the address block is the inside address of the form letter. An address block automatically includes fields for the street, city, state, and postal code, but you can select the format for the recipient's name and indicate whether to include a company name or country in the address.

3. **Scroll the list of formats for a recipient's name to get a feel for the kinds of formats you can use, then click Mr. Joshua Randall Jr. if it is not already selected**

   The selected format uses the recipient's title, first name, and last name.

4. **Make sure the Only include the country/region if different than: option button is selected, select United States in the text box, type US, then deselect the Format address according to the destination country/region check box**

   You only need to include the country in the address block if the country is different from the United States, so you indicate that all entries in the Country field except "US" should be included in the printed address.

   > **QUICK TIP**
   > You cannot simply type chevrons around a field name. You must insert merge fields using the Mail Merge task pane or the buttons on the Mail Merge toolbar.

5. **Click OK, then press [Enter] twice**

   The merge field AddressBlock is added to the main document. Chevrons (<< and >>) surround a merge field to distinguish it from the boilerplate text.

6. **Click Greeting line in the Mail Merge task pane**

   The Greeting Line dialog box opens. You want to use the format "Dear Mr. Randall:" (the recipient's title and last name, followed by a colon) for a greeting. The default format uses a comma, so you have to change the comma to a colon.

7. **Click the , list arrow, click :, click OK, then press [Enter]**

   The merge field GreetingLine is added to the main document.

   > **QUICK TIP**
   > You can also click the Insert Merge Fields button 🔳 on the Mail Merge toolbar to insert a merge field.

8. **In the body of the letter select STORE, then click More items in the Mail Merge task pane**

   The Insert Merge Field dialog box opens and displays the list of field names included in the data source.

9. **Make sure Store is selected, click Insert, click Close, press [Spacebar] to add a space between the merge field and Coffee if there is no space, save your changes, then click ¶ to turn off the display of formatting marks**

   The merge field Store is inserted in the main document, as shown in Figure H-10. You must type spaces and punctuation between merge fields if you want spaces and punctuation to appear between the data in the merged documents. You preview the merged data and perform the merge in the next lesson.

FIGURE H-9: Insert Address Block dialog box

Formats for the recipient's name

Click to match the default address field names to the field names used in your data source

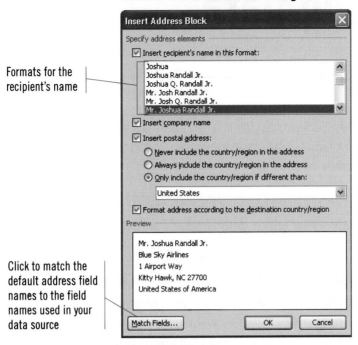

FIGURE H-10: Merge fields in the main document

Merge fields

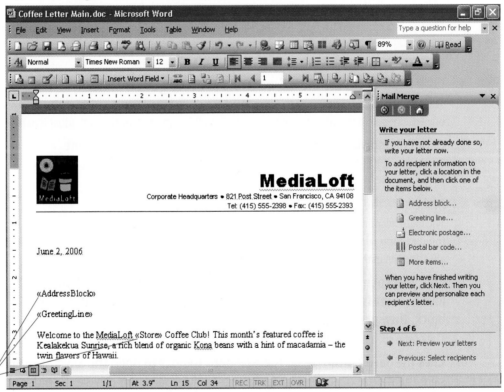

Clues to Use

Matching fields

The merge fields you insert in a main document must correspond with the field names in the associated data source. If you are using the Address Block merge field, you must make sure that the default address field names correspond with the field names used in your data source. If the default address field names do not match the field names in your data source, click Match Fields in the Insert Address Block dialog box, then use the list arrows in the Match Fields dialog box to select the field name in the data source that corresponds to each default address field name.

Merging Data

Once you have added records to your data source and inserted merge fields in the main document, you are ready to perform the merge. Before merging, it's a good idea to preview the merged data to make sure the printed documents will appear as you want them to. You can preview the merge using the task pane or the View Merged Data button on the Mail Merge toolbar. When you merge the main document with the data source, you must choose between merging to a new file or directly to a printer. ▰▰▰▰ Before merging the form letter with the data source, you preview the merge to make sure the data appears in the letter as you intended. You then merge the two files to a new document.

STEPS

QUICK TIP

To adjust the main document, click the View Merged Data button ▨ on the Mail Merge toolbar, then make any necessary changes. Click ▨ again to preview the merged data.

1. **Click Next: Preview your letters in the Mail Merge task pane**

   The data from the first record in the data source appears in place of the merge fields in the main document, as shown in Figure H-11. Always check the preview document to make sure the merge fields, punctuation, page breaks, and spacing all appear as you intend before you perform the merge.

2. **Click the Next Recipient button ⟩⟩ in the Mail Merge task pane**

   The data from the second record in the data source appears in place of the merge fields.

3. **Click the Go to Record text box on the Mail Merge toolbar, press [Backspace], type 4, then press [Enter]**

   The data for the fourth record appears in the document window. The non-US country name, in this case Canada, is included in the address block, just as you specified. You can also use the First Record ⏮, Previous Record ◀, Next Record ▶, and Last Record ⏭ buttons on the Mail Merge toolbar to preview the merged data. Table H-1 describes other buttons on the Mail Merge toolbar.

QUICK TIP

If your data source contains many records, you can merge directly to a printer to avoid creating a large file.

4. **Click Next: Complete the merge in the Mail Merge task pane**

   The options for Step 6 of 6 appear in the Mail Merge task pane. Merging to a new file creates a document with one letter for each record in the data source. This allows you to edit the individual letters.

5. **Click Edit individual letters to merge the data to a new document**

   The Merge to New Document dialog box opens. You can use this dialog box to specify the records to include in the merge.

QUICK TIP

To restore a main document to a regular Word document, click the Main document setup button ▨ on the Mail Merge toolbar, then click Normal Word document. Restoring a main document removes the associated data source from it.

6. **Make sure the All option button is selected, then click OK**

   The main document and the data source are merged to a new document called Letters1, which contains a customized form letter for each record in the data source. You can now further personalize the letters without affecting the main document or the data source.

7. **Click the Zoom list arrow on the Standard toolbar, click Page Width, scroll to the fourth letter (addressed to Ms. Anne Butler), place the insertion point before V6F in the address block, then press [Enter]**

   The postal code is now consistent with the proper format for a Canadian address.

8. **Click the Save button ▨ on the Standard toolbar to open the Save As dialog box, then save the merge document as Coffee Letter Merge to the drive and folder where your Data Files are located**

   You may decide not to save a merged file if your data source is large. Once you have created the main document and the data source, you can create the letters by performing the merge again.

9. **Click File on the menu bar, click Print, click the Current Page option button in the Page range section of the Print dialog box, click OK, then close all open Word files, saving changes if prompted**

   The letter to Anne Butler prints.

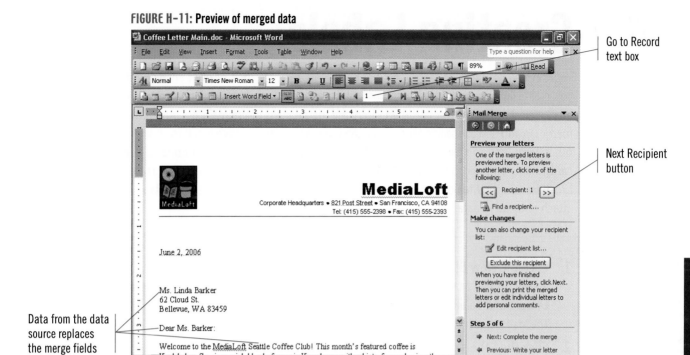

FIGURE H-11: Preview of merged data

Go to Record text box

Next Recipient button

Data from the data source replaces the merge fields

TABLE H-1: Buttons on the Mail Merge toolbar

button	use to	button	use to
	Change the main document to a different type, or convert it to a normal Word document		Highlight the merge fields in the main document
	Select an existing data source		Match address fields with the field names used in the data source
	Edit, sort, or filter the associated data source		Search for a record in the merged documents
	Insert an Address Block merge field		Check for errors in the merged documents
	Insert a Greeting Line merge field		Merge the data to a new document and display it on screen
	Insert a merge field from the data source		
	Switch between viewing the main document with merge fields and with merged data		Print the merged documents without first reviewing them on screen

Creating Labels

You can also use the Mail Merge task pane to create mailing labels or print envelopes for a mailing. When you create labels or envelopes, you must select a standard label or envelope size to use as the main document, select a data source, and then insert the merge fields in the main document before performing the merge. In addition to mailing labels, you can use mail merge to create labels for diskettes, CDs, videos, and other items, and to create documents that are based on standard or custom label sizes, such as business cards, nametags, and postcards.  You use the Mail Merge task pane to create mailing labels for a brochure you need to send to all members of the Coffee Club. You create a new label main document and attach an existing data source.

STEPS

1. **Click the** New Blank Document button ▯ **on the Standard toolbar, click the** Zoom list arrow **on the Standard toolbar, click** Page Width, **click** Tools **on the menu bar, point to** Letters and Mailings, **then click** Mail Merge

   The Mail Merge task pane opens.

   > **TROUBLE**
   > If your dialog box does not show Avery standard, click the Label products list arrow, then click Avery standard.

2. **Click the** Labels option button **in the Mail Merge task pane, click** Next: Starting document **to move to Step 2 of 6, make sure the** Change document layout option button **is selected, then click** Label options

   The Label Options dialog box opens, as shown in Figure H-12. You use this dialog box to select a label size for your labels and to specify the type of printer you plan to use. The default brand name Avery standard appears in the Label products list box. You can use the Label products list arrow to select other label products or a custom label. The many standard types of Avery labels for mailings, file folders, diskettes, post cards, and other types of labels are listed in the Product number list box. The type, height, width, and paper size for the selected product are displayed in the Label information section.

   > **TROUBLE**
   > If your gridlines are not visible, click Table on the menu bar, then click Show Gridlines.

3. **Scroll down the Product number list, click** 5161 – Address, **then click** OK

   A table with gridlines appears in the main document, as shown in Figure H-13. Each table cell is the size of a label for the label product you selected.

4. **Save the label main document with the filename** Coffee Labels Main **to the drive and folder where your Data Files are located**

   Next you need to select a data source for the labels.

5. **Click** Next: Select recipients **to move to Step 3 of 6, make sure the** Use an existing list option button **is selected, then click** Browse

   The Select Data Source dialog box opens.

6. **Use the** Look in list arrow **to navigate to the drive and folder where your Data Files are located, then open the file** WD H-2.mdb

   The Mail Merge Recipients dialog box opens and displays all the records in the data source. In the next lesson you sort and filter the records before performing the mail merge.

FIGURE H-12: Label Options dialog box

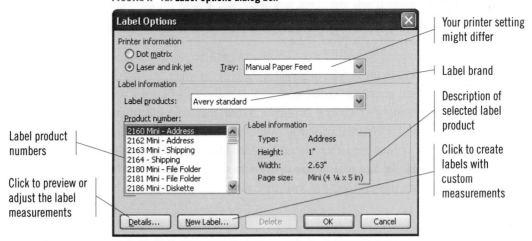

Label product numbers

Click to preview or adjust the label measurements

Your printer setting might differ

Label brand

Description of selected label product

Click to create labels with custom measurements

FIGURE H-13: Label main document

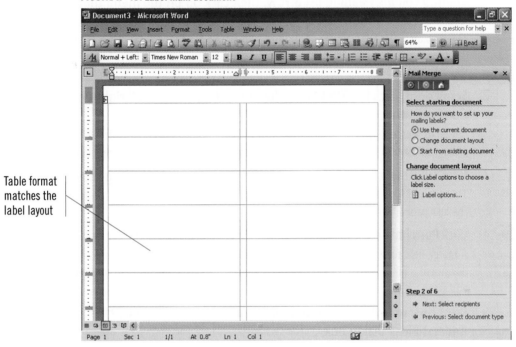

Table format matches the label layout

Clues to Use

Printing individual envelopes and labels

The Mail Merge task pane enables you to easily print envelopes and labels for mass mailings, but you can also quickly format and print individual envelopes and labels using the Envelopes and Labels dialog box. To open the Envelopes and Labels dialog box, point to Letters and Mailings on the Tools menu, then click Envelopes and Labels. On the Envelopes tab, shown in Figure H-14, type the recipient's address in the Delivery address box and the return address in the Return address box. Click Options to open the Envelope Options dialog box, which you can use to select the envelope size, add a postal bar code, change the font and font size of the delivery and return addresses, and change the printing options. When you are ready to print the envelope, click Print in the Envelopes and Labels dialog box. The procedure for printing an individual label is similar to printing an individual envelope: enter the recipient's address on

the Labels tab, click Options to select a label product number, click OK, then click Print.

FIGURE H-14: Envelopes and Labels dialog box

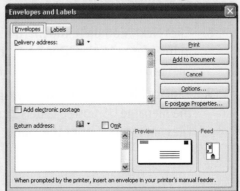

Word 2003

Sorting and Filtering Records

If you are using a large data source, you might want to sort and/or filter the records before performing a merge. Sorting the records determines the order in which the records are merged. For example, you might want to sort an address data source so that records are merged alphabetically by last name or in zip code order. Filtering the records pulls out the records that meet specific criteria and includes only those records in the merge. For instance, you might want to filter a data source to send a mailing only to people who live in the state of New York. You can use the Mail Merge Recipients dialog box both to sort and to filter a data source. ▰▰▰▰ You apply a filter to the data source so that only United States addresses are included in the merge. You then sort those records so that they merge in zip code order.

STEPS

QUICK TIP

For more advanced sort and filter options, click Filter and Sort in the New Address List dialog box when you create or edit the data source.

1. **In the Mail Merge Recipients dialog box, scroll right to display the Country field, click the Country column heading list arrow, then click US on the menu that opens**

   A filter is applied to the data source so that only the records with "US" in the Country field will be merged. The blue arrow in the Country column heading indicates that a filter has been applied to the column. You can filter a data source by as many criteria as you like. To remove a filter, click a column heading list arrow, then click "All."

2. **Scroll right, click the ZIP Code column heading, then scroll right again to see the ZIP Code column**

   The Mail Merge Recipients dialog box now displays only the records with a US address sorted in zip code order, as shown in Figure H-15. If you want to reverse the sort order, you can click a column heading again.

3. **Click OK, then click Next: Arrange your labels in the Mail Merge task pane**

   The sort and filter criteria you set are saved for the current merge, and the options for Step 4 of 6 appear in the task pane.

QUICK TIP

You use the Insert Postal Bar Code dialog box to select the field names for the zip code and street address in your data source. Postal bar codes can be inserted only for U.S. addresses.

4. **Click Postal bar code in the task pane, then click OK in the Insert Postal Bar Code dialog box**

   A merge field for a U.S. postal bar code is inserted in the first label in the main document. When the main document is merged with the data source, a customized postal bar code determined by the recipient's zip code and street address will appear on every label.

5. **Press [→], press [Enter], click Address block in the task pane, then click OK in the Insert Address Block dialog box**

   The Address Block merge field is added to the first label.

6. **Point to the down arrow at the bottom of the task pane to scroll down, then click Update all labels in the task pane**

   The merge fields are copied from the first label to every label in the main document.

QUICK TIP

To change the font or paragraph formatting of merged data, format the merge fields before performing a merge.

7. **Click Next: Preview your labels in the task pane**

   A preview of the merged label data appears in the main document. Only U.S. addresses are included, and the labels are organized in zip code order.

8. **Click Next: Complete the merge in the task pane, click Edit individual labels, then click OK in the Merge to New Document dialog box**

   The merged labels document is shown in Figure H-16.

9. **Replace Ms. Clarissa Landfair with your name in the first label, save the document with the filename US Coffee Labels Zip Code Merge to the drive and folder where your Data Files are located, print the labels, save and close all open files, then exit Word**

FIGURE H-15: US records sorted in zip code order

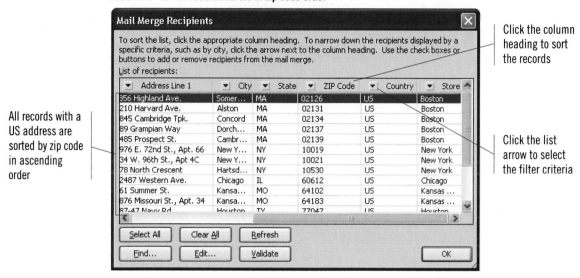

Click the column heading to sort the records

All records with a US address are sorted by zip code in ascending order

Click the list arrow to select the filter criteria

FIGURE H-16: Merged labels

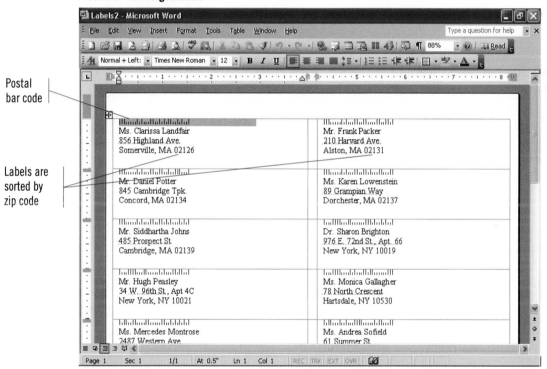

Postal bar code

Labels are sorted by zip code

Clues to Use

Inserting individual merge fields

You must include proper punctuation, spacing, and blank lines between the merge fields in a main document if you want punctuation, spaces, and blank lines to appear between the data in the merge documents. For example, to create an address line with a city, state, and zip code, you insert the City merge field, type a comma and a space, insert the State merge field, type a space, and then insert the Zip Code merge field: <<City>>, <<State>> <<Zip Code>>.

You can insert an individual merge field by selecting the field name in the Insert Merge Fields dialog box, clicking Insert, and then clicking Close. You can also insert several merge fields at once by clicking a field name in the Insert Merge Field dialog box, clicking Insert, clicking another field name, clicking Insert, and so on. When you have finished inserting the merge fields, click Close. You can then add spaces, punctuation, and lines between the merge fields you inserted in the main document.

Practice

▼ CONCEPTS REVIEW

Label each toolbar button shown in Figure H-17.

Figure H-17

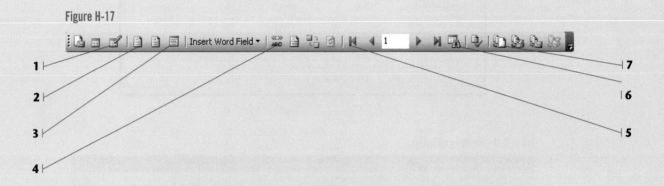

Match each term with the statement that best describes it.

8. **Main document**
9. **Merge field**
10. **Data field**
11. **Boilerplate text**
12. **Data source**
13. **Data record**
14. **Filter**
15. **Sort**

a. To organize records in a sequence
b. A file that contains customized information for each item or individual
c. To pull out records that meet certain criteria
d. A category of information in a data source
e. The standard text that appears in every version of a merged document
f. A complete set of information for one item or individual
g. A file that contains boilerplate text and merge fields
h. A placeholder for merged data in the main document

Select the best answer from the list of choices.

16. **In a mail merge, which type of file contains the information that varies for each individual or item?**
    a. Data source
    b. Main document
    c. Label document
    d. Merge document

17. **Which of the following buttons can be used to insert a merge field for an inside address?**
    a.
    b.
    c.
    d.

18. **Which of the following buttons can be used to preview the merged data in the main document?**
    a.
    b.
    c.
    d.

19. **To change the font of merged data, which element should you format?**
    a. Data record
    b. Merge field
    c. Field name
    d. Boilerplate text

20. **Which of the following is included in a data source?**
    a. Records
    b. Boilerplate text
    c. Labels
    d. Merge fields

▼ SKILLS REVIEW

1. Create a main document.

a. Start Word, then open the Mail Merge task pane.

b. Use the Mail Merge task pane to create a letter main document, click Next, then select the current (blank) document.

c. At the top of the blank document, press [Enter] four times, type today's date, press [Enter] five times, then type **We are delighted to receive your generous contribution of AMOUNT to the New England Humanities Council (NEHC).**

d. Press [Enter] twice, then type **Whether we are helping adult new readers learn to read or bringing humanities programs into our public schools, senior centers, and prisons, NEHC depends upon private contributions to ensure that free public humanities programs continue to flourish in CITY and throughout the REGION region. I hope we will see you at a humanities event soon.**

e. Press [Enter] twice, type **Sincerely**, and press [Enter] four times, type your name, press [Enter], then type **Executive Director**.

f. Save the main document as **Donor Thank You Main** to the drive and folder where your Data Files are located.

2. Design a data source.

a. Click Next, select the Type a new list option button in the Step 3 of 6 Mail Merge task pane, then click Create.

b. Click Customize in the New Address List dialog box, then remove these fields from the data source: Company Name, Address Line 2, Country, Home Phone, Work Phone, and E-mail Address.

c. Add an **Amount** field and a **Region** field to the data source. Be sure these fields follow the ZIP Code field.

d. Rename the Address Line 1 field **Street**, then click OK to close the Customize Address List dialog box.

3. Enter and edit records.

a. Add the following records to the data source:

Title	First Name	Last Name	Street	City	State	Zip Code	Amount	Region
Mr.	John	Conlin	34 Mill St.	Exeter	NH	03833	$250	Seacoast
Mr.	Bill	Webster	289 Sugar Hill Rd.	Franconia	NH	03632	$1000	Seacoast
Ms.	Susan	Janak	742 Main St.	Derby	VT	04634	$25	North Country
Mr.	Derek	Gray	987 Ocean Rd.	Portsmouth	NH	03828	$50	Seacoast
Ms.	Rita	Murphy	73 Bay Rd.	Durham	NH	03814	$500	Seacoast
Ms.	Amy	Hunt	67 Apple St.	Northfield	MA	01360	$75	Pioneer Valley
Ms.	Eliza	Perkins	287 Mountain Rd.	Dublin	NH	03436	$100	Pioneer Valley

b. Save the data source as **Donor Data** to the drive and folder where your Data Files are located.

c. Change the region for record 2 (Bill Webster) from Seacoast to **White Mountain**.

d. Click OK to close the Mail Merge Recipients dialog box.

4. Add merge fields.

a. Click Next, then in the blank line above the first body paragraph, insert an Address Block merge field.

b. In the Insert Address Block dialog box, click Match Fields.

c. Click the list arrow next to Address 1 in the Match Fields dialog box, click Street, then click OK.

d. In the Insert Address Block dialog box, select the Never include the country/region in the address option button, then click OK.

e. Press [Enter] twice, insert a Greeting Line merge field using the default greeting line format, then press [Enter].

f. In the first body paragraph, replace AMOUNT with the Amount merge field.

g. In the second body paragraph, replace CITY with the City merge field and REGION with the Region merge field. (*Note*: Make sure to insert a space before or after each merge field as needed.)

h. Save your changes to the main document.

sidebar
Word 2003

5. Merge data.

 a. Click Next to preview the merged data, then scroll through each letter.

 b. Click the View Merged Data button on the Mail Merge toolbar, place the insertion point before "I hope" in the second sentence of the second body paragraph, then press [Enter] twice to create a new paragraph.

 c. Combine the first and second body paragraphs into a single paragraph.

 d. Make any other necessary adjustments to the letter, save your changes, then click the View Merged Data button to return to the preview of the document.

 e. Click Next, click Edit individual letters, then merge all the records to a new file.

 f. Save the merged document as **Donor Thank You Merge** to the drive and folder where your Data Files are located, print a copy of the first letter, then save and close all open files.

6. Create labels.

 a. Open a new blank document, then open the Mail Merge task pane.

 b. Create a label main document, click Next, then select the Change document layout option button if necessary in the Step 2 of 6 Mail Merge task pane.

 c. Open the Label Options dialog box, select Avery standard 5162 – Address labels, then click OK.

 d. Save the label main document as **Donor Labels Main** to the drive and folder where your Data Files are located, then click Next.

 e. Select the Use an existing list option button, click Browse, then open the Donor Data.mdb file you created.

7. Sort and filter records.

 a. Filter the records so that only the records with NH in the State field are included in the merge.

 b. Sort the records in zip code order, then click OK.

 c. If the Mail Merge toolbar is not open, point to Toolbars on the View menu, then click Mail Merge.

 d. Click Next, insert a Postal bar code merge field using the default settings, press [→], then press [Enter].

 e. Insert an Address Block merge field using the default settings, click the View Merged Data button on the Mail Merge toolbar, then notice that the street address is missing and the address block includes the region.

 f. Click the View Merged Data button again, click the Address Block merge field in the upper-left table cell to select it if necessary, then click Address block in the Mail Merge task pane.

 g. Click Match Fields in the Insert Address Block dialog box to open the Match Fields dialog box.

 h. Click the list arrow next to Address 1, click Street, scroll down, click the list arrow next to Country or Region, click (not matched), click OK, then click OK again.

 i. Click the View Merged Data button to preview the merged data, and notice that the address block now includes the street address and the region name is missing.

 j. Click Update all labels in the Mail Merge task pane, then click Next to move to Step 5.

 k. Examine the merged data for errors, then click Next to move to Step 6.

 l. Click Edit individual labels, merge all the records, then save the merged file as **NH Donor Labels Merge** to the drive and folder where your Data Files are located.

 m. In the first label, change Ms. Eliza Perkins to your name, save the document, then print it.

 n. Save and close all open Word files, then exit Word.

▼ INDEPENDENT CHALLENGE 1

You are the director of the Emerson Arts Center (EAC). The EAC is hosting an exhibit of ceramic art in the city of Cambridge, Massachusetts, and you want to send a letter advertising the exhibit to all EAC members with a Cambridge address. You'll use Mail Merge to create the letter. If you are performing the ACE steps and are able to print envelopes on your printer, you will also use Word to print an envelope for one letter.

a. Start Word, then use the Mail Merge task pane to create a letter main document using the file WD H-3.doc, found on the drive and folder where your Data Files are located.

b. Replace Your Name with your name in the signature block, then save the main document as **Member Letter Main** to the drive and folder where your Data Files are located.

c. Use the file WD H-4.mdb, found on the drive and folder where your Data Files are located, as the data source.

d. Sort the data source by last name, then filter the data so that only records with Cambridge as the city are included in the merge.

e. Insert an Address Block and a Greeting Line merge field in the main document, preview the merged letters, then make any necessary adjustments.

f. Merge all the records to a new document, then save it as **Member Letter Merge** to the drive and folder where your Data Files are located.

g. Print the first letter.

Advanced Challenge Exercise

- If you can print envelopes, select the inside address in the first merge letter, click Tools on the menu bar, point to Letters and Mailings, then click Envelopes and Labels.
- On the Envelopes tab, verify that no check mark appears in the check box next to Omit, type your name in the Return address text box, type **60 Crandall Street, Concord, MA 01742**, click Options, make sure the Envelope size is set to Size 10, then change the font of the Delivery address and the Return address to 12-point Times New Roman.
- On the Printing Options tab, select the appropriate Feed method for your printer, then click OK.
- Click Print, then click No to save the return address as the default.

h. Close all open Word files, saving changes, and then exit Word.

▼ INDEPENDENT CHALLENGE 2

One of your responsibilities at JDE Enterprises, a growing information technology company, is to create business cards for the staff. You use mail merge to create the cards so that you can easily produce standard business cards for future employees.

a. Start Word, then use the Mail Merge task pane to create labels using the current blank document as the main document.

b. Select Avery standard 3612 – Business Card labels.

c. Create a new data source that includes the following fields: Title, First Name, Last Name, Phone, Fax, E-mail, and Hire Date. Add the following records to the data source:

Title	First Name	Last Name	Phone	Fax	E-mail	Hire Date
President	Sandra	Bryson	(312) 555-3982	(312) 555-6654	sbryson@jde.com	1/12/01
Vice President	Philip	Holm	(312) 555-2323	(312) 555-4956	pholm@jde.com	1/12/01

d. Add six more records to the data source, including one with your name as the Administrative Assistant.

e. Save the data source with the filename **Employee Data** to the drive and folder where your Data Files are located, then sort the data by Title.

▼ INDEPENDENT CHALLENGE 2

f. In the first table cell, create the JDE Enterprises business card. Figure H-18 shows a sample JDE business card, but you should create your own design. Include the company name, a street address, and the Web site address www.jde.com. Also include a First Name, Last Name, Title, Phone, Fax, and E-mail merge fields. (*Hint*: If your design includes a graphic, insert the graphic before inserting the merge fields. Use the Insert Merge Field dialog box to insert each merge field, adjusting the spacing between merge fields as necessary.)

FIGURE H-18

JDE Enterprises

Sandra Bryson
President

234 Walden Street, Dublin, PA 32183
Tel: (312) 555-3982; Fax: (312) 555-6654
E-mail: sbryson@jde.com
www.jde.com

g. Format the business card with fonts, colors, and other formatting features. (*Note*: Use the Other Task Panes list arrow to reopen the Mail Merge task pane if necessary.)

h. Update all the labels, preview the data, make any necessary adjustments, then merge all the records to a new document.

i. Save the merge document with the filename **Business Cards Merge** to the drive and folder where your Data Files are located, print a copy, then close the file.

j. Save the main document with the filename **Business Cards Main** to the drive and folder where your Data Files are located, close the file, then exit Word.

▼ INDEPENDENT CHALLENGE 3

You need to create a team roster for the children's softball team you coach. You decide to use mail merge to create the team roster. If you are completing the ACE steps, you will also use mail merge to create mailing labels.

a. Start Word, then use the Mail Merge task pane to create a directory using the current blank document.

b. Create a new data source that includes the following fields: First Name, Last Name, Age, Position, Parent First Name, Parent Last Name, Address, City, State, Zip Code, and Home Phone.

c. Enter the following records in the data source:

First Name	Last Name	Age	Position	Parent First Name	Parent Last Name	Address	City	State	Zip Code	Home Phone
Sophie	Wright	8	Shortstop	Kerry	Wright	58 Main St.	Camillus	NY	13031	555-2345
Will	Jacob	7	Catcher	Bob	Jacob	32 North Way	Camillus	NY	13031	555-9827
Brett	Eliot	8	First base	Olivia	Eliot	289 Sylvan Way	Marcellus	NY	13032	555-9724
Abby	Herman	7	Pitcher	Sarah	Thomas	438 Lariat St.	Marcellus	NY	13032	555-8347

d. Add five additional records to the data source using the following last names and positions:
O'Keefe, Second base
George, Third base
Goleman, Left field
Siebert, Center field
Choy, Right field
Make up the remaining information for these five records.

e. Save the data source as **Softball Team Data** to the drive and folder where your Data Files are located.

f. Sort the records by last name, then click Next in the Mail Merge task pane.

g. Insert a table that includes five columns and one row in the main document.

h. In the first table cell, insert the First Name and Last Name merge fields, separated by a space.

i. In the second cell, insert the Position merge field.

j. In the third cell, insert the Address and City merge fields, separated by a comma and a space.

k. In the fourth cell, insert the Home Phone merge field.

l. In the fifth cell, insert the Parent First Name and Parent Last Name merge fields, separated by a space.

m. Preview the merged data and make any necessary adjustments. (*Hint*: Only one record is displayed at a time when you preview the data.)

n. Merge all the records to a new document, then save the document with the filename **Softball Roster Merge** to the drive and folder where your Data Files are located.

o. Press [Ctrl][Home], press [Enter], type **Wildcats Team Roster** at the top of the document, press [Enter], type **Coach:**, followed by your name, then press [Enter] twice.

p. Insert a new row at the top of the table, then type the following column headings in the new row: **Name, Position, Address, Phone, Parent Name**.

q. Format the roster to make it attractive and readable, save your changes, print a copy, then close the file.

r. Close the main document without saving changes.

Advanced Challenge Exercise

■ Open a new blank document, then use the Mail Merge task pane to create mailing labels using Avery standard 5162 – Address labels.

■ Use the Softball Team Data data source you created, and sort the records in zip code order.

■ In the first table cell, create your own address block using the Parent First Name, Parent Last Name, Address, City, State, and Zip Code merge fields. Be sure to include proper spacing and punctuation.

■ Update all the labels, preview the merged data, merge all the records to a new document, then type your name centered in the document header.

■ Save the document with the filename **Softball Labels Merge ACE** to the drive and folder where your Data Files are located, print a copy, close the file, then close the main document without saving changes.

s. Exit Word.

▼ INDEPENDENT CHALLENGE 4

Your boss has given you the task of purchasing mailing labels for a mass mailing of your company's annual report. The annual report will be sent to 55,000 people. Your company plans to use Avery standard 5160 white labels for a laser printer, or their equivalent, for the mailing. In this independent challenge, you will search for Web sites that sell Avery labels, compare the costs, and then write a memo to your boss detailing your purchasing recommendations.

a. Use your favorite search engine to search for Web sites that sell Avery labels or the equivalent. Use the keywords **Avery labels** to conduct your search.

b. Find at least three Web sites that sell Avery 5160 white labels for a laser printer, or their equivalent. Note the URL of the Web sites and the price and quantity of the labels. You need to purchase enough labels for a mailing of 55,000, plus enough extras in case you make mistakes.

c. Start Word, then use the Professional Memo template to create a memo to your boss. Save the memo as **5160 Labels Memo** to the drive and folder where your Data Files are located.

d. In the memo, make up information to replace the placeholder text in the memo header, be sure to include your name in the memo header, then type the body of your memo.

e. In the body, include a table that shows the URL of each Web site, the product name, the unit cost, the number of labels in each unit, the number of units you need to purchase, and the total cost of purchasing the labels. Also make a brief recommendation to your boss.

f. Format the memo so it is attractive and readable, save your changes, print a copy, close the file, then exit Word.

▼ VISUAL WORKSHOP

Using the Mail Merge task pane, create the post cards shown in Figure H-19. Use Avery standard 3611 – Post Card labels for the main document and create a data source that contains at least four records. Save the data source as **Party Data**, save the main document as **Party Card Main**, and save the merge document as **Party Card Merge**, all to the drive and folder where your Data Files are located. (*Hint:* Use a table to lay out the postcard; the clip art graphic uses the keywords "party cake balloon"; and the font is Comic Sans MS.) Print a copy of the postcards.

FIGURE H-19

You're invited to a
surprise party!

⫿⫿⫿⫿⫿⫿⫿⫿⫿⫿⫿⫿⫿
Grace Pappas
186 Buena Vista Terrace
Apt. 5C
San Francisco, CA 94117

For: Claudette Summer
When: August 3rd, 7:00 p.m.
Where: The Wharf Grill
Given by: Your Name

You're invited to a
surprise party!

⫿⫿⫿⫿⫿⫿⫿⫿⫿⫿⫿⫿⫿
Mika Takeda
456 Parker Ave.
San Francisco, CA 94118

For: Claudette Summer
When: August 3rd, 7:00 p.m.
Where: The Wharf Grill
Given by: Your Name

Working with Styles and Templates

OBJECTIVES

Explore styles and templates
Create custom paragraph styles
Modify paragraph styles
Create and modify custom character styles
Create custom list and table styles
Rename, delete, and copy styles
Create a template
Revise and attach a template

If you have a SAM user profile, you may have access to hands-on instruction, practice, and assessment of the skills covered in this unit. Log in to your SAM account and go to your assignments page to see what your instructor has assigned.

The sophisticated styles and templates available in Word allow you to format your documents quickly, efficiently, and professionally. In this unit, you learn how to apply existing styles to selected text in a document and how to create new custom styles. You also learn how to apply a template to a document and how to create a new template that contains styles. The MediaLoft Marketing Department has hired you to produce author profiles for distribution at book-signing events. To save time, you decide to develop a template on which to base each author profile. This template will include several custom styles, which you can periodically update. You use styles and templates to create and modify the author profiles.

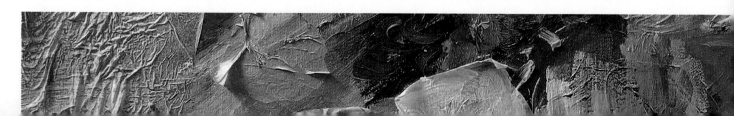

Exploring Styles and Templates

You use styles and templates to automate document-formatting tasks and to ensure consistency among related documents. A **style** consists of various formats such as font style, font size, and alignment that are combined into one set that you can name. For example, a style called "Main Head" could be used to apply the Arial font, 14-point font size, bold, and a border style to selected text. A **template** is a file that contains the basic structure of a document, such as the page layout, headers and footers, styles, and graphic elements. ▓▓▓▓ You want to include styles in the template you plan to create for the author profiles. You familiarize yourself with how you can use styles to automate formatting tasks and how you can use templates to create unified sets of documents.

DETAILS

Styles

- Using styles helps you save time because you can update styles quickly and easily. For example, suppose you have applied a style named "Section Head" to each section head in a document. When you change the formatting in the Section Head style, Word automatically updates all the text formatted with that style. Imagine how much time you would save if your document contains 50 or 100 section headings that are all formatted with the Section Head style!

- Word includes four style categories: paragraph, character, list, and table. A **paragraph** style includes both character formats, such as font style, and paragraph formats, such as line spacing. You use a paragraph style when you want to format all the text in a paragraph at once. A **character** style includes character formats only. You use a character style to apply character format settings only to selected text within a paragraph. A **list** style allows you to format a series of lines with numbers or bullets and with selected font and paragraph formats. Finally, you create a **table** style to specify how you want both the table grid and the text in a table to appear. Figure I-1 shows a document formatted with the four kinds of styles.

- You work in the Styles and Formatting task pane to create, apply, and modify all four types of styles. In this task pane, you can use the list arrow next to each style name to select all text that has been formatted with a specific style, as shown in Figure I-2, to modify the style, to delete the style, or to create a new style.

- Text you type into a blank document is formatted with the paragraph style called **Normal style** until you specify otherwise. By default, text formatted with the Normal style uses 12-point Times New Roman as the font and the text is left-aligned and single spaced.

Templates

- Every document you create in Word is based on a template. Most of the time, this template is the **Normal template** because the Normal template is loaded automatically when you start a new document. The styles assigned to the Normal template, such as Normal style, are available to all documents.

- You can create your own template or you can use one of the preset templates available in Word. When you create a new document based on a template, the styles included with the template are automatically assigned to the new document. You can also attach a template to an existing document and then apply the styles in the attached template to selected text in the document.

Clues to Use

Exploring AutoFormats and the Style Gallery

AutoFormat and the Style Gallery are two Word features that allow you to apply styles quickly. When you use the AutoFormat feature, Word analyzes each paragraph in your completed document and then applies an appropriate style, depending on where the paragraph appears in the document. To access the AutoFormat feature, click Format on the menu bar, and then click AutoFormat. When you use the Style Gallery feature, you select a template and all styles included in that template override the styles in the existing document. To access the Style Gallery, click Format on the menu bar, click Theme, then click Style Gallery in the Theme dialog box.

FIGURE I-1: Document formatted with styles

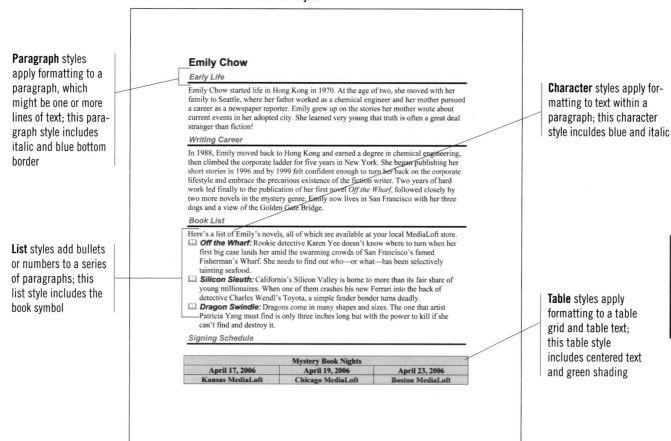

Paragraph styles apply formatting to a paragraph, which might be one or more lines of text; this paragraph style includes italic and blue bottom border

List styles add bullets or numbers to a series of paragraphs; this list style includes the book symbol

Character styles apply formatting to text within a paragraph; this character style incldues blue and italic

Table styles apply formatting to a table grid and table text; this table style includes centered text and green shading

FIGURE I-2: Styles and Formatting task pane

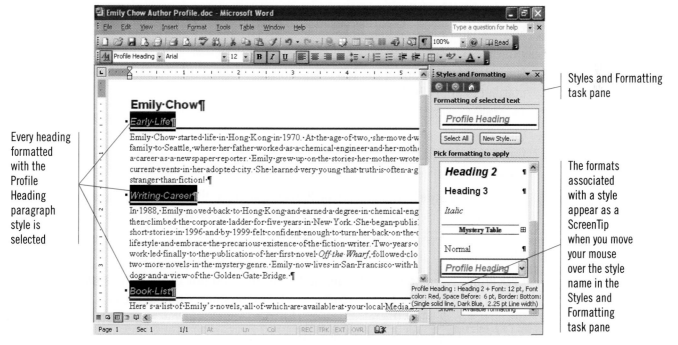

Every heading formatted with the Profile Heading paragraph style is selected

Styles and Formatting task pane

The formats associated with a style appear as a ScreenTip when you move your mouse over the style name in the Styles and Formatting task pane

Creating Custom Paragraph Styles

A **paragraph style** is a combination of character and paragraph formats that you name and store as a set. You can create a paragraph style and then apply it to any paragraph. Remember that any line of text followed by a hard return is considered a paragraph—even if the line consists of only one or two words. ███████ You have written a profile of mystery author Jonathon Grant. You decide to create your own custom paragraph styles for the headings and subheadings included in the profile.

STEPS

QUICK TIP

This unit assumes Show/Hide ¶ is on.

1. **Start Word, open the file WD I-1.doc from the drive and folder where your Data Files are located, save the file as Jonathon Grant Author Profile, then click the Styles and Formatting button 🔳 on the Formatting toolbar**

   The Styles and Formatting task pane opens. The Normal paragraph style is applied to the author's name at the top of the document and to the paragraphs of text, and the Heading 2 style is applied to section heads such as Early Life.

2. **Click the New Style button in the Styles and Formatting task pane**

   The New Style dialog box opens, as shown in Figure I-3. In this dialog box, you enter a name for the new style, select a style type, and then select the formatting options you want applied to text formatted with the new style.

3. **Type Profile Title as the custom style name in the Name text box, press [Tab], then make sure that "Paragraph" appears in the Style type list box**

   The default style type is Paragraph. When you create a new paragraph style, you can base it on another style by selecting a style in the Style based on list box, or you can create a new style that is based on no preset style. When you base a style on an existing style, the settings for the existing style, as well as any changes you make to the settings, are included with the new style. By default, a new style is based on the Normal style.

QUICK TIP

The name of each color appears as a ScreenTip when you move the pointer over a color.

4. **Select Arial, 16 point, Bold, and the Blue font color as shown in Figure I-4, then click OK**

   The Profile Title style appears in the Pick formatting to apply list box.

5. **Select Jonathon Grant at the top of the document, then click Profile Title in the Pick formatting to apply list box**

   The heading Jonathon Grant is formatted with the new Profile Title style.

TROUBLE

The list arrow appears when you move the pointer over a style name in the Pick formatting to apply list box.

6. **Click anywhere in the Early Life heading, click the Heading 2 list arrow in the Pick formatting to apply list box, then click Select All 4 Instance(s)**

   The four headings formatted with the Heading 2 style are selected.

7. **Click the New Style button, then type Profile Heading as the style name in the Name text box**

   Notice that the Profile Heading style is based on the Heading 2 style because this style was applied to the text you selected before opening the New Style dialog box.

8. **Change the font size to 12 point and the font color to Red, then click OK**

9. **Click Profile Heading in the Pick formatting to apply list box to apply the Profile Heading style to the selected headings, scroll up and click Jonathon Grant at the beginning of the document to deselect the selected text, click the Show list arrow at the bottom of the Styles and Formatting task pane, click Formatting in use, then save the document**

   The document appears as shown in Figure I-5. When you show only the formatting in use, you can quickly identify which styles you used to format your document.

FIGURE I-3: New Style dialog box

By default, a new style is based on the Normal style

Enter a name for the new style in the Name text box

By default, the Paragraph style type is selected

By default, after you format a paragraph with the new style, the new style is applied to the next paragraph when you press [Enter]

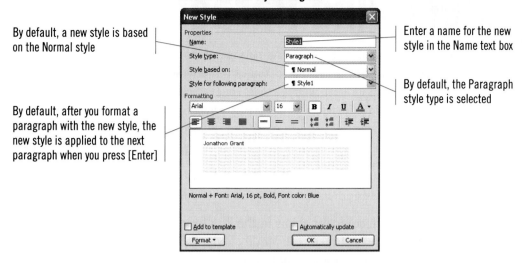

FIGURE I-4: Settings for Profile Title style

Arial font style selected

Bold selected

Blue font color selected

16-point font size selected

Appearance of text formatted with the Profile Title style

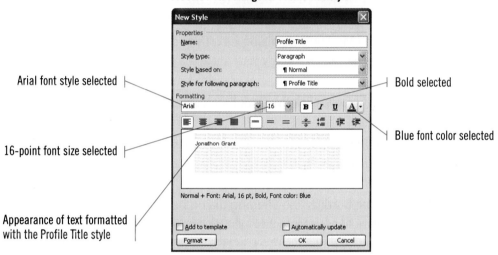

FIGURE I-5: Document formatted with custom styles

The style in the Style list box on the Formatting toolbar names the style applied to text at the location of the insertion point

Profile Title style applied

Profile Heading style applied

Only the styles currently in use are displayed in alphabetical order

Paragraph symbol indicates a paragraph style

Show list arrow

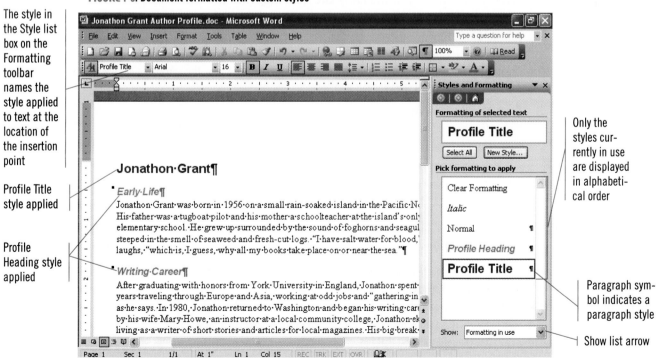

Modifying Paragraph Styles

A paragraph style is composed of character formats such as bold and italic and of paragraph formats such as line spacing before and after a paragraph. You can modify an existing or a custom paragraph style to change the set of formats included with the style. For example, you might decide to change the font style to Britannic Bold and add a border line under the paragraph. You can also change paragraph formats such as line spacing and alignment. Finally, you can include numbers or bullets with text formatted with a paragraph style. You decide to modify the Profile Heading style by reducing the Before paragraph spacing and by adding a bottom border.

STEPS

1. **Click the Profile Heading list arrow in the Pick formatting to apply list box, click Modify, click Format at the bottom of the Modify Style dialog box, then click Paragraph**
   The Paragraph dialog box opens with the Indents and Spacing tab selected.

2. **Click the down arrow next to the Before text box in the Spacing section one time to reduce the Spacing Before a paragraph to 6 point as shown in Figure I-6, then click OK**

3. **Click Format in the Modify Style dialog box, then click Border**
   The Borders and Shading dialog box opens. You want to add a single line under each heading formatted with the Profile Heading style.

4. **Click the Color list arrow, click the Dark Blue color, click the Width list arrow, then click the 2 ¼ pt width**

   QUICK TIP
   You can also click the paragraph borders in the Preview section to select a border option.

5. **Click the Bottom Border button ⊞ in the Preview section as shown in Figure I-7**
   Figure I-7 shows the format settings for the bottom border line. The Preview section shows the placement of the bottom border.

6. **Click OK to exit the Borders and Shading dialog box, then click OK**
   All four of the headings formatted with the Profile Heading style are automatically updated. You can view all the format settings included with the Profile Heading style—or any currently selected text—by viewing the Reveal Formatting task pane.

7. **Click the word Early in the Early Life heading, click the Other Task Panes list arrow at the top of the Styles and Formatting task pane, then click Reveal Formatting**
   All the formatting associated with the text at the position of the insertion point appears in the Reveal Formatting task pane, as shown in Figure I-8. Information about text, paragraph, and section formatting is organized into categories in the Reveal Formatting task pane. Use the scroll bar as needed to view all of the formatting assigned to the selected text.

8. **Save the document**

Clues to Use

Clearing formats

To quickly remove all the formatting from selected text, click Clear Formatting in the Pick formatting to apply list box in the Styles and Formatting task pane. All the styles and any other formats that have been applied to the selected text are instantly removed. This feature is most useful when you need to reformat text that has been formatted several times with various styles and options. To avoid unexpected results when working with styles, you may want to get into the habit of clearing the existing styles and then starting with a new style that you have created yourself and which includes only the formats you want.

FIGURE I-6: Before paragraph spacing reduced

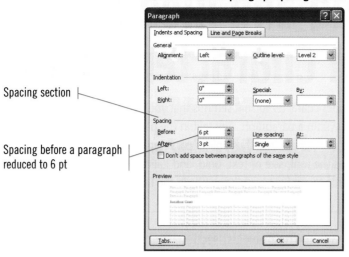

Spacing section

Spacing before a paragraph reduced to 6 pt

FIGURE I-7: Border options selected

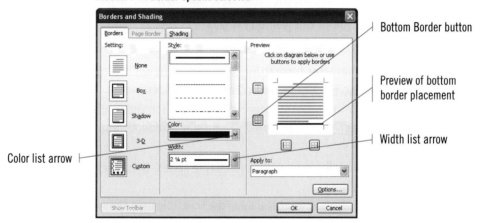

Bottom Border button

Preview of bottom border placement

Width list arrow

Color list arrow

FIGURE I-8: Reveal Formatting pane with modified Profile Heading style applied

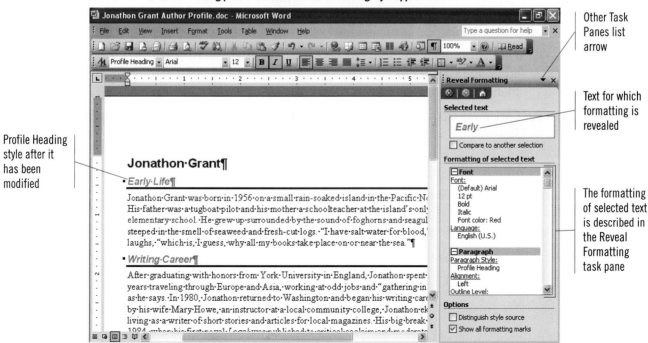

Other Task Panes list arrow

Text for which formatting is revealed

The formatting of selected text is described in the Reveal Formatting task pane

Profile Heading style after it has been modified

Creating and Modifying Custom Character Styles

A **character style** includes character format settings that you name and store as a set. You apply a character style to selected text within a paragraph. Any text in the paragraph that is not formatted with the character style is formatted with the currently applied paragraph style. You use a character style to apply character formats such as the font, size of text, bold, and italic. You want to create a custom character style called Book Title to apply to each book title in the Book List section of Jonathon's profile.

1. Scroll down the page to the Book List section, then select the book title Sea Swept:, including the colon

2. Click the Other Task Panes list arrow in the Reveal Formatting task pane, click Styles and Formatting, then click the New Style button in the Styles and Formatting task pane

3. Type Book Title in the Name text box

4. Click the Style type list arrow, then select Character

5. Select the character formatting settings as shown in Figure I-9: Arial, 14 point, Bold, Italic, and the Dark Blue font color, then click OK

   The Book Title style does not appear in the Pick formatting to apply list box because the Styles and Formatting task pane is set to show the Formatting in use option, and you have not yet applied the Book Title style to text in the document.

6. Click the Show list arrow, click Available styles, then click Book Title in the Pick formatting to apply list box

   Notice that Sea Swept is formatted using the Book Title style. Only the selected characters Sea Swept: are formatted in the Book Style because you selected only them and not the entire paragraph.

7. Apply the Book Title style to Mystery Tug: and Shell Game:

   Notice that the font size assigned to the Book Title style is larger than the font size assigned to Book List, which is the section head. You modify the font size assigned to the Book Title style to follow acceptable design practices.

8. With Shell Game: still selected, click the Book Title list arrow in the Pick formatting to apply list box, click Modify, change the font size to 12 point and the font color to Blue, then click OK

9. Click away from Shell Game: to deselect it, compare the three book titles to Figure I-10, then save the document

FIGURE I-9: Formatting options selected for Book Title character style

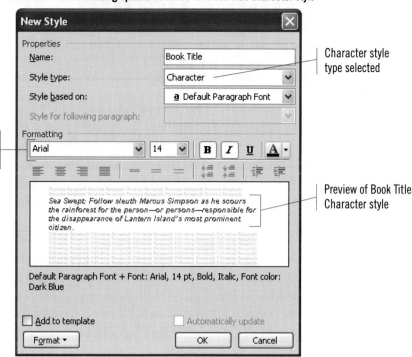

Character style type selected

Character formatting set as Arial font, 14-point font size, Bold, Italic, and Dark Blue font color

Preview of Book Title Character style

FIGURE I-10: Modified Book Title style applied

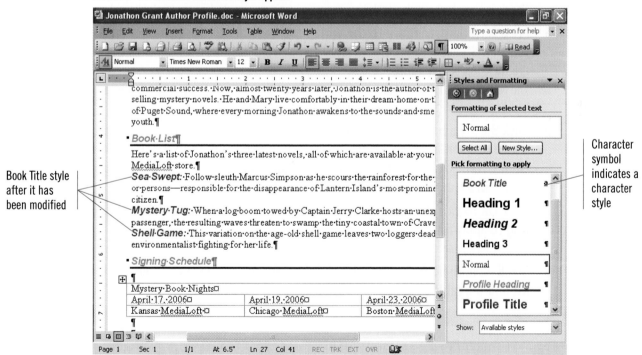

Book Title style after it has been modified

Character symbol indicates a character style

Word 2003

Creating Custom List and Table Styles

A **list style** includes paragraph format settings that you use to format a series of paragraphs when you want the paragraphs to appear related in some way. For example, you can create a list style that adds bullet characters to a series of paragraphs or sequential numbers to a list of items. A **table style** includes formatting settings for both the table grid and the table text. ▓▓▓▓ You want to create a custom list style called Book List to format the list of books with a special bullet character, and then you want to create a custom table style called Mystery Table to format the table at the end of the document.

STEPS

1. **Click the New Style button in the Styles and Formatting task pane, type Book List in the Name text box, click the Style type list arrow, then select List**
   The New Style dialog box changes to show the formatting options for a list style, as shown in Figure I-11. You want to select a symbol as the bullet character for your bulleted list.

> **TROUBLE**
> You may need to scroll up to find the Book symbol.

2. **Click the Insert Symbol button Ω to open the Symbol dialog box, click the Font list arrow, scroll down and select Wingdings if it is not already selected, then click the Book symbol as shown in Figure I-12**

3. **Click OK to exit the Symbol dialog box, then click OK to exit the New Style dialog box**

4. **Click in the paragraph that describes Sea Swept, click Book List in the Pick formatting to apply list box, then apply the Book List style to the paragraph that describes Mystery Tug and the paragraph that describes Shell Game**
   The three paragraphs in the Book List section are formatted with the new Book List style.

> **TROUBLE**
> If you do not see the table gridlines, click Table, then click Show Gridlines.

5. **Press [Ctrl][End] to move to the end of the document, click anywhere in the table, click the New Style button, type Mystery Table in the Name text box, click the Style type list arrow, then select Table**
   The New Style dialog box changes to show formatting options for a table. You can base the style on one of Word's preset table styles or you can modify the default table style.

6. **Click the Style based on list arrow, scroll to select Table Grid, click the Bold button, click the Font Color list arrow, select the Dark Blue color, click the Fill Color list arrow, select the Light Green color, click the Alignment button list arrow, then click the Align Center button**
   The format settings required for the table are selected.

7. **Click OK to exit the New Style dialog box, then click Mystery Table in the Pick formatting to apply list box**
   The Mystery Table style is applied to the table.

8. **Scroll up until both the book list and the table appear on the screen, compare the book list and the table with Figure I-13, then save the document**

FIGURE I-11: Formatting options for a list in the New Style dialog box

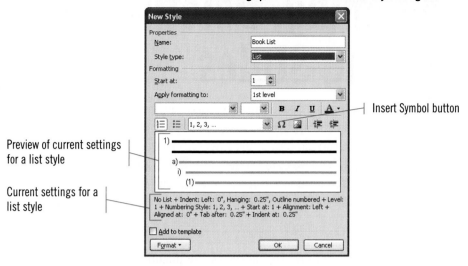

Insert Symbol button

Preview of current settings for a list style

Current settings for a list style

FIGURE I-12: Book symbol selected

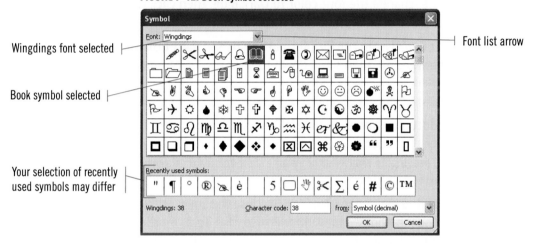

Font list arrow

Wingdings font selected

Book symbol selected

Your selection of recently used symbols may differ

FIGURE I-13: Custom List and Table styles applied

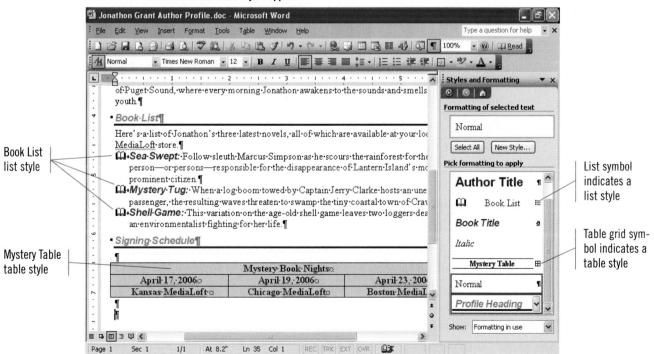

Book List list style

Mystery Table table style

List symbol indicates a list style

Table grid symbol indicates a table style

Renaming, Deleting, and Copying Styles

In the Styles and Formatting task pane, you can change the name of a style and even delete it altogether. Sometimes you might want the styles you've created for one document to be available in another document. In the Organizer dialog box, you can copy all the styles you've saved with one document to another document, where you can then apply those styles to selected text. ▨▨▨▨ You decide to change the name of the Profile Title style to Author Title. You also decide to remove the Book List style. Finally, you copy the styles to a document containing an author profile that you've written for Emily Chow, a mystery author from San Francisco.

STEPS

1. **Press [Ctrl][Home] to move to the top of the document, click the Profile Title list arrow in the Pick formatting to apply list box (you may need to scroll down), click Modify, type Author Title, change the font color to Dark Blue, then click OK**

   The text "Jonathon Grant" is formatted with the Author Title style.

   TROUBLE
   Use the Pick formatting to apply scroll bar if necessary to view a style.

2. **Right-click Book List in the Pick formatting to apply list box, click Delete, click Yes to accept the warning, then scroll down to view the list of book titles**

   The book descriptions are formatted with the Normal style. After removing the Book List style, the text may be formatted with a hanging indent. That is acceptable; just continue with the next step.

3. **Save the document, open the file WD I-2.doc from the drive and folder where your Data Files are located, then save it as Emily Chow Author Profile**

   Some of the headings in Emily's author profile are formatted with a default heading style and the book titles are formatted with a character style called Books.

4. **Click File on the menu bar, click Close to close the Emily Chow Author Profile document and return to the Jonathon Grant Author Profile, click Tools on the menu bar, click Templates and Add-Ins, then click the Organizer button in the Templates and Add-ins dialog box**

   In the Organizer dialog box, you need to open the file called Emily Chow Author Profile.doc and make it the Target file.

   QUICK TIP
   By default, only templates are listed.

5. **Click Close File under the list box on the right side in the Organizer dialog box, then click Open File, click the Files of type list arrow, select All Word Documents, navigate to the drive and folder where your Data Files are located, click Emily Chow Author Profile.doc, then click Open**

   The styles assigned to the Emily Chow Author Profile document appear in the list box on the right side.

6. **Confirm that Author Title is selected at the top of the list of styles in the Jonathon Grant Author Profile document (left side of the Organizer dialog box), press and hold the [Shift] key, scroll down the list, then click the last style listed Table Normal to select all the styles as shown in Figure I-14**

7. **Click Copy, click Yes to All, click Close File on the right side, click Yes to save the document, then click Close to exit the Organizer dialog box**

8. **Open the file Emily Chow Author Profile.doc, click the Styles and Formatting button 🔠 on the Formatting toolbar, apply styles as shown in Figure I-15, press [Ctrl][End], type Compiled by followed by your name, save the document, print a copy, then close the document**

   The file Jonathon Grant Author Profile is again the active document.

FIGURE I-14: Styles selected in the Organizer dialog box

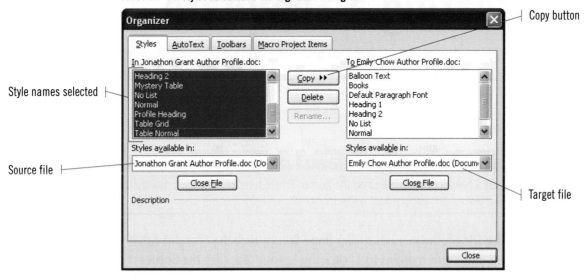

Copy button

Style names selected

Source file

Target file

FIGURE I-15: Document after new styles applied

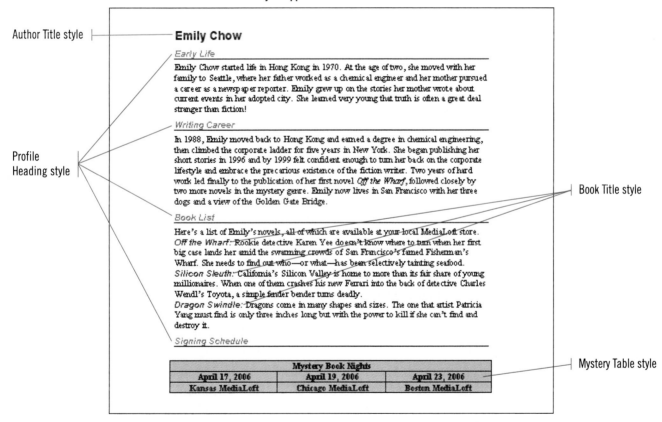

Author Title style

Profile Heading style

Book Title style

Mystery Table style

Creating a Template

A template is a document that contains the basic structure of a document, including styles. You can create a template from an existing document, or you can create the template from scratch. Templates that you create yourself are called **user templates**. To base a document on a template, you select On my computer in the New Document task pane, and then double-click the template to open a new document that contains all the formats stored in the template. You can enter text into the document and then save it, just as you would any document. The original template is not modified. ▰▰▰ You decide to modify some of the document settings, replace text related to Jonathon Grant with instructions, then save the document as a template called Author Profile. You then open a new document based on the Author Profile template and start modifying it for a new author.

STEPS

QUICK TIP
Be sure Jonathon Grant Author Profile.doc is the active document.

1. **Click File on the menu bar, click Page Setup, click the Margins tab if necessary, change the Left and Right margins to 1" click the Layout tab, click the Borders button, click Box, verify that the border color is Dark Blue and the border width is 2¼ point, then click OK**

2. **Press [Ctrl][Home], select Jonathon Grant, type [Enter Author Title Here], then enter the placeholder text as shown in Figure I-16**
   The Word document is ready to save as the Author Profile template. You can save the template in the default location on your computer's hard drive or you can select a new location.

3. **Minimize Word, right-click My Computer on your computer desktop, click Explore, navigate to the drive and folder where your Data Files are located, click File on the menu bar, point to New, click Folder, type Your Name Templates as the folder name, then press [Enter]**
   You want this new folder to be the default location for user templates. When you save the template, it is saved to this folder by default.

4. **Close Explorer, return to Word, click Tools on the menu bar, click Options, click File Locations, click User templates, click Modify, click the Look in list arrow, navigate to the Your Name Templates folder, click the folder to select it, click OK, then click OK**
   Now you can save the document on your screen as a template into the new folder.

5. **Click File on the menu bar, click Save As, click the Save as type list arrow, then click Document Template**
   When you select Document Template as the file type, Word switches to the default location for user templates—which you set as the folder called Your Name Templates.

6. **Delete the text in the File name box, type Author Profile as the filename, then click Save**
   The file is saved as Author Profile.dot to your default template location, which is the folder you called Your Name Templates. The .dot filename extension identifies this file as a template file. You can create new documents based on this template.

7. **Click File on the menu bar, click Close, click File on the menu bar, click New, then click On my computer in the Templates section of the New Document task pane**
   The default Templates folder opens and the template you saved to the Your Name Templates folder is available.

QUICK TIP
If text you enter appears in a style other than Normal, select the text, then click Clear Formatting in the Pick formatting to apply list box.

8. **Click Author Profile.dot, be sure the Document option button in the Create New section is selected, then click OK**
   The template opens as a new document. Note that Document2 appears in the title bar. You can enter text into this document just as you would any document.

9. **Replace the placeholder text with text as shown in Figure I-17**

10. **Click File, click Save as, navigate to the drive and folder where your Data Files are located, type Monique Deville Author Profile, then click Save**
    The file Monique Deville Author Profile is the active document.

FIGURE I-16: Template text entered

Placeholder text

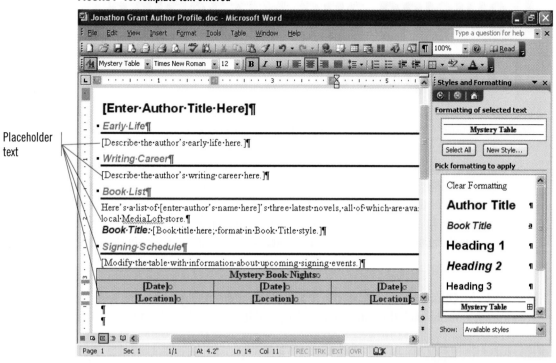

FIGURE I-17: Information about a new author

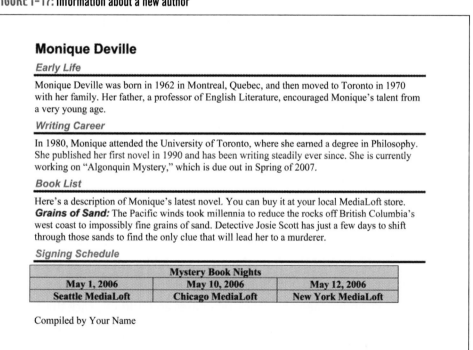

Clues to Use

Changing the default file location for user and workgroup templates

By default, user templates are stored in the Templates folder. The path for this folder is: C:/Documents and Settings/Administrator/Application Data/Microsoft/Templates. Note that a different folder might appear for Administrator, depending on how your computer system is set up. If the default location where user templates are saved has been changed, you can change back to the default location by selecting the Templates folder path in the File Locations tab of the Options dialog box.

You can also create templates to distribute to others. These templates are called **workgroup templates**. You select the location of a workgroup template in the File Locations tab of the Options dialog box, just as you select the location of a user template. To open the Options dialog box, click Tools on the Standard toolbar, then select Options.

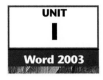
Revising and Attaching a Template

You can modify a template just as you would any Word document. All new documents you create from the modified template will use the new settings. All documents that you created before you modified the template are not changed unless you open the Templates and Add-ins dialog box and direct Word to update styles automatically. Note that when you attach a template to an existing document, structural settings such as margins and page layouts originally included with the template are not attached to the new document. These structural settings affect only new documents that you create from a template. You decide to change the font style, size, and color of the Author Title style, update Monique Deville's author profile with the revised template, and then add the template to the author profile you've already written for veteran mystery author Charles Sheldon.

STEPS

1. **Click the Open button 📂 on the Standard toolbar, navigate to the Your Name Templates folder, double-click the folder name to open it, click Author Profile.dot, then click Open**
   The file opens.

2. **Click the Styles and Formatting button 🖺 on the Formatting toolbar, right-click Author Title in the Pick formatting to apply list box, click Modify, change the font to Bodoni MT Black (or a similar font), change the font size to 18 point, change the font color to Dark Teal, then click OK**

3. **Modify the Profile Heading style so that the color is Teal and the font size is 14 point, click File on the menu bar, click Save As, click the Save as type list arrow, select Document Template, click Save, then close the template**
   The modified template is saved and the Monique Deville Author Profile document is the active document.

4. **Click Tools on the menu bar, click Templates and Add-Ins, click the Automatically update document styles option button to select it if it is not already selected, then click OK**
   The Author Title and Profile Heading styles in the Monique Deville Author Profile are updated, as shown in Figure I-18.

   TROUBLE
   All of the page border might not print on some printers. Remove the page border if your printer cannot accommodate it.

5. **Be sure your name is on the document, save it, print a copy, then close the file**
   The document prints and the file closes. You can also attach the template to a new document.

6. **Open the file WD I-3.doc from the drive and folder where your Data Files are located, then save it as Charles Sheldon Author Profile**

7. **Click Tools on the menu bar, click Templates and Add-Ins, click the Templates tab, click Attach, select the Author Profile.dot template, click Open, click the Automatically update document styles check box, then click OK**

8. **Open the Styles and Formatting task pane if necessary, then apply styles as shown in Figure I-19**
   The text is formatted with the styles, but the page border does not appear and the left and right margins are still set at 1.25". When you add the template to an existing document or update an existing document with a modified template, structural changes do not appear.

9. **Press [Ctrl][End], type Compiled by followed by your name, save the document, print a copy, close the file, then exit Word**

FIGURE I-18: Updated document

Author Title style updated

Profile Heading style updated

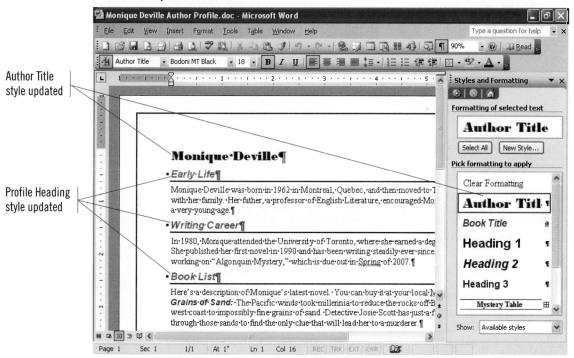

FIGURE I-19: Charles Sheldon Author Profile formatted

Author Title style

Profile Heading style

Charles Sheldon

Early Life

Charles Sheldon was born in 1921 near a Kansas town so small that it doesn't show up on most maps. He grew up on the family farm, where his earliest memories of the Depression left a life-long mark. At the age of 13, Charles quit school and took a job as a copy boy for the local newspaper. The pay was barely enough to feed the family, but the experience taught him a deep love for the power of words.

Writing Career

When war broke out, Charles served in the Pacific as a war correspondent and then moved to Washington in 1947 to begin his career as a political analyst. His marriage to Sally Morris in 1949 produced three children, all of whom have grown up to be writers. In 1962, Charles moved to New York where he began writing crime novels. Fifty books later and at the age of 82, Charles Sheldon is a legend who shows no signs of slowing down. His latest novel, "Gas Bar" features Darlene Drew, one of his most popular and endearing sleuths.

Book List

Charles Sheldon has invented three wonderful sleuths. You can buy all of Charles's books at your local MediaLoft store.

Darlene Drew: With her teased hair, short skirts, and smart mouth, Darlene epitomizes the stereotype of a "blonde bombshell." Where she goes, trouble follows. An offbeat sense of humor coupled with razor-sharp insights into the workings of the criminal mind, make Darlene a sleuth that always gets her man.

Tory Rankin: He's the archetypal gumshoe with the heart of gold and the voice of a hacksaw. Tory stalks criminals through the back alleys of 1950's New York and never comes up empty-handed.

Aldus Quigley: His cultured British accent, balding pate, and mild-mannered mien fool clients and criminals alike. But the local police in Cornwall's St. Alice-by-the-Sea have learned to rely on Aldus to solve even the most baffling of crimes.

Signing Schedule

Book Title style

Mystery Table style

Mystery Book Nights		
April 17, 2006	**April 19, 2006**	**April 23, 2006**
Kansas MediaLoft	**Chicago MediaLoft**	**Boston MediaLoft**

Practice

▼ CONCEPTS REVIEW

Identify each type of style shown in Figure I-20.

FIGURE I-20

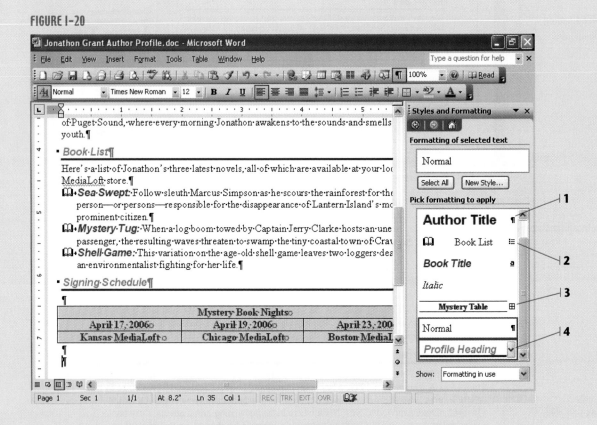

Match each term with the statement that best describes it.

5. **AutoFormat**

6. **Paragraph style**

7. **Template**

8. **Normal template**

9. **Character style**

10. **Style**

a. A combination of character and paragraph formats that are named and stored as a set

b. Character formats that you name and store as a set

c. Various formats that are combined into one set, which is named

d. A file that contains the basic structure of a document in addition to selected styles

e. A file that contains the settings available to all documents

f. Used to apply formatting quickly to a completed document

Select the best answer from the list of choices.

11. **What is the name of the template that is loaded automatically when you start a new document?**
    a. Global template
    b. User template
    c. Normal template
    d. Paragraph template

12. **What is the purpose of AutoFormat?**
    a. To remove extra spacing from a document
    b. To apply styles to text in a template
    c. To change the document type
    d. To apply a preset theme to a document

13. Which of the following definitions best describes a paragraph style?

  a. Format settings applied only
     to selected text within a paragraph

  b. Format settings applied to a table grid

  c. Format settings applied to the structure
     of a document

  d. Format settings applied to all the text in a paragraph

14. How do you modify a style?

  a. Double-click the style in the
     Styles and Formatting task pane

  b. Right-click the style in the Styles and
     Formatting task pane, then click Modify

  c. Right-click the style in the Styles and
     Formatting task pane, then click Revise

  d. Click the style in the Styles and Formatting
     task pane, then click New Style

15. In which dialog box do you copy styles from one document to another?

  a. Organizer dialog box

  b. New Document dialog box

  c. Styles dialog box

  d. Modify Styles dialog box

16. Which selection from the Tools menu do you click to attach a template to a document?

  a. Templates

  b. New templates

  c. General template

  d. Templates and Add-Ins

▼ SKILLS REVIEW

1. Create custom paragraph styles.

  a. Start Word, open the file WD I-4.doc from the drive and location where your Data Files are stored, save it as **Shaped Jigsaw Puzzles**, then open the Styles and Formatting task pane.

  b. Create a new paragraph style called **Puzzle Title** with the Arial Black font, 16 point, and the Green font color.

  c. Apply the Puzzle Title style to Shaped Jigsaw Puzzles.

  d. Click the Animal Puzzles heading, then select all the headings formatted with the Heading 3 style.

  e. Create a new style called **Puzzle Heading** that is based on the Heading 3 style, but that changes the font size to 14 point, adds Underlining, and changes the font color to Brown.

  f. Apply the Puzzle Heading style to the three selected headings, then deselect the text to view the change.

  g. Show only the formatting currently in use in the document, then save the document.

2. Modify paragraph styles.

  a. Click the Puzzle Heading list arrow in the Pick formatting to apply list box, then click Modify.

  b. Click the Format button, open the Paragraph dialog box, change the After spacing to 4 point, then click OK.

  c. Click the Format button, open the Font dialog box, then select the Shadow font effect.

  d. Exit the Modify Style dialog box, then verify that the modified Puzzle Heading style is applied to text formatted with the Puzzle Heading style.

  e. Click any text formatted with the Puzzle Heading style, open the Reveal Formatting task pane and view the formatting currently applied to the text, then save the document.

3. Create and modify custom character styles.

  a. Show the Styles and Formatting task pane, then create a new character style named **Puzzle Theme**.

  b. Select the Arial Black font, 12 point, Italic, Underlining, and the Brown font color, then exit the New Style dialog box.

  c. Show the Available styles, apply the Puzzle Theme style to the text Elephant puzzle and Whale puzzle.

  d. Apply the Puzzle Theme style to the text Italy puzzle and Great Britain puzzle in the Map Puzzles section.

  e. Modify the Puzzle Theme style by changing the font size to 11 point and the color to Green, then save the document.

4. Create custom list and table styles.

  a. Create a List style called **Puzzle List**.

  b. Select the right-pointing solid arrow symbol (➔) from the Wingdings character set. (*Hint*: Character code 232.)

  c. Accept the symbol, select the 14-point font size for the bullet character, then apply the style to each paragraph that describes a puzzle (for example, Elephant puzzle, Whale puzzle).

  d. Click the table at the bottom of the document, then create a Table style called **Puzzle Table** based on the Table Grid style.

  e. Select Dark Green for the font color, select Light Yellow for the fill color, change the font size to 14 point, select the Align Top Center alignment, then accept the style specifications to close the New Style dialog box.

    f. Apply the Puzzle Table style to the table, then save the document.

5. Rename, delete, and copy styles.

    a. Change the name of the Puzzle Title style to **Puzzle Category**, then change the font color to Dark Yellow, which is just above Lime. Check that the formatted text Shaped Jigsaw Puzzles at the beginning of the document is changed.

    b. Delete the Puzzle List style. (*Note*: After removing the Puzzle List style, the text may be formatted with a hanging indent. That is acceptable; just continue with the next step.)

    c. Save the document, then open the file WD I-5 and save it as **3-D Jigsaw Puzzles**.

    d. Close the 3-D Jigsaw Puzzle file, make sure Shaped Jigsaw Puzzles is the active document, click Tools on the menu bar, click Templates and Add-Ins, then click the Organizer button.

    e. Close the file in the right of the Organizer dialog box, then open the 3-D Jigsaw Puzzles document. Remember to change the Files of type to Word documents.

    f. Select all the styles in the Shaped Jigsaw Puzzles document, then copy them to the 3-D Jigsaw Puzzles document. Click Yes to All to overwrite existing style entries with the same name.

    g. Close the 3-D Jigsaw Puzzles document in the Organizer dialog box, click Yes to save when prompted, then close the Organizer dialog box.

    h. Open the file 3-D Jigsaw Puzzles.doc, then open the Styles and Formatting task pane. Apply the Puzzle Category style to the document title, apply the Puzzle Heading style to all text formatted with the Heading 3 style, apply the Puzzle Theme style to the name of each individual puzzle (for example, Willow Tree puzzle, Tulips puzzle, Palazzo puzzle, and Chalet puzzle), then apply the Puzzle Table style to the table.

    i. Type **Prepared by your name** at the end of the document, save the document, print it, then close it.

6. Create a template.

    a. Make sure that Shaped Jigsaw Puzzles is the active document.

    b. Change the left and right margins to 1.5", and then add a 3-point Dark Yellow page border.

    c. Select Shaped Jigsaw Puzzles at the top of the page, type **[Enter Puzzle Category Here]**, then delete text and enter directions so the document appears as shown in Figure I-21.

    d. In Explorer, create a new folder called **Your Name Skills Review** in the drive and folder where your Data Files are located.

    e. Change the file location for user templates to the new folder you named Your Name Skills Review.

    f. Save the file as a template called **Puzzle Description** to the Your Name Skills Review folder, then close the template.

    g. Create a new file based on the Puzzle Description template.

    h. Replace the title of the document with the text **Brain Teaser Puzzles**, then save the document as **Brain Teaser Puzzles**.

FIGURE I-21

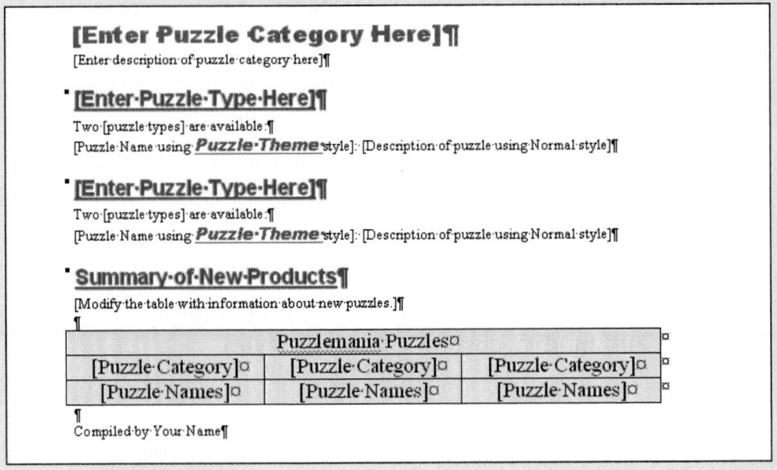

[Enter Puzzle Category Here]¶
[Enter·description·of·puzzle·category·here]¶

■ **[Enter·Puzzle·Type·Here]¶**
Two·[puzzle·types]·are·available.¶
[Puzzle·Name·using ***Puzzle·Theme*** style]: [Description·of·puzzle·using·Normal·style]¶

■ **[Enter·Puzzle·Type·Here]¶**
Two·[puzzle·types]·are·available.¶
[Puzzle·Name·using ***Puzzle·Theme*** style]: [Description·of·puzzle·using·Normal·style]¶

■ **Summary·of·New·Products¶**
[Modify·the·table·with·information·about·new·puzzles.]¶
¶

Puzzlemania·Puzzles□		
[Puzzle·Category]□	[Puzzle·Category]□	[Puzzle·Category]□
[Puzzle·Names]□	[Puzzle·Names]□	[Puzzle·Names]□

¶
Compiled·by·Your·Name¶

7. Revise and attach a template.

    a. Open the Puzzle Description.dot template, change the font color in the Puzzle Category style to Dark Red, open the Save As dialog box and verify that the Save as type is Document Template, then save and close the template.

    b. With the Brain Teaser Puzzles document active, click Tools on the menu bar, click Templates and Add-ins, click the Automatically update document styles check box, then click OK.

c. Verify that the font color of text formatted with the Puzzle Category style has changed to Dark Red.

d. Save the document, then close it.

e. Open the file WD I-6.doc, then save it as **Landscape Puzzles**.

f. Attach the Puzzle Description template to the document. Remember to click the Automatically update document styles check box in the Templates and Add-ins dialog box to select it.

g. Apply styles from the Puzzle Description template so that the Landscape Puzzles document resembles the other documents you have formatted for this Skills Review.

h. Type **Prepared by** followed by **your name** at the end of the document, save the document, print a copy, close all documents, then exit Word.

INDEPENDENT CHALLENGE 1

You are the office manager of Digital Learning, a company that creates learning materials for delivery over the Internet. The annual company softball game is coming soon and you need to inform the employees about the date and time of the game. To save time, you've decided to type the text of the memo without formatting and then to use the AutoFormat and Style Gallery features to format the memo attractively.

a. Start Word, open the file WD I-7.doc from the drive and folder where your Data Files are located, then save it as **Softball Memo**.

b. Use the AutoFormat feature to apply styles to the document. (*Hint*: To apply an AutoFormat, click Format on the menu bar, click AutoFormat, click the AutoFormat now option button, then click OK.)

c. Open the Style Gallery and apply the Professional Memo template. (*Hint*: To open the Style Gallery, click Format on the menu bar, click Theme, then click the Style Gallery button. Select the Professional Memo template from the list of templates, click the Document option button to see how the template appears when applied to the current document, then click OK.)

d. Open the Styles and Formatting task pane, then refer to Table I-1 to make the following changes to selected styles. If you do not have the fonts listed, select other fonts. (*Hint*: To identify the style assigned to specific text, click the text and then notice which style name is framed in the Pick formatting to apply list box.)

TABLE I-1

style name	changes
Document	Berlin Sans FB font, 22-pt font size, Centered
Message Header	Arial font, 12-point font size, Before paragraph spacing to 6 point
Heading 1	Berlin Sans FB font, 14-point font size, Bold

e. Select Your Name in the message header, type **your name**, save the document, print it, close it, then exit Word.

▼ INDEPENDENT CHALLENGE 2

As the owner of Le Bistro Café in Montreal, you need to create two menus—one for winter and one for summer. You've already created an unformatted version of the winter menu. Now you need to format text in the winter menu with styles, open and save a new document for the summer menu, copy the styles from the winter menu document to the summer menu document, then use the styles to create a summer version of the menu. You will type your own entries for appetizers, entrees, salads, and desserts for the summer menu.

a. Start Word, open the file WD I-9.doc from the drive and location where your Data Files are located, then save it as **Winter Menu**.

b. Create the styles as described in Table I-2.

c. Apply the Menu Title style to the document title.

TABLE I-2

style name and type	formats
Menu Title: paragraph	Arial, 18-point font size, Bold, Dark Teal, Center Alignment
Menu Categories: paragraph	Arial, 14-point font size, Bold Italic, Top and bottom border in 1 point and Dark Teal
Prices: paragraph	Right tab at 6" (*Hint*: Select Tabs from the Format menu in the New Style dialog box)
Menu Items: list	The Flower bullet character ({) from Wingdings (*Hint*: The character code is 123)

d. Apply the Menu Categories style to each menu category (for example, Appetizers, Soups and Salads).

e. Select all the menu items in the Appetizers category, apply the Prices style, then apply the Menu Items style. (*Note*: You must apply the styles in this order.)

f. Apply the Prices and the Menu Items styles to the remaining menu items in the document.

g. At the bottom of the document, press [Enter] twice, type **your name**, a **comma**, and **Owner**, apply the Normal style, center the text, save the document, then print it.

h. Create a new document, save it as **Summer Menu**, then close it.

i. Open the Organizer dialog box, copy the styles from the Winter Menu document to the Summer Menu document, then close the Organizer dialog box, saving files where prompted.

j. Open the Summer Menu document.

k. Create a menu similar to the winter menu, but with menu items more suitable for summer fare. For example, instead of Winter squash medley, you could include Mint-Raspberry Compote.

Advanced Challenge Exercise

- Modify the Menu Title style so that it includes the Britannic Bold font, 20-point font size, and Brown.
- Modify the Menu Categories style so it includes Orange text and Brown top and bottom border lines.
- Modify the Menu Items list style so that the bullet is diamond shape and Orange. (*Hint*: To change the color of the bullet, click the Font Color button; the font is already orange from the previous step).
- Modify the Prices style so that the Right tab includes the 2 leader style (*Hint*: Select Tabs from the Format menu in the Modify Style dialog box).

l. Apply styles to appropriate text.

m. Two lines below the last entry in the menu, type **your name**, a **comma**, and **Owner**, apply the Normal style, center the text, save the document, print it, close the document, then exit Word.

▼ INDEPENDENT CHALLENGE 3

You have enrolled in a new e-commerce program at your local community college. You have volunteered to create a design for the class newsletter and another classmate has volunteered to write text for the first newsletter. First, you create a template for the newsletter, then you apply the template to the document containing the newsletter text.

FIGURE I-22

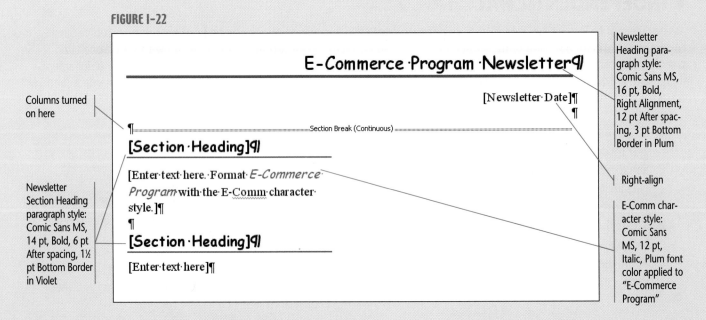

▼ INDEPENDENT CHALLENGE 3 (CONTINUED)

a. Start Word, then create the document shown in Figure I-22. Enter the content first, then create the styles shown in Figure I-22. (*Hint*: To create two columns, click to the left of the first occurrence of the text Section Heading, click Format on the menu bar, then click Columns. In the Columns dialog box, click two in the Presets section, click the Apply to list arrow, select This point forward, then click OK.)

b. Modify the default location for user templates so that they are saved in the folder you created previously named Your Name Templates. This folder should be in the drive and folder where your Data Files are located.

c. Save the document as a template named **E-Commerce Newsletter.dot**, then close the template.

d. Open the file WD I-8.doc from the drive and folder where your Data Files are stored, then save it as **October E-Commerce Newsletter**.

e Attach the E-Commerce Newsletter template to the document.

f. Change the left and right margins to 1.1", then apply the two-column format starting at the Class Projects heading. (*Note*: You need to apply the two-column format because options related to the structure of a document saved with a template are lost when you attach the template to an existing document.)

g. Apply styles to the appropriate text. (*Note*: The text E-Commerce Program appears four times in the newsletter.)

h. Insert a column break to the left of the Cool Sites heading so the second column starts with the section on Cool Sites.

Advanced Challenge Exercise

- Create a Table style called **Schedule**.
- Click the Apply formatting to list arrow, click Header row, then select Violet as the shading color, White as the font color, and Bold.
- Click the Apply formatting to list arrow, click Whole Table, then select Lavender as the shading color and Dark Blue as the font color.
- Apply the Schedule style to the table in the Class Projects section.

i. Type **Editor:** followed by your name so it is right-aligned at the end of the second column, save the document, print a copy, close the document, then exit Word.

▼ INDEPENDENT CHALLENGE 4

From the Microsoft Office Templates Web site, you can access a variety of templates. You can import any template from the Web site directly into Word and then modify it for your own purposes. You decide to find and then modify a template for a sales letter.

a. Open the New Document task pane, then click Templates on Office Online in the Templates section.

b. In a few seconds, the Microsoft Office Online Templates Home Web site opens in your browser.

c. Explore some of the documents available, then click Letters to Customers in the Marketing section (scroll down, if necessary).

d. Scroll through the sales letters listed. You need to select one that you can adapt for a business of your choice.

e. Select the letter you want to adapt, then click Download Now.

f. If necessary, read and accept the licensing agreement, click Yes to accept the Security warning, then click Continue. If another message box appears, click No. In a few moments, the letter appears in Word.

g. Modify the content of the sales letter in Microsoft Word so it contains information relevant to a company of your choice.

h. Use AutoFormat to format the document as a letter.

i. From the Style Gallery, select a letter style to apply to the letter.

j. In the Styles and Formatting task pane, modify two styles to reflect settings you prefer.

k. Save the sales letter as **Sales Letter from Microsoft Office Templates**, be sure your name appears in the signature block, print a copy, close the document, then exit Word.

Create a new document, then type the text and create the tables shown in Figure I-23. Do not include any formatting. Apply the Heading 1 style to the title, then modify it so that it appears as shown in Figure I-23. Apply the Heading 2 style to the names of the price lists, then modify them so that they appear as shown in Figure I-23. Create a table style called **Price Table** that formats each table as shown in Figure I-23. Save the price list as **Essential Essence**, be sure your name appears at the end of the document, print a copy, then close the document.

FIGURE I-23

Essential Essence

Essential Oils Price List

Product #	Essential Oil	Price
6590	Fir	$7.90
6592	Clove	$6.50
6593	Ginger	$8.00
6596	Lavender	$6.50

Perfume Oils Price List

Product #	Perfume Oil	Price
7880	Cinnamon	$7.00
7882	Jasmine	$7.50
7990	Marigold	$6.00
7995	Peppermint	$6.95
7998	Musk	$7.00

Compiled by Your Name

UNIT
J
Word 2003

Developing Multipage Documents

OBJECTIVES

Build a document in Outline view
Work in Outline view
Add footnotes and endnotes
Navigate a document
Generate a table of contents
Generate an index
Modify pages in multiple sections
Work with master documents

If you have a SAM user profile, you may have access to hands-on instruction, practice, and assessment of the skills covered in this unit. Log in to your SAM account and go to your assignments page to see what your instructor has assigned.

In Outline view, you use headings and subheadings to organize multipage documents, such as reports and manuals. These documents can include footnotes, cross-references, multiple sections, and even an index. You can also combine several documents—called subdocuments—into one master document.
Alice Wegman in the MediaLoft Marketing Department asks you to help her develop a set of guidelines to help MediaLoft store managers host events such as Meet the Authors, book reading clubs, and children's story fun sessions. You start by working in Outline view to revise the structure for the guidelines and then you use several advanced Word features to format the document for publication.

Building a Document in Outline View

You work in Outline view to organize the headings and subheadings that identify topics and subtopics in multipage documents. In Outline view, each heading is assigned a level from 1 to 9, with Level 1 being the highest level and Level 9 being the lowest level. In addition, you can assign the Body text level to the paragraphs of text that enhance or clarify the document headings. Each level is formatted with one of Word's preset styles. For example, Level 1 is formatted with the Heading 1 style and the Body text level is formatted with the Normal style. You work in Outline view to develop the structure of the Meet the Author Guidelines.

STEPS

QUICK TIP
Close the Getting Started task pane if it opens.

1. **Start Word, click the Show/Hide ¶ button ¶ on the Standard toolbar if necessary to show the paragraph marks, then click the Outline View button ▤ in the lower-left corner of the program window**

   The document appears in Outline view. Notice the Outlining toolbar below the Formatting toolbar at the top of the program window and the minus symbol in the document window. Table J-1 describes the buttons on the Outlining toolbar.

2. **Type Meet the Author Guidelines**

   Figure J-1 shows the text in Outline view. By default, the text appears at the left margin, is designated as Level 1, and is formatted with the Heading 1 style.

3. **Press [Enter], click the Demote button ➡ on the Outlining toolbar to move to Level 2, then type Manual Structure**

   The text is indented, designated as Level 2, and formatted with the Heading 2 style.

4. **Press [Enter], then click the Demote to Body Text button ➡➡ on the Outlining toolbar**

5. **Type the following text: Three principal activities relate to the organization and running of a Meet the Author event. You need to gather the appropriate personnel, advertise the event, and arrange the physical space. This manual will cover each of these activities in turn., then press [Enter]**

   The text is indented, designated as Body text level, and formatted with the Normal style. Notice that both the Level 1 and Level 2 text are preceded by a plus symbol ✚. This symbol indicates that the heading includes subtext, which could be a subheading or a paragraph of body text.

6. **Click the Promote to Heading 1 button ◄◄ on the Outlining toolbar**

   The insertion point returns to the left margin and the Level 1 position.

7. **Type Personnel, press [Enter], then save the document as Author Event Guidelines to the drive and folder where your Data Files are located**

   When you create a long document, you often enter all the headings and subheadings first to establish the overall structure of your document.

QUICK TIP
You can press [Tab] to move from a higher level to a lower level and you can press [Shift][Tab] to move from a lower level to a higher level.

8. **Use the Promote, Demote, and Promote to Heading 1 buttons to complete the outline shown in Figure J-2**

9. **Place the insertion point after Guidelines, press [Enter], click ➡➡, type Prepared by Your Name, save the document, print a copy, then close it**

   The printed copy does not include the outline symbols.

FIGURE J-1: Level 1 text in Outline view

Level of current heading

Outlining toolbar

Minus outline symbol means that no other heading or text appears below the current heading

Outline View button

Show/Hide ¶ button selected

Buttons for working with a table of contents and master document

Show Formatting button

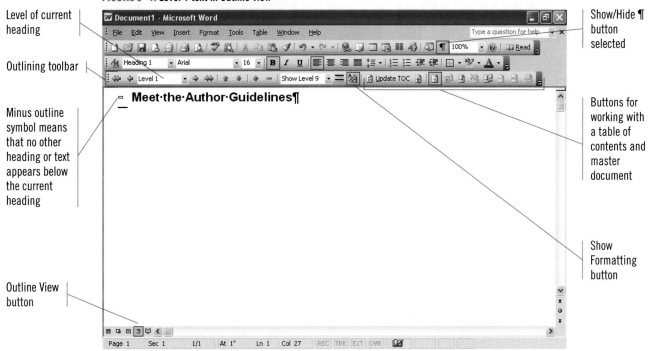

FIGURE J-2: Updated outline

Level 1 heading

Body text

Level 2 heading

Level 3 headings

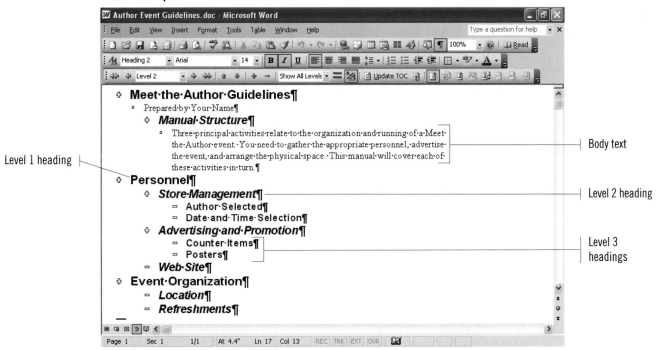

TABLE J-1: Outlining buttons on the Outlining toolbar

button	use to	button	use to
⇐⇐	Promote text to level 1	⬇	Move a heading and its text down one line
⇐	Promote text one level	✚	Expand text
Body text ▼	Show outline level at insertion point placement	▬	Collapse text
⇒	Demote text one level	Show All Levels ▼	Show a specific level or levels
⇒⇒	Demote to body text	═	Show only the first line of each paragraph
⬆	Move a heading and its text up one line	ᴬ⁄ₐ	Show text formatting

Working in Outline View

In Outline view, you can promote and demote headings and subheadings and move or delete whole blocks of text. When you move a heading, all the text and subheadings under that heading move with the heading. You also can use the Collapse, Expand, and Show Level buttons on the Outlining toolbar to view all or just some of the headings and subheadings. For example, you can choose to view just the Level 1 headings so that you can quickly evaluate the main topics of your document. ▓▓▓ Alice has written a draft of her guidelines for running a Meet the Author event. She asks you to work in Outline view to reorganize the structure of the document.

STEPS

1. **Open the file** WD J-1.doc **from the drive and folder where your Data Files are located, save it as** Meet the Author Guidelines, **scroll through the document to get a sense of its content, then click the** Outline View button 🔳

2. **Click the** Show Level list arrow **on the Outlining toolbar, then click** Show Level 1
   Only the Level 1 headings appear, as shown in Figure J-3.

3. **Click the** plus outline symbol ✚ **to the left of Advertising and Promotion**
   The heading and all its subtext (which is hidden because the topic is collapsed) are selected.

4. **Press and hold** [Shift], **select the headings:** Personnel, Event Organization, **and** Summary, **then click the** Demote button 🔳 **on the Outlining toolbar**
   You use [Shift] to select multiple headings at once. The selected headings are demoted one level to Level 2.

5. **Press** [Ctrl][A] **to select all the headings, click the** Expand button 🔳 **on the Outlining toolbar to expand the outline one level, then click** 🔳 **two more times**
   The outline expands to show all the subheadings and body text associated with each of the selected headings. You can also expand a single heading by selecting only that heading, then clicking the Expand button until all the associated subheadings and body text appear.

QUICK TIP
You can also use your pointer to drag a heading up or down to a new location in the outline. A horizontal line indicates the placement.

6. **Click the** Collapse button 🔳 **on the Outlining toolbar three times to collapse the outline, click** ✚ **next to** Personnel **to select it, click the** Move Up button 🔳 **on the Outlining toolbar once, then double-click** ✚ **next to** Personnel
   The outline for Personnel expands. When you move a heading in Outline view, all subtext and text associated with the heading also move.

7. **Click the** Show Level list arrow, **select** Show Level 3, **double-click** ✚ **next to** Equipment **under the Event Organization heading, then press** [Delete]
   The Equipment heading and its associated subtext are deleted from the document. The revised outline is shown in Figure J-4.

8. **Click the** Show Level list arrow, **click** Show All Levels, **press** [Ctrl][End] **to move to the bottom of the document, press** [Enter] **twice, then type** Revised by **followed by your name.**

9. **Save the document**

FIGURE J-3: Level 1 headings

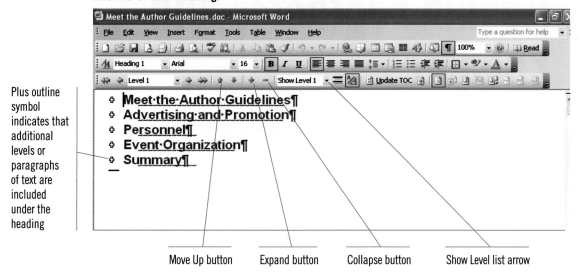

Plus outline symbol indicates that additional levels or paragraphs of text are included under the heading

Move Up button   Expand button   Collapse button   Show Level list arrow

FIGURE J-4: Revised outline

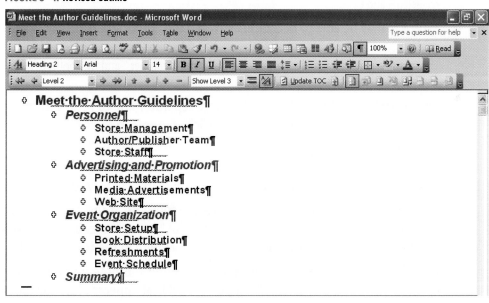

Adding Footnotes and Endnotes

You use **footnotes** and **endnotes** to provide additional information or to acknowledge sources for text in a document. Footnotes appear at the bottom of the page on which the footnote reference appears; endnotes appear at the end of the document. You can use footnotes and endnotes in the same document. For example, a footnote can cite the source and an endnote can comment on information provided in the text. Every footnote and endnote consists of a **note reference mark** and the corresponding note text. When you add, delete, or move a note, any additional notes in the document are renumbered automatically. ▰▰▰ You work in Print Layout view to add a footnote to the Meet the Author Guidelines document and to edit footnotes you inserted earlier. You use the Find command to move quickly to the text you want to reference.

STEPS

1. **Click the Print Layout View button ▣, press [Ctrl][Home] to move to the beginning of the document, click Edit on the menu bar, click Find, type agent and/or publisher in the Find what text box, click Find Next, click Cancel to close the Find dialog box, then press [→] once to position the insertion point just before the period following publisher**

2. **Click Insert on the menu bar, point to Reference, then click Footnote**
   The Footnote and Endnote dialog box opens, as shown in Figure J-5.

3. **Click Insert**
   The insertion point moves to the footnote area at the bottom of the page, and the existing footnotes are relabeled B and C.

4. **Type You may be able to deal directly with some authors, particularly local or self-published authors.**
   The footnote reference marker appears after the word "publisher," and the footnote text appears in the footnote area, as shown in Figure J-6.

5. **Click anywhere in the text above the note separator line to return to the document text, click Edit on the menu bar, click Go To, click Footnote in the Go to what list box, click in the Enter footnote number text box, type E, click Go To, then click Close**
   The insertion point moves to the footnote reference marker for E.

TROUBLE

If the footnote does not appear in a comment text box, click Tools on the menu bar, click Options, click the ScreenTips check box to select it, then click OK.

6. **Move the pointer over the footnote reference marker to view the footnote text**

7. **Double-click the footnote marker to view the footnote at the bottom of the page, position the insertion point after the word "special," press [Spacebar], type sidewalk, scroll up until the document is visible, then click anywhere in the text above the note separator**

8. **Press [Ctrl][G], verify that E is selected in the Enter footnote number text box, type B, click Go To, click Close, select the superscript B that appears after cookbooks, then press [Delete]**
   The footnote reference marker and its associated footnote are deleted. The footnote reference markers and the footnotes in the footnote area are relabeled.

9. **Click Insert on the menu bar, point to Reference, click Footnote, click the Number format list arrow, select the 1, 2, 3 number format, click Apply, then save the document**
   The footnote reference markers and the footnotes are relabeled, as shown in Figure J-7.

FIGURE J-5: Footnote and Endnote dialog box

Footnotes selected by default

Format options

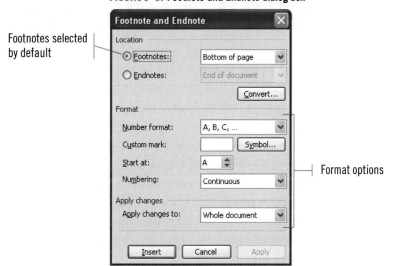

FIGURE J-6: Footnote text inserted in the footnote area

Footnote reference marker

Note separator

Footnotes automatically re-lettered sequentially

New footnote text

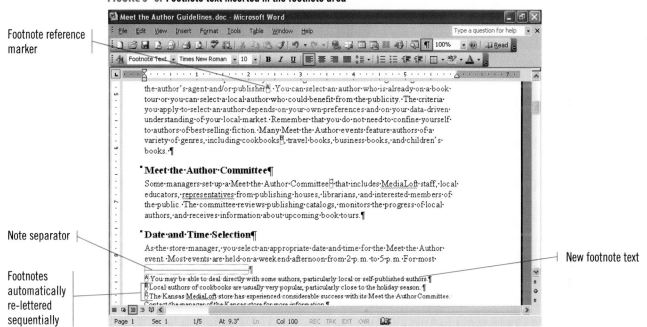

FIGURE J-7: Revised footnotes

New footnote format

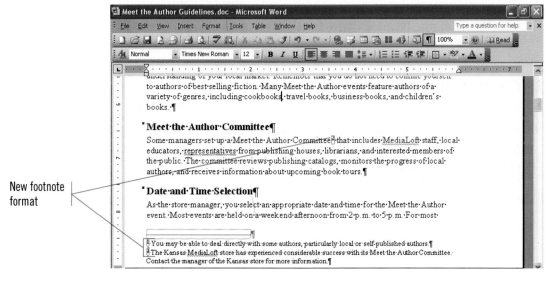

Navigating a Document

You can use the document map, thumbnails, and cross-references to navigate through a multipage document. The **Document Map** pane shows all the headings and subheadings in the document and opens along the left side of the document window. You can quickly move through a document by clicking headings and subheadings in the Document Map pane. You can also view a thumbnail of each page in your document. A **thumbnail** is a smaller version of a page that appears in the Thumbnails pane to the left of the document window when you select thumbnails on the View menu. A **cross-reference** is text that electronically refers the reader to another part of the document, such as a numbered paragraph, a heading, or a figure. For example, if you make the text "below" an active hyperlink in "See Figure 1 below," then when "below" is clicked, the reader moves directly to Figure 1. You use the Document Map to navigate to a specific heading in the document so you can make a quick editing change. You use the Thumbnails feature to jump quickly to a specific page in the document, and finally you add a caption to the graphic of a pie chart and create a cross-reference to the pie chart.

STEPS

TROUBLE
If you do not see Counter Items, click the plus symbol next to Printed Materials to expand the list, then click Counter Items.

1. **Press [Ctrl][Home], click the Document Map button 🔲 on the Standard toolbar to open the Document Map, then click Counter Items in the Document Map pane**
   The Counter Items subheading is selected in the Document Map pane and the insertion point moves to the subheading Counter Items in the document.

2. **Select flyers in the first line of text under the Counter Items heading, type author profiles, then click 🔲 to close the Document Map pane**

3. **Click View on the menu bar, click Thumbnails, scroll down the Thumbnails pane if necessary, then click the page containing the pie chart as shown in Figure J-8**

4. **Click View on the menu bar, click Thumbnails to close the Thumbnails pane, click the pie chart to select it, click Insert on the menu bar, point to Reference, click Caption, then click OK to enter the default caption text "Figure 1"**
   The caption "Figure 1" appears below the pie chart and is the element you want to cross-reference.

5. **Press [Ctrl][F], type children's books, click Find Next, click Cancel, press [→] three times so the insertion point moves just to the left of the ¶ mark, type the text See Figure 1 as the beginning of a new sentence, then press [Spacebar] once**

6. **Click Insert on the menu bar, point to Reference, then click Cross-reference**
   In the Cross-reference dialog box, you select the Reference type, such as a Numbered item or Figure, and the cross-reference text, such as the words above or below.

7. **Click the Reference type list arrow, select Figure, click the Insert reference to list arrow, then select Above/below**
   Figure J-9 shows the options selected in the Cross-reference dialog box.

8. **Click Insert, then click Close**
   The word below is inserted because the figure appears below the cross-reference.

9. **Type a period after below, move the pointer over below to show the [Ctrl] + click message, press and hold [Ctrl] to show ᕀ, click the left mouse button to move directly to the pie chart caption, scroll up to see the figure, then save the document**

FIGURE J-8: **Selecting a page in the Thumbnails pane**

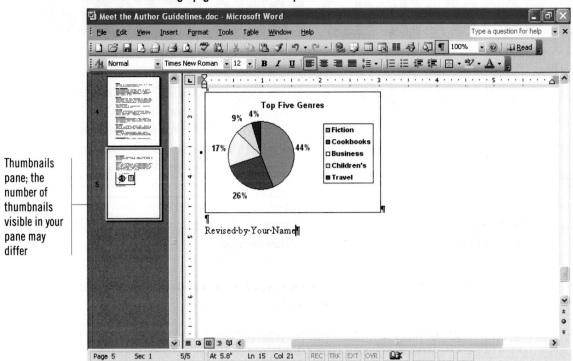

Thumbnails pane; the number of thumbnails visible in your pane may differ

FIGURE J-9: **Cross-reference dialog box**

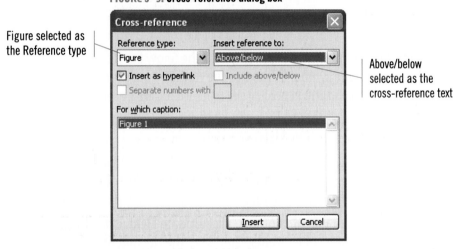

Figure selected as the Reference type

Above/below selected as the cross-reference text

Clues to Use

Using bookmarks

A **bookmark** identifies a location or a selection of text in a document. To create a bookmark, you first move the insertion point to the location in the text that you want to reference. This location can be a word, the beginning of a paragraph, or a heading. Click Insert on the menu bar, then click Bookmark to open the Bookmark dialog box. In this dialog box, you type a name for the bookmark, then click Add. To find a bookmark, press [Ctrl][G] to open the Go To dialog box, click Bookmark in the Go to what list box, click the Enter bookmark name list arrow to see the list of bookmarks in the document, select the bookmark you require, click Go To, then close the Go To dialog box.

Generating a Table of Contents

Readers refer to a table of contents to obtain an overview of the topics and subtopics covered in a multipage document. When you generate a table of contents, Word searches for headings, sorts them by heading levels, and then displays the completed table of contents in the document. By default, a table of contents lists the top three heading levels in a document. Consequently, before you create a table of contents, you must ensure that all headings and subheadings are formatted with heading styles. ████ You are pleased with the content of the document and are now ready to create a new page that includes a table of contents. Because you organized the document in Outline view, you know that all headings are assigned a Word heading style.

STEPS

1. **Press [Ctrl][Home], click** Insert **on the menu bar, click** Break, **click the** Next page option button **in the Section break types area, then click** OK

2. **Press [Ctrl][Home], press [Enter] twice, select the** top paragraph mark **as shown in Figure J-10, click the** Style list arrow **on the Formatting toolbar, then click** Clear Formatting
   The formatting associated with the paragraph is removed.

3. **Type** Table of Contents, **center it, select and enhance it with** Bold **and the** 18 pt **font size, click after** Contents, **press [Enter] twice, then clear the current formatting**
   The insertion point is positioned at the left margin where the table of contents will begin.

4. **Click** Insert **on the menu bar, point to** Reference, **click** Index and Tables, **then click the** Table of Contents tab
   The Table of Contents tab in the Index and Tables dialog box opens.

QUICK TIP
Depending on your computer settings, your Table of Contents (TOC) may appear with a gray background. The gray shading does not print.

5. **Click the** Formats list arrow, **click** Formal, **select** 3 **in the Show levels text box, type** 4, **compare the dialog box to Figure J-11, then click** OK
   A complete table of contents that includes all the Level 1, 2, 3, and 4 headings appears.

6. **Click the** Outline View button 🗐, **click the** Show Level list arrow, **click** Show Level 3, **click the** plus outline symbol ⊕ **next to the** Author/Publisher Team **heading, then press [Delete]**
   The Author/Publisher Team heading and its related subtext are deleted from the document.

7. **Click the** Print Layout View button 🗐, **then press [Ctrl][Home]**
   Error messages appear in the table of contents next to the items you deleted.

TROUBLE
The TOC should appear black with white text when selected. If the background is gray with black text, repeat Step 8.

8. **Move the mouse to the left of** Meet the Author Guidelines **at the top of the table of contents until the** ⟍ **appears, then click** ⟍ **to select the entire table of contents at once**
   With the table of contents selected, you can update it to show the new page numbers.

9. **Right-click the** table of contents, **click** Update Field, **click the** Table of Contents title **to deselect the table of contents, then save the document**
   The completed table of contents appears, as shown in Figure J-12. Each entry in the table of contents is a hyperlink to the entry's corresponding heading in the document.

10. **Move the pointer over the heading** Media Advertisements, **press [Ctrl], then click the** left mouse button
    The insertion point moves automatically to the Media Advertisements heading in the document.

FIGURE J-10: Paragraph mark selected

Style list arrow

Top paragraph mark

Section break

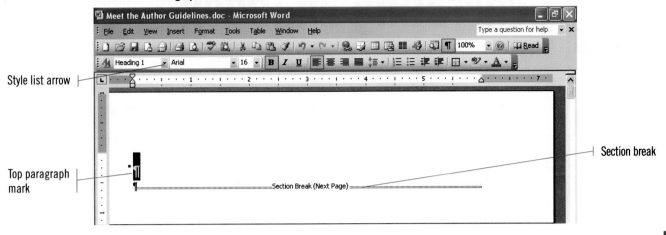

FIGURE J-11: Index and Tables dialog box

Table of Contents tab

Preview of Formal format

Formats list arrow

Formal format selected

Number of heading levels included in the table of contents

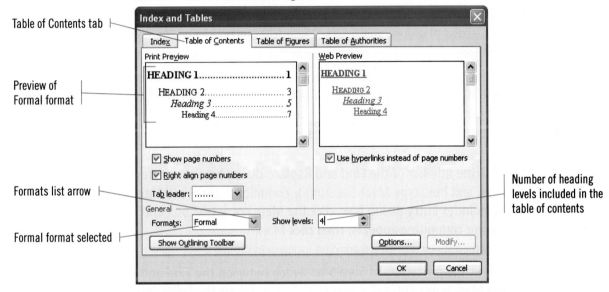

FIGURE J-12: Updated table of contents

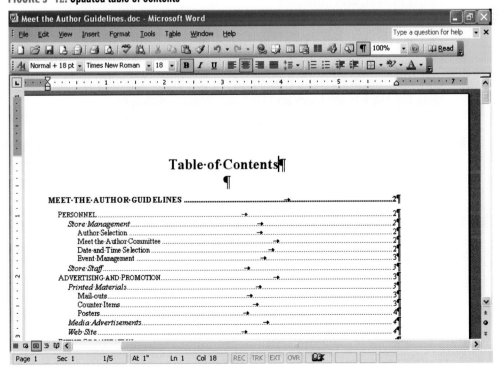

Generating an Index

An **index** lists many of the terms and topics included in a document, along with the pages on which they appear. An index can include main entries, subentries, and cross-references. Once you have marked all the index entries, you select a design for the index, and then you generate it. ■■■■■ You mark terms that you want to include in the index, create a new last page in the document, and then generate the index.

STEPS

1. **Press [Ctrl][Home], press [Ctrl] and click** Meet the Author Guidelines **in the table of contents, then select the text** Meet the Author event **in the first paragraph**

2. **Click** Insert **on the menu bar, point to** Reference, **click** Index and Tables, **click the** Index tab, **then click** Mark Entry

   The Mark Index Entry dialog box appears, as shown in Figure J-13.

QUICK TIP
The XE field code appears when Show/ Hide ¶ is on. By default, the code does not print in your final document.

3. **Click** Mark All

   All instances of "Meet the Author event" are marked with the XE field code. "XE" stands for "Index Entry." The Mark Index Entry dialog box remains open so that you can continue to mark text for inclusion in the index.

4. **Click twice anywhere in the document to deselect the** current index entry, **press [Ctrl][F], type** store manager **in the Find what text box, click** Find Next, **click** Yes **if a message appears, click the** title bar **of the Mark Index Entry dialog box, then click** Mark All

   All instances of "store manager" are marked for inclusion in the index. By default, selected text is entered in the Main entry text box and treated as a main entry in the index.

TROUBLE
Click Yes if a message appears asking you to continue the search from the beginning of the document.

5. **Click the** title bar **of the Find and Replace dialog box, select** store manager **in the Find what text box, type** Meet the Author committee, **click** Find Next, **click the** title bar **of the Mark Index Entry dialog box, click the Main entry text box and verify that Meet the Author committee appears, then click** Mark

   Only the text you selected is marked for inclusion in the index.

6. **Follow the procedure in Step 5 to switch between the Find and Replace dialog box and the Mark Index Entry dialog box to find and mark the following main entries:** rain checks, target market, **and** publisher

   In addition to main entries, an index often has a subentry included under a main entry.

7. **Click the** title bar **of the Find and Replace dialog box, find the text** shopping cart, **click the** title bar **of the Mark Index Entry dialog box, select** shopping cart **in the Main entry text box, type** Web site, **press [Tab], type** shopping cart **in the Subentry text box, click** Mark All, **then close the Mark Index Entry and Find and Replace dialog boxes**

   The text "shopping cart" is marked as a subentry to appear following the Main entry, Web site.

8. **Press [Ctrl][End], click to the left of** Revised by your name, **click** Insert **on the menu bar, click** Break, **click the** Next page option button, **click** OK, **type** Index, **press [Enter] three times to move your name down, enhance** Index **with** 18 pt **and** Bold **and** center alignment, **then click at the left margin above your name**

QUICK TIP
Depending on your computer settings, your index may appear with a gray background. The gray shading does not print.

9. **Click** Insert **on the menu bar, point to** Reference, **click** Index and Tables, **click the** Formats list arrow, **click** Fancy, **click** OK, **then save the document**

   As shown in Figure J-14, Word has collected all the index entries, sorted them alphabetically, included the appropriate page numbers, and removed duplicate entries. If you add or delete index entries, you can update the index by right-clicking the index and clicking Update Field.

FIGURE J-13: Mark Index Entry dialog box

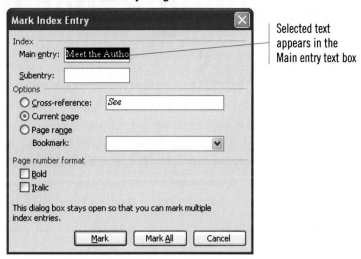

Selected text appears in the Main entry text box

FIGURE J-14: Completed index

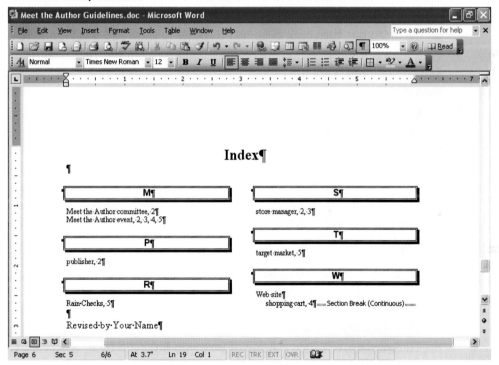

Clues to Use

Creating a cross-reference in the index

A cross-reference in an index refers the reader to another entry in the index. For example, a cross-reference in an index might read, "London. *See* Europe." Readers then know to refer to the Europe entry in the index to find the page number that contains information about London, presented in the context of its relationship to Europe. To create a cross-reference in an index, find the text in the document you want to cross-reference. In the Mark Index Entry dialog box, click after *See* in the Cross-reference text box, then type the text you want readers to refer to when they see the marked entry. For example, you could mark the text "London" as a main entry and then enter "Europe" after *See* in the Cross-reference text box.

Modifying Pages in Multiple Sections

Multipage documents often consist of two or more sections—each of which can be formatted differently. For example, you can include different text in the header for each section, or change how page numbers are formatted from section to section. ░░░░░ You want to format the page number on the table of contents page in lowercase Roman numerals and format the page numbers for the guidelines in regular numbers, starting with page 1. You also want to include a header that starts on the second page of the guidelines. The diagram in Figure J-15 shows the header and footer for each of the three document sections.

STEPS

1. **Press [Ctrl][Home], click Insert on the menu bar, click Page Numbers, click the Alignment list arrow, select Center, click Format, click the Number format list arrow, click i, ii, iii, click OK to close the Page Number Format dialog box, click OK to close the Page Numbers dialog box, then scroll to the bottom of the page**
   Notice the "i" inserted in the footer area at the bottom of the table of contents page.

2. **Scroll to the top of the next page, click the Meet the Author Guidelines heading, click View on the menu bar, then click Header and Footer to show the Header and Footer toolbar**

3. **Click the Page Setup button ⊞ on the Header and Footer toolbar to open the Page Setup dialog box, click the Layout tab, click the Different first page check box to select it, then click OK**

> **QUICK TIP**
> When you want the first page in a section to be different from the other pages in the same section, you must be sure to select the Different first page option.

4. **Click the Switch Between Header and Footer button ▤ on the Header and Footer toolbar, click the Link to Previous button ▦ on the Header and Footer toolbar to deselect it, click the Center button ▤ on the Formatting toolbar, then click the Insert Page Number button ▣**
   The number 2 appears in the First Page Footer - Section 2 because by default, the numbering is continuous from the first page in the document.

5. **Click the Format Page Number button ▣ on the Header and Footer toolbar, click the Start at option button, verify that 1 appears, click OK, then click the Show Next button ▦ on the Header and Footer toolbar**
   Clicking the Show Next button moves the insertion point to the header or footer on the next page of the document when the Different first page option is selected in the Page Setup dialog box. Clicking the Show Next button moves the insertion point to the header or footer of the next section of a document when the Different first page option is *not* selected.

6. **Click ▤, click ▦ to deselect it, type Meet the Author Guidelines, press [Tab] twice, type the current date, enhance the line of text with Bold and Italic, then click Guidelines to deselect the text**
   The header appears as shown in Figure J-16. You deselected the Link to Previous button to make sure that only the header in this section contains the text you type into the header. You must deselect the Link to Previous button when you want the header in a section to be unique.

7. **Click ▦, click ▦, delete Meet the Author Guidelines and the current date, then click Close on the Header and Footer toolbar**
   When you click the Show Next button, the header for Section 3, which contains the index, appears. You delete the header text in section 3 so that it does not appear on the index page.

8. **Press [Ctrl][Home], right-click the table of contents, click Update Field, click the Update entire table option button, then click OK**

9. **Press [Ctrl][End], scroll as needed to view the Index, right-click the index, click Update Field, save the document, print a copy, then close it**
   The headers and footers appear in the printed document as indicated in Figure J-15.

FIGURE J-15: Diagram of headers and footers by section

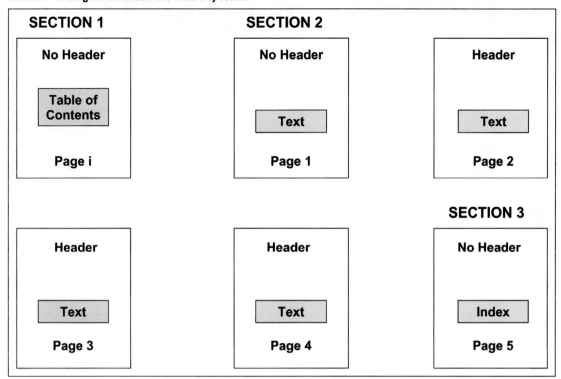

FIGURE J-16: Completed header

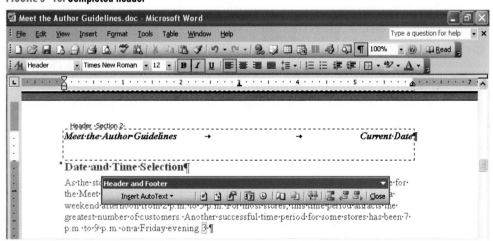

Clues to Use

Using text flow options

You adjust text flow options to control how text in a multipage document breaks across pages. To change text flow options, open the Paragraph dialog box on the Format menu, and then select the Line and Page Breaks tab. In the Pagination section of this tab, you can choose to select or deselect four text flow options. For example, you select the Widow/Orphan control option to prevent the last line of a paragraph from printing at the top of a page (a widow) or the first line of a paragraph from printing at the bottom of a page (an orphan). By default, Widow/Orphan is turned on. You can also select the Keep lines together check box to keep a paragraph from breaking across two pages.

Working with Master Documents

A **master document** is a Word document that contains links to two or more related documents called **subdocuments**. You create a master document to organize and format long documents such as reports and books into manageable subdocuments, each of which you can open and edit directly from the master document. ▨▨▨ Alice has written guidelines for story time sessions and book clubs. She has also created a new version of the Meet the Author Guidelines. She asks you to create a master document that contains all three sets of guidelines.

STEPS

1. **Open a new blank Word document, type** MediaLoft Event Guidelines, **center the text and enhance it with** Bold **and** 26 pt, **press** [Enter] **two times, change the font size to** 14 pt, **type** Prepared by Your Name, **press** [Enter] **twice, clear the formatting, then save the document as** MediaLoft Event Guidelines **to the drive and folder where your Data Files are located**

QUICK TIP

The files should be in the drive and folder where your Data Files are located.

2. **Open the file** WD J-2.doc, **save it as** Guidelines_Meet the Author, **close the document, open the file** WD J-3.doc, **save it as** Guidelines_Reading Club, **close the document, open the file** WD J-4.doc, **save it as** Guidelines_Story Fun, **then close the document**

   The MediaLoft Event Guidelines document is again the active document.

3. **Switch to** Outline view, **if it is not selected click the Show Formatting button** 🔲, **click the Insert Subdocument button** 🔲 **on the Outlining toolbar, click** Guidelines_Meet the Author **in the list of files, then click** Open

   By default, each subdocument is contained in its own section so a section break is added automatically at the end of the Meet the Author Guidelines text.

TROUBLE

If you see a message about installing a converter, click No. If you see a message about saving in Word, click Yes.

4. **Use** 🔲 **to insert** Guidelines_Reading Club **and** Guidelines_Story Fun **as the second and third subdocuments, click the Collapse Subdocuments button** 🔲 **on the Outlining toolbar, then click** OK **to save the master document if prompted**

   The three subdocuments appear, as shown in Figure J-17. To make changes to a subdocument, you open the subdocument in the master document or open the subdocument file.

TROUBLE

If the Web toolbar opens, close it.

5. **Press** [Ctrl] **and click the link** Guidelines_Reading Club, **switch to** Outline view **when the document opens, show the top three levels, delete the** Store Setup **subheading and its subtext, then save and close the document**

   You are returned to the master document.

6. **Click the** Expand Subdocuments button 🔲 **on the Outlining toolbar, switch to Print Layout view, then scroll to the table of contents, right-click the table of contents, click** Update Field, **click the** Update entire table option button, **then click** OK

   The table of contents includes the headings for the Reading Club Guidelines and the Story Fun Guidelines.

7. **Press** [Ctrl] **and click the** Reading Club Guidelines **heading, double-click in the header, click the** Link to Previous button 🔲 **to deselect it, change the header text to** Reading Club Guidelines, **then click** Close

8. **Scroll down to the Story Fun Guidelines document on page 8, double-click in the header, click** 🔲 **to deselect it, type** Story Fun Guidelines, **then click** Close

   Each section of the guidelines now includes an appropriate header.

9. **Save the document, print a copy of the title page, page 5 and page 8, close the document, then exit Word**

   The title page and pages 5 and 8 are printed, as shown in Figure J-18.

FIGURE J-17: Inserting a subdocument

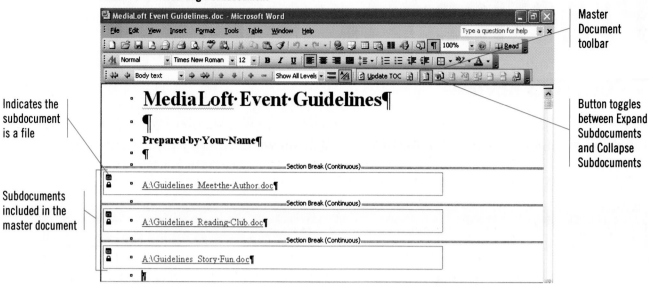

Indicates the subdocument is a file

Subdocuments included in the master document

Master Document toolbar

Button toggles between Expand Subdocuments and Collapse Subdocuments

FIGURE J-18: Pages from the printed document

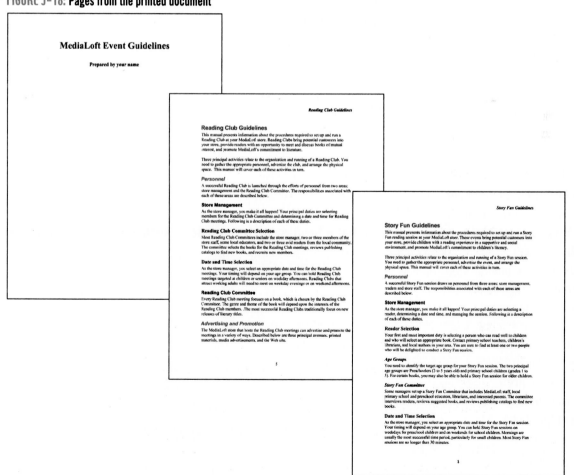

Practice

▼ CONCEPTS REVIEW

Label the numbered items on the Outlining toolbar shown in Figure J-19.

FIGURE J-19

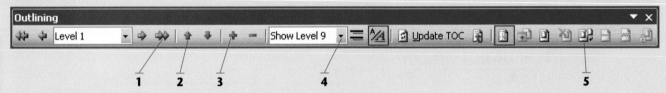

Match each term with the statement that best describes it.

6. **Table of contents**
7. **Demote button**
8. **Mark Index Entry dialog box**
9. **Footnote**
10. **Insert Subdocument button**
11. **Cross-reference**
12. **Demote to Body Text button**

a. Used to enter a lower-level heading in Outline view
b. Provides additional comments on information provided in the text
c. Included on the Master Document toolbar
d. Used to enter a paragraph of text in Outline view
e. List of topics and subtopics included at the beginning of a document
f. Text that refers the reader to another part of the document
g. Where you enter text for inclusion in an index

Select the best answer from the list of choices.

13. **In Outline view, which button do you click to move to Level 1?**
    a. Demote to Body Text button
    b. Promote to Level 1 button
    c. Promote to Heading 1 button
    d. Promote subtext button
14. **Which symbol in Outline view indicates that a heading includes subtext such as subheadings or paragraphs of text?**
    a. Plus outline symbol
    b. Minus outline symbol
    c. Slash outline symbol
    d. Level outline symbol
15. **Which feature can you use to navigate a document?**
    a. Thumbnails
    b. Cross-reference
    c. Document map
    d. All of the above

16. **On the Insert menu, which item do you select when you want to insert a table of contents?**
    a. Tools
    b. Index and Tables
    c. Reference
    d. Supplements

17. **Which button on the Header and Footer toolbar do you deselect to make sure that text you enter in a header or footer is unique from that section forward?**
    a. Same as Next button
    b. Same as Previous button
    c. Link to Previous button
    d. Show Formatting button

18. **What is a master document?**
    a. A document formatted in Outline view
    b. A short document included as part of a primary document
    c. A document containing two or more subdocuments
    d. A document containing two or more secondary documents

▼ SKILLS REVIEW

1. **Build a document in Outline view.**
    a. Start Word, switch to Outline view, type **Introduction by Your Name** as a Level 1 heading, press [Enter], type **Partnership Requirements** as another Level 1 heading, then press [Enter].
    b. Type **Background Information**, then use the Demote button to demote it to a Level 2 heading.
    c. Type the text shown in Figure J-20 as body text under Background Information.
    d. Use the Promote button to type the heading **Benefits** as a Level 2 heading, then complete the outline, as shown in Figure J-20.
    e. Save the document as **Partnership Agreement Outline** to the drive and folder where your Data Files are located, print a copy, then close the document.

2. **Work in Outline view.**
    a. Open the file WD J-5.doc from the drive and folder where your Data Files are located, save it as **Partnership Agreement Proposal**, switch to Outline view, then show all Level 1 headings.

FIGURE J-20

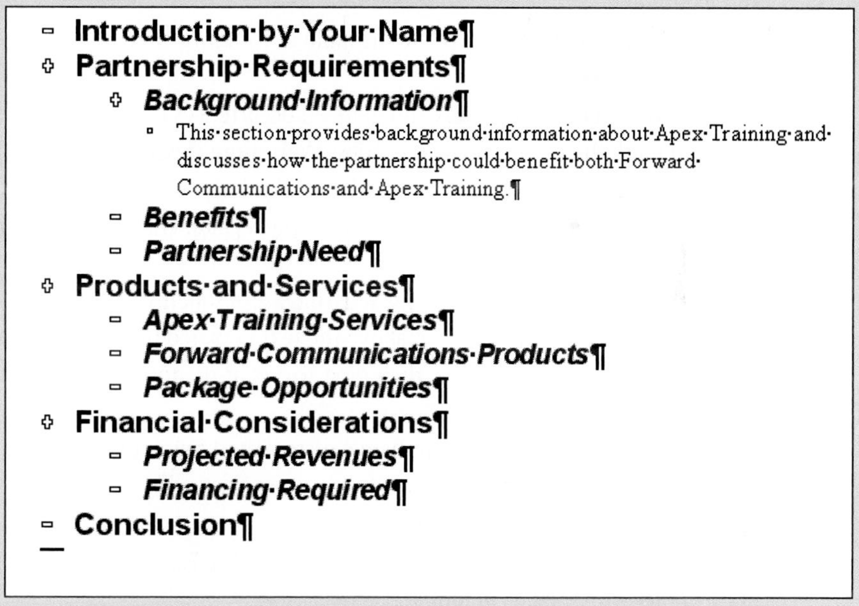

- Introduction·by·Your·Name¶
- Partnership·Requirements¶
  - Background·Information¶
    - This·section·provides·background·information·about·Apex·Training·and·discusses·how·the·partnership·could·benefit·both·Forward·Communications·and·Apex·Training.¶
  - Benefits¶
  - Partnership·Need¶
- Products·and·Services¶
  - Apex·Training·Services¶
  - Forward·Communications·Products¶
  - Package·Opportunities¶
- Financial·Considerations¶
  - Projected·Revenues¶
  - Financing·Required¶
- Conclusion¶

    b. Move the heading Financial Considerations below Products and Services.
    c. Select the Partnership Requirements heading, click the Expand button twice, collapse Benefits, collapse Partnership Need, then move Benefits and its subtext below Partnership Need and its subtext.
    d. Collapse the Partnership Requirements section to show only the Level 1 heading.
    e. Expand Products and Services, then delete Crystal Communications Products and its subtext.
    f. Show all levels of the outline, press [Ctrl][End], press [Enter] twice, type **Prepared by** followed by your name, then save the document.

▼ SKILLS REVIEW (CONTINUED)

3. Add footnotes and endnotes.

  a. In Print Layout view, find the words **computer labs**, then position the insertion point before the period.

  b. Insert a footnote, which will be Footnote 2, with the default settings and the text: **The principal competitor is Great West Trainers, which offers clients a choice of three computer training labs for a total of 120 workstations.**

  c. In the document, go to Footnote 4, click in the footnote area, then change Appendix B to **Appendix C.**

  d. Click in the document, then find, read, and delete Footnote 1.

  e. Apply the a, b, c format to the footnotes, view the footnote area, then save the document.

4. Navigate a document.

  a. Open the Document Map and then navigate to Package Opportunities.

  b. Change custom to **customizable** under the Package Opportunities heading, then close the Document Map.

  c. Open the Thumbnails pane, click the page containing the column chart graphic, close the Thumbnails pane, select the column chart in the document, then add **Figure 1** as a caption.

  d. Find the text **See Figure 1**, then insert a cross-reference to the figure using above/below as the reference text.

  e. Insert a period after the word **below**, test the cross-reference, scroll to see the figure, then save the document.

5. Generate a table of contents.

  a. Press [Ctrl][Home]. Use the Next page section break command to insert a new page above the first page.

  b. Press [Ctrl][Home], press [Enter] twice, select the top paragraph mark, clear the current formatting, enter **Table of Contents** at the top of the new first page, press [Enter] twice, enhance the text with 18 pt and Bold, then center it.

  c. Two lines below Table of Contents at the left margin, generate a table of contents using the Distinctive format and showing two levels.

  d. Use [Ctrl] + click to navigate to Partnership Need in the document, switch to Outline view, then delete Partnership Need and its subtext.

  e. Return to Print Layout view, update the table of contents, then save the document.

6. Generate an index.

  a. Find the words **computer labs** and mark all occurrences for inclusion in the index.

  b. Find and mark the following main entries: **Web page design**, **Networking**, and **PowerPoint**.

  c. Find **online publishing**, click in the Mark Index Entry dialog box, select online publishing in the Main entry text box, type **Crystal Communications Products**, press [Tab], type **online publishing** in the Subentry text box, then click Mark All.

  d. Repeat the process to insert **writing seminars** as a subentry of Crystal Communications Products.

  e. Insert a new page in a new section above the text Prepared by Your Name at the end of the document, press [Enter] twice at the top of the new page, then type **Index** at the top of the page and format it with Bold and 18 pt and center alignment.

  f. Click at the left margin above your name, press [Enter] twice, press the up arrow once, generate the index in the Bulleted format, then save the document.

7. Modify pages in multiple sections.

  a. Move to the beginning of the document, then open the Page Numbers dialog box and insert a right-aligned page number in the footer with the i, ii, iii format.

  b. Scroll down and click the title of the next page, then show the Header and Footer toolbar.

  c. Select Different first page in the Page Setup dialog box, then move to the header that will start on page 2, which is page 1 of Section 2.

  d. Deselect the Link to Previous button, type **Partnering Agreement: Tri-Mark Training**, center it, then format the text in Bold and Italic.

  e. Insert a right-aligned page number in the footer starting on the first page of Section 2. Use the 1, 2, 3 number format starting at 1. (*Hint*: Don't forget to deselect the Link to Previous button.)

  f. Remove the header from the index page.

  g. Update the table of contents and the index, save the document, print a copy, then close the document.

▼ SKILLS REVIEW (CONTINUED)

8. Work with master documents.

a. In a new blank document, type **Crystal Communications Partnership Agreements** as a centered title formatted with Bold and 20 pt font size, press [Enter] twice, type **Prepared by** followed by your name in 14 pt and centered, press [Enter] twice, then clear the formatting.

b. Save the document as **Partnership Agreements**.

c. Open the files from the drive and folder where your Data Files are located, save them as follows, and close them: WD J-6.doc as **Partnering_Tri-Mark Training**; WD J-7.doc as **Partnering_Verbally Yours**; and WD J-8.doc as **Partnering_Golden Gate College**.

d. In Outline view, insert the three files as subdocuments in the following order: Tri-Mark Training, Verbally Yours, and Golden Gate College.

e. Collapse and save the master document so just the filenames appear.

f. Use Ctrl + click to open the subdocument Partnering_Tri-Mark Training. (*Note*: Click No if a message opens asking you to install a converter.)

g. Remove the subheading Partnership Need and its subtext and save and close the document. (*Note*: Click Yes if a message opens asking if it is OK to save in Word format.)

h. Expand the subdocuments, show all levels, switch to Print Layout view, then update the table of contents.

i. In Print Layout view, view the Header and Footer toolbar, change the header starting on the first page of the Partnering_Verbally Yours subdocument to **Partnering Agreement: Verbally Yours**, then change the header starting on the first page of the Partnering_Golden Gate College subdocument to **Partnering Agreement: Golden Gate College**.

j. Update the table of contents, print a copy of the table of contents page, the first page of the Verbally Yours subdocument (page 4), and the first page of the Golden Gate College subdocument (page 7), save the document, close it, then exit Word.

▼ INDEPENDENT CHALLENGE 1

You work in the Finance Department of Super Strength, a successful fitness and spa facility in Orlando, Florida. Recently, Super Strength's owners began selling franchises. Your supervisor asks you to format a report that details the development of these franchise operations.

a. Start Word, open the file WD J-9.doc from the drive and folder where your Data Files are located, then save it as Super Strength Franchises.

b. In Outline view, organize the document as shown in the following table, starting with Introduction, followed by Scope of the Report, and then moving column by column. Note that the headings are formatted with the green font color.

Heading	Level	Heading	Level	Heading	Level
Introduction	1	Elinor Shore	2	Naples Clientele	3
Scope of the Report	2	Franchise Locations	1	Fort Lauderdale	2
Owner Information	1	Orlando	2	Fort Lauderdale Clientele	3
John Johnson	2	Orlando Clientele	3	Opening Schedules	1
Maria Sanchez	2	Naples	2		

c. Switch the order of Naples and its accompanying subtext so it follows Fort Lauderdale and its subtext.

Advanced Challenge Exercise

- Switch to Print Layout view, use the Document Map to move directly to the Opening Schedules heading, then create a bookmark called **Dates** using the first of the three dates listed. (*Hint*: Select the first date, click Insert on the menu bar, click Bookmark, type Dates, then click Add.)
- Move to the beginning of the document and go to your bookmark. (*Hint*: Press [Ctrl][G], click Bookmark, click Go To, then click Close.)
- Follow the same process to create a bookmark named **Location** that goes to the Franchise Locations heading, then close the Document Map.

▼ INDEPENDENT CHALLENGE 1 (CONTINUED)

d. Insert a footnote following the text **gourmet restaurants** that reads **One of these restaurants specializes in vegetarian and health-conscious cuisines.**

e. Create an index with appropriate Main entries and subentries. You could mark all locations and owners' names as Main entries and cross-reference owners with their specialties. For example, the owner Maria Sanchez could be listed as a cross-reference under the main entry **Massage Therapist** because Maria's specialty is massage therapy.

f. Create a new page in a new section at the end of the document, enter and format **Index** as the page title, then generate an index in the Modern format.

g. Create a footer with your name left-aligned and the page number right-aligned. The footer can print on every page.

h. Save the document, print a copy, close the document, then exit Word.

▼ INDEPENDENT CHALLENGE 2

You work for an author who has just written a series of vignettes about her travels in France and Italy. The author hopes to publish the vignettes and accompanying illustrations in a book called *Pastel and Pen*. She has written a short proposal that she plans to present to publishers. As her assistant, your job is to combine the proposal into a master document that includes three of the vignettes as subdocuments.

a. Start Word, open these files from the drive and folder where your Data Files are located, save them as follows, and close them: WD J-10.doc as **Pastel and Pen Proposal**, WD J-11.doc as **Pastel_Lavender**, WD J-12.doc as **Pastel_Ocher**, WD J-13.doc as **Pastel_Roman Rain**.

b. Open Pastel and Pen Proposal, switch to Outline view, press [Ctrl][End], then add the other three files as subdocuments under the body text for Sample Vignettes. Use the order: Lavender, Ocher, Roman Rain.

c. With the subdocuments expanded, switch to Print Layout view, press [Ctrl][Home], then scroll down to the Sample Vignettes heading and the list of the three titles (Lavender, Ocher, and Roman Rain) on page 1.

Advanced Challenge Exercise

- Make Lavender a cross-reference to its corresponding subdocument title. Select the text **Lavender**, open the Cross-reference dialog box, select Heading as the reference type, then select the **Lavender** heading as the reference text. (*Note*: After pressing Insert, click between Lavender and Ocher, then press [Enter] so the titles continue to appear as a list in the document.)
- Follow the same process to make Ocher and Roman Rain cross-references to their corresponding subdocuments.
- Test the Lavender cross-reference. Move the pointer over the title, then use [Ctrl] + click to follow the link. Once your insertion point moves to the Lavender subdocument, open the Document Map. Click the title Sample Vignettes in the Document Map to navigate back to the list of titles.
- Repeat the previous step to test the other two cross-references.

d. Insert a new page with a section break at the beginning of the document, enter and format **Table of Contents** as the page title (*Hint*: Make sure Table of Contents is not formatted as Heading 1), then generate a table of contents with two levels in the Formal style.

e. On the Table of Contents page, add your name left-aligned in the footer, and the page number **i** right-aligned in the footer. On the Proposal Overview page, add your name left-aligned in the footer, and the page number **1** right-aligned in the footer.

f. Update the table of contents, save the document, print page 1, which prints a copy of the table of contents page and page 1 of the proposal, close the document, then exit Word.

▼ INDEPENDENT CHALLENGE 3

As the program assistant at Green Gables College on Prince Edward Island, you are responsible for creating and formatting reports about programs at the college. You work in Outline view to create one program report.

    a. Create a new document and save it as **Program Information Report**.

    b. In Outline view, enter the headings and subheadings for the report as shown in the table starting with **Program Overview**, followed by **Career Opportunities**. You need to substitute appropriate course names for Course 1, Course 2, and so on. For example, courses in the first term of E-Business Studies could be **Introduction to E-Business**, **Online Marketing**, and so on.

Heading	Level	Heading	Level
Program Overview	1	[Enter name for Course 1]	3
Career Opportunities	2	[Enter name for Course 2]	3
Admission Requirements	2	Second Term	2
Program Content	1	[Enter name for Course 1]	3
First Term	2	[Enter name for Course 2]	3

    c. Enter appropriate body text for each heading. For ideas, refer to college catalogs.

    d. In Print Layout view, add a title page: include the name of the program, your name, and any other pertinent information. Format the title page text.

    e. If necessary, insert a page break in the body of the report to spread it over two pages. Format the title page with no header and no page number. Format Page 1 of the report with no footer and a right-aligned page number in the header starting with 1 using the 1, 2, 3 format. Format page 2 and the following pages of the report with the name of the program left-aligned in the footer, your name right-aligned in the footer, and a right-aligned page number in the header.

    f. Save the document, print a copy, then close it.

▼ INDEPENDENT CHALLENGE 4

Many large online businesses post job opportunities on their Web sites. You can learn a great deal about opportunities in a wide range of fields just by checking out the job postings on these Web sites. You decide to create a document that describes a selection of jobs available on two Web sites of your choice.

    a. Use your favorite search engine and the search phrase **job search** to find two Web sites that post jobs online.

    b. On two Web sites, find a page that lists current job opportunities.

    c. Identify two job categories (e.g., Marketing and Web Page Development) on each Web site.

    d. Create a new document in Word, then save it as **Online Job Opportunities**.

    e. In Outline view, set up the document starting with the name of the Web site, and followed by Job Category 1 as shown in the table. (*Note*: You need to enter specific text for headings such as Marketing Jobs for Job Category 1 and Marketing Assistant for Job Posting 1.)

Heading	Level	Heading	Level
Name of Web site 1	1	Job Posting 2	3
(for example, Yahoo.com)		Job Category 2	2
Job Category 1	2	Job Posting 1	3
Job Posting 1	3	Job Posting 2	3

    f. Repeat the outline for the other Web site.

    g. Complete the Word document with information you find on the Web sites. Include a short description of each job you select.

    h. Double-space the document text so that the document prints over at least two pages. Use Page Formatting options to keep headings with their paragraph text and lines of text in a paragraph together.

    i. Format the document so that a header starts on page 1 and includes the text **Online Job Opportunities for Your Name**. Include a page number on each page of the document in either the header or the footer.

    j. Save the document, print a copy, close the document, then exit Word.

▼ VISUAL WORKSHOP

Open the file WD J-14.doc, then save it as **E-Business Term Paper**. Modify the outline so that it appears as shown in Figure J-21. You need to change the order of some sections as well as rename some topics. In Print Layout view, insert a new page in a new section at the beginning of the document, clear the formatting, enter and enhance the title **Table of Contents**, then generate a table of contents in the Distinctive style with three heading levels as shown in Figure J-22. Be sure your name is on the document, then print one copy of the table of contents page and one copy of the first three levels of the document in Outline view, then save the document.

FIGURE J-21

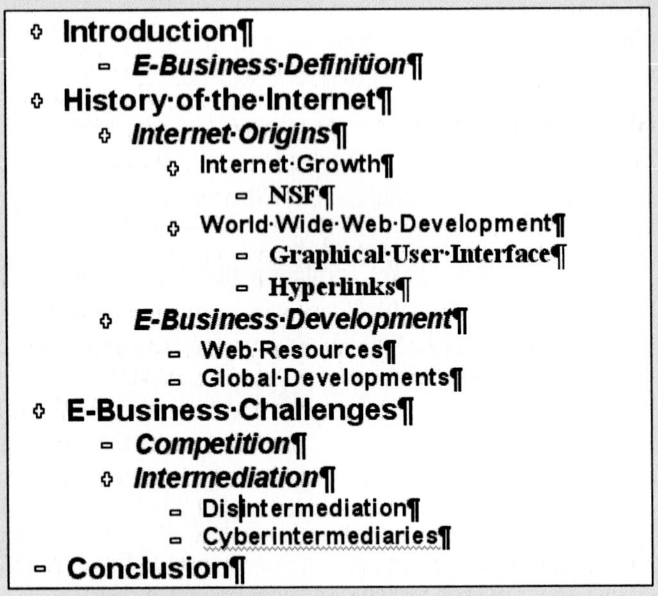

FIGURE J-22

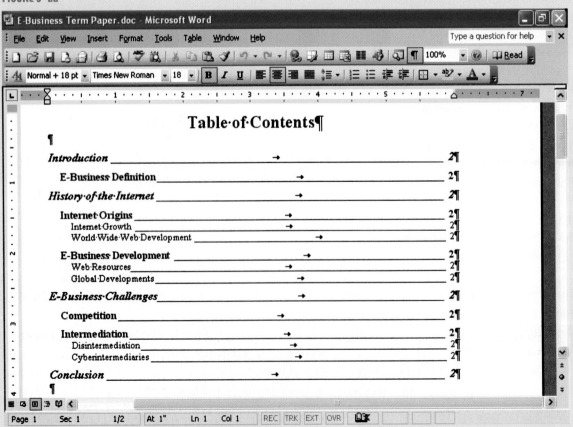

Integrating Word with Other Programs

OBJECTIVES

Explore integration methods
Embed an Excel worksheet
Link an Excel chart
Embed a PowerPoint slide
Insert a Word file
Import a table from Access
Manage document links
Merge with an Access data source

If you have a SAM user profile, you may have access to hands-on instruction, practice, and assessment of the skills covered in this unit. Log in to your SAM account and go to your assignments page to see what your instructor has assigned.

The Office suite includes several programs, each with its own unique purpose and characteristics. Sometimes information you want to include in a Word document is stored in files created with other Office programs such as PowerPoint or Excel. For example, the report you are writing in Word might need to include a pie chart from a worksheet created in Excel. You can embed information from other programs in a Word document or you can create links between programs. ▓▓▓ Nazila Sharif in the Marketing Department has started a report on how to market Media-Loft.com, MediaLoft's home on the World Wide Web. She asks you to supplement the report with information contained in another Word file and in files she created in Excel, PowerPoint, and Access. You then need to merge an Access data source with the cover letter you'll send along with the report to all the MediaLoft store managers.

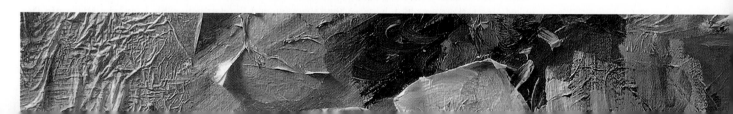

Exploring Integration Methods

You can integrate information created with other Office programs into a Word document in a variety of ways. Figure K-1 shows a six-page Word document containing shared information from PowerPoint, Excel, Access, and another Word document. The methods available for sharing information between programs include copy and paste, drag and drop, Object Linking and Embedding, and inserting files. Table K-1 describes each Office program and includes its associated file extension and icon. Each program uses a unique **file extension**, the three letters that follow the period in a filename. ▓▓▓▓ Before you integrate information created in other programs into the report contained in a Word document, you review the various ways in which information is shared between programs.

DETAILS

You can share information in the following ways:

- **Copy and paste**

  You use the Copy and Paste commands to copy information from one program and paste it into another program, usually when you need to copy a small amount of text.

- **Drag and drop**

  You can position documents created in two programs side by side in separate windows and then use drag and drop to copy or move selected text or objects from one document (the source file) into another document (the destination file).

- **Insert a Word file**

  You can use the File command on the Insert menu to insert an entire file. The file types you can insert include Word documents (.doc) or templates (.dot), documents saved in rich text format (.rtf), and documents created as .mht or .htm files for Web pages.

- **Object Linking and Embedding**

  The ability to share information with other programs is called **Object Linking and Embedding (OLE)**. Two programs are involved in the OLE process. The **source program** is the program in which information is originally created, and the **destination program** is the program to which the information is copied. With OLE, you use the source program to create a **source file** and you use the destination program to create a **destination file**.

- **Objects**

  An **object** is defined as self-contained information that can be in the form of text, spreadsheet data, graphics, charts, tables, or even sound and video clips. Objects provide a means of sharing information between programs. You can create objects by selecting Object on the Insert menu or by selecting Paste Special on the Edit menu.

- **Embedded objects**

  An **embedded object** is created within the destination file or copied from the source file. You can edit an embedded object within the destination program using the editing features of the source program. Any changes you make to an embedded object appear only in the destination file; the changes are *not* made to the information in the source file.

- **Linked objects**

  A **linked object** is created in a source file, then inserted into a destination file and linked to the source file. When you link an object, changes made to the data in the source file are reflected in the destination file. In a linked object, the connection between the source file and the destination file is called a **Dynamic Data Exchange (DDE)** link.

PowerPoint slide
created as an
embedded object
in Word

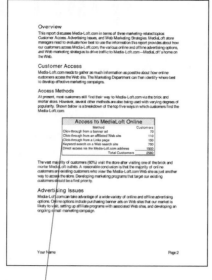

Excel worksheet
inserted as an
embedded object
into Word

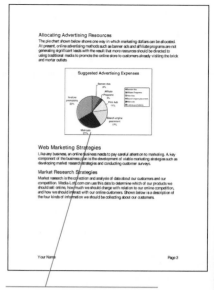

Excel pie chart inserted into Word as a
linked object; the linked chart in Word
can be updated to reflect changes
made to the chart in Excel

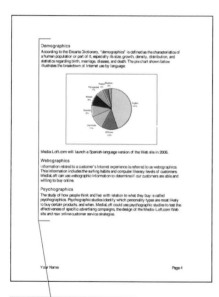

Word file inserted into the Word
document with formatting and
chart image intact

Access table copied
from Access and
then formatted

TABLE K-1: Office programs

icon	program	extension	purpose
W	Word	.doc	To create documents and share information in print, e-mail, and on the Web
X	Excel	.xls	To create, analyze, and share spreadsheets and to analyze data with charts, PivotTable dynamic views, and graphs
P	PowerPoint	.ppt	To organize, illustrate, and deliver materials in an easy-to-understand graphics format for delivery in a presentation or over the Internet
A	Access	.mdb	To store, organize, and share database information
F	FrontPage	.htm or .html	To create and manage the files required for a Web site

Embedding an Excel Worksheet

An embedded object uses the features of another program such as Excel, but is stored as part of the Word document. You embed an object, such as an Excel worksheet or a PowerPoint slide, in Word when you do *not* need changes made in the source file to be updated in the embedded Word object. You edit an embedded object directly in Word using the source program toolbars. For example, you can embed a worksheet created in Excel into a Word document, double-click the embedded worksheet object to enter edit mode and show the Excel toolbars, and then edit the embedded object using the Excel toolbars. The Online Marketing Report that Nazila created in Word contains placeholder text and bookmarks to designate where information created in other programs should be inserted. Your first task is to embed an Excel worksheet that contains data related to the top five methods customers use to find Media-Loft.com.

STEPS

1. **Start Word, open the file** WD K-1.doc **from the drive and folder where your Data Files are located, save it as** Online Marketing Report, **click the Show/Hide ¶ button** ¶ **to select it, then scroll through the report to note where you will insert content from other programs**

2. **Click** Edit **on the menu bar, click** Go To, **click** Bookmark **in the Go to what list box, verify that** Customers **appears in the Enter bookmark name text box, click** Go To, **click** Close, **then delete the placeholder text** Excel Worksheet Here **but** *not* **the ¶ mark following Here**

3. **Click** Insert **on the menu bar, then click** Object
    You use the Object dialog box to create a new object using the tools of a program other than Word or to insert an object created in another program.

4. **Click the** Create from File tab, **click the** Browse button, **navigate to the drive and folder where your Data Files are located, click** WD K-2.xls, **then click** Insert
    The Object dialog box opens. Because you want to create an embedded object, you leave the Link to file check box blank, as shown in Figure K-2.

5. **Click** OK
    The Excel worksheet is inserted as an embedded object in Word.

6. **Double-click the embedded worksheet object**
    The embedded object opens in an Excel object window and the Excel toolbars appear under the Word menu bar. You can use the Excel toolbars to format the cells or change the data in the Excel worksheet object.

7. **Click the** value **in cell B3 as shown in Figure K-3, type** 70, **click the** value **in cell B8, then click the** Bold button **B** **on the Excel Formatting toolbar**
    The total number of customers shown in cell B8 increases by 32 from 2548 to 2580.

8. **Click to the right of the embedded Excel worksheet object**
    The Excel toolbars close and the Word toolbars open.

9. **Click the worksheet object again to select it, click the** Center button **≡** **on the Formatting toolbar, click the** Outside Border button **⊞** **on the Formatting toolbar, click below the worksheet object, then save the document**
    The modified embedded Excel worksheet object appears in the Word document, as shown in Figure K-4.

FIGURE K-2: Object dialog box

Use this tab to create a new object

Object embedded in Word will be based on this Excel file

Description of current action

Click to navigate to location (the drive and folder) of the file to insert

Link to file is *not* selected when embedding the file in Word

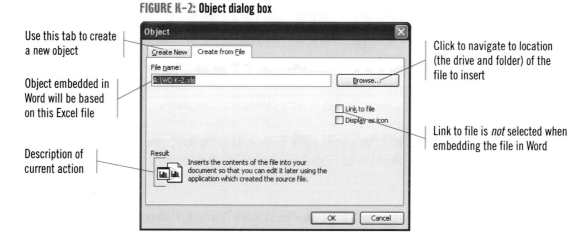

FIGURE K-3: Editing the embedded worksheet object

Microsoft Word title bar

Excel Standard and Formatting toolbars

Embedded worksheet appears in an Excel object window

Bold button

Cell B3

Cell B8

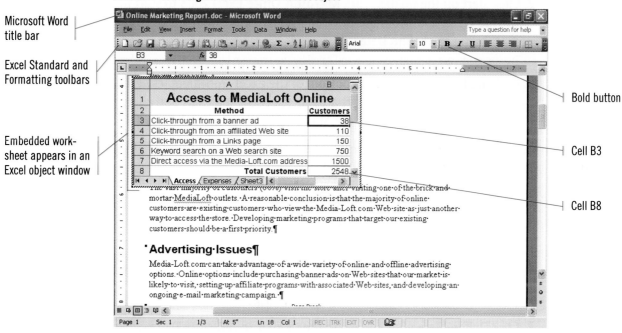

FIGURE K-4: Modified embedded worksheet object

Word toolbars

Excel worksheet embedded in Word document; formatted using Word toolbars

Outside Border button

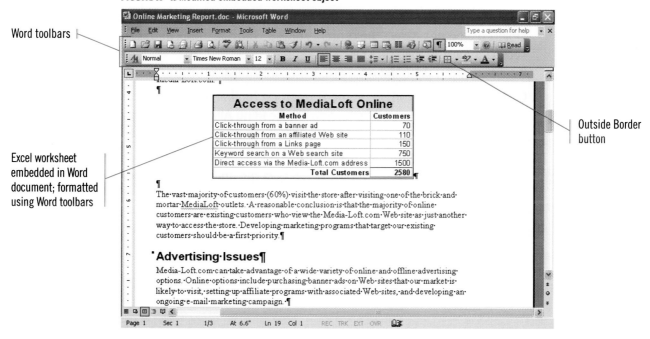

Linking an Excel Chart

You can use the Paste Special command on the Edit menu to integrate data from a source file into a destination file. When you use the Paste Special command, you create a linked object by copying data from the source file in one program and pasting the data into the destination file in another program. If you make a change to the data in the source file, the data in the linked object in the destination file is updated. Any changes you make to the data in the destination file are *not* made to the data in the source file. **∅∅∅∅∅** You use the Paste Special command to insert a pie chart you created in Excel into the Word report as a linked object.

QUICK TIP

The data in cell B3 is outdated because of the change you made in the previous lesson. You do not need to update the data.

1. **Press [Ctrl][G], click the** Enter bookmark name list arrow, **select** Resources, **click** Go To, **click** Close, **then delete the text** Excel Pie Chart Here **but** *not* **the ¶ mark following** Here

2. **Click** Start **on the taskbar, click** Microsoft Office Excel 2003 **to start Microsoft Excel, open the file** WD K-2.xls **from the drive and folder where your Data Files are located, then save it as** Online Marketing Data

   Two programs are currently open, as indicated by the program buttons on your taskbar.

TROUBLE

Be sure a border with sizing handles surrounds the pie chart and all its related components. If only one component is selected, click outside the chart area, then repeat Step 3.

3. **Click the** Expenses tab **at the bottom of the Excel worksheet, click the** white space **in the lower-right corner of the chart area to select the pie chart and all its components, then click the** Copy button 🖺 **on the Standard toolbar**

4. **Click the** Microsoft Word **program button on the taskbar to return to Word, click** Edit **on the menu bar, then click** Paste Special

   You use the Paste Special dialog box, shown in Figure K-5, to identify whether the data you want to paste will be inserted as an embedded object or a linked object.

5. **Click the** Paste link option button, **then click** OK

   The pie chart is inserted. Notice that Banner Ads account for 2% of suggested advertising expenses.

6. **Click the** Microsoft Excel program button **on the taskbar to return to Excel, scroll up to see the top of the worksheet, click cell B2, type** 9000, **then press [Enter]**

   The Banner Ads slice increases to 9%, as shown in Figure K-6.

TROUBLE

If your link did not update automatically, you can right-click the chart, then click Update Link on the shortcut menu.

7. **Click** Online Marketing Report **on the taskbar to return to Word, then verify that the Banner Ads slice now shows 9%**

8. **Right-click the** pie chart object, **click** Format Object, **click the** Size tab **in the Format Object dialog box, select the contents of the** Width **text box in the Size and rotate section, type** 3.8, **then click** OK

   You use the Format Object dialog box to format embedded and linked objects.

9. **Click the** Center button 🢃 **on the Formatting toolbar, click away from the pie chart object to deselect it, scroll up to view the heading Allocating Advertising Resources, compare the pie chart object to Figure K-7, then save the document**

10. **Click the** Microsoft Excel **program button on the taskbar to return to Excel, click** File **on the menu bar, click** Exit, **then click** Yes **to save the updated worksheet**

    The Online Marketing Report in Word is again the active document.

FIGURE K-5: Paste Special dialog box

Use the Paste option button to create an embedded object

Use the Paste link option button to create a linked object

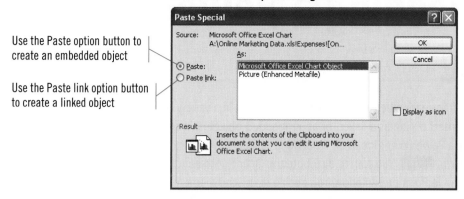

FIGURE K-6: Modified pie chart in Excel

Microsoft Excel title bar

Banner Ads slice increased to 9%

Word file open

Cell B2

Excel file active window

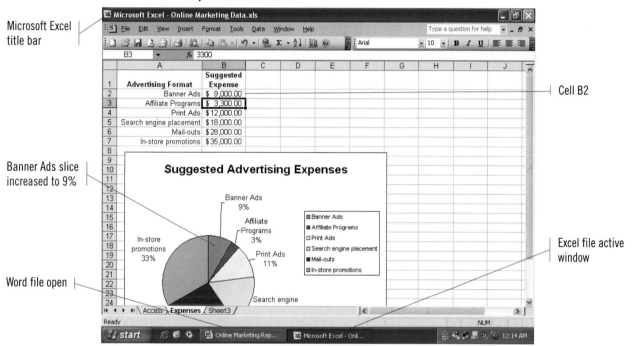

FIGURE K-7: Updated pie chart in Word

Banner Ads slice increased to 9%

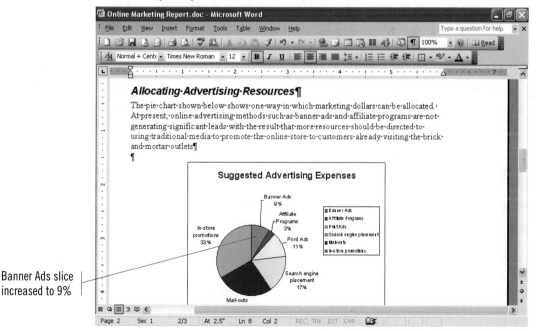

Embedding a PowerPoint Slide

You can share information between Word and PowerPoint in a variety of ways. You can use the Paste Special command to insert a slide as a linked or an embedded object into a Word document. You can use Create New to create a PowerPoint slide as an embedded object in Word, and then use PowerPoint tools to modify the slide in Word. ▰▰▰▰▰ You plan to distribute the Online Marketing Report at a conference where you will also deliver a PowerPoint presentation. You decide to use the theme you've chosen for the PowerPoint presentation on the title page of the report. You create a new PowerPoint slide and embed it in the title page, then you use PowerPoint tools to format the embedded object.

STEPS

1. **Press [Ctrl][Home], then press [Ctrl][Enter]**
   A page break appears. You want to embed a PowerPoint slide on the new blank page.

2. **Press [Ctrl][Home], click Insert on the menu bar, then click Object**
   The Object dialog box opens. The types of objects that you can create new in Word are listed in the Object type list box.

3. **Scroll down, select Microsoft PowerPoint Slide in the Object type list box, then click OK**
   A blank PowerPoint slide appears along with the PowerPoint toolbars.

4. **Click in the Click to add title text box, type Marketing Online Report, click in the Click to add subtitle text box, type Media-Loft.com, press [Enter], then type your name**

TROUBLE
If the slide design is not applied to the slide, double-click Stream.pot in the Available for Use list box.

5. **Click the Slide Design button ⧉ Design on the PowerPoint Formatting toolbar, then scroll down and click the Stream.pot design (see Figure K-8)**

6. **Click Color Schemes at the top of the Slide Design task pane, then scroll down and click the beige color scheme (see Figure K-9)**
   Figure K-9 shows the beige color scheme applied to the slide. You can apply new color schemes to any of the slide designs included with PowerPoint.

7. **Click the Zoom list arrow on the Standard toolbar, click Whole Page, click below the embedded slide object, click the object to select it if necessary, click Format on the menu bar, click Object, click the Size tab, type 6 in the Width text box in the Size and rotate section, then click OK**

8. **Click Format on the menu bar, click Borders and Shading, click Box on the Borders tab, select the double border style, the Brown color, and the 3 pt width, then click OK**

9. **Click to the right of the slide object to deselect it, then save the document**
   The embedded PowerPoint slide appears in a Word document, as shown in Figure K-10.

Clues to Use

Creating a PowerPoint presentation from a Word outline

When you create a PowerPoint presentation from a Word outline, the Word document is the source file and the PowerPoint document is the destination file. In the Word source file, headings formatted with heading styles are converted to PowerPoint headings in the PowerPoint destination file. For example, each Level 1 heading becomes its own slide. To create a PowerPoint presentation from a Word outline, create the outline in Word, click File on the menu bar, point to Send To, then click Microsoft Office PowerPoint. In a few moments the Word outline is converted to a PowerPoint presentation, where you can modify it just like any PowerPoint presentation. Any changes you make to the presentation in PowerPoint are *not* reflected in the original Word document.

FIGURE K-8: Stream.pot design applied to slide

Microsoft Word title bar

PowerPoint Standard and Formatting toolbars

Slide Design button on the PowerPoint Formatting toolbar

Stream.pot selected; list arrow appears when pointer moves over slide design

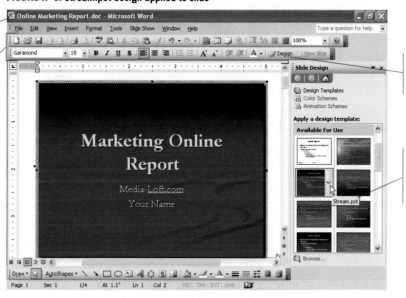

FIGURE K-9: Beige color scheme applied to slide

Beige color scheme

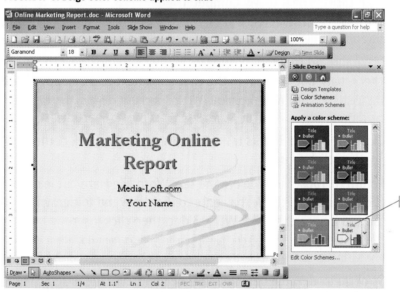

FIGURE K-10: Completed embedded PowerPoint slide object in Word

Microsoft Word title bar

Word Standard and Formatting toolbars

PowerPoint Stream.pot design applied to embedded PowerPoint slide using PowerPoint toolbars in Word

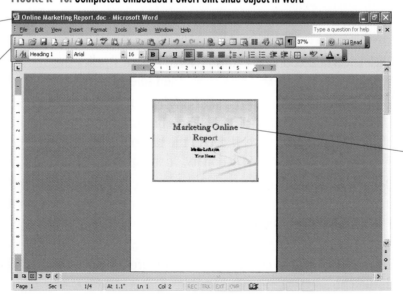

Inserting a Word File

When you need the contents of an entire Word document, you can insert an entire Word file rather than copy and paste the document into your current Word document. The formatting of the current document can be applied to the text in the inserted file. When you insert a Word file into a Word document, you cannot return to the original document from the inserted file; instead, the inserted file becomes an integral part of the Word document. ◼◼◼ You previously created a Word document that contains information about methods used to conduct market research. You use the File Search function to find the Word file containing the information you need to include in the report and then you use the Research function to look up a definition of the word "Demographics."

STEPS

1. Click File on the menu bar, click File Search to open the Basic File Search task pane, then type Webographics in the Search text box

2. Click the Results should be list arrow, click the Anything check box, click the Search in list arrow, click the Expand button ⊞ next to Everywhere to expand the menu if necessary, then click ⊞ next to My Computer

    By default, the Search function looks for the search text in several locations, including your computer's hard drive and any network drives. You want to search the contents of your Data Files only.

TROUBLE

If your Data Files are *not* located in drive A, select the check box next to the drive where your Data Files are located.

3. Make sure no check mark appears in the check box next to My Computer, make sure a check mark does appear in the check box next to 3½ Floppy (A:), then click Go two times

    The filename for the Word document (WD K-3.doc) that contains the search text "Webographics" appears. You can click a filename listed in the Search Results task pane to open that file in its associated program.

4. Close the Search Results task pane, press [Ctrl][G], select the Research bookmark, click Go To, then click Close

5. Return to 100% view, delete the text Word File Here but leave the ¶ mark, click Insert on the menu bar, click File, navigate to the drive and folder where your Data Files are located if necessary, click WD K-3.doc, then click Insert

    The contents of the WD K-3.doc file appear in your current document. If you make changes to the text you inserted in this destination file, the changes will *not* be reflected in the WD K-3.doc source file.

6. Scroll up to view the Demographics heading, click the Research button 📖 on the Standard toolbar, click in the Search for text box, type Demographics, then click the list arrow next to All Reference Books

    A selection of the references you can search appears. You can find word definitions and synonyms or search various research sites for information about specific topics.

TROUBLE

This lesson assumes you have an active Internet connection. If you do not, you will need to type the definition shown in Figure K-11.

7. Click Encarta Dictionary: English (North America), click the Start searching button ➡, scroll down the Research task pane, then select the definition as shown in Figure K-11

8. Right-click the selected text, click Copy, click to the left of the first line of text under the Demographics heading, click the Paste button 📋 on the Standard toolbar, type a period (.), press [Spacebar] once, move to the beginning of the sentence and add the text According to the Encarta Dictionary, "demographics" is defined as, then press [Spacebar]

9. Delete the title Market Research Methods including the ¶, select the Demographics heading, apply the Heading 3 style, then apply the Heading 3 style to the Webographics and Psychographics headings

10. Scroll up and insert a page break to the left of the Demographics heading, close the Research task pane, scroll down and compare the document to Figure K-12, then save the document

FIGURE K-11: Selecting a definition in the Research task pane

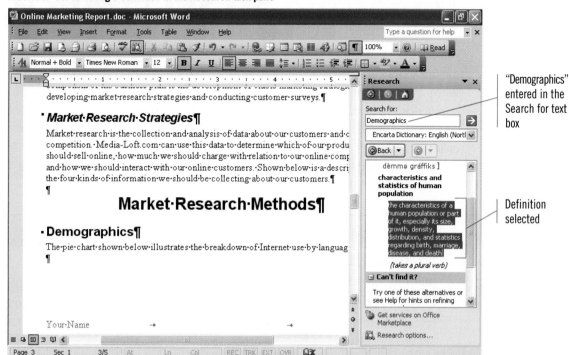

"Demographics" entered in the Search for text box

Definition selected

FIGURE K-12: Word file inserted into a Word document and formatted

Heading 3 style applied

Text copied from the Research task pane

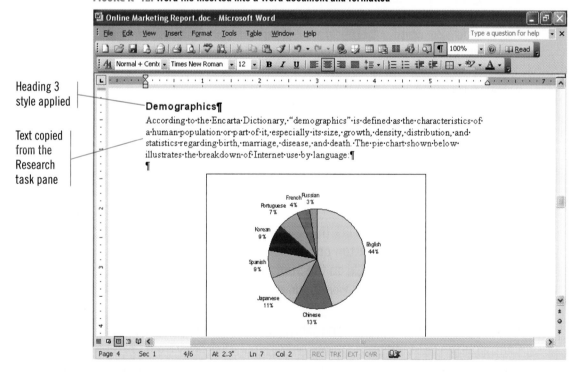

Clues to Use

Conducting a search

Using the File Search command on the File menu opens the Basic Search task pane, where you can search for specific text in files located on your computer hard drive, your local network, your Microsoft Outlook mailbox, and your network places. When you conduct a search from the Basic Search task pane, all the files that contain the search text you specified are displayed according to their location. For example, a search for the text "book club" yields a list of all the files that contain the text "book club" in the filename, contents, or properties in the locations you specified. When you find the file you want, you can open and edit the file in its program, you can create a new document based on the file, you can copy a link to the file to the Office Clipboard, or you can view the file's properties.

Importing a Table from Access

You can share information between Access and Word in a variety of ways. The most common method is to use the Access Publish It with Microsoft Office Word command, which publishes an Access table into Word. When you publish an Access table, Access launches Word and then copies the Access table to a Word window in rich text format (.rtf). Once the Access table is published to Word, you can use Word's table features to format it. ██████ You have already created an Access database that contains information related to online survey results. You open the Access database, then use the Publish It command in Access to publish one of the Access database tables into Word. You format it with one of Word's preset Table AutoFormats, and then copy the Word table into the Marketing Online Report.

STEPS

1. Press [Ctrl][G], select the Survey bookmark, go to and then delete the placeholder text Access Table Here but *not* the ¶ mark, click Start on the taskbar, point to All Programs, point to Microsoft Office, then click Microsoft Office Access 2003

> **TROUBLE**
> If warning messages appear, click Yes, then click Open.

2. Click the Open button 🗁 on the Standard toolbar in Access, navigate to the drive and folder where your Data Files are located, click WD K-4.mdb, then click Open

   The database file opens in Microsoft Access. You publish the Online Survey table in a Word document.

3. Click Online Survey in the Tables window as shown in Figure K-13, click the OfficeLinks list arrow 🖳 ▾ on the Access Standard toolbar, then click Publish It with Microsoft Office Word

   In a few moments, a Word window opens with a new document named Online Survey.rtf, as shown in Figure K-14. The "rtf" extension stands for "rich text format." Notice that the taskbar indicates you have two Word documents open. You may see one Word button with the number 2 (as shown in Figure K-14), or you may see two Word buttons. When you use the Publish It with Microsoft Office Word command in Access, the Access data is always copied into a new Word window.

4. Click the table move handle ⊞ in the upper-left corner of the table to select the entire table, click Table on the menu bar, click Table AutoFormat, click Table List 7, then click Apply

   The Online Survey table is formatted with the Table List 7 style.

5. With the entire table still selected, move the pointer over any column border in the gray area of the first row to show the ✛‖✛ pointer, then double-click to automatically resize the columns to fit the data

6. With the table still selected, click the Copy button 🗐 on the Standard toolbar, click the Microsoft Word program button on the taskbar, select Online Marketing Report.doc, then click the Paste button 🛱 on the Standard toolbar

   The Word table is copied into your Word document. The Word table is just that—a Word table; it is *not* an embedded object or a linked object.

7. Scroll up to see the first row of the table, click ⊞ to select the entire table, click the Center button ☰ on the Formatting toolbar, then click away from the table to deselect it

   Figure K-15 shows the formatted table in Word.

8. Save the Word Online Marketing Report document, click the Microsoft Word button on the taskbar, select Online Survey.rtf, then close the document without saving it

   You don't need to save the Online Survey.rtf file because you've already copied the table.

9. Click the Microsoft Access button on the taskbar, click File on the menu bar, then click Exit

   The Online Marketing Report is the active document.

FIGURE K-13: Online Survey table selected in Access

Microsoft Access
title bar

Access toolbar

Open button

Tables selected

OfficeLinks
list arrow

Online Survey
table selected

Tables window

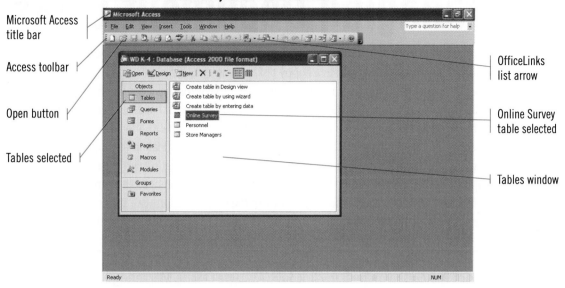

FIGURE K-14: Online Survey.rtf file published in Word

Microsoft Word
Online Survey.rtf

Click to show
menu that
includes Microsoft
Word Online
Marketing
Report.doc

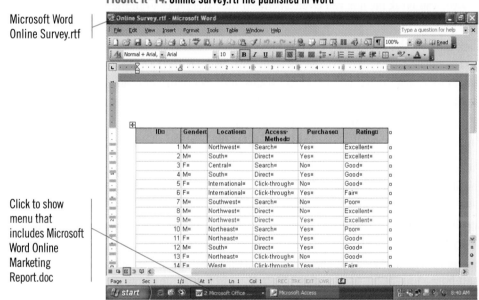

FIGURE K-15: Access table published to Word, then formatted and copied to a Word document

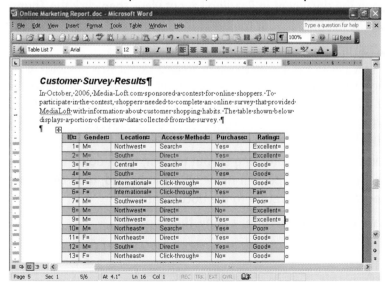

Managing Document Links

When you create a document that contains linked objects, you must include all source files when you copy the document to a new location, such as a floppy disk, or when you e-mail the document to a colleague. If you do *not* include source files, you (or your colleague) will receive error messages when trying to open the destination file. If you do *not* want to include source files when you move or e-mail a document containing links, then you should break the links before moving or e-mailing the document. After you break the links, the Update Links command cannot be used to update information in your destination file. Any changes you make to the source files after breaking the links will *not* be reflected in the destination file. The objects in the destination file will appear as they do at the time the links are broken.  You need to distribute the Word report to all the MediaLoft store managers. You keep a copy of the original report with the links intact and then you save the report with a new name and break the links. You also view the entire report in Reading Layout view.

STEPS

1. **Click File on the menu bar, click Save As, type Online Marketing Report_Managers, then click Save**

   Now you can break the link you created between the Excel pie chart in the Word destination file and the Excel pie chart in the Excel source file.

2. **Click Edit on the menu bar, then click Links**

   The Links dialog box opens, as shown in Figure K-16. You can use the Links dialog box to update links, open source files, change source files, and break existing links. Notice that only one source file is listed in the Links dialog box—the Excel file called "Online Marketing Data.xls."

3. **With the Excel file selected, click Break Link**

   A message appears asking if you are sure you want to break the selected link.

4. **Click Yes**

   The link between the Excel source file and the pie chart in the Word destination file is broken. Now if you make a change to the pie chart in the Excel source file, the pie chart in Word will *not* change.

5. **Scroll up until the Suggested Advertising Expenses pie chart is visible, then double-click the pie chart**

   The Format Picture dialog box opens. When you broke the link to the source file, Word converted the pie chart from a linked object to a picture object. You can format the picture object using the Format Picture dialog box, but you cannot change the content of the pie chart.

6. **Click Cancel, click the Reading Layout button 📖 to the left of the horizontal scroll bar to open the document in Reading Layout view, then click the Thumbnails button 🔲 Thumbnails on the Reading Layout toolbar if the Thumbnails pane is not open**

TROUBLE
Your total number of pages may differ depending on your monitor and printer settings.

7. **Scroll up the Thumbnails pane, then click page 3**

   Screen 3 of 16 and 4 of 16 appear in Reading Layout view as shown in Figure K-17. In Reading Layout view, you can comfortably read the document text and scroll from page to page by clicking thumbnails or using the Document Map. As you scroll through the report in Reading Layout view, you notice that some elements, such as the Access table on screen 12, appear less attractively formatted then they did in Print Layout view. Page breaks also appear in different places.

8. **Click Close on the Reading Layout toolbar, scroll down to view the footer, double-click in the footer area, type your name where indicated, then click Close on the Header and Footer toolbar to return to the document**

9. **Save the document, print a copy, then close it**

FIGURE K-16: Links dialog box

Excel file

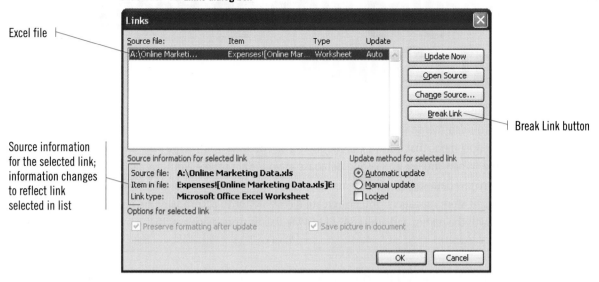

FIGURE K-16: Links dialog box

Source information for the selected link; information changes to reflect link selected in list

Break Link button

FIGURE K-17: Completed report in Reading Layout view

Reading Layout toolbar

Thumbnails button

Page 3 selected in the Thumbnails pane; text placement on your thumbnails and pages may differ

Total number of pages; yours may differ

Page number

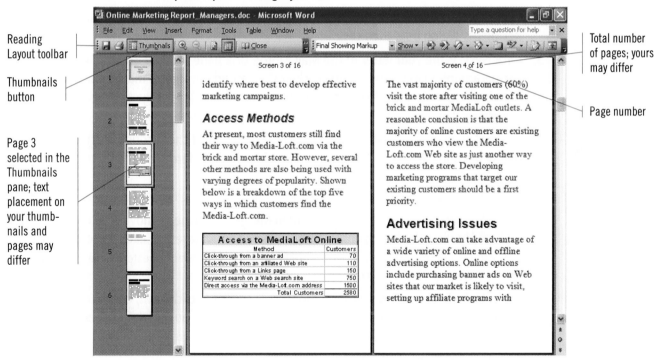

Merging with an Access Data Source

Many businesses store the names and addresses of contacts, employees, and customers in an Access database. You can merge information contained in an Access database with a letter, a sheet of labels, or any merge document that you've created in Word. The data you merge with the destination file is the **data source**. When you use an existing database as your data source, you save time because you do *not* need to create a new data source.  You need to mail a printed copy of the Online Marketing Report to all the MediaLoft store managers. You first create a cover letter to accompany the report and then you merge the letter with the names and addresses of the MediaLoft store managers that are stored in an Access database.

STEPS

1. Open the file WD K-5.doc from the drive and folder where your Data Files are located, save it as Online Marketing Cover Letter, replace Current Date with today's date, scroll down, then type your name in the complimentary closing

2. Click Tools on the menu bar, point to Letters and Mailings, then click Mail Merge

   The Mail Merge task pane opens at Step 3 of 6.

   > **TROUBLE**
   > If the Mail Merge task pane does not open at Step 3 of 6, click Next two times.

3. Click Browse, navigate to the drive and folder where your Data Files are located, select the Access database called WD K-4.mdb, then click Open

   The Select Table window lists the tables available in the WD K-4.mdb Access database.

4. Click Store Managers in the Select Table window, click OK to open the Mail Merge Recipients dialog box, then click OK

5. Click Next: Write your letter in the Mail Merge task pane to move to Step 4 of 6, show the paragraph marks, if necessary, click at the second paragraph mark below the current date in the cover letter, then click Address block in the Mail Merge task pane

   A preview of the default address block appears in the Preview area in the Insert Address Block dialog box.

6. Click OK to accept the default settings, click to the left of the second paragraph mark below the address block, click Greeting line in the Mail Merge task pane, select Joshua as shown in Figure K-18, then click OK

   The field code for the Address block and the field code for the Greeting Line are inserted in your letter.

7. Click Next: Preview your letters in the Mail Merge task pane to move to Step 5 of 6, then click >> to view the letters containing the name and address of each store manager

   You've successfully merged the cover letter with the names and addresses of the store managers. Now you can print just a selection of the letters.

8. Click Next: Complete the merge to move to Step 6 of 6, click Print, click the From option button, enter 1 in the From text box and 2 in the To text box, click OK, then click OK

   The letters to Harriet Gray and Sandra Barradas print, as shown in Figure K-19.

9. Save the document in Word, close it, then exit Word

FIGURE K-18: Greeting Line dialog box

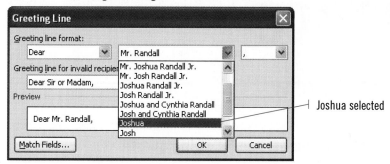

Joshua selected

FIGURE K-19: Merged cover letters

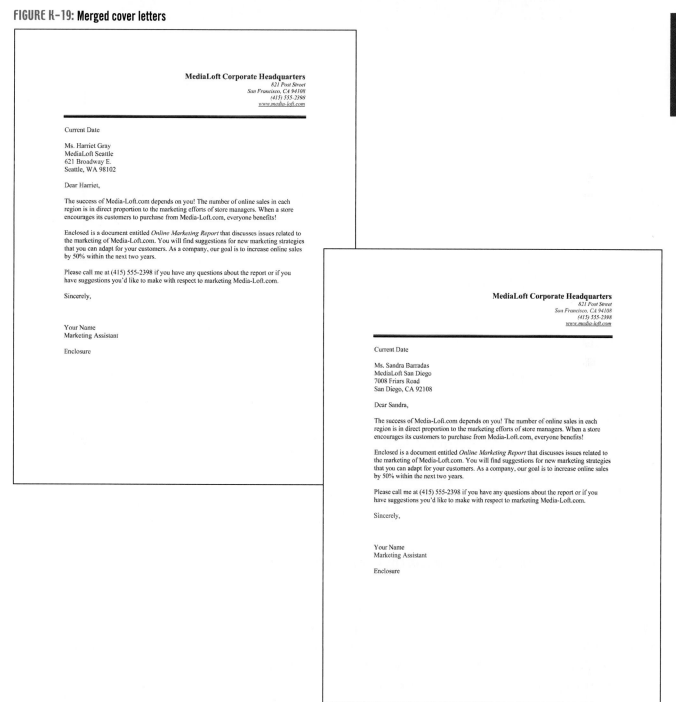

Practice

▼ CONCEPTS REVIEW

Refer to Figure K-20 to answer the following questions.

FIGURE K-20

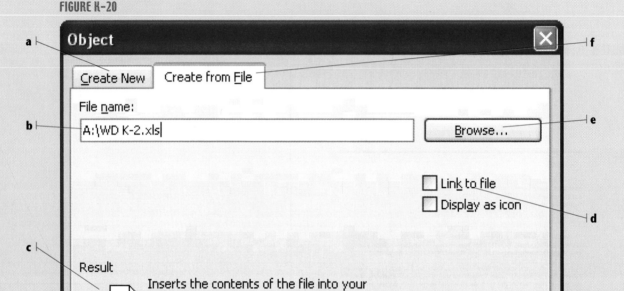

1. Which element do you click to insert a file created in another program?
2. Which element do you click to create an Excel worksheet or PowerPoint slide directly in Word?
3. Which element describes the action being taken?
4. Which element points to the name of the file that will be inserted?
5. Which element do you click to link the inserted file to its source program?
6. Which element do you click to find the file you want to insert?

Match each term with the statement that best describes it.

7. OLE	**a.** Describes the connection between linked objects
8. Object	**b.** Program to which information is copied
9. DDE	**c.** Doesn't change if the source document is edited
10. Embedded object	**d.** Self-contained information that can be in the form of text, graphics, and so on
11. Source program	**e.** Program from which information is copied
12. Destination program	**f.** Provides a means of exchanging information between programs

Select the best answer from the list of choices.

13. What is the destination program?
- **a.** The program from which the information is copied
- **b.** The program to which the information is copied
- **c.** The program in which the information is created
- **d.** The program containing new information

14. What is the source program?
- **a.** The program from which the information is copied
- **b.** The program to which the information is copied
- **c.** The program containing new information
- **d.** None of the above

15. What does DDE stand for?
- **a.** Dedicated Data Exchange
- **b.** Dynamic Data Extension
- **c.** Dynamic Data Exchange
- **d.** Dynamic Data Enhancements

16. Which of the following statements is *not* true about an embedded object?
- **a.** An embedded object can be created in a source file and inserted into a destination file.
- **b.** An embedded object becomes part of the destination file.
- **c.** Changes you make to an embedded object are reflected in the destination file.
- **d.** Changes you make to an embedded object are reflected in the source file.

17. Which of the following statements is *not* true about a linked object?
- **a.** A linked object is created in a source file and inserted into a destination file, while maintaining a connection between the two files.
- **b.** Source files must accompany destination files with linked objects when the destination files are moved.
- **c.** Changes made to a linked object in the destination file are also reflected in the source file.
- **d.** The linked object can be updated in the destination file by right-clicking it, then clicking Update Link.

18. Which command can be used to insert a linked object?
- **a.** Paste
- **b.** Paste Special
- **c.** Link Paste
- **d.** Insert Link

19. Which command do you use in Access to create a Word version of a selected table?
- **a.** Publish It with Access
- **b.** Publish It with Microsoft Office Word
- **c.** Publish It
- **d.** Insert

20. Which view do you access to scroll through a document screen by screen so you can easily read the text?
- **a.** Window view
- **b.** Screen view
- **c.** Thumbnails view
- **d.** Reading Layout view

▼ SKILLS REVIEW

1. Embed an Excel worksheet.
- **a.** Start Word, open the file WD K-6.doc from the drive and folder where your Data Files are located, then save it as **Untamed Tours Report**.
- **b.** Use the Go To command to find the Categories bookmark, then delete the placeholder text **Insert Excel Worksheet Here** but do *not* delete the ¶ mark.
- **c.** Click Insert on the menu bar, then click Object.
- **d.** Click the Create from File tab, then use the Browse feature to insert the file WD K-7.xls from the drive and folder where your Data Files are located into the Word document.
- **e.** Edit the worksheet object. Change the value in cell B7 from 1500 to **2400**, then enhance the value in cell B8 with Bold.
- **f.** In Word, center the worksheet object, apply an outside border, then save the document. (*Hint*: You may need to change the border style to a single black line.)

2. Link an Excel chart.
- **a.** Use the Go To command to find the Popularity bookmark, then delete the placeholder text **Insert Excel Chart Here**, but do *not* delete the ¶ mark.
- **b.** Start Microsoft Office Excel, open the file WD K-7.xls from the drive and folder where your Data Files are located, then save it as **Untamed Tours Data**.

    c. Show the Popularity worksheet, copy the column chart, switch to Word, then use the Paste Special command in Word to paste the column chart as a link in the Word document.

    d. Switch to Excel, scroll up to view the data used to create the column chart, then change the value in cell C2 from 1800 to **3400**.

    e. Save the worksheet in Excel, then exit Excel.

    f. In Word, right-click the chart, then click Update Link.

    g. Reduce the width of the chart in Word to **5**", center the chart, then save the document.

3. Embed a PowerPoint slide.

    a. Insert a blank page at the top of the document, then insert a PowerPoint slide as an embedded object on the new blank page.

    b. Enter the text **Untamed Tours** as the slide title, then enter **your name** as the subtitle.

    c. Apply the Mountain Top.pot slide design to the embedded slide object.

    d. Select the turquoise color scheme.

    e. Switch to Whole Page view, click below the embedded slide object, then change the width of the object to **6**".

    f. Save the document.

4. Insert a Word file.

    a. Use the File Search command to find the Data File that contains the text **Queen Charlotte Islands**.

    b. Make note of the Data File filename, close the Search Results task pane, then use the Go To command to find the Tours bookmark in the Untamed Tours Report Word document.

    c. Return to 100% view, remove the placeholder text but not the ¶, then insert the file WDK-8.doc from the drive and folder where your Data Files are located.

    d. Scroll up, click the second paragraph mark below the paragraph describing sea kayaking tours, then open the Research task pane.

    e. Enter the text Queen Charlotte Islands in the Search for text box, click the list arrow to the right of All Reference Books, then select Encarta Encyclopedia: English (North America) as the reference source to search. (*Note:* You must be connected to the Internet to complete this step and the following two steps.)

    f. When a description of the Queen Charlotte Islands appears in the Research task pane, scroll down the Research task pane and click the link called Dynamic Map-Encarta Encyclopedia. In a few moments a map of the Queen Charlotte Islands will open in your Web browser.

    g. Right-click the map in the Web browser, click Save Picture As, navigate to the drive and folder where your Data Files are located, then click Save.

    h. Close the Web browser, then in Word, close the Research task pane.

    i. Click Insert on the menu bar, point to Picture, click From File, select the MapImg file, click Insert, be sure the heading Backpacking is on a line by itself, then reduce the width of the map to 3.5" and center it between the left and right margins of the page.

    j. Scroll up, delete the centered title, **Untamed Tours**, then remove the extra ¶ above Sea Kayaking.

    k. Apply the Heading 3 style to the five headings: Sea Kayaking, Backpacking, Wildlife Photography, Wilderness Canoeing, and Mountain Biking.

    l. Save the document.

5. Import a table from Access.

    a. Use the Go To command to find the Profile bookmark, then remove the placeholder text **Insert Access Table Here**.

    b. Start Microsoft Access, then open the file WD K-9.mdb from the drive and folder where your Data Files are located.

    c. Publish the Customer Profile table to Word.

    d. Apply the Table Columns 3 AutoFormat to the table in Word, then automatically reduce the column widths to fit the column content.

    e. Copy the formatted table to the Untamed Tours Report Word document.

    f. Save the Untamed Tours Report Word document, switch to and close the Customer Profile.rtf file without saving it, then switch to and exit Access.

▼ SKILLS REVIEW (CONTINUED)

6. **Manage document links.**
   a. Open the Links dialog box, then break the link to the Untamed Tours Data.xls file.
   b. Insert a page break to the left of the Tour Popularity heading.
   c. Insert a page break to the left of the Sea Kayaking heading.
   d. Enter your name where indicated at the end of the document.
   e. Switch to Reading Layout view, show the thumbnails, then scroll through the screens.
   f. Save the document, print a copy, then close it.

7. **Merge with an Access data source.**
   a. Open the file WD K-10.doc from the drive and folder where your Data Files are located, save it as **Untamed Tours Cover Letter**, then replace the placeholder text **Current Date** and **Your Name** with the appropriate information.
   b. Open the Mail Merge task pane, then move to Step 3 of 6, if necessary.
   c. Browse to the drive and folder where your Data Files are located, then select the Access file WD K-9.mdb.
   d. Select the Tour Guides table from the Access database, click OK, then click OK to select all the tour guides listed in the Mail Merge Recipients dialog box.
   e. Move to Step 4 of 6, insert the Address block at the second paragraph mark below the date, use the default format, then insert the Greeting line with the first name selected to follow **Dear** at the second paragraph mark below the Address block. Insert blank paragraphs as needed to ensure proper letter format.
   f. Move to Step 5 of 6, then preview each letter.
   g. Move to Step 6 of 6, print a copy of letters 2 and 3, save and close the document, then exit Word.

▼ INDEPENDENT CHALLENGE 1

As a member of the Rainforest Recreation Commission in the Great Bear Rainforest in British Columbia, you are responsible for compiling the minutes of the monthly meetings. You have already written most of the text required for the minutes. Now you need to insert information from two sources. First, you insert a worksheet from an Excel file that shows the monies raised from various fundraising activities and then you insert a Word file that the director of the commission has sent you for inclusion in the minutes.

   a. Start Word, open the file WD K-11.doc from the drive and folder where your Data Files are located, then save it as **Recreation Commission Minutes**.
   b. Go to the Fundraising bookmark, then insert the Data File WD K-12.xls from the drive and folder where your Data Files are located as an embedded object. (*Hint*: Click the Create from File tab in the Object dialog box.)
   c. Edit the worksheet object by changing the value in cell D5 from 800 to **700**, and then by using the Excel Formatting toolbar to enhance the contents of cells A5 and A6 with Bold.
   d. Center the worksheet in Word, then enclose it with a border.
   e. Press [Ctrl][End], then insert the file WD K-13.doc from the drive and folder where your Data Files are located.
   f. Use Format Painter to apply the formatting of the current headings to the text **Director's Report**, then delete the paragraph mark above **Director's Report**.
   g. Type **Prepared by** followed by your name at the bottom of the document.

Advanced Challenge Exercise

   ■ Double-click the embedded Excel worksheet, click cell A1, change the shading color to Light Turquoise, then change the shading color of cells B4 to F4 to Tan.
   ■ Click cell A6, then press [↓] once to view another row in the worksheet.
   ■ Click cell A7, type **Per Person**, click cell B7, enter the formula **=B6/B5**, then press [Enter].
   ■ Drag the lower-right corner of cell B7 across to cell F7 to fill cells C7 to F7 with the formula, then with the cells still selected, click the Currency Style button on the Formatting toolbar.
   ■ Bold and right-align the label in cell A7, use the vertical scroll bar at the right edge of the worksheet object to scroll up to view cell A1, then drag the lower-right corner of the worksheet object down slightly so that the new row 7 is visible.
   ■ Click outside the worksheet object.

   h. Print, save, and close the document, then exit Word.

▼ INDEPENDENT CHALLENGE 2

You run a summer camp in Grand Canyon National Park in Arizona for teenagers interested in taking on leadership roles at their schools and in their communities. You need to create a report in Word and a presentation in PowerPoint that describes the camp for potential investors. You start by creating an outline of the report in Word, then sending it to PowerPoint as a presentation.

a. Start Word, open the file WD K-14.doc from the drive and folder where your Data Files are located, then save it as **Grand Canyon Camp Report**.

b. Send the outline to PowerPoint as a presentation. (*Hint*: Click File on the menu bar, point to Send To, then click Microsoft Office PowerPoint.)

c. In PowerPoint, apply the Capsules.pot design template and select the maroon color scheme (last selection in the first column).

FIGURE K-21

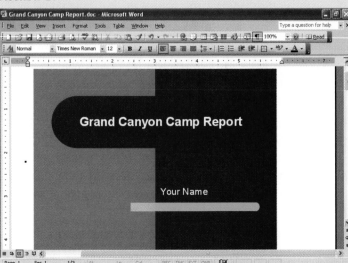

d. Save the PowerPoint presentation as **Grand Canyon Camp Presentation**, close it, then exit PowerPoint.

e. In Word, insert a new page above the first page in the document, then insert an embedded PowerPoint slide formatted with the Capsules design and the maroon color scheme. Include **Grand Canyon Camp Report** as the title and **your name** as the subtitle.

f. In Whole Page view, center and resize the slide object to fit the space. See Figure K-21.

g. Press [Ctrl][End], scroll up to the Student Enrollment heading, click after the subheading that begins **The chart shows**, then press [Enter] twice.

h. Insert the Excel file WD K-15.xls from the drive and folder where your Data Files are located as an embedded object.

i. Double-click the worksheet object, then change the value in cell B3 from 1500 to **1900**.

j. Exit the worksheet object, then center it.

Advanced Challenge Exercise

- Go to the beginning of the document, then double-click about 1" below the embedded slide on page 1.
- Open the Research task pane, be sure your Internet connection is active, then search the Encarta Encyclopedia using the search text "Grand Canyon."
- When the search results appear, scroll to the Media section, click any of the links that appear, then find and save a picture of your choice.
- Insert the picture you've selected below the embedded PowerPoint slide in the Word report.
- Center the picture, resize the picture if necessary, then add a note under the picture with information about the source of the picture.

k. View the document in Print Preview, save the document, print a copy, close the document, then exit Word.

▼ INDEPENDENT CHALLENGE 3

You own a small Web-based business that sells art materials online. The business is growing—thanks in large part to the help you're receiving from several art stores in your area. The store managers are promoting your Web site in exchange for commissions paid to them when a customer from their target market purchases art materials from your Web site. You've decided to send a memo to the store managers every few months to keep them informed about the growth of the Web site. The memo will include a linked Excel worksheet and a table published to Word from Access. Once you have completed the memo, you will merge it with a database containing the names of all the store managers who are helping to promote the Web site.

a. Start Word, open the file WD K-16.doc from the drive and folder where your Data Files are located and save it as **Arts Online Memo**.

b. Start Access, then open the file WD K-17.mdb from the drive and folder where your Data Files are located.

c. Publish the Access table called May 1 Sales to Word.

d. In Word, apply the table AutoFormat of your choice, automatically adjust the column widths, copy the formatted table, then paste it to the second paragraph mark below the paragraph The table illustrated below in the Arts Online Memo Word document. Center the table.

e. Start Excel and open the file WD K-18.xls from the drive and folder where your Data Files are located, then save the Excel file as **Arts Online Data.**

f. Scroll down the worksheet, click the pie chart to select it, copy the pie chart, switch to the Arts Online Memo file in Word, then paste the worksheet as a link at the second paragraph mark below the paragraph **The pie chart shown below**.

g. In Excel, click cell F4, change the sale generated by the Delaware customer from 240.62 to **320.15**, press [Enter], then save and close the worksheet.

h. Switch to the Arts Online Memo Word document, then update the link to the pie chart. Change the width of the chart to **3"**, then center it and add a border.

i. Scroll to the top of the document, then replace the placeholder text with your name and today's date in the Memo heading.

j. Click after the **To:** → in the Memo heading, open the Mail Merge task pane, navigate to Step 3 of 6 in the Mail Merge task pane, browse to the drive and folder where your Data Files are located, select the file WD K-17.mdb, then select the Retail Outlets table and all the recipients listed in the table.

k. Insert an Address Block following To: that contains only the recipient's name. (*Hint:* Deselect the Insert postal address check box and the Insert company name check box in the Insert Address Block dialog box.)

l. View the recipients, then print copies of the memos from Tara Winston through Richard Harwood.

m. Save and close the document in Word, close the published table without saving it, then exit all open applications.

▼ INDEPENDENT CHALLENGE 4

The Internet is a great resource for gathering information about products and services. If you are starting a new business or even if you run an established business, you can always gain new ideas by checking out the ways competing businesses use the Internet to advertise and sell products and services. You decide to evaluate the contents of a Web site that sells a product or service of your choice and write a report. You plan to integrate information from the Web site into your report. To integrate the information, you will use Copy and Paste commands or the drag-and-drop method to copy excerpts from the Web site you've selected so that you can comment on them.

a. Select a product or service that interests you and that you might even want to sell as part of your own business. For example, if you are interested in mountain biking, you could decide to find a Web site that sells mountain bikes and related equipment.

b. Open your Web browser and conduct a search for a company that sells the product or service that interests you. You can try entering related keywords such as **mountain biking**, **cycling**, and **mountain bikes** into your favorite search engine, or you can try entering generic domain names such as www.bikes.com or www.mountainbiking.com in the Address box of your Web browser.

c. Open the file WD K-19.doc from the drive and folder where your Data Files are located, then save it as **Competition Research**. This document contains questions about the Web site you've selected.

d. Complete the Competition Research document with the information requested. Follow the directions in the document. Note that you will be directed to integrate information from the Web site into your document. You might need to modify the formatting of the copied information. Be sure to always cite your source.

e. Type your name at the bottom of the document, print a copy, save and close it, then exit Word.

▼ VISUAL WORKSHOP

In Word, enter the headings and text for the document shown in Figure K-22. Start Excel, open the file WD K-20.xls from the drive and folder where your Data Files are located, then save it as **Cell Phone Data**. Copy the pie chart, then paste it as a link to the Word document. Center the pie chart in Word. In Excel, change the value in cell B2 to **180**, then save the worksheet. In Word, verify that the pie chart appears as shown in Figure K-22, update the pie chart in Word as needed, then break the link to the Excel file. Save the document as **Missouri Arts Cell Phone Report**, type your name under the chart, print a copy, then close the document and exit Word. Close the worksheet in Excel, then exit Excel.

FIGURE K-22

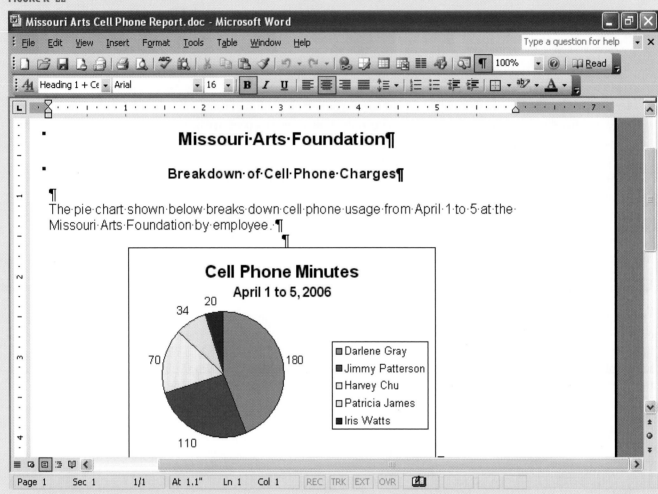

Exploring Advanced Graphics

OBJECTIVES

Insert drop caps
Edit clip art
Work with the drawing canvas
Use layering options
Align, distribute, and rotate graphics
Use advanced positioning options
Adjust shadow and 3-D settings
Insert a watermark and a page border

If you have a SAM user profile, you may have access to hands-on instruction, practice, and assessment of the skills covered in this unit. Log in to your SAM account and go to your assignments page to see what your instructor has assigned.

Word includes features you can use to create and modify pictures and other objects such as shapes and text boxes. In addition, you can enhance a document with drop caps, a watermark, and a page border. You can use shadow and 3-D effects to add pizzazz to all kinds of graphics objects. You can also create your own pictures in the drawing canvas by modifying clip art pictures and combining them with other pictures and drawn objects. ▚▚▚ The Seattle MediaLoft is excited about holding a series of Mystery Book Nights featuring authors who will sign their books and meet readers. You work in the Marketing Department at MediaLoft and have offered to provide the Seattle MediaLoft store with sample posters for advertising the events. You have already written the text for the posters. Now you will enhance the posters with a variety of graphics objects.

Inserting Drop Caps

A **drop cap** is a large dropped character that appears as the first character in a paragraph. By default, a drop cap that you insert from the Format menu is three lines high and appears in its own text box. You can modify the size of a drop cap and its position relative to the paragraph of text. You can also select a font style for the drop cap that differs from the font style of the surrounding text. The poster you created to advertise the first Mystery Book Night featuring Emily Chow includes a description of three of Ms. Chow's novels. You decide to make the first letter of each novel title a drop cap. You experiment with different looks for the drop caps, decide on the best drop cap format, and then edit the drop caps so that they all contain the same formatting.

STEPS

1. **Start Word, open the file WD L-1.doc from the drive and folder where your Data Files are located, then save the file as Mystery Book Night Poster_Emily Chow**
   A WordArt object appears at the top of the poster and two clip art pictures (also called clip art objects) appear at the bottom. You will use these pictures in later lessons.

2. **Click in the paragraph that starts with the book title On the Wharf**
   Word automatically assigns the drop cap to the first letter of the paragraph containing the insertion point.

3. **Click Format on the menu bar, then click Drop Cap**
   The Drop Cap dialog box opens. You use this dialog box to insert a drop cap in the margin or as part of the current paragraph. You can also use it to select a font style for the drop cap and to specify the number of lines to drop.

4. **Click Dropped, click the Font list arrow, select Arial Black, click the Lines to drop down arrow once to reduce the lines to drop to 2 as shown in Figure L-1, then click OK**
   The letter O in On the Wharf appears as a drop cap in its own text box, as shown in Figure L-2. The drop cap looks good, but you format the next drop cap differently so you can decide which effect you prefer.

5. **Click in the paragraph that begins Silicon Sleuth, click Format, click Drop Cap, click Dropped, click the Font list arrow, select Arial Black, click the Lines to drop list arrow two times to reduce the lines to drop to 1, then click OK**
   The letter S in Silicon is a drop cap that drops 1 line. You decide that dropping 1 line is not enough. You format the next drop cap as 2 lines dropped and experiment with the distance from text option.

6. **Click in the paragraph that begins Dragon Swindle, click Format, click Drop Cap, click Dropped, select the Arial Black font, select 2 for the lines to drop, click the Distance from text up arrow one time to set the distance from the text at 0.1", then click OK**
   The D in Dragon Swindle is a drop cap and exactly what you want. You modify the other two drop caps.

7. **Click the drop cap O, then click the shaded border**

8. **Right-click the drop cap, click Drop Cap, change the distance from text to 0.1", click OK, then revise the drop cap for Silicon Sleuth to drop 2 lines and appear 0.1" from the text**

9. **Click away from the selected drop cap, scroll up slightly so that the poster appears as shown in Figure L-3, then save the document**
   Notice that a portion of the paragraph mark appears next to each drop cap because the Show/Hide ¶ button on the Standard toolbar is selected. Remember that the ¶ marks do not print.

FIGURE L-1: Drop Cap dialog box

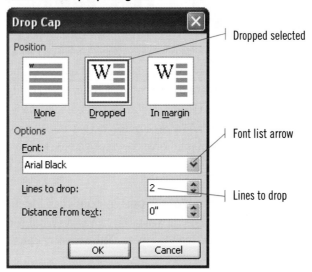

Dropped selected

Font list arrow

Lines to drop

FIGURE L-2: Drop cap inserted

Text box containing the drop cap

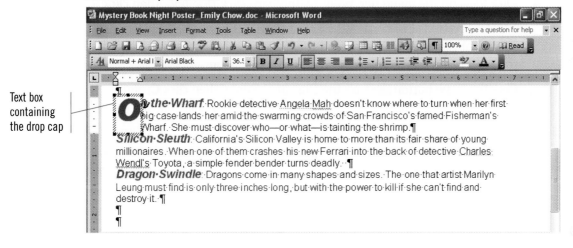

FIGURE L-3: Paragraphs with drop caps

Paragraph marks will not print

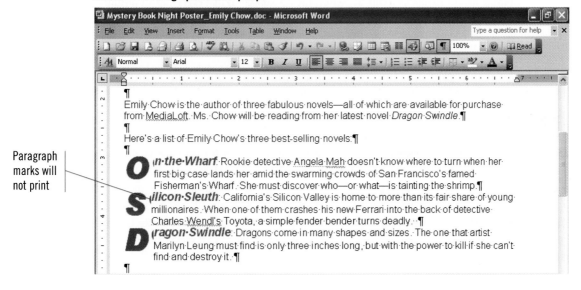

Word 2003

Editing Clip Art

The pictures included in the poster document are all clip art pictures obtained from the Clip Organizer. When you first import a clip art picture into a document, all of the objects that make up the clip art picture are grouped together into one picture. When you edit a clip art picture, you are really editing the objects that make up the picture. Because clip art pictures are composed of many objects, you work with the Group and Ungroup commands. You have already inserted two clip art pictures from the Clip Organizer into the poster. You decide to combine them with some drawn objects to create a new picture.

STEPS

TROUBLE
If the Drawing Canvas toolbar does not appear, right-click the selected picture, then click Show Drawing Canvas Toolbar.

1. **Scroll to the bottom of the poster, right-click the picture of the bridge, then click Edit Picture**
   The picture is contained in a drawing canvas. A shaded border encloses the edge of the drawing canvas and the Drawing Canvas toolbar appears. The **drawing canvas** is an area upon which you can draw multiple shapes and insert clip art.

2. **Click the blue shape that represents the sky as shown in Figure L-4, then press [Delete]**

3. **Click the Expand Drawing button ⊞ Expand on the Drawing Canvas toolbar three times**
   Each time you click, the drawing canvas enlarges, creating more white space around the picture.

4. **Click View on the menu bar, point to Toolbars, click Drawing, then click the Select Objects button ⬚ on the Drawing toolbar**

5. **Point ⬚ at the upper-left corner of the drawing canvas, then click and drag to select all the objects that make up the bridge as shown in Figure L-5**

6. **Click the Draw button Draw ▾ on the Drawing toolbar, then click Group**
   The Group command combines all the objects that make up the bridge into one object.

TROUBLE
If you see Format Drawing Canvas, click outside the drawing canvas to deselect it, click the bridge to select it, and then repeat Step 7.

7. **With the bridge still selected, click the right mouse button, click Format Object, click the Size tab, enter 2.5 in the Height text box, enter 4 in the Width text box, then click OK**
   The bridge is resized. Notice that the area under the bridge consists of two objects: one black object that represents the skyline of San Francisco and one turquoise object that represents the frigid waters of San Francisco Bay.

8. **Right-click the bridge, point to Grouping, click Ungroup, click outside the drawing canvas to deselect all the objects, click just the skyline object to select it, then press [Delete]**

9. **Right-click a blank area of the drawing canvas, point to Grouping, click Regroup, then save the document**
   The bridge picture appears, as shown in Figure L-6. While you can spend many hours using the tools on the Drawing toolbar to modify a clip art picture, the key concept is that every clip art picture is composed of two or more drawn objects—all of which can be modified or removed.

Clues to Use

Converting clip art pictures

You can use two methods to convert a clip art picture into a drawing object. First, you can right-click a clip art picture and select Edit Picture from the menu. You used this method to convert the clip art picture of the bridge into a clip art object. Second, you can change a clip art picture from an inline graphic to a floating graphic. In the next lesson you will use this second method to convert a clip art picture of a dragon into a clip art object that you can ungroup and modify. Which method you choose depends on how you wish to modify the graphic. If your main purpose is to change components of a graphic (for example, change the fill color of one of the elements), then use the Edit Picture method. If your main purpose is to change the layout of the graphic so that you can wrap text around it or use your mouse to move the graphic to another location in the document, then use the Layout dialog box to change the graphic from an inline graphic to a floating graphic.

FIGURE L-4: Sky object selected

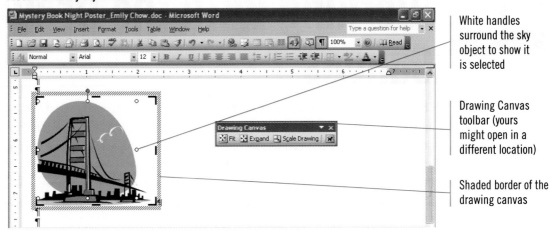

White handles surround the sky object to show it is selected

Drawing Canvas toolbar (yours might open in a different location)

Shaded border of the drawing canvas

FIGURE L-5: Selecting the bridge objects

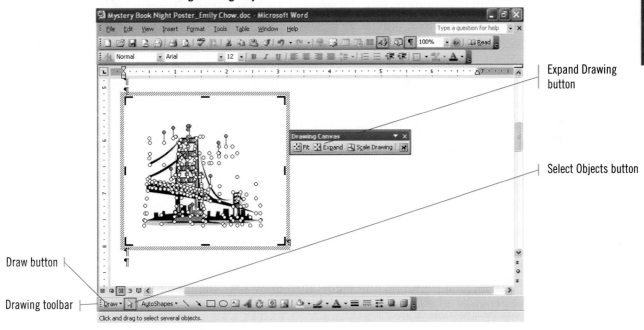

Expand Drawing button

Select Objects button

Draw button

Drawing toolbar

FIGURE L-6: Modified bridge picture

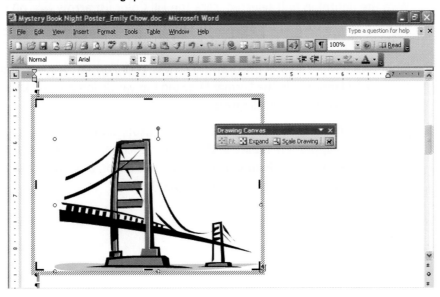

Working with the Drawing Canvas

The drawing canvas appears when you right-click a clip art picture and select Edit Picture or when you draw an AutoShape. You can add new objects such as clip art pictures or shapes you draw yourself to an existing drawing canvas. You also can change the size of the drawing canvas, move it anywhere in the document, and format it with an attractive fill color and border, just as you would any graphics object. When you move the drawing canvas, all the pictures and objects contained within it also move. ▰▰▰ You want to include a picture of a dragon next to the Golden Gate Bridge, draw a lightning bolt shape, and change the size and fill color of the drawing canvas.

STEPS

1. **With the bridge picture still selected, click the** Expand Drawing button 🔲 Expand **on the Drawing Canvas toolbar three times, then drag the bridge picture down and to the lower-left corner of the drawing canvas**

2. **Scroll down the document to the top of page 2, click the** dragon **to select it, right-click the** dragon**, click** Format Picture**, click the** Layout tab **in the Format Picture dialog box, click the** Square **wrapping style, then click** OK

3. **Click the** Zoom list arrow **on the Standard toolbar, click** Two pages**, drag the** dragon **onto the bridge, click the** Zoom list arrow **and select** Page Width**, then position the dragon as shown in Figure L-7**

4. **Make sure the dragon picture is selected, click the** More Brightness button 🔲 **on the Picture toolbar three times, then click a blank area in the drawing canvas to deselect the dragon**

   You can add objects that you draw yourself to the drawing canvas.

5. **Click the** AutoShapes button AutoShapes ▼ **on the Drawing toolbar, point to** Basic Shapes**, select the** Lightning Bolt **shape, then draw a lightning bolt that appears as shown in Figure L-8**

6. **Right-click the** lightning bolt**, click** Format AutoShape**, click the** Size tab**, change the Height to** 1.3" **and the Width to** 0.8"**, then click** OK

7. **With the** lightning bolt **selected, click the** Fill Color list arrow 🔲 ▼ **on the Drawing toolbar, click the** Yellow **color in the second row from the bottom, position the lightning bolt relative to the bridge as shown in Figure L-9, then click a blank area of the drawing canvas**

8. **Right-click a white area of the drawing canvas, click** Format Drawing Canvas**, click the** Colors and Lines tab **in the Format Drawing Canvas dialog box, click the** Color list arrow **in the Fill section, then click** Fill Effects

9. **In the Gradient tab, click the** Preset option button**, click the** Preset colors list arrow**, select** Fog**, click the** upper-left square **in the Variants section, click** OK **to exit the Fill Effects dialog box, click** OK **to exit the Format Drawing Canvas dialog box, then save the document**

   The picture appears in the poster, as shown in Figure L-10.

FIGURE L-7: Dragon and bridge pictures positioned

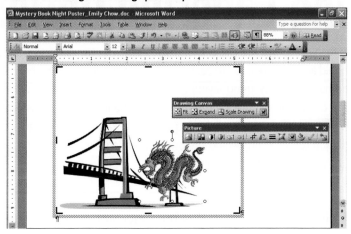

FIGURE L-8: Lightning bolt drawn

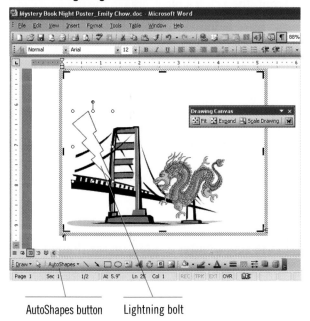

AutoShapes button Lightning bolt

FIGURE L-9: Lightning bolt sized and positioned

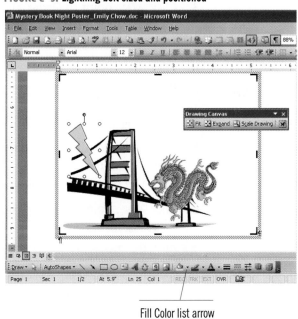

Fill Color list arrow

FIGURE L-10: Formatted drawing canvas

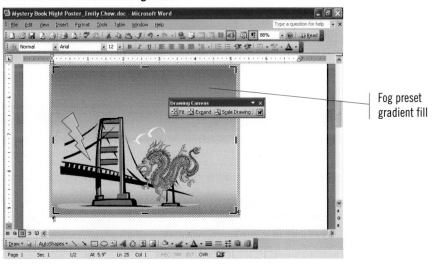

Fog preset gradient fill

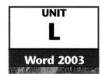
Using Layering Options

The Draw menu includes the Order command, which in turn includes several options for specifying how objects should appear in relation to each other. For example, you can choose to show one object partially on top of another object. By using layering commands in combination with the group and ungroup commands, you can achieve some interesting effects. The layering options available in Word are explained in Table L-1. ▒▒▒▒▒ You want the lightning bolt to strike between the two suspension cables of the bridge and the dragon to slither up behind the bridge roadbed. Your first task is to use the Ungroup command to separate the bridge into its various objects.

STEPS

1. **Click the** bridge **to select it, click the** Draw button `Draw ▾` **on the Drawing toolbar, click** Ungroup, **then click a blank area in the drawing canvas to deselect the bridge objects**

2. **Click the lower of the two** suspension cables **as shown in Figure L-11 to select it**
   You want this lower cable to appear in front of the lightning bolt.

3. **Click** `Draw ▾`, **point to** Order, **click** Bring to Front, **then click a blank area in the drawing canvas to deselect the suspension bridge**
   The lightning bolt appears to be striking between the suspension cables.

4. **Click the** Zoom list arrow **on the Standard toolbar, click** 200%, **then scroll down to view the bridge roadbed**
   The bridge roadbed consists of numerous black objects. You want just the solid black line that represents the roadbed and one of the suspension cables to appear in front of the dragon.

5. **Press and hold [Ctrl], then click the solid black roadbed object and the suspension cable nearest the dragon**
   Figure L-12 shows the two objects selected.

6. **Click** `Draw ▾`, **point to** Order, **click** Bring to Front
   Notice that the dragon appears to slither up behind the bridge roadbed.

7. **Click the** Zoom list arrow, **click** 100%, **then use your pointer to position the dragon as shown in Figure L-13**

8. **Click away from the dragon to deselect it, click the** Fit Drawing to Contents button `⊞Fit` **on the Drawing Canvas toolbar, then save the document**
   The contents of the drawing canvas now fit the drawing canvas.

TABLE L–1: Layering options in Word

command	function	command	function
Bring to Front	Places the object in front of all other objects	Send Backward	Moves the object backward one layer at a time
Send to Back	Places the object behind all other objects	Bring in Front of Text	Moves the object on top of text
Bring Forward	Moves the object forward one layer at a time; use to show an object overlapping one object and then being overlapped by another object	Send Behind Text	Moves the object behind text; often used to show a lightly shaded picture behind relevant text

FIGURE L-11: Lower suspension cable selected

Click here to
select the
correct cable

Handles appear
just around the
lower suspension
cable

FIGURE L-12: Roadbed and suspension cable objects selected

Two sets of sizing handles are visible, which indicate that both the roadbed
object and the suspension cable closest to the dragon are selected

FIGURE L-13: Dragon positioned

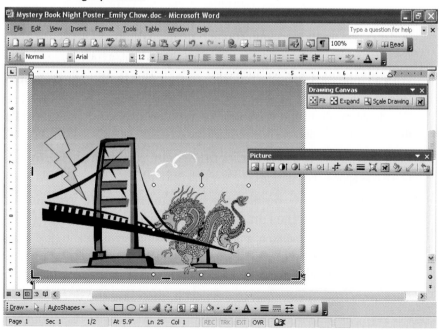

Aligning, Distributing, and Rotating Graphics

The Align or Distribute option on the Draw menu includes commands you can use to change the relative positioning of two or more objects. For example, you can use the Left Align command to align several drawn objects along their left sides. You can use the Distribute Vertically or the Distribute Horizontally command to display three or more objects so that the same amount of space appears between each object. The Rotate or Flip option on the Draw menu includes commands you can use to rotate or flip an object. For example, suppose you insert a clip art picture of a cat stalking to the right. You can use the Flip Horizontal command to flip the cat so that it stalks to the left, or you can use the Rotate option to make the cat stalk uphill or downhill. 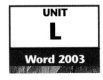 You decide to include a series of stars that are aligned and distributed vertically above the dragon along the right side of the drawing canvas. You also want to rotate the dragon by 30 degrees.

STEPS

1. **Click the drawing canvas to select it, click the AutoShapes button** `AutoShapes ▾` **on the Drawing toolbar, point to Stars and Banners, click 5-Point Star, then draw a star similar to the star shown in Figure L-14**

2. **With the star selected, click the Fill Color list arrow** `⬧ ▾` **on the Drawing toolbar, select Red, click the Line Color list arrow** `✐ ▾` **on the Drawing toolbar, then click No Line**
   The star is filled with the color red and is no longer outlined in black.

> **QUICK TIP**
> If you want to specify both a height and a width that are not necessarily proportional, then clear the Lock aspect ratio check box.

3. **Right-click the star, click Format AutoShape, click the Size tab, click the Lock aspect ratio check box to select it, set the Height at 0.3", press [Tab] to set the Width automatically, then click OK to exit the Format AutoShape dialog box**
   By selecting the Lock aspect ratio check box, you make sure that the Width is calculated in proportion to the Height you enter (or vice versa).

4. **Drag the star to the left so it appears above the dragon's head and towards the top of the drawing canvas, press [Ctrl][C], press [Ctrl][V] three times, then drag the bottom star right so that it appears just above the dragon's tail**
   Four red stars are visible.

5. **Press and hold [Ctrl], then click each star until all four stars are selected, click the Draw button** `Draw ▾` **on the Drawing toolbar, point to Align or Distribute, then click Align Right**
   The four stars are aligned along the right side of the drawing canvas.

6. **With all four stars still selected, click** `Draw ▾`, **point to Align or Distribute, then click Distribute Vertically**
   The aligned and distributed stars appear, as shown in Figure L-15. The Distribute Vertically command places the stars so that the distance between each star is equal.

7. **Click the dragon to select it, click Draw, point to Rotate or Flip, then click Free Rotate**
   Green dots appear at each corner of the selected picture.

8. **Press and hold [Shift], position the** `⟲` **over the upper-left green dot, drag to the right so the dragon rotates, then drag to the right again**
   Each time you drag the dragon, a dotted box shows the new position. Holding the [Shift] key rotates the dragon 15 degrees each time you drag, in this case, to the right. The dragon is rotated 30 degrees to the right, as shown in Figure L-16.

9. **Click away from the dragon to deselect it, then save the document**

FIGURE L-14: Star drawn in the drawing canvas

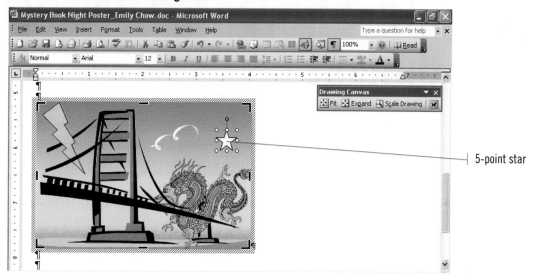

5-point star

FIGURE L-15: Aligned and distributed stars

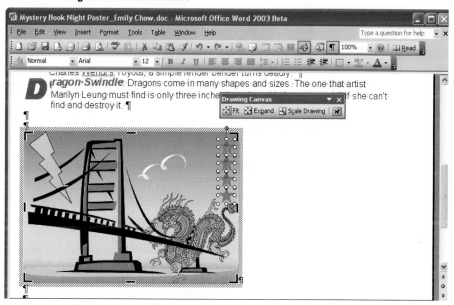

FIGURE L-16: Rotated dragon

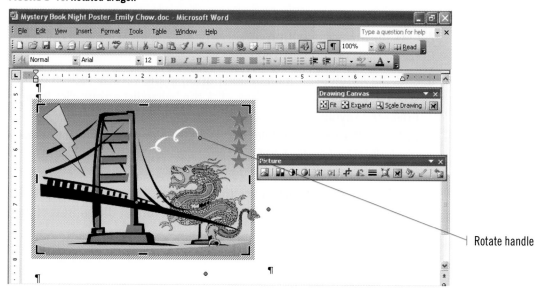

Rotate handle

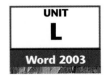

Using Advanced Positioning Options

Word offers a variety of ways to position objects. You can use your pointer to position an object anywhere on the page in a Word document, including on the drawing canvas, or you can use the Nudge command on the Draw menu to move an object by very small increments. You can also use the Layout tab in the Format Object dialog box to position an object precisely in relation to the page, margin, column, paragraph, or line in a Word document. Finally, you can use the Advanced Layout dialog box in the Format Drawing Canvas dialog box to position an object precisely on the drawing canvas. You decide to group the stars into one object and then position the object precisely in relation to the upper-right corner of the drawing canvas. You then use the Nudge option to position the dragon in relation to the bridge.

STEPS

1. **Use [Ctrl] to select each of the four stars, click the Draw button Draw ▾ on the Drawing toolbar, then click Group**

   You group the stars into one object so that you can position the group of stars easily.

2. **Right-click the grouped object, click Format Object, then click the Layout tab**

   The Layout tab in the Format Object dialog box appears. In this dialog box you can set an exact horizontal and vertical position for the selected object in relation to either the upper-left corner or the center of the drawing canvas.

3. **Set the Horizontal position at 3.6, set the Vertical position at .1 as shown in Figure L-17, then click OK**

   The star object is positioned precisely, based on the measurements you entered.

4. **Click the dragon to select it, click Draw ▾, point to Nudge, then click Left**

   The dragon moves 1 pixel to the left. The Nudge command moves an object one pixel at a time. You can also use the arrow keys to nudge an object up, down, left, or right.

5. **With the dragon still selected, use the arrow keys to move it up, down, left, or right so that its final position appears similar to Figure L-18**

6. **Right-click the border of the drawing canvas, click Format Drawing Canvas, click the Square wrapping style, then click the Center option button in the Horizontal alignment section**

   You select the Square wrapping style to transform the drawing canvas from an inline graphic to a floating graphic. Now you can apply advanced positioning options.

7. **Click the Advanced button**

   The Advanced Layout dialog box opens.

8. **Click the Absolute Position option button in the Vertical section of the dialog box to select it, enter 6 in the text box, click the below list arrow, click Page, click OK to exit the Advanced Layout dialog box, then click OK**

   The Format Drawing Canvas dialog box closes. The drawing canvas is centered horizontally and positioned exactly six inches from the top of the page. You can use the Click and Type feature to position the insertion point below the drawing canvas.

9. **Scroll down, double-click below the drawing canvas, click the Center button ▤ on the Formatting toolbar if necessary, then type and format the address of the Seattle MediaLoft as shown in Figure L-19**

10. **Save the document**

FIGURE L-17: Format Object dialog box

Use to set exact horizontal and vertical placement of an object in relation to a diagram or a drawing canvas

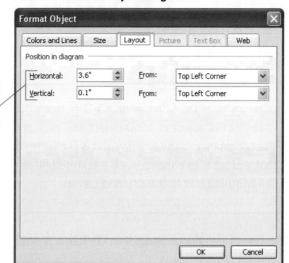

FIGURE L-18: Dragon nudged into position

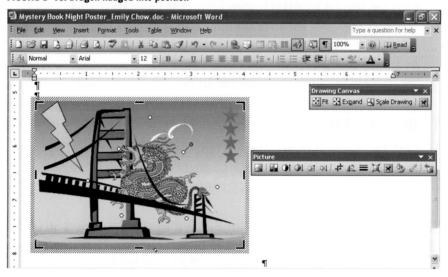

FIGURE L-19: Address information entered

Enhance Seattle MediaLoft with bold and italic

Address text centered

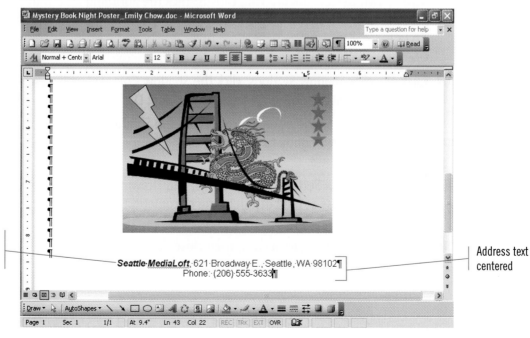

Adjusting Shadow and 3-D Settings

The Drawing toolbar includes the Shadow and 3-D buttons that you can use to enhance a graphics object. You can change a flat object to a 3-D object and you can add a shadow effect to an object. You can also modify the appearance of the shadow and 3-D effects you apply. The poster includes a WordArt object that you want to enhance with a textured fill and a 3-D effect. You also want to add a blue shadow to the lightning bolt in the drawing canvas.

STEPS

TROUBLE
Click toward the top of the "B" in "Book" to select the WordArt object.

1. **Scroll to the top of the document, then click the WordArt object to select it**
   When you select the WordArt object, the WordArt toolbar opens. If the WordArt toolbar does not appear, right-click the WordArt object, then click Show WordArt Toolbar.

2. **Click the Format WordArt button 🖌 on the WordArt toolbar, click the Colors and Lines tab, click the Color list arrow in the Fill section, click Fill Effects, click the Texture tab, select Blue tissue paper as shown in Figure L-20, click OK to exit the Fill Effects dialog box, then click OK**
   The Format WordArt dialog box closes and the WordArt object is formatted with the Blue tissue paper texture.

QUICK TIP
As you move the pointer over the 3-D styles, the style name appears in a ScreenTip.

3. **With the WordArt object selected, click the 3-D Style button 🔲 on the Drawing toolbar, then select 3-D Style 2**

4. **With the WordArt object still selected, click 🔲, then click 3-D Settings**
   The 3-D Settings toolbar appears. Table L-2 describes the buttons on the 3-D Settings toolbar. These buttons are used to change the appearance of the 3-D effect. For example, you can change the depth and lighting of the 3-D effect.

5. **Click the Depth button 🗔 on the 3-D Settings toolbar, select 36.00 pt in the Custom text box, type 18, press [Enter], click the Lighting button 🗔 on the 3-D Settings toolbar, then click the Lighting Direction button in the lower-left corner**
   The WordArt is modified based on the style, depth, and shadow settings you set.

6. **Scroll down to view the drawing canvas, click the lightning bolt in the drawing canvas to select it, click the Shadow Style button 🔲 on the Drawing toolbar, then click Shadow Style 1**
   One way to enhance a shadow effect is to change the shadow color.

7. **Click 🔲, click Shadow Settings, click the Shadow Color list arrow 🔲, verify that Semitransparent Shadow is selected, then select Dark Red**

8. **Click the Nudge Shadow Left button 🔲 on the Shadow Settings toolbar three times to move the shadow slightly to the left**
   Your poster is completed.

9. **Close the Shadow Settings, 3-D Settings, and Drawing Canvas toolbars, double-click below the address at the bottom of the document, then type Contact Your Name for assistance.**

10. **Save the document, print a copy, then close the document**
    The completed poster is shown in Figure L-21.

FIGURE L-20: Blue tissue paper texture selected

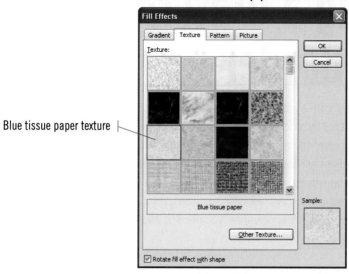

Blue tissue paper texture

FIGURE L-21: Completed poster

TABLE L-2: The 3-D Settings toolbar

button	use to	button	use to
	Turn the 3-D effect on or off		Change the depth of the 3-D effect
	Tilt the 3-D effect down		Change the direction of the 3-D effect
	Tilt the 3-D effect up		Select a lighting direction
	Tilt the 3-D effect to the left		Select a surface texture for the 3-D effect
	Tilt the 3-D effect to the right		Select a 3-D color

Inserting a Watermark and a Page Border

You can enhance a document with a watermark and a page border. A **watermark** is a picture or other type of graphics object that appears lightly shaded behind text in a document. For example, you could include a company logo as a watermark on every page of a company report, or you could create "Confidential" as a WordArt object that appears in a very light gray behind the text of an important letter or memo. A **page border** encloses one or more pages of a document. You can create a box border using a variety of line styles and colors, or you can insert one of Word's preset art borders. You have promised to supply two poster designs. To finish the poster advertising Jonathon Grant's appearance, you need to add a watermark and a page border.

STEPS

1. **Open the file** WD L-2.doc **from the drive and folder where your Data Files are located, then save it as** Mystery Book Night Poster_Jonathon Grant

   The picture that you want to make into a watermark appears at the bottom of the document.

2. **Scroll to the end of the document, then click the picture of the** magnifying glass and pipe **to select it**

3. **Click the** Color button 🔳 **on the Picture toolbar, then click** Washout

   The colors of the picture now appear very lightly tinted. You can use the More Brightness, Less Brightness, More Contrast, and Less Contrast buttons on the Picture toolbar to further modify the appearance of the picture. However, you are pleased with the default settings.

4. **Click the** Text Wrapping button 🔳 **on the Picture toolbar, then click** Behind Text

5. **Use the** Zoom list arrow **to select** Whole Page, **click the** Format Picture button 🔳 **on the Picture toolbar, click the** Size tab, **click the** Lock aspect ratio check box **to clear it, change the Height to** 6" **and the Width to** 4", **click** OK, **then use the pointer to position the picture behind the text as shown in Figure L-22**

6. **Click away from the picture to deselect it, click** Format **on the menu bar, click** Borders and Shading, **then click the** Page Border tab

   In the Page Border tab of the Borders and Shading dialog box you can add a simple box border, a shadow border, or a 3-D border.

7. **Click** Box, **scroll down the Style list box, then select the** Thick-Thin border style, **the** Teal border color, **and the** 4½ pt border width **(see Figure L-23)**

TROUBLE
If your page border does not appear as expected, read the Clues to Use on the next page.

8. **Click** OK **to exit the Borders and Shading dialog box, return to** 100% view, **then type your name in place of Your Name at the bottom of the document**

9. **Save the document, print a copy, close the document, then exit Word**

   The completed poster appears as shown in Figure L-24.

Clues to Use

Printing a page border

Sometimes a document formatted with a page border will not print correctly on certain printers because the page border falls outside the print area recognized by the printer. For example, the bottom border or one of the side borders might not print. To correct this problem, open the Borders and Shading dialog box, click Options on the Page Border tab, then increase the point size of the top, bottom, left, or right margins. Or, you can specify that the border be measured from the text, not from the edge of the page, and set the points to measure from the text. Experiment until you find the settings that work with your printer.

FIGURE L-22: Watermark sized and positioned

Watermark

FIGURE L-23: Borders and Shading dialog box

Line style selected

Color selected

Width selected

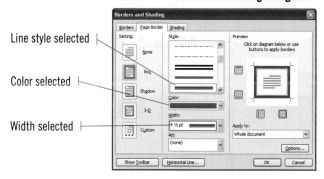

FIGURE L-24: Completed poster

Practice

Refer to the pictures in the drawing canvas shown in Figure L-25, then answer the following questions.

FIGURE L-25

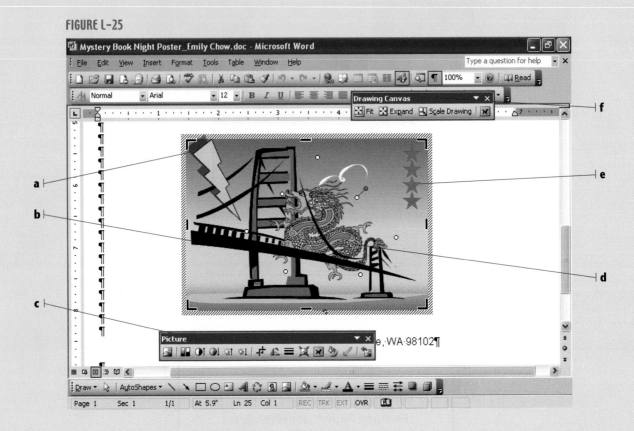

1. Which items are vertically distributed?
2. Which item is enhanced with a shadow?
3. A layering option was applied to which item?
4. Which item is currently ready to rotate?
5. Which item contains the tools used to modify a picture?
6. Which item contains the button used to expand the drawing canvas?

Match each term with the statement that best describes it.

7. **Drawing canvas**
8. **Drop cap**
9. **Ungroup**
10. **Distribute Vertically**
11. **Align Left**
12. **Gradient Fill Effect**

a. Large single letter that appears at the beginning of a paragraph
b. Color shading that ranges from light to dark in various patterns
c. Evenly spaces three or more objects
d. Used to separate a clip art picture into its component objects
e. Arrange two or more objects along the same plane
f. Enclosed box that contains a variety of graphics objects

Select the best answer from the list of choices.

13. Which of the following options is *not* available in the Drop Cap dialog box?

   a. Distance from text

   b. Vertical alignment

   c. Lines to drop

   d. Font style

14. What is the purpose of the Expand button on the Drawing Canvas toolbar?

   a. To increase the size of the drawing canvas, but not the contents of the drawing canvas

   b. To increase the size of the drawing canvas and its contents

   c. To increase only the contents of the drawing canvas

   d. To expand the contents to fit the drawing canvas

15. Which of the following fill effects is *not* available in the Fill Effects dialog box?

   a. Texture

   b. Gradient

   c. Picture

   d. Color

16. How do you select two or more objects?

   a. Press and hold [Ctrl], then click each object in turn.

   b. Click each object in turn.

   c. Press and hold [Alt], then click each object in turn.

   d. Click Edit on the menu bar, then click Select.

17. Which option from the Draw menu do you select to modify how two or more objects appear in relation to each other?

   a. Align or Distribute

   b. Nudge

   c. Edit AutoShape

   d. Distribute

18. How far does a Nudge button move an object?

   a. 2 pixels

   b. 1 inch

   c. 1 pixel

   d. 10 pixels

19. Which option in the Color button on the Picture toolbar do you select to turn an object into a watermark?

   a. Washout

   b. Grayscale

   c. Watermark

   d. More Brightness

▼ SKILLS REVIEW

1. Insert drop caps.

   a. Start Word. Open the file WD L-3.doc from the drive and folder where your Data Files are located, then save it as **Story Time Poster_Joanne**.

   b. Click in the paragraph that begins with the text **Joanne Preston has been delighting....**

   c. Insert a drop cap that is dropped three lines and uses the Britannic Bold font (or an alternate font if this one is not available).

   d. Insert a drop cap at the beginning of the next paragraph that is dropped two lines and uses the Britannic Bold font.

   e. Insert a drop cap at the beginning of the next paragraph that is dropped two lines, uses the Britannic Bold font, and is positioned 0.1" from the text.

   f. Modify the **J** drop cap and the **M** drop cap to match the **A** drop cap, then save the document.

2. Edit clip art.

   a. Scroll to the bottom of the poster, right-click the picture of the Eiffel Tower, then click Edit Picture.

   b. Ungroup the picture.

   c. Delete all the objects that make up the sky, including the pink object behind the bridge toward the bottom of the picture. (*Hint*: You will need to delete quite a few objects so that the tower appears against a white background.)

   d. Use the Drawing Canvas toolbar to expand the drawing canvas four times, then change to 75% zoom or whatever zoom setting allows you to see the entire drawing canvas.

   e. Use the Select Objects tool on the Drawing toolbar to select all the objects that make up the Eiffel Tower picture.

   f. Group the picture into one object.

   g. With the object selected, open the Format Object dialog box, click the Size tab if necessary, then change the Height of the object to 2.5" and the width to 3.5".

3. **Work with the drawing canvas.**

   a. Drag the Eiffel Tower picture down so that its lower-left sizing handle is even with the lower-left corner of the drawing canvas. (*Note*: If the entire picture does not move, use the Select Objects tool to select and group the picture again.)

   b. Use the Zoom list arrow to view Two Pages, click the picture of the bicycle, then change it to an object with the Square wrapping style.

   c. Ungroup the bicycle, answer Yes if prompted, delete the blue background object, then select all the elements of the bicycle and group them into one object.

   d. Drag the bicycle picture into the drawing canvas, then switch to a zoom setting that allows you to see the entire drawing canvas. (*Note*: If the wheels on the bike are black, you did not group all of the objects successfully in Step 3c. Undo the move object command, and then regroup all the elements of the bike.)

   e. Position the bicycle so the back wheel is even with the right side of the Eiffel Tower picture and the front wheel is on the bridge. You don't need to be exact at this stage.

   f. Draw a crescent moon AutoShape that is 0.8" high with the lock aspect ratio check box selected. Position the moon in the sky to the left of the Eiffel Tower.

   g. Fill the moon shape with a light yellow color and delete the black outline.

   h. Fill the drawing canvas with the Daybreak preset gradient, using the top-right variant (light pink at the top). Save the document.

4. **Use layering options.**

   a. Use the Send Backward command to position the bicycle behind the Eiffel Tower picture so that part of the wheels are hidden.

   b. Use the Fit button on the Drawing Canvas toolbar to fit the picture inside the drawing canvas.

   c. Save the document.

5. **Align, distribute, and rotate graphics.**

   a. Make sure the drawing canvas is selected, draw a heart AutoShape that is 0.3" wide and 0.3" in height, then fill it with pink.

   b. Copy the heart twice so that you have a total of three hearts, then move the selected heart near the right edge of the picture.

   c. Align the hearts along their bottom edges.

   d. Use the Distribute Horizontally feature to distribute the hearts, then position them so that they appear about an inch above the bicycle. You do not have to position them precisely yet.

   e. Select the bicycle, then flip it horizontally. (*Hint*: Click Draw, point to Rotate or Flip, then click Flip Horizontal.)

6. **Use advanced positioning options.**

   a. Group the hearts into one object.

   b. Position the grouped hearts in the drawing canvas so that the horizontal position is 1.8" from the top left corner and the vertical position is 0.5" from the top left corner. (*Note*: If a warning appears, enter the measurements suggested.) Refer to the picture of the completed drawing in Figure L-26.

   c. Position the moon so that the horizontal position is .38" from the top left corner and the vertical position is 0.24" from the top left corner.

   d. Nudge the bike so it appears as shown in the completed drawing in Figure L-26.

   e. Change the layout of the drawing canvas to select the Square wrapping style and Center horizontal alignment.

   f. In the Advanced Layout dialog box, set the Absolute Vertical position of the drawing canvas to 5.8" below the page.

   g. Double-click below the drawing canvas, then type with center alignment the following text:

   MediaLoft Houston, 2118 Westheimer Road, Houston, TX 77098

   Phone: (281) 555-8233

   Contact Your Name for assistance.

   h. Enhance **MediaLoft Houston** with bold, then save the document.

7. Adjust Shadow and 3-D settings.

  a. Click the WordArt object at the top of the document to select it.

  b. Fill the WordArt object with the Papyrus texture.

  c. Add the 3-D Style 3 to the WordArt object.

  d. Change the 3-D settings so that the depth is 18 points and change the lighting so it comes from the center right.

  e. Scroll down, click the crescent moon in the drawing canvas to select it, then add the Shadow Style 5.

  f. Make the shadow semitransparent and light orange. The completed drawing appears as shown in Figure L-26.

  g. Save the document, view it in Print Preview, print a copy, then close the document.

FIGURE L-26

8. Insert a watermark and a page border.

  a. Open the file WD L-4.doc from the drive and folder where your Data Files are located, then save it as **Story Time Poster_Hayley**.

  b. Click the picture at the top of the document, then use the Color button on the Picture toolbar to change its color to the Washout setting.

  c. Click the More Brightness button twice to further increase the washed out effect.

  d. Change the text wrapping of the picture to Behind Text.

  e. Use the Zoom list arrow to view the Whole Page, change the Height of the picture to 5" with the Lock Aspect ratio check box selected so that the Width is calculated automatically.

  f. Center the picture and position it 4" below the top of the page.

  g. Add a green page border in the 3 pt, double-line box style.

  h. In 100% view, replace Your Name at the bottom of the document with your name.

  i. Save the document, print a copy, close the document, then exit Word.

▼ INDEPENDENT CHALLENGE 1

You work as a teacher's aide at an elementary school. Your supervisor has asked you to create an attractive picture that includes a variety of elements that children can color, according to the labels. You've already downloaded the clip art pictures you plan to use to create the picture. Now you need to work in the drawing canvas to modify the pictures you've downloaded, draw some AutoShapes, then add some text objects.

  a. Start Word, open the file WD L-5.doc from the drive and folder where your Data Files are located, and save it as **Learning Colors Picture**.

  b. Edit the picture of the balloons, then expand the drawing canvas eight times. (*Note*: Change the zoom setting as needed to meet your needs as you work.)

  c. Remove the colored shape from each balloon, then group the balloons into one object.

  d. Increase the Height of the balloons to 5" with the Lock aspect ratio check box selected.

  e. Scroll down the page to find the picture of the hat and balloon, edit the picture, then remove all the objects that make up the single balloon.

  f. Expand the drawing canvas containing the hat two times, then group all the objects that make up the hat into one object.

  g. Drag the grouped hat picture into the drawing canvas that contains the three balloons. Position the hat picture in the lower-left corner of the drawing canvas, then increase its Height to 3" with the Lock aspect ratio check box selected so the Width is calculated automatically.

▼ INDEPENDENT CHALLENGE 1 (CONTINUED)

FIGURE L-27

h. Rotate the hat picture by 15 degrees to the left. (*Hint*: Press and hold [Shift] while dragging a rotate handle to constrain the rotation to 15-degree increments.)

i. Nudge the hat to position it as shown in the completed drawing in Figure L-27.

Advanced Challenge Exercise

- Refer to Figure L-27 to complete the picture, according to the following instructions.
- Add the Sun AutoShape, then use rotate and layering options to show the sun just behind the two balloons on the right.
- Position all the objects so they are placed similarly to how they are shown in Figure L-27. Use the pointer, as well as the order, rotate, and size commands as needed.
- Add text boxes and draw lines. Type text in the text boxes and format it in 16 pt, Arial, and Bold. (*Note*: Remove the border around each text box and move text boxes as needed to ensure they do not block other parts of the picture.)

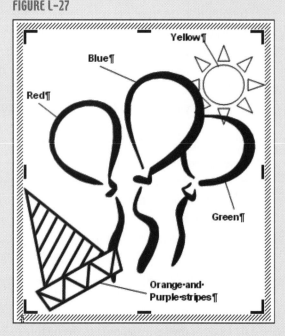

j. Click the Fit button to fit the canvas to the objects, then create a page border that is a dark red single line.

k. Change the layout of the drawing canvas to a Square floating graphic, then center the drawing canvas.

l. Use Click and Type to enter **Prepared by** followed by your name centered below the Drawing canvas.

m. View the document in Whole Page view, delete the blank drawing canvas below the picture, save the document, print a copy, close the document, then exit Word.

▼ INDEPENDENT CHALLENGE 2

You have just been hired to create a series of templates for the menus and other documents produced by Grains & Greens—a new vegetarian café in your neighborhood. Your first task is to create the logo for Grains & Greens that appears as shown in Figure L-28. Refer to this figure as you work.

FIGURE L-28

a. Start Word. Open a new blank Word document, show the Drawing toolbar, if necessary, click the Insert WordArt button on the Drawing toolbar, select the upper-left WordArt style (the default style), then enter the text G & G. Select the Bauhaus 93 font style (or alternate font if this one is not available).

b. Change the WordArt object to a floating graphic with the Square wrapping style and left-aligned. (*Hint*: Right-click the WordArt object, then click Format WordArt to open the Format WordArt dialog box.)

c. Set the Width of the WordArt object to 2" with the Lock aspect ratio check box unselected, then fill the object with the Green marble texture.

d. Apply the Shadow Style 1 to the WordArt object, then add a semitransparent lime to the shadow.

e. Refer to Figure L-28 to insert and modify the pea pod clip art picture. (*Hint*: Click the Insert Clip Art button on the Drawing toolbar, then enter the search term **pea pod** to find the clip art picture). You need to change the layout of the drawing canvas with the pea pod picture to square and right, then ungroup the pea pod and change the background color to bright green. Use your mouse to resize, rotate, and reposition the pea pod so that it appears as shown in Figure L-28.

▼ INDEPENDENT CHALLENGE 2 (CONTINUED)

Advanced Challenge Exercise

- Insert a horizontal line graphic below the WordArt object and pea pod picture as follows:
- Position the insertion point below the logo, then open the Page Border tab in the Borders and Shading dialog box.
- Click Horizontal Line, select the middle line style in the second row of the line style selections, then click OK.
- Right-click the horizontal line, click Format Horizontal Line, change the height to 10 pt, then click OK.

f. Type your name right-aligned below the logo, save the document as **Grains and Greens Logo** to the drive and folder where your Data Files are located, print a copy, save and close the document, then exit Word.

▼ INDEPENDENT CHALLENGE 3

You are the owner of a small home-based business in Halifax, Nova Scotia. You determine the kinds of products and services you sell. For example, you could operate a small catering business that specializes in company parties, or you could operate a Web site design service for other home-based businesses. You use Word's graphics features to create an attractive flyer to advertise your business.

a. On a piece of paper, plan the contents of your flyer. Your flyer must include four of the following five elements: WordArt object containing the name of the company or a slogan, clip art picture that has been modified in some way, three or more AutoShapes that are aligned and distributed, a formatted drawing canvas containing the modified clip art picture and AutoShapes, along with additional graphics if appropriate, and two or more drop caps used appropriately.

b. Start Word. Open a new blank Word document, show the Drawing toolbar if necessary, then create the text for your flyer. You should include the following information: company name, company address and contact information, including the URL of a Web site, and two or three short paragraphs describing the products or services offered.

c. Add the graphics objects required. Use Drawing tools as you create and edit the graphics. Experiment with some of the tools you did not use in this unit. Make sure you use at least five of the following Drawing tools: align and distribute; group and ungroup; fill colors, textures, or gradients—use at least one fill effect somewhere in your document; advanced positioning to set the position of an object within the drawing canvas; layering options; rotate; and 3-D and Shadow effect.

d. Enter your name in an appropriate location on your flyer.

e. View the flyer in Whole Page view, then make any final spacing and sizing adjustments to ensure all the text and graphics elements appear attractively on the page.

f. Save your flyer as **My Company Flyer** to the drive and folder where your Data Files are located.

g. Print a copy of the flyer, close the document, then exit Word.

▼ INDEPENDENT CHALLENGE 4

Many of the Web pages on the World Wide Web are beautifully designed with attractive graphics that entice the Web surfer to explore further. Other Web pages are less well designed, and sometimes have clashing colors, unattractive graphics, and hard-to-read text. To increase your understanding of the role graphics play in enhancing—or detracting from—the effectiveness of a document, you decide to evaluate design elements on the home pages of two Web sites that sell similar products or services.

a. Open your Web browser and search for two companies that sell a product or service of interest to you. You can try entering product-related keywords, such as **art supplies**, **pastels**, and **watercolors**, or you can try entering generic domain names, such as www.art.com or www.artsupplies.com, in the Address box of your Web browser.

b. Open the file WD L-6.doc from the drive and folder where your Data Files are located, then save it as **Web Page Design Evaluations**. This document contains criteria for ranking the design elements on the Web pages you've chosen.

c. As directed in the Web Page Design Evaluations document, enter the company name and copy the URL of each Web site to the spaces provided.

d. Assign a ranking to each site as directed, then complete the two questions at the bottom of the document.

e. Type your name at the bottom of the document, print a copy, save and close it, then exit Word.

▼ VISUAL WORKSHOP

You have been hired by Fur and Feathers, a local pet store, to design an attractive letterhead. The graphics you need to create the letterhead are already included in a Word file. Open the file WD L-7.doc from the drive and folder where your Data Files are located, then save it as **Fur and Feathers Letterhead**. Use the graphics to create the letterhead shown in Figure L-29. Note that you need to fill the WordArt object with the Woven Mat texture and then add the 3-D Style 3 with a depth of 18 pt and brown as the 3-D color. To modify the pictures, start by editing the parrot and changing the color of the blue feathers on the parrot to red. Change the layout of the puppy to Square, then drag the puppy into the same drawing canvas inhabited by the parrot. Modify, size, and position the puppy and parrot, then fit the drawing canvas to the two pictures and position the drawing canvas so that the completed letterhead appears as shown in Figure L-29. Use Click and Type to enter the contact information. Save the document, then print a copy.

FIGURE L-29

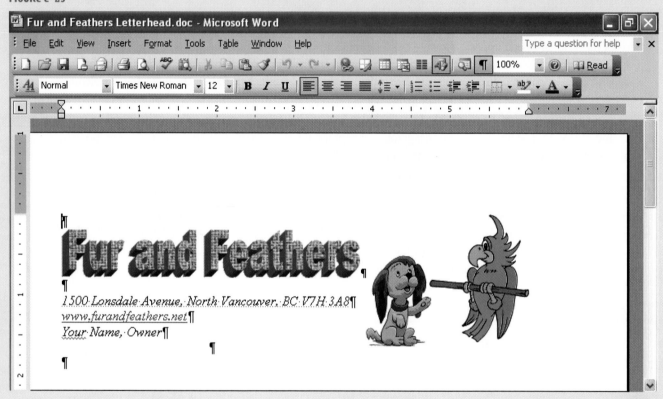

Building Forms

OBJECTIVES

Construct a form template
Add and modify text form fields
Add drop-down and check box form fields
Use calculations in a form
Add Help to a form
Insert form controls
Format and protect forms
Fill in a form as a user

If you have a SAM user profile, you may have access to hands-on instruction, practice, and assessment of the skills covered in this unit. Log in to your SAM account and go to your assignments page to see what your instructor has assigned.

Word provides the tools you need to build forms that users can complete within a Word document. A **form** is a structured document with spaces reserved for entering information. You create a form as a template that includes labeled spaces—called **form fields**—into which users type information. The form template can include check boxes, drop-down lists, formulas used to perform calculations, Help messages, and other form controls to make the form interactive. Finally, you can protect a form so that users can enter information into the form, but they cannot change the structure of the form itself. ▨▨▨ Alice Wegman in the Marketing Department wants to create a form to survey MediaLoft store managers. You start by creating the form template.

Constructing a Form Template

A Word form is created as a **form template**, which contains all the components of the form. As you learned in an earlier unit, a template is a file that contains the basic structure of a document, such as the page layout, headers and footers, and graphic elements. In the case of a form template, the structure usually consists of a table form that contains field labels and form fields. Figure M-1 shows a completed form template containing several different types of form fields. A **field label** is a word or phrase such as "Date" or "Location" that tells users the kind of information required for a given field. A **form field** is the location where the data associated with a field label is stored. Information that can be stored in a form field includes text, an X in a check box, a number, or a selection in a drop-down list.  You need to create the basic structure of the form in Word and then save the document as a template. You start by creating the form in Word, then saving it as a template to a new folder that you create in the drive and folder where your Data Files are located.

STEPS

1. **Start Word, click** File **on the menu bar, then click** New **to open the New Document task pane**

2. **Click** On my computer **in the Templates section of the New Document task pane**
   The Templates dialog box opens.

3. **Verify** Blank Document **is selected, click the** Template option button **in the Create New section, then click** OK
   A new document appears in the document window and Template1 appears on the title bar.

4. **Type** Marketing Survey, **center the text, enhance it with** Bold **and the** 18 pt **font size, press** [Enter] **twice, then clear the formatting**

5. **Click** Table **on the menu bar, point to** Insert, **click** Table, **enter** 2 **for the number of columns and** 13 **for the number of rows, then click** OK

6. **Type** Name:, **press** [Tab], **type** Date:, **press** [Tab], **then enter the remaining field labels and merge selected cells as shown in Figure M-2**
   Once you have created the structure for your form, you can save it as a template. First, you create a new folder to contain the template and then you specify this folder as the location of user templates so that Word can find it.

   > **TROUBLE**
   > To merge cells, click to the left of the row to select it, click Table on the menu bar, then click Merge Cells.

7. **Minimize Word, right-click** My Computer **on your computer desktop, click** Explore **to open Windows Explorer, navigate to the drive and folder where your Data Files are located, click** File, **point to** New, **click** Folder, **type** Your Name Form Templates **as the folder name, then press** [Enter]
   In order to have your templates stored in the same location, you set this new folder as the default location for user templates. A **user template** is any template that you create yourself.

8. **Close** Windows Explorer, **click** Template1 **on the taskbar, click** Tools **on the menu bar, click** Options, **click** File Locations, **click** User templates **in the list of File types, click** Modify, **click the** Look in list arrow, **select the** location **where you created the Your Name Form Templates folder, click the** folder **to select it, click** OK, **then click** OK

9. **Click the** Save button **on the Standard toolbar, verify that "Marketing Survey.dot" appears in the File name text box as shown in Figure M-3, then click** Save
   Word saves the template to the new folder you created.

FIGURE M-1: Form construction

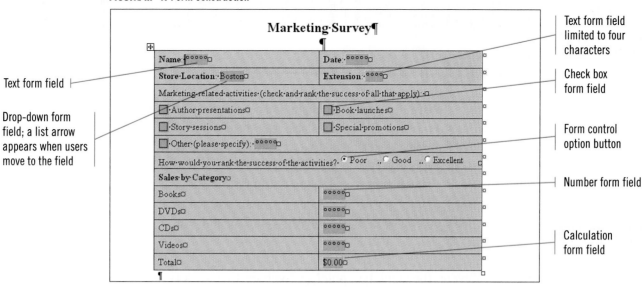

Text form field

Drop-down form field; a list arrow appears when users move to the field

Text form field limited to four characters

Check box form field

Form control option button

Number form field

Calculation form field

FIGURE M-2: Table form

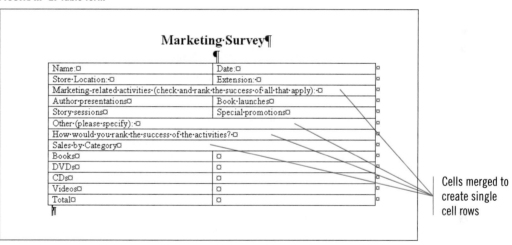

Cells merged to create single cell rows

FIGURE M-3: Saving a user template

Save location is the folder you identified as the default location for template files

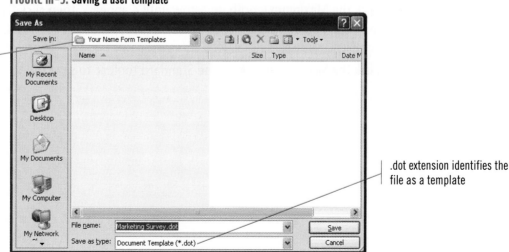

.dot extension identifies the file as a template

Adding and Modifying Text Form Fields

Once you have created a structure for your form, you need to designate form fields where users enter information. You insert **text form fields** in the table cells where users will enter text information, such as their names or the current date. A text form field allows you to control the kind of information users can enter. For example, you can specify that a text form field accepts only a numeric value, limits the number of characters entered, or requires dates to be entered in a specified format. You insert text form fields in the table cells where you need users to enter text or numbers. You then work in the Text Form Field Options dialog box to specify the kind of information required for each text form field.

STEPS

1. **Click View on the menu bar, point to Toolbars, then click Forms**
   The Forms toolbar contains the buttons used to create and modify the various elements of a form. Table M-1 describes each button on the Forms toolbar.

> **TROUBLE**
> If dots do not appear in the shaded rectangle, click the Show/Hide ¶ button on the Formatting toolbar.

2. **Click after Name:, press [Spacebar] one time, then click the Text Form Field button [abl] on the Forms toolbar**
   A gray shaded rectangle with five dots appears following Name. When completing the form, the user will be able to enter text into this form field.

3. **Press [Tab], click after Date:, press [Spacebar] one time, then click [abl]**

4. **Repeat step 3 to insert a text form field after Extension: and after Other (please specify):**
   Figure M-4 shows the form with text form fields inserted in four table cells. You want each user who completes the form to enter a date in a specific format in the text form field following the Date label.

5. **Click the text form field next to Date:, then click the Form Field Options button [icon] on the Forms toolbar**
   The Text Form Field Options dialog box opens. In this dialog box, you specify options related to the format and content of the selected text form field.

> **QUICK TIP**
> If the user types 03/03/06, the date entered will appear as March 3, 2006.

6. **Click the Type list arrow, click Date, click the Date format list arrow, click MMMM d, yyyy as shown in Figure M-5, then click OK**
   The text form field looks the same. In a later lesson, you will add a Help message to inform users how to enter the date.

7. **Click the text form field next to Extension:, then click [icon]**

8. **Click the Maximum length up arrow until 4 appears, then click OK**
   You specify the number of characters a field can contain when you want to restrict the length of an entry. For example, a user completing this form can enter a phone extension of no more than four digits.

9. **Click the Save button [icon] on the Standard toolbar to save the template**

FIGURE M-4: Text form fields inserted

Forms toolbar

Text form field

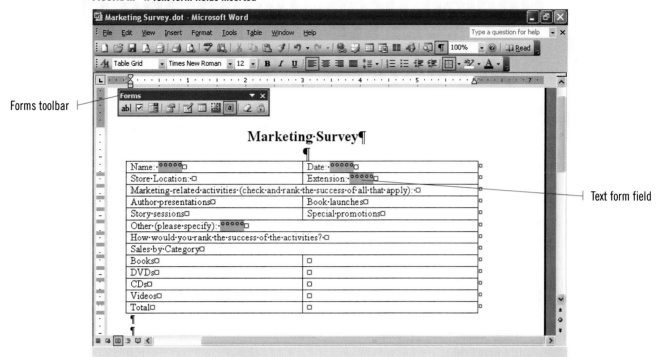

FIGURE M-5: Text Form Field Options dialog box

Type list arrow

Date format list arrow

Date format selected

Indicates the number of the text form field in the form; Text2 indicates that the current text form field was the second field you entered while creating the form

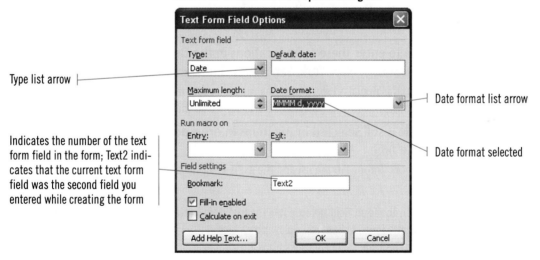

TABLE M-1: Buttons on the Forms toolbar

button	use to	button	use to
abl	Insert a text form field		Insert a table/cell to contain form fields
☑	Insert a check box form field		Insert a frame to contain a form
	Insert a drop-down form field	a	Insert or remove shading from form fields
	Open the Form Field Options dialog box, then modify the options of an inserted form field		Reset form fields to their default settings
	Draw a table to contain form fields		Protect a form so that users can enter only data required for the form fields

Adding Drop-Down and Check Box Form Fields

In addition to text form fields, Word forms can include check box form fields and drop-down form fields. Users can use the pointer to make selections in check box or drop-down form fields. For example, users can click a check box to select it or they can select an item from a drop-down list. You want to provide store managers an easy way to select the location of their MediaLoft store. You decide to provide a drop-down list of the MediaLoft store locations so that store managers can select the location of their MediaLoft store. You also want the store managers to identify which marketing-related activities listed in the form they engaged in during the past month. You provide check boxes next to the activities so store managers can quickly make their selections.

STEPS

1. **Click after** Store Location:, **press [Spacebar] one time, then click the** Drop-Down Form Field button **on the Forms toolbar**

   A gray shaded rectangle without dots appears, indicating that the field is a drop-down form field and not a text form field.

2. **Click the** Form Field Options button **on the Forms toolbar**

   The Drop-Down Form Field Options dialog box opens. In this dialog box, you enter the selections you want to appear in the drop-down list.

3. **Type** Boston **in the Drop-down item text box, then click** Add

   Boston becomes the first entry in the drop-down list.

QUICK TIP
You can press [Enter] after typing each entry, or you can click Add.

4. **Repeat Step 3 to enter these store locations in the Drop-down item text box:** Chicago, Houston, Kansas City, New York, San Diego, San Francisco, Toronto, **and** Seattle

   Figure M-6 shows the MediaLoft store locations entered in the Drop-Down Form Field Options dialog box. You can change the order in which the locations are presented so that the entire list appears in alphabetical order.

5. **Be sure** Seattle **is still selected in the Items in drop-down list box, then click the** Move up button **one time**

   Seattle moves above Toronto in the list and the list is in alphabetical order.

6. **Click** OK

   Boston appears in the form field because it is the first item in the drop-down form field list. In a later lesson, you will protect the form. When you open the protected form to complete it as a user, a list arrow appears next to Boston to indicate that other selections are available.

7. **Click to the left of** Author presentations, **click the** Check Box Form Field button **on the Forms toolbar, then press [Spacebar] one time to insert a space between the check box and the text**

   A gray shaded box appears before the text "Author presentations." After the form is protected, an X will appear in the box when a user selects it.

8. **Repeat Step 7 to insert check boxes next to** Book launches, Story sessions, Special promotions, **and** Other (please specify):

   Figure M-7 shows the form with the text form fields, a drop-down form field, and check box form fields.

9. **Save the template**

FIGURE M-6: Drop-Down Form Field Options dialog box

Drop-down item text box

Boston and Chicago appear above Houston

Move up button

Move down button

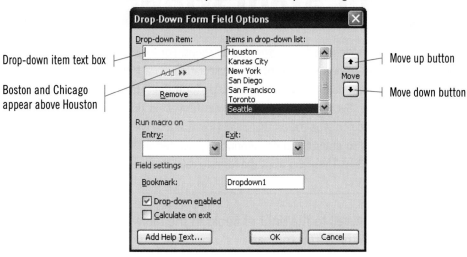

FIGURE M-7: Form fields inserted in a Word form

Text form field

Drop-down form field

Check box form fields

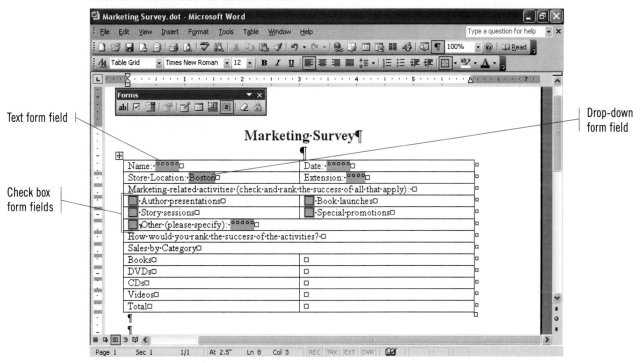

Word 2003

Using Calculations in a Form

A Word form can be designed to perform calculations. For example, you can specify that a text form field should add a series of numbers. To perform calculations in a form, you must follow two steps. First, you specify each text form field that will be used to perform the calculation as Number type so that a user can only enter numbers. Second, you specify the text form field that contains the result of the calculation as Calculation type and you type the mathematical formula that will perform the calculation. █████ You want the store managers to enter the dollar amounts generated in the current month from the sale of books, DVDs, CDs, and videos. Then you want the form to calculate the total sales automatically.

STEPS

1. **Click the blank** cell **to the right of Books in the table form, then click the** Text Form Field button ᵃᵇˡ **on the Forms toolbar**

2. **Click the** Form Field Options button 🗒 **on the Forms toolbar, click the** Type list arrow, **then select** Number

   You change the text form field type to Number because you want users to be able to enter only a number.

3. **Click the** Number format list arrow, **select the number format shown in Figure M-8, click the** Calculate on exit check box, **then click** OK

   You select the Calculate on exit check box because you want the number that users enter into the text form field to be included as part of a calculation. The three table cells under the current cell require the same text form field as the one you just created. You can save time by copying and pasting the text form field you just created.

4. **With the** form field **selected, click the** Copy button 🖹 **on the Standard toolbar, click the blank** cell **to the right of DVDs, click the** Paste button 🖺 **on the Standard toolbar, then paste the text form field into the blank cells to the right of CDs and Videos**

   You want the cell to the right of Total to display the total of the values users enter in the four cells immediately above it.

5. **Click the blank** cell **to the right of Total, click** 🖺, **click** 🗒 **to open the Text Form Field Options dialog box, click the** Type list arrow, **then click** Calculation

6. **Click in the** Expression text box **to the right of the = sign, type** SUM(ABOVE), **then compare the Text Form Field Options dialog box to Figure M-9**

   The formula =SUM(ABOVE) is a standard calculation expression that is recognized by programs such as Word and Excel. The =SUM(ABOVE) calculation expression calculates all the values entered in the designated text form fields. The designated text form fields must be above the text form field that contains the calculation expression, and the text form fields must use a Number format.

7. **Click** OK

   The $0.00 entered next to Total indicates that the cell contains a calculation form field.

8. **Compare your form to Figure M-10, then save the template**

FIGURE M-8: Number format selected

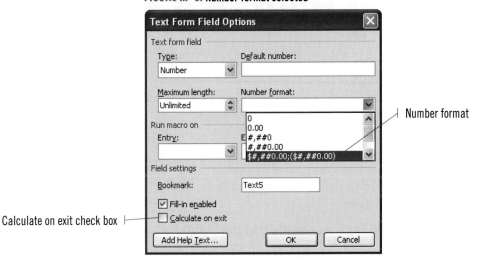

Number format

Calculate on exit check box

FIGURE M-9: Calculation options selected

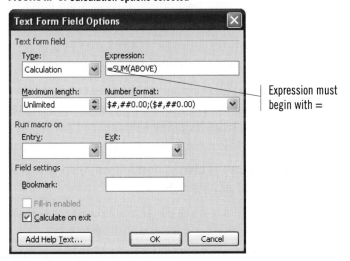

Expression must begin with =

FIGURE M-10: Calculation form field inserted

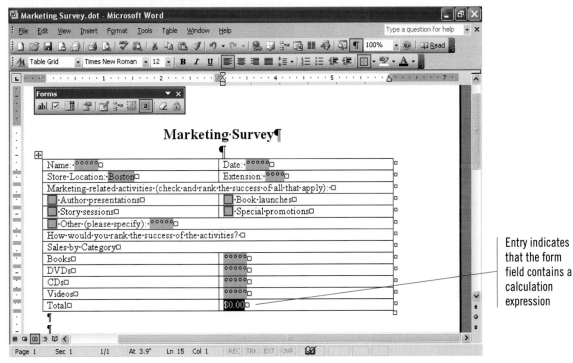

Entry indicates that the form field contains a calculation expression

Adding Help to a Form

You can help users fill in a form quickly and easily by attaching Help messages to selected form fields. For example, you can include a Help message in the Date form field that advises users how to enter a correctly formatted date. Help messages can be set to appear on the status bar or when the user presses the [F1] function key. You want to include instructions that advise store managers how to enter the date. You also want to add instructions about how to complete the Other (please specify): form field.

STEPS

1. **Click the text form field to the right of Date:, then click the Form Field Options button on the Forms toolbar**

2. **Click Add Help Text, then verify that the Status Bar tab is selected**
   You can choose to include an AutoText entry such as a page number or the word "Confidential," or you can type your own Help message.

3. **Click the Type your own option button, then enter the Help text shown in Figure M-11**
   The text entered in the Status Bar text box will appear on the status bar when a user clicks the text form field next to Date.

4. **Click OK to exit the Form Field Help Text dialog box, then click OK to exit the Text Form Field Options dialog box**

5. **Click the text form field to the right of Other (please specify):, click , click Add Help Text, then click the Help Key (F1) tab**
   You can enter a Help message containing up to 225 characters in the Help Key (F1) text box.

6. **Click the Type your own option button, then type the Help text shown in Figure M-12**

7. **Click OK, then click OK**
   The text form fields to which you have added Help messages do not appear to change. You will see the Help messages in the last lesson when you fill in the form as a user.

8. **With the text form field to the right of Other (please specify): still selected, click the Italic button I on the Formatting toolbar, then click to the right of the text form field**
   The text form field does not appear to have changed. However, the Italic button on the Formatting toolbar is selected to indicate that any text entered in the text form field will appear in italic.

9. **Save the template**

FIGURE M-11: Status Bar Help

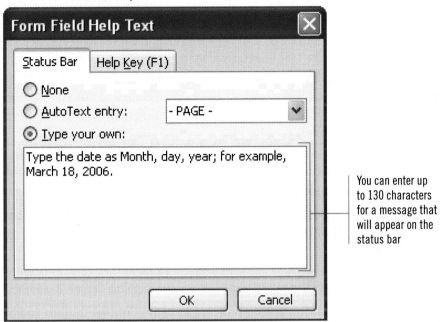

You can enter up to 130 characters for a message that will appear on the status bar

FIGURE M-12: Help Key (F1) text

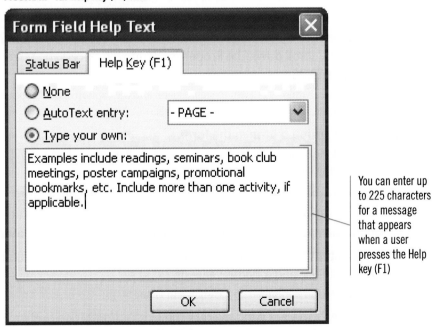

You can enter up to 225 characters for a message that appears when a user presses the Help key (F1)

Inserting Form Controls

The Forms toolbar contains the tools most commonly used to create a form that users complete in Word. You can further enhance a form by including some of the controls available on the Control Toolbox toolbar. These controls are referred to as ActiveX controls and are used to offer options to users or to run macros or scripts that automate specific tasks. One of the easiest controls to use in a form that users complete in Word is the Option button control. When you want users to select just one of several available options, you insert a series of Option button controls. ▓▓▓▓ You want the store managers to rank the effectiveness of the month's marketing activities. You decide to create a series of labeled Option buttons so that store managers can select one to indicate if the marketing activities yielded poor, good, or excellent results.

STEPS

1. **Click View on the menu bar, point to Toolbars, then click Control Toolbox**

   The Control Toolbox toolbar opens.

2. **Click the Design Mode button 🔲 on the Control Toolbox toolbar, click the blank area to the right of How would you rank the success of the activities?, then press the [Spacebar] one time**

   The Design Mode button becomes a floating toolbar, indicating that you are in Design Mode. You must be in Design Mode when you want to insert a control from the Control Toolbox toolbar to a selected cell.

3. **Click the Option Button button 🔘 on the Control Toolbox toolbar to insert an option button control into the selected cell**

   Figure M-13 shows the option button with the button caption "OptionButton1" inserted in the selected cell. You need to change the properties of the control so that the label next to the option button shows the caption "Poor." A **property** is a named attribute of a control that you set to define one of the control's attributes such as its size, its color, and its behavior in response to user input.

4. **Click the Properties button 🗔 on the Control Toolbox toolbar**

   The Properties window opens with the Alphabetic tab selected. The properties are listed in alphabetical order on the Alphabetic tab. In this window, you can identify properties such as the height and width of the option button and designate the label text to appear next to the option button.

5. **Select the text OptionButton1 next to Caption, type Poor, select 21.75 next to Height, type 17.25, scroll down the Properties window if necessary, select 108 next to Width, then type 50.25**

   The Properties window is shown in Figure M-14, and the caption "Poor" appears next to the option button in the Word form. The measurements are in pixels.

6. **Click the option button in the form**

   The size of the option button changes to match the Properties (Height = 17.25 and Width = 50.25) that you entered in the Properties window.

7. **With the option button box still selected, press [→] once, press [Spacebar] two times, click 🔘, replace OptionButton2 next to Caption in the Properties window with the word Good, change the Height to 17.25, then change the Width to 50.25**

8. **Repeat Steps 6 and 7 to enter an option button with the caption text Excellent, a Height value of 17.25, and a Width value of 75**

   The three option buttons appear, as shown in Figure M-15.

9. **Close the Properties window, click the Exit Design Mode button 🔲 on the Design Mode floating toolbar, close the Control Toolbox toolbar, then save the template**

   You must exit Design Mode after you insert a form control so that you can continue working with the form.

FIGURE M-13: OptionButton1 inserted

Control Toolbox toolbar

Design Mode button

Option Button button

Option Button control inserted

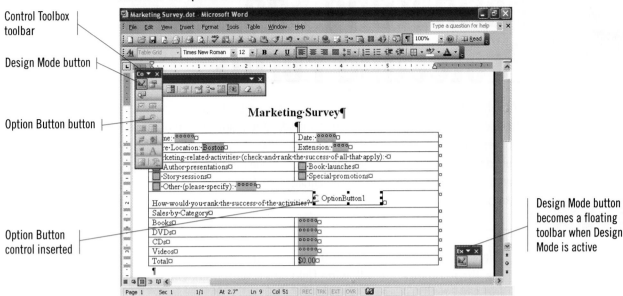

Design Mode button becomes a floating toolbar when Design Mode is active

FIGURE M-14: Properties window

Alphabetic tab selected

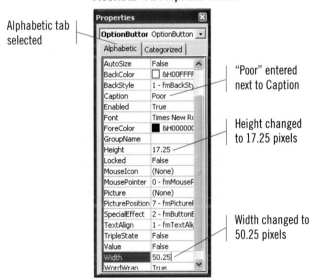

"Poor" entered next to Caption

Height changed to 17.25 pixels

Width changed to 50.25 pixels

FIGURE M-15: Option buttons inserted

Drag toolbars and arrange as needed so you can see options while you work

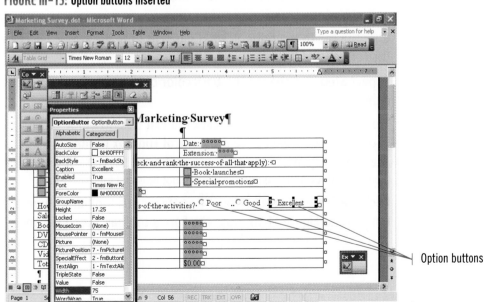

Option buttons

Formatting and Protecting Forms

Forms should be easy to read onscreen so that users can fill them in quickly and accurately. You can enhance a table containing form fields and you can modify the magnification of a document containing a form so that users can easily see the form fields. You can then protect a form so that users can enter only the data required and *not* be able to change the structure of the form. When a form is protected, information can be entered only in form fields. ░░░░░ You enhance the field labels, add shading to the form, and change the background color of the option button controls. Finally, you protect and then save the form template.

STEPS

1. Select Name in the first cell of the table, click the Bold button **B** on the Formatting toolbar, then enhance the following field labels with bold: Date, Store Location, Extension, and Sales by Category

TROUBLE
If the table move handle is not visible, click Table on the menu bar, point to Select, then click Table.

2. Click the table move handle ⊞ at the upper-left corner of the table to select the table, click Table on the menu bar, click Table Properties, click the Row tab, click the Specify height check box, enter .3 in the text box, then click OK

3. Click View on the menu bar, point to Toolbars, then click Tables and Borders
   The Tables and Borders toolbar appears. You can use this toolbar to fill the entire table with shading.

4. With the entire table still selected, click the Shading Color list arrow ░ ▾ on the Tables and Borders toolbar, click More Fill Colors, click the Custom tab, enter settings in the Red, Green, and Blue text boxes as shown in Figure M-16, then click OK

5. With the entire table still selected, click the Align Top Left list arrow ▤ on the Tables and Borders toolbar, click the Align Center Left button ▤, click away from the table to deselect it, then close the Tables and Borders toolbar
   The option buttons still have white backgrounds. You can change the background color of an ActiveX form control in the Properties window.

6. Click View on the menu bar, point to Toolbars, click Control Toolbox, click the Design Mode button ▨, click the Poor option button to select it, then click the Properties button ▤ on the Control Toolbox toolbar to open the Properties window for the Poor option button

TROUBLE
After changing a control property, click the option button, then press [→] to deselect the option button.

7. Click the cell to the right of BackColor, click the list arrow, select the Light Green color in the top row as shown in Figure M-17

8. Repeat Step 7 to change the back color of the Good and Excellent option buttons to light green

9. Close the Properties window, click the Exit Design Mode button ▨ on the Control Toolbox toolbar, then close the Control Toolbox toolbar
   After you modify an ActiveX control, you need to exit Design Mode so that you can protect the form. When the Design Mode button is selected, you cannot protect a form.

10. Click the Protect Form button ▤ on the Forms toolbar, compare the completed form template to Figure M-18, close the Forms toolbar, then save and close the template

FIGURE M-16: **Custom fill color**

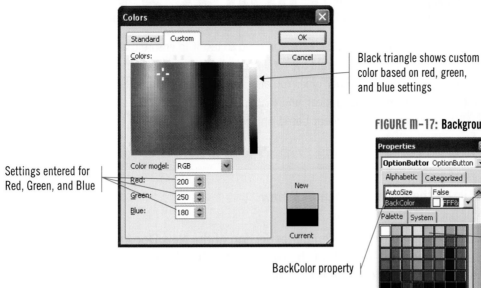

Black triangle shows custom color based on red, green, and blue settings

Settings entered for Red, Green, and Blue

FIGURE M-17: **Background color selected**

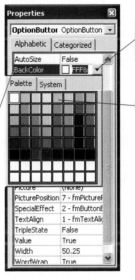

BackColor list arrow appears after clicking in cell to the right of BackColor

Light Green

BackColor property

FIGURE M-18: **Completed form template**

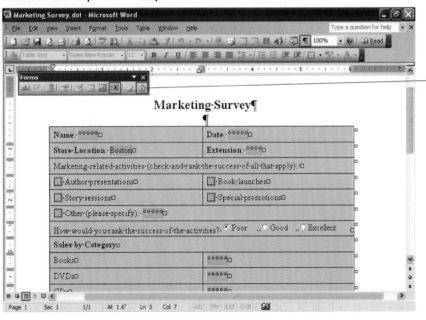

Protect Form button selected indicating that the form is protected

Clues to Use

Locking form fields

When you protect a form using the Protect Form button on the Forms toolbar, the form information, such as field labels, is protected or locked. A user can input information only in form fields and the input information must match the type specified by the person who originated the form. Sometimes, however, instead of protecting an entire form, you might want to lock certain form fields. For example, if you are entering numbers in a form for a budget and you want to be sure that the numbers do not inadvertently get changed, you can lock the form field after you enter the numbers. To lock a form field, and prevent changes to the current field results, click the field, then press [Ctrl][F11]. If you need to unlock a field to update the field results, click the field, then press [Ctrl][Shift][F11].

Filling in a Form as a User

Before you distribute a form template to users, you need to test it to ensure that all the elements work correctly. For example, you want to make sure the total is calculated properly when numbers are entered in the form fields formatted with the Number type. You also want to make sure that selections appear in the list box, that the correct Help messages appear, and that you can easily select the check boxes and option buttons. ▰▰▰▰ You open a new document based on the template, then fill in the form as if you were the Houston store manager.

1. **Click File on the menu bar, then click New**

   The New Document task pane opens.

2. **Click On my computer in the Templates section of the New Document task pane, click Marketing Survey.dot, verify that the Document option button in the Create New section of the Templates window is selected, then click OK**

   Notice that the Marketing Survey.dot file opens as a Word document, as indicated by the filename that appears on the title bar. The insertion point highlights the space following Name. The form is protected, so you can enter information only in spaces that contain text form fields, check boxes, drop-down lists, or option buttons.

3. **Type Your Name, then press [Tab]**

   The insertion point moves to the space following Date. Notice the Help message that appears in the status bar, telling you how to enter the date.

4. **Enter the current date in the required format, press [Tab], click the list arrow next to Boston, click Houston, then press [Tab]**

5. **Type 4455, press [Tab], then click the check box next to Author presentations, the check box next to Book launches, and the check box next to Other (please specify):**

6. **Press [Tab], then press [F1]**

   The Help message appears, as shown in Figure M-19.

7. **Click OK, type Mystery Book Night readings by Jonathon Grant, click the Good option button, press [Tab] two times to move the insertion point to the text form field next to Books, type 58000, then press [Tab]**

   The amount is automatically formatted with a dollar sign and the amount in the cell to the right of Total is updated automatically when you press [Tab] to move the insertion point out of the cell.

8. **Enter the remaining sales amounts shown in the completed form in Figure M-20; press [Tab] after you enter each value**

   The total—$112,000—is calculated automatically because this text field is a calculation type with the =SUM(ABOVE) formula. When you press [Tab] after entering the last value, the insertion point moves to the next text form field that accepts user input, which is the text form field after Name.

9. **Save the document with the name Houston Survey to the drive and folder where your Data Files are located, print a copy, then close the document**

   After you use the Monthly Marketing Survey template, it will be listed in the New from template section of the New Document task pane.

FIGURE M-19: F1 Help message

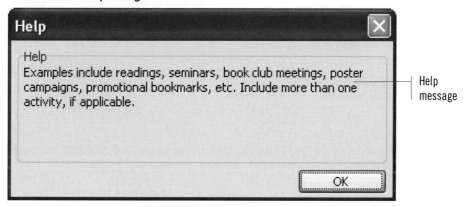

Help message

FIGURE M-20: Sales amounts entered

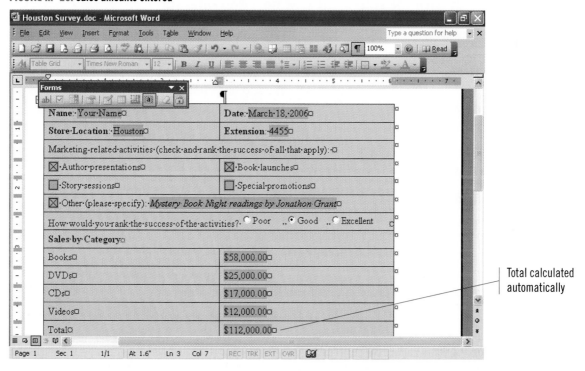

Total calculated automatically

Clues to Use

Editing a form template

To edit the structure of a form, you need to open the template, then click the Protect Form button on the Forms toolbar to deselect it. You can then make changes to the form by adding or removing form fields and modifying the appearance of the form. When you have finished modifying the form template, click the Protect Form button again, then save the template.

Practice

▼ CONCEPTS REVIEW

Identify each of the numbered buttons on the Forms toolbar shown in Figure M-21.

FIGURE M-21

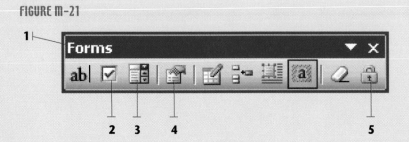

Match each term with the statement that best describes it.

6. **Drop-down form field**	**a.** An area of a form into which users can enter information
7. **Control Toolbox**	**b.** A list of options in a form
8. **Text form field**	**c.** Contains a mathematical expression
9. **[F1]**	**d.** Contains a selection of ActiveX controls that can be inserted in a form
10. **Calculation form field**	**e.** One type of ActiveX control
11. **Option button**	**f.** Help key

Select the best answer from the list of choices

12. **What is a field label?**
   a. A space for users to enter variable information
   b. A placeholder for text such as a user's name or the current date
   c. A word or phrase, such as the user's current address, that is entered into a blank cell
   d. A word or phrase such as "Date" or "Location" that tells users the kind of information required for a given field

13. **What happens when you insert a text form field into a table cell?**
   a. A blank check box appears.
   b. A shaded rectangle with five dots appears.
   c. A blank bar outlined in black appears.
   d. A Help message appears to inform users what information to enter in the form field.

14. **How do you view the list of choices available in a drop-down form field?**
   a. Double-click the drop-down form field to insert a list arrow.
   b. Open the form as a user, click the drop-down form field, then click the list arrow.
   c. Right-click the drop-down form field, then click Activate.
   d. View the form in the Print Preview screen.

15. **How would you enter a Help message containing 200 characters?**
   a. Enter the Help message in the Type your own text box in the Status Bar tab of the Help Text dialog box.
   b. Enter the Help message in the form field.
   c. Edit the Help message so it contains only 130 characters, the accepted limit.
   d. Enter the Help message in the Type your own text box in the Help Key (F1) tab of the Help Text dialog box.

1. Construct a form template.

   a. Start Word, open the New Document task pane if necessary, click the On my computer link, then create a new blank document as a template.

   b. Check to ensure that Your Name Form Templates is designated as the folder to contain user templates. If necessary, refer to the lesson on Constructing a form template.

   c. Type **Change of Grade Notification** as the title, then center the text and enhance it with Bold and a 20-point font size.

   d. Two lines below the title, clear the formatting, then create a table consisting of four columns and 13 rows.

   e. Refer to Figure M-22. Type the text as shown. Merge cells in rows 2, 10, 11, 12, and 13 as shown. Apply bold to field labels as shown. (*Note*: You will align text later in the exercise.)

   f. Save the template as **Change of Grade Notification** to the Your Name Form Templates folder.

FIGURE M-22

Change·of·Grade·Notification¶

Student·Number	▢	Date	▢	▢
Student·Name	▢			
Course·Title	▢	Course·Number	▢	▢
Original·Letter·Grade	Revised·Letter·Grade	Courses	Points	▢
A·—4▢	A·—4▢	Accounting	▢	▢
B·—3▢	B·—3▢	Business·English	▢	▢
C·—2▢	C·—2▢	Excel·Level·1	▢	▢
D·—1▢	D·—1▢	Marketing	▢	▢
F·—0▢	F·—0▢	Word·Level·1	▢	▢
		Grade·Point·Average	▢	▢
Reason·for·Grade·Change·(check·one)	▢			
▢			▢	▢
Other·(specify):	▢			▢

2. Add and modify text form fields.

   a. Show the Forms toolbar, if necessary.

   b. Insert text form fields in the blank cells to the right of the following field labels: Student Number, Date, Student Name, Course Number, and Other (specify).

   c. Modify the text form field next to Student Number so that users can enter up to six numbers.

   d. Modify the text form field next to Date so that users must enter a date formatted as M/d/yyyy.

   e. Save your changes to the template.

3. Add drop-down and check box form fields.

   a. Insert a drop-down form field after Course Title.

   b. In the Drop-Down Form Field Options dialog box, enter the following list of items: **Accounting**, **Excel Level 1**, **Marketing**, **Business English**, and **Word Level 1**.

   c. Move Business English up so that it appears immediately after Accounting.

   d. Insert a check box form field and a space to the left of each letter grade in the Original Letter Grade and Revised Letter Grade columns.

   e. Save the template.

4. Use calculations in a form.

   a. Insert a text form field in the blank cell to the right of Accounting with the Number type, the Number format set to 0, and the Calculate on exit check box selected.

   b. Copy the text form field with number formatting to the next four cells (Business English through Word Level 1).

   c. Insert a text form field with the type set to Calculation in the blank cell to the right of Grade Point Average.

   d. Type the expression **=SUM(ABOVE)/5**. This formula will add the numbers in the Points cells, then divide the total by 5 to determine the average.

   e. Make sure the Number format is set to 0 and the Calculate on exit check box is selected before you exit the Text Form Field Options dialog box, then save the template.

5. Add Help to a form.

   a. Add a status bar Help message in the Date form field that states: **Type the date in numerals as month, day, year; for example, 03/18/2006.**

   b. Add a Help key (F1) Help message in the Other (specify): field that states: **Acceptable reasons include completion of work outstanding and acceptance of medical documentation.**

   c. Save the template.

6. Insert form controls.

    a. Show the Control Toolbox toolbar. Make sure the Design Mode button is selected, then click the blank cell below the Reason for Grade Change field label.

    b. Insert an Option Button control with the following properties: Caption is **Calculation Error** and height is **18**.

    c. Insert an Option Button control in the next blank cell with the caption **Exam Retake** and a height of **18**.

    d. Close the Properties window, then exit Design Mode.

    e. Close the Control Toolbox toolbar, then save the template.

7. Format and protect a form.

    a. With the table selected, change the row height to **.35"**.

    b. Show the Tables and Borders toolbar, then change the text alignment for the entire table to Align Center Left.

    c. Align Top Center all four field labels in the row beginning with Original Letter Grade.

    d. Align Center all the form fields in the six cells under the cell with the Points label.

    e. Align Center Right the Grade Point Average field label.

    f. Select the table again, then change the colors in the Custom tab of the Colors dialog box to Red: **240**, Green: **220**, and Blue: **250**. (*Hint*: You should see a light lavender color.)

    g. View the Control Toolbox toolbar, then select Design Mode.

    h. With the Calculation Error option button selected, change the BackColor in the Properties window to light pink (last box in the top row of the color selections), which creates a two-tone effect—lavender for the form background and light pink for the option button.

    i. Repeat the preceding procedure to change the BackColor to light pink for the Exam Retake option button.

    j. Close the Properties window, then exit Design Mode. (*Note*: You must click the Design Mode button on the Control Toolbox toolbar to exit Design Mode.)

    k. Protect the form, then close the Forms toolbar, the Tables and Borders toolbar, and the Control Toolbox toolbar.

    l. Save and close the template.

8. Fill in a form as a user.

    a. Open a new document based on the Change of Grade Notification template. (*Hint*: Make sure the Document option button in the Create New section of the Templates dialog box is selected.)

    b. Type **337888** as the Student Number, press [Tab], type the **current date**, press [Tab], type your name, select Business English as the Course Title, enter **626** as the Course Number, select B as the Original Letter Grade, then select A as the Revised Letter Grade.

    c. Enter the points for each course as follows: Accounting: **3**, Business English: **4**; Excel Level 1: **4**; Marketing: **2**; and Word Level 1: **2**.

    d. Press [Tab] and verify that the value in the Grade Point Average cell is 3.

    e. Select the Exam Retake option button.

    f. Check the F1 Help Message in the Other (specify): field.

    g. Save the document with the filename **Business English Grade Change** to the drive and folder where your Data Files are located, print a copy, close the document, then exit Word.

▼ INDEPENDENT CHALLENGE 1

You work for the owner of Sun Sensations—a new company that sells tours to exotic sun spots around the world. The owner and some of the sales representatives have begun taking frequent business trips to tropical resorts in the South Pacific to set up tours. Your boss asks you to help expedite the bookkeeping by creating an expense report form that can be completed online in Word.

    a. Start Word and open the file WD M-1.doc from the drive and folder where your Data Files are located. Save it as a template called **Expense Report Form** to the Your Name Form Templates folder that you created to complete the lessons in this unit. (Refer to the first lesson in this unit, if necessary.)

    b. View the Forms toolbar.

    c. Insert text form fields for the Name, Report Date, Extension, and Purpose of Travel field labels.

d. Specify the date format of your choice for the Report Date form field.

e. Change the type of the text form field next to Extension to Number and specify a maximum of four numbers.

f. Add a status bar Help message to the Purpose of Travel form field that states: **Specify the location(s) you visited and the business goals accomplished**.

g. Insert a drop-down form field in the blank cell to the right of Department that includes the following entries: **Management**, **Marketing**, and **Sales**.

h. Insert a text form field in the first blank cell in the Date column, select Date as the type, specify the M/d/yy date format, then copy the text form field and paste it to all the blank cells in the Date column.

i. Insert a drop-down form field in the first blank cell in the Category column. Include the following entries in the drop-down list: **Meals**, **Hotel**, **Air Fare**, and **Other**. Put the entries in alphabetical order.

j. Copy the drop-down form field and paste it to all the blank cells in the Category column.

k. Insert a text form field in the first blank cell in the Details column, then copy the text form field and paste it to all the blank cells in the Details column.

l. Insert a text form field in the blank cell below Amount, then change the text form field options so the type is Number, the format is 0.00, and the Calculate on exit check box is selected. Copy the text form field with Number formatting and paste it to all the blank cells in the Amount column, except the cell next to Total.

m. Insert a text form field in the blank cell to the right of Total, then change the form field options so the type is Calculation, the format is 0.00, the Expression is =SUM(ABOVE), and the Calculate on exit check box is selected.

n. Right-align the form fields in the Amount column and Total cell.

o. Protect the form, then save and close the template.

p. Open a new document based on the template.

q. Type **your name** and the **current date**, select the Marketing Department, type **5555** for the extension, then describe the Purpose for Travel as **Evaluating the Paradise Palms Resort in Tahiti**.

r. Enter the following dates and expenses: **April 10: Return Air Fare from Seattle to Tahiti: $1800, April 11: Meals at Paradise Palms Resort: $200, April 12: Meals in various locations: $200, April 13: Meals including hosted dinner for Paradise Palms Resort Managers, $550, April 13: Hotel accommodation for three nights at the Paradise Palms Resort: $1200**, and **April 13: Other described as Taxis and Miscellaneous Expenses: $300**.

s. Verify the total expenses are 4250.00, then save the document as **Completed Expense Report** to the drive and folder where your Data Files are located.

Advanced Challenge Exercise

FIGURE M-23

- Unprotect the form on the Expense Report Form.dot.
- Click below the form, press [Enter], then clear the formatting.
- Click the Insert Frame button on the Forms toolbar, draw a box approximately 4" wide and 1" tall, then enter text

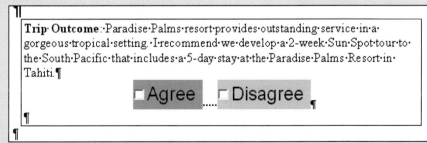

and the two check box controls as shown in Figure M-23. Note that you need to select True for the AutoSize property for both controls and change the font of the caption to Arial and 18 point. (Note: Adjust the boxes manually as needed.)

- Exit design mode, protect the form, then click the Agree check box.

t. Print a copy of the completed form, then close the document.

▼ INDEPENDENT CHALLENGE 2

You are the Office Manager at Atlantic Regional Securities, a company that has just instituted parking regulations for staff wanting to park in the new staff parking lot. Any staff member who wants to park in the lot must purchase a parking permit. You decide to create a Word form that staff members complete to purchase a parking permit. You will create the form as a Word template saved on the company's network. Staffers can open a new Word document based on the template, then complete the form in Word, or they can print the form and fill it in by hand.

a. Start Word, open the file WD M-2.doc from the drive and folder where your Data Files are located, and save it as a template called **Parking Permit Requisition** to the Your Name Form Templates folder that you created to complete the lessons in this unit. (Refer to the first lesson in this unit, if necessary.)

b. View the Forms toolbar.

c. Insert a text form field in the blank cell to the right of Date. Format the text form field to accept dates entered in the format you prefer. Include a Help message that appears on the status bar and tells users how to enter the date.

d. Enter a text form field in the blank cell to the right of Name.

e. Insert a drop-down form field in the blank cell to the right of Department that includes the following entries: **Accounting**, **Administration**, **Finance**, **Marketing**, **Sales**, and **Information Technology**.

f. Move entries so they appear in alphabetical order.

g. Insert a text form field in the blank cell to the right of Extension, then modify the text form field so that it accepts a maximum of four numbers. Include a status bar Help message that advises users to enter their four-digit telephone extension.

h. Insert check box form fields to the left of the selections in the fourth column (Full-time, Part-time, etc.). Leave a space between the check box and the first letter of each selection.

i. Insert an option button control in each of the blank cells in the last row of the form. The captions for the option buttons are as follows: **Check**, **Cash**, and **Pay Debit**.

j. Click the Exit Design Mode button on the Control Toolbox, then close the Control Toolbox.

k. Apply the Table Columns 5 Table AutoFormat to the table.

l. Show the Tables and Borders toolbar, then remove the shading from the cell that contains the Check option button.

Advanced Challenge Exercise

- Revise each of the three option buttons as follows:
- Change the foreground color (ForeColor) of each option button to Bright Blue. Note that the ForeColor is the text color.
- Change the Font to Impact and 16 point.
- Change the SpecialEffect to 0 – fmButtonEffectFlat.
- Change the TextAlign to 2 – fmTextAlignCenter.
- Set the width at 75 for the Check and Cash buttons and 100 for the Pay Debit button.
- Exit Design Mode.

m. Protect the form, then save and close the template.

n. Open a new document based on the template, then complete the form as a user. Type the **current date** and **your name**, select Executive status, select the Information Technology Department, enter any **four-digit extension**, then select Cash as the payment method.

o. Save the document as **Completed Parking Requisition** to the drive and folder where your Data Files are located, print a copy, close the document, then exit Word.

▼ INDEPENDENT CHALLENGE 3

You work for a company called Asian History Tours that specializes in taking small groups of people on educational tours to various areas in China, Southeast Asia, Korea, and Japan. One way you can measure the success of the tours is to ask customers to complete a feedback form after participating in a tour. You decide to create a Word form that you can e-mail to customers. Your customers can complete the form in Word, then send it back to you as an e-mail attachment.

a. Start Word, type **Asian History Tours** as the title and **Tour Feedback** as the subtitle, then enhance both titles attractively.

b. Save the document as a template named **Feedback Form** to the Your Name Form Templates folder you created to contain the form templates you created in this unit.

c. Plan a form that contains the following field labels: **Name**, **Tour Date**, **Tour Guide**, and **Tour Name** and a section for ranking tour components similar to Figure M-24.

FIGURE M-24

Asian History Tours Tour Feedback					
Name		Tour Date			
Tour Guide		Tour Name			
Please rank each of the following components on a scale from 1 (Poor) to 4 (Incredible)					
		1	2	3	4
Meals					
Accommodations					
Tour Guide					
Educational Interest					
Overall					
Additional Comments					
May we contact you regarding new tours that may interest you?					

d. Enter text form fields in the cell to the right of Name, Tour Date, and Tour Guide, then enter a drop-down form field in the Tour Name cell that lists five tours. Type sample tour names such as Yangtze Odyssey, Great Wall Trek, and Temples of Japan. Be sure the names appear in alphabetical order in the drop-down list. Also be sure to assign the Date type to the Date form field, using a format of your choice.

e. Insert check box form fields in the ranking section of your form.

f. In the last row of the table, insert two Option Button controls: one labeled **YES!** and one labeled **No thanks**. Format the option buttons so that they fit the table cell.

g. Format the form attractively, using one of the Table AutoFormats if you wish. (*Hint*: You might need to increase the row height so that the option buttons fit.)

h. Protect the form, save it, then close the template.

i. Open a new document based on the form template, then save it as **Completed Feedback Form** to the drive and folder where your Data Files are located.

j. Fill in the form as if you had participated in one of your tours. Enter your name in the Name field.

k. Save the form, print a copy, close the form, then exit Word.

▼ INDEPENDENT CHALLENGE 4

Many companies and organizations that maintain Web sites include online forms that visitors can complete to participate in a survey, provide payment information, select products or services, and request information. You can learn a great deal about form design by studying some of the forms included on Web sites. You decide to search for Web sites that include forms, identify the form controls used in the forms, and then describe two unusual or creative ways in which form controls are used to request information.

a. Open your Web browser and conduct a search for companies that are likely to include forms that are used to gather information. Good choices include shopping Web sites such as an online bookstore that request payment information or travel site Web sites that request travel information.

b. Select two Web sites that include forms that users complete to provide information.

c. Open the file WD M-3.doc, then save it as **Form Evaluation** to the drive and folder where your Data Files are located.

d. Type **your name** and the **current date** in the spaces provided.

e. As directed in the Form Evaluation document, type the company name and copy the Web site address to the spaces provided, then follow the directions in the document to insert the required information.

f. Save the document, print a copy, then close it.

▼ VISUAL WORKSHOP

You are in charge of the audio-visual department at a local community college. Faculty members come to you to borrow projectors, DVD players, and computers to use in class presentations. You decide to make up a simple form that faculty members can complete online and then e-mail to you when they want to borrow audio-visual equipment. Create and enhance a form template, as shown in Figure M-25. Save the template as **Audio Visual Request Form** to the Your Name Form Templates folder containing all the form templates you've created for this unit. The items in the drop-down list for Department are **Arts**, **Business**, **Sciences**, **Education**, and **Technology**. The items in the drop-down list for Equipment are **DVD Player**, **Projector**, **Computer**, and **Television**. Protect the form, close the template, then open a new document based on the template. Complete the form with **your name**, the **current date**, the Business Department, Extension **4433**, a Projector, a **date** one week after the current date, a time of **2:00 p.m.**, one day checked, and special instructions of **Please deliver to Room 233**. Save the completed form as **My Audio Visual Form** to the drive and folder where your Data Files are located, print a copy, and close the document.

FIGURE M-25

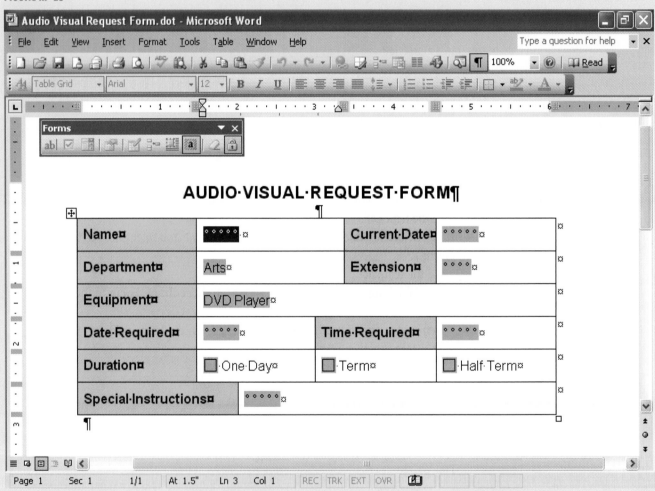

Working with Charts and Diagrams

OBJECTIVES

Define charts and diagrams
Create a column chart
Edit a chart
Create a pie chart
Import spreadsheet data into a chart
Create a diagram
Create an organization chart
Modify an organization chart

If you have a SAM user profile, you may have access to hands-on instruction, practice, and assessment of the skills covered in this unit. Log in to your SAM account and go to your assignments page to see what your instructor has assigned.

Word provides the tools you need to create and modify numerically based charts, such as bar charts, pie charts, and area charts. You can also create and modify diagrams such as Venn diagrams and cycle diagrams to show conceptual relationships that are not numerically based. Finally, you can create and modify an organization chart that shows hierarchical relationships, such as those among employees in a corporation. Graham Watson has just started working in the Marketing Department at MediaLoft. One of his first jobs is to prepare an analysis for MediaLoft management that highlights the success of online marketing efforts on MediaLoft's Web site at www.Media-Loft.com. Most of the data he needs is already entered in a Word document. You will help him present the information in chart and diagram form.

Defining Charts and Diagrams

A **chart** illustrates the trends, relationships, or patterns represented by a series of numbers in various combinations. Charts should clarify data for the reader. For example, when viewing a column chart about sales, a reader can see at a glance the relationship between the column representing the current year's sales and the column representing the previous year's sales, and then make decisions and draw conclusions accordingly. You can create different kinds of charts in Word, as shown in Figure N-1. You can also create six types of diagrams, as shown in Figure N-2. The Drawing toolbar includes the Insert Diagram or Organization Chart button, which you use to create diagrams and organization charts.  You are intrigued by the various charts and diagrams available in Word. You decide to investigate the purpose of each type of chart and diagram so that you can make appropriate choices when working with the data in the Marketing report.

DETAILS

You can create the following types of charts and diagrams:

- **Charts**

  Column charts compare values side by side, usually over time. For example, you can use a column chart to show total sales generated in each of four years, with each year represented by one column. Several variations on the column chart are available. You can select a **bar chart** to show values as horizontal bars; you can select **cylinder**, **cone**, and **pyramid charts** to show values in either horizontal or vertical format, similar to the rectangles used in column and bar charts.

  Circular charts show how values relate to each other as parts of a whole. For example, you can create a **pie chart** to show the breakdown of sales by product category for a store that specializes in sporting goods. Each product category, such as skis, boots, snowboards, and clothing, is represented by a slice of the pie chart. The most commonly used circular charts are pie charts and 3-D pie charts.

  Line style charts illustrate trends, where each value is connected to the next value by a line. An **area chart** shows data similarly to a line chart, except that the space between the lines and the bottom of the chart is filled, and a different band of color represents each value.

  Point-to-point charts are used to identify patterns or to show values as clusters. **XY charts** (also called **scatter charts**) are the most commonly used point-to-point charts.

- **Diagrams**

  An **organization chart** illustrates a hierarchy, most often in terms of how functional areas in a company or organization relate to each other. For example, you can use an organization chart to show relationships among executives, managers, supervisors, and employees in a company.

  A **Venn diagram** illustrates areas of overlap between two or more elements. You can use a Venn diagram to show how three departments in a company have individual responsibilities in addition to shared responsibilities.

  A **cycle diagram** illustrates a process that has a continuous cycle. You can use a cycle diagram to show the life cycle of a product from manufacturing to sales to consumer use to recycling into raw materials to manufacturing back into the same or a new product.

  A **pyramid diagram** illustrates a hierarchical relationship. Probably the most familiar pyramid diagram is the food diagram, which shows the food groups you should eat the most at the base of the pyramid and the food groups you should eat the least at the top.

  A **target diagram** illustrates steps toward a goal. You can use a target diagram to show the steps required to complete a specific project represented by the target area of the diagram.

  A **radial diagram** illustrates the relationships of several related elements to a core element. You can use a radial diagram to show how a group of individuals all report to the same supervisor.

FIGURE N-1: Sample chart types in Word

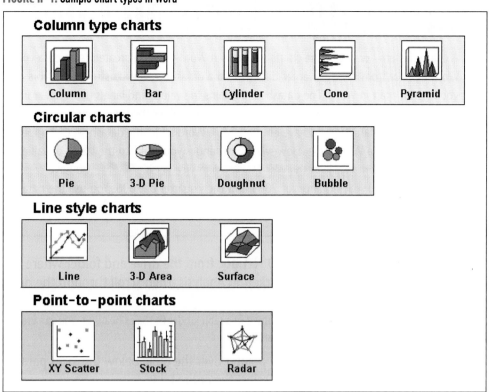

FIGURE N-2: Diagram Gallery

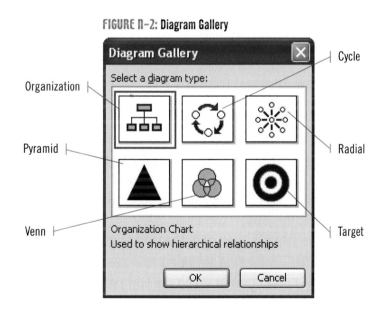

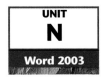

Creating a Column Chart

A column chart—or any of the charts available in Word—can be created from data you have entered into a Word table or from data you enter directly into a datasheet. A **datasheet** is a table grid that opens when you insert a chart in Word. The datasheet contains the values and labels that appear in the chart. A **value** is a number and a **label** is a word or two of text that describes the significance of the number. When you create a chart from data that you have entered into a Word table, the datasheet that appears contains the same information as the Word table. However, any changes you make to the labels or values in the datasheet are not reflected automatically in the Word table—and vice versa. ▰▰▰ You have created a Word table that shows the sales for each quarter of 2005 and each quarter of 2006. You use the data in this Word table to create a column chart.

STEPS

1. **Start Word, open the file** WD N-1.doc **from the drive and folder where your Data Files are located, save it as** Online Marketing Analysis, **then scroll through the document to get a sense of its contents**

   The data you want to chart is contained in a table under the Sales heading. You can create a chart from all the data in the table or just a portion of the data.

2. **Press [Ctrl][Home], move the pointer over the table below the Sales paragraph, then click the** table move handle ⊞ **to select the entire table**

   > **TROUBLE**
   > If the datasheet covers the chart, click the datasheet title bar and drag the datasheet to a new location.

3. **Click** Insert **on the menu bar, point to** Picture, **then click** Chart

   A column chart opens in the document, as shown in Figure N-3, because the default chart type is column. In addition, a datasheet opens that contains the same data shown in the Word table. The buttons required for working with charts appear on the Standard toolbar.

4. **Click** Chart **on the menu bar, click** Chart Options, **click the** Titles tab **if necessary, click in the** Chart title text box, **type** Media-Loft.com Sales, **then press** [Tab]

   The Chart title appears in the preview window in the Chart Options dialog box, as shown in Figure N-4.

5. **Click the** Legend tab, **click the** Bottom option button, **then click** OK

   The **legend** identifies the patterns or colors assigned to the data series in a chart.

6. **Click** cell B1 **in the datasheet (contains $70,000), type** 50000, **then click an** empty cell **in the datasheet**

   The value is formatted as currency and the column that illustrates the data in cell B1 changes to reflect the new data.

7. **Click** outside the chart area **to return to your Word document, click the** cell **below 2nd Quarter in the table, then change $70,000 to** $50,000

   You change the value in the Word table because the values in the table do not update automatically to reflect changes made to the datasheet.

   > **QUICK TIP**
   > If necessary, click View, then click Ruler to show the ruler bars.

8. **Click the** chart **to select it, then drag the lower-right corner down diagonally until the bottom of the chart aligns approximately with** 6.5 **on the vertical ruler**

9. **Click the** Outside Border button ▦ **on the Formatting toolbar, click away from the chart, then save the document**

   Figure N-5 shows the completed column chart.

FIGURE N-3: Inserted column chart

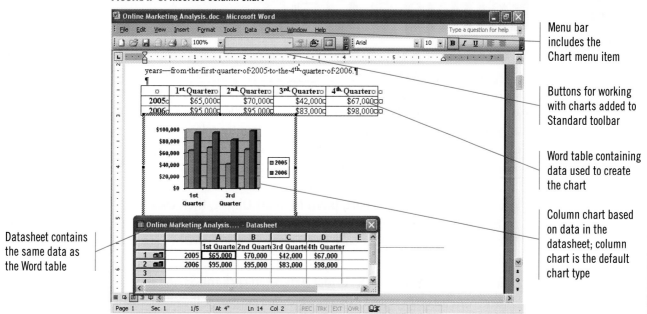

Menu bar includes the Chart menu item

Buttons for working with charts added to Standard toolbar

Word table containing data used to create the chart

Column chart based on data in the datasheet; column chart is the default chart type

Datasheet contains the same data as the Word table

FIGURE N-4: Chart Options dialog box

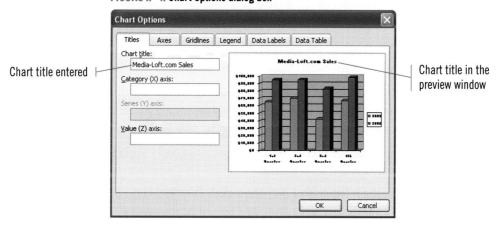

Chart title entered

Chart title in the preview window

FIGURE N-5: Completed column chart

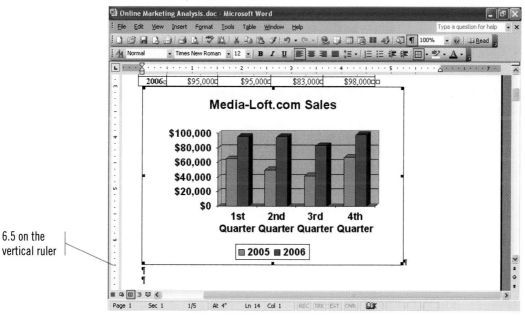

6.5 on the vertical ruler

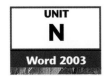

Editing a Chart

You can edit a chart in a variety of ways. For example, you can change the appearance of the columns representing each data series and you can change the font sizes of the various chart labels. You can also change the scale and appearance of each chart axis. In a two-dimensional chart, the **y-axis** is the vertical axis and the **x-axis** is the horizontal axis. ▰▰▱▱ You modify the y-axis and the x-axis of the chart and then change the font size of selected data labels. You also change the color of one of the data series and then change the column chart into a cone chart.

STEPS

1. **Right-click the column chart, point to Chart Object, then click Edit**
   The chart and datasheet open so that you can modify the chart. The y-axis of the chart is represented by the numbers to the left of the chart and the x-axis is represented by the text below the chart (1st Quarter, 2nd Quarter, and so forth).

2. **Right-click the y-axis, click Format Axis, then click the Scale tab**
   In the Scale tab of the Format Axis dialog box, you can change the values shown on the y-axis by changing the value of the major and minor units. For example, you can select the maximum value to appear on the y-axis and then you can set unit increments such as 5,000 or 50 between each value.

3. **Select the contents of the Major unit text box, then type 15000 as shown in Figure N-6**
   The check mark is removed from the Major unit check box when you set a specific unit.

4. **Click the Font tab in the Format Axis dialog box, change the font size to 10, then click OK**
   The information in the y-axis changes to reflect the settings you selected.

5. **Right-click the x-axis, click Format Axis, select the 10-point font size, then click OK**
   The information in the x-axis changes to reflect the settings you selected.

QUICK TIP
The maroon bars represent the year 2006.

6. **Click one of the maroon bars in the column chart**
   All the maroon bars are selected. When you point to a bar in a column chart a ScreenTip appears with information about what that bar represents.

7. **Click Format on the menu bar, then click Selected Data Series**
   You use the Format Data Series dialog box to modify the appearance of a data series. For example, you can select a new fill color or pattern.

8. **In the Format Data Series dialog box, select the Red color as shown in Figure N-7, then click OK**
   The bars representing the selected data series are now red.

QUICK TIP
You can also convert a column chart into a cylinder chart or a pyramid chart.

9. **Click Chart on the menu bar, click Chart Type, scroll down the Chart type list box, then click Cone**

10. **Click OK to exit the Chart Type dialog box, click outside the chart area to exit Edit mode, then save the document**
    The modified cone chart appears, as shown in Figure N-8. Notice that the columns representing each data series now appear as 3-D cones.

FIGURE N-6: Format Axis dialog box

Check mark removed
to show value set
manually

Major unit
changed to 15000

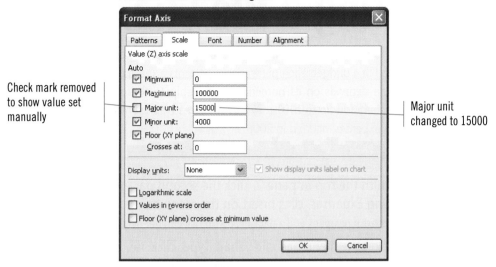

FIGURE N-7: Format Data Series dialog box

Red color selected

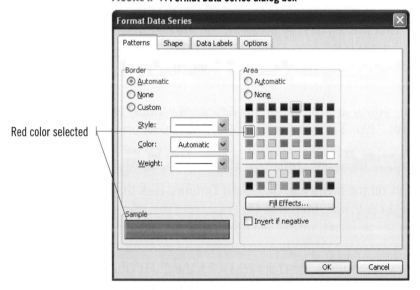

FIGURE N-8: Modified cone chart

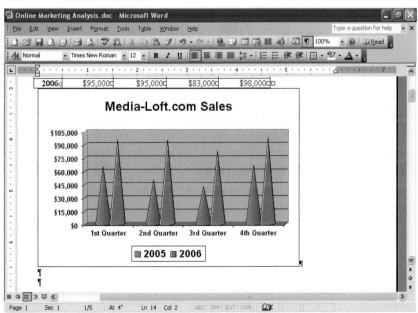

Creating a Pie Chart

Pie charts show data as parts of a whole. For example, you can create a pie chart to show the various expenses included in a budget. Each pie wedge represents a specific expense, such as Rent or Salaries. The size of the wedge depends on its numerical relationship to the overall budget. Taken together, all the wedges of a pie chart add up to 100%. You create a pie chart to show the breakdown by category of the marketing expenses incurred in 2006.

STEPS

TROUBLE
If you don't see the paragraph marks, click the Show/Hide ¶ button to show formatting marks.

1. **Scroll down to the top of page 2, click the** second paragraph mark **below the paragraph on Marketing Expenses, click** Insert **on the menu bar, point to** Picture, **then click** Chart
   The default chart type opens and a datasheet with placeholder data and labels appears.

2. **Click** Chart **on the menu bar, click** Chart Type, **click** Pie, **then click** OK
   A pie chart based on the default data in the datasheet appears. In a pie chart, only the column labels and the values in the first row of the datasheet are used.

3. **Click the** upper-left white cell **in the datasheet, drag to select the** default data, **press** [Delete], **click the** cell **directly below "A" on the datasheet (contains "Slice 1"), type** Brochures, **press** [Tab], **type** Magazine Ads, **press** [Tab], **type** Flyers, **press** [Tab], **type** Radio Ads, **press** [Tab], **type** E-Mail Marketing, **then press** [Enter]
   The pie chart includes five wedges—one for each value represented by the labels.

4. **Drag the** horizontal scroll bar **on the datasheet window to the left, click the** cell below **"Brochures," type** $15,000, **press** [Tab], **type** $10,000, **press** [Tab], **type** $5,000, **press** [Tab], **type** $2,400, **press** [Tab], **type** $900, **then press** [Enter]
   Figure N-9 shows the completed datasheet.

5. **Click** Chart **on the menu bar, click** Chart Options, **click the** Data Labels tab, **click the** Percentage check box, **then click** OK
   The size of the pie chart is reduced and labels appear to indicate the percentage represented by each pie wedge. For example, the $15,000 Brochure expense is labeled 45%.

6. **Click any** white space in the chart area, **click the** Chart Objects list arrow **on the Standard toolbar, select** Plot Area as shown in Figure N-10, **then press** [Delete]
   You can select any component of a chart by clicking it or by selecting it from the Chart Objects list.

7. **Click** Chart **on the menu bar, click** Chart Type, **select the** middle chart **in the top row of the Chart sub-type section, then click** OK
   After changing a pie chart from a two-dimensional to a three-dimensional view, you can modify the appearance of the 3-D view.

8. **Click** Chart **on the menu bar, click** 3-D View, **type** 45 **in the Elevation text box, then click** OK

9. **Click** outside the chart area, **click the** pie chart **to select it, click** Format **on the menu bar, click** Object, **click the** Size tab, **change the Width to** 4", **click** OK, **click the** Center button ▤ **on the Formatting toolbar, click the** Outside Border button ▦, **click away from the pie chart, then save the document**
   The completed pie chart is shown in Figure N-11.

FIGURE N-9: Data labels and values entered

Color wedge matches the color in the legend and the pie chart

Use the scroll bar to view all columns

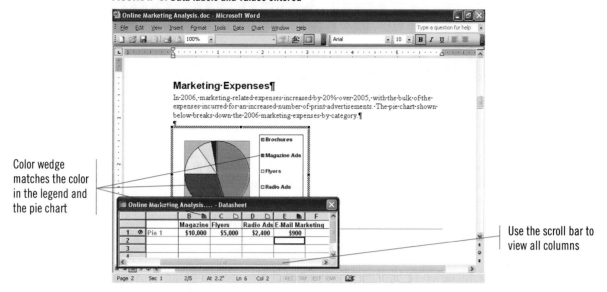

FIGURE N-10: Selecting the plot area

Chart Objects list arrow

Components of the pie chart

Plot area is the gray shaded square that appears behind the pie chart

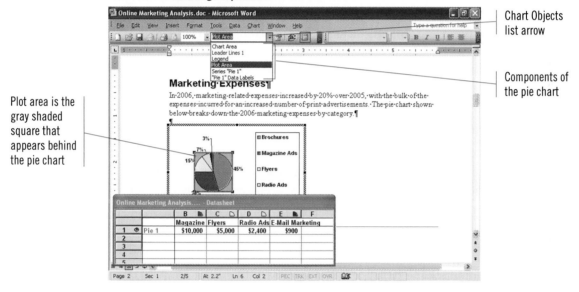

FIGURE N-11: Completed pie chart

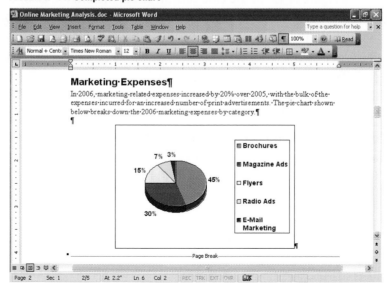

Importing Spreadsheet Data into a Chart

As you have learned, you can create a chart from data entered into a Word table or from data you enter in a datasheet. You can also create a chart from data you import from an Excel worksheet. You often choose this option when you have used Excel to enter data suitable for a chart and do not wish to re-create the data in Word. Importing the data in the Excel worksheet directly into the datasheet for a chart you create in Word can save you time. ▰▰▱▱▱ You have created an Excel worksheet containing data about the number of visitors Media-Loft.com has attracted over a two-year period. You import the Excel file into a datasheet for a chart you create in Word. You then change the chart type to a line chart.

STEPS

1. **Scroll down to the top of page 3, click the** second paragraph mark **below the Web Site Visitors paragraph, click** Insert **on the menu bar, point to** Picture, **then click** Chart

QUICK TIP

If you don't see the Import File button, click the Toolbar Options button, then click the Import File button on the palette that opens.

2. **Click the** Import File button 📇 **on the Standard toolbar, navigate to the drive and folder where your Data Files are located, click** WD N-2.xls, **click** Open, **verify that** Web Site **in the Import Data Options dialog box is selected, then click** OK

   The Web Site worksheet from the WD N-2.xls file is imported into the Word datasheet and the column chart changes to reflect the information in the datasheet. You can also choose to import specific cells from an Excel worksheet by selecting the Range Option button and identifying the cells to import.

3. **Refer to Figure N-12: use ✛ to select the** framed cells **(three rows of five cells each) in the datasheet**

4. **Move the pointer over the left edge of the selected cells to show** ⬚, **use** ⬚ **to drag the** selected cells **left one column, click the** top border **of column E, then press** [Delete]

   The placement of the columns shifts to reflect the change in the datasheet.

5. **Click** Chart **on the menu bar, click** Chart Type, **click** Line, **then click** OK **to accept the default line chart style**

   The column chart changes to a line chart with markers at each data value.

QUICK TIP

If you see Format Gridlines, click the pink line to select it, right click the selected line, then click Format Data Series.

6. **Right-click the** pink line **in the line chart, then click** Format Data Series

   The Format Data Series dialog box opens with the Patterns tab selected.

7. **Refer to Figure N-13: in the Line section select the** orange **color for the Line color, in the Marker section select the** triangle **style and the** orange **color for both the Foreground and the Background color of the marker, then click** OK

   With the chart data completed, you can format the chart object so that it appears attractively in the Word document.

8. **Click** outside the chart area, **right-click the** chart, **click** Format Object, **click the** Size tab, **change the Height to** 3" **if necessary, then click** OK

9. **Center the chart and add an outside border, click away from the chart, then save the document**

   The completed line chart is shown in Figure N-14.

FIGURE N-12: Moving imported data in the chart datasheet

Select framed cells

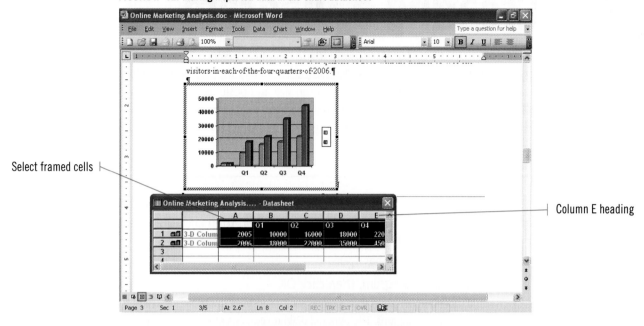

Column E heading

FIGURE N-13: Selecting options in the Format Data Series dialog box

Orange line color selected

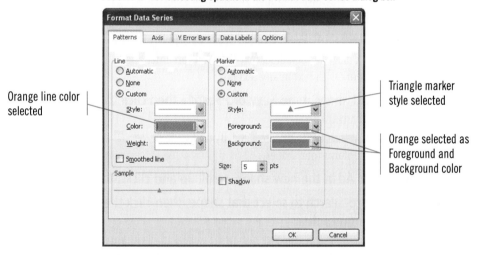

Triangle marker style selected

Orange selected as Foreground and Background color

FIGURE N-14: Completed line chart

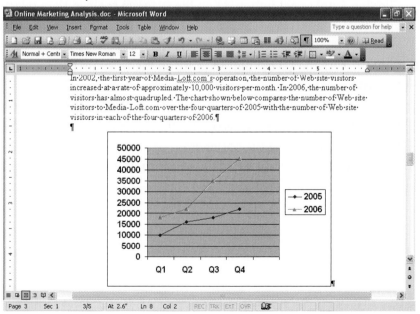

Creating a Diagram

You can create six kinds of diagrams with the Diagram tool. After you select a diagram type, you can enter text into the various sections of the diagram, then modify the size and fill color of the diagram. The diagram appears in a drawing canvas that you can size and position, just like you would any graphics object. 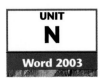 You want to provide MediaLoft management a visual comparison of the four ways in which users access MediaLoft's Web site. You start by showing the Drawing toolbar and then creating and labeling a pyramid diagram.

STEPS

1. **Scroll down to the top of page 4, click the** second paragraph mark **below the Access Methods paragraph, show the Drawing toolbar, then click the** Insert Diagram or Organization Chart button 🔯 **on the Drawing toolbar**

   The Diagram Gallery dialog box opens.

2. **Click the** Pyramid Diagram, **then click** OK

   A pyramid diagram opens and the Diagram toolbar appears. Table N-1 describes the buttons on the Diagram toolbar for pyramid diagrams. The pyramid diagram consists of a series of shapes. The Insert Shape and Move Shape buttons change, depending on the diagram you create.

3. **Scroll down to see the bottom shape of the pyramid diagram, click the** bottom shape, **then type** MediaLoft Web Site Address **as shown in Figure N-15**

   Each shape in a diagram includes a text box. You can enter and then format text in each shape text box just as you would work with text in any text box.

4. **Click the next** shape, **type** Keyword Search, **then click the** Insert Shape button A Insert Shape **on the Diagram toolbar**

   The new shape is inserted to fit automatically under the shape that contains the insertion point. The pyramid diagram now contains four shapes.

5. **Type** Banner Ad **in the new shape, scroll up and click the** top shape, **then type** Links

6. **Click** Keyword Search **to select that shape, then click the** Move Shape Forward button 🔼 **on the Diagram toolbar**

   You use the Move Shape Forward button to switch the positions of the Keyword Search and Banner Ad shapes. The Banner Ad shape moves above the Keyword Search shape.

7. **Click the** AutoFormat button 🔳 **on the Diagram toolbar, then select** Primary Colors

   In the Diagram Style Gallery dialog box, you can select from a variety of interesting diagram formats. When you select a format, a preview of the selected format appears to the right of the Diagram Style list.

8. **Click** OK, **click the** Layout button Layout ▾ **on the Diagram toolbar, then click** Fit Diagram to Contents

   The Primary Colors scheme is applied to the diagram and the diagram is adjusted to fit the content.

9. **Click** outside the drawing canvas, **click the** Zoom list arrow, **click** 50% **and scroll to view the pyramid, then save the document**

   The completed pyramid diagram appears, as shown in Figure N-16.

FIGURE N-15: Text entered in the bottom shape of the pyramid diagram

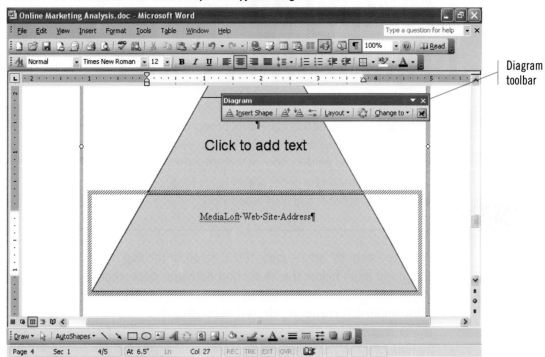

Diagram toolbar

FIGURE N-16: Completed pyramid diagram

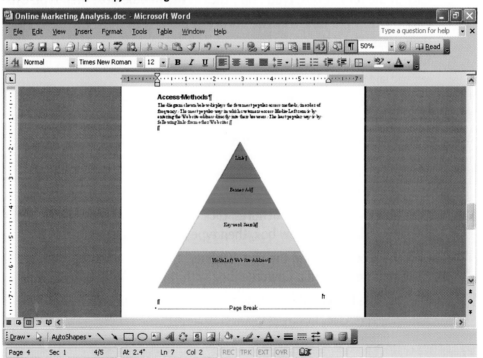

TABLE N-1: Buttons on the Diagram toolbar

button	use to	button	use to
Insert Shape	Insert a new shape in the diagram	Layout	Change the layout of the diagram
	Move a selected shape backward		Apply an AutoFormat
	Move a selected shape forward	Change to	Change the diagram to another diagram type
	Reverse the diagram		Adjust the text wrapping

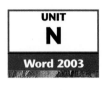
Creating an Organization Chart

An organization chart shows information in the form of a hierarchy—the top box in the organization chart represents a top position, such as a president or supervisor, and the subordinate boxes represent secondary positions, such as vice presidents or clerks. You can also create an organization chart to show the relationships among related components, such as Web pages in a Web site. ░░░░ You want to create a visual representation of the marketing activities related to the MediaLoft Web site. You create an organization chart to show two principal activities and their subactivities.

STEPS

1. **Click the** Zoom list arrow, **click** 100%, **scroll to the top of page 5, click the** second paragraph mark **below the Marketing Activities paragraph, click the** Insert Diagram or Organization Chart button 🔅 **on the Drawing toolbar, verify that the** organization chart **in the upper-left corner is selected, then click** OK

    An organization chart with two levels opens in a drawing canvas and the Organization Chart toolbar appears. The boxes in the organization chart contain placeholder text.

2. **Click in the** top box, **then type** Marketing Activities

3. **Click in the** far left box, **type** Print, **click in the** middle box, **then type** Online

4. **Click the** far right box, **click the** border **of the box to show the handles as in Figure N-17, then press** [Delete]

    When you delete a box in an organization chart, the remaining boxes increase in size, shift position, and are centered under the top box.

5. **Click the** box **containing the text "Print," click the** Insert Shape list arrow ⚏ Insert Shape ▾ **on the Organization Chart toolbar, then click** Subordinate **as shown in Figure N-18**

    A new box appears under the Print box. You select Subordinate when you want to show a component beneath another component in the organization chart. You select Coworker when you want to show a component on the same level as another component. You select Assistant when you want a component to appear off to the side, indicating a supportive role, rather than a subordinate or equal role.

> **TROUBLE**
> If you insert a Subordinate below the Brochures text box, click Edit, then click Undo.

6. **Click the** new box, **type** Brochures, **click the** Insert Shape list arrow ⚏ Insert Shape ▾, **select** Coworker, **click in the** new box, **then type** Bookmarks

7. **Click the** box **containing the text "Online," then add a** Subordinate **box with the text** E-Mail Marketing **and a** Coworker **box with the text** Affiliate Programs

8. **Click** outside the drawing canvas, **then save the document**

    The organization chart appears, as shown in Figure N-19.

FIGURE N-17: Organization chart box selected

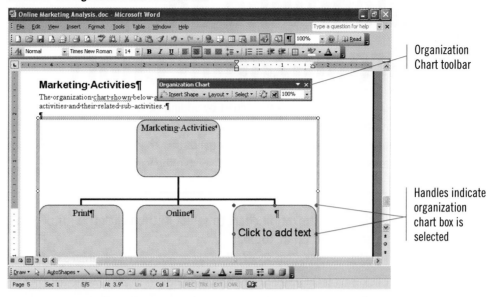

Organization Chart toolbar

Handles indicate organization chart box is selected

FIGURE N-18: Insert Shape menu options

Each diagram shows the placement of where a new box would be placed in relation to the selected box

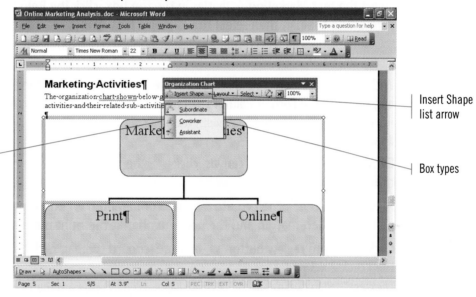

Insert Shape list arrow

Box types

FIGURE N-19: Completed organization chart

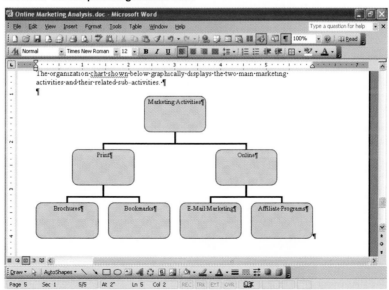

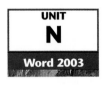

Modifying an Organization Chart

You can modify an organization chart by adding boxes to represent new coworkers or subordinates, or by removing boxes. You can also change the fill color of the boxes and modify the text. Finally, you can increase or decrease the size of the organization chart. ░░░░░ You apply one of the AutoFormats to the organization chart and then modify the text in the various boxes.

STEPS

1. **Click the organization chart to select it, then click the AutoFormat button 🜲 on the Organization Chart toolbar**

   The Organization Chart Style Gallery opens. You can choose from a variety of interesting styles.

2. **Click Beveled Gradient as shown in Figure N-20, then click OK**

   The Beveled Gradient style is applied to the organization chart.

3. **Select the text Marketing Activities in the top box, click the Bold button B on the Formatting toolbar, then select the 12-point font size**

   You use the buttons on the Formatting toolbar to modify text in an organization chart box, just as you would modify any text in a Word document.

4. **With the text still selected, double-click the Format Painter button 🖌 on the Standard toolbar, then use the Format Painter to apply formatting to the text in all of the chart boxes**

   You can use the Format Painter to modify text in an organization chart, just as you would in a regular Word document.

5. **Click outside the drawing canvas, click 🖌, then compare the completed organization chart to Figure N-21**

6. **Press [Ctrl][Home], then create a footer containing the text Prepared by followed by your name at the left margin and the page number at the right margin**

7. **Click the Print Preview button 🔍 on the Standard toolbar, click the Multiple Pages button, then click 2 × 3 pages**

   The completed marketing analysis document appears on five pages, as shown in Figure N-22.

8. **Click Close on the Print Preview toolbar, save the document, print a copy, close the document, then exit Word**

> **TROUBLE**
> If the top border is missing on the first three charts in the printed document, change the text wrapping for each chart from inline to floating.

FIGURE N-20: Organization Chart Style Gallery

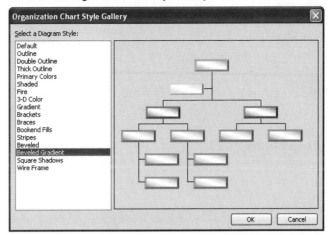

FIGURE N-21: Formatted organization chart

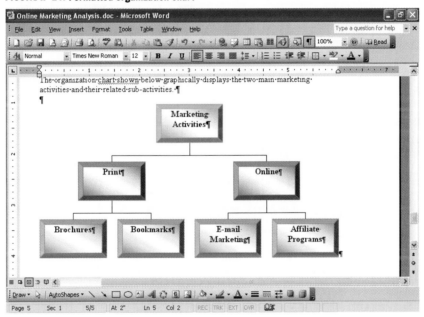

FIGURE N-22: Completed document in Print Preview

The top borders of some charts may not appear in Print Preview; however, they should appear in the printed document

Cone chart

Pyramid diagram

Line chart

Pie chart

Organization chart

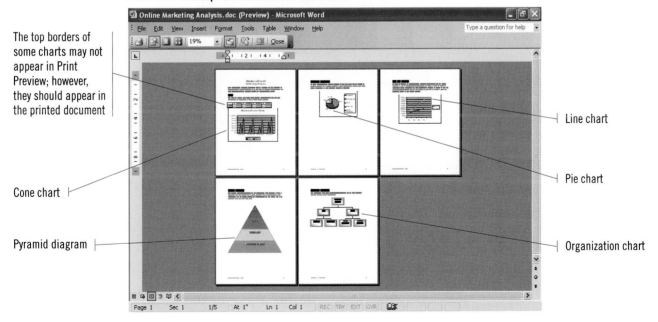

Practice

▼ CONCEPTS REVIEW

Label each of the elements in Figure N-23.

FIGURE N-23

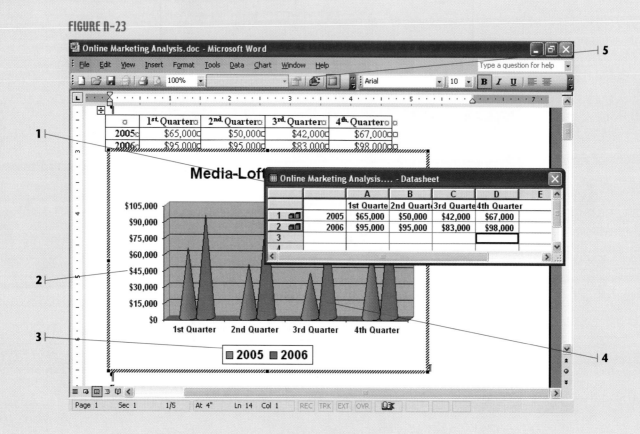

Match each term with the statement that best describes it.

6. Cone

7. Radial

8. Legend

9. Label

10. Datasheet

11. Coworker

a. Contains the data for a chart

b. Type of column chart

c. The key to the chart data

d. A diagram that shows relationships to a core element

e. A kind of box included in an organization chart

f. Describes the significance of a value

Select the best answer from the list of choices.

12. **Which of the following chart types shows data as part of a whole?**
    a. Column chart
    b. Pie chart
    c. Scatter XY chart
    d. Cylinder chart

13. **Which term refers to a number represented by a data series in a chart?**
    a. Label
    b. Legend
    c. Value
    d. Datasheet

14. **Which tab in the Format Axis dialog box do you select to change the increments shown on an x-axis or y-axis?**
    a. Scale
    b. Font
    c. Data series
    d. Legend

15. **How many rows or columns of data can be represented in a pie chart?**
    a. One
    b. Two
    c. Three
    d. Four

16. **How do you import Excel spreadsheet data into a chart you create in Word?**
    a. Click Insert on the menu bar, then select Chart Data.
    b. Click the Import File button on the Standard toolbar.
    c. Click the Insert File button on the Standard toolbar.
    d. Right-click a chart, then click Insert Data.

17. **Which type of diagram do you use to show areas of overlap between elements?**
    a. Venn diagram
    b. Target diagram
    c. Organization chart
    d. Pyramid diagram

18. **Where does a Subordinate shape appear in an organization chart?**
    a. Above the selected shape
    b. Below the selected shape
    c. To the right of the selected shape
    d. To the left of the selected shape

19. **How do you enhance an organization chart with a preset format?**
    a. Click the AutoFormat button on the Organization Chart toolbar.
    b. Click the Format Chart button on the Organization Chart toolbar.
    c. Double-click the top box in the organization chart, then click AutoFormat.
    d. Double-click the organization chart to enter Edit mode, then select a format from the AutoFormat gallery.

▼ SKILLS REVIEW

1. Create a column chart.

a. Start Word, open the file WD N-3.doc from the drive and folder where your Data Files are located, then save it as **Pacific Rim Trading Report**.

b. Select the table below the Sales paragraph near the top of the document, then insert a column chart.

c. Open the Chart Options dialog box, then enter **Pacific Rim Trading Sales** as the chart title.

d. Move the legend to the bottom of the chart.

e. Change the 1st Quarter sales for 2004 to **$35,000** in the datasheet and in the table.

f. Drag the lower-right corner sizing handle of the chart down to approximately the 7" mark on the vertical ruler bar and the 5" mark on the horizontal ruler.

g. Enclose the chart with an outside border, center the chart, deselect the chart, then save the document

2. Edit a chart.

a. Select the chart, double-click it, then change the Major unit of the y-axis from 20000 to **30000**.

b. Change the font size of the y-axis to **10** point.

c. Change the font size of the x-axis to **10** point.

d. Change the font size of the legend to **10** point.

e. Change the color of the data series representing 2005 to bright pink.

f. Change the chart to a cylinder chart, then save the document.

3. Create a pie chart.

a. Insert a chart below the Sales Expenses paragraph on the second page of the document.

b. Convert the chart to a pie chart, then clear the placeholder data.

c. Click Slice 1 in the datasheet, type **Web Site**, then enter **Print Ads**, **Radio Ads**, **Travel Expenses**, and **Special Events** as the labels for columns B through E.

d. Click the cell below Web Site, type **$45,000**, then enter **$20,000**, **$15,000**, **$10,000**, and **$5,000** as the values for columns B through E.

e. Open the Chart Options dialog box, then show the data labels as percentages.

f. Click any white area in the chart, select Plot Area from the Chart Objects list, then delete the plot area.

g. Convert the pie chart to a 3-D pie chart.

h. Change the 3-D elevation of the chart to **35** degrees.

i. Use the Format Object dialog box to change the width to **4"**, center the chart, add a border, then save the document.

4. Import spreadsheet data into a chart.

a. Insert a chart at the second paragraph mark below the Retail Outlet Visitors paragraph on page 3 of the document.

b. Import the file WD N-4.xls from the drive and folder where your Data Files are located, then click OK.

c. Use the pointer to select cells with data under the columns labeled A–E in the datasheet (15 cells total), move the selected cells to the left, then delete column E.

d. Convert the chart to a line chart. Accept the default chart subtype for a line chart.

e. Format the data series that represents 2006 so that the line color and the foreground and background marker colors are light orange and the marker style is a circle.

f. Use the Format Object dialog box to change the height of the chart to **3"**, center the chart, apply a border, then save the document.

5. Create a diagram.

a. Scroll down to the top of page 4, click the second paragraph mark below the Supplier Countries paragraph, then show the Drawing toolbar, if necessary.

b. Insert a radial diagram.

c. Click the top circle, type **Japan**, then click the Insert Shape button twice so that the total number of circles is six, including the middle circle.

d. Enter text in the circles, as shown in Figure N-24.

e. Click the Thailand circle, then click the Move Shape Forward button so that Thailand and China change places.

f. Change the AutoFormat style to Fire.

g. Change the text Pacific Rim Trading to bold, 14 point, and white, then use the Format Painter to format the text in the remaining circles.

h. Save the document.

6. Create an organization chart.

a. Scroll to the top of page 5, click the second paragraph mark below the Store Management Structure paragraph, then insert an organization chart.

b. In the top box, type **Anita Chau**, press [Enter], then type **Store Manager**.

c. In the far left box, type **George West** followed by **Day Supervisor**; in the middle box, type **Yvonne Howe** followed by **Evening Supervisor**, then delete the far right box.

d. Insert a Subordinate below the George West box that contains the text **Marion Leung** followed by **Clerk**.

e. Insert a Coworker next to Marion Leung that contains the text **Sue Ng** followed by **Clerk**.

f. Insert a Subordinate below the Yvonne Howe box that contains the text **Sam Ramos** followed by **Clerk**.

g. Save the document.

7. Modify an organization chart.

a. Open the Organization Chart Style Gallery, then select the Stripes style.

b. Apply bold and 16 point to the name Anita Chau in the top box.

c. Use the Format Painter to apply the formatting to just the names in the remaining boxes.

d. Click outside the organization chart, create a footer that includes the text **Prepared by** followed by your name at the left margin and the page number at the right margin, then view all five pages in the Print Preview screen.

e. Close the Print Preview screen, print a copy of the document, save and close it, then exit Word.

FIGURE N-24

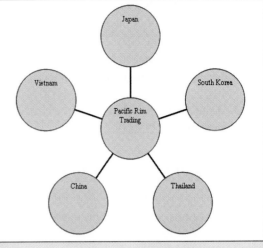

▼ INDEPENDENT CHALLENGE 1

As the assistant manager of a local art gallery, you are responsible for keeping track of how many people visit the gallery each month. At the end of six months, you compile the results into a column chart that you include in the gallery's semiannual report. The data for the column chart is already contained in an Excel worksheet.

a. Start Word, open a new blank document, then save it as **Gallery Attendance** to the drive and folder where your Data Files are located.

b. Type the text **Prairie View Art Gallery** as a heading formatted with bold, 16 point, and center alignment.

c. Press [Enter] twice after the heading, clear the formatting, then enter the following sentence: **The column chart shown below presents the gallery attendance figures for adults and children from July to December, 2006.**

d. Press [Enter] twice after the sentence, then create a column chart with the default settings.

e. Click the Import File button, then import the data from the Attendance worksheet in the file WD N-5.xls, which is stored in the drive and folder where your Data Files are located.

f. Edit the chart to change the color of the Adults data series.

g. Change the chart type to pyramid.

h. Enter **Gallery Attendance 2006** as the chart title, then move the legend to the bottom of the chart.

i. Use the Format Object dialog box to change the width to **6"** wide, then include a border line.

j. Edit the chart, change the font size of the y-axis, x-axis, and the legend text to **10** point.

▼ INDEPENDENT CHALLENGE 1 (CONTINUED)

Advanced Challenge Exercise

- Remove the gray walls from the chart. (*Hint*: Right-click an area of the gray wall, click Format Walls, then change the color to None.)
- Change the 3-D view to an elevation of **20** and a rotation of **30**. (*Hint*: Right-click the chart, then click 3-D View).
- Add the value to each data point. (*Hint*: Click the Data Labels tab in the Chart Options dialog box).
- Reduce the font size of both sets of value labels to **10** point.

k. Double-click two lines below the chart, type **Prepared by** followed by your name left-aligned, save the document, print a copy, close the document, then exit Word.

▼ INDEPENDENT CHALLENGE 2

Six months ago, you started a new online business called Linen Barn that sells designer towels and linens. As part of a report for your investors, you want to include a pie chart that shows online sales of your products by category.

a. Start Word, open a new document, then save it as **Linen Barn Sales** to the drive and folder where your Data Files are located.

b. Create a 3-D pie chart based on the data that follows.

Category	Sales
Bath Towels	**$87,000**
Bed Linens	**$71,000**
Bedspreads	**$46,000**
Hand Towels	**$18,000**
Bath Accessories	**$12,000**

c. Add the title **Online Sales by Category**, position the legend at the top of the chart, below the title, then add data labels to show the percentage represented by each slice of the pie.

d. Remove the shaded plot area, then change the color of the Bath Towels data point to bright green. (*Hint*: You need to click the pie chart, then click just the pie slice that represents Bath Towels.)

e. Increase the 3-D tilt to 45 degrees.

f. Use the Format Object dialog box to increase the width of the chart to **5"**, enclose the chart in an outside border, then center the chart.

g. Edit the chart by changing Bath Accessories to **$18,000**, then change the font size of the legend text to **10** point and the data labels to **9** point.

h. Double-click below the chart, type **Prepared by** followed by your name left-aligned, save the document, print a copy, close the document, then exit Word.

▼ INDEPENDENT CHALLENGE 3

You have just started working for Masterworks Tours, an English-language tour company based in Vienna, Austria, that specializes in tours to sites frequented by classical composers such as Beethoven and Mozart. One of your jobs is to help prepare the company's annual report. Included in the report will be a page that describes the company personnel. You suggest creating an organization chart to show the hierarchy of positions.

a. Start Word, open a new document, then save it as **Masterworks Tours** to the drive and folder where your Data Files are located.

b. Type **Masterworks Tours Organization Chart** as a title enhanced with 18 point, bold, and center alignment.

c. Two blank lines below the title, insert an organization chart.

d. Refer to Figure N-25 to enter the text and add the boxes required for your organization chart.

e. Apply the Stripes AutoFormat, then apply bold to the names.

▼ INDEPENDENT CHALLENGE 3 (CONTINUED)

Advanced Challenge Exercise

- Add an Assistant box to the top box.
- Type **Jason Kane** as the name and **Executive Assistant** as the title.
- Remove the Stripes AutoFormat and restore the Default AutoFormat.
- Click just the border of the top box, click the Fill Color list arrow on the Drawing toolbar, then select the Gold fill color.

FIGURE N-25

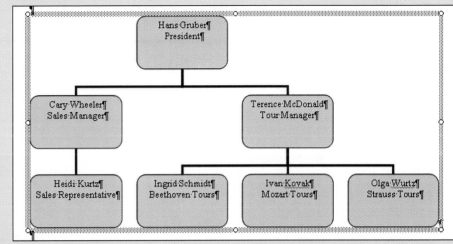

- Fill the assistant's box with Light Turquoise, then fill the two boxes related to Sales positions with Light Orange and the four boxes related to Tour positions with Sky Blue.
- Open the Clip Art task pane, search for **Beethoven** (you must be connected to the Internet to find suitable clip art), then insert one of the Beethoven pictures that appears.
- Change the layout of the picture to Square, then move the picture into the blank area of the organization chart to the right of the top box. Resize the picture if necessary, then position it so that the bottom-left corner is slightly overlapped by Terence McDonald's box. Note that you will need to change the stacking order of the picture to Send to Back.

f. Double-click below the organization chart, type **Prepared by** followed by your name left-aligned, print a copy of the document, save and close the document, then exit Word.

▼ INDEPENDENT CHALLENGE 4

You use radial diagrams to illustrate relationships of several related elements to a core element. As a Web designer in the process of designing a new Web site for a company of your choice, you have been checking out your competitors' Web sites. To help you determine the features you want your new Web site to have, you create a radial diagram that shows six features included on a competitor's Web site that sell similar products or services.

a. Open your Web browser and conduct a search for a company that sells a product or service that interests you. You can enter keywords related to the product, such as **lawn furniture**, **garden tools**, and **hiking tours**, and you can enter generic domain names such as **www.garden.com** or **www.hiking.com** in the Address box of your Web browser.

b. Explore the Web site you have selected and identify six features. Features include a search tool, shopping cart, free gift offer, product-related content, and a Frequently Asked Questions page.

c. Start Word. In a new Word document, enter a title such as **Radial Diagram of an Online Garden Store**. In place of the word **Garden** use a word that describes the type of stores you researched.

d. Insert a radial diagram that contains the name of the Web site in the center circle and one feature in each of the six surrounding circles. (*Note*: You need to add three new circles.)

e. Format the diagram with the AutoFormat of your choice.

f. Format the text so that it appears attractive and easy to read. (*Note*: You might need to scale the diagram and then drag the sizing handles so that the text doesn't wrap inappropriately.)

g. Type **Prepared by** and your name below the diagram.

h. Save the document as **Web Site Radial Diagram** to the drive and folder where your Data Files are located, print a copy, close the document, then exit Word.

▼ VISUAL WORKSHOP

You are working with the Web Development Group at ZooPlace.com to plan and launch a new Web site that sells a wide assortment of exotic stuffed animals—from manatees to moose. To help your investors understand the development process, you've created a target diagram that illustrates the steps toward the goal of launching the Web site. The largest circle of the target diagram represents the first step in the process and the target area of the diagram represents the final goal. In a new Word document, enter the title and create the target diagram shown in Figure N-26. Note that you will need to fill each of the five circles and enhance the corresponding text with the colors shown in Figure N-26 or of your own choosing. Save the document with the name **Web Launch Target Diagram**, print a copy, then close the document.

FIGURE N-26

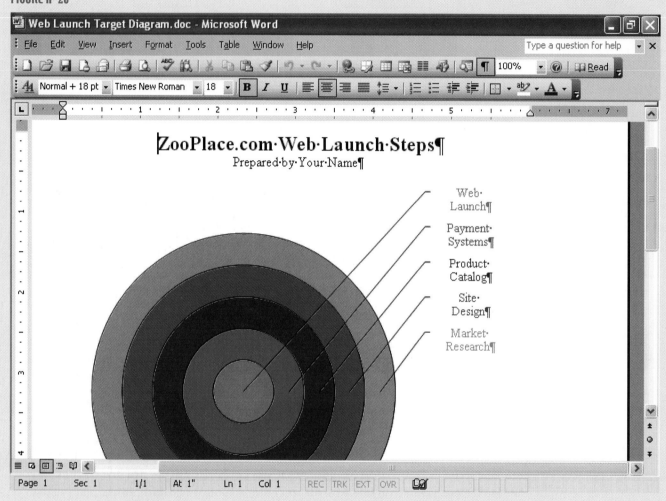

Collaborating with Workgroups

OBJECTIVES

Explore collaboration options
Include comments in a document
Track changes
Accept and reject changes
Create document versions
Compare documents and merge changes
Use Find and Replace options
Protect documents

If you have a SAM user profile, you may have access to hands-on instruction, practice, and assessment of the skills covered in this unit. Log in to your SAM account and go to your assignments page to see what your instructor has assigned.

Word includes a variety of functions designed to let you work on a document as part of a team. You can include comments in a document, highlight the changes you've made to the document text, create different versions of a document, compare these versions, and then merge changes to create a finished document that all members of the team can approve. You can also use Find and Replace options to find special characters and formatting. Finally, you can protect documents against unauthorized changes and set permission options. Nazila Sharif in the Marketing Department at MediaLoft has written several questions for an online survey that visitors to MediaLoft's Web site can complete. You collaborate with Nazila to develop a version of the survey that you can submit to Alice Wegman, the department manager, for final approval.

Exploring Collaboration Options

You can collaborate with colleagues in different ways. For example, you can distribute printed documents that show all the changes made by one or more colleagues, along with the comments they've made, or you can share the electronic file of the document, which also shows the changes and comments. ▰▰▰ Before you start working with colleagues to develop questions for an online survey, you investigate collaborative features available in Word.

DETAILS

The collaborative features in Word include the following:

- **Reviewing toolbar**
  You use the buttons on the Reviewing toolbar to access commands that allow you to share a document between two or more people. Table O-1 describes the buttons on the Reviewing toolbar.

- **Insert comments**
  You insert comments into a document when you want to ask questions or provide additional information. When several people work on the same document, their comments appear in different colored balloons along the right side of the document in Print Layout view. Figure O-1 shows a document containing comments made by two people.

- **Track changes**
  When you share documents with colleagues, you need to be able to show them where you have inserted and deleted text. In Word, inserted text appears in the document as underlined text in the color assigned to the person who made the insertion. This same color identifies that person's deletions and comment text. For example, if Nazila's comment balloons are green, then the text she inserts or deletes in a document will also be green. Text that is deleted appears in a balloon along the right side of the document in Print Layout view, along with the comment balloons. Figure O-1 includes new text inserted in the document and two balloons containing deleted text.

- **Create versions**
  Sometimes you might want to maintain two or three versions of the same document so you can keep an ongoing record of changes. To save disk space, you can save several versions of one document within the same document file. You can then view each version of the document at any time.

- **Compare and merge documents**
  You use the Compare and Merge Documents feature to compare any two documents to show the differences between the two. Compare and Merge is often used to show the differences between an original document and an edited copy of the original. It is also used to merge the changes and comments of multiple reviewers into a single document when each reviewer edits the document using a separate copy of the original. When you compare and merge two documents, you have the option of merging the changes into one of the documents or of merging the changes into a new third document. Figure O-2 shows the three locations possible for displaying the compare and merge results. The differences between the two documents are shown in the merged document as tracked changes. You can then examine the merged document, edit it, and save it with a new filename.

TABLE O-1: Buttons on the Reviewing toolbar

button	use to	button	use to
⊕	Show the previous change in a document	aby ▾	Highlight selected text
⊕	Show the next change in a document	🔲	Insert voice comment
⊘ ▾	Accept the highlighted change	📝	Turn Track Changes on/off
⊗ ▾	Reject the highlighted change or delete the currently selected comment	🔲	Open the Reviewing Pane
🔲	Insert a new comment		

FIGURE O-1: Document showing tracked changes and comments

Reviewing toolbar

Inserted text

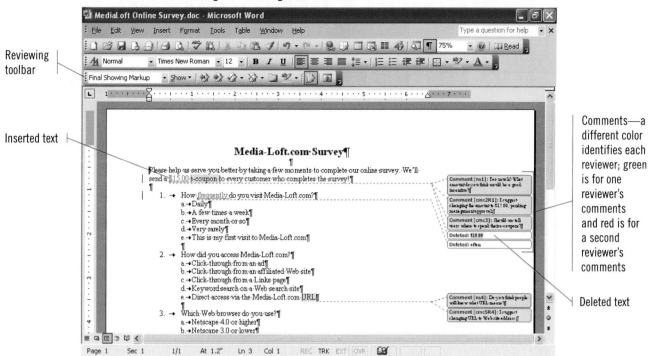

Comments—a different color identifies each reviewer; green is for one reviewer's comments and red is for a second reviewer's comments

Deleted text

FIGURE O-2: Options for merging document changes

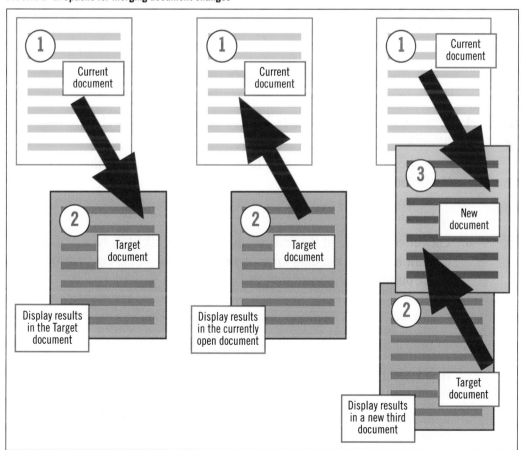

Display results in the Target document

Display results in the currently open document

Display results in a new third document

Including Comments in a Document

Sometimes when you review a document that someone else has written, you want to insert a comment relating to the document text, the document formatting, or any number of related issues. A **comment** is text you insert in a comment balloon that appears, by default, along the right side of your document in Print Layout view. A comment mark appears in the document at the point where you inserted the comment. A line leads from the comment mark to the comment balloon. ▓▓▓▓▓ Your colleague Nazila has already inserted some comments in the document containing the list of survey questions. You open the document, add a new comment and then edit one of the comments that Nazila inserted. You work in Page Layout view so you can see the comments in comment balloons in the right margin.

STEPS

1. **Start Word, open the file** WD O-1.doc **from the drive and folder where your Data Files are located, then verify that the Show/Hide ¶ button** ▓ **is selected**

TROUBLE
If you do not see the Reviewing toolbar, repeat Step 2.

2. **Verify that you are in Print Layout view, click** View **on the menu bar, point to** Toolbars, **click** Reviewing, **click the** Zoom list arrow **on the Standard toolbar, click** Page Width, **scroll the document to view its contents, then save it as** MediaLoft Online Survey
   The Reviewing toolbar opens above the document window and the two comments that Nazila inserted appear in colored balloons in the right margin of the document. Comment markers appear in the document itself.

QUICK TIP
Comments appear in a ScreenTip when you move the insertion point over the area enclosed by the comment markers.

3. **Select the word** e-coupon **in the first paragraph, then click the** Insert Comment button ▓ **on the Reviewing toolbar**
   Comment markers appear around the word "e-coupon" and a comment balloon appears in the right margin in a color that is different from Nazila's comment. When inserting a comment, you select a word or two of the text so that the comment markers enclose the selected words and the words are shaded with the same color as the corresponding comment balloon.

4. **Click the** Zoom list arrow, **click** 100%, **then if necessary scroll right to view the comment balloon**

5. **Type** Should we tell users where to spend their e-coupons?, **then click anywhere outside the balloon**
   You increase the zoom percentage so you can read text in a balloon. Your comment appears in a new balloon, as shown in Figure O-3.

QUICK TIP
When you click in a comment balloon, the balloon becomes a darker shade of its original color.

6. **Click after** incentive **in the first comment balloon, click** ▓, **type** I suggest changing the amount to $15.00, pending management approval. **in the new balloon, then click anywhere outside the comment balloon**
   A comment balloon with your response appears between the two existing comments. You click in a comment balloon and then click the Insert Comment button on the Reviewing toolbar to keep the original comment and the response together.

7. **Scroll down, click in Nazila's** second comment balloon, **click** ▓, **then in the new balloon type** I suggest changing URL to Web site address.
   You can also choose to view comments in the Reviewing Pane.

8. **Click the** Reviewing Pane button ▓ **on the Reviewing toolbar, then scroll down the Reviewing Pane to view the comments**
   Figure O-4 shows comments in the Reviewing Pane.

9. **Click** ▓ **to close the Reviewing Pane, then save the document**

FIGURE O-3: Comment balloons

Insert Comment button

Comment marker in text

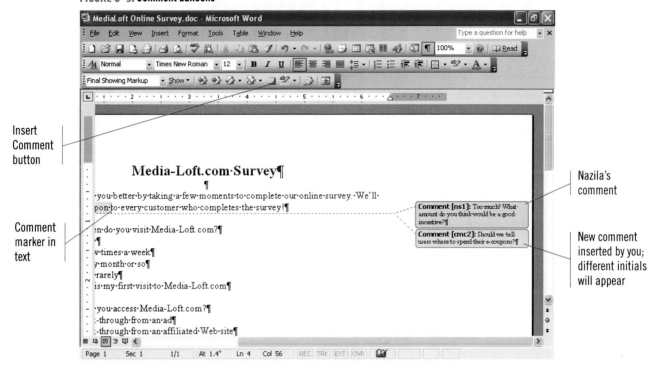

Nazila's comment

New comment inserted by you; different initials will appear

FIGURE O-4: Comments in the Reviewing Pane

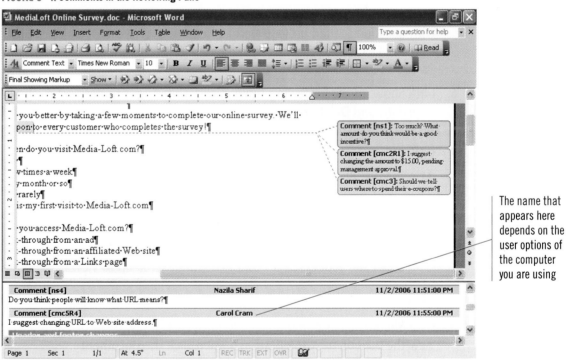

The name that appears here depends on the user options of the computer you are using

Clues to Use

Changing user information

The initials that appear in the markup balloons and the name that appears in the Reviewing Pane are based on content in the User Information tab. To change the user information, open the Tools menu, click Options, then click the User Information tab. In this tab, you can enter a name in the Name text box and the corresponding set of initials in the Initials text box. You modify user information when two or more people share access to the same computer and you want each person's comments and changes to appear in separate colors. If you are working in a lab setting, do not change the user information on the User Information tab without permission.

Tracking Changes

When you work on a document with two or more people, you want to be able to see where changes have been made. You use the Track Changes command to show inserted text and deleted text. In Page Layout view, the deleted text appears in a balloon, similar to a comment balloon, and the inserted text appears in the color assigned to the reviewer and underlined in the document. ████████ You go through the survey that Nazila prepared and make some editing changes. You then review changes by type and reviewer.

STEPS

1. **Press [Ctrl][Home] to move to the top of the document, then click the Track Changes button ▣ on the Reviewing toolbar**

   Now that Track Changes is turned on, every change you make to the document will appear in colored text.

2. **Select $10.00 in the first paragraph (but not the space following it), then press [Delete]**

   The deleted text appears in a balloon in the right margin. The ballon outline is the same color as your comment balloon; the text in the balloon matches Nazila's color because her comment is associated with the deleted text.

3. **Type $15.00**

   As shown in Figure O-5, the inserted text appears underlined and in the same color as the color of the comment you inserted in the previous lesson.

4. **Select often in question 1, then type frequently**

   The deleted text appears in a new balloon and the text "frequently" appears in colored underlined text.

5. **Scroll down the document to question 6, select all the text (Have you...No ¶) included with question 6, then press [Delete] twice**

   The deleted text appears in a balloon in the right margin along with a balloon that shows the formatting associated with the deleted text.

6. **Click Show on the Reviewing toolbar, click Comments to deselect it, click Show, click Insertions and Deletions to deselect it, click Show, then click Formatting to deselect it**

   You deselect all tracked changes and comment balloons so that you can review changes by type and reviewer.

7. **Click Show, then point to Reviewers**

   A menu opens listing the reviewers and showing the color assigned to each, as shown in Figure O-6. You can choose to view comments either for all reviewers or for individual reviewers. A check mark next to a reviewer's name means that the comments and tracked changes for that reviewer appear in the document window. If you do not want to view a reviewer's comments and tracked changes, click the check box next to that reviewer's name to deselect that reviewer and remove the check mark. You leave All Reviewers selected.

8. **With Show still active, select Comments, then scroll up to view the comment balloons**

   Since you left All Reviewers selected, comment balloons for all reviewers appear in the right margin. The different colors match the colors assigned to the reviewers in the reviewers list.

9. **Click Show, click Insertions and Deletions, click Show, click Formatting, scroll down to view the balloon next to question 6, then save the document**

   The insertions appear as underlined text in the document and the deletions appear in balloons in the right margin. Formatting changes appear in their own balloons.

FIGURE O-5: Text inserted with Track Changes feature active

New inserted text

Track Changes button (also available on the Tools menu)

Deleted text appears in a new balloon

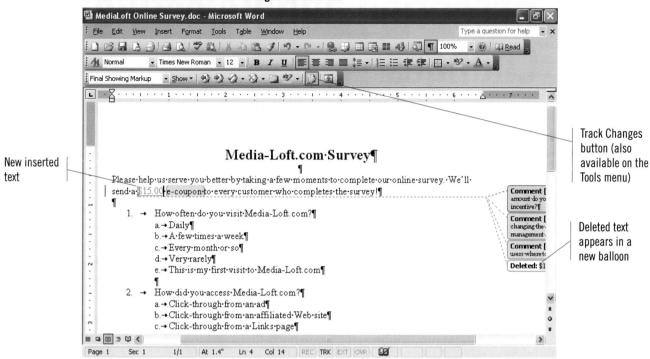

FIGURE O-6: List of Reviewers

Your name may appear here

Additional names may appear, depending on reviewing actions performed by others using your computer

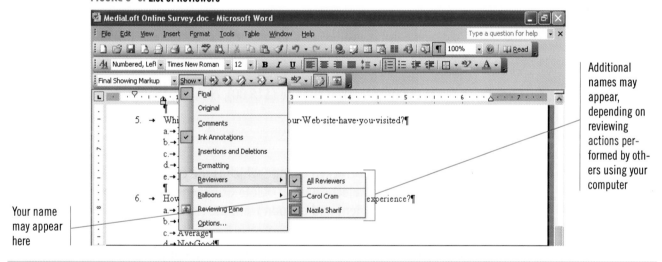

Clues to Use

Modifying Track Changes options

You modify the appearance of tracked changes using the Track Changes dialog box, which is shown in Figure O-7. To open this dialog box, click Show on the Reviewing toolbar, then click Options. In the Track Changes dialog box, you can change the formatting of insertions and select a specific color for them, and you can modify the appearance of the comment balloons. For example, you can increase or reduce the width of the balloons and you can choose to display the balloons in either the left or the right margin of the document.

FIGURE O-7: Track Changes dialog box

Accepting and Rejecting Changes

When you receive a document containing tracked changes, you will want to accept or reject the changes before you print the document as a final copy. When you accept a change, inserted text becomes part of the document and deleted text is permanently removed. You use the Reviewing toolbar to accept and reject changes in a document and to find and remove comments. ▰▰▰▰ Now that you've added your own changes to the document, you use the Reviewing toolbar to accept or reject the tracked changes and to remove the comments.

STEPS

1. **Press [Ctrl][Home], click the** Zoom list arrow **on the Standard toolbar, click** Page Width, **click the** Display for Review list arrow **on the Reviewing toolbar, then click** Original Showing Markup

   In this view, the inserted text appears in a balloon, as shown in Figure O-8.

2. **Click the** Display for Review list arrow, **click** Final Showing Markup, **then click the** Next **button** ⎆ **on the Reviewing toolbar to move to the first tracked change ($10.00) in the document**

   The insertion point moves to the balloon containing the deleted text $10.00.

3. **Click the** Accept Change button ⎙ **on the Reviewing toolbar**

   The balloon containing the deleted text and the comments associated with that deletion are removed from the right margin. The insertion point appears in the document before the next tracked change, which is $15.00.

4. **Click** ⎆ **to select the next tracked change ($15.00), click** ⎙, **then click** e-coupon **to deselect the text**

   The amount $15.00 appears in black text in the document, which indicates that it has been accepted as the new amount.

5. **Click** ⎆ **to move to the next tracked change which is the comment you inserted in a previous lesson, then click the** Reject Change/Delete Comment button ⎘ **on the Reviewing toolbar to remove the comment and balloon from the right margin**

6. **Click** ⎆ **to move to the next change (often), click** ⎘ **to restore the word "often", click** ⎆, **then click** ⎘ **to reject the insertion of the text "frequently"**

   Question 1 is restored to its original wording. You can continue to review and accept or reject changes individually, or you can choose to accept the remaining changes in the document.

7. **Click** ⎙, **then click** Accept All Changes in Document

   All the tracked changes in the document are accepted.

8. **Click the** Reject Change/Delete Comment list arrow ⎘ ▾, **then click** Delete All Comments in Document

   Scroll through the document. Notice that all tracked changes and comments are removed from the document. See Figure O-9.

9. **Click the** Track Changes button ⎚ **on the Reviewing toolbar to turn off Track Changes, then save the document**

FIGURE O-8: Original Showing Markup view

Original Showing Markup selected

Display for Review list arrow

Deleted text appears in strikethrough formatting

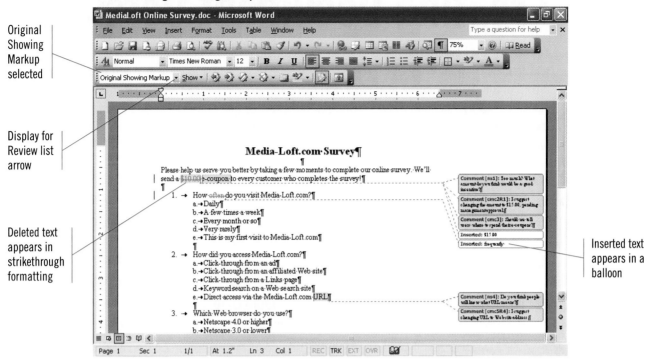

Inserted text appears in a balloon

FIGURE O-9: Tracked changes and comments accepted or rejected

Accept Change button

Reject Change/Delete Comment button

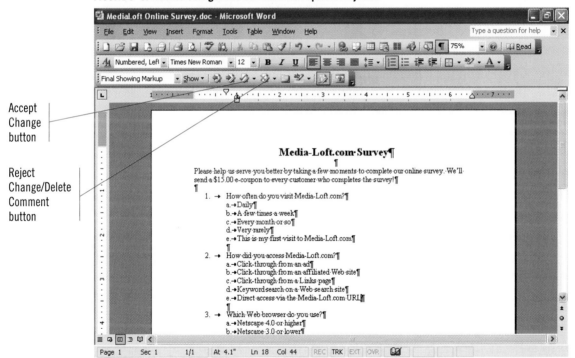

Clues to Use

Distributing documents for revision

When you work with several people on a document, you can e-mail each person a copy of the document and ask for their input. To save time, you can use the Send To command that automatically asks a recipient to review the attached document. To send the active document, click File on the menu bar, point to Send To, then click Mail Recipient (for Review). In a few moments, the default e-mail client window opens. If you are already connected to the Internet, you just enter the e-mail address of the recipient in the To: text box, and then click Send.

Creating Document Versions

You can use the Versions command to create two or more versions of a document. Each version can contain text that differs from every other version. You create versions of a document when you want to keep a record of the changes you've made to a document and store all versions of the document within the same filename. ▉▉▉▉ Although you are pleased with the revised questions, you decide to create two versions of the survey document. One version will contain the changes you have just accepted and the other version will contain a new question.

STEPS

1. **Click** File **on the menu bar, then click** Versions

   The Versions in MediaLoft Online Survey.doc dialog box opens. Depending on your computer settings, you may see a version with the comment "Auto version for sharing."

2. **Click** Save Now

   The Save Version dialog box opens. In this dialog box, you can type a short description of the version.

3. **Type** Survey with 6 questions **as shown in Figure O-10, then click** OK

   The Versions dialog box closes and the version of the document containing six survey questions is saved to the drive and folder where the original document is located.

4. **Switch to** 100% **view**

5. **Click at the end of item** e. **in Question 2, press** [Enter] **twice, type** 3., **press** [Tab], **type** Have you ever visited a MediaLoft real world store?, **press** [Enter], **press** [Tab], **type** Yes, **press** [Enter], **then type** No

   The new question appears in the document, as shown in Figure O-11.

6. **Click** File **on the menu bar, then click** Versions

   The Versions in MediaLoft Online Survey.doc dialog box opens and information about the document version you've already saved appears in the Existing versions area.

7. **Click** Save Now, **type** Survey with 7 questions, **then click** OK

   A second version of the MediaLoft Online Survey document is saved.

8. **Click** File **on the menu bar, then click** Versions

   Both versions of the document appear in the Versions in MediaLoft Online Survey.doc dialog box, as shown in Figure O-12.

9. **Click** Close, **then save and close the document**

Clues to Use

Using versions

To work on a version of a document, be sure that document is the active document, click File on the menu bar, then click Versions to open the Versions dialog box. In the Versions dialog box, all versions of the document that you've saved are listed. The versions are listed with the most recently saved version first. You select the version you want to work on, and then click Open. When you open a version, two Word windows are open at the same time. The document you are working on appears in the top part of the window and the version you just opened appears in the bottom of the window. The title bar of the window containing the version includes the date and time the version was created.

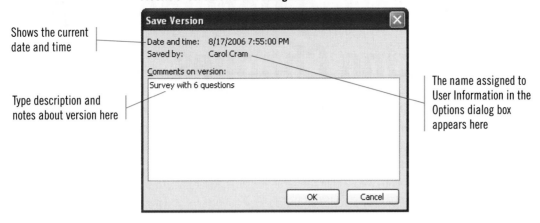

FIGURE O-10: Save Version dialog box

Shows the current date and time

Type description and notes about version here

The name assigned to User Information in the Options dialog box appears here

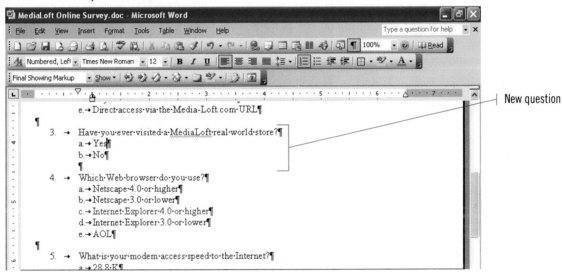

FIGURE O-11: New question inserted

New question

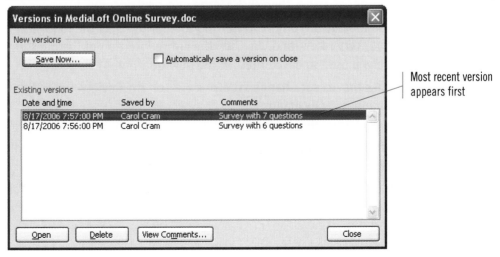

FIGURE O-12: Versions in MediaLoft Online Survey.doc dialog box

Most recent version appears first

Comparing Documents and Merging Changes

The Compare and Merge Documents feature in Word allows you to merge two documents at a time so you can compare the documents and determine where changes have been made. Word shows the differences between the documents as tracked changes. To use the Compare and Merge Documents feature, the files you want to compare must be the same document saved using different filenames. You cannot use the feature to compare versions of the document saved within the same filename. Refer back to Figure O-2 to review options for merging documents. ▓▓▓▓▓ Alice has reviewed the document and sent you her revision of the survey questions. In addition, Chris Williams in Customer Service has sent his revision of the survey questions. After opening and saving these documents, you use the Compare and Merge Documents features to check the changes Alice and Chris have made.

STEPS

1. **Open the file** WD O-2.doc **from the drive and folder where your Data Files are located, then save the document as** MediaLoft Online Survey_Alice

QUICK TIP

In order to merge these documents, these files must be saved to the drive and folder that contains the MediaLoft Online Survey document.

2. **Open the file** WD O-3.doc, **then save it as** MediaLoft Online Survey_Chris

   MediaLoft Online Survey_Chris is the active document. In the Compare and Merge process, the active document is called the **current document**.

3. **Click** Tools **on the menu bar, then click** Compare and Merge Documents

   The three survey documents appear in the Compare and Merge Documents dialog box. First, you want to merge the document from Alice into the MediaLoft Online Survey document created by Chris. After reviewing that merge, you will merge the original document with the merged document you just created into a new document.

4. **Click** MediaLoft Online Survey_Alice, **then click the** Merge list arrow **to view the list of Merge options as shown in Figure O-13**

   You use the Merge command to display results in the target document, which is the document created by Alice. You use the Merge into current document command to display the results in the currently open document, which is the document created by Chris. You use the Merge into new document command to display results in a new document.

QUICK TIP

Scroll through the document to get a feel for its contents.

5. **Click** Merge into current document

   The document appears, as shown in Figure O-14.

6. **Click** Tools, **click** Compare and Merge Documents, **click** MediaLoft Online Survey, **click the** Merge list arrow, **then click** Merge into new document

QUICK TIP

To reject specific changes, click the Next button until the text to delete is highlighted, then click the Reject Change/Delete Comment button.

7. **Use the buttons on the Reviewing toolbar to reject the following tracked changes:** A few, two, Very rarely, find, an, URL, the entire insertion of the question Which Web browser do you use?, **and** Favorites (in the new question 4)

8. **Click the** Accept Change list arrow ▨ ▾ **on the Reviewing toolbar, click** Accept All Changes in Document

   After accepting the combined tracked changes, the new document contains five questions.

9. **Scroll to the bottom of the document, type your name where indicated, then save the document as** MediaLoft Online Survey_Final

10. **Click** Window **on the menu bar, click** MediaLoft Online Survey_Alice, **close the document, click** Window **on the menu bar, click** MediaLoft Online Survey_Chris, **then save and close it**

    MediaLoft Online Survey_Final is the only active Word document.

FIGURE O-13: Compare and Merge Documents dialog box

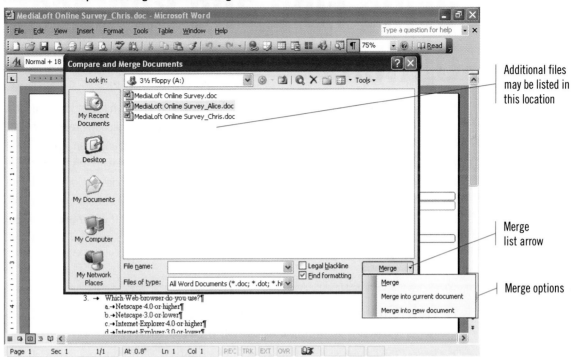

Additional files may be listed in this location

Merge list arrow

Merge options

Word 2003

FIGURE O-14: Document showing merged changes

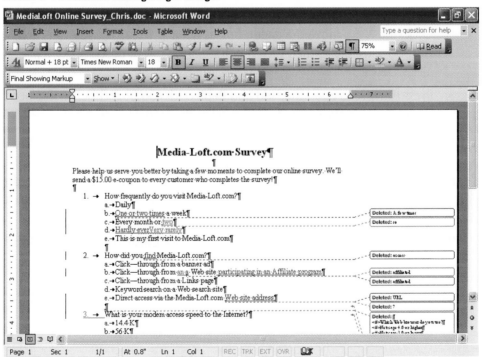

Using Find and Replace Options

Word offers advanced find and replace options that allow you to search for and replace formats, special characters, and even nonprinting elements such as paragraph marks (¶) and section breaks. For example, you can direct Word to find every occurrence of a word or phrase of unformatted text and then replace it with the same text formatted in a different font style and font size. ▓▓▓ You are pleased with the final version of the survey questions. Now you need to consider how best to format the questions for delivery over the Internet. You decide that every instance of the Web site name Media-Loft.com should appear in bold and italic. You use the Find and Replace feature to find every instance of Media-Loft.com and replace it with ***Media-Loft.com***. You then notice that an em dash (—) appears between the words "Click" and "through" in three entries in question 2. You decide to replace the em dash with the smaller en dash (–).

STEPS

1. **Press [Ctrl][Home] to move to the top of the document, click** Edit **on the menu bar, click** Replace, **then type** Media-Loft.com **in the Find what text box**

2. **Press [Tab], type** Media-Loft.com **in the Replace with text box, then click** More
   The Find and Replace dialog box expands.

3. **Click in the** Replace with text box

4. **Click** Format **at the bottom of the Find and Replace dialog box, click** Font **to open the Replace Font dialog box, select** Bold Italic **in the Font style list, then click** OK
   The format settings for the replacement text Media-Loft.com appear in the Find and Replace dialog box, as shown in Figure O-15.

5. **Click** Find Next, **move the dialog box as needed to see the selected text, click** Replace All, **click** OK, **click** Close, **then click the** first paragraph **to deselect the text**
   All instances of Media-Loft.com are replaced with ***Media-Loft.com***.

6. **Press [Ctrl][F] to open the Find and Replace dialog box, click the** Replace tab, **then press [Delete] to remove** Media-Loft.com **from the Find what text box**

7. **Click** Special, **click** Em Dash, **press [Tab], click** Special, **then click** En Dash
   Codes representing the em dash and en dash are entered in the Replace tab in the Find and Replace dialog box.

8. **Click the** No Formatting button **at the bottom of the Find and Replace dialog box to remove the formatting assigned to the text in the Replace with text box so the Find and Replace dialog box appears as shown in Figure O-16**

9. **Click** Find Next, **click** Replace All, **click** OK, **click** Close, **then save the document**

FIGURE O-15: Expanded Find and Replace dialog box

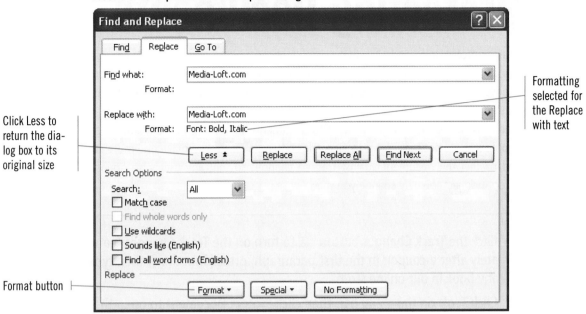

Click Less to return the dialog box to its original size

Formatting selected for the Replace with text

Format button

FIGURE O-16: Special characters inserted in the Find and Replace dialog box

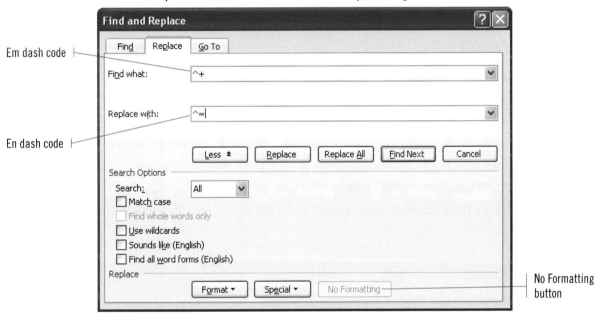

Em dash code

En dash code

No Formatting button

Protecting Documents

You can protect a document so that no one else can make changes or insert comments. When you protect a document, you choose the level of protection you want to impose on the document and then you can choose to enter a password. A user then needs to enter this password to make the permitted editing or formatting changes to the document. For a higher level of security, you can use the new Information Rights Management feature to restrict access to documents and ensure that documents cannot be distributed to people who do not have rights to view the content. ▓▓▓▓ You make one more change to the document and protect the document against tracked changes so that any user who opens the document cannot accept or reject the new change you made.

STEPS

1. **Click the** Track Changes button 🗎 **to turn on the Track Changes feature, click immediately after** e-coupon **in the first paragraph, press [Spacebar], then type** redeemable for any book in our online store

2. **Click** Tools **on the menu bar, then click** Protect Document **to open the Protect Document task pane**

   In the Protect Document task pane, you can select the formatting and editing restrictions you want to place on the document.

3. **Click the** check box **in the Editing restrictions section of the Protect Document task pane, then click the** No changes (Read only) list arrow **to view the editing restrictions you can choose as shown in Figure O-17**

QUICK TIP

Passwords generally consist of letters and numbers in a combination that is almost impossible to decipher.

4. **Select** Tracked changes, **click** Yes, Start Enforcing Protection, **enter** mrk2$7# **as the password, press [Tab], type** mrk2$7# **again, then click** OK

   For security reasons, the password you entered appears as a series of bullets. Now that you have protected the document, the Track Changes button on the Reviewing toolbar is dimmed. With the document protected, users can no longer accept or reject changes unless they enter the password.

5. **Save and close the document, open** MediaLoft Online Survey_Final.doc, **then click the** Next button 🗎 **on the Reviewing toolbar**

   The tracked change is highlighted, but you cannot accept or reject the change because the document is protected.

6. **Click** Tools **on the menu bar, click** Unprotect Document, **type** mrk2$7#, **click** OK, **click the** Accept Change button 🗎, **then press [→] to deselect the text**

   With the document unprotected, you can again accept or reject changes.

7. **Save the document, print a copy, close the document, then exit Word**

Clues to Use

Understanding Information Rights Management (IRM)

You use the IRM feature when you want to specify exactly who can access a document and what activities they are authorized to perform. You can specify three access levels. Users with Read access can read the document, but they cannot edit, print, or copy the document. Users with **Change** access can read, edit, and save changes to a document, but they cannot print the document. Users with **Full Control** access can do anything with the document that the document author can do. By default, you have Full Control access to a document that you create. To specify an access level for a document, you click Restrict permission at the bottom of the Protect Document task pane or you click the Permission (Unrestricted Access) button 🗎 on the Standard toolbar. You will then be asked to install the Windows Rights Management client, which you use to set access levels. You can install the IRM client only if you have administrative rights to your computer.

FIGURE O-17: Protect Document task pane

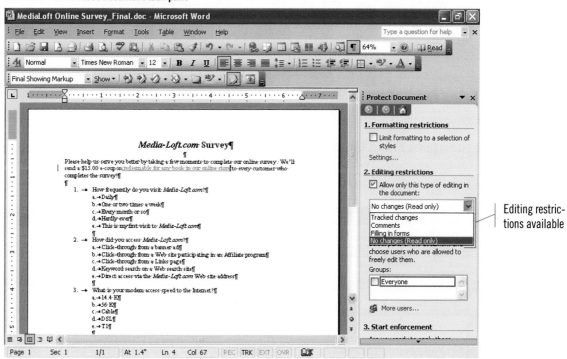

Editing restric-
tions available

Clues to Use

Obtaining and attaching a digital signature

You can authenticate yourself as the author of a document by inserting a digital signature. A **digital signature** is an electronic stamp
that you attach to a document to authenticate the document. The
highest-level digital signature is encryption-based and secure, which
assures the recipient that the document originated from the signer
and has not been altered. To obtain a secure digital signature, you
need to first obtain a digital certificate from a certificate authority
such as VeriSign, Inc. A digital certificate is an attachment for a file
that vouches for the authenticity of the file, provides secure encryption, or supplies a verifiable signature. You or your organization must
submit an application to obtain a digital certificate from a commer-
cial certification authority. You must obtain a digital certificate in
order to generate an authenticated digital signature.

To attach a digital signature, click Tools on the menu bar, click
Options, click the Security tab, click Digital Signatures, and then
click Add in the Digital Signatures dialog box. Read the message
boxes that open, clicking "Yes" or "OK" as needed to accept the
default certificate. Click View Certificate to see the default digital
certificate attached to your document. See Figure O-18.

FIGURE O-18: Digital Signature information

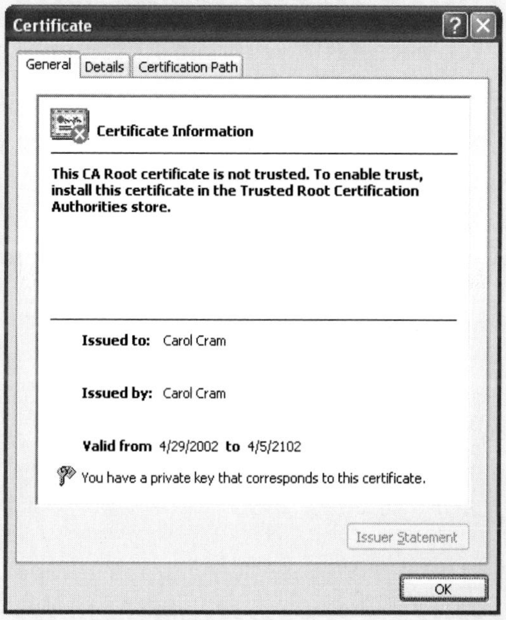

Certificate

General | Details | Certification Path

Certificate Information

**This CA Root certificate is not trusted. To enable trust,
install this certificate in the Trusted Root Certification
Authorities store.**

Issued to: Carol Cram

Issued by: Carol Cram

Valid from 4/29/2002 **to** 4/5/2102

You have a private key that corresponds to this certificate.

Issuer Statement

OK

Practice

▼ CONCEPTS REVIEW

Label each of the elements in Figure O-19.

FIGURE O-19

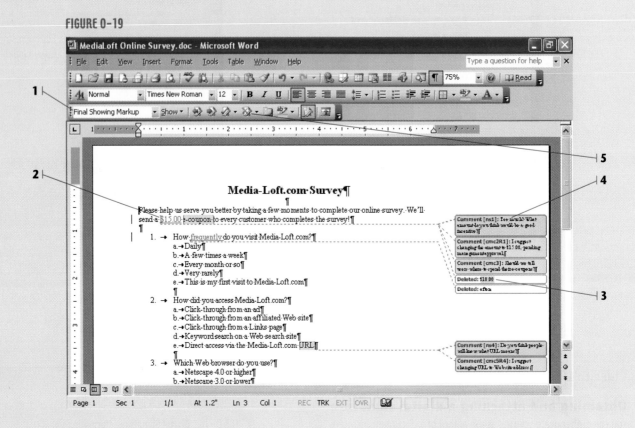

Match each term with the statement that best describes it.

6. Balloon
7. Next button
8. Original Showing Markup
9. Digital signature
10. Reviewing Pane
11. Tracked Changes dialog box

a. Use to move to another change
b. View that shows deleted text in strikethrough form
c. Contains a comment and appears in the right margin
d. Use to verify the identity of the person who created the document
e. Use to view comments at the bottom of the document window
f. Use to change the appearance of tracked changes.

Select the best answer from the list of choices.

12. **How are comments inserted by two or more individuals differentiated in a document?**
    a. The initials of the individual are inserted in the document next to the comment.
    b. The comment balloon is a different color for each individual.
    c. The comment balloon appears in a different location for each individual.
    d. The full name of the individual appears at the end of the comment text.

13. **Which view do you choose when you want the text of the document and the comment balloons to be visible on the screen at the same time?**
    a. Original Showing Markup view
    b. Final Showing Markup view
    c. Page Width view
    d. 100% view

14. **Where can you see the name of an individual associated with a specific comment?**
    a. In the Reviewing Pane
    b. In the comment balloon
    c. At the location where the comment was inserted
    d. In the Track Changes pane

15. **In Print Layout view, how is deleted text shown in the Final Showing Markup view?**
    a. As strikethrough text that ~~looks like this~~
    b. As bold and colored text in the document
    c. As double-underlined text in the document
    d. In a balloon along the right side of the document

16. **Which of the following merge options do you select when you want to display results in the target document?**
    a. Merge
    b. Merge into current document
    c. Merge into target document
    d. Merge into new document

17. **How do you e-mail document revisions to a colleague?**
    a. Select Mail Recipient from the Send To menu.
    b. Select Mail Recipient (for Review) from the Send To menu.
    c. Select Reviewers from the Show menu.
    d. Select Mail Reviewers from the File menu.

18. **How do you protect a document against tracked changes?**
    a. Select Document Protection from the File menu.
    b. Select Protect Document from the Edit menu.
    c. Select Protect Document from the Tools menu.
    d. Select Protect Document on the Safety tab in the Options dialog box.

19. **Which of the following statements best describes a digital signature?**
    a. It confirms that the document originated from the signer and has not been altered.
    b. It confirms that the document originated from a certification authority.
    c. It confirms that the document is password protected.
    d. It confirms that the document has been approved by VeriSign.

20. **Using the Information Rights Management (IRM) feature, which of the following permissions is *not* an option?**
    a. Read access
    b. Write access
    c. Full Control access
    d. Change access

▼ SKILLS REVIEW

1. **Include comments in a document.**
   a. Start Word, open the file WD O-4.doc from the drive and folder where your Data Files are located.
   b. Change the zoom to 90% or whatever value allows you to see the document and the comments without having to scroll horizontally, and then scroll vertically to view the two comments.
   c. Select **service** at the end of the second line in the Company Overview section, return to 100% view, then insert this comment: **We need to change this sentence to mention Demarco Designs.**

▼ SKILLS REVIEW (CONTINUED)

   d. Scroll to the end of the paragraph in the Company Background section, click in the comment, then insert a new comment with the text **Good idea.**

   e. Open the Reviewing Pane to view the names of the two reviewers.

   f. Close the Reviewing Pane.

   g. Save the file as **Design Signs Company Description.**

2. Track changes.

   a. Press [Ctrl][Home], then turn on Track Changes.

   b. Delete **no other design consultation services operates** in the first paragraph, then type **the only local competition comes from Demarco Designs, a small consulting firm that opened just three months ago**.

   c. Replace **objects d'art** at the end of the first paragraph with **collectibles**.

   d. Scroll down to the Expansion Plans section of the document, then replace **$50,000** with **$75,000.**

   e. Save the document.

3. Accept and reject changes.

   a. Change the Display for Review view to Original Showing Markup view, note the deletions made to the document, then return to Final Showing Markup view.

   b. Use the Reviewing toolbar to accept the changes in the first paragraph and to delete the comment associated with the first paragraph.

   c. Delete the comments associated with the Company Background paragraph. (*Hint*: Right-click a comment, then click Delete Comment on the shortcut menu.)

   d. Reject deleting the original amount of $50,000 and reject inserting $75,000 in the third paragraph.

   e. Save the document.

4. Create document versions.

   a. Save the active document as a version with the comment **Three new employees**. (*Note:* You will be able to save document versions only if you are saving to a hard drive.)

   b. Scroll to the Expansion Plans sections, then select the text **two apprentice designers and an administrative assistant** and type **three designers and an office manager**.

   c. Save the document as a version with the comment **Four new employees.**

   d. Accept all tracked changes, save the document, then close the document.

5. Compare documents and merge changes.

   a. Open the file WD O-5.doc from the drive and folder where your Data Files are located and save the document as **Design Signs_Donald**, open WD O-6.doc, then save it as **Design Signs_Julia**.

   b. Be sure Design Signs_Julia is the active document, then select Compare and Merge Documents from the Tools menu.

   c. Select the document Design Signs Company Description, click the Merge list arrow, then select Merge into a new document.

   d. With the new document the active document, select Compare and Merge Documents from the Tools menu, select Design Signs_Donald, then select Merge into current document. (Note: If a warning box appears, be sure Your Document is selected, then click Continue with Merge.)

   e. Show all the reviewers who have worked on the document. In addition to yourself, you'll see Donald Vogt and Julia Pirelli.

   f. Show changes by type: comments only, insertions and deletions only, formatting only, and then all three types again.

   g. Use the Reviewing toolbar to remove the following text: **a** before **an**, **consulting**, **three**, **antiques** and **ten**, and then delete all comments.

   h. Scroll to the bottom of the document, insert your name where indicated, then accept all the changes to the document.

   i. Reduce the top and bottom margins to **.5** so that all the text fits on one page.

   j. Save the document as **Design Signs_Final**, close the other Word documents so only Design Signs_Final is open.

6. Use Find and Replace options.

   a. Open the Find and Replace dialog box, select any text in the Find what text box and type **Design Signs**, expand the Find and Replace dialog box if necessary, then assign Italic formatting to the text in the Find what text box.

▼ SKILLS REVIEW (CONTINUED)

    b. Select any text in the Replace with text box and type **Design Signs**, then assign Bold Italic formatting to the text in the Replace with text box.

    c. Find and replace all instances of Design Signs formatted in Italic with Design Signs formatted in Bold and Italic.

    d. Click in the Find what text box, delete Design Signs, show the list of Special characters, select Manual Line Break, then clear the formatting assigned to text in the Find what text box. (*Hint*: Click the No Formatting button at the bottom of the Find and Replace dialog box.)

    e. Click in the Replace with text box, delete **Design Signs**, show the list of Special characters, select Paragraph Mark, then clear the formatting assigned to text in the Replace with text box.

    f. Find and replace all instances of a Manual Line Break with a Paragraph Mark. (*Note*: If a message box appears, click Yes to continue the search.)

    g. Close the Find and Replace dialog box, then save the document.

7. Protect documents.

    a. Turn on Track Changes, then delete **freelance** in the Company Background section.

    b. Protect the document for Tracked changes with the password **R2D3%12**.

    c. Save the document.

    d. Press [Ctrl][Home], then move to the tracked change and try to accept it.

    e. Unprotect the document with the **R2D3%12** password, then accept the change.

    f. Save the document, print a copy, close the document, then exit Word.

▼ INDEPENDENT CHALLENGE 1

You work for Adelphi Solutions, a large application service provider based in Durham, England. The company is sponsoring a conference called E-Business Solutions for local businesses interested in developing or enhancing their online presence. Two of your coworkers have been working on a preliminary schedule for the conference. They ask for your input.

    a. Start Word, open the file WD O-7.doc from the drive and folder where your Data Files are located, then save it as **E-Business Solutions Conference**.

    b. Save a version of the document with the comment **Changes by Mark and Winnifred**. (*Note*: You will be able to save document versions only if you are saving to a hard drive.)

    c. Scroll through the document to read the comments and view the changes made by Mark Smythe and Winnifred Reese.

    d. In the 9:00 to 10:00 entry, select E-Payment Systems, then insert a comment with the text **I suggest we change the name of this session to E-Cash in the New Millennium.**

    e. Be sure the Track Changes feature is active. In the 3:00 to 4:00 entry, delete the text Nirvana, and then type **Heaven**.

    f. Type your name where indicated at the bottom of the document, then accept all the changes, but do not delete the comments.

    g. Save a new version of the document with the comment **Changes by** followed by your name.

Advanced Challenge Exercise

    ■ Open the Versions dialog box, then delete the version with the comment Changes by Mark and Winnifred.

    ■ Open the version you created, then maximize the window containing the version. (*Note*: A new window opens containing the version.)

    ■ With Track Changes turned on, select the text **Library Building University of Durham**, then apply highlighting to the text.

    ■ Accept the formatting change you just made.

    ■ Save the document as **E-Business Solutions Conference ACE**. (*Hint*: Click the Save button to open the Save as dialog box.)

    h. Print a copy of the document, close all open Word files, and then exit Word.

▼ INDEPENDENT CHALLENGE 2

You work as an editor for Rex Harding, a freelance author currently writing a series of articles related to e-commerce. Rex sent you the first draft of his article titled **Web Security Issues**. You edited the article, then sent it back to Rex, who reviewed your changes, accepted or rejected them, inserted some new changes of his own, responded to some of your comments, and then added some new comments. You've just received this latest revision of the article. Now you need to review Rex's new changes and then prepare the final document. Rex has also asked you to use the Find and Replace feature to apply formatting to selected text included throughout the article.

a. Start Word, open the file WD O-8.doc from the drive and folder where your Data Files are located, then save it as **Web Security Issues Article**.

b. Turn on Track Changes, then scroll through the document to get a feeling for its contents.

c. Open the Reviewing Pane. Notice there were two reviewers—Rex and you, as indicated by Your Name in the Reviewing Pane. Close the Reviewing Pane.

d. Find and accept the first change (the formatting of Rex's name as the author of the article at the top of the document).

FIGURE O-20

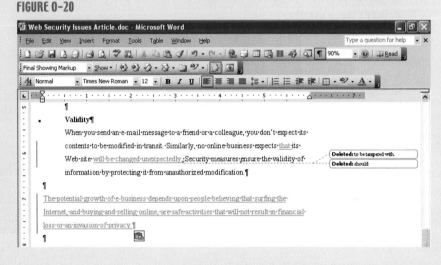

e. Move to the first comment, read it, delete it, then move to the next comment and delete it. As requested in the comments, move the last sentence in paragraph 1 to the end of the article (following the paragraph on Validity), as shown in Figure O-20. (*Note*: As you cut and paste text, the text is tracked as a change. You will accept the change later.)

f. Move to the comment that states Could you switch the Protection and Access Control sections?, then perform the action requested. (*Hint*: Select the Protection section (including the heading), press [Ctrl][X], click to the left of the Access Control section, then press [Ctrl][V].)

g. Accept all the remaining changes in the document, delete all the comments from the document, then turn off the Track Changes feature.

h. Scroll to the top of the document, then use the Find and Replace feature to find all instances of **Web** and replace it with **Web** formatted in Italic. You should make nine replacements.

i. Clear formatting assigned to the text in the Replace with text box, and then close the Find and Replace dialog box.

Advanced Challenge Exercise

- Click Show on the Reviewing toolbar, then click Options.
- Change Markup options as follows: Double-underline for insertions and Italic for deletions.
- Change the width of the comment balloons to 1".
- Show balloons in the Left margin, then close the Track Changes dialog box.
- Turn on track changes, select harm in the second sentence and add the comment **Should we also mention financial harm?**
- Select the word harm in the last sentence of the introduction (in the phrase from potential harm or failure), and change it to **danger**.
- Switch to the Original Showing Markup view to verify that harm appears in italic, then switch back to Final Showing Markup view.
- Print a copy of the document, then reject the change you just made and delete the comment.
- Open the Track Changes dialog box again and return the settings to their defaults: Underline for insertions, Strikethrough for Deletions, and 2.5" balloon width appearing in the right margin.

j. Create a header that includes your name and the date, proofread the document making formatting changes as needed, save the document, print a copy, close the document, then exit Word.

▼ INDEPENDENT CHALLENGE 3

The Southern Alps Institute in Wanaka, New Zealand, offers teens and young adults courses in various winter and summer mountain sports. As the course programmer, you are responsible for approving all the course descriptions included on the school's Web site. Three of your colleagues, Malcolm Pascal, Teresa Lopez, and Gregg Luecke have each revised descriptions of the three summer courses offered at the school. You use the Compare and Merge Documents feature to merge the documents so that you can see the changes made by the reviewers. You review the changes and add some additional changes. Finally, you protect the document so that only you or your colleagues with access to your password may accept or reject your changes.

a. Start Word, open these files from the drive and folder where your Data Files are located, then save them as indicated: WD O-9.doc as **Summer Courses_Malcolm**, WD O-10.doc as **Summer Courses_Teresa**, and WD O-11.doc as **Summer Courses_Gregg**.

b. Use the Compare Documents and Merge feature to merge the Summer Courses_Malcolm (target file) and the Summer Courses_Gregg (active) documents into the current document (accept the default setting to keep formatting changes from your document), then merge Summer Courses_Teresa into a new document (again, accept the default to keep the formatting changes from your document).

c. Review the changes in the merged version of the document.

d. Accept all the changes and delete any comments, then save the document as **Summer Courses_Final**.

e. If you have e-mail capability, e-mail this revision to yourself and then continue revising the e-mailed document; otherwise, continue revising the current document.

f. Be sure the Track Changes feature is active, then change the name of the Mountaineering Course to **Wilderness Survival**.

g. Password protect the document for Tracked Changes with a password of your choice, then try to accept the tracked change to verify that the file is protected.

h. Unprotect the document, then accept the changes.

i. Add a digital signature, if available.

j. Create a header containing your name and the date, save the document, print a copy, close all documents without saving changes, then exit Word.

▼ INDEPENDENT CHALLENGE 4

You are thinking about launching a small business that sells a product or service of your choice. As part of your start-up, you decide to find out more about digital signatures and digital certificates.

a. Open your Web browser and conduct a search for information on digital signatures and digital certificates. You can try entering the keywords **digital signature definition** and **digital certificate definition**.

b. Start Word, open the file WD O-12.doc from the drive and folder where your Data Files are located, then save it as **Digital Signatures**.

c. Use information from the Web sites you accessed as well as the Word Help system to answer the questions.

d. Type your name and the current date in the header section.

e. Close your browser when you have completed your research.

f. Print a copy of the Word document, close the document, then exit Word.

▼ VISUAL WORKSHOP

You work for a company called Paradise Found that sells gardening supplies and plants. Your coworker has prepared a mission statement for the company and she asks you to edit it. Open the file WD O-13.doc, then save it as **Paradise Found Mission Statement**. Turn on the Track Changes feature, then insert comments and add changes so that the edited mission statement appears as shown in Figure O-21. Ensure that your name and the current date appear in the footer, save the document, print a copy, then close the document.

FIGURE O-21

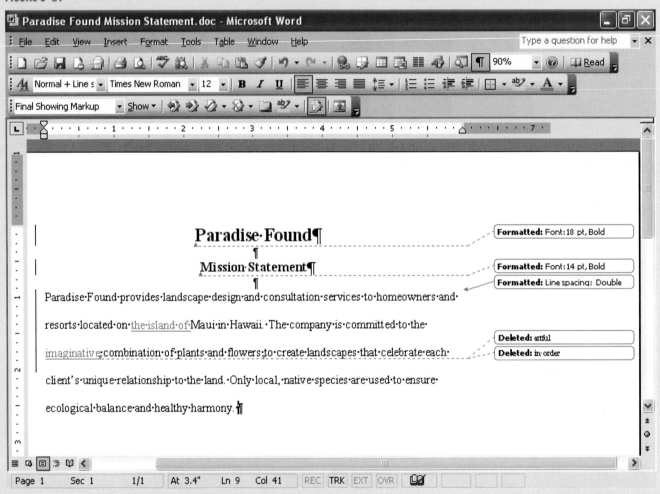

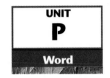

UNIT P
Word

Customizing Word

OBJECTIVES

Plan a macro
Create a macro
Run a macro
Edit a macro in Visual Basic
Rename, delete, and copy macros
Create a custom toolbar
Customize menus
Modify options
Summarize content using automated tools

If you have a SAM user profile, you may have access to hands-on instruction, practice, and assessment of the skills covered in this unit. Log in to your SAM account and go to your assignments page to see what your instructor has assigned.

You can customize Word to suit your working style by creating macros to automate a series of tasks and procedures that you perform frequently, selecting only the options you use frequently on customized toolbars and menus, and even changing default options such as measurement units and custom dictionaries. Finally, you can use the AutoSummarize feature to examine a document, highlight the main points, and even create a summary. Graham Watson in the Marketing Department at MediaLoft has asked you to produce a booklet containing excerpts from novels featured at book signing events. You have already received excerpts from several authors, but each excerpt is formatted differently. You decide to create a macro to automate the formatting and saving tasks. Then you modify menus and default settings to help you work more efficiently. Finally, you use the AutoSummarize feature to quickly summarize the contents of a guidelines document.

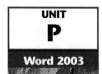

Planning a Macro

If you perform a task repeatedly in Microsoft Word, you can automate the task by using a macro. A **macro** is a series of Word commands and instructions that you group together as a single command to accomplish a task automatically. You create a macro when you want to quickly perform multiple tasks usually by clicking a button or using a shortcut key. For example, you can create a macro that inserts a table with a specific number of rows and columns and with a particular border style, or you can create a macro to perform a series of complex tasks that involve multiple keystrokes. You want to create a macro to format each book excerpt document consistently, enter a title at the top of each document, and then save and close each document. You carefully plan the steps you will perform to create the macro.

DETAILS

- **Macro tasks**

  When planning a macro, the first step is to determine the tasks you want the macro to accomplish. For example, the macro could apply consistent formatting such as size, text wrapping, and borders to a series of graphics in a document, insert a fill-in text field so you can enter a caption for each graphic, and then perform commands such as saving, printing, and closing the document. Table P-1 lists all the tasks that you want your macro to perform when you open a document containing a book excerpt.

- **Macro steps**

  Table P-1 also lists all the steps required to accomplish each task. You plan and practice these steps before you create a macro so that you can perform the steps without error when you create the macro. If you make an error while recording the steps in the macro, you usually need to stop recording and start over because the recorded macro will include not only the correct steps but also the errors. By rehearsing the steps required before recording the macro, you ensure accuracy. While recording a macro, you can only use keystrokes or mouse clicks to complete all the macro steps, except selecting text. To select all the text in a document, you use the [Ctrl][A] or Edit, Select All commands. To select just a portion of text, first you use arrow keys to move the insertion point to the text, then you press the [F8] key to turn on select mode, and finally you use arrow keys to select the required text.

- **Macro information**

  Once you have practiced the steps required for the macro, you are ready to determine the information related to the macro. Figure P-1 shows the Record Macro dialog box. You use this dialog box to name the macro, assign the macro to a button to be placed on a toolbar or to a keyboard shortcut, and enter a short description of the macro. This description is usually a summary of the tasks the macro will perform. You also use this dialog box to assign the location where the macro should be stored. The default location is in the Normal template so that the macro is accessible in all documents that use the Normal template. The date and name of the person who created the macro appear in the description section. The name of the person is based on the user information listed on the User Information tab in the Options dialog box.

- **Record macro procedure**

  When you click OK after completing the Record Macro dialog box, the Stop Recording toolbar opens, as shown in Figure P-2. The buttons on the Stop Recording toolbar are toggle buttons. You click the Pause button if you want to pause recording temporarily to fix an error; you click the Stop button when you have completed all the steps required for the macro. You must click the Stop button before you close the Stop Recording toolbar because simply closing the toolbar does not stop the macro recording function.

FIGURE P-1: Record Macro dialog box

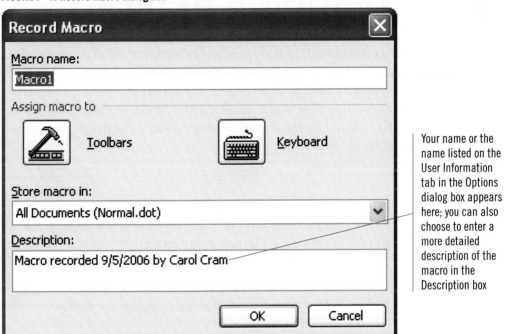

Your name or the name listed on the User Information tab in the Options dialog box appears here; you can also choose to enter a more detailed description of the macro in the Description box

FIGURE P-2: Stop Recording toolbar

Toolbar options list arrow

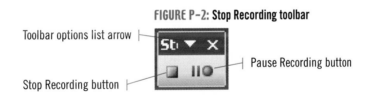

Pause Recording button

Stop Recording button

TABLE P-1: Macro tasks and steps to complete the tasks

tasks	steps
Select all the text	Press [Ctrl][A]
Change the line spacing to 1.5 lines	Click Format on the menu bar, click Paragraph, click the Line spacing list arrow, click 1.5 lines, click OK
Select the Comic Sans MS font and 14 pt	Click Format on the menu bar, click Font, select the Comic Sans MS font, select 14 pt, click OK
Insert a fill-in field text box into which a page title can be typed	Press [↑] once to deselect the text and move to the top of the document, click Insert on the menu bar, click Field, scroll down the list of Field names, click Fill-in, click OK, click OK
Save and close the document	Click the Save button, click File on the menu bar, click Close

Creating a Macro

You can create a macro by using the macro recorder or by entering codes into the Visual Basic Editor. For most routine macros, you use the macro recorder. For complex macros, you use the Visual Basic Editor and enter macro steps as a series of Visual Basic codes. In this lesson, you use the macro recorder to create a macro. The macro recorder actually records each step you perform as a sequence of Visual Basic codes. ▓▓▓▓ Now that you have planned the macro, you are ready to create and record the macro steps. You create the macro in a new blank document.

STEPS

QUICK TIP
You create the macro in its own blank document so that if you make errors, you do not affect the formatting of a completed document.

1. **Start Word, close the Getting Started task pane, verify that the** Show/Hide ¶ button ▐¶▌ **on the Standard toolbar is selected, save the blank document as** Macro Setup **to the drive and folder where your Data Files are located, then press** [Enter] **four times**

   With the paragraph marks visible, you can see the formatting changes you make as part of your macro steps.

2. **Click** Tools **on the menu bar, point to** Macro, **then click** Record New Macro

   The Record Macro dialog box opens. In this dialog box, you enter information about the macro, including the name, the location where you want to store the macro, and a description.

3. **Type** FormatExcerpts, **then press** [Tab] **three times to move to the Store macro in list box**

   You can store the macro in the Normal.dot template so that it is available to all new documents or you can store the macro in the current document. Since you want the new macro to format several different documents, you accept the default storage location, which is the Normal.dot template.

4. **Press** [Tab] **to move to the Description box, then type the description shown in Figure P-3**

   By default, the Description box contains the name of the person who is recording the macro and the date the macro is recorded. You can keep this information, you can add to it, or you can overwrite it as you did in Step 4.

5. **Click** OK

   The Stop Recording toolbar opens, the pointer changes to ▐▓, which indicates that you are in record macro mode.

6. **Press** [Ctrl][A], **click** Format **on the menu bar, click** Paragraph, **click the** Line spacing list arrow, **click** 1.5 lines, **then click** OK

   The line spacing between the paragraph marks changes to 1.5 spacing.

7. **Click** Format **on the menu bar, click** Font, **select the** Comic Sans MS **font, select** 14 pt, **then click** OK

   The size of the paragraph marks changes to show 14 pt Comic Sans MS.

8. **Press** [↑] **once to move to the top of the document, click** Insert **on the menu bar, click** Field, **select** Fill-in **from the list of Field names, then click** OK

   A fill-in field text box appears, as shown in Figure P-4. If necessary, you can move the Fill-in Text box so that the Stop Recording toolbar is still visible. When you run the macro, you will enter text in the fill-in field text box.

QUICK TIP
You should no longer see ▐▓.

9. **Click** OK, **click the** Save button ▐▌ **on the Standard toolbar, click** File **on the menu bar, click** Close, **then click the** Stop Recording button ▐▌ **on the Stop Recording toolbar**

   The Macro Setup file is saved and closed. The macro steps are completed and the Stop Recording toolbar closes. When you run the macro on a document that you open, the Save command saves the document with the filename already assigned to it. When you run the macro on a document that has not been saved, the Save command opens the Save As dialog box so that you can enter a filename in the File name text box, click Save, and then continue running the macro.

FIGURE P-3: Description entered in the Record Macro dialog box

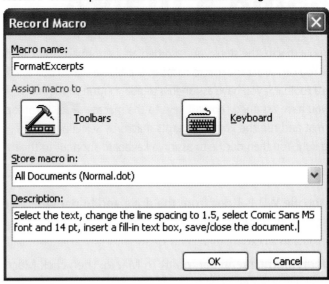

Stop Recording toolbar

FIGURE P-4: Fill-in field text box

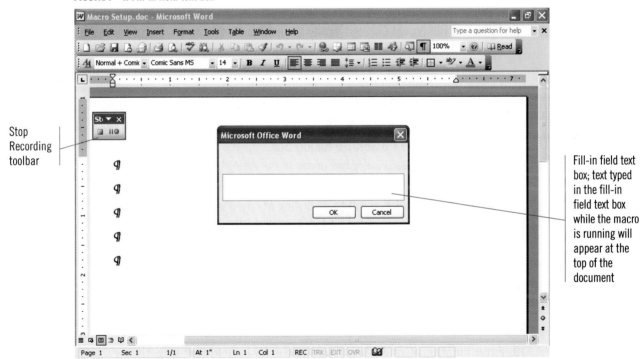

Fill-in field text box; text typed in the fill-in field text box while the macro is running will appear at the top of the document

Running a Macro

When you run a macro, the steps you recorded are performed. You can choose to run a macro in three different ways. You can select the macro name in the Macro dialog box and click the Run button, you can click a button on a toolbar if you have assigned a toolbar button to the macro, or you can press a keystroke combination if you have assigned shortcut keys to the macro. ░▓▓▒▒ You open one of the novel excerpts you want to format and run the FormatExcerpts macro by selecting the macro name in the Macro dialog box and clicking Run. You then decide to assign a keyboard shortcut to the macro.

STEPS

TROUBLE
The document contains spelling errors that you will correct later.

1. **Open the file** WD P-1.doc **from the drive and folder where your Data Files are located, then save it as** Novel Excerpt_Emily Chow

   The file contains an excerpt from Emily Chow's new novel *Dragon Swindle*.

2. **Click** Tools **on the menu bar, point to** Macro, **then click** Macros

   The Macros dialog box opens. In this dialog box, you select a macro and then the action you want to perform such as running, editing, or deleting the macro. The FormatExcerpts macro is listed, as well as any other macros that other users created in the Normal template. The name of the macro selected in the list box appears in the Macro name text box.

3. **Be sure** FormatExcerpts **is selected, then click** Run

   The macro selects all the text, changes the line spacing to 1.5, selects the Comic Sans MS font and 14 pt, then opens a fill-in field text box.

4. **Type** Emily Chow's Dragon Swindle **in the fill-in field text box, then click** OK,

   The macro saves and then closes the document.

TROUBLE
If the title is not shaded, your computer is not set to display field shading. You display field shading by selecting options on the View tab of the Options dialog box.

5. **Open the file** Novel Excerpt_Emily Chow.doc **from the drive and folder where your Data Files are located, then compare it to Figure P-5**

   The text you entered in the fill-in field text box appears at the top of the page. The document text uses 1.5 line spacing and 14-pt Comic Sans MS. The title text you typed appears shaded because you entered it in a fill-in field text box. The shading will not appear in the printed document.

6. **Close the document, click** Tools **on the menu bar, click** Customize, **then click** Keyboard **at the bottom of the Customize dialog box**

   The Customize Keyboard dialog box opens. In this dialog box, you can assign a keystroke combination to a macro or you can create a button for the macro and identify on which toolbar to place the button.

7. **In the Categories list, scroll to and click** Macros, **verify that** FormatExcerpts **is selected, click in the** Press new shortcut key **text box, then press** [Alt][E]

   Figure P-6 shows the settings assigned to the FormatExcerpts macro to create a keyboard shortcut.

8. **Click** Assign, **click** Close, **then click** Close

9. **Open the file** WD P-2.doc **from the drive and folder where your Data Files are located, save it as** Novel Excerpt_Jonathon Grant, **then press** [Alt][E]

   The macro runs to the point where the fill-in field text box appears.

10. **Enter** Jonathon Grant's Sea Swept **in the fill-in field text box, then click** OK

    The macro saves and closes the document.

FIGURE P-5: Document formatted with the FormatExcerpts macro

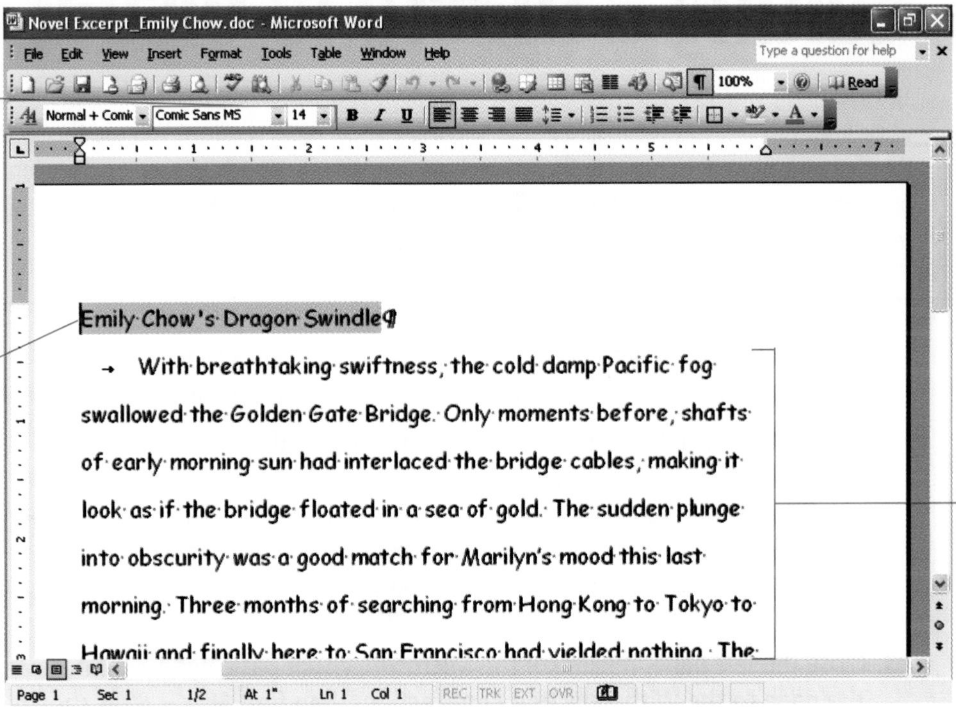

Comic Sans
MS font
and 14 pt
formatting
applied
to text

Title created
by entering
text in the
Fill-in field
text box

1.5 line spacing
applied

FIGURE P-6: Customize Keyboard dialog box

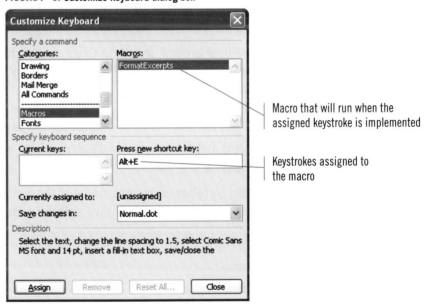

Macro that will run when the
assigned keystroke is implemented

Keystrokes assigned to
the macro

Editing a Macro in Visual Basic

You can make changes to a macro in two ways. First, you can delete the macro and record the steps again, or second, you can edit the macro in the Microsoft Visual Basic window. You use the second method when the change you want to make to the macro is relatively minor—such as changing the font style or font size, or removing one of the commands. You decide to increase the font size that the macro applies to text from 14 pt to 16 pt and then remove the close document command.

STEPS

1. **Click** Tools **on the menu bar, point to** Macro, **then click** Macros
   The FormatExcerpts macro appears in the list of available macros in the Macros dialog box.

2. **Verify that** FormatExcerpts **is selected, then click** Edit
   The Microsoft Visual Basic window opens. The green text in the right pane is the description of the macro you entered when you created the macro. A list of codes appears in the right pane below the description. These codes were created as you recorded the steps for the FormatExcerpts macro. The text that appears to the left of the equal sign represents the code for a specific attribute such as SpaceBefore or KeepWithNext. The text to the right of the equal sign represents the attribute setting.

3. **Close the left pane, maximize the Microsoft Visual Basic window if necessary, scroll down the page to the With Selection.Font section, then find** Size = 14 **as shown in Figure P-7**

4. **Select** 14, **then type** 16

5. **Scroll down to the last End With section, then find** ActiveDocument.Close **shown in Figure P-8**

6. **Select the** ActiveDocument.Close **command, then press** [Delete]
   With the Close document code removed from the Visual Basic window, the macro will no longer close the document after saving it.

7. **Click the** Save Normal button ⊟ **on the Standard toolbar in the Microsoft Visual Basic window, then click the** View Microsoft Word button 🖾 **on the Standard toolbar**

8. **Open the file** Novel Excerpt_Jonathon Grant.doc **from the drive and folder where your Data Files are located, press** [Alt][E] **to run the macro, then click** Cancel **to close the fill-in field text box**
   The second time you run the macro you don't need to enter a title in the fill-in field text box. The font size of the document is now increased to 16 pt and the document is saved, but not closed.

9. **Click** Microsoft Visual Basic **on the taskbar, then click the** Close **button on the Microsoft Visual Basic window title bar**

10. **Type** Formatted by **followed by your name at the bottom of the Novel Excerpt_Jonathon Grant document, print a copy, then save and close the document**

Clues to Use

Locating Visual Basic codes

Sometimes you might want to insert a Visual Basic code into a macro. You find the correct code by searching Microsoft Visual Basic Help. To access Help, click Tools on the menu bar, point to Macro, click Visual Basic Editor, then click the Microsoft Visual Basic Help button on the Standard toolbar in the Microsoft Visual Basic window. You may then be prompted to install the required Help files. The Visual Basic Help task pane opens, which includes a Table of Contents and a Search feature. You use the Table of Contents to select links to various topics and you use the Search feature to generate a list of links to information about a specific action you want to perform. To use the Search feature, you type a brief description of the action you want to perform and then search for the required codes. Once you have found the code you want to use, you must paste the code above the "End Sub" code and either above or below any of the codes related to other tasks. All codes related to a specific task, such as format paragraph spacing, must stay together in their own sections.

FIGURE P-7: Font size code in Visual Basic

With Selection.Font section

Code to change the font size

All codes in this section relate to font selection attributes

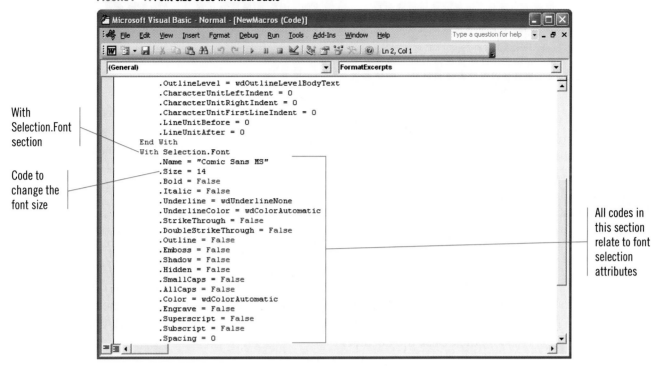

```
            .OutlineLevel = wdOutlineLevelBodyText
            .CharacterUnitLeftIndent = 0
            .CharacterUnitRightIndent = 0
            .CharacterUnitFirstLineIndent = 0
            .LineUnitBefore = 0
            .LineUnitAfter = 0
        End With
    With Selection.Font
            .Name = "Comic Sans MS"
            .Size = 14
            .Bold = False
            .Italic = False
            .Underline = wdUnderlineNone
            .UnderlineColor = wdColorAutomatic
            .StrikeThrough = False
            .DoubleStrikeThrough = False
            .Outline = False
            .Emboss = False
            .Shadow = False
            .Hidden = False
            .SmallCaps = False
            .AllCaps = False
            .Color = wdColorAutomatic
            .Engrave = False
            .Superscript = False
            .Subscript = False
            .Spacing = 0
```

FIGURE P-8: ActiveDocument.Close code in Visual Basic

Save Normal button

View Microsoft Word button

Code to save the active document

Code to close the active document

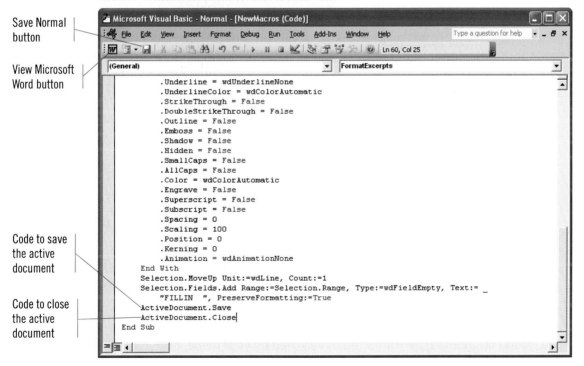

```
            .Underline = wdUnderlineNone
            .UnderlineColor = wdColorAutomatic
            .StrikeThrough = False
            .DoubleStrikeThrough = False
            .Outline = False
            .Emboss = False
            .Shadow = False
            .Hidden = False
            .SmallCaps = False
            .AllCaps = False
            .Color = wdColorAutomatic
            .Engrave = False
            .Superscript = False
            .Subscript = False
            .Spacing = 0
            .Scaling = 100
            .Position = 0
            .Kerning = 0
            .Animation = wdAnimationNone
        End With
    Selection.MoveUp Unit:=wdLine, Count:=1
    Selection.Fields.Add Range:=Selection.Range, Type:=wdFieldEmpty, Text:= _
        "FILLIN ", PreserveFormatting:=True
    ActiveDocument.Save
    ActiveDocument.Close
End Sub
```

Renaming, Deleting, and Copying Macros

If you save a macro in the current document, you can choose to copy the macro to other documents in which you wish to run the macro. You can also choose to copy the macro to the Normal.dot template so that the macro is available to all documents. You use the Organizer dialog box to copy macros from one document to another document. ▰▰▰ Graham Watson, your supervisor, asks you to use a different macro to format the novel excerpts. He sends you a document containing a new macro, which you copy to an unformatted novel excerpt

STEPS

QUICK TIP

If the security setting was not Medium when you opened the Security dialog box, you can return to the original security setting when you have completed this lesson.

1. **Click Tools, point to Macro, click Security, then click the Medium option button**

   With the security level set to Medium, you can choose whether or not to open documents containing macros.

2. **Click OK, open the file WD P-3.doc from the drive and folder where your Data Files are located, click Enable Macros when the Security Warning appears, save the document as Novel Excerpt Macro, open the file WD P-4.doc, save it as Novel Excerpt_Charles Sheldon, then close the document**

   The Novel Excerpt Macro document is the active document. You will copy the macro from the Novel Excerpt Macro document to the Novel Excerpt_Charles Sheldon document.

3. **Click Tools on the menu bar, point to Macro, click Macros, then click Organizer**

   In the Organizer dialog box, shown in Figure P-9, you copy macros from a source file to a target file.

QUICK TIP

If you save your solution files in a location that is different from where your Data Files are located, navigate to that location.

4. **Click Close File under the right-hand list in the Organizer dialog box, click Open File, navigate to the drive and folder where your Data Files are located, click the Files of type list arrow, click All Word Documents, click Novel Excerpt_Charles Sheldon.doc, then click Open**

5. **Be sure NewMacros is selected in the list box on the left (see Figure P-9), click Copy, click Close in the lower right corner of the Organizer dialog box, then click Yes to save the document**

6. **Close the Novel Excerpt Macro document, open Novel Excerpt_Charles Sheldon.doc, click Enable Macros, click Tools on the menu bar, point to Macro, click Macros, select NovelExcerptMacro, then click Run**

   The macro formats the text with 1.5 line spacing and 14-pt Arial Narrow, and then saves the document.

7. **Press [Alt][E], type Charles Sheldon's Spade Murders, then click OK**

   The original FormatExcerpts macro reformats the document.

8. **Click Tools on the menu bar, point to Macro, click Macros, click NovelExcerptMacro, click Delete, then click Yes**

9. **Click FormatExcerpts, click Edit, replace FormatExcerpts in two places with Book (see Figure P-10), then click the Close button on the Microsoft Visual Basic title bar to close Microsoft Visual Basic and return to Word**

   The FormatExcerpts macro is renamed Book.

10. **Press [Ctrl][End], type Formatted by followed by your name, print a copy, then save and close the document**

FIGURE P-9: Organizer dialog box

Source file (file to copy macro from)

Target file (file to copy macro to)

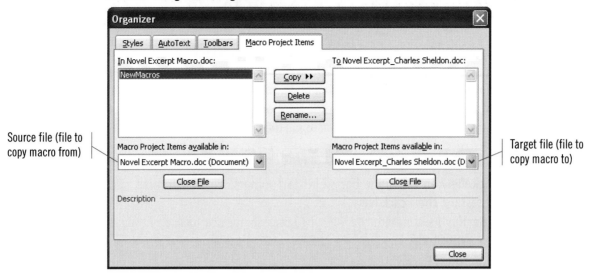

FIGURE P-10: Renaming the macro in Visual Basic

Book entered here

Book entered here

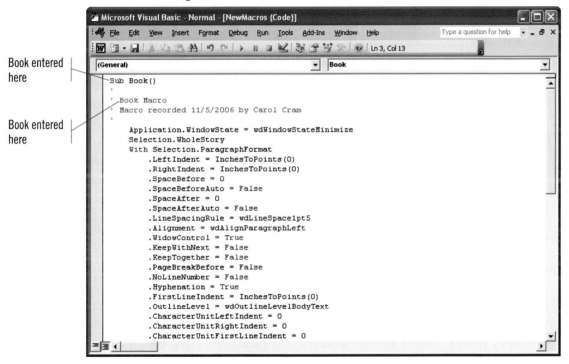

Clues to Use

Setting security levels

If you frequently receive documents containing macros, you might need to change the security level, depending on the source of the macros. A macro can introduce a virus into your system. As a result, you want to ensure that any macro included with documents you open in Word are created by sources you trust. You can select three security levels. A High security level (the default setting) allows you to open only digitally signed macros from trusted sources. Any macro that is not digitally signed will be automatically disabled. A Medium security level provides you with a prompt when you open a document containing a macro. You can then choose to enable or disable the macros. A Low security level accepts any document containing any number of macros, and you are not protected from unsafe macros.

Creating a Custom Toolbar

You can create a custom toolbar that contains only the buttons you want to use to perform a specific number of tasks. The custom toolbar can include a button that you click to run a macro, along with buttons for other functions such as checking spelling or drawing an AutoShape. You decide to create a toolbar that includes a button to count the words in the document, a button to add an outside border at the position of the insertion point, and a button to run the Book macro.

STEPS

1. **Click** View **on the menu bar, point to** Toolbars, **click** Customize, **click the** Toolbars tab **if necessary, then click** New

   In the New Toolbar dialog box, you type a name for the new toolbar and you assign a location in which to store the toolbar.

2. **Type** Novel Excerpts, **then click** OK

   The new toolbar appears next to the Customize dialog box and contains no buttons.

3. **Click the** Commands tab **in the Customize dialog box, select** Tools **in the Categories list, scroll down the list of commands, click** Word Count, **then drag** Word Count **to the Novel Excerpts toolbar as shown in Figure P-11**

   The I-beam shows where the command you are dragging to the toolbar will be placed.

4. **Scroll down the Categories list, click** Borders, **scroll down the Commands list, click** Outside Borders, **then drag the** Outside Borders **button to the Novel Excerpts toolbar**

5. **Scroll down the Categories list, click** Macros, **click** Normal.NewMacros.Book **in the Commands list, then drag** Normal.NewMacros.Book **to the Novel Excerpts toolbar**

6. **Click** Modify Selection **in the Customize dialog box, point to** Change Button Image, **click the** red diamond **shape, click** Modify Selection, **click** Text Only (in Menus), **click** Close **to close the Customize dialog box, then click the** New Blank Document button 🗋 **on the Standard toolbar**

   The selections on the Novel Excerpts toolbar are activated as shown in Figure P-12.

7. **Close the new document without saving it, open the file** Novel Excerpt_Emily Chow.doc **from the drive and folder where your Data Files are located, then click** Word Count **on the Novel Excerpts toolbar**

   The Word Count dialog box opens, as shown in Figure P-13.

8. **Click** Close **to close the Word Count dialog box, click the** red diamond **on the Novel Excerpts toolbar to run the macro, click** Cancel **to close the fill-in field text box, select** Emily Chow's Dragon Swindle **including the paragraph mark, click the** Outside Border button 🔲 **on the Novel Excerpts toolbar, click anywhere in the first paragraph, save the document, then compare it to Figure P-14**

9. **Click** View **on the menu bar, point to** Toolbars, **click** Customize, **click the** Toolbars tab, **scroll to the bottom of the list to view** Novel Excerpts, **click the** check box **to deselect it, click** Delete, **click** OK, **then click** Close

   The customized toolbar is deleted. Next, you delete the macros you created.

10. **Click** Tools, **point to** Macro, **click** Macros, **select** Book **if necessary, click** Delete, **click** Yes, **then close the dialog box**

FIGURE P-11: Word Count dragged to the Novel Excerpts toolbar

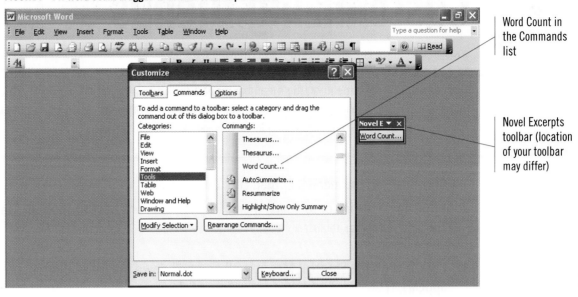

Word Count in the Commands list

Novel Excerpts toolbar (location of your toolbar may differ)

FIGURE P-12: Novel Excerpts custom toolbar

Your toolbar buttons may appear in a different order

FIGURE P-13: Word Count dialog box

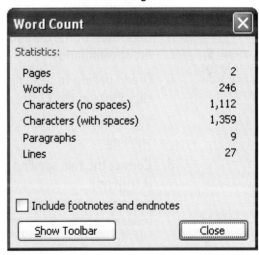

FIGURE P-14: Title enhanced with an outside border

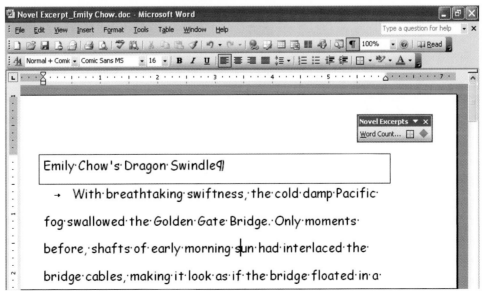

Customizing Menus

You can customize any menu in Word by removing commands, by renaming commands, and by displaying an icon and text for a command. You can also copy a command from one menu to another menu. You can choose to customize a menu on the menu bar, or you can customize a shortcut menu. ████ You decide that you want the Spelling command to appear on the shortcut menu when you right-click the mouse. Then you can quickly check the spelling in each novel excerpt you format.

STEPS

1. **Click Tools on the menu bar, then click Customize**

2. **Scroll down the list of toolbars, then click the check box next to Shortcut Menus**
   The Shortcut Menus toolbar appears, as shown in Figure P-15. You can modify Text, Table, and Draw shortcut menus.

3. **Click Text on the Shortcut Menus toolbar, scroll down the list of shortcut menus that appears, then click Text as shown in Figure P-16**
   The Text shortcut menu appears when you right-click a line of text.

4. **Drag the Customize dialog box title bar as needed so you can see the Commands tab, then click the Commands tab in the Customize dialog box**

QUICK TIP
Be sure to select Spelling, not Spelling and Grammar, in the list of commands.

5. **Click Tools in the Categories list, scroll down the Commands list, then click Spelling in the list of commands**

6. **Drag Spelling to below Hyperlink in the shortcut menu as shown in Figure P-17, then click Close in the Customize dialog box**

7. **Right-click anywhere in the document to show the modified shortcut menu, then click Spelling**

8. **Correct the two spelling errors ("sholders" and "radioe"), save the document, then press [Ctrl][End]**
   Notice that the word "copyright" at the bottom of the document is misspelled as COPYWRIGHT. That is because one of the default options in Word is to not check the spelling of a word if it is in all uppercase letters. You will change the option setting and correct this spelling error in the next lesson.

FIGURE P-15: Shortcut Menus toolbar

Shortcut Menus toolbar

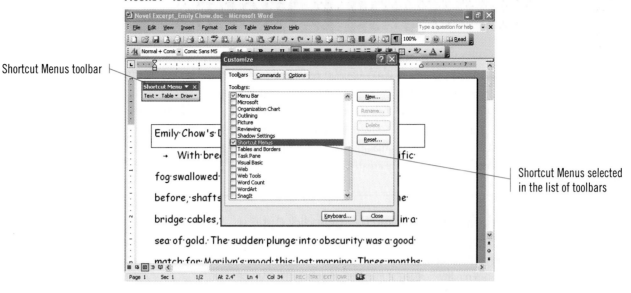

Shortcut Menus selected
in the list of toolbars

FIGURE P-16: Text shortcut menu selected

FIGURE P-17: Spelling added to the Text shortcut menu

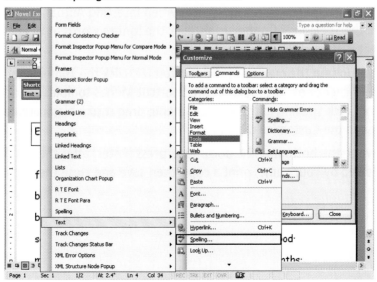

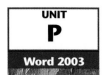

Modifying Options

Word includes many default settings designed to meet the needs of most users. For example, the default setting for entering text is black text on a white background. You can change this default to enter text another way, such as white text on a blue background. You modify default settings by selecting or deselecting options in the Options dialog box from the Tools menu. After working with Word for several months, you have identified some default options that do not suit your working style. You decide to change these options in the Options dialog box. First, you modify one of the Spelling options and then you deselect the option that automatically creates a drawing canvas each time you insert an AutoShape.

1. **Click Tools on the menu bar, then click Options**

   In the Options dialog box, you can change settings in eleven categories. For example, you can enter new information via the User Information tab, you can change the location where files are stored via the File Locations tab, and you can modify how a document is printed via the Print tab.

2. **Click the Spelling & Grammar tab, then click the Ignore words in UPPERCASE check box to deselect it**

   Now when you use the Spelling command to check the spelling of a document, Word will check the spelling of words entered in uppercase.

3. **Click the General tab, click the Automatically create drawing canvas when inserting AutoShapes check box to deselect it, then click OK**

   Now you can draw an AutoShape independent of the drawing canvas—something you often need to do when you want to draw just one AutoShape such as a horizontal line or a small geometric shape.

4. **Right-click anywhere in the document, click Spelling, then change COPYWRIGHT to the correct spelling—COPYRIGHT**

5. **Move to the top of the document, show the Drawing toolbar if necessary, click AutoShapes on the Drawing toolbar, point to Callouts, click the Rounded Rectangular Callout, then draw a callout shape as shown in Figure P-18**

6. **Type Nominated for Mystery Book of the Year!, then enhance the text with Bold, center the text, then size and position the callout shape (see Figure P-19)**

   If you are working on a computer that other users access, you should restore the default options and remove the Spelling command from the shortcut menu.

7. **Click outside the callout shape, click Tools on the menu bar, click Options, click the Automatically create drawing canvas when inserting AutoShapes check box to select it, click the Spelling & Grammar tab, click the Ignore words in UPPERCASE check box to select it, then click OK**

8. **Click Tools on the menu bar, click Customize, click the Toolbars tab, click the Shortcut Menus check box, click Text on the Shortcut Menus toolbar, select the Text shortcut menu, click Spelling in the shortcut menu, drag it to a blank area of the screen, then click Close in the Customize dialog box**

9. **Move to the bottom of the document, press [Enter] after the last line, type Formatted by followed by your name, print a copy, then save and close the document**

FIGURE P-18: Callout shape drawn

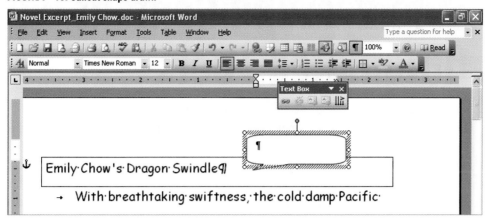

FIGURE P-19: Completed callout shape

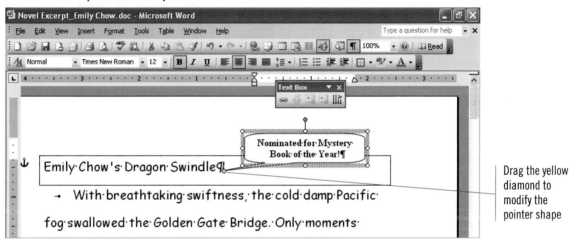

Drag the yellow diamond to modify the pointer shape

Clues to Use

Creating and using custom dictionaries

You can use a custom dictionary to prevent Microsoft Word from flagging words that are spelled correctly, but that do not appear in Word's main dictionary. For example, you can create a custom dictionary to contain terms you use frequently, such as medical terms, technical terms, or surnames. You use this dialog box to change the default dictionary, add a dictionary, and edit a dictionary. To create a new custom dictionary, you open the Spelling & Grammar tab in the Options dialog box, click Custom Dictionaries, click New, type a name for the custom dictionary, save it, then click Modify to add words to it. Each custom dictionary, including the default dictionary, appears in the list of dictionaries shown in the Custom Dictionaries dialog box. If you do not want a custom dictionary to be activated for a particular document, you can remove the green check box that appears next to it in the Custom Dictionaries dialog box. Figure P-20

shows the Custom Dictionaries dialog box containing the default dictionary and a new custom dictionary called Names.

FIGURE P-20: Custom Dictionaries dialog box

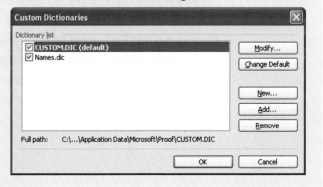

Summarizing Content with Automated Tools

You can use AutoSummarize to identify the key points in a document and then present them in the form of an easy-to-read summary. AutoSummarize produces the summary by analyzing a document and assigning a score to each sentence. High scores are assigned to sentences that contain words used frequently in the document. You can choose how you want AutoSummarize to display the summary. For best results, you use AutoSummarize to analyze documents such as reports, proposals and scientific or academic papers that already have a definite structure. ▀▄▅▆▅ You realize that AutoSummarize is designed to analyze business and academic documents, rather than fiction. As a result, you decide to use AutoSummarize to produce an executive summary of the Meet the Author Guidelines you created in a previous unit.

STEPS

1. **Open the file** WD P-5.doc **from the drive and folder where your Data Files are located, save it as** Author Guidelines, **then scroll through the document to get a sense of the content**

2. **Return to the top of the document, click** Tools **on the menu bar, then click** AutoSummarize

   The AutoSummarize dialog box appears as shown in Figure P-21. In this dialog box, you can choose to highlight key points or insert an executive summary or abstract at the top of the document, in a new document, or in the same document but with the principal text hidden.

3. **Click** OK **to accept the** Highlight key points **option**

   The key sentences that AutoSummarize has identified are highlighted and the AutoSummarize tool bar appears as shown in Figure P-22. By default, 25% of the sentences are highlighted.

4. **Scroll through the document to view the highlighted sentences, then click** Close **on the AutoSummarize toolbar to remove the highlighting**

5. **Click** Tools **on the menu bar, click** AutoSummarize, **select the** Insert an executive summary or abstract at the top of the document **option, then click** OK

6. **Read the summary**

7. **Click** File **on the menu bar, click** Properties, **click the** Summary tab **if necessary, then read the text inserted in the Comments section**

   By default, AutoSummarize updates the document properties to include keywords and comments related to the document contents as shown in Figure P-23. You can edit these keywords and comments in the Properties dialog box, just as you would any text.

8. **Click** OK, **click the** Undo button 🔄▾ **on the Standard toolbar to remove the summary, click** Tools **on the menu bar, click** AutoSummarize, **select the option next to** Create a new document and put the summary there, **click the** Percent of original list arrow, **click** 20 sentences, **then click** OK

9. **Press** [Ctrl][End], **type** Summarized by **followed by your name, save the document as** Author Guidelines Summary, **print a copy, save and close the document, save and close the Author Guidelines document, then exit Word**

FIGURE P-21: AutoSummarize dialog box

FIGURE P-22: AutoSummarize applied to a document

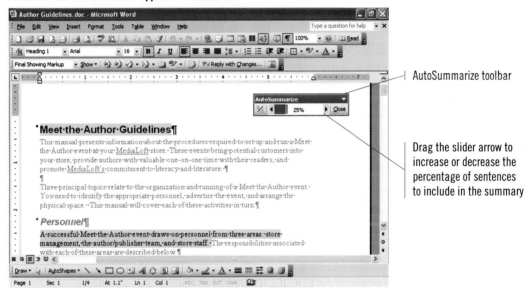

AutoSummarize toolbar

Drag the slider arrow to increase or decrease the percentage of sentences to include in the summary

FIGURE P-23: Document Properties

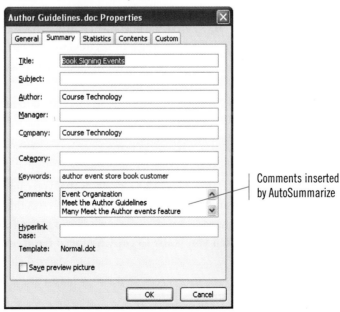

Comments inserted by AutoSummarize

Practice

▼ CONCEPTS REVIEW

Label each of the elements in Figure P-24.

FIGURE P-24

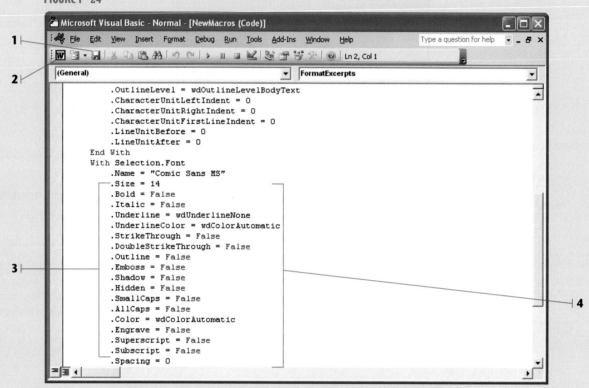

Match each term with the statement that best describes it.

5. **Stop Recording toolbar**
6. **AutoSummarize**
7. **Custom toolbar**
8. **Customize**
9. **Options**
10. **Macros dialog box**

a. Contains the buttons of your choice
b. Analyze the document and assign a score to each sentence
c. Contains the buttons used to stop and pause a macro
d. Command selected to modify a shortcut menu
e. Used to run macros
f. Selection on the Tools menu used to modify default settings

Select the best answer from the list of choices.

11. What is a macro?

a. A series of procedures
b. A series of Word commands and instructions that you group together as a single command

c. Tasks that you cannot perform manually
d. A series of tasks that Word performs when you select Run Macro from the Tools menu

12. Which dialog box do you open when you want to copy a macro from one document to another document?

a. Organizer dialog box
b. Organizing Macros dialog box

c. Record Macro dialog box
d. Copy Macro dialog box

▼ SKILLS REVIEW

1. **Create a macro.**
   a. Start Word, open the file WD P-6.doc from the drive and folder where your Data Files are located, then save it as **Press Release_Lake Towers Hotel**.
   b. Open the Record Macro dialog box, then type **PressReleaseFormat** as the macro name.
   c. Enter the following description after the identification information: **Select all the text, change the Before and After spacing to 3 pt, enhance the title with Arial Black, 24 pt, Bold, then apply the Table List 8 AutoFormat to the table.**
   d. Click OK, press [Ctrl][A] to select all the text, open the Paragraph dialog box, then change the Before spacing to **3 pt** and the After spacing to **3 pt**.
   e. Exit the Paragraph dialog box, press [→] once, press [Ctrl][Home], press [F8] to turn on text select mode, then press [End] to select the document title (Lake Towers Hotel).
   f. Open the Font dialog box, then select the Arial Black font, Bold, and 24 pt.
   g. Exit the Font dialog box, press [Ctrl][End], press [↑] to move into the table, click Table on the menu bar, click Table AutoFormat, then apply the Table List 8 AutoFormat.
   h. Click [↓] once, then click the Stop Recording button on the Stop Recording toolbar.
   i. Scroll up to view the formatted document, then save and close the document.

2. **Run a macro.**
   a. Open the file WD P-7.doc from the drive and folder where your Data Files are located, then save it as **Press Release_Saskatoon Classic Hotel**.
   b. Open the Macros dialog box, select the PressReleaseFormat macro, then click Run.
   c. Type **Formatted by** followed by your name at the bottom of the document, scroll up and view the formatted document, print a copy, then save and close it.
   d. Open the Customize dialog box from the Tools menu, click Keyboard, select Macros from the Categories list, select the PressReleaseFormat macro, assign the [Alt][H] keystrokes to the FormatPressRelease macro, then close the dialog boxes.
   e. Open the file WD P-8.doc from the drive and folder where your Data Files are located, save it as **Press Release_Atlantica Hotel**, press [Alt][H] to run the macro, scroll up to view the formatted document, then save the document.

3. **Edit a macro in Visual Basic.**
   a. Open the Macros dialog box, verify the PressReleaseFormat macro is selected, then click Edit.
   b. Find the .SpaceAfter = 3 in the paragraph format section, then change the spacing to **6**.
   c. Scroll down as needed to find the .Size = 24 code in the Font section, then change the size to **36**.
   d. Save the macro, close the Visual Basic window, verify Press Release_Atlantica Hotel is the active document, then use the [Alt][H] keystrokes to run the revised macro.
   e. Verify that the security level for macros is set to Medium. (*Note:* If the security setting was *not* Medium, return to the original security setting when you have completed this Skills Review.)
   f. Save the document, then close it.

4. **Rename, delete, and copy macros.**
   a. Open the file WD P-9.doc from the drive and folder where your Data Files are located, click Enable Macros, then save the document as **Hotel Macro Sample**.
   b. Open the Macros dialog box, then open the Organizer dialog box.
   c. Close the file in the list on the right side, then open the Press Release_Atlantica Hotel.doc file. (*Note:* You must change the Files of type to All Word Documents.)
   d. Copy the macro from the Hotel Macro Sample file to the Press Release_Atlantica Hotel file, then close the Organizer dialog box and click Yes to save the Press Release_Atlantica Hotel file.
   e. Close the Hotel Macro Sample file, open the Press Release_Atlantica Hotel.doc file, click Enable Macros, then run the HotelMacro using the Macros dialog box.
   f. Scroll through the document to view the results of the HotelMacro, then run the [Alt][H] macro.
   g. Delete the HotelMacro macro from the Macros dialog box.

    h. Click PressReleaseFormat in the Macro name list if necessary, click Edit, change the name of the macro PressReleaseFormat to **Hotel** in two places, save, then close Visual Basic to return to Word.

    i. Type **Formatted by** followed by your name at the bottom of the Press Release_Atlantica Hotel document, print a copy, then save and close the document.

5. Create a custom toolbar.

    a. Click View on the menu bar, point to Toolbars, click Customize, click the Toolbars tab if necessary, then click New.

    b. Enter **Hotels** as the name of the new custom toolbar.

    c. From the Commands tab, select Drawing in the Categories list, scroll down the list of commands, then drag the Shadow Style button to the Hotels toolbar. (*Note*: When you drag a button that includes a black list arrow at the right side of the Commands list, the options associated with the list arrow move with the button.)

    d. Select Macros in the Categories list, then select Normal.NewMacros.Hotel in the Commands list and drag it to the toolbar.

    e. Modify the Macro button so that it shows the key shape and appears as text only in menus, then close the Customize dialog box.

    f. Open the file Press Release_Lake Towers Hotel.doc from the drive and folder where your Data Files are located, click the picture of the waiter, click the Shadow Style button on the Hotel toolbar, select Shadow Style 2, then deselect the image.

    g. Click the Hotel macro button on the Hotel toolbar to run the revised macro.

    h. Delete the Hotel toolbar from the Customize Toolbars dialog box, then save the document.

6. Customize menus.

    a. Open the Customize dialog box, then click the check box next to Shortcut Menus in the Toolbars tab to select it.

    b. Click Table on the Shortcut Menus toolbar, then select the Table Text shortcut menu.

    c. Click the Commands tab in the Customize dialog box, click Table in the Categories list, select the Sort Ascending button from the list of commands, drag it to the Table Text shortcut menu so that it appears above Borders and Shading, then close the Customize dialog box.

    d. Scroll to the bottom of the document, click anywhere in the Price column (contains the room rates) of the table, right-click to show the modified Table Text shortcut menu, click Sort Ascending, then save the document.

7. Modify options.

    a. Open the Options dialog box from the Tools menu, click the General tab, click the Measurement units list arrow, then select Centimeters.

    b. Close the Options dialog box, right-click the picture at the top of the document, click Format Picture, click the Size tab, change the Height of the picture to **8** centimeters, then exit the Format Picture dialog box.

    c. Open the Options dialog box, then change the Measurement unit in the General tab back to inches.

    d. Open the Customize dialog box, then remove the Sort Ascending button from the Table Text shortcut menu. (*Hint*: Repeat steps 6a–6b. When the Table Text shortcut menu appears, drag Sort Ascending to a blank area of the screen.)

    e. Scroll to the bottom of the document, type **Formatted by** followed by your name, print a copy of the document, then save and close it.

    f. Open the Macros dialog box, delete the Hotel macro, close the Macros dialog box, then exit Word.

8. Summarize Content Using Automated Tools

    a. Open the file WD P-10.doc from the drive and folder where your Data Files are located, then save the document as **Back Country Tours**.

    b. Read through the document, then use AutoSummarize to highlight key points.

    c. Use AutoSummarize to insert an executive summary at the top of the document, then read the summary.

    d. Remove the three bulleted points: Sea Kayaking, Wildlife Photography, and Mountain Biking.

    e. Add a page break below the summary, then type **Summarized by** followed by your name at the bottom of the summary page.

    f. Center "Summary" at the top of the page and increase its font size to 24 pt.

    g. Save and close the document, then exit Word.

▼ INDEPENDENT CHALLENGE 1

You've just started working for Organics Forever, a company that delivers fresh, organic fruits and vegetables to its customers throughout Wellington, New Zealand. Your supervisor wants you to automate some tasks related to the company documentation. First, he asks you to use AutoSummarize to create a summary of the company description for use on the company's Web site. He then asks you to create a macro that will speed up the tasks required to prepare each week's price lists.

a. Start Word, open the file WD P-11.doc from the drive and folder where your Data Files are located, then read through the document to get a sense of the contents.

b. Use AutoSummarize to insert an executive summary in a new document.

c. Save the new document as **Organics Forever_About Us**, type **Summarized by** followed by your name at the end of the document, print a copy, then save and close it.

d. Close WD P-11.doc without saving it.

e. In a new Word document, type **Starting Date**, press [Enter], type **Date**, press [Enter] two times, type **Special of the Week**, press [Enter], type **Weekly Special**, then press [Enter]. This text is sample text that you can use as you create the macro.

f. Press [Ctrl][Home], open the Record Macro dialog box, then enter **PriceList** as the macro name.

g. Click the Store macro in list arrow and select Document1 (document).

h. Enter the following description for the macro: **Macro created by [your name] on [the current date]. Select Date, insert the current date, select Weekly Special, then insert a fill-in text box.**

i. Click Keyboard in the Record Macro dialog box and assign the [Alt][P] shortcut key combination.

j. Click Assign and Close, then perform the steps required for the macro as follows:
   - Press [▼], press [F8], then press [End] to select Date.
   - Press [Delete], click Insert on the menu bar, click Date and Time, click the format corresponding to March 29, 2006, verify that the Update automatically check box is selected, then click OK.
   - Press [Enter], press the [▼] twice, press [F8], press [End] to select Weekly Special, click Insert on the menu bar, click Field, click Fill-in, click OK, then click OK.
   - Click the Stop Recording button on the Stop Recording toolbar.

k. Save the document as **Price List Macro**.

l. Open the file WD P-12.doc from the drive and folder where your Data Files are located, save it as **Organics Forever Price List_[Current Date]**, then close the document.

m. Copy the macro in the Price List Macro document to the Organics Forever Price List_[Current Date] document.

n. Set the Security setting to Medium if necessary, close the Price List Macro document, open the file Organics Forever Price List_[Current Date].doc, click Enable Macros, then run the [Alt][P] macro. In the fill-in box, type **Papayas on sale: $2.00 each**, then click OK.

o. Change the name of the PriceList macro in the Visual Basic window to SalePrice, then close Visual Basic and return to the document.

Advanced Challenge Exercise

- Open a new blank document, then create a table consisting of 4 rows and 4 columns.
- Position the insertion point in the table, then create a new macro called FormatTable stored in all documents that selects the entire table, changes the table fill to light yellow, changes the vertical alignment of each cell to Center, and changes the row height to .3. Be sure to save the document after you stop recording. (*Hint*: Practice the steps before you create the macro. Remember that you need to use menus to perform all the steps, including selecting the table.)
- Create a new table, place the insertion point in the table, and then run the macro to test it.
- Close the document without saving it, then run the macro in the tables in the Organics Forever Price List.

p. Type **Formatted by** followed by your name at the bottom of the document, print a copy of the document, save it, close it, then exit Word.

▼ INDEPENDENT CHALLENGE 2

As the office manager of the Black Belt Academy, you prepare a gift certificate that you can give to new members. Since you will need to create several of these certificates each week, you decide to create a custom toolbar that contains the buttons you'll use most often to personalize each certificate.

a. Start Word, then open the Customize dialog box.

b. Click the Toolbars tab, then create a new toolbar named **Gift Certificate** and save in the Normal.dot template.

c. Click the Commands tab in the Customize dialog box. From the Drawing category, add the Change AutoShape button and the Fill Color button; from the AutoShapes category, add the Line button. (*Note*: Make sure you select the "Line" button, *not* the Lines button.)

d. Compare the completed Gift Certificate toolbar to Figure P-25, then close the Customize dialog box.

FIGURE P-25

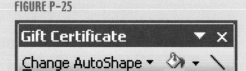

e. Open the Options dialog box from the Tools menu, click the General tab if necessary, then click the Automatically create drawing canvas when inserting AutoShapes check box to deselect it.

f. Open the file WD P-13.doc, then save it as **Gift Certificate_George Price**.

g. Click the hexagon shape, click the Change AutoShape button on the Gift Certificate toolbar, point to Stars and Banners, then select the Change Shape to Explosion 2 shape.

h. Right-click the explosion shape, click Add Text, type **George Price** on two lines, then enhance the text with Bold, 14 pt, and center alignment.

i. Click the Fill Color list arrow on the Gift Certificate toolbar, then select the Light Turquoise fill color.

j. Click next to To:, click the Line button, click the straight line, press and hold the [Shift] key, draw a line approximately six inches from To: to the right margin, then draw a line next to Date:.

k. Click next to To:, type **George Price, 202 West 4ᵗʰ Street, Milwaukee, WI**, then remove Bold.

l. Click next to Date:, then type the current date. If necessary, adjust the line so that it appears under the date.

Advanced Challenge Exercise

■ Open the Customize dialog box, then click Commands.

■ Select Built-in Menus, then drag Font to the Gift Certificate toolbar.

■ Click Rearrange Commands in the Customize dialog box, then click the Toolbar option button and select the Gift Certificate toolbar.

■ Move the Change AutoShape button on the Gift Certificate toolbar to the bottom of the list of four buttons.

■ Click Line, click Modify Selection, then change the name of the Line button to Info Line.

■ Select Edit Button Image from the list of selections, then click squares below the current line to make a thicker line. See Figure P-26.

FIGURE P-26

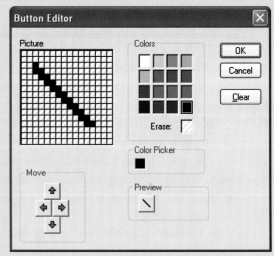

■ Exit all dialog boxes.

■ Select the text **George Price** in the explosion shape, click the Font button on the Gift Certificate toolbar, then select the BrushScript MT font (or a similar script-like font).

■ Click the new Line button, then draw a line under Gift Certificate. Use Shift to keep the line straight.

m. Type **Prepared by** followed by your name at the bottom of the document, print a copy, then save and close the document.

n. Delete the Gift Certificate toolbar from the toolbars list in the Customize dialog box, close the document, then exit Word.

▼ INDEPENDENT CHALLENGE 3

You work for Blossom Inc., a florist shop in Nashville, Tennessee. The company has moved recently. As a result, several letters include an incorrect address in the letterhead. You decide to create a macro that replaces the address, phone number, and fax number of the old location with the correct contact information.

a. Start Word, open the file WD P-14.doc from the drive and folder where your Data Files are located, then save it as **Catalog Request_Farrell.**

b. Open the Record Macro dialog box, name the new macro **BlossomLetterhead**, then enter the following text in the Description text box: **Select the address, type a new address, change the zip code, change the phone and fax numbers, apply italic**. Close the dialog box.

c. Press [▼] once, then press [◄] once to position the insertion point at the beginning of the address line.

d. Press [F8] to turn on select mode, then press [►] repeatedly to select just 1801 Bower Avenue.

e. Press [Delete], then type **150 Mainline Avenue**.

f. Press [►] to move just before the 0 in the zip code, type **22**, then press [Delete] two times to delete 01.

g. Press [▼] two times, then press [Home] to move to the beginning of the Phone number line.

h. Press[►] to move to the last four digits of the phone number (7766), type **4455**, press [Delete] four times to delete 7766, press [►] to move to the last four digits of the fax number (7768), type **6641**, then press [Delete] four times to delete 7768.

i. Press [Home] to move to the beginning of the line, press [F8], then press [End].

j. Press [Ctrl][I] to turn on italic, press [▼] once, then click the Stop Recording button on the Stop Recording toolbar.

k. Enter your name in the closing where indicated, print a copy of the letter, then save and close it.

l. Open the Macros dialog box, click BlossomLetterhead in the list of macros, click Edit to enter the Visual Basic window, then change the name of the macro to **Letterhead** (in two places).

m. Scroll down toward the end of the Letterhead code to find the code Selection.Font.Italic = wdToggle, then delete the line of code. (*Note*: If you make a mistake, click Edit Undo.)

n. Save the revised macro, then close the Visual Basic window.

o. Open the file WD P-15.doc from the drive and folder where your Data Files are located, save it as **Catalog Request_Deville**, run the Letterhead macro, press [▼] to remove highlighting if necessary, enter your name in the complimentary closing, print a copy of the letter, save, then close the document.

p. Delete the Letterhead macro, then exit Word.

 ## ▼ INDEPENDENT CHALLENGE 4

You can obtain custom dictionaries from many Web sites on the World Wide Web and then add them to Microsoft Word so that you can check documents that contain specialized terms such as medical or scientific terms. You decide to check out some of the resources available on the Web with respect to custom dictionaries that you can use with Spell Checker.

a. Conduct a search for keywords such as "spelling dictionaries" and "spell checking dictionaries."

b. Find two Web sites that provide spelling dictionaries you can download and add as custom dictionaries to Microsoft Word. Some of the Web sites will offer spelling dictionaries for free and some will sell them.

c. Open WD P-16.doc from the drive and folder containing your Data Files, then save it as **Spelling Dictionaries**.

d. Complete the document with the required information about the spelling dictionaries available from the Web sites you've selected.

e. Add a summary paragraph explaining the steps you would follow to make one of these custom dictionaries the default dictionary.

f. Enter your name where indicated in the document, print a copy, then save and close the document and exit Word.

▼ VISUAL WORKSHOP

Open the file WD P-17.doc from the drive and folder where your Data Files are located, click Enable Macros, then save the file as **Birthday Card_Sara**. The file contains text and a macro called BirthdayCard. Open the Visual Basic window for the BirthdayCard macro (see Figure P-27), then edit the code as follows: Change the font attribute from Arial to **Georgia**, scroll down, then change the line spacing attribute from wdLineSpaceDouble to wdLineSpaceSingle. (*Note*: You only need to replace Double with Single in the attribute code.) Save the revised macro, close the Visual Basic window, then run the revised macro and enter **Sara** in the fill-in box. Switch to Whole Page view, then compare the completed birthday card to Figure P-28, adjust formatting as needed. Type **Formatted by** followed by your name at the bottom of the document, print a copy, then save and close the document.

FIGURE P-27

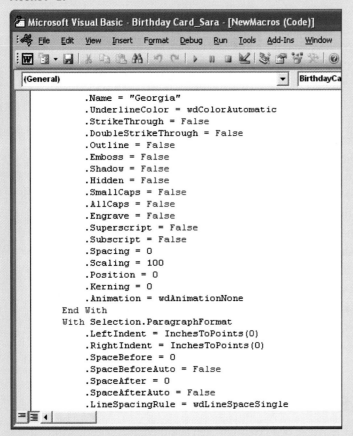

FIGURE P-28

Working with XML

OBJECTIVES

Work with XML Schema

Manage XML Documents and Options

If you have a SAM user profile, you may have access to hands-on instruction, practice, and assessment of the skills covered in this unit. Log in to your SAM account and go to your assignments page to see what your instructor has assigned.

Word 2003 includes the features needed to create and work with XML documents. **XML** stands for eXtensible Markup Language and is used to structure, store, and send information. You can attach an XML schema to a document, select XML options, and save a document in XML format. Information about customers, suppliers, and products currently contained in documents can, through the use of XML, be coded, extracted, and stored, and then distributed across the Internet to facilitate a variety of business operations from marketing to strategic planning. In the past, information, such as customer names and addresses, could be accessed easily only if it was stored in a database. Now XML can be used to extract and use information that can be contained in a wide variety of documents. ▓▓ Graham Watson in the Marketing Department at MediaLoft asks you to learn more about how XML can be used to code documents in Word.

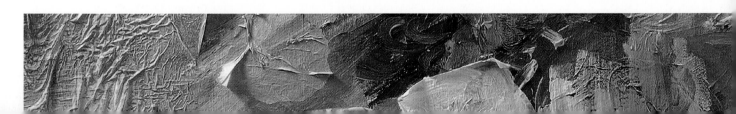

Working with XML Schema

Before you can convert a Word document into an XML document, you need to attach an XML schema. An **XML schema** is a formal specification that is written in XML code. When attached to a document, an XML schema defines the structure of an XML document. The schema includes the names of **elements** that can be defined in the document and defines which **attributes** are available for each element. XML is based on user-defined tags and XML schemas are usually created within a company for use with the company's documents. Companies develop their own custom schemas that they then apply to documents containing information required for a wide variety of business operations. 🕮🕮🕮 Graham Watson has received an XML schema from MediaLoft's XML experts and asks you to attach it to a Word document containing a list of authors and their books. The file containing the schema is called BookList_Schema. Figure XML-1 shows the Book List schema in Notepad. You attach this schema to a Word document in Word and then you attach XML tags to relevant content.

STEPS

TROUBLE

Make sure that the Show/Hide ¶ button ¶ is selected so that paragraph marks are visible.

1. **Start Word, open the file** WD XML-1.doc **from the drive and folder where your Data Files are located, then save it as** Book List

   The document contains the names of three authors and the titles of their books.

2. **Click** View **on the menu bar, click** Task Pane, **click the** Other Task Panes list arrow **in the task pane, then click** XML Structure

   The XML Structure task pane opens and advises you that you need to select a schema before you can apply XML elements to a Word document.

3. **Click** Templates and Add-Ins, **then click the** XML Schema tab **if it is not already selected**

   Using options available on the XML Schema tab, you can add a schema, access the schema library where you can modify schema settings and delete schemas you no longer need, and modify XML options.

4. **Click** Add Schema, **navigate to the drive and folder where your Data Files are located, click** BookList_Schema.xsd, **then click** Open

   The .xsd extension identifies the file as an XML schema.

TROUBLE

If Book List already appears in the dialog box, type Book List1 or another number to give the schema a unique name.

5. **In the Schema Settings dialog box, type** Book List, **press [Tab], type** Book List, **then click** OK

6. **Click** OK **to attach the Book List schema to the document**

   The XML Structure task pane appears as shown in Figure XML-2. Next you add XML tags to selected text in your document.

TROUBLE

If you do not see {Book List}, click Book and continue.

7. **Click** Books {Book List} **in the Choose an element to apply to your current selection list box, then click** Apply to Entire Document **in the Apply to entire document message box**

   The Books tag defines the content of the entire document.

8. **Click [▼] once to deselect the text, then save the document**

   In the next lesson you will finish adding the required tags from the XML schema to the Book List document.

FIGURE XML-1: Book List schema viewed in Notepad

Code to create an element

```
BookList_Schema.xsd - Notepad
File  Edit  Format  View  Help
<?xml version="1.0"?>

<!-- File Name: books.xsd -->

<xsd:schema xmlns:xsd="http://www.w3.org/2001/XMLSchema">

    <xsd:element name="Books">
        <xsd:complexType>
            <xsd:sequence>
                <xsd:element name="Book" type="BookType"
                     minOccurs="0" maxOccurs="unbounded"/>
            </xsd:sequence>
        </xsd:complexType>
    </xsd:element>

    <xsd:complexType name="BookType">
        <xsd:sequence>

            <xsd:element name="Author_First" type="xsd:string"/>
            <xsd:element name="Author_Last" type="xsd:string"/>
            <xsd:element name="Title" type="xsd:string"/>

        </xsd:sequence>


    </xsd:complexType>

</xsd:schema>
```

FIGURE XML-2: XML Structure task pane

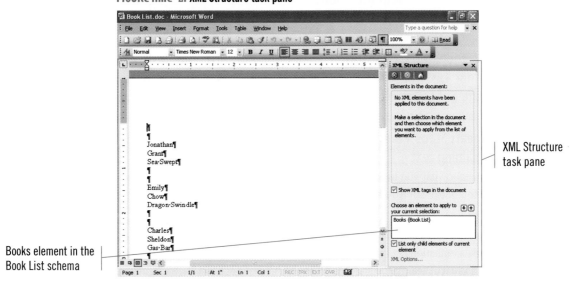

XML Structure task pane

Books element in the Book List schema

Clues to Use

Understanding XML

With XML you can define your own tags. Consider the following very simple example:

```
<Tour>
<Tour_Title>Antarctica Marathon</Tour_Title>
    <Tour_Date>April 2 to April 20</Tour_Date>
    <Guides>
    <Guide_Name>Harriet Knutson</Guide_Name>
    </Guides>
</Tour>
```

This document contains five XML tags: Tour, Tour_Title, Tour_Date, Guides, and Guide_Name. The author of the XML document chose these tag names because they accurately describe the data they represent. These XML tags are defined in an XML schema attached to the document. Imagine that the document contains a list of 500 tours. After coding information about each tour with the appropriate tags,

the author of the document could extract a list of tours, tour guides, or tour dates. Then, the extracted data could be used to update the database profiles of clients or users so a record of their preferences could be maintained, or a request could be sent to the tour operator for more information or for a reservation for a particular tour with choices of guide, tour location, etc. If this data is already included in a database, then extraction would be easy. XML provides users with the means of easily extracting data stored in documents so it can be used in other documents or in other applications without having to be rekeyed. You can handle an XML document in two ways. First, you can use a style sheet to display the content of an XML document in an Internet browser such as Explorer or Netscape and second, you can use a programming language such as JavaScript and Java to read and process the contents of an XML document, usually in a browser.

Managing XML Documents and Options

You have completed the first step in creating an XML document, which is to attach an XML schema to a document from which you want to extract specific information. The next step is to add tags from the XML schema that identify the information you want to be able to access. Once you have added XML tags from the XML schema to the Word document, you can save the document as an XML document. You can also modify XML options and work further with schemas in the Schema Library. ◼◼◼◼ You add XML tags from the Book List schema to the Book List document, save the document as an XML document, then view XML options and the Schema Library.

STEPS

1. **Select from the line above Jonathon to the line below Sea Swept, click the check box next to List only child elements of current element in the XML Structure task pane to deselect it, then click Book in the Choose an element to apply to your current selection list box**

   The Book tag is inserted above and below the information relating to Jonathon Grant and his book called *Sea Swept*.

2. **Select Jonathon, click Author_First in the XML Structure task pane, select Grant, click Author_Last in the XML Structure task pane, select Sea Swept, scroll down and click Title in the Choose an element to apply to your current selection list box, then press [↓] once**

   The information related to Jonathon Grant and his book is tagged, as shown in Figure XML-3.

3. **Repeats Steps 1 and 2 to apply the required XML tags shown in Figure XML-4 to the remaining text**

   Remember that you need to select the required text first and then select the tag. You start by selecting from the line above Emily to the line below Dragon Swindle and then selecting the Book tag.

4. **Click XML Options at the bottom of the XML Structure task pane**

   As shown in Figure XML-5, the XML Options dialog box contains options related to saving XML, applying Schema validation options, and changing XML view options. You accept the default setting, which is to validate the document against the attached schema. When this option is selected, a wavy pink line appears next to text that is tagged incorrectly. As you were applying tags to the document, the wavy pink line did appear. However, once the entire document is tagged as instructed, the wavy pink line that indicates violations no longer appears. From the XML Options dialog box you can also access options related to working with the Schema Library.

5. **Click Schema Library, then click Book List in the list of schemas**

   The options available for working with schemas appear. As you can see, you can choose to add another schema or you can delete the current schema. You can also change the name attached to the schema by selecting the Schema Settings button.

QUICK TIP
You should delete a schema when you share a computer with other users.

6. **Click Delete Schema, click OK to close the Schema Library dialog box, then click OK to close the XML Options dialog box**

7. **Click File on the menu bar, click Save As, click the Save as type list arrow, click XML Document, then click Save**

   The document is saved as Book List.xml.

8. **Press [Ctrl][End] to move to the bottom of the document, press [Enter], type your name, click File on the menu bar, click Print, click Options, click the check box next to XML tags to select it, click OK, then click OK**

   The document is printed along with the XML tags.

9. **Save and close the document, then exit Word**

FIGURE XML-3: Tags applied to Jonathon Grant information

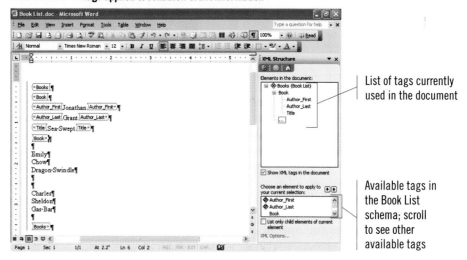

List of tags currently used in the document

Available tags in the Book List schema; scroll to see other available tags

FIGURE XML-4: Tags applied to Emily Chow and Charles Sheldon information

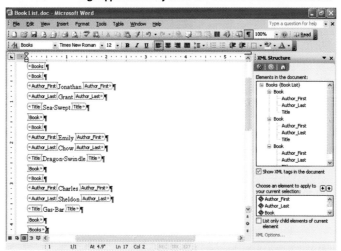

FIGURE XML-5: XML Options dialog box

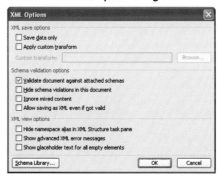

Clues to Use

HTML and XML

XML is a meta-markup language; that is, a language that you use to create languages. As you have learned, you use XML to design your own tags. HTML is a markup language that you use to format data so that it can be displayed on the Internet. The HTML tags used to format the data are predefined. In other words, you must use the <b> and </b> HTML tags to indicate that selected text is to be displayed in bold. With XML, the focus is on content, *not* format. You can define your own tags that describe different types of data, depending on the nature of the information you wish to extract from a document. For example, you can define a tag called <author> and then create related children such as <authorfirst>, <authorlast>, etc. The fact that you can select your own names for XML tags makes XML an incredibly versatile language that you can use to process and share an almost limitless variety of information.

▼ SKILLS REVIEW

1. Work with XML Schema.

a. Start Word, open the file WD XML-2.doc from the drive and folder where your Data Files are located, then save it as **Adventure Tours**.

b. Show the XML Structure task pane.

c. Open the Templates and Add-ins dialog box.

d. Click Add Schema, navigate to the drive and folder containing your Data Files, then open AdventureTours_Schema.xsd.

e. Type **Adventure Tours** for both the name and the alias of the schema, then attach the Adventure Tours schema to the document.

f. Click Tours {Adventure Tours} in the XML Structure task pane, then click Apply to Entire Document.

g. Deselect the text, then save the document.

2. Manage XML documents and options.

a. Select from the line above Antarctica Marathon to the line below April 2 to April 20, then deselect the List only child elements of current element check box in the XML Structure task pane.

b. Select the Tour tag.

c. Apply the Tour_Title tag to Antarctica Marathon.

d. Apply the Guide_Name tag to Harriet Knutson.

e. Apply the Tour_Date tag to April 2 to April 20.

f. Apply the Tour tag to the information about the Costa Rica Rainforest Odyssey tour.

g. Apply the Tour_Title, Guide_Name and Tour_Date tags to the required information about the Rainforest tour.

h. Open the XML Options dialog box.

i. Open the Schema Library dialog box and click the Adventure Tours schema.

j. Delete the Adventure Tours schema, then close the dialog boxes.

k. Save the document as an XML document called **Adventure Tours**.

l. Type your name at the bottom of the document, then print a copy of the document with the XML tags showing.

m. Save and close the document, then exit Word

Glossary

Adjustment handle The yellow diamond that appears when certain AutoShapes are selected; used to change the shape, but not the size, of an AutoShape.

Alignment The position of text in a document relative to the margins.

Anchored The state of a floating graphic that moves with a paragraph or other item if the item is moved; an anchor symbol appears with the floating graphic when formatting marks are displayed.

Application *See* Program.

Area chart A chart similar to a line chart; however the space between the lines and the bottom of the chart is filled, and a different band of color represents each value.

Ascending order Lists data alphabetically or sequentially (from A to Z, 0 to 9, or earliest to latest).

Attribute In XML, extra information about an element that is stored in the start tag; for example, an assigned default value for the element is an attribute of that element.

AutoComplete A feature that automatically suggests text to insert.

AutoCorrect A feature that automatically detects and corrects typing errors, minor spelling errors, and capitalization, or inserts certain typographical symbols as you type.

Automatic page break A page break that is inserted automatically at the bottom of a page.

AutoShape A drawing object, such as a rectangle, oval, triangle, line, block arrow, or other shape that you create using the tools on the Drawing toolbar.

AutoText A feature that stores frequently used text and graphics so they can be easily inserted into a document.

Bar chart A chart that shows values as horizontal bars; Cylinder, Cone, and Pyramid charts can also show values in horizontal format, similar to the rectangles used in bar charts.

Bitmap graphic A graphic that is composed of a series of small dots called "pixels."

Boilerplate text Text that appears in every version of a merged document.

Bold Formatting applied to text to make it thicker and darker.

Bookmark Text that identifies a location or a selection of text in a document.

Border A line that can be added above, below, or to the sides of a paragraph, text, or a table cell; a line that divides the columns and rows of a table.

Browser A software program used to access and display Web pages.

Bullet A small graphic symbol used to identify items in a list.

Cell The box formed by the intersection of a table row and table column.

Cell reference A code that identifies a cell's position in a table; each cell reference contains a letter (A, B, C, and so on) to identify its column and a number (1, 2, 3, and so on) to identify its row.

Center Alignment in which an item is centered between the margins.

Character spacing Formatting that changes the width or scale of characters, expands or condenses the amount of space between characters, raises or lowers characters relative to the line of text, and adjusts kerning (the space between standard combinations of letters).

Character style A named set of character format settings that can be applied to text to format it all at once.

Chart A visual representation of numerical data, usually used to illustrate trends, patterns, or relationships.

Circular chart A chart that shows how values relate to each other as parts of a whole; a pie chart is an example of a circular chart.

Click and Type A feature that allows you to automatically apply the necessary paragraph formatting to a table, graphic, or text when you insert the item in a blank area of a document in Print Layout or Web Layout view.

Click and Type pointer A pointer used to move the insertion point and automatically apply the paragraph formatting necessary to insert text at that location in the document.

Clip A media file, such as a graphic, photograph, sound, movie, or animation, that can be inserted into a document.

Clip art A collection of graphic images that can be inserted into documents, presentations, Web pages, spreadsheets, and other Office files.

Clip Organizer A library of the clips that come with Word.

Clipboard A temporary storage area for items that are cut or copied from any Office file and are available for pasting. *See also* Office Clipboard and System Clipboard.

Column break A break that forces text following the break to begin at the top of the next column.

Column chart A chart that compares values side-by-side, usually over time; Cylinder, Cone, and Pyramid charts can also show values in vertical format, similar to the rectangles used in column charts.

Comment An embedded note or annotation that an author or a reviewer adds to a document; appears in a comment balloon when working in Page Layout view.

Copy To place a copy of an item on the Clipboard without removing it from a document.

Crop To trim away part of a graphic.

Cross-reference Text that electronically refers the reader to another part of the document.

Cut To remove an item from a document and place it on the Clipboard.

Cut and paste To move text or graphics using the Cut and Paste commands.

Cycle diagram A diagram that illustrates a process that has a continuous cycle.

Data field A category of information, such as last name, first name, street address, city, or postal code.

Data record A complete set of related information for a person or an item, such as a person's name and address.

Data source In mail merge, the file with the unique data for individual people or items; the data merged with a main document to produce multiple versions.

Datasheet A table grid that opens when a chart is inserted in Word.

Delete To permanently remove an item from a document.

Descending order Lists data in reverse alphabetical or sequential order (Z to A, 9 to 0, or latest to earliest).

Destination file The file to which data is copied.

Destination program The program to which the data is copied.

Digital certificate An attachment for a file that vouches for the authenticity of the file, provides secure encryption, or supplies a verifiable signature.

Digital signature An electronic stamp attached to a document to authenticate the document.

Document The electronic file you create using Word.

Document map A pane that shows all the headings and subheadings in a document.

Document properties Details about a file, such as author name or the date the file was created, that are used to organize and search for files.

Document window The workspace in the program window that displays the current document.

Drag and drop To move text or a graphic by dragging it to a new location using the mouse.

Drawing canvas A workspace for creating graphics; an area within which multiple shapes can be drawn and clip art or pictures inserted.

Drop cap A large dropped initial capital letter that is often used to set off the first paragraph of an article.

Dynamic Data Exchange (DDE) The connection between the source file and the destination file.

Element In XML, the unit of content that forms the basic structure of an XML document; an element consists of an element name and element content, and can also includes the attributes (extra information) related to the element.

Embedded object An object contained in a source file and inserted into a destination file; an embedded object becomes part of the destination file that is no longer linked to the source file.

Endnote Text that provides additional information or acknowledges sources for text in a document and that appears at the end of a document.

Field A code that serves as a placeholder for data that changes in a document, such as a page number.

Field label A word or phrase that tells users the kind of information required for a given field.

Field name The name of a data field.

File An electronic collection of information that has a unique name, distinguishing it from other files.

Filename The name given to a document when it is saved.

Filename extension Three letters that follow the period in the filename; for example, .doc for a Word file and .xls for Excel files.

Filter In a mail merge, to pull out records that meet specific criteria and include only those records in the merge.

First line indent A type of indent in which the first line of a paragraph is indented more than the subsequent lines.

Floating graphic A graphic to which a text wrapping style has been applied, making the graphic independent of text and able to be moved anywhere on a page.

Font The typeface or design of a set of characters (letters, numbers, symbols, and punctuation marks).

Font effect Font formatting that applies a special effect to text, such as a shadow, an outline, small caps, or superscript.

Font size The size of characters, measured in points (pts).

Footer Information, such as text, a page number, or a graphic, that appears at the bottom of every page in a document or a section.

Footnote Text that provides additional information or acknowledges sources for text in a document and that appears at the bottom of the page on which the footnote reference appears.

Form field The location where the data associated with a field label is stored.

Form template A file that contains the structure of a form. Users create new forms from a form template; data entered into new forms based on a form template do not affect the structure of the template file.

Format Painter A feature used to copy the format settings applied to the selected text to other text you want to format the same way.

Formatting marks Nonprinting characters that appear on screen to indicate the ends of paragraphs, tabs, and other formatting elements.

Formatting toolbar A toolbar that contains buttons for frequently used formatting commands.

Frame A section of a Web page window in which a separate Web page is displayed.

Full screen view A view that shows only the document window on screen.

Getting Started task pane A task pane that contains shortcuts for opening documents, for creating new documents, and for accessing information on the Microsoft Web site.

Gridlines Nonprinting lines that show the boundaries of table cells.

Gutter Extra space left for a binding at the top, left, or inside margin of a document.

Hanging indent A type of indent in which the second and subsequent lines of a paragraph are indented more than the first.

Hard page break *See* Manual page break.

Header Information, such as text, a page number, or a graphic, that appears at the top of every page in a document or a section.

Header row The first row of a table that contains the column headings.

Highlighting Transparent color that can be applied to text to call attention to it.

Home page The main page of a Web site and the first Web page viewers see when they visit a site.

Horizontal ruler A ruler that appears at the top of the document window in Print Layout, Normal, and Web Layout view.

HTML (Hypertext Markup Language) The programming language used to code how each element of a Web page should appear when viewed with a browser.

Hyperlink Text or a graphic that opens a file, Web page, or other item when clicked. Also known as a link.

I-beam pointer The pointer used to move the insertion point and select text.

Indent The space between the edge of a line of text or a paragraph and the margin.

Indent marker A marker on the horizontal ruler that shows the indent settings for the active paragraph.

Index Text that lists many of the terms and topics in a document, along with the pages on which they appear.

Inline graphic A graphic that is part of a line of text in which it was inserted.

Insertion point The blinking vertical line that shows where text will appear when you type in a document.

Italic Formatting applied to text to make the characters slant to the right.

Justify Alignment in which an item is flush with both the left and right margins.

Keyboard shortcut A combination of keys or a function key that can be pressed to perform a command.

Label Text that describes the significance of a value in a chart.

Landscape orientation Page orientation in which the page is wider than it is tall.

Left indent A type of indent in which the left edge of a paragraph is moved in from the left margin.

Left-align Alignment in which the item is flush with the left margin.

Legend A chart element that identifies the patterns or colors that are assigned to the data series or categories in a chart.

Line spacing The amount of space between lines of text.

Line chart A chart that illustrates trends, where each value is connected to the next value by a line.

Linked object An object created in a source file and inserted into a destination file that maintains a connection between the 2 files; changes made to the data in the source file are reflected in the destination file.

List style A named set of format settings, such as indents and outline numbering, that can be applied to a list to format it all at once.

Macro A series of Word commands and instructions grouped together as a single command to accomplish a task automatically.

Mail Merge Combines a standard document, such as a form letter, with customized data, such as a set of names and addresses, to create a set of personalized documents.

Main document In a mail merge, the document with the standard text.

Manual page break A page break inserted to force the text following the break to begin at the top of the next page.

Margin The blank area between the edge of the text and the edge of a page.

Master document A Word document that contains links to two or more related documents called subdocuments.

Menu bar The bar beneath the title bar that contains the names of menus; clicking a menu name opens a menu of program commands.

Merge To combine adjacent cells into a single larger cell.

Merge field A placeholder that you insert in the main document to indicate where the data from each record should be inserted when you perform a mail merge.

Mirror margins Margins used in documents with facing pages, where the inside and outside margins are mirror images of each other.

Negative indent A type of indent in which the left edge of a paragraph is moved to the left of the left margin.

Nested table A table inserted in a cell of another table.

Normal style The paragraph style that is used by default to format text typed into a blank document.

Normal template The template that is loaded automatically when a new document is inserted in Word.

Normal view A view that shows a document without margins, headers and footers, or graphics.

Note reference mark A number or character that indicates additional information is contained in a footnote or endnote.

Nudge To move a graphic a small amount in one direction using the arrow keys.

Object Self-contained information that can be in the form of text, spreadsheet data, graphics, charts, tables, or sound and video clips.

Object Linking and Embedding (OLE) The ability to share information with other programs.

Office Assistant An animated character that offers tips and provides access to the program's Help system.

Office Clipboard A temporary storage area shared by all Office programs that can be used to cut, copy and paste multiple items within and between Office programs. The Office Clipboard can hold up to 24 items collected from any Office program. *See* Clipboard and System Clipboard.

Open To use one of the methods for opening a document to retrieve it and display it in the document window.

Organization chart A chart that illustrates a hierarchy, most often showing how functional areas in a company or organization relate to each other.

Outdent *See* Negative indent.

Outline view A view that shows the headings of a document organized as an outline.

Overtype mode A feature that allows you to overwrite existing text as you type.

Page border A graphical line that encloses one or more pages of a document.

Paragraph spacing The amount of space between paragraphs.

Paragraph style A named set of paragraph and character format settings that can be applied to a paragraph to format it all at once.

Paste To insert items stored on the Clipboard into a document.

Pixels Small dots that define color and intensity in a graphic.

Point The unit of measurement for text characters and the space between paragraphs and characters; 1/72 of an inch.

Point-to-point chart A chart used to identify patterns or to show values as clusters; the most commonly used type of point-to-point charts is the XY chart, also known as a Scatter chart.

Portrait orientation Page orientation in which the page is taller than it is wide.

Print Layout view A view that shows a document as it will look on a printed page.

Print Preview A view of a file as it will appear when printed.

Program Task-oriented software (such as Excel or Word) that enables you to perform a certain type of task such as data calculation or word processing.

Property A named attribute of a control set to define one of the control's attributes such as its size, its color, and its behavior in response to user input.

Pyramid diagram A diagram that illustrates a hierarchical relationship.

Radial diagram A diagram that illustrates the relationships of several related elements to a core element.

Reading Layout view A view that shows a document so that it is easy to read and annotate.

Right indent A type of indent in which the right edge of a paragraph is moved in from the right margin.

Right-align Alignment in which an item is flush with the right margin.

Sans serif font A font, such as Arial, whose characters do not include serifs, which are small strokes at the ends of letters.

Save To store a file permanently on a disk or to overwrite the copy of a file that is stored on a disk with the changes made to the file.

Save As Command used to save a file for the first time or to create a new file with a different filename, leaving the original file intact.

Scale To resize a graphic so that its height to width ratio remains the same.

ScreenTip A label that appears on the screen to identify a button or to provide information about a feature.

Scroll To use the scroll bars or the arrow keys to display different parts of a document in the document window.

Scroll arrows The arrows at the ends of the scroll bars that are clicked to scroll a document one line at a time.

Scroll bars The bars on the right edge (vertical scroll bar) and bottom edge (horizontal scroll bar) of the document window that are used to display different parts of the document in the document window.

Scroll box The box in a scroll bar that can be dragged to scroll a document.

Section A portion of a document that is separated from the rest of the document by section breaks.

Section break A formatting mark inserted to divide a document into sections.

Select To click or highlight an item in order to perform some action on it.

Serif font A font, such as Times New Roman, whose characters include serifs, which are small strokes at the ends of letters.

Shading A background color or pattern that can be applied to text, tables, or graphics.

Shortcut key *See* Keyboard shortcut.

Sizing handles The black squares or white circles that appear around a graphic when it is selected; used to change the size or shape of a graphic.

Smart tag A purple dotted line that appears under text that Word identifies as a date, name, address, or place.

Smart Tag Actions button The button that appears when you point to a smart tag.

Soft page break *See* Automatic page break.

Sort To organize data, such as table rows, items in a list, or records in a mail merge, in ascending or descending order.

Source file The file in which data is originally saved.

Source program The program in which data is originally created.

Split To divide a cell into two or more cells.

Standard toolbar A toolbar that contains buttons for frequently used operating and editing commands.

Status bar The bar at the bottom of the Word program window that shows the vertical position, section, and page number of the insertion point, the total number of pages in a document, and the on/off status of several Word features.

Style A named collection of character and/or paragraph formats that are stored together and can be applied to text to format it quickly.

Subdocument A document contained within a master document.

Subscript A font effect in which text is formatted in a smaller font size and placed below the line of text.

Superscript A font effect in which text is formatted in a smaller font size and placed above the line of text.

Symbols Special characters that can be inserted into a document using the Symbol command.

System Clipboard A clipboard that stores only the last item cut or copied from a document. *See* Clipboard and Office Clipboard.

Tab *See* Tab stop.

Tab leader A line that appears in front of tabbed text.

Tab stop A location on the horizontal ruler that indicates where to align text.

Table A grid made up of rows and columns of cells that you can fill with text and graphics.

Table style A named set of table format settings that can be applied to a table to format it all at once.

Tags HTML codes placed around the elements of a Web page to describe how each element should appear when viewed with a browser.

Target diagram A diagram that illustrates steps toward a goal.

Task pane An area of the Word program window that contains shortcuts to Word formatting, editing, research, Help, clip art, mail merge, and other features.

Template A formatted document that contains placeholder text you can replace with your own text; a file that contains the basic structure of a document.

Text box A container that you can fill with text and graphics.

Text form field A location in a form where users enter text.

Theme A set of complementary design elements that you can apply to Web pages, e-mail messages, and other documents that are viewed on screen.

Thumbnail Smaller version of a page that appears in the Thumbnails pane to the left of the document window when you select thumbnails on the View menu.

Title bar The bar at the top of the program window that indicates the program name and the name of the current file.

Toggle button A button that turns a feature on and off.

Toolbar A bar that contains buttons that you can click to perform commands.

Tracked change A mark that shows where an insertion, deletion, or formatting change has been made in a document.

Type a question for help box The list box at the right end of the menu bar that is used to query the Help system.

Undo To reverse a change by using the Undo button or command.

URL (Uniform Resource Locator) A Web address.

User template Any template created by the user.

Value A number in a chart.

Venn diagram A diagram that illustrates areas of overlap between two or more elements.

Vertex The point where two straight lines meet or the highest point in a curve.

Vertical alignment The position of text in a document relative to the top and bottom margins.

Vertical ruler A ruler that appears on the left side of the document window in Print Layout view.

View A way of displaying a document in the document window; each view provides features useful for editing and formatting different types of documents.

View buttons Buttons to the left of the horizontal scroll bar that are used to change views.

Watermark A picture or other type of graphics object that appears lightly shaded behind text in a document.

Web Layout view A view that shows a document as it will look when viewed with a Web browser.

Web page A document that can be stored on a computer called a Web server and viewed on the World Wide Web or on an intranet using a browser.

Web site A group of associated Web pages that are linked together with hyperlinks.

Wizard An interactive set of dialog boxes that guides you through a task.

Word processing program A software program that includes tools for entering, editing, and formatting text and graphics.

Word program window The window that contains the Word program elements, including the document window, toolbars, menu bar, and status bar.

Word-wrap A feature that automatically moves the insertion point to the next line as you type.

WordArt A drawing object that contains text formatted with special shapes, patterns, and orientations.

Workgroup Templates Templates created for distribution to others.

X-axis The horizontal axis in a two-dimensional chart.

XML Acronym that stands for eXtensible Markup Language, which is a language used to structure, store, and send information.

XML Schema A formal specification that is written in XML code and then attached to an XML document to define the structure of the document.

Y-axis The vertical axis in a two-dimensional chart.

Index

Microsoft Office Specialist Program

WHAT DOES THIS LOGO MEAN?

It means this courseware has been approved by the Microsoft® Office Specialist Program to be among the finest available for learning one or more of the applications of the Microsoft Office 2003 Suite. It also means that upon completion of this courseware, you may be prepared to take an exam for Microsoft Office Specialist qualification. If "1 of 2" or "2 of 2" appears below the logo on the cover, this indicates this courseware has been approved as part of a sequence of texts for preparation to become a Microsoft Office Specialist. See the table below for more information.

WHAT IS A MICROSOFT OFFICE SPECIALIST?

A Microsoft Office Specialist is an individual who has passed exams for certifying his or her skills in one or more of the Microsoft Office desktop applications such as Microsoft Word, Microsoft Excel, Microsoft PowerPoint®, Microsoft Outlook®, Microsoft Access, or Microsoft Project. The Microsoft Office Specialist Program is the only program in the world approved by Microsoft for testing proficiency in Microsoft Office desktop applications and Microsoft Project. This testing program can be a valuable asset in any job search or career advancement.

ILLUSTRATED TITLES FOR OFFICE 2003 MICROSOFT OFFICE SPECIALIST CERTIFICATION

The Illustrated Series offers a growing number of Microsoft-approved courseware products that cover the objectives required to pass a Microsoft Office Specialist exam. After studying with any of the books listed below, you should be prepared to take the Microsoft office Specialist Program exam indicated. The following titles have certification approval as courseware for the Microsoft Office Specialist program:

Exam	Course Technology Illustrated Series Textbook
Microsoft Office Access 2003	Microsoft Office Access 2003 - Illustrated Introductory, CourseCard Edition (1-4188-4298-2) or Microsoft Office Access 2003 - Illustrated Complete, CourseCard Edition (1-4188-4299-0)
Microsoft Office Excel 2003	Microsoft Office Excel 2003 – Illustrated Introductory, CourseCard Edition (1-4188-4295-8)
Microsoft Office Excel 2003 Expert	Microsoft Office Excel 2003 – Illustrated Complete, CourseCard Edition (1-4188-4296-6)
Microsoft Office PowerPoint 2003	Microsoft Office PowerPoint 2003 – Illustrated Introductory, CourseCard Edition (1-4188-4304-0)
Microsoft Office Word 2003	Microsoft Office Word 2003 – Illustrated Introductory, CourseCard Edition (1-4188-4301-6)
Microsoft Office Word 2003 Expert	Microsoft Office Word 2003 – Illustrated Complete, CourseCard Edition (1-4188-4302-4)
Microsoft Office 2003 (separate exams for Word, Excel, Access and PowerPoint)	Microsoft Office 2003 – Illustrated Introductory (0-619-05789-0) and Microsoft Office 2003 – Illustrated Second Course (0-619-18826-X) when used in a sequence, meet the requirements for Microsoft Office Specialist for Word, Excel Access and PowerPoint.

MORE INFORMATION:

To learn more about becoming a Microsoft Office Specialist, visit www.microsoft.com/officespecialist

To learn about other Microsoft Office Specialist approved courseware from Course Technology, visit www.course.com.

Some of the exercises in this book require that you begin by opening a Data File. Follow one of the procedures below to obtain a copy of the Data Files you need.

Instructors

- A copy of the Data Files is on the Instructor Resources CD under the category Data Files for Students, which you can copy to your school's network for student use.

- Download the Data Files via the World Wide Web by following the instructions below.

- Contact us via e-mail at reply@course.com.

- Call Course Technology's Customer Service Department for fast and efficient delivery of the Data Files if you do not have access to a CD-ROM drive.

Students

- Check with your instructor to determine the best way to obtain a copy of the Data Files.

- Download the Data Files via the World Wide Web by following the instructions below.

Instructions for Downloading the Data Files from the World Wide Web

1. Start your browser and enter the URL www.course.com.

2. When the course.com Web site opens, click Student Downloads, and then search for your text by title or ISBN.

3. If necessary, from the Search results page, select the title of the text you are using.

4. When the textbook page opens, click the Download Student Files link, and then click the link of the compressed files you want to download.

5. If the File Download dialog box opens, make sure the Save this program to disk option button is selected, and then click the OK button. (NOTE: If the Save As dialog box opens, select a folder on your hard disk to download the file to. Write down the folder name listed in the Save in box and the filename listed in the File name box.)

6. The filename of the compressed file appears in the Save As dialog box (e.g., 3500-8.exe, 0361-1d.exe).

7. Click either the OK button or the Save button, whichever choice your browser gives you.

8. When a dialog box opens indicating the download is complete, click the OK button (or the Close button, depending on which operating system you are using). Close your browser.

9. Open Windows Explorer and display the contents of the folder to which you downloaded the file. Double-click the downloaded filename on the right side of the Windows Explorer window.

10. In the WinZip Self-Extractor window, specify the appropriate drive and a folder name to unzip the files to. Click Unzip.

11. When the WinZip Self-Extractor displays the number of files unzipped, click the OK button. Click the Close button in the WinZip Self-Extractor dialog box. Close Windows Explorer.

12. Refer to the Read This Before You Begin page(s) in this book for more details on the Data Files for your text. You are now ready to open the required files.

Macintosh users should use a program to expand WinZip or PKZip archives. Students, ask your instructors or lab coordinators for assistance.

Keep Your Skills Fresh with Quick Reference CourseCards!

Thomson Course Technology CourseCards allow you to easily learn the basics of new applications or quickly access tips and tricks long after your class is complete.

Each highly visual, four-color, six-sided CourseCard features:

- **Basic Topics** enable users to effectively utilize key content.

- **Tips and Solutions** reinforce key subject matter and provide solutions to common situations.

- **Menu Quick References** help users navigate through the most important menu tools using a simple table of contents model.

- **Keyboard Shortcuts** improve productivity and save time.

- **Screen Shots** effectively show what users see on their monitors.

- **Advanced Topics** provide advanced users with a clear reference guide to more challenging content.

Over 75 CourseCards are available on a variety of topics! To order, please visit *www.courseilt.com/ilt_cards.cfm*

IF THIS BOOK DOES NOT HAVE A COURSECARD ATTACHED TO THE BACK COVER, YOU ARE NOT GETTING THE FULL VALUE OF YOUR PURCHASE.